Mergers, Acquisitions, and Other Restructuring Activities

MERGERS, ACQUISITIONS, AND OTHER RESTRUCTURING ACTIVITIES

An Integrated Approach to Process, Tools, Cases, and Solutions

DONALD DEPAMPHILIS

College of Business Administration
Loyola Marymouth University
Los Angeles, California

ACADEMIC PRESS

A Harcourt Science and Technology Company

San Diego   San Francisco   New York   Boston   London   Sydney   Tokyo

Copyright © 2001 by ACADEMIC PRESS

All Rights Reserved.
No part of this publication may be reproduced or transmitted in any form or by any
means, electronic or mechanical, including photocopy, recording, or any information
storage and retrieval system, without permission in writing from the publisher.

Requests for permission to make copies of any part of the work should be mailed to:
Permissions Department, Harcourt Inc., 6277 Sea Harbor Drive,
Orlando, Florida 32887-6777

Academic Press
A Harcourt Science and Technology Company
525 B Street, Suite 1900, San Diego, California 92101-4495, USA
http://www.academicpress.com

Academic Press
Harcourt Place, 32 Jamestown Road, London NW1 7BY, UK
http://www.academicpress.com

Library of Congress Catalog Card Number: 00-111084

International Standard Book Number: 0-12-210735-7

PRINTED IN THE UNITED STATES OF AMERICA
00   01   02   03   04   05   EB   9   8   7   6   5   4   3   2   1

*I extend my heartfelt gratitude to my wife, Cheryl,
and my daughter, Cara, without whose patience and understanding
this book could not have been completed, and to
my brother, Mel, without whose encouragement this book
would never have been undertaken.*

CONTENTS

2

REGULATORY CONSIDERATIONS

3

COMMON TAKEOVER TACTICS AND DEFENSES

PART II

THE MERGERS AND ACQUISITIONS PROCESS: PHASES 1–10

4

PLANNING: DEVELOPING BUSINESS AND ACQUISITION PLANS—PHASES 1 AND 2 OF THE ACQUISTION PROCESS

5

IMPLEMENTATION: SEARCH THROUGH CLOSING— PHASES 3 TO 10

6

INTEGRATION: MERGERS, ACQUISITIONS, AND BUSINESS ALLIANCES

PART III

MERGER AND ACQUISITION TOOLS AND CONCEPTS

7

A PRIMER ON MERGER AND ACQUISITION VALUATION

8

APPLYING FINANCIAL MODELING TECHNIQUES TO VALUE AND STRUCTURE MERGERS AND ACQUISITIONS

9

ANALYSIS AND VALUATION OF PRIVATELY HELD COMPANIES

10

STRUCTURING THE DEAL: PAYMENT, LEGAL, TAX, AND ACCOUNTING CONSIDERATIONS

PART IV

ALTERNATIVE STRATEGIES AND STRUCTURES

11

LEVERAGED BUYOUT STRUCTURES AND VALUATION

12

SHARED GROWTH AND SHARED CONTROL STRATEGIES: JOINT VENTURES, PARTNERSHIPS, AND ALLIANCES

13

ALTERNATIVE EXIT AND RESTRUCTURING STRATEGIES: DIVESTITURES, SPIN-OFFS, CARVE-OUTS, SPLIT-UPS, BANKRUPTCY, AND LIQUIDATION

PART V

PUTTING IT ALL TOGETHER

14

THE ACQUISITION PROCESS: THE GEE WHIZ MEDIA CASE

PREFACE

The explosive growth in the number, size, and complexity of mergers, acquisitions, and alliances during the 1990s demonstrates how ingrained business combinations have become in the global business community. Despite these developments, studies show that a disproportionately large number of such combinations fail to satisfy their participants' expectations, suggesting a need to think and act differently in conceiving and implementing corporate restructuring activities.

The increasing sophistication of transactions demands that managers and analysts alike clearly understand how the various activities contributing to successful business combinations fit together in an integrated framework. Because business combinations often entail a common set of activities, the manager or analyst is able to view mergers, acquisitions, or business alliances in the context of a process or logical sequence of activities. A properly articulated process disciplines the manager or analyst to consider all relevant activities in an orderly manner, to understand how the various activities interact, to review the range of reasonable options, and to select the option that best satisfies the primary needs of all parties involved.

Moreover, the manager or analyst must also draw upon varied skills to resolve the numerous and diverse challenges that inevitably arise in any business combination. These skills include strategic and operations management; project administration; organizational dynamics; accounting, economics, and finance; business, tax, and securities law; and negotiation. For example, the process of structuring a merger or acquisition requires understanding the nuances of different tax, legal, accounting, and payment forms and their impact on other aspects of the deal to satisfy the key objectives of the participants through negotiation.

INTEGRATING THE SUBJECT MATTER

Most books on mergers, acquisitions, and other forms of corporate restructuring focus on process management, human resource management, or the financial aspects of the deal. In contrast, this book brings together the essential elements of each domain, including postmerger integration; business alliances as alternatives to mergers and acquisitions (M&As); the application of basic financial modeling techniques to analyzing and valuing M&As; and assumptions-driven planning—subjects often overlooked or treated only superficially in many corporate restructuring texts. This unique book covers a broad array of subjects critical to understanding how to implement different types of business combinations successfully within an integrated framework.

Integration is addressed in three important ways. First, activities common to the formation of most business combinations are discussed in the context of a process rather than as a series of discrete, independent events (process-related integration). Second, the tools and concepts required to solve common problems faced in the M&A process are discussed in contexts in which they normally occur (context-related integration). Finally, all aspects of the M&A process are integrated into a highly realistic business case, Gee Whiz Media (Chapter 14), which enables the reader to understand how normal business challenges are resolved through a transaction described from conception through completion.

Process-Related Integration

Process-related integration refers to a coherent description of the logical sequence of M&A activities, including key interactions among various components of the process. The M&A process outlined in this book consists of 10 interrelated phases and is sufficiently flexible to be applicable to businesses of various sizes and in different industries. The first two phases make up the planning stage and comprise the development of a business plan, defining where and how a firm chooses to compete, and an acquisition plan—if management believes that an acquisition is the most desirable option for implementing the business plan. The remaining eight phases make up the implementation stage, comprising such activities as search, screen, first contact, negotiation, integration planning, and closing, as well as postmerger integration and evaluation.

The negotiation phase is highlighted as the most dynamic aspect of the M&A process, consisting of a continuous refinement of the preliminary valuation, deal structure, and financing plan based on information obtained through due diligence. This iteration continues until a decision is made either to proceed to closing or to "walk away." In this crucial negotiation phase, all elements of the purchase price are actually determined.

Contextual Integration

Contextual integration is best understood through illustration. For example, deal structuring is most often treated as a series of largely independent events most often handled by lawyers. In practice, deal structuring is a highly interactive process supported by numerous analysts possessing different types of expertise. Deal structuring is conceptualized as a process consisting of six interdependent components discussed in Chapter 10. These include the acquisition vehicle, the post-closing organization, the form of payment, the form of accounting, the form of acquisition, and the tax structure. Another example of contextual integration involves the discussion of takeover tactics and defenses in Chapter 3, which emphasizes that the takeover tactics employed often reflect the defenses in place at the target company. Similarly, the defenses initiated following the initial bid for the target company often depend on the type of takeover tactics employed by the suitor.

PUTTING IT ALL TOGETHER IN A REALISTIC BUSINESS CASE

Although largely fictional, the Gee Whiz Media case study reflects the relevant aspects of my experience in managing more than 30 transactions in nine different industries through closing. The case illustrates the application of the planning-based approach to M&As presented in this book. Although the case takes place in a rapidly changing high-technology environment, the approach transfers across industries, and the challenges described are common to most transactions. The case illustrates the importance of "up-front planning," techniques for searching for and screening potential acquisition candidates, and initiating contact. In addition, the case explores the concurrent phases of the negotiation process, methods for identifying sources and destroyers of value, events common to the closing activity, and the hazards of postclosing integration.

WHO MIGHT BE INTERESTED IN THIS BOOK

The text is intended for students of M&As, corporate restructuring, business strategy, industrial organization, and entrepreneurship courses at both the undergraduate and the master in business administration level. Moreover, the material has worked effectively in executive development and training programs. The book should also interest those actively pursuing careers as financial analysts, chief financial officers, corporate treasurers, operating managers, investment bankers, business brokers, portfolio managers, or investors, as well as corporate development and strategic planning managers. Others who may have an interest include bank lending officers, venture capitalists, business appraisers, actuaries, government regulators and policy makers, and entrepreneurs. Hence, from the classroom to the boardroom, this text offers something for anyone with an interest in M&As,

business alliances, and other forms of corporate restructuring.

TO THE INSTRUCTOR

This book equips the instructor with the information and tools needed to communicate effectively with students from diverse backgrounds and levels of preparation. The generous use of examples and contemporary business cases makes the text suitable for distance learning and self-study programs as well as large, lecture-focused courses. Prerequisites for this text include familiarity with basic accounting, finance, and general management concepts.

PRACTICAL, TIMELY, AND DIVERSE EXAMPLES AND BUSINESS CASES WITH SOLUTIONS

Each chapter begins with a vignette based on my own experience, intended to illustrate a key point or points that will be described in more detail as the chapter unfolds. Hundreds of examples, business cases, and figures illustrate the application of key concepts and tools. The many tables summarize otherwise diffuse information and the results of numerous empirical studies substantiating key points made in each chapter. Each chapter concludes with a series of 10 discussion questions and an integrative Chapter Business Case intended to stimulate critical thinking and test the readers's understanding of the material. Solutions to the Chapter Business Cases are found in the back of the book.

The case studies used throughout the text include business combinations in 15 different industries as well as cross-border deals, highly leveraged transactions, and other types of corporate restructuring activities. Many case studies and illustrations focus on transactions involving e-commerce businesses. Chapter 14, the Gee Whiz Media business case, ties it all together and is conveniently divided into two parts: planning and implementation. Of the 10 discussion questions at the end of the case, the initial 5 relate to the first part of the case and the remaining 5 to the second part. This format enables instructors to customize the case study discussion to their specific pedagogical style.

COMPREHENSIVE YET FLEXIBLE ORGANIZATION

Although the text is sequential, each chapter was developed as a self-contained unit to enable adaptation of the text to various types of students and teaching strategies. The flexibility of the organization also makes the material suitable for courses of various lengths, from one quarter to two full semesters. Table 1 suggests the approximate amount of time that might be devoted to each chapter. The amount of time required depends on the students' level of sophistication and the desired focus of the instructor.

TABLE 1   Suggested Approaches to Teaching Content

Chapter title	Estimated hours to teach material
1. Introduction to Mergers and Acquisitions	3–4
2. Regulatory Considerations	3–4
3. Common Takeover Tactics and Defenses	4–6
4. Planning: Developing Business and Acquisition Plans— Phases 1 and 2 of the Acquisition Process	4–6
5. Implementation: Search through Closing—Phases 3–10	3–6
6. Integration: Mergers, Acquisitions, and Business Alliances	3–4
7. A Primer on Merger and Acquisition Valuation	4–6
8. Applying Financial Modeling Techniques to Value and Structure Mergers and Acquisitions	3–4
9. Analysis and Valuation of Privately Held Companies	3–4
10. Structuring the Deal: Payment, Legal, Tax, and Accounting Considerations[a]	4–6
11. Leveraged Buyout Structures and Valuation[a]	3–4
12. Shared Growth and Shared Control Strategies: Joint Ventures, Partnerships, and Alliances	3–4
13. Alternative Exit and Restructuring Strategies: Divestitures, Spin-offs, Carve-outs, Split-ups, Bankruptcy, and Liquidation[a]	4–6
14. The Acquisition Process: The Gee Whiz Media Case[a]	2–3

[a] Recommended for graduate level or MBA students only.

ACKNOWLEDGMENTS

I extend my heartfelt gratitude to my wife, Cheryl, and my daughter, Cara, without whose patience and understanding this book could not have been completed, and to my brother, Mel, without whose encouragement it would never have been undertaken. In addition, I express my sincere appreciation for the many helpful suggestions received from eight anonymous reviewers and the many resources of Academic Press. Finally, I thank John Mellen for his many constructive comments and J. Scott Bentley, a senior editor at Academic Press, for his ongoing support.

THE MERGERS AND ACQUISITIONS ENVIRONMENT

1

INTRODUCTION TO MERGERS AND ACQUISITIONS

Murphy's Law: "If anything can go wrong, it will."

O'Toole's Commentary on Murphy's Law: "Murphy was an optimist."

Watch the evening news or read the business section of any major city newspaper and it's not hard to be swept up in merger mania. Chief executive officers (CEOs) confidently communicate their visions for the combined businesses to assure shareholders that the transaction is in their best interests. The infectious camaraderie of the CEOs of the companies involved in the transaction radiates from the podium as they, sometimes almost giddily, announce the emergence of the latest behemoth. The CEOs seem to revel in the limelight, as they are asked how it feels to be running the largest firm in the industry. The press loves the big story. It gives them an opportunity to once again give mainstream America a glimpse of the arcane world of high finance. Wall Street, never inclined to ignore an oncoming gravy train, nods approvingly.

Amidst the euphoria surrounding the event, there are few willing to question the record-breaking purchase price. After all, everyone seems to want to enjoy the moment. For those at the top, it is often their "fifteen minutes of fame." But reality soon sets in as the studio lights are dimmed and investors' attention turns to the next big merger announcement. Away from the glare of the cameras, the CEOs and their subordinates hunker down to meet the challenge of making it all work.

OVERVIEW

In terms of the intensity of merger and acquisition (M&A) activity, the decade of the 1990s was unlike any other in U.S. history. Following a drop in both the number of transactions and the total dollar volume during the 1990 recession, M&A activity has rebounded sharply since 1992. By 1995, the number and dollar volume exceeded their previous record levels set in the mid-1980s, when many transactions were largely financially motivated. The five largest transactions completed during the 1990s averaged $77 billion, about five times the average of the five largest deals completed during the previous decade. The average purchase price continued to set new records year after year. During the 1990s, cumulative M&A transactions totaled $6.5 trillion in the United States, with more than one-half of the transactions during this period taking place during the last 2 years of the decade.

Today's deals tend to be more strategic in nature and use a lot less debt than in the 1980s. As was true of the 1990s, M&A activity continues to be motivated by intensifying global competition, rapid industry consolidation, deregulation, as well as increasingly complex and rapidly changing technologies. The overall antitrust regulatory environment has also been generally supportive, as exemplified by the rapid consolidation in the cable, telephone, defense, and radio industries. In evaluating the competitive effects of mergers, regulators are increasingly looking beyond simply the size of the transaction and more toward their potential for improving operating efficiency. The financial environment has also been highly favorable, with soaring stock market multiples and relatively low interest rates.

The intent of this chapter is to provide the reader with a working knowledge of the relevant vocabulary, the role of the various participants in the M&A process, and the wide range of factors influencing M&A activity historically. The dynamics of the five major merger waves that have taken place since the close of the 19th century are also described. Moreover, the chapter addresses the question of whether mergers pay off for target and acquiring company shareholders as well as for society. The most frequently cited reasons for many M&A's failure to meet expectations are also discussed. The chapter concludes with a case study of America Online's acquisition of Time Warner, the largest acquisition in U.S. history and an interesting combination of "old" and "new" economy companies.

BUILDING A COMMON VOCABULARY

Any field of endeavor tends to have its own jargon. The study of buying and selling entire businesses or parts of businesses is no exception. Understanding the field requires a familiarity with the vocabulary. In this section, terms are defined that will be used frequently throughout the book without any further explanation.

CORPORATE RESTRUCTURING

Actions taken to expand or contract a firm's basic operations or fundamentally change its asset or financial structure are referred to as *corporate restructuring* activities. Corporate restructuring is a catchall term that refers to a broad array of activities from mergers, acquisitions, and business alliances to divestitures and spin-offs.

In the literature, corporate restructuring activities are often broken into two specific categories: operational and financial restructuring. *Operational restructuring* usually refers to the outright or partial sale of companies or product lines or to downsizing by closing unprofitable or nonstrategic facilities. *Financial restructuring* describes actions by the firm to change its total debt and equity structure. An example of financial restructuring would be to add debt to either lower the corporation's overall cost of capital or as part of an antitakeover defense (see Chapter 3).

ACQUISITIONS, DIVESTITURES, AND BUYOUTS

Generally speaking, an *acquisition* occurs when one company takes a controlling interest in another firm, a legal subsidiary of another firm, or selected assets of another firm such as a manufacturing facility. In contrast, a *divestiture* is the sale of all or substantially all of a company or product line to another party for cash or securities. A *leveraged buyout* (LBO) is the purchase of a company financed primarily by debt. The term is often applied to a firm borrowing funds to buy back its stock to convert from a publicly owned to a privately owned company (see Chapter 11). A *management buyout* is a LBO in which managers of the firm to be taken private are also equity investors. A firm that attempts to acquire or merge with another company is called an *acquiring company*. The *target company* is the firm that is being solicited by the acquiring company. A *takeover* refers to a change in the controlling interest of a corporation.

MERGERS AND CONSOLIDATIONS

Mergers can be described from a structural or from an industrial–operational perspective. This distinction is relevant to later discussions in this book of deal structuring, regulatory issues, and strategic planning.

A Structural Perspective

From a structural standpoint, a *merger* is a combination of two firms in which only one firm's identity survives. A *statutory merger* is one in which the acquiring company assumes the assets and liabilities of the target company in accordance with the statutes of the state in which it is incorporated. A *subsidiary merger* of two companies occurs when the target becomes a subsidiary of the parent (e.g., General Motors and Electronic Data Systems [EDS]).

Although the terms *mergers* and *consolidations* are often used interchangeably, a *consolidation,* which involves two or more companies joining to form a new company, is technically not a merger. All legal entities that are consolidated are dissolved during the formation of the new company. In a merger, either the acquirer or the target company survives. The 1999 combination of Daimler-Benz and Chrysler to form Daimler-Chrysler is a recent example of a consolidation. The new corporate entity created as a result of consolidation or the surviving entity following a merger usually assumes ownership of the assets and liabilities of the merged or consolidated organizations. Stockholders in merged companies typically exchange their shares for shares in the new company.

An Industrial–Operational Perspective

Business combinations may also be classified as horizontal, vertical, and conglomerate mergers. How a merger is classified depends on whether the merging firms are in the same or different industries and on their positions in the corporate value chain.

Horizontal and Conglomerate Mergers

Horizontal and conglomerate mergers are best understood in the context of whether the merging firms are in the same or different industries. A *horizontal merger* occurs between two firms within the same industry. Examples of horizontal acquisitions include Exxon and Mobil (1999), SBC Communications and Ameritech (1998), and NationsBank and BankAmerica (1998). *Conglomerate mergers* are those in which the acquiring company purchases firms in largely unrelated industries. An example would be U.S. Steel's acquisition of Marathon Oil to form USX.

Vertical Mergers

Vertical mergers are best understood operationally in the context of the corporate value chain (see Figure 1-1). Vertical mergers are those in which the two firms participate at different stages of the production or value chain. A simple value chain in the basic steel industry may distinguish between raw materials, such as coal or iron ore; steel making, such as hot metal and rolling operations; and metals distribution. Similarly, a value chain in the oil and gas industry would separate exploration activities from production, refining, and marketing. An Internet value chain might distinguish between infrastructure providers such as Cisco and MCI WorldCom, content providers such as Bloomberg and Dow Jones, and portals such as Yahoo and AOL.

Companies that do not own operations in each major segment of the value chain may choose to backward integrate by acquiring a supplier or to forward integrate by acquiring a distributor. An example of forward integration is the 1993 merger between Merck, then the world's largest pharmaceutical company, and Medco, the nation's largest seller of discount drugs. An example of backward integration in the natural resources industry is Chevron Oil's 1984 purchase of

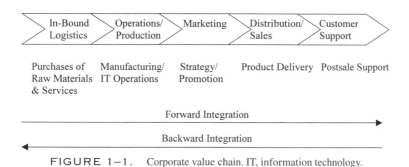

FIGURE 1–1. Corporate value chain. IT, information technology.

Gulf Oil to augment its reserves. A more recent example in the technology industry is America Online's 1999 $1.1 billion purchase of content provider MapQuest.com, a provider of online access to digital maps.

FRIENDLY VERSUS HOSTILE TAKEOVERS

In a *friendly* takeover of control, the target company's management is receptive to the idea and recommends shareholder approval. To gain control, the acquiring company must offer a premium to the current price of the stock. The excess of the offer price over the target company's current share price is called a *control premium.* If the stockholders approve, the transaction is consummated through a purchase of the target company's shares for cash, stock, debt, or some combination of all three.

In contrast, an *unfriendly* or *hostile takeover* occurs when the target company's management does not support a solicitation from a potential acquirer, often due to the perceived inadequacy of the proposed purchase price. The acquirer may attempt to circumvent management by going directly to the target's shareholders and by buying shares in the marketplace. This is accomplished by a *tender offer,* which is an offer to buy the shares of a company for cash, securities, or both with the intent to take control of the corporation.

Bidders usually find friendly takeovers preferable to hostile transactions, because they can often be consummated at a lower purchase price. A hostile takeover attempt may put the target company "into play" and attract new bidders. In the ensuing auction environment, the final purchase price may be bid up to a point well above the initial offer price. In addition, acquirers prefer friendly takeovers, because the postmerger integration process can usually be accomplished more expeditiously and effectively when both parties are fully cooperating.

Although the number of bids classified as hostile and unsolicited has been on the rise, most deals of this type are ultimately unsuccessful and subsequently withdrawn. According to Thomson Financial Securities Data Corporation, only about 17% of such M&A transactions in the United States over the last decade were successful. However, almost 40% of the targeted firms were ultimately sold to another bidder and 6% were sold to White Knights, firms perceived as friendly by the target firm. The remaining target firms remained independent.

G. William Schwert (1999) argues that the distinction between hostile and friendly takeovers is largely perceptual and often cannot be substantiated based on accounting and stock price data. The perceived differences between the two may depend on how information is released to the public. Transactions in which negotiations are not made public until an agreement is reached are often viewed as friendly. In contrast, transactions may be viewed as hostile when negotiations are made public before all issues are resolved. To put pressure on the target company's management, such information may be leaked to the public by the bidder (Schwert: 1999).

THE ROLE OF HOLDING COMPANIES IN MERGERS AND ACQUISITIONS

A *holding company* is a legal entity having a controlling interest in one or more companies. The primary function of a holding company is to own stock in other corporations. In general, it has no wholly owned operating units of its own. The segments owned by the holding company are separate legal entities, which in practice are controlled by the holding company. This differs from firms having multiple divisions or profit centers reporting to a single corporate headquarters.

The Holding Company as an Investment Vehicle

The primary advantage of the holding company structure is the potential leverage that can be achieved by gaining effective control of other companies' assets at a lower overall cost than would be required if the firm were to acquire 100% of the target's outstanding shares. Effective control can sometimes be achieved by owning as little as 20% of the voting stock of another company. This is possible when the target company's ownership is highly fragmented, with few shareholders owning large blocks of stock. Consequently, the holding company is frequently able to cast the deciding votes by voting its shares as a block on important issues of corporate strategy and governance. In this manner, investors through a holding company structure are able to gain control of substantially more assets than they could through a merger.

Effective control largely determines how a subsidiary's financial performance will be treated for accounting purposes. Gaining effective control of assets with relatively little equity investment can magnify fluctuations in the holding company's earnings, because the firm's consolidated statements, for financial reporting purposes, reflect 100% of a subsidiary's earnings, but less than 100% of the subsidiary's assets. The amount of the subsidiary's assets included on the parent's consolidated statements will generally be equal to the holding company's percentage share of the subsidiary's equity. Effective control is generally achieved by acquiring less than 100% but usually more than 50% of another firm's equity. One firm is said to have effective control over another when control has been achieved through the purchase of voting stock, it is not likely to be temporary, there are no legal restrictions on control such as from a bankruptcy court, and there are no powerful minority shareholders.

Companies controlled by the holding company are generally referred to as wholly or partially owned subsidiaries depending upon the percentage of voting shares held by the holding company. As explained in Chapter 10, the percentage of ownership has significant implications for accounting and tax purposes.

Disadvantages of Holding Companies

Despite the potential for gaining control of another company at a lower cost than through an acquisition, the holding company structure can create significant management challenges. Because the holding company can gain effective control with less than 100% ownership, the holding company is left with a significant number of minority shareholders, who may not always agree with the strategic direction of the company. Consequently, implementing holding company strategies may become very contentious. Furthermore, in highly diversified holding companies, managers may also have difficulty in making optimal investment decisions because of their limited understanding of the different competitive dynamics of each business.

The holding company structure can also create significant tax problems for shareholders of the holding company. Subsidiaries of holding companies pay taxes on their operating profits. The holding company then pays taxes on dividends they receive from their subsidiaries. Finally, holding company shareholders pay taxes on dividends they receive from the holding company. This amounts to triple taxation of subsidiary operating earnings.

THE ROLE OF EMPLOYEE STOCK OWNERSHIP PLANS IN MERGERS AND ACQUISITIONS

An employee stock ownership plan (ESOP) is a mechanism whereby a corporation can make tax-deductible contributions of cash or stock into a trust. The assets are allocated to employees and are not taxed until withdrawn by employees. Both interest and principal payments on ESOP loans are tax deductible by the firm sponsoring the ESOP. Dividends paid on stock contributed to ESOPs are also deductible, if they are used to repay ESOP debt. The sponsoring firm could use tax credits equal to .5% of payroll, if contributions in that amount were made to the ESOP.

There are also tax advantages to lenders making loans to ESOPs owning more than 50% of the sponsoring firm's stock. Only one-half of the interest earned on such loans is taxable to the lender.

Although early studies (U.S. General Accounting Office: 1987) were not able to establish a direct link between gains in worker productivity and the profitability of the sponsoring firms, a recent study found that the financial returns of public companies with ESOPs are significantly higher than comparable firms without ESOPs (Conte, Biasi, Kruse, and Jampani: 1996).

Establishing an ESOP

The steps involved in establishing an ESOP are illustrated in Figure 1-2. The ESOP borrows from financial institutions (1), and the employer sponsoring the ESOP guarantees the loan (2). The ESOP uses the borrowed funds to purchase stock from the sponsoring employer, and the stock is used to provide collateral for the loan (3). The employer then makes periodic cash contributions to the ESOP (4). The interest and principal on the loan are repaid by cash contributions to the ESOP from the sponsoring firm (5). Because it has a contingent liability (loan guarantee), the sponsoring firm transfers ownership of the stock to the ESOP only as portions of the loan principal are repaid (6).

ESOPs as an Alternative to Divestiture

If a subsidiary cannot be sold at what the parent firm believes to be a reasonable price, and liquidating the subsidiary would be disruptive to customers, the parent may initiate a sale directly to employees through a shell corporation. A *shell corporation* is one that is incorporated but has no significant assets or operations. The shell corporation sets up the ESOP, which borrows the money to buy the subsidiary. The parent guarantees the loan. The shell corporation operates the subsidiary while the ESOP holds the stock. As income is generated from the subsidiary, tax-deductible contributions are made by the shell to the ESOP to service the debt. As the loan is paid off, the shares are allocated to employees who eventually own the firm.

ESOPs and Management Buyouts

ESOPs are commonly used by employees in leveraged or management buyouts to purchase the shares of owners of privately held firms. This is particularly common where the owners have most of their net worth tied up in their firms. The mechanism is similar to a sale initiated by the owner to employees.

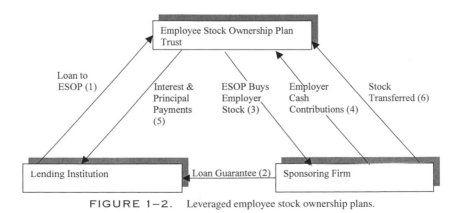

FIGURE 1-2.   Leveraged employee stock ownership plans.

ESOPs as an Antitakeover Defense

A firm concerned about the potential for a hostile takeover creates an ESOP. The ESOP borrows with the aid of the sponsoring firm's guarantee and uses the loan proceeds to buy stock issued by the sponsoring firm. While the loan is outstanding, the ESOP's trustees retain voting rights on the stock. Once the loan is paid off, it is generally assumed that employees will tend to vote against bidders who they perceive as jeopardizing their jobs.

BUSINESS ALLIANCES

In addition to mergers and acquisitions, businesses may also combine through joint ventures (JVs), strategic alliances, minority investments, franchises, and licenses. These alternative forms of combining businesses are addressed in more detail in Chapter 12. The term *business alliance* will be used to refer to all forms of business combination other than mergers and acquisitions.

Alternative Structures

Joint Ventures

JVs are cooperative business relationships formed by two or more separate parties to achieve common strategic objectives. The JV is usually an independent legal entity in the form of a corporation or partnership. JV corporations have their own management reporting to a board of directors consisting of representatives of those companies participating in the JV. The JV is generally established for a limited period of time. Each of the JV partners continues to exist as separate entities.

Strategic Alliances

Alliances generally fall short of creating a separate legal entity. They can be an agreement to sell each firm's products to the other's customers or to co-develop a technology, product, or process. Such agreements are often cancelable without significant penalties.

Minority Investments

Passive minority investments require little commitment of management time and may be highly liquid if the investment is in a publicly traded company. Investing companies may choose to assist small or start-up companies in the development of products or technologies useful to the investing company.

Franchises

From a legal perspective, a franchise is a privilege given to a dealer by a manufacturer or franchise service organization to sell the franchiser's products or services in a given area, with or without exclusivity. Such arrangements are sometimes formalized with franchise agreements. Under the agreement, the franchiser may offer the franchisee consultation, promotional assistance, financing, and other benefits in exchange for a share of the franchise's revenue. Franchises represent a low-cost way to expand, since the capital is usually provided by the franchisee; however, the success of franchising has been limited largely to such industries as fast food services and retailing.

License Agreements

Licenses require no up-front capital and represent a convenient way for a company to extend its brand to new products and new markets by licensing their brand name to others. Alternatively, a company may gain access to a proprietary technology through the licensing process.

Advantages and Disadvantages

The major attraction of these alternatives to outright acquisition is the opportunity for each partner to gain access to the other's skills, products, and markets at a lower commitment of management time and financial resources. The JV also allows for the sharing of ongoing operating expenses. Major disadvantages include limited control and, in the case of JVs, independent management that may have divided loyalties between the various owners of the JV, the requirement that each party share the profits, and the potential for loss of trade secrets and skills. The latter exposure is greatest in license arrangements, in which controls tend to be very limited.

PARTICIPANTS IN THE MERGERS AND ACQUISITIONS PROCESS

Even the best ideas founder if they are not executed properly. Moving from the concept stage to a completed transaction requires an array of highly skilled advisors. Each advisor specializes in a specific aspect of the M&A process. Understanding the roles of the various players is helpful in sorting out what types of resources will be required for a specific transaction.

Good advice is worth its weight in gold; bad advice can be a disastrous. Like all professions, the quality of advisors can very widely. Although major financial institutions may provide "one-stop" M&A advisory services, they are unlikely to have highly competent people to support all aspects of a transaction. Even though investment bankers and lawyers frequently get the greatest press in the largest transactions, there are many other professionals who play an essential role in the successful completion of the deal.

INVESTMENT BANKERS

Investment bankers are often at the forefront of the acquisition process. They offer strategic and tactical advice and acquisition opportunities, screen potential buyers and sellers, make initial contact with a seller or buyer, and provide negotiation support, valuation, and deal structuring. Investment bankers help to identify the firm's strategic objectives and assist in evaluating alternative strategies for achieving these objectives. According to Thompson Financial Securities Data Corporation, the top three investment banks in terms of their share of the dollar value of 1999 M&A transactions include Goldman Sachs (39.1%), Morgan Stanley (26.5%), and Merrill Lynch (22.3%).

Fairness Opinion

In large transactions, investment bankers are almost always used to evaluate competing proposals for a target company to minimize the potential for shareholder lawsuits that might arise if there is any appearance that the board of directors is not adequately fulfilling its fiduciary obligations to the shareholder. Their opinion is often stated in a "fairness letter," which indicates that a specific offer represents fair market value for the target company. In small to medium-sized transactions, investment bankers may play a central role in structuring the transaction and in negotiating the agreement of purchase and sale.

Large versus Small Investment Banks

The size of the transaction will often determine the size of the investment bank that can be used as an advisor. The largest investment banks are unlikely to consider any transaction valued at less than $100 million. Large investment banks do not necessarily provide the best advice. So-called investment boutiques can be very helpful in providing specialized industry knowledge. However, the larger firms are likely to offer easier entrée at higher levels in potential corporate buyers and sellers. Investment banks often provide large databases of recent transactions, which are critical in valuing potential target companies. For highly specialized transactions, the investment boutiques are apt to have more relevant data. Finally, the large investment banks are more likely to be able to assist in funding large transactions because of their current relationships with institutional lenders and broker distribution networks.

Financing Services

In large transactions, a group of investment banks, also referred to as a syndicate, agrees to purchase a new issue of securities (e.g., debt, preferred, or common stock) from the acquiring company for sale to the investing public. Within the syndicate, the banks underwriting or purchasing the issue are often different from the group selling the issue. The selling group often consists of those firms with the best broker distribution networks.

Following registration with the Securities and Exchange Commission (SEC), such securities may be offered to the investing public as an *initial public offering* (IPO) at a price agreed upon by the issuer and the investment banking group or *privately placed* with institutional investors, such as pension funds and insurance companies. Unlike a public offering, a private placement does not have to be registered with the SEC if the securities are purchased for investment rather than for resale.

LAWYERS

The legal framework surrounding a typical transaction has become so complex that no one individual can have sufficient expertise to address all the issues. On large, complicated transactions, legal teams can consist of more than a dozen attorneys, each of whom represents a specialized aspect of the law. Areas of expertise include M&As, corporate, tax, employee benefits, real estate, antitrust, securities, and intellectual property. In a hostile transaction, the team may grow to include litigation experts. According to Thomson Financial Securities Data Corporation, the leading law firms in terms of their share of the dollar value of 1999 M&A transactions include Simpson Thatcher & Bartlett (35%); Skadden, Arps, Slate, Meagher & Flom (27.5%); and Sherman & Sterling (24.4%).

ACCOUNTANTS

Services provided by accountants include advice on the optimal tax structure, financial structuring, and on performing financial due diligence. Tax accountants or tax attorneys are vital in determining the appropriate tax structure. A transaction can be structured in many different ways, with each having different tax implications for the parties involved. The structure of the transaction can also impact the form of accounting employed, which may impact the reported earnings of the combined companies (see Chapter 10). In conducting due diligence for a friendly takeover, accountants perform the role of auditors by reviewing the target's financial statements and operations through a series of on-site visits and interviews with senior and middle-level managers.

PROXY SOLICITORS

Proxy battles are attempts to change management control of a company by gaining the right to cast votes on behalf of other shareholders. In contests for the control of the board of directors of a target company, it is often difficult to compile mailing lists of stockholders' addresses, since many are held by brokerage houses. Proxy solicitation companies are often hired by an acquiring company or dissident shareholder for this purpose. Proxy solicitors can represent both dissident shareholders and management.

Contests for control, particularly unsolicited tender offers, are a critical test of a company's leadership. For corporations defending themselves against takeover bids or making tender offers, success depends on the ability to quickly identify shareholders and to communicate effectively with these shareholders. Whether a hostile bid or an unsolicited tender offer, the proxy solicitation company designs strategies to educate shareholders and communicate why shareholders should follow the Board's recommendations. The major companies in this business are Georgeson & Company and D. F. King & Company. Georgeson & Company (1999) claims to have won 77% of the proxy contests representing management (66 of 86) and 65% representing dissident shareholders (57 of 88).

PUBLIC RELATIONS

Communicating a consistent position during a takeover attempt is vital. Inconsistent messages reduce the credibility of the parties involved. From the viewpoint of the acquiring company in a hostile takeover attempt, the message to the shareholders must be that their plans for the company will increase shareholder value more than the plans of incumbent management. The target company's management will frequently hire private investigators, such as Kroll Associates acquired by O'Gara in 1997, to look into the backgrounds and motives of those managing the takeover attempt. Private investigators may be hired to develop detailed financial data on the company and to do background checks on key personnel. Such information may be used by the target firm to discredit publicly the management of the acquiring firm. Major public relations firms with significant experience in the M&A arena include Kekst & Company, Hill & Knowlton, and Robinson Lerer & Montgomery.

INSTITUTIONAL INVESTORS

Institutional investors include public and private pension funds, insurance companies, investment companies, bank trust departments, and mutual funds. Although a single institution generally cannot influence a company's actions, a collection of institutions can. Prior to 1992, for an institutional investor to submit a slate of candidates for the board of directors and to get support for its candidates, it had to file a proxy statement with the SEC and mail copies to all other shareholders of the company. Today, however, federal regulations require only institutional shareholders who are seeking actual proxies or who hold a large percentage of a company's stock to file a proxy statement with the SEC. Shareholders may announce how they intend to vote on a matter and advertise their position in order to seek support. Consequently, institutional shareholders now have more influence than ever before.

ARBITRAGEURS

When a bid is made for a target company, the target company's stock price often trades at a small discount to the actual bid. This reflects the risk that the offer may not be accepted. Arbitrageurs ("Arbs") buy the stock and make a profit on the difference between the bid price and the current stock price if the deal is consummated. Arbs may accumulate a substantial percentage of the stock held outside of institutions to place themselves in a position to influence the outcome of

the takeover attempt. For example, if other offers appear, arbs promote their positions directly to managers and institutional investors with phone calls and
through leaks to the financial press. Arbs also provide market liquidity during
transactions. Arbs make it possible for institutional investors, who are willing to
accept less rather than risk losing their entire profit if the transaction is not completed, to sell their holdings of the target company shares prior to completion of
the transaction.

With the number of merger arbitrageurs increasing, arbs are becoming more
proactive in trying to anticipate takeover situations (i.e., firms that appear to be
undervalued). Arbs monitor rumors and share price movements to determine if
investors are accumulating a particular stock. Their objective is to identify the
target before the potential acquirer is required by law to announce its intentions.
Empirical studies show that the price of a target company's stock starts to rise in
advance of the announcement of a takeover attempt. Also, if one firm in an industry is acquired, it is commonplace for the share prices of other firms in the same
industry to also increase as they are viewed as potential targets. Exhibit 1-1 illustrates the implementation of a typical arbitrage strategy.

EXHIBIT 1-1. MERGER ARBITRAGE
IN PRACTICE

Normally following an announced merger, the price of the target's stock
rises but not to the offering price because of the uncertainty associated with
completing the transaction. A transaction may not be consummated, because it does not receive regulatory or shareholder approval or the acquirer
cannot arrange financing. The difference between the target's trading price
and the offer price is called the discount. The amount of the discount increases with the expected length of time until closing and the likelihood that
the deal will not close. The arb seeks to lock in this spread. To do this when
the offer is a cash offer, the arbitrageur merely has to buy the stock of the
target. However, when the offer is an exchange of securities, the investor
must also hedge against the possibility of the acquirer's stock falling. This
can be accomplished by selling the acquirer's stock short.[1]

Assume an acquirer offers to exchange one share of its stock for each
share of the target's stock, the acquirer and target's stocks are currently trading at $90 and $70 per share, respectively, and an arb buys the target's stock
at $85. This is the price the target's share reached immediately following
the announcement. The arb hedges his position by selling the acquirer's
stock short at $90. As the merger date approaches, this $5 spread between
the arb's purchase price for the target's stock and the acquirer's share price
(i.e., the offer price) will diminish as the prices of the target's and acquirer's
stock converge.

Once the merger is consummated and the target's stock is converted to the acquirer's stock, the arb locks in the $5 gain regardless of the current price of the acquirer's stock. The arb covers his short sale with the acquirer's stock valued at $90. If during the interim the market has declined, sending the acquirer's stock down to $70, the investor makes $20 on the short sale of the acquirer's stock at $90 less the loss of $15 on the target's shares for which he paid $85.

Arbitrage Strategy: Buy 1 share of target at $85/sell short 1 share of acquirer stock at $90.

Scenarios after merger	Gain (loss) on long position of $85	Gain (loss) on short position of $90	Total gain (loss)
Rise in acquirer's stock to $110:	$25	($20)	$5
Fall in acquirer's stock to $70:	($15)	$20	$5

If the merger takes 6 months to complete from the announcement date, the 5% profit realized in this example equates to an annualized gain of 10%. If the arb had borrowed half of the total investment in the arbitrage transaction, the annualized return would double.

The risk is that the merger will not be completed. The target's stock price should return to its original price of $70. The result would be a loss of $15 on the purchase of the target's stock at $85. Similarly, even if the acquirer's share price had fallen after the merger announcement, the acquirer's share price should return to its previous price of $90 after the transaction is called off. This occurs as short sellers cover their positions buying the acquirer's stock. Any investor who sold the acquirer's stock short at less than $90 would incur a loss on their short position in addition to the loss incurred on the target's shares.

[1] In a short sale, the arb instructs her broker to sell the acquirer's shares at a specific price. The broker loans the arb the shares and obtains the stock from its own inventory or borrows it from a customer's margin account or from another broker. If the acquirer's stock declines in price, the short seller can buy it back at the lower price and make a profit; if the stock increases, the short seller incurs a loss.

HISTORICAL MOTIVATIONS FOR MERGERS AND ACQUISITIONS

There are numerous theories of why mergers and acquisitions take place. For example, Arthur D. Little, Inc., identified 21 motives in a 1978 report to the Financial Executives Institute (Lajoux: 1998). In 1980, a U.S. Federal Trade Commission panel report based on a focus group of ten executives counted 31 motives for mergers and acquisitions (Rock, Rock and Sikora: 1994). Table 1-1 lists some

TABLE 1-1.   Common Theories of What Causes Mergers and Acquisitions

Theory	Motivation
Synergy	$1 + 1 = 3$

Operating synergy
      Economies of scale
      Economies of scope
	Improve operating efficiency through economies of scale or scope by acquiring a customer, supplier, or competitor

Financial synergy	Lower cost of capital by smoothing cash flow, realizing financial economies of scale, and better matching of investment opportunities with internal cash flows

Diversification
   New products/current markets
   New products/new markets
   Current products/new markets
	Position the firm in higher growth products or markets

Market power	Increase market share to improve ability to set and maintain prices above competitive levels

Strategic realignment
   Technological change
   Regulatory and political change
	Acquire needed capabilities to adapt more rapidly to environmental changes than developing them internally

Hubris (managerial pride)	Acquirers believe that their valuations of targets are more accurate than the market's causing them to overpay by overestimating the gains from synergy
Buying undervalued assets (Q-Ratio)	Acquire assets more cheaply when the stock of existing companies is less than the cost of buying or building the assets
Agency problems and mismanagement	Replace marginally competent managers or managers who are not acting in the best interests of the owners
Managerialism	Increase the size of a company to increase the power and pay of managers
Tax considerations	Obtain unused net operating losses and tax credits, asset write-ups, and substitute capital gains for ordinary income

of the more prominent theories about why mergers happen. Each of these theories is discussed in greater detail in the remainder of this section.

SYNERGY

Synergy is a widely used, albeit often misused, justification for making acquisitions. Synergy is the rather simplistic notion that the combination of two businesses can create greater shareholder value than if they are operated separately. There are two basic types of synergy: operating and financial.

Operating Synergy

Operating synergy consists of both economies of scale and economies of scope. Gains in efficiency can come from either factor as well as improved managerial practices. Both economies of scale and scope assume a level of management talent in place to realize the benefits of operating synergy.

Economies of Scale

Economies of scale refer to the spreading of fixed costs over increasing production levels. Scale is defined by such fixed costs as depreciation of equipment and amortization of capitalized software; normal maintenance spending; obligations such as interest expense, lease payments, and union, customer and vendor contracts; and taxes. Such costs are fixed in the sense that they cannot be altered in the short-run. Consequently, for a given scale or level of fixed expenses, the dollar value of fixed expenses per dollar of revenue decreases as output and sales increase.

Economies of scale are most frequently seen in manufacturing operations, although they can be important in any business having substantial fixed overhead expenses. Declining per-unit expenses reflect improving labor productivity as workers and managers learn how to improve workflow. Per-unit costs continue to fall until the firm begins to experience inefficiencies associated with managing very large organizations. Economies of scale are most evident in very high fixed-cost industries such as utilities, steel making, pharmaceutical, chemical, and aircraft manufacturing.

There is only marginal empirical support for using mergers to achieve economies of scale. Some research suggests a correlation between changes in ownership and improvements in efficiency (Lictenberg and Siegel: 1987). However, simple correlation does not demonstrate a causal link between corporate takeovers and lower operating costs due to economies of scale. There is some evidence that operating efficiencies in vertical integration may be significant. By combining firms at different stages of production, better communication and coordination as well as less customer–vendor bargaining may result in improved product planning and implementation (Klein, Crawford, and Alchian: 1978). By acquiring a supplier, a firm may avoid potential disruptions in supply that might occur when independent supplier agreements expire (Carlton and Perloff: 1994).

Economies of Scope

Economies of scope refer to using a specific set of skills or an asset currently employed in producing a specific product or service to produce related products or services. For example, Proctor and Gamble, the consumer products giant, uses its highly regarded consumer marketing skills to market a full range of personal care as well as pharmaceutical products. Honda utilizes its skills in enhancing internal combustion engines to develop motorcycles, lawn mowers, and snow blowers, as well as automobiles. Sequent Technology lets customers run applications on UNIX and NT operating systems on a single computer system. Citigroup uses the same computer center to process loan applications, deposits, trust services, and mutual fund accounts for its bank's customers. Small banks, which do not have sufficient revenue to provide trust services and investment advice, may be able to afford to provide such services if they merge (Mester: 1987).

Financial Synergy

Financial synergy refers to the impact of mergers and acquisitions on the cost of capital of the acquiring firm or the newly formed firm resulting from the merger or acquisition. Theoretically, the cost of capital could be reduced if the merged firms have uncorrelated cash flows, realize financial economies of scale, or result in a better matching of investment opportunities with internally generated funds.

Financial Economies of Scale

Another example of financial synergy is the reduction in cost of capital resulting from lower securities and transactions costs (Levy and Sarnat: 1970). Larger firms should be able to issue debt at a lower average interest rate and also lower average cost to issue the debt because SEC registration fees, legal fees, and printing costs are spread over the firm's larger bond issue. Similar logic applies to issuing common equity.

Better Matching of Opportunities with Internally Generated Funds

Combining a firm with excess cash flows with one whose internally generated cash flow is insufficient to fund its investment opportunities may result in a lower cost of borrowing (Nielsen and Melicher: 1973). A firm in a mature industry whose growth is slowing may produce cash flows well in excess of available investment opportunities. Another firm in a high-growth industry may have more investment opportunities than the cash to fund them. Reflecting their different growth rates and risk levels, the firm in the mature industry may have a lower cost of capital than the one in the high-growth industry. Combining the two firms might result in a lower cost of capital for the merged firms because of lower perceived risk by investors, savings in flotation and transactions costs, and a more efficient allocation of capital as the higher growth opportunities are funded by cash generated by the more mature business.

DIVERSIFICATION

Diversification refers to a strategy of buying firms outside of a company's current primary lines of business. There are two commonly used justifications for diversification.

Firms often justify diversification on the basis of reducing shareholder risk by stabilizing overall revenue through shifting a portion of the firm's assets from a cyclical to what is perceived to be a more stable industry. If the two firms have cash flows that are uncorrelated, their combined cash flow may be less volatile than their cash flows viewed separately. Consequently, investors may believe that the combined firms are less likely to default on their obligations than the firms viewed separately and require a lower rate of return to invest in the combined firm's securities. This is also referred to as "co-insurance." This was the announced motivation for U.S. Steel's mid-1980s acquisition of Marathon Oil to form USX. At the time, oil and gas revenues appeared to be considerably more predictable than steel industry revenues. This justification for diversification by firms has always been on shaky theoretical grounds (Levy and Sarnat: 1970). Shareholders can efficiently spread their investments and risk among industries, thus obviating the need for companies to diversify on behalf of their shareholders.

The second common argument for diversification is for firms to shift from their core product lines or markets into product lines or markets that have higher growth prospects. The product–market matrix illustrated in Table 1-2 illustrates this strategy. If a company's current products are not selling well due to increased competition, or if the overall growth rate of its current markets is slowing, the firm may accelerate growth by assuming somewhat more risk in shifting current products it already understands how to produce to new markets that are somewhat unfamiliar and therefore more risky. Similarly, the firm may attempt to achieve higher growth rates by developing new products, untested in the marketplace, and selling them into familiar and less risky current markets.

Diversified Company Performance

The performance of diversified companies has changed dramatically over time. In a study of the highly diversified conglomerates of the 1960s, Schipper and Thompson (1983) found that the share prices of such firms responded positively to announcements of new acquisitions prior to 1967. After 1967, legislation such as the Williams Act of 1968 and the Tax Reform Act of 1969 created new challenges to the types of M&A activity that took place during the 1960s (see Chapters 2 and 10).

TABLE 1-2. Product–Market Matrix

Markets:	Current	Related	New
Products			
Current	Lower growth/ lower risk		Higher growth/ higher risk
Related			
New	Higher growth/ higher risk		Highest growth/ highest risk

With the passage of time, the perceived value of diversification diminished significantly. In a comparison of the stock performance of 13 conglomerates with the Standard and Poor's (S&P) 500, Ravenscraft and Scherer (1988) showed that investments in conglomerates made prior to 1968 dramatically outperformed the overall market through 1983. However, investments made in 1968, the peak in conglomerate share prices, underperformed the S&P 500 through 1983. These findings were contradicted in a study of 337 mergers between 1957 and 1975 in which the share prices of conglomerate mergers outperformed nonconglomerate mergers in the sample (Elgers and Clark: 1980).

More recent studies have supported the conclusion that investors do not benefit from diversification. Investors perceive companies diversified in unrelated areas as riskier because they are difficult for management to understand (Morck, Schleiffer, and Vishny: 1990). Empirical studies also show that unrelated acquisitions are four times more likely to be divested than those related to the acquirer's core business (Kaplan and Weisbach: 1992). Berger and Ofek (1995) reported that between 1986 and 1991, for a sample of 100 large firms, that the average diversified firm destroyed about 13 to 15% of its market value and that the loss of value tended to be larger the greater the degree of unrelated diversification.

Corporate Focus versus Diversification

In a study of corporate performance during the 1980s, Comment and Jarrell (1993) found that stock returns tended to increase as firms increased their focus, and concluded that greater corporate focus is consistent with shareholder wealth maximization. This conclusion was supported in a study of corporate spin-offs, a process in which a parent will dividend the stock in a wholly owned subsidiary to its shareholders (see Chapter 13). The increase in market value of firms spinning off businesses in unrelated industries was substantially greater than for firms getting rid of businesses operating in the same industry as the parent firm's core business (Daley, Mehrotra, and Sivakumar, 1996). Berger and Ofek (1996) found that asset sales lead to an improvement in operating performance in the year following the sale; the improvement occurs mainly in firms that increase their focus.

STRATEGIC REALIGNMENT

This theory suggests that firms use M&As as ways of rapidly adjusting to changes in their external environments. Although change can come from many different sources, I consider only changes in the regulatory environment and technological innovation. During the 1990s these two factors have been major forces in creating new opportunities for growth or threats to a firm's primary line of business.

Regulatory Change

M&A activity in recent years has centered in industries that have been subject to significant deregulation. These industries include financial services, health care, utilities, media, telecommunications, and defense.

The advent of deregulation broke down artificial barriers in these industries and stimulated competition. In some states, utilities are now required to sell power to competitors, which can resell the power in the utility's own marketplace. Some utilities are responding to this increased competition by attempting to achieve greater operating efficiency through mergers and acquisitions. In financial services, commercial banks are moving well beyond their historical role of accepting deposits and granting loans and into investment banking, insurance, and mutual funds. The Financial Services Modernization Act of 1999 repealed depression-era legislation that prevented banks, securities firms, and insurance companies from merging. The legislation could accelerate the trend toward mega-financial services companies typified by the 1998 Citicorp-Travelers merger.

Historically, local and long-distance phone companies were not allowed to compete against each other. Cable companies were essentially monopolies. Following the Telecommunications Reform Act of 1996, local and long-distance companies are actively encouraged to compete in each other's markets (Case Study 1-1). AT&T, confined in the 1980s largely to the long-distance market, is now among the leading suppliers of cable, wireless, and Internet access services as well as long-distance services. Cable companies are moving to offer Internet access as well as local telephone service. Radio and television broadcasters are now permitted to own far more stations. During the first half of the 1990s, the U.S. Department of Defense actively encouraged consolidation of the nation's major defense contractors to improve their overall operating efficiency.

CASE STUDY 1-1. AT&T'S RESURGENCE IN TELECOMMUNICATIONS

Following the break-up of "Ma Bell" in 1984, it appeared that there would never again be a behemoth dominating the telecommunications industry. This is the position that AT&T had for almost 100 years until a changing political and regulatory climate exploded AT&T into a series of independent operating companies.

Once again, the competitive landscape changed radically in 1999. Shortly after completing a $70 billion acquisition of the cable company, Tele-Communications Inc., AT&T announced the $54 billion acquisition of MediaOne Group. These transactions make AT&T the biggest player in the cable industry, with customers in 60% of U.S. households currently using cable television. The strategy is to give AT&T high speed access into millions of U.S. households, through which customers can be offered bundled services such as voice (telephone), video (television), and Internet access.

Source: "AT&T and MediaOne Group Sign Definitive Merger Agreement," AT&T Press Release, May 6, 1999.

Technological Change

Technology has disrupted the status quo throughout history. Certain technological advances have created new competitors, products, markets, and industries at a blinding pace. The advent of the railroad opened up the western United States, allowing a more rapid and less expensive flow of products between the eastern and western states. The development of the airplane provided faster, easier access to more distant geographic areas and created new industries, such as the passenger airline, avionics, and satellite industries. The vacuum tube, transistor, and microchip provided the basis for the television, radio, and the personal computer. The telephone ultimately evolved into wireless communication. The emergence of satellite delivery of cable network to local systems ignited explosive growth in the cable industry. Today, with the expansion of broadband technology, we are witnessing the convergence of voice, data, and video technologies on the Internet.

Although the pace of technological progress has been rapid in the past, there is evidence that it is likely to accelerate in the future. Today, the so-called digital world is driving the nation's economic growth and dramatically changing the global workplace. The U.S. Commerce Department notes that the information technology (IT) industries accounted for only 8% of the U.S. gross domestic product (GDP) between 1995 and 1998. However, the IT sector of the economy contributed one-third of the nation's economic growth during this period. IT industries include firms that produce computers, communication hardware, and software and services. From 1995–1998, investment in computers and communication equipment accounted for one-half of all business spending (U.S. Department of Commerce: 1998, p. 19). By 2006, almost half of all U.S. workers will be employed in industries that either produce IT or are major IT users (U.S. Department of Commerce: 1998, p. 37).

The acceleration in the use of IT is likely to boost technology's role in motivating corporate takeovers and restructuring. Large, more bureaucratic firms are often unable to exhibit the creativity and speed smaller, more nimble, niche players display. With engineering talent often in short supply and product life cycles shortening, firms often do not have the luxury of time or the resources to innovate. Consequently large companies often look to mergers and acquisitions as a fast and sometimes less expensive way to acquire new technologies and proprietary know-how to fill gaps in their current product offering or to enter entirely new businesses. Cisco Systems, the well-known network router company, made 42 acquisitions between 1997 and 1999 to add new products, update their current portfolio of technologies, and to add emerging technologies. Acquiring technologies can also be used as a defensive weapon to keep important new technologies out of the hands of competitors.

The growing importance of technological change will modify the way we evaluate and value target companies, increase the importance of intangible assets such as intellectual property, and the way in which deals are structured. The accelerating pace of new technology will also tend to drive the pace of deregulation, because the speed of technological change makes it increasingly unlikely that any one company can continue to remain a monopoly. This is the basis on which many argue that Microsoft should not be viewed as a monopoly. These issues are explored in more detail in Chapters 2, 5, 7, and 10 of this book.

HUBRIS AND THE "WINNER'S CURSE"

The hubris hypothesis is an explanation of why mergers may happen even if the current market value of the target firm reflects its true economic value. As a result of hubris, managers believe that their own valuation of a target firm is superior to the market's valuation. Thus, the acquiring company tends to overpay for the target because of over-optimism in evaluating potential synergies.

Even in the presence of significant synergies, competition among bidders is likely to result in the winner overpaying because of hubris, even if significant synergies are present (Roll: 1986). Senior managers tend to be very competitive and sometimes self-important. The desire not to lose can result in a bidding war that can drive the purchase price of an acquisition well in excess of the actual economic value of that company.

Hubris or ego-driven decision making is a factor contributing to the so-called "winner's curse." In an auction environment where there are many bidders, there is likely to be a wide range of bids for a target company. The winning bid is often substantially in excess of the expected value of the target company, given the difficulty all participants have in estimating the actual value of the target company and the competitive nature of the process. The winner is cursed in the sense that he paid more than the company is worth (Capen, Clapp, and Campbell: 1971).

THE Q-RATIO AND BUYING UNDERVALUED ASSETS

The q-ratio is defined as the ratio of the market value of the acquiring firm's stock to the replacement cost of its assets. Firms interested in expansion have a choice of investing in new plant and equipment or obtaining the assets by acquiring a company whose market value is less than the replacement cost of its assets (i.e., q-ratio <1). This theory was very useful in explaining M&A activity during the 1970s when high inflation and interest rates depressed stock prices well below the book value of many firms. High inflation also caused the replacement cost of assets to be much higher than the book value of assets.

AGENCY PROBLEMS

Agency problems arise when there is a difference between the interest of incumbent managers and the firm's shareholders. This happens when management owns a small fraction of the outstanding shares of the firm. These managers are more inclined to focus on maintaining job security and a lavish lifestyle than maximizing shareholder value. When the shares of a company are widely held, the cost of mismanagement is spread across a large number of shareholders. Each shareholder bears only a small portion of the cost. This allows for such misman-agement to be tolerated for long periods of time. According to this theory, mergers take place to correct situations where there is a separation between what the man-agers may want and what the owners want. Low stock prices put pressure on managers to take actions to raise the share price or become the target of acquirers, who perceive the stock to be undervalued (Fama and Jensen: 1983).

TAX CONSIDERATIONS

There are two important issues in discussing the role of taxes as a motive for M&As. The first involves the tax benefits associated with the target's unused net operating losses and tax credits as well as the revaluation or write-up of acquired assets. The second concerns the tax-free status of the deal. These issues are dis-cussed in greater detail in Chapter 10.

Tax benefits such as loss carry forward, and investment tax credits can be used to offset the combined firms' taxable income. Additional tax shelter is created if the acquisition is recorded under the purchase method of accounting, which re-quires the book value of the acquired assets to be revalued to their current market value. The resulting depreciation of these generally higher asset values also shel-ters future income generated by the combined companies (see Chapter 10).

The taxable nature of the transaction will frequently play a more important role in determining if the merger takes place than any tax benefits that accrue to the acquiring company. The tax-free status of the transaction may be viewed by the seller as a prerequisite for the deal to take place. A properly structured transaction can allow the target shareholders to defer any capital gain resulting from the trans-action. If the transaction is not tax-free, the seller will normally want a higher purchase price to compensate for the tax liability resulting from the transaction.

MARKET POWER

This theory suggests that firms merge to improve their monopoly power to set product prices at levels not sustainable in a more competitive market. Early em-pirical studies failed to support this theory. In one study of 11 mergers challenged by antitrust authorities, only 2 of the 11 mergers examined displayed statistically significant (i.e., results not due to chance) abnormal positive financial returns (Stillman: 1983). Another study hypothesized that if the market power theory is correct, mergers that are likely to be challenged as anticompetitive should show abnormal negative financial returns when they are first announced. In a sample of 126 horizontal and vertical mergers, the study found statistically significant posi-tive abnormal returns when the merger was first announced, but no negative re-turns when investigations were undertaken by the regulatory authorities (Eckbo: 1981). These results suggest that investors apparently did not believe that the regu-latory authorities would find these business combinations anticompetitive. Pre-sumably, the motivation for these mergers was something other than a desire to gain market power.

More recent studies do show that market power may be a motive in some instances. According to one study, mergers in the airline industry in the late 1980s did result in higher ticket prices (Kim and Singal: 1993). A study by Judith Chevalier (Gaughan: 1999, p. 150) found that supermarket chains that had undergone leveraged buyouts tended to have the highest price increases in their regional markets.

MANAGERIALISM

Self-serving managers are presumed to make poorly planned acquisitions to increase the size of the acquiring firm and their own compensation. This theory assumes that compensation received by senior management is determined by the size of their firm (D. C. Mueller: 1969). However, this basic premise may be incorrect, as there is empirical evidence that management compensation is determined more by profitability than size (Lewellen and Huntsman: 1970).

HISTORICAL MERGER AND ACQUISITION WAVES

M&A activity in the United States came in five identifiable waves in the last century (see Figure 1-3). Two preceded and three followed World War II (Gaughan: 1996).

THE FIRST WAVE: HORIZONTAL CONSOLIDATION, 1897–1904

This period was marked by a Darwinian struggle of survival of the fittest. M&A activity was spurred by a drive for efficiency, lax enforcement of the Sherman Anti-Trust Act, westward migration, and technological change. Mergers during this period were largely horizontal and resulted in increased concentration in primary metals, transportation, and mining. Fraudulent financing and the stock market crash of 1904 ended this boom.

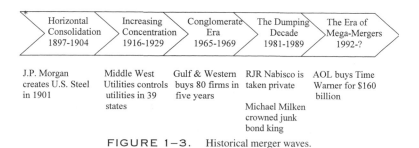

FIGURE 1–3.   Historical merger waves.

During this period, mergers were characterized by large companies absorbing small ones. In 1901, J. P. Morgan created America's first billion-dollar corporation, U.S. Steel. U.S. Steel was formed by the combination of 785 separate companies, the largest of which was Carnegie Steel. Other giants that were formed during this era included Standard Oil, Eastman Kodak, American Tobacco, and General Electric.

THE SECOND WAVE:
INCREASING CONCENTRATION, 1916–1929

Activity during this period was a result of the entry of the United States into World War I and the postwar economic boom. Mergers also tended to be horizontal and further increased industry concentration. For example, Samuel Insull built his utilities' empire consisting of operations in 39 states. This era came to a close as a consequence of the stock market crash of 1929 and the passage of the Clayton Act, which further defined what constituted monopolistic practices.

THE THIRD WAVE:
THE CONGLOMERATE ERA, 1965–1969

This period of M&A activity was spawned by the desire to diversify and was characterized by the emergence of financial engineering and conglomeration. A rising stock market and the longest period of uninterrupted growth in the nation's history up to that time resulted in record price-to-earnings (P/E) ratios. Companies given high P/E ratios by investors learned how to grow earnings per share (EPS) through acquisition, rather than through reinvestment. Stock-for-stock transactions became increasingly commonplace.

Companies with high P/E ratios would often acquire firms with lower P/E ratios and increase the EPS of the combined companies. The increase in EPS boosted the share price of the combined companies, as long as the P/E applied to the stock price of the combined companies did not fall below the P/E of the acquiring company before the transaction. However, for this pyramiding effect to continue, target companies had to have earnings growth rates sufficiently attractive to convince investors to apply the higher multiple of the acquiring company to the combined companies. In time, the number of high-growth, relatively low P/E companies declined, as conglomerates bid their P/Es up. The higher prices paid for the targets, coupled with the increasing leverage of the conglomerates, caused the pyramids to collapse (see Exhibit 1-2).

Companies such as ITT, Litton Industries, and LTV acquired firms in totally diverse industries that had absolutely nothing to do with one another. Because so much of this period's merger activity was by conglomerates, there was relatively little increase in concentration within industries. This was in marked contrast to the earlier merger waves in which industry concentration increased dramatically.

EXHIBIT 1-2. THE PYRAMID GAME

Assume that a diversified growth company selling at 25 times earnings[a] acquires a firm selling at 15 times earnings[b] and that it has to pay a premium[c] of 20 times earnings to acquire a controlling interest in the target company. Each firm has 5 million shares outstanding and after-tax earnings of $10 million. The market value of the combined firms increases if the P/E multiple applied to the acquirer is also applied to the combined firms following the acquisition.

	Acquirer	Target	Combined firms
P/E	25	15	25
After-tax earnings	$10 million	$10 million	$20 million
Shares outstanding	5 million	5 million	9 million[d]
E/S	$2.00	$2.00	$2.22
Price per share (P/E applied to combined firms = 25)	$50.00	$40.00	$55.50
Price per share (P/E applied to combined firms = 20)	$50.00	$40.00	$44.40

[a] Current share price: Acquirer = (25 × $10 million) / 5 million shares outstanding = $50; target = (15 × $10 million) / 5 million shares outstanding = $30.

[b] Offer price: Because the acquiring firm has agreed to pay 20 times the target's after-tax earnings of $10 million to acquire all of the target's five million shares outstanding, the offer price per share of the target company is (20 × $10 million) / 5 million shares = $40.

[c] Premium: Offer price / target's current price = $40 / $30 = 33%.

[d] New shares issued: The number of new shares issued by the acquirer is ($40/$50) × 5 million shares outstanding = 4 million in exchange for the 5 million target shares outstanding.

There were many famous deal makers during the third wave. Among the most famous included Harold Geneen of ITT, Ben Heineman of Northwest Industries, Larry Tisch of Loews, and Charles Bludhorn of Gulf & Western. However, the personality most associated with this period was James Joseph Ling (see Case Study 1-2).

By the early 1970s, conglomerates were largely out of favor with investors. Their stock prices frequently traded at a discount from the overall market. Some observers believe that this "conglomerate discount" reflected the perception by investors that conglomerates were difficult to manage because of the diversity of businesses in their portfolios and the difficulty Wall Street analysts had in evaluating and understanding the value of the individual operations.

CASE STUDY 1-2. JAMES LING, MASTER
OF FINANCIAL ENGINEERING

Widely viewed as a financial wizard, Ling mastered the art of complicated financial transactions. Although Ling understood the leveraged buyout strategy, he was largely opposed to turning a quick profit by selling off assets. He bought companies with a long-term strategy in mind. Ling's prowess as a deal maker reached legendary proportions as he transformed a $2,000 investment in a small electronics firm into the fourteenth largest corporation in the United States. Ling's company, LTV, was the epitome of sprawling conglomerates and included major U.S. businesses such as Jones & Laughlin Steel, the nation's sixth largest steel company; Braniff Airways, a domestic and international carrier; and Tempco and Vought Aircraft, major defense contractors. LTV went through a period of poor financial performance, which ultimately forced Ling to restructure the business. Ling was finally forced out of the company by dissident shareholders and bondholders due to inconsistent financial results and an antitrust lawsuit by the Justice Department. LTV eventually went through a long period of bankruptcy, eventually emerging as a shadow of its former self.

Source: Brown, 1972.

THE FOURTH WAVE: THE DUMPING DECADE, 1981–1989

While James Ling was among the most famous deal makers of the 1960s, the 1980s saw the rise of such corporate raiders as Carl Icahn and T. Boone Pickens and the emergence of the hostile takeover. Prior to this period, there were relatively few hostile takeovers. They were viewed as unethical, and large, reputable companies engaged only in friendly takeovers in which the target's management embraced the acquirer's proposal. If the target's management rejected the offer, the takeover effort was generally dropped. This changed in 1974 with the takeover of Electronic Storage Battery (ESB), the world's largest maker of batteries, by International Nickel of Canada.

The decade of the 1980s was characterized by a break-up of many of the major conglomerates and a proliferation of financial buyers using the hostile takeover and the LBO as their primary acquisition strategies (see Case Study 1-3). Management buyouts and takeovers of U.S. companies by foreign acquirers became more common. Conglomerates began to divest unrelated acquisitions made in the 1960s and early 1970s. Sixty percent of acquisitions made outside of the acquiring company's primary industry between 1970 and 1982 were sold by 1989 (Wasserstein: 1998). In 1988, the mega-railroad Burlington Northern spun off Burlington

Resources, its energy properties, for $4.2 billion. The same year Mobil Oil sold retailer Montgomery Ward for $3.8 billion. In 1989, Paramount, formerly Gulf and Western Industries, sold its finance company, Associates First Capital, for $3.4 billion.

CASE STUDY 1-3. THE GIBSON GREETING CARDS' LEVERAGED BUYOUT

The success of the LBO of Gibson Greeting Cards by an investor group headed by William Simon, former Secretary of the Treasury, in the early 1980s sparked considerable interest in this takeover technique. Wesray, under the direction of Simon, purchased Gibson Greeting Cards from RCA for $81 million. Using Gibson's assets as collateral, Wesray investors provided only $1 million in equity capital and borrowed the rest. Three years later, Wesray sold 50% of the company for $87 million.

Source: Melicher and Norton (1999).

For the first time, takeovers of U.S. companies by foreign firms in the 1980s exceeded in number and dollars the acquisitions by U.S. firms of companies in Europe, Canada, and the Pacific Rim, excluding Japan. The motivation for foreign purchases of U.S. companies stemmed from the size of the market, limited restrictions on takeovers, the sophistication of U.S. firm's technology, and the weaknesses of the dollar against major foreign currencies. Foreign companies also tended to pay substantial premiums for U.S. companies since the strength of their currencies lowered the effective cost of acquisitions. Moreover, favorable accounting practices allowed foreign buyers to write off goodwill in the year in which it occurred, unlike U.S. firms which had to charge goodwill expense against earnings for many years. The largest cross-border deals of the 1980s included the Beecham Group PLC (UK) purchase of the SmithKline Beckman Corporation for $16.1 billion in 1989. In 1987, British Petroleum Corporation acquired the remaining 45% of Standard Oil Corporation for $7.8 billion. Campeau Corporation of Canada purchased Federated Department Stores for $6.5 billion in 1988.

During the 1980s, LBOs were used to finance hostile takeovers, whereas today they are more likely to be used to finance management buyouts. Among the most famous of the financiers of the time was Drexel Burnham's junk bond king, Michael Milken, named for his prowess in arranging financing for highly leveraged and largely unsecured transactions.

The fortunes of LBOs waned during the second half of the decade. RJR Nabisco exemplifies the challenges faced by LBOs during this period. Kohlberg, Kravis & Roberts (KKR) paid $24.5 billion for the company in 1988, a record purchase price at the time. Despite going public in 1991, RJR Nabisco struggled under the burden of its massive debt until the mid-1990s, when improving cash flow enabled the firm to pay off a significant portion of its debt. Other LBO transactions also fell upon hard times. Campeau Corporation's leveraged buyouts of Allied Store and Federated Department Stores resulted in Federated's declaring bankruptcy.

Toward the end of the decade, the level of merger activity slowed in line with a slowing economy and widely publicized LBO bankruptcies. Moreover, the junk bond market dried up as a major source of financing with the demise of Drexel Burnham, the leading underwriter and "market-maker" for high-yield securities.

THE FIFTH WAVE:
THE AGE OF THE MEGA-MERGER, 1992–?

Following the 1980s, many believed that the M&As during the 1980s were largely overpriced and overleveraged. Moreover, junk bond or high-yield financing was thought unlikely to recover from its pummeling during the late 1980s. Consequently, many assumed that takeovers would not return to their levels of the late 1980s.

While M&A activity did taper off during the 1990 recession, the number of transactions and the dollar volume has rebounded sharply since 1992. The combination of the IT revolution, continued deregulation, reductions in trade barriers, and the global trend toward privatization powered the longest economic expansion and stock market boom in U.S. history.

By 1999, the announced dollar volume of global M&A activity set a new record of $3.43 trillion. This figure was 36% above 1998's dollar value of $2.52 trillion. The total number of announced transactions reached 31,528 in 1999. The bulk of this robust increase came in Europe where the announced dollar volume of $1.2 trillion was more than double its 1998 level.

In the United States, 1999's announced dollar volume rose by a more modest 7.4% over its 1998 level of $1.63 trillion to $1.75 trillion, its seventh consecutive annual record. This increase in the dollar volume of activity came despite a decline in the number of U.S. transactions from 1998's record level of 12,300 to 10,800 in 1999 (Thompson Financial Securities Data Corporation, 2000). The average purchase price paid for U.S. businesses jumped approximately 22% from $13.3 million in 1998 to $16.2 million in 1999.

The surge in the average purchase price reflected both the declining number of transactions and the lofty stock market. Stock prices usually serve as a floor on merger prices, because target company shareholders are rarely willing to accept a buyout offer at less than the current market value of their stock. In the mid-1990s, the average P/E ratio for S&P 500 companies hovered at 18 times earnings over the prior 52 weeks. In 1999, P/E ratios averaged more than 30 times trailing 52-week earnings. Moreover, the average premium paid by an acquirer above the target's current stock price rose in 1999 to about 40%, up from 35% in 1998 (*Wall Street Journal,* October 12, 1999). Consequently, not only were current share prices for many businesses at extraordinarily high levels, but acquirers, whose share prices may also have been overvalued, were willing to pay more to get a controlling interest.

The impact of this escalation in purchase prices during the 1990s is apparent in a comparison of the top five "completed" transactions ranked by purchase price for each decade from the 1950s through the 1990s (Table 1-3). Completed transactions are those that actually closed in the decade in which they were

TABLE 1-3. Largest "Completed" Transactions by Decade—1950s through the 1990s (Ranked by Dollar Value)[a]

Decade	Buyer	Target	Value
1990s			
1999	Exxon	Mobil	$85.2 billion
1999	SBC Communications	Ameritech	$80.6 billion
1999	Vodafone	AirTouch	$74.4 billion
1998	Travelers Group	Citicorp	$72.6 billion
1998	AT&T	TCI	$69.9 billion
1980s			
1988	Kohlberg Kravis Roberts	RJR Nabisco	$24.6 billion
1989	Beecham Group PLC	SmithKline Beckman	$16.1 billion
1984	Chevron	Gulf	$13.2 billion
1988	Phillip Morris	Kraft	$13.1 billion
1989	Bristol-Meyers	Squibb	$12.0 billion
1970s			
1979	Shell Oil	Belridge Oil	$3.7 billion
1979	Exxon	Reliance Electric	$1.4 billion
1978	United Technologies	Carrier Corp.	$1.3 billion
1978	RJRNabisco	DelMonte	$936 million
1979	Mobil	General Crude Oil	$763 million
1960s			
1969	Atlantic Richfield	Sinclair Oil	$1.9 billion
1969	Rapid-American	Glen Alden Corp	$1.3 billion
1968	Ling-Temco-Vought	Jones & Laughlin	$1.1 billion
1969	Lykes Corp.	Youngstown Sheet & Tube	$1.0 billion
1967	McDonnell	Douglas Aircraft	$850 million
1950s			
1959	General Telephone	Sylvania	$265 million
1954	Mathieson Chemical	Olin Industries	$233 million
1955	Sperry Corp.	Remington Rand	$208 million
1955	Sunray Oil	Mid-Continental Petroleum	$186 million
1956	Gulf Oil	Warren Petroleum	$164 million

[a] From: "1990s—Securities Data Corporation; 1980s—Mergerstat; 1950s–1970s—Forbes, "A Century of Deals," April 10, 1999, www.forbes.com.

proposed. The average purchase price of the top five transactions during the 1990s was about 4 times the average during the 1980s but 400 times the average of the 1950s.

A number of other mergers and acquisitions have been announced, but have not yet been completed, that are substantially larger than those listed in Table 1-4. In February 2000, U.K.-based Vodafone AirTouch announced that it had reached agreement to buy Mannesmann of Germany for $183 billion to create the world's largest cellular phone company. This came thirty days after AOL announced its intentions to acquire Time Warner for $160 billion (see Case Study 1-5).

The buoyant market for corporate transactions during the late 1990s seemed reminiscent of the 1960s "pyramid game." In the 1960s, many believed that companies with high P/Es acquiring lower P/E companies were able to boost the market value of the combined firms as long as investors were willing to value the new company's earnings using the acquirer's P/E. The difference in the late 1990s was that the shares of many companies were selling at huge multiples of revenue because they had no reported earnings. This was particularly apparent in the feeding frenzy for Internet-related companies (see Case Study 1-4).

DO MERGERS AND ACQUISITIONS PAY OFF FOR SHAREHOLDERS?

Unfortunately, the answer to this question is ambiguous. The answer seems to depend on for whom and over what period of time. Around the announcement date of the transaction, average returns to target firm shareholders are about 30%. In contrast, the shareholders of acquiring firms generally show returns that range from slightly negative to modestly positive around the announcement date. Over longer periods of time, many M&As either underperform their industry peers or destroy shareholder value.

Two approaches have been employed to measure the impact of takeovers on shareholder value. The first approach, premerger returns, involves the examination of abnormal stock returns to the shareholders of both bidders and targets around the announcement of an offer and includes both successful and unsuccessful takeovers. The second approach, postmerger returns, measures the impact on shareholder value after the merger has been completed.

PREMERGER RETURNS TO SHAREHOLDERS

Positive abnormal returns represent gains for shareholders, which could be explained by such factors as improved efficiency, pricing power, or tax benefits. To measure the effect on stock value of an announcement of a tender offer, analysts calculate the expected price for each day by regressing the return on a firm's stock

CASE STUDY 1-4. CMGI USES HIGHLY INFLATED STOCK TO BUY STOCKS THAT ARE HIGHLY INFLATED

David S. Wetherell, the founder and CEO of Internet holding company and venture capital fund CMGI, has become something of a guru when it comes to picking the next winner on the Internet. His approach has been conceptually simple. Take small stakes in emerging Internet companies, grow them until they become commercially viable, and then sell them to strategic buyers. CMGI uses its lofty stock price to acquire Internet companies Wetherell believes have excellent growth prospects not yet apparent to other investors.

Reflecting his success, CMGI's stock has skyrocketed on a split-adjusted basis from 33¢ when it was initially offered in February 1994 to $165 in April 1999. A $100 investment in CMGI's IPO would have been worth $31,500 at its April high. The company has a market value of $10 billion, despite its 1999 revenues of only $176 million and an operating loss of $127 million.

His successes have been legendary. In 1995, he paid $2 million for 80% of the Internet portal Lycos. CMGI sold portions of its holdings in 1997 and 1998; nonetheless, its remaining 17% stake was worth $900 million at the end of 1999. In 1996, CMGI bought a one-third stake in GeoCities, a home page-building website, for about $6 million. In 1998, CMGI sold its stake to Yahoo for more than $1 billion.

Escalating stock prices for Internet companies may imperil CMGI's business model. The continued success of the company is heavily dependent on finding high potential companies whose price-to-sales[1] ratios are low relative to CMGI's, because their inherent value has not yet been "discovered" by other investors. The dilemma the company faces is much the same as that faced by the conglomerate acquirers of the 1960s who used their inflated stock to purchase high-growth, low P/E companies. As investor scrutiny of Internet IPOs and start-ups intensifies, the share prices of those with the highest potential will appreciate rapidly, making it increasingly difficult for companies like CMGI to find "undervalued" firms.

Despite this concern, CMGI took minority positions in sixty Internet companies in 1999 alone. The expectation is that 10–15% of these companies can be taken public during the subsequent 1–2 years. To fund these new ventures, CMGI continues to sell stakes in its ten most highly successful majority-owned businesses.

[1] Note that many Internet companies without earnings are valued based on the ratio of their market value to revenue.

Source: CMGI 1998 10K filing, and *Business Week,* 1999.

price against the return on a stock market index. The difference each day between the firm's actual return and the return predicted by the regression model is the abnormal rate of return for that day. The difference is then averaged across all firms in the sample to minimize the effects of factors specific to individual firms that could distort the returns. The final step is to cumulate the average abnormal returns for each day to create the cumulative average return.

The results of numerous studies of returns to shareholders of both bidding and target firms, computed over a preacquisition period starting immediately before the announcement and ending on or before the effective date of the tender offer, for both successful and unsuccessful tender offers, are summarized in Table 1-4. Despite the difficulty in distinguishing between the two different types of take-overs (Schwert: 1999), these studies often associate tender offers and mergers with hostile and friendly takeovers, respectively. Moreover, these studies usually assume that share prices fully adjust to anticipated synergies that could materialize as a result of the acquisition; and, therefore, they reflect both the short- and long-term effects of the acquisition.

Returns to Target Shareholders: Successful and Unsuccessful Offers

These studies suggest that during the 1970s and 1980s successful tender offers resulted in significant abnormal returns ranging from 30–45% reflecting the frequent bidder strategy of offering a substantial premium to preempt other potential bidders and the potential for revising the initial offer due to competing bids. These returns compare to about 20% for presumed friendly mergers during the same period. Returns from tender offers typically exceed those from mergers, which are characterized by less contentious negotiated settlements between the boards and management of the bidder and the target firm. Moreover, mergers often do not receive competing bids.

Premerger returns to target shareholders in successful takeovers have increased substantially since the 1960s, reflecting the 1968 Williams Act requirement to disclose "toehold" investments in target firms and the proliferation of state anti-takeover laws providing for a delay before a tender offer can be completed. This delay enables targets to add takeover defenses (see Chapters 2 and 3 for more details).

Unsuccessful takeovers may also result in significant returns for target company shareholders around the announcement date, but much of the gain quickly dissipates within 60 days if another bidder does not appear. Bradley, Desai, and Kim (1988) showed that abnormal gains realized by target companies after the announcement of a tender offer disappear if the bid does not succeed and no subsequent bid materializes within 5 years. Asquith (1983) concluded that the announcement of a merger bid that is eventually unsuccessful generates an immediate increase in the price of the target's shares, but the entire gain disappears within a year after the termination of the bid.

TABLE 1-4.   Empirical Evidence on Returns to Bidders
and Targets around Announcement Dates

Outcome of takeover attempt	Impact on shareholder value	
	Target	Bidder
Successful		
Jensen and Ruback (1983) (Review of 13 studies during 1970s)	30% (Tender offers only) 20% (Mergers only)	4% (Tender offers only) 0% (Mergers only)
Asquith (1983) (Sample = 211 successful tender offers)	20% (1962–1976)	2% (1962–1976)
You, Caves, Smith, and Henry (1986) (Sample = 133 mergers)	20% (1975–1984)	1% (1975–1984)
Jarrell, Brickley, and Netter (1988) (Sample = 663 successful tender offers)	19% (1962–1965) 30% (1970–1979) 35% (1980–1985)	4% (1962–1965) 2% (1970–1979) (1)% (1980–1985)
Bradley, Desai, and Kim (1988) (Sample = 236 successful tender offers)	19% (1963–1969) 35% (1968–1980) 35% (1981–1984)	4% (1963–1969) 1.3% (1968–1980) (3)% (1981–1984)
Cotter, Shivdasani, and Zenner (1997) (Sample = 169 successful tender offers)	62% (1989–1992) Highly independent board 41% (1989–1992) Less independent board	Not applicable
Bhagat and Hirshleifer (1996) (Sample = 290 successful tender offers)	45% (1958–1984)	1.3% (1958–1984)
Schwert (1996) (Sample size = 1814 tender offers)	35% (1975–1991)	0% (1975–1991)
Range (tenders & mergers 1960s–1980s)	19–45%	(3)–4%
Range (tenders only 1970s–1980s)	30–45%	(3)–4%
Range (mergers only 1970s–1980s)	20%	0–1%
Unsuccessful		
Bradley, Desai, and Kim (1988) (Sample = 112 unsuccessful takeovers)	Cumulative average 66% (Target acquired by another bidder within 60 days)	Cumulative average (8)% of pre-offer price (Target taken over by another bidder within 6 months)
Asquith (1983) (Sample = 91 unsuccessful takeovers)	2%–3% (1962–1976) (Most of 10% gain in 60 days preceding announcement lost in 60 day postannounce- ment period)	(5)–(7)%
Range	Not applicable	(5)–(8)%

Returns to Bidder's Shareholders: Successful and Unsuccessful Offers

For successful takeovers, returns are modest to slightly negative for both tender offers and mergers. In a perfectly competitive market, bidding firms should not receive returns in excess of what is normal for the amount of risk being assumed. Therefore, the empirical studies suggest that the market for "corporate control" is highly competitive. For unsuccessful takeovers, returns are moderately negative. Bidder returns have generally declined over time, as the premiums paid for targets have increased.

POSTMERGER RETURNS TO SHAREHOLDERS

The second approach to measuring the performance of M&As has been to examine accounting or other performance measures, such as cash flow and operating profit, during the 3–5-year period following completed transactions. Unfortunately, these studies provide conflicting evidence about the long-term impact of M&A activity. Although some find a better than average chance that M&As create shareholder value, others have found that as many as 50–80% underperform their industry peers or fail to earn their cost of capital. The diversity of conclusions strongly suggests that evaluations of postmerger returns are highly sensitive to sample selections and the methodology employed in the studies (Table 1-5).

TABLE 1-5.   Postmerger Performance Studies: Returns to Merged Companies versus Industry Average Returns

Underperform industry average	Approximate industry average (3–5 years following announcement date)	Overperform industry average
McKinsey & Company (1990)	Mueller (1985)	Healy, Palepu, and Ruback (1991)
Mangenheim and Mueller (1988)	Ravenscraft and Sherer (1986)	Kaplan and Weisbach (1992)
Franks, Harris, and Titman (1991)	Bradley and Jarrell (1988)	Rau and Vermaelen (1998)[a]
Agrawal, Jaffe, and Mandelker (1992)		
Sirower (1997)		
Loughran and Vijh (1997)		
Rau and Vermaelen (1998)[b]		
Sanford C. Bernstein & Company (2000)		

[a] Pertains to business combinations involving tender offers.
[b] Pertains to business combinations involving mergers.

Performance to Industry Averages

Some studies find that merging firms tend to do no better and, in some cases worse, than comparable firms that do not merge (Mueller: 1985; Ravenscraft and Sherer: 1987b). McKinsey & Company (1990) found in a 1987 study that 61% of 112 companies studied failed to earn their estimated cost of capital during the 3 years following the closing of the deal. Although noting that postmerger shareholder returns are sensitive to the choice of the performance benchmark, Franks, Harris, and Titman (1991) also found negative postmerger performance in the years immediately following closing. In a comprehensive study of 937 mergers and 227 tender offers, Agrawal, Jaffe, and Mandelker (1992) concluded that acquiring company shareholders experience a reduction in wealth of about 10% during the 5-year period following the completion of the merger.

Loughran and Vijh (1997) found that in the case of stock mergers, the gains experienced around the announcement date tend to dissipate within 5 years even if the acquisition succeeds. These findings imply that shareholders, who sell immediately following the closing date of transactions, realize the largest gains from either tender offers or mergers. Those who hold onto the acquirer's stock received in payment for their shares see their gains diminish over time.

Other studies also document the risk associated with takeovers, but there is some indication that the chances for success are improving. Mark Sirower (1997) analyzed 168 deals between 1979 and 1990 and concluded that two-thirds of them destroyed shareholder value. Sanford Bernstein & Company (2000) found that merged companies tended to underperform the S&P 500 stock index by an average of 15% during the 3 years following the merger. In a 1997 study of 215 acquisitions, each valued at more than $500 million, Mercer Management Consulting (MMC) found that 52% of the mergers completed during the 1990s achieved above industry-average shareholder returns during the 3 years following closing, as compared to only 37% completed during the 1980s. MMC attributes this favorable trend to improved postmerger integration.

In contrast to these findings, Bradley and Jarrell (1988) did not find any significant deterioration in returns to shareholders in the 3 years following closing. Studies by Healy, Palepu, and Ruback (1992) and Kaplan and Weisbach (1992) showed statistically significant improvements in the bidders' accounting performance measures. Although bidders in mergers underperform their peers, Rau and Vermaelen (1998) show that bidders in tender offers overperform in the 3 years following the acquisition. The authors believe that the long-term underperformance of acquiring firms is mainly due to the poor postacquisition performance of so-called "glamour" companies (i.e., those with high market-to-book ratios). The authors attribute this underperformance to the tendency of investors in and the management of bidder firms to have excessive expectations about their acquisition targets based on the bidder's past performance. Such expectations contribute to a propensity to overpay for an acquisition.

Experience Improves Performance

Not surprisingly, cumulative experience increases the likelihood that M&As will create shareholder value. The importance of experience was documented in a 1995 joint study by MMC and *Business Week* of 248 acquirers, which purchased 1,045 companies from January 1990 through July 1995. Experienced acquirers tended to substantially outperform less experienced acquirers in terms of returns to shareholders during the 3 years following the transaction when they were compared to their industry peers (Lajoux, 1998, p. 8).

Experienced acquirers were defined as those that had completed six or more transactions annually; less experienced buyers were those that completed less than one to five transactions per year. Experienced buyers constituted 24% of the entire sample. Of the firms in this group, 72% generated returns in excess of their industry average. In contrast, only 55% of those firms in the less experienced group earned financial returns above their industry average.

The Impact of the Method of Payment on Valuation

The use of stock to acquire a firm seems to negatively impact the return to the bidders' shareholders during the 3–5 years following the transaction. Travlos (1987) finds negative abnormal returns for firms financing a takeover with common stock, but no impact for firms using cash. This may suggest that investors are concerned about potential long-term dilution in earnings per share of the combined companies resulting from the issuance of new shares by the acquiring company. Using stock to acquire a target firm is equivalent to public equity offerings, which frequently show negative returns to shareholders around the equity issue announcement dates (Smith: 1986).

The use of stock may also cause the bidder to overpay for the target company to take advantage of a favorable accounting treatment known as pooling of interests (see Chapter 10). This accounting treatment requires the bidder to use its stock to buy at least 90% of the target's shares. To induce the target to accept its stock, the bidder may have to offer a higher price than would have been necessary using some other form of payment (Sanford Bernstein & Company: 2000; Sirower: 1997; Loughran and Vijh: 1997). In particular, the Sanford Bernstein & Company study found that large stock-for-stock transactions tended to underperform the S&P 500 the most because the degree of overpayment tends to be the greatest.

WHY DO MERGERS AND ACQUISITIONS OFTEN FAIL TO MEET EXPECTATIONS?

There are many reasons given for the failure of takeovers to meet expectations. Table 1-6 identifies 11 of the most commonly cited reasons ranked by the number

TABLE 1-6.　Commonly Cited Reasons for Merger and Acquisition Failure[a]

Overestimating synergy	Chapman, Dempsey, Ramsdell, & Bell (1998)
	Sirower (1997)
	Mercer Management Consulting (1998)
	Bradley, Desai, and Kim (1988)
	McKinsey & Company (1987)
Slow pace of integration	Coopers & Lybrand (1996)
	Mitchell (1998)
	Business Week (1995)
	McKinsey & Company (1987)
Poor strategy	Mercer Management Consulting (1998)
	Bogler (1996)
	McKinsey & Company (1987)
	Salter & Weinhold (1979)
Payment in stock	Loughran & Vijh (1997)
	Sirower (1997)
	Sanford Bernstein & Company (2000)
Overpaying[b]	Sirower (1997)
	McKinsey & Company (1987)
	Rau and Vermaelen (1998)
Poor postmerger communication	Mitchell (1998)
	Chakrabarti (1990)
Conflicting corporate cultures	Mercer Management Consulting (1995 & 1997)
	Hillyer & Smolowitz (1996)
Weak core business	McKinsey & Company (1987)
Large size of target company	McKinsey & Company (1987)
Inadequate due diligence	Mercer Management Consulting (1998)
Poor assessment of technology	Bryoksten (1965)

[a] Factors are ranked by the number of times they have been mentioned in studies.

[b] It is difficult to determine if overpayment is a cause of merger failure or a result of other factors such as overestimating synergy, the slow pace of integration, a poor strategy, or simply the bidder overextrapolating past performance.

of studies in which they are mentioned. The top three include overestimation of synergy, the slow pace of postmerger integration, and a flawed strategy.

DO MERGERS PAY OFF FOR SOCIETY?

Available evidence suggests that M&A activity tends to improve aggregate shareholder value (i.e., the shareholder value of both the target and acquiring firms' shareholders) without increasing industry concentration. Although the evidence is compelling that target company shareholders benefit, gains to acquiring firm shareholders depend largely on the ability to realize potential synergies and to improve overall operating efficiency.

Moreover, there is little evidence that the gains in aggregate shareholder value are attributable to enhanced market power rather than improved operating efficiency following consolidation. If a transaction is due to an increase in monopoly power, the price paid by customers of the new firm should rise. Profit margins should also increase if operating expenses do not change. Reflecting these developments, competitor share prices should rise in anticipation of higher product or service selling prices. In contrast, if the new firm is more efficient following consolidation, the share prices of competitors should decline with the prospect of increased competition. Studies indicate that rival firms' share prices do not rise when mergers are announced (Stillman: 1983) or do not decline when proposed mergers are blocked by regulatory authorities (Eckbo: 1981). Benerjee and Eckard (1998) also support the notion that improved efficiency rather than market power explains the gain in total shareholder value. In their study of the 1897–1904 merger wave, they found that competitors experienced significant operating losses inconsistent with monopoly-induced output reductions and price increases.

Merger activity has not increased industry concentration in terms of the share of output or value produced by the largest firms in the industry either in manufacturing or in the overall economy. There has been little increase in concentration since 1970 (Carlton and Perloff: 1999).

THINGS TO REMEMBER

Deals in the 1990s tended to be more strategically focused and used substantially less debt than the financially driven takeovers of the 1980s. Deals were motivated by corporations wanting to realign strategies to exploit new opportunities created by changing government regulation or accelerating technological innovation. Intensifying global competition contributed to rapid industry consolidation to achieve cost savings through economies of scale and scope. Government antitrust regulatory authorities seemed less concerned about the size of a transaction and more interested in its implications for improving the overall efficiency of the combined businesses. Finally, soaring stock prices and relatively low interest rates throughout most of the 1990s contributed greatly to the stratospheric prices paid in the megadeals of the decade.

There are myriad theories of why M&As take place. Operating and financial synergies are commonly used rationales for takeovers. *Operating synergy* consists of both economies of scale, the spreading of fixed costs over increasing production levels, and economies of scope, the use of a specific set of skills or an asset currently employed to produce a specific product to produce related products. *Financial synergy* is the reduction in the cost of capital as a result of more stable cash flows, financial economies of scale, or a better matching of investment opportunities with available funds. *Diversification* is a strategy of buying firms outside of the company's primary line of business. There is little evidence that shareholders benefit from a company's efforts to diversify on their behalf, since investors can more efficiently spread their investments and risk among industries on their own. Recent studies suggest that corporate strategies emphasizing focus deliver more benefit to shareholders.

Strategic realignment suggests that firms use takeovers as a means of rapidly adjusting to changes in their external environment such as deregulation and technological innovation. *Hubris* is an explanation for takeovers that attributes a tendency to overpay to excessive optimism about the value of a deal's potential synergy or excessive confidence in management's ability to manage the acquisition. The *undervaluation of assets* theory states that takeovers occur when the market value of a target is less than the replacement value of its assets. The *agency theory* postulates that mergers take place when there are differences between what managers and shareholders want. Low share prices of such firms pressure managers to take action to either raise the share price or become the target of an acquirer.

Tax considerations are generally not the driving factor behind acquisitions. The value of tax benefits may represent a significant but relatively small percentage of the target's total value. A more important factor is the tax status of the deal. The seller may make a tax-free transaction a prerequisite for the deal to take place. The *market power* hypothesis suggests that firms merge to gain greater control over pricing, but the empirical support for this notion is mixed. According to the *managerialism* theory, managers acquire companies to increase the acquirer's size and their own remuneration. In practice, management compensation seems to be more determined by profitability than size.

Most acquisitions require a broad array of different skills to complete a corporate takeover. Few firms have all of the needed skills in-house. Investment bankers offer strategic and tactical advice, acquisition opportunities, screening of potential buyers and sellers, making contact with a buyer or seller, negotiation support, valuation, and deal structuring. Legal expertise is often required in such specialized areas as mergers and acquisitions, corporate, tax, employee benefits, real estate, antitrust, securities, and intellectual property law. Accountants provide advice on financial structuring, tax issues, and on performing due diligence. Proxy solicitation companies are often hired to compile lists of stockholder mailing addresses. Public relations advisors ensure that both the target and acquiring companies present a compelling and consistent message to their respective constituencies.

Although there is substantial evidence that mergers pay off for target company shareholders around the time the takeover is announced, shareholder wealth creation in the 3–5 years following closing is problematic. Studies suggest as many as 50 to almost 80% fail to outperform their peers or to earn their cost of capital. Not surprisingly, the performance for more experienced acquirers is much better. The most commonly cited reasons for failure is the overestimation of synergies, the slow pace of postmerger integration, and the lack of a coherent business strategy. Empirical studies also suggest that M&As tend to pay off for society, because on average the summation of bidder and target shareholder value tends to increase. More often than not, this increase seems to be related to improved operating efficiency of the combined firms rather than an increase in market power.

Although M&As took center stage during the 1990s, it is important not to lose sight of alternative types of business combinations. These include JVs, strategic alliances, minority investments, franchises, and licenses. Corporations, holding companies, ESOPs, and JVs represent alternative vehicles for engaging in various types of business combinations.

CHAPTER DISCUSSION QUESTIONS

1-1. Discuss why mergers and acquisitions occur.

1-2. What are the advantages and disadvantages of a holding company structure in making acquisitions?

1-3. How might a leveraged ESOP be used as an alternative to a divestiture, to take a company private, or as a defense against an unwanted takeover?

1-4. What is the role of the investment banker in the M&A process?

1-5. Describe how arbitrage typically takes place in a takeover of a publicly traded company.

1-6. In your judgment, why is potential synergy often overestimated by acquirers in evaluating a target company?

1-7. What are the major differences between the merger waves of the 1980s and 1990s?

1-8. In your opinion, what are the motivations for two mergers or acquisitions currently in the news?

1-9. What are the arguments for and against corporate diversification through acquisition? Which do you support and why?

1-10. What are the primary differences between operating and financial synergy? Give examples to illustrate your statements.

CHAPTER BUSINESS CASE

CASE STUDY 1-5: AMERICA ONLINE (AOL) ACQUIRES TIME WARNER

Time Warner, itself the product of the world's then largest media merger in a $14.1 billion deal a decade ago, celebrated its 10th birthday by announcing on January 10, 2000, that it had agreed to be taken over by AOL. AOL had proposed the acquisition in October 1999; in less than 3 months, the $160 billion deal ($178 billion including Time Warner debt assumed by AOL) became the largest on record up to that point in time. To some it looked as if the minnow had swallowed the shark. AOL had less than one-fifth of the revenue and workforce of Time Warner, but AOL had almost twice the market value. As if to confirm the move to the new electronic revolution in media and entertainment, the ticker symbol of the new company is AOL.

Time Warner

Time Warner is the world's largest media and entertainment company, which views its primary business as the creation and distribution of branded content throughout the world. Its major business segments include cable networks, magazine publishing, book publishing and direct marketing, recorded music and music publishing, and filmed entertainment consisting of TV production and broadcasting as well as interests in other film companies. Its major brands include, among others, *Time,* CNN, Warner Bros., *Sports Illustrated, People,* HBO, TBS, and TNT.

Time Warner owns the nation's largest collection of cable companies. Subscribers by the end of 2000 will be able to receive broadband technology. Such technology divides a frequency range into multiple independent channels, allowing voice, video, and data signals to be transmitted at the same time. Broadband technology is 10 to 80 times faster than standard telephone dial-up services. Many believe that the proliferation of this technology will promote electronic commerce, interactive TV, and Internet phone service.

Time Warner had authorized more than $500 million to create an online information infrastructure to facilitate and standardize the promotion and delivery of its products over the Internet. The company's efforts to date to market on the Internet have had mixed results. Existing sites have a significantly different "look and feel" and the cross-promotion of the various Time Warner products has been limited.

The 1990 merger between Time Inc, and Warner Communications was supposed to create a seamless marriage of magazine publishing and film production, but the company was never able to put that vision into place. Time Warner's stock underperformed the market through much of the 1990s until the company bought Turner Broadcasting System in 1996.

America Online

Founded in 1985, AOL views itself as the world leader in providing interactive services, Web brands, Internet technologies, and electronic commerce services. AOL operates two subscription-based Internet services: AOL with greater than 20 million subscribers and CompuServe with more than 2 million. Other leading brands include ICQ (Internet telephony service), AOL Instant Messenger (an online e-mail alert service), Digital City, Netscape, AOL.com, AOL MovieFone (the nation's largest movie listing guide and ticketing service), and Spinner and Nullsoft (leaders in providing music on the Internet). Through a strategic alliance with Sun Microsystems, AOL provides hardware and systems support for companies doing business on the Internet. AOL believes that its cumulative investment in its information infrastructure and network enables it to design, develop, and operate websites because of its huge investment in IT and infrastructure. AOL claims that this investment enables it to design, implement, and operate websites at about one-fifth the cost of major competitors such as Yahoo.

Prior to the announcement, AOL had been pushing the regulatory authorities to require all cable TV operators to open their systems to Internet service provider (ISP) subscribers. At that time, cable companies usually had exclusive relationships with ISPs (e.g., AT&T cable subscribers had to use Excite @Home as their ISP). AOL was also developing alliances with local phone companies to enable AOL subscribers to access the Internet using the digital subscriber line (DSL) capabilities of these companies and had a minority interest in DirectTV's satellite business as alternative broadband technologies.

AOL is no stranger to doing deals. In 1999, it acquired Netscape Communications, MovieFone, CompuServe, and a stake in Hughes Electronics DirecTV operation. AOL has had continuous success ever since it went public in 1992. By the end of 1999, its stock rose more than 800-fold, giving it a market value of $165 billion, greater than Time Warner and Disney combined.

AOL's growth has benefited greatly from the relatively benign government policies to protect Internet user privacy and the decision to impose a moratorium on taxing e-commerce transactions. Moreover, the Federal Communications decision not to subject ISPs to the same local telephone company access fees that are paid by long-distance carriers has promoted e-commerce activity. However, pending privacy legislation could severely restrict how personal information is used for marketing and promotional purposes, and state and local government pressure mounts to tax the growing volume of transactions on the Internet. Differences in European Union and U.S. privacy policies may make it impossible to share consumer information to engage in cross-border promotion activities.

Comparative Corporate Profiles

	America Online	Time Warner
Headquarters	Dulles, Virginia	New York
Founded	1985	1990
Employees	12,100	82,000
1999 revenue	$4.8 billion (FY 6/30/99)	$26.8 billion
Shares outstanding	2.35 billion	1.5 billion
Market value, year-end 1999	$165 billion	$97 billion
Strengths	World's largest online service	World's foremost news brand
	Services in 15 countries and 7 languages	Most successful premium TV network, HBO
	No. 1 and No. 2 in instant messaging products	Foremost creator of publishing brands

Strategic Fit

On the surface, the two companies look quite different. Time Warner is a media and entertainment content company dealing in movies, music, and magazines, whereas AOL is largely an ISP offering access to content and commerce. There is very little overlap between the two businesses. AOL says it is buying access to both rich and varied branded content, a huge potential subscriber base, and to broadband technology.

Time Warner cable systems serve 20% of the country, giving AOL a more direct path into broadband transmission than it has with its ongoing efforts to upgrade local telephone lines using a technology called DSL and satellite TV. The cable connection will facilitate the introduction of AOL TV, a service introduced in 2000 and designed to deliver access to the Internet through the TV transmission.

The Time Warner deal solves AOL's cable-access problem. AOL had been lobbying for open access, under which cable-system operations would open their systems and their large subscriber bases to ISPs for a negotiated fee. Most cable operators have deals that make Excite @Home Corp, which is majority owned by AT&T, the exclusive ISP for their subscribers. Time Warner's Roadrunner is the second largest cable modem ISP behind Excite @Home.

With all this bandwidth, AOL Time Warner will be able to deliver a broad array of content directly to consumers (Figure 1-4). Together, the two companies have relationships with almost 100 million consumers. AOL has 23 million subscribers and Time Warner has 28 million subscribers to its magazines, 13 million cable subscribers, and 35 million HBO subscribers. The combined companies will also have a huge customer database to assist in the cross promotion of each other's products.

Content		Distribution	
Print	(33 publications including *Time, Fortune, Money,* and *People*)	Cable	(Time Warner Cable)
Films	(Warner Bros.; Turner Broadcasting; New Line Cinema)	Internet	(AOL, CompuServe; Roadrunner)
TV	(CNN, TNT, TBS, HBO; WB Network)	Telephony	(Digital subscriber line deals with Baby Bells)
Music	(Warner Music)	Satellite	(AOL's stake in DirecTV)
Digital	(AOL sites, CNNi, Magazine sites, Moviefone MapQuest)		

FIGURE 1-4.   The pyramid game.

The acquisition is expected to be completed by the end of 2000. AOL Time Warner is projecting the combined businesses to have $40 billion in revenue and earnings before interest, taxes, depreciation, and amortization of $10 billion during the first full year of operation. The companies will be combining sales forces and back-end functions, such as sales and customer service call centers. The new company expects to generate at least $1 billion in operating cash flow from realizing these synergies.

Terms of the Transaction

To secure the deal, AOL paid a 71% premium over the value of Time Warner's stock price prior to the announcement. AOL shareholders received one share in the new company for each of their shares, and Time Warner shareholders received 1.5 shares for each of their Time Warner shares. As such, AOL shareholders will own 55% and Time Warner shareholders 45% of the combined companies. AOL agreed to assume $18 billion in debt on the balance sheet of Time Warner.

Market Confusion following the Announcement

AOL's stock was immediately hammered following the announcement, losing about 19% of its market value in two days. Despite a greater than 20% jump in Time Warner's stock during the same period, the market value of the combined companies was actually $10 billion lower two days after the announcement than it had been immediately prior to making the deal public. Investors appeared to be confused about how to value the new company.

The two companies' shareholders represented investors with different motivations, risk tolerances, and expectations. AOL shareholders bought their company as a pure play in the Internet, while investors in Time Warner were interested in a media company. Prior to the announcement, AOL's shares traded at 55 times earnings before interest, taxes, depreciation, and amortization have been deducted. Reflecting its much lower growth rate, Time Warner traded at 14 times the same measure of its earnings. Could the new company achieve growth rates comparable to the 70% annual growth that AOL had achieved prior to the announcement? In contrast, Time Warner had been growing at less than one-third of this rate. The final multiple placed on the combined companies depends on whether investors see the new company as more like AOL or Time Warner.

Organizational Considerations

During the 1990s, Time Warner executives did not demonstrate a sterling record in achieving their vision of leveraging the complementary elements of their vast empire of media properties. The diverse set of businesses never seemed to reach agreement on how to handle online strategies among the various businesses.

Top management of the combined companies includes icons of the digital world such as Steve Case and Robert Pittman of the digital world and Gerald Levin and Ted Turner of the media and entertainment industry. Steve Case, former

Chairman and CEO of AOL, was appointed chairman of the new company, while Gerald Levin, former chairman and CEO of Time Warner, remained as chairman. Levin cannot be removed until at least 2003, unless at least three-quarters of the new board consisting of eight directors from each company agree. Ted Turner was appointed as Vice-Chairman. The presidents of the two companies, Bob Pittman of AOL and Richard Parsons of Time Warner, were named co-chief operating officers of the new company, although their roles remain unclear.

Monopoly Potential?

Embroiled in a bitter contract dispute with Time Warner, Disney Corporation accused Time Warner of exerting monopoly power that would only become more onerous when the planned merger with AOL was completed. In early May 2000 Disney officials urged the federal government to consider appropriate remedies. These included blocking the merger, separating AOL/Time Warner's creative content from its delivery system, or imposing strong regulations to ensure that companies that own their own delivery system do not use it to favor their own programming. Disney accused Time Warner of giving its own channels preferred placement and of showing program guides that favor shows it produces.

Time Warner countered by noting that Disney was simply using such accusations as a ploy to extract extra payments for its ABC and other Disney channel programs that are accessible through the Time Warner cable system. This dispute led to a 24-hour blackout on May 1, 2000, of access to ABC programs via Time Warner's cable system. The blackout was short-lived, since both companies ran the risk of tarnishing their images and of having the government intervene to impose a solution that neither party liked. Access was restored to ABC programs, at least until July 15, as both parties agreed to diligently work toward a settlement. (Sources: America Online, 2000; Time Warner 10Q SEC filing, 11/23/99; *Business Week,* 2000; *Wall Street Journal,* 2000; and Bloomberg.com, 2000.)

Case Study Discussion Questions

1. What were the primary motives for this transaction? How would you categorize them in terms of the historical motives for mergers and acquisitions discussed in this chapter?
2. Although the AOL–Time Warner deal is referred to as an acquisition in the case, why is it technically more correct to refer to it as a consolidation? Explain your answer.
3. Would you classify this business combination as a horizontal, vertical, or conglomerate transaction? Explain your answer.
4. What are some of the reasons AOL Time Warner may fail to satisfy investor expectations?
5. What would be an appropriate arbitrage strategy for this all-stock transaction?

Solutions to these questions are found in the Appendix at the back of the book.

REFERENCES

Agrawal, Anup, Jeffrey F. Jaffe, and Gershon N. Mandelker, "The Post-Merger Performance of Acquiring Firms: A Re-examination of an Anomaly," *Journal of Finance, 47,* September 1992, pp. 1605–1621.

America Online, Securities & Exchange Commission Filing, 8K, January, 2000, p. 15.

Asquith, Paul, "Merger Bids and Stock Returns," *Journal of Financial Economics, 11* (1-4), 1983, pp. 51–83.

Benerjee, Ajeyo, and E. Woodrow Eckard, "Are Mega-Mergers Anti-Competitive? Evidence from the First Great Merger Wave," *Rand Journal of Economics, 29,* Winter 1998, pp. 803–827.

Berger, Phillip G., and Eli Ofek, "Bustup Takeovers of Value Destroying Diversified Firms," *Journal of Finance, 51,* September 1996, pp. 1175–1200.

Berger, Phillip G., and Eli Ofek, "Divestification's Effect on Firm Value," *Journal of Financial Economics, 37* (1), January 1995, pp. 39–65.

Bhagat, Sanfai, and David Hirshleifer, "Do Takeovers Create Value?: An Intervention Approach," University of Michigan Business School, Working Paper 9505-03-R, http://eres,bus.umich.edu/docs/workpap/wp9505-03-R.pdf, December 1996, p. 35.

Bloomberg.com., "America Online to Buy Time Warner," January 10, 2000.

Bogler, Daniel, "Post-Takeover Stress Disorder," Summary of a PA Consulting Study in *Financial Times,* May 22, 1996, p. 11.

Bradley, Michael, Anand Desai, and E. Han Kim, "Synergistic Gains from Corporate Acquisitions and Their Division Between the Stockholders of Target and Acquiring Firms," *Journal of Financial Economics, 21,* 1988, p. 3.

Bradley, Michael, and Gregg Jarrell, "Comment," Chapter 15 in John Coffee, Jr., Louis Lowenstein, and Susan Rose-Ackerman, eds., *Knights, Raiders, and Targets,* Oxford, England: Oxford University Press, 1988, pp. 253–259.

Brown, Stanley H., *Ling: The Rise, Fall and Return of a Texas Titan,* Atheneum Publishing Company, 1972.

Bryoksten, Johan, "Merger lemons," *Mergers & Acquisitions,* Fall 1965, pp. 36–41.

Business Week, "The Case Against Mergers," October 31, 1995, p. 122.

Business Week, "21st Century," January 15, 2000, pp. 37–47.

Business Week, "Internet Evangelist," October 25, 1999, pp. 141–148.

Capen, E. C., R. V. Clapp, and W. M. Campbell, "Competitive Bidding in High Risk Situations," *Journal of Petroleum Technology, 23,* June 1971, pp. 641–653.

Carlton, Dennis, and Jeffrey Perloff, *Modern Industrial Organization* (2nd ed.), New York: Harper Collins, 1994, p. 502.

Carlton, Dennis, and Jeffrey Perloff, *Modern Industrial Organization* (3rd ed.), New York: Addison Wesley Longman, 1999, p. 27.

Chakrabarti, Alok K., "Organizational Factors in Post-Acquisition Performance," *IEEE Transactions on Engineering Management, 37* (4), November 1990, p. 135.

Chapman, Timothy L., Jack J. Dempsey, Glenn Ramsdell, and Trudy J. Bell, "Purchasing's Big Moment—After a Merger," *The McKinsey Quarterly, 1,* 1998, pp. 56–65.

Comment, Robert, and Gregg A. Jarrell, "Corporate Focus and Stock Returns," *Journal of Financial Economics, 37* (1), 1993, pp. 67–87.

Conte, Michael A., Joseph Biasi, Douglas Kruse, and Rama Jampani, "Financial Returns of Public ESOP Companies: Investor Effects vs. Manager Effects," *Financial Analysts Journal, 52,* July/August 1996, pp. 51–61.

Coopers & Lybrand, "Most Acquisitions Fail, C&L Study Says," *Mergers & Acquisitions,* Report 7, No. 47, November 1996, p. 2.

Cotter, James F., Anil Shivdasani, and Marc Zenner, "Do Independent Directors Enhance Target Shareholder Wealth during Tender Offers?," *Journal of Financial Economics, 43* (2), February 1997.

Daley, Lane, Vikas Mehrotra, and Ranjini Sivakumar, "Corporate Focus and Value Creation: Evidence from Spin-Offs," *Journal of Financial Economics, 45* (2) 1996, pp. 257–281.

Eckbo, B. E., "Examining the Anti-Competitive Significance of Large Horizontal Mergers," Unpublished Ph.D. dissertation, University of Rochester, 1981.

Elgers, Pieter T., and John J. Clark, "Merger Types and Shareholder Returns: Additional Evidence," *Financial Management,* Summer, 1980, pp. 66–72.

Fama, E. F., and M. C. Jensen. "Separation of Ownership and Control," *Journal of Law and Economics, 26,* 1983, pp. 301–325.

Franks, Julian R., Robert S. Harris, and Sheridan Titman, "The Post-Merger Share-Price Performance of Acquiring Firms," *Journal of Financial Economics, 29,* 1991, pp. 81–96.

Gaughan, Patrick A., *Mergers, Acquisitions and Corporate Restructurings,* John Wiley & Sons, Inc., 1996, pp. 18–53.

Gaughan, Patrick A., *Mergers, Acquisitions, and Corporate Restructurings* (2nd ed.), John Wiley & Sons, Inc., 1999, p. 150.

Georgeson & Company, "Proxy Solicitation," www.georgeson.com/proxy/proxy.html, 1999.

Healy, Paul M., Krishna G. Palepu, and Richard S. Ruback, "Does Corporate Performance Improve After Mergers?," *Journal of Financial Economics, 31,* 1992, pp. 135–175.

Hillyer, Clayton, and Ira Smolowitz, "Why Do Mergers Fail to Achieve Synergy?" *Director's Monthly,* January 1996, p. 13.

Hubbard, R. Glenn, and Darius Palia, "Benefits of Control, Managerial Ownership, and the Stock Returns of Acquiring Firms," *RAND Journal of Economics, 26,* pp. 782–792.

Jarrell, Gregg A., James A. Brickley, and Jeffry M. Netter, "The Market for Corporate Control: The Empirical Evidence Since 1980," *Journal of Economic Perspectives, 2,* 1988, pp. 49–68.

Jensen, Michael C., and Robert S. Ruback, "The Market for Corporate Control: The Scientific Evidence," *Journal of Financial Economics, 11,* 1983, pp. 5–53.

Kaplan, Steven N., and Michael N. Weisbach, "The Success of Acquisitions: Evidence from Divestitures," *Journal of Finance, 47* (1), March 1992, pp. 107–138.

Kim, E. Han, and Vijay Singal, "Mergers and Market Power: Evidence from the Airline Industry," *American Economic Review, 83* (3), June 1993, pp. 549–569.

Klein, B., R. Crawford, and A. Alchian, "Vertical Integration, Appropriate Rents, and the Competitive Contracting Process," *Journal of Law and Economics, 21,* October 1978, pp. 207–326.

Lajoux, Alexandra Reed, *The Art of M&A Integration,* New York: McGraw-Hill, 1998, p. 8.

Lewellen, W. G., and B. Huntsman, "Managerial Pay and Corporate Performance," *American Economic Review, 60,* September 1970, pp. 710–720.

Levy, Haim, and Marshall Sarnat, "Diversification, Portfolio Analsis and the Uneasy Case for Conglomerate Mergers," *Journal of Finance, 25,* September 1970, pp. 795–802.

Lictenberg, Frank, and Donald Siegel, "Productivity and Changes in Ownership of Manufacturing Plants," *Brookings Papers on Economic Activity, 3,* 1987, pp. 643–683.

Loughran, Tim, and Anand M. Vijh, "Do Long-Term Shareholders Benefit from Corporate Acquisitions?," *Journal of Finance,* April 1997.

Mangenheim, Ellen B., and Dennis C. Mueller, "Are Acquiring Firm Shareholders Better Off After an Acquisition," Chapter 11 in John Coffee Jr., Louis Lowenstein, and Susan Rose-Ackerman, eds., *Knight, Raiders, and Targets,* Oxford, England: Oxford University Press, 1988, pp. 171–193.

McKinsey & Company, "Creating Shareholder Value through Merger and / or Acquisition: A McKinsey & Company Perspective," an internal 1987 memorandum cited in Tom Copeland, Tim Koller, and Jack Murrin, *Valuation: Measuring and Managing the Value of Companies,* New York: John Wiley & Sons, 1990, p. 321.

Melicher, Ronald W., Edgar A. Norton, *Finance: Introduction to Institutions, Investments, and Management,* Cincinnati, OH: Southwestern College Publishing, 1999, p. 320.

Mercer Management Consulting, 1995 and 1997 surveys cited in Alexandra Reed Lajoux, *The Art of Integration,* New York: McGraw-Hill, 1998, pp. 19–21.

Mester, Loretta L. "Efficient Product of Financial Services: Scale and Scope Economies." *Review,* Federal Reserve Bank of Philadelphia, January/February 1987, pp. 15–25.

Mitchell, David, survey conducted by Economist Intelligence Unit, cited in Alexandra Reed Lajoux, *The Art of M&A Integration,* New York: McGraw-Hill, 1998, p. 19.

Morck, Randall, Andrei Shleifer, and Robert W. Vishny, "Do Managerial Objectives Drive Bad Acquisitions?" *Journal of Finance, 45* (1), March 1990, pp. 31–48.

Mueller, Dennis, "Mergers and Market Share," *Review of Economics and Statistics, 47,* 1985, pp. 259–267.

Mueller, D. C., "A Theory of Conglomerate Mergers," *Quarterly Journal of Economics, 83,* 1969, pp. 643–659.

Nielsen, J. F., and R. W. Melicher, "A Financial Analysis of Acquisitions and Merger Premiums," *Journal of Financial and Quantitative Analysis, 8,* March 1973, pp. 139–162.

Rau, P. Raghavendra, and Theo Vermaelen, "Glamour, Value, and the Post-Acquisition Performance of Acquiring Firms," *Journal of Financial Economics, 49,* Issue 2, August, 1998, pp. 223–253.

Ravenscraft, David, and Frederic Scherer, *Mergers, Selloffs and Economic Efficiency,* Washington, DC: Brookings Institution, 1987a.

Ravenscraft, David, and Frederick Scherer, "Life After Takeovers," *Journal of Industrial Economics, 36,* 1987 (b), pp. 147–156.

Ravenscraft, David, and Frederick Scherer, "Mergers and Managerial Performance," in John Coffee, Louis Lowenstien, and Susan Rose Ackerman, eds., *Knights and Targets,* New York: Oxford University Press, 1988, pp. 194–210.

Rock, Milton L., Robert H. Rock, and Martin Sikora, eds., *The Mergers & Acquisitions Handbook* (2nd ed.), New York: McGraw-Hill, 1994, p. 51.

Roll, Richard. "The Hubris Hypothesis of Corporate Takeovers," *Journal of Business, 59* (2), April 1986, pp. 197–216.

Salter, Malcolm S., and Wolf A. Weinhold, *Diversification Through Acquisition: Strategies for Creating Economic Value,* New York: The Free Press, 1979, pp. 30–31.

Sanford Bernstein & Company, "Net Equation," *Business Week,* January 31, 2000, pp. 39–41.

Schipper, Katherine, and Rex Thompson, "Evidence on the Capitalized Value of Merger Activity for Merging Firms," *Journal of Financial Economics, 11,* 1983, pp. 85–119.

Schwert, G. William, "Hostility in Takeovers: In the Eyes of the Beholder," *NBER Working Paper,* W7085, April 1999.

Schwert, William, "Markup Pricing in Mergers and Acquisitions," *Journal of Financial Economics, 41,* 1996, pp. 153–192.

Sirower, Mark, *The Synergy Trap,* New York: The Free Press, 1997.

Smith, Clifford W., Investment Banking and the Capital Acquisition Process, *Journal of Financial Economics, 15,* 1986, pp. 3–30.

Stillman, R. S., "Examining Anti-Trust Policy Towards Horizontal Mergers," *Journal of Finance, 11,* April 1983, pp. 225–240.

Thompson Financial Securities Data Corporation, "The World is Not Enough . . . To Merge," press release, January 5, 2000.

Travlos, Nicholas G., "Corporate Takeover Bids, Methods of Payment, and Bidding Firm's Stock Returns," *Journal of Finance, 42,* 1987, pp. 943–963.

U.S. Department of Commerce, "The Emerging Digital Economy," Economics and Statistics Administration, 1998.

United States General Accounting Office, "Employee Stock Ownership Plans: Little Evidence of Effects on Corporate Performance," Washington DC, 1987.

Wall Street Journal, "AOL to Acquire Time Warner in $160 Billion Deal," January 10, 2000, www.wsj.com.

Wall Street Journal, "Mergers: Windfalls or Pitfalls?," October 12, 1999, www.wsj.com.

Wasserstein, Bruce. *Big Deal: the Battle for Control of America's Leading Corporations,* Warner Books, New York, 1998, pp. 113–116.

You, Victor, Richard Caves, Michael Smith, and James Henry, "Mergers and Bidders' Wealth: Managerial and Strategic Factors," Chapter 9 in Lacy Glenn Thomas, III, ed., *The Economics of Strategic Planning,* Lexington, MA: Lexington Books, 1986, pp. 201–220.

2

REGULATORY
CONSIDERATIONS

"Have you ever been convicted of a major crime?"
"Convicted? No!"

—*Bill Murray*

As chief executive officer (CEO) of one of the nation's largest direct marketing companies, Maria was convinced that the proposed merger between her firm and the third largest competitor in the industry would result in substantial cost savings and expanded geographic coverage. Lower overall operating expenses for the combined companies would result from the elimination of overlapping administrative and support positions at the corporate level and the elimination of one of the two data centers currently operated by the two companies. Moreover, the increased leverage of the combined companies would result in significant savings in purchasing mailing addresses and certain demographic information such as age or marital status from regional vendors specializing in the collection of such data. Finally, because the target company owned information on both consumers and small businesses in geographic areas not covered by Maria's firm, the combined companies would have a truly national database suitable for developing and selling mailing lists to retailers and financial service companies interested in conducting national marketing campaigns.

The merger would not come cheap. Maria knew that she would have to pay at least $1 billion, resulting in a premium of almost 50% over the target's current share price. "But it would be worth it," she reasoned, "if the anticipated synergy could be realized in a timely manner." Although Maria was confident that she could get shareholder approval for the proposed transaction, she was less sanguine about receiving regulatory approval without making significant concessions to the Federal Trade Commission (FTC). The FTC was concerned that the combined firms would own the most comprehensive database in the industry and could effectively exclude other direct marketing firms from gaining access to certain types of data highly valued by retailers and financial services companies. Maria worried that the FTC might make approval of the transaction conditional on her willingness to license such information to others. She knew that such a requirement could materially reduce the value of the data by creating competitors.

Maria was a veteran of a number of transactions. She knew that completing the deal would ultimately depend on receiving FTC approval under conditions that would be acceptable to all parties involved. She was prepared to walk away from the transaction if the requirements to receive regulatory approval threatened her ability to achieve the synergy necessary to justify the purchase price.

OVERVIEW

Regulations that affect merger and acquisition (M&A) activity exist at all levels of government. Regulatory considerations can be classified as either general or industry-specific. General considerations are those that affect all firms, whereas industry-specific considerations impact only certain types of transactions in specific industries. General considerations include federal security, antitrust, environmental, racketeering, and employee benefits laws.

Examples of industries that are subject to substantial regulation include the following: insurance, banking, broadcasting, telecommunications, defense contracting, transportation, and public utilities. M&A activities in these industries may require government approvals to transfer government-granted licenses, permits, and franchises. For example, the Federal Communications Commission (FCC) must grant approval to transfer a communications license.

In addition to federal regulations, numerous state statutes have to be considered in M&As. For example, state antitakeover statutes place limitations on how and when a hostile takeover may be implemented. Moreover, approval may have to be received to make deals in certain industries at both the state and federal levels.

This chapter will focus on the key elements of selected federal and state regulations and their implications for M&As. Considerable time is devoted to discussing the prenotification and disclosure requirements of current legislation and how decisions are made within the key securities law and antitrust enforcement agencies. Finally, this chapter provides only an overview of the labyrinth of environmental, labor, and benefit laws affecting M&As. Because a detailed discussion is well beyond the scope of this book, the intent of this overview is simply to make the reader aware of the challenges of complying with all of the applicable laws.

FEDERAL SECURITIES LAWS

Whenever either the acquiring or the target company is publicly traded, the firms are subject to the substantial reporting requirements of the current federal securities laws. Passed in the early 1930s, these laws were a direct result of the loss of confidence in the securities markets following the crash of the stock market in 1929.[1]

SECURITIES ACT OF 1933

Originally administered by the FTC, the Securities Act of 1933 requires that all securities offered to the public must be registered with the government. Registration requires, but does not guarantee, that the facts represented in the registration statement and prospectus are accurate. However, the law makes providing false or misleading statements in the sale of securities to the public punishable with a fine, imprisonment, or both. The registration process requires the description of the company's properties and business, a description of the securities, information about management, and financial statements certified by public accountants. The legislation is intended to enable investors to have an opportunity to realistically evaluate the worth of securities they are being offered.

SECURITIES EXCHANGE ACT OF 1934

The Securities Exchange Act of 1934 established the Securities and Exchange Commission (SEC) to regulate the public securities markets. The Securities Exchange Act extends disclosure requirements stipulated under the Securities Act of 1933 covering new issues to include securities already trading on the national exchanges. In 1964, coverage was expanded to include securities traded on the Over-the-Counter (OTC) Market. Moreover, the Act prohibits a company's securities brokerage firms and others related to the securities transaction from engaging in fraudulent and unfair behavior such as insider trading. The Act also covers proxy solicitations by a company or shareholders.

Registration Requirements

Companies that are required to register are those with assets of more than $1 million and with more than 500 shareholders. Even if both parties are privately owned, an M&A transaction is subject to federal securities laws if a portion of the purchase price is going to be financed by an initial public offering of stock or a public offering of debt by the acquiring firm.

---

[1] For a comprehensive discussion of federal securities laws, see the Securities Exchange Commission Website (www.sec.gov), Loss and Seligman (1995), and Gilson and Black (1995).

Frequency of Filings

Following registration of securities, companies must file annual and other periodic reports to update data in the original filing. Section 13 of the Securities and Exchange Act covers periodic reporting requirements. These include the 10-K or annual report, the Form 10-Q or quarterly report, and the Form 8-K. The 8K must be submitted within 15 days of the occurrence of certain specified events, such as the acquisition or divestiture of a significant amount of assets. Acquisitions and divestitures are deemed significant if the equity interest in the acquired assets or the amount paid or received exceeds 10% of the total book assets of the registrant and its subsidiaries.

Section 13: Periodic Reports

The Form 10K or annual report summarizes and documents the firm's financial activities during the preceding year. The four key financial statements that must be included are the income statement, balance sheet, statement of retained earnings, and the statement of cash flows. The statements must be well documented with information on accounting policies and procedures, calculations, and transactions underlying the entries on the financial statements. The Form 10K also includes a relatively detailed description of the business, the markets served, major events and their impact on the business, key competitors, and competitive market conditions. The Form 10Q is a highly succinct quarterly update of this information.

In the event an acquisition or divestiture is deemed significant, the Form 8K must describe the assets acquired or disposed, the nature and amount of consideration given or received, and the identity of the persons for whom the assets were acquired. In the case of an acquisition, the Form 8K must also identify the source of funds used to finance the purchase and the financial statements of the acquired business.

Section 14: Proxy Solicitations

Where proxy contests for control of corporate management are involved, the act requires the names and interests of all participants in the proxy contest. Proxy materials must be filed in advance of their distribution to ensure that they are in compliance with disclosure requirements. If the transaction involves the shareholder approval of either the acquirer or target firm, any materials distributed to shareholders must conform to the SEC's rules for proxy materials.

WILLIAMS ACT: REGULATION OF TENDER OFFERS

Until the late 1960s, most M&A activity involved negotiated settlements between the management of the acquirer and the target companies. During the era of conglomerate mergers in the late 1960s, mergers grew more hostile. Tender offers were becoming more commonplace. Regulatory officials became increasingly concerned about whether target shareholders had sufficient time to make informed decisions about such offers.

Passed in 1968, the Williams Act consists of a series of amendments to the Securities Act of 1934. The Williams Act was intended to protect target firm shareholders from lightning fast takeovers in which they would not have enough information or time to adequately assess the value of an acquirer's offer. This was to be achieved by requiring more disclosure by the bidding company, establishing a minimum period during which a tender offer must remain open, and authorizing targets to sue bidding firms. The disclosure requirements of the Williams Act apply to anyone, including the target company asking shareholders to accept or reject a takeover bid.

The major sections of the Williams Act as they impact M&As are in Sections 13(d) and 14(d). Note that the procedures outlined in the Williams Act for prenotification must be followed diligently. Failure to deliver copies of the required documents to all parties stipulated in the law can result in a violation of U.S. securities laws.

Section 13(d)

This section of the Williams Act is intended to regulate "substantial share" or large acquisitions and serves to provide an early warning for a target company's shareholders and management of a pending bid. Any person or firm acquiring 5% or more of the stock of a public corporation must file a Schedule 13D with the SEC within 10 days of reaching that percentage ownership threshold. The disclosure is necessary even if the accumulation of the stock is not followed by a tender offer.

Under Section 13(g), any stock accumulated by related parties such as affiliates, brokers or investment bankers working on behalf of the person or firm are counted toward the 5% threshold. This prevents an acquirer from avoiding filing by accumulating more than 5% of the target's stock through a series of related parties. Institutional investors such as registered brokers and dealers, banks, and insurance companies can choose to file a Schedule 13G, a shortened version of the Schedule 13D, if the securities were acquired in the normal course of business.

Schedule 13D Disclosure Requirements

The information required by the Schedule 13D includes the identities of the acquirer, their occupation and associates, sources of financing, and the purpose of the acquisition. If the purpose of the acquisition of the stock is to take control of the target firm, the acquirer must reveal his business plan for the target firm. The plans could include the break-up of the firm, the suspension of dividends, a recapitalization of the firm, or the intention to merge it with another firm. Otherwise, the purchaser of the stock could indicate that the accumulation was for investment purposes only.

Whenever a material change in the information on the Schedule 13D occurs, a new filing must be made with the SEC and the public securities exchanges. The Williams Act is vague when it comes to defining what constitutes a material change. Filing within 10 days of the material change is generally considered acceptable.

Section 14(d)

Section 14(d) applies to public tender offers only. The 5% notification threshold also applies.

Obligations of the Acquirer

An acquiring firm must disclose its intentions and business plans as well as any agreements between the acquirer and the target firm in a Schedule 14D-1. The schedule is called a *tender offer statement*. The commencement date of the tender offer is defined as the date on which the tender offer is published, advertised, or submitted to the target.

Schedule 14D-1 must contain the identity of the target company and the type of securities involved, the identity of the person, partnership, syndicate, or corporation that is filing, and any past contracts between the bidder and the target company. The schedule must also include the source of the funds used to finance the tender offer, its purpose, and any other information material to the transaction.

Obligations of the Target Firm

The management of the target company cannot advise its shareholders how to respond to a tender offer until it has filed a Schedule 14D-9 with the SEC within 10 days after the tender offer's commencement date. This schedule is called a *tender offer solicitation/recommendation statement*. Target management is limited to telling its shareholders to defer responding to the tender offer until it has completed its consideration of the offer. The target must also send copies of the Schedule 14D-9 to each of the public exchanges on which its stock is traded.

Shareholder Rights: 14(d) (4)–(7)

The tender offer must be left open for a minimum of 20 trading days. The acquiring firm must accept all shares that are tendered during this period. The firm making the tender offer may get an extension of the 20-day period if it believes that there is a better chance of getting the shares its needs. The firm must purchase the shares tendered at the offer price, at least on a prorata basis, unless the firm does not receive the total number of shares it requested under the tender offer. The tender offer may also be contingent on attaining the approval of such regulatory agencies as the Department of Justice (DoJ) and the FTC. Shareholders have the right to withdraw shares that they may have tendered previously. They may withdraw their shares at any time during which the tender offer remains open.

ANTITRUST LAWS

Federal antitrust laws exist to prevent individual corporations from assuming too much market power such that they can limit their output and raise prices without concern for any significant competitor reaction. The DoJ and the FTC have the primary responsibility for enforcing federal antitrust laws. The FTC was established in the Federal Trade Commission Act of 1914 with the specific purpose of enforcing antitrust laws such as the Sherman, Clayton, and Federal Trade Commission Acts.

The attitude of the government regulatory agencies has changed dramatically over the years. In the 1960s, mergers were often challenged by the FTC and DoJ even though they were only remotely related. During the Reagan and Bush Administrations, antitrust challenges to M&As were relatively infrequent, as regulators assumed a more pro-free-market stance.

During the second half of the 1990s, the pendulum shifted once again to a more aggressive enforcement of antitrust laws. This shift is illustrated by the government's blocking of Microsoft's attempted acquisition of Intuit in 1995, Rite Aid's proposal to purchase Revco in 1996, the Office Depot and Staples merger in 1997, and MCT WorldCom's attempt to purchase Sprint in 2000.[2]

SHERMAN ACT

Passed in 1890, the Sherman Act makes illegal all contracts, combinations, and conspiracies, which "unreasonably" restrain trade (U.S. Department of Justice: 1999). Examples include agreements to fix prices, rig bids, and allocate customers or to monopolize any part of interstate commerce.

Section I of the Sherman Act prohibits business combinations that result in monopolies or in a significant concentration of pricing power in a single firm. Section II applies to firms that are already dominant in their targeted markets. The Sherman Act remains the most important source of antitrust law today.

The act applies to all transactions and businesses involved in interstate commerce, or if the activities are local, all transactions and business "affecting" interstate commerce. The latter phrase has been interpreted to allow broad application of the Sherman Act. Most states have comparable statutes prohibiting monopolistic conduct, price fixing agreements, and other acts in restraint of trade having strictly local impact.

The sheer breadth of these sections of the act underscore Congress' intent to cover all types of anticompetitive activities. However, the breadth of the wording of the act reduced its effectiveness since it stated that all contracts that restrained trade were illegal. This implies that virtually all contracts are illegal. Historically, courts have had substantial difficulty in enforcing this part of the law.

[2] For an excellent discussion of antitrust law, see the DoJ (www.usdoj.gov) and FTC (www.ftc.gov) wetsites, Gaughan (1999), and Ton and Lyssky (1992).

CLAYTON ACT

Passed in 1914 to strengthen the Sherman Act, the Clayton Act made it illegal for one company to purchase the stock of another company if their combination results in reduced competition within the industry. The act also made price discrimination among customers illegal, unless it could be justified by economies associated with bulk purchases. Tying of contracts was also prohibited in which a firm refused to sell certain important products to a customer unless the customer agreed to buy other products from the firm. Finally, interlocking directorates were made illegal when the directors were on the boards of competing firms.

Unlike the Sherman Act, which contains criminal penalties, the Clayton Act is a civil statute. The Clayton Act allows private parties injured by the antitrust violation to sue in federal court for three times their actual damages. State attorneys general may also bring civil suits. These are costs that must be borne by the party violating prevailing antitrust law if the plaintive wins in addition to the criminal penalties imposed under the Sherman Act.

In the Celler–Kefauver Act of 1950, the Clayton Act was amended to give the FTC the power to prohibit asset as well as stock purchases. The FTC may also block mergers if it believes that the combination will result in increased market concentration as measured by the sales of the largest firms.

HART–SCOTT–RODINO ANTITRUST IMPROVEMENTS ACT

Acquisitions involving companies of a certain size cannot be completed until certain information is supplied to the federal government and until a specified waiting period has elapsed. The premerger notification allows the FTC and the DoJ to have sufficient time to challenge acquisitions believed to be anticompetitive before they are completed. Once the merger has taken place, it is often exceedingly difficult to break it up. See Table 2-1 for a summary of prenotification filing requirements

Bidding firms must execute a Hart–Scott–Rodino (HSR) filing at the same time as they make an offer to a target firm. The target firm is also required to file within 15 days following the bidder's filing. Filings consist of information on the operations of the two companies and their financial statements. The required forms also request any information on internal documents, such as the estimated market share of the combined companies made prior to the offer being made. Consequently, any such analyses should be undertaken with the understanding that the information will ultimately be shared with the antitrust regulatory authorities.

If the regulatory authorities suspect anticompetitive effects, they will file a lawsuit to block completion of the proposed transaction. Although it is rare that either the bidder or the target contest the lawsuit because of the expense involved, it does happen (see Case Study 2-1). If fully litigated, a government lawsuit can result in substantial legal expenses as well as a significant use of management time and attention. Even if the FTC's lawsuit is ultimately overturned, the perceived benefits of the merger often have disappeared by the time the lawsuit has been decided. This is especially true in the fast changing environment of high-technology businesses. Nevertheless, both the combining companies and the regulatory authorities may choose to file lawsuits as part of the negotiation process.

CASE STUDY 2-1. BP AMOCO AND ARCO VOW TO CONTEST THE FTC'S RULING

Reflecting their concern about the effect on gasoline prices on the West Coast, the FTC commissioners rejected on February 3, 2000 the merger of BP Amoco and Atlantic Richfield Corporation (Arco) and directed its staff to file a court injunction to block the proposed $30 billion transaction. If it had been allowed, the combination would have resulted in the second largest nongovernment-owned oil company at the time, behind Exxon Mobil, whose merger had been approved by the FTC in November 1999.

The primary concern of the Commission is that the combined companies would have too much control over Alaskan oil production. BP Amoco and Arco together account for 70% of the oil on Alaska's North Slope. That accounts for 45% of the oil refined in California, Oregon, and Washington. The FTC's staff recommended against the proposed acquisition in December 1999, suggesting that the combination would lead to higher gasoline prices on the West Coast. This allegation had been strongly denied by BP Amoco and Arco. During negotiations with the FTC, BP Amoco sought to allay antitrust concerns by agreeing to reduce its North Slope production by 13% by selling interests in the oil fields. However, these concessions were not enough for the FTC, which noted that even with the sales BP Amoco and Arco would still control 55% of Alaska's oil production.

BP Amoco has said that despite FTC opposition, it is determined to move ahead with the merger. Although a settlement is possible, the prognosis in early February was for a lengthy court battle.

The rejection of this highly visible merger seems to represent the introduction of a more stringent application of current antitrust laws. Recent comments by Robert Pitofsky, Chairman of the FTC, suggested as much. On February 18, 2000, Pitofsky stated in a speech before international antitrust lawyers that the agency's reviews of M&As are going to be more rigorous than in the past. In particular, Pitofsky noted that, "We [the agency] have seen more frequent proposals that are so extensive and complex that it is impossible to predict with any confidence that competition will be restored and consumer welfare will be protected." The harsher stance is being taken for two reasons. First, deals are currently more strategic in nature and are capable of changing the competitive landscape. Second, regulators now believe that despite efforts to require companies to sell off operations to protect competition, it often does not work that way. Currently, the FTC reviews about 4% of all M&As and challenges about 2%.

By March 2000, the posturing by both sides seems to have resulted in substantial progress toward receiving regulatory approval. Both sides assumed a more conciliatory position following further action taken by BP Amoco and Arco. The FTC voted to approve the proposed merger between Arco and BP Amoco following the announcement of the pending sale of Arco's Alaskan operations to Phillips Petroleum. This would bring the amount of oil on the North Slope of Alaska controlled by the combined companies to less than 50%. However, the completion of the transaction was still dependent on BP Amoco reaching some accommodation with Exxon Mobil, which claims to have a right of first refusal to purchase the Arco reserves in Alaska. By late April, this issue was resolved and the transaction was completed.

Source: Bloomberg.com, 2000a and 2000b.

Who Must File?

If the transaction is reportable, both the acquiring and target companies must submit reports to the Pre-Merger Notification Office of the FTC and the director of operations of the Antitrust Division of the DoJ. Transactions are generally reportable if both of the following conditions are met. First, one party to the transaction has sales or assets of at least $100 million and the other party has sales or assets of at least $10 million. Second, the acquirer will own more than $15 million in stock or assets of the target firm or more than 50% of the voting stock of a company with sales or assets of more than $15 million.

What Must Be Filed?

The reporting requirements of the prenotification form are extensive. They include background information on the "ultimate parent" of the acquiring and target parents, a description of the transaction, as well as all background studies relating to the transaction. The "ultimate parent" will be the corporation that is at the top of the chain of ownership, if the actual buyer is a subsidiary. In addition, the reporting firm must supply detailed product line breakdowns, a listing of competitors, and an analysis of sales trends.

By receiving background studies relating to the proposed transaction, the government is gaining access to such information as internal memoranda describing the deal. In Microsoft's proposed acquisition of Intuit in 1994, the DoJ uncovered several communications, including one in which Intuit's CEO, Scott Wood, noted that the transaction would leave financial institutions "with one clear option" for financial software and would eliminate a "bloody (market) share war." In another communication, a Microsoft executive noted that "as a combination [Microsoft and Intuit] would be dominant" (Wasserstein: 1998, p. 758). Such information was used by the DoJ to eventually block the proposed acquisition on the grounds that the combined companies would have too much market power in the personal financial software market (see Case Study 2-4).

Waiting Period

For an all-cash offer, the waiting period begins when the acquirer has filed the required forms; for offers including all or some securities, the waiting period begins when both the acquirer and target have filed. Before the takeover can be completed, a 30-day waiting period for transactions involving securities and 15 days for cash tender offers is required. Either the FTC or the DoJ may request a 20-day extension of the waiting period for transactions involving securities and 10 days for cash tender offers. If the acquiring firm believes that there is little likelihood of anticompetitive effects, it can request early termination. However, the decision is entirely at the discretion of the regulatory agencies.

PROCEDURAL RULES

When the DoJ files an antitrust suit, it is adjudicated in the federal court system. When the action is initiated by the FTC, it is heard before an administrative law judge at the FTC. The results of the hearing are subject to review by the commissioners of the FTC. Criminal actions are reserved for the DoJ, which may seek fines or imprisonment for violators. Individuals and companies may also file antitrust lawsuits.

The FTC reviews complaints that have been recommended by its staff and approved by the commission. Each complaint is reviewed by one of the FTC's hearing examiners. The commission as a whole then votes whether to accept or reject the hearing examiner's findings. The decision of the commission can then be appealed in the federal circuit courts.

Historically, once a filing has been challenged by the FTC, it has taken years to work through the commission's review process from complaint to final commission ruling. Recently, the FTC has implemented new "fast-track" guidelines that commit the FTC to making a final decision on a complaint within 13 months. The 12-month resolution of the challenge of the $81 billion Exxon-Mobil merger suggests that the new guidelines may be working. (See Case Study 2-8).

As an alternative to litigation, a company may seek to negotiate a voluntary settlement of its differences with the FTC. Such settlements are usually negotiated during the review process and are called *consent decrees*. The FTC then files a complaint in the federal court along with the proposed consent decree. The federal court judge routinely approves the consent decree.

THE CONSENT DECREE

A typical consent decree requires the merging parties to divest overlapping businesses or to restrict anticompetitive practices. If a potential acquisition is

TABLE 2-1.   Summary of Regulatory Prenotification Filing Requirements[a]

	Williams Act	Hart-Scott-Rodino Act
Required filing	1. Schedule 13D within 10 days of acquiring 5% stock ownership in another firm 2. Ownership includes stock held by affiliates or agents of bidder 3. Schedule 14D-1 for tender offers 4. Disclosure required even if 5% accumulation not followed by a tender offer	HSR filing necessary when both of the following conditions are met: 1. One firm has assets/sales of $100 million and the other $10 million 2. Ownership of target stock or assets is $15 million; or greater than 50% of firm with stock or assets of more than $15 million
File with whom	Schedule 13D 1. 6 copies to SEC 2. 1 copy via registered mail to target's executive office 3. 1 copy via registered mail to each public exchange on which target stock traded Schedule 14D-1 1. 10 copies to SEC 2. 1 copy hand delivered to target's executive offices 3. 1 copy hand delivered to other bidders 4. 1 copy mailed to each public exchange on which target stock traded (each exchange must also be phoned)	1. Premerger Notification Office of the FTC 2. Director of Operations of the DoJ Antitrust Division
Time period	1. Tender offers must stay open a minimum of 20 business days 2. Begins on date of publication, advertisement, or submission of materials to target	1. Review/waiting period: 30 days (15 days for all cash tender offer) 2. Target must file within 15 days of bidder's filing 3. Period begins for all cash offer when bidder files; for cash/stock bids, period begins when both bidder and target have filed 4. Regulators can request 20 day extension (10 days for cash tender offers)

[a] SEC, Securities and Exchange Commission; FTC, Federal Trade Commission.

likely to be challenged by the regulatory authorities, an acquirer may seek to negotiate a consent decree in advance of consummating the deal. In the absence of a consent decree, a buyer often requires that an agreement of purchase and sale includes a provision that allows the acquirer to back out of the transaction if it is challenged by the FTC or the DoJ on antitrust grounds.

In a report evaluating the results of 35 divestiture orders entered between 1990 and 1994, including licensing of intellectual property, the FTC concluded that the use of consent decrees as a means of limiting the increase in market power resulting from a business combination has proven to be successful (Federal Trade Commission, Bureau of Competition: 1999). Most divestitures have created viable competitors in the markets that the FTC felt were most likely to be affected if it approved the merger without requiring the divestiture of one of the businesses that had been direct competitors prior to the merger announcement. The study also found that the success of the divestiture is more likely with the divestiture of an ongoing business than with the divestiture of a single product line or proprietary technology. Moreover, the divestiture is also likely to be more successful if it is made to a firm in a related business rather than a new entrant into the business.

CASE STUDY 2-2. JUSTICE DEPARTMENT REQUIRES ALLIEDSIGNAL AND HONEYWELL TO DIVEST OVERLAPPING BUSINESSES

AlliedSignal Inc. and Honeywell Inc. were ordered to divest significant portions of their avionics (airplane electronics systems) businesses in 1999 in order to resolve the DoJ's competitive concerns involving their proposed $16 billion merger. Both companies are major providers of avionics and other advanced technology products to a broad range of commercial, space, and U.S defense customers. The DoJ concluded that the transaction as originally proposed would have been anticompetitive, resulting in higher prices and lower quality for these products.

The DoJ's Antitrust Division filed a lawsuit and proposed a consent decree in U.S. District Court in Washington, D.C. The consent decree, if approved by the Court, would resolve the issue. According to the complaint, the proposed merger would have substantially lessened competition in four product areas: traffic alert and collision avoidance systems, search and surveillance weather radar, reaction and momentum wheels, and inertial systems. In each of these product areas, the merger would leave at most two or three major competitors. Consequently, the DoJ alleged that these competitors would have been able to coordinate their pricing and more easily raise prices to customers.

Under the consent decree, AlliedSignal must divest its search and surveillance weather radar business in Olathe, Kansas; its space and navigation business in Teterboro, New Jersey; its MRG business in Cheshire, Connecticut, and a related repair business in Newark, Ohio; its MEMs business in Redmond, Washington, and related MEMS licenses. Also, Honeywell must divest its traffic alert and collision avoidance systems business located in Glendale, Arizona.

Source: Department of Justice, 1999.

ANTITRUST MERGER GUIDELINES FOR HORIZONTAL MERGERS

Understanding an industry begins with understanding its market structure. Market structure may be defined in terms of the number of firms in an industry, their concentration, cost, demand and technological conditions, and ease of entry and exit. The size of individual competitors does not tell one much about the nature of competition within an industry. Some industries give rise to larger firms than do other industries due to the importance of economies of scale or huge capital and research and development requirements. For example, Boeing and Airbus dominate the commercial airframe industry but the nature of industry rivalry is intense.

Beginning in 1968, the DoJ issued guidelines indicating the types of M&As the government would oppose. Intended to clarify the provisions of the Sherman and Clayton Acts, the largely quantitative guidelines were presented in terms of specific market share percentages and concentration ratios. Concentration ratios were defined in terms of the market shares of the top four or eight firms in an industry. Due to their initial rigidity, the guidelines have been revised over the years to reflect the role of both quantitative and qualitative data. Qualitative data includes factors such as the enhanced efficiency that might result from a combination of firms, the financial viability of potential merger candidates, and the ability of U.S. firms to compete globally.

In 1992, both the FTC and the DoJ announced a new set of guidelines indicating that they would challenge mergers creating or enhancing market power, even if there are measurable efficiency benefits. Market power is defined as a situation in which the combined firms will be able to profitably maintain prices above competitive levels for a significant period of time. M&As that do not increase market power are acceptable.

The 1992 guidelines were revised in 1997 to reflect the regulatory authorities' willingness to recognize that improvements in efficiency over the long-term could more than offset the effects of increases in market power. Consequently, a combination of firms, which enhances market power, would be acceptable to the regulatory authorities if it could be shown that the increase in efficiency resulting from the combination more than offsets the increase in market power.

In general, horizontal mergers, those between current or potential competitors, are most likely to be challenged by regulators. Vertical mergers or customer–supplier mergers are considered much less likely to result in anticompetitive effects, unless they deprive other market participants of access to an important resource. The antitrust regulators seldom contest conglomerate mergers, involving the combination of dissimilar products into a single firm.

The 1992 guidelines describe the process the antitrust authorities go through to make their decisions. This process falls into five discrete steps.

Step 1: Market Definition, Measurement, and Concentration

Although a number of factors are examined to determine if a proposed transaction will result in a violation of law, calculating the respective market shares of the combining companies and the degree of industry concentration in terms of the number of competitors is the starting point for any investigation.

Defining the Market

The market is generally defined by the regulators as a product or group of products offered in a specific geographic area. Market participants are those currently producing and selling these products in this geographic area as well as potential entrants. Regulators calculate market shares for all firms or plants identified as market participants based on total sales or capacity currently devoted to the relevant markets. In addition, the market share estimates include capacity that is likely to be diverted to this market in response to a small, but significant and sustainable, price increase.

In certain cases, the regulatory agencies have chosen to segment a market more narrowly by size or type of competitor. This is the approach adopted in the FTC's investigation of Staple's acquisition of Office Depot (Case Study 2-3).

Determining Market Concentration

The number of firms in the market and their respective market shares determines market concentration (i.e., the extent to which a single or a few firms control a disproportionate share of the total market). Concentration ratios are an incomplete measure of industry concentration. Such ratios measure how much of the total output of an industry is produced by the "n" largest firms in the industry. The shortcomings of this approach include the frequent inability to define accurately what constitutes an industry, the failure to reflect ease of entry or exit, foreign competition, regional competition, and the distribution of firm size.

In an effort to account for the distribution of firm size in an industry, the FTC measures concentration by using the Herfindahl-Hirschman Index (HHI), which is calculated by summing the squares of the market shares for each firm competing in the market. For example, a market consisting of five firms with market shares of 30, 25, 20, 15, and 10% would have an HHI of 2250 ($30^2 + 25^2 + 20^2 + 15^2$

CASE STUDY 2-3. FTC PREVENTS STAPLES FROM ACQUIRING OFFICE DEPOT

As the leading competitor in the office supplies superstore market, Staples' proposed $3.3 billion acquisition of Office Depot received close scrutiny from the FTC immediately after its announcement in September 1996. The acquisition would create a huge company with annual sales of $10.7 billion. Following the acquisition, only one competitor, OfficeMax with sales of $3.3 billion, would remain. The FTC requested documents to determine whether superstores lower prices in cities where they compete with other superstores.

Staples pointed out that the combined companies would comprise only about 5% of the total office supply market. However, the FTC considered the superstore market as a separate segment within the total office supply market. Using the narrow definition of market, the FTC concluded that the combination of Staples and Office Depot would control more than three-quarters of the market and substantially increase the pricing power of the combined firms. Despite Staples willingness to divest 63 stores to Office Max in markets in which its concentration would be the greatest following the merger, the FTC could not be persuaded to approve the merger.

Staples continued its insistence that there would be no harmful competitive effects from the proposed merger, because office supply prices would continue their long-term decline. Both Staples and Office Depot had a history of lowering prices for their customers due to the efficiencies associated with their "superstores." The companies argued that the merger would result in more than $4 billion in cost savings over 5 years that would be passed onto their customers. However, the FTC argued and the federal court concurred that the product prices offered by the combined firms would still be higher, as a result of reduced competition, than they would have been had the merger not taken place. The FTC relied on a study showing that Staples tended to charge higher prices in markets in which it did not have another superstore as a competitor.

In early 1997, Staples withdrew its offer for Office Depot.

Source: CNNfn, 1996; The Motley Fool Lunchtime News, 1996.

$+ 10^2$). Note that an industry consisting of five competitors with market shares of 70, 10, 5, 5, 5 will have a much higher HHI score of 5,075, because the process of squaring the market shares gives the greatest weight to the firm with the largest market shares. The HHI measure takes into consideration all firms in the industry and is therefore more complete than traditional concentration ratios.

Likely FTC Actions Based on the Herfindahl–Hirschman Index

The HHI ranges from 10,000 for an almost pure monopoly to approximately zero in the case of a highly competitive market. The index gives proportionately more weight to the market shares of larger firms to reflect their relatively greater market power. The FTC has developed a scoring system described in Figure 2-1, which is used as one factor in determining whether the FTC will challenge a proposed merger or acquisition.

Step 2: Potential Adverse Competitive Effects of Mergers

Market share and concentration data alone do not provide a complete picture of the ability of a single firm, or a small group of firms, to exercise market power. Market concentration and market share data are based on historical data. Consequently, changing market conditions may overstate the significance of market share.

Suppose a new technology that is important to the long-term competitive viability of the firms within a market has been licensed to other firms within the market but not to the firm with the largest market share. Regulators may conclude that market share information overstates the potential for an increase in the market power of the firm with the largest market share. Therefore, before determining whether to challenge a proposed transaction, regulators will consider factors other than simply market share and concentration to determine if a proposed merger will have "adverse competitive effects." These other factors include evidence of coordinated interaction, differentiated products, and similarity of substitute products.

Coordinated Interaction

Regulators consider the extent to which a small group of firms may exercise market power collectively by cooperating in restricting output or setting prices. Tacit collusion is not necessarily illegal unless competitors have the ability to detect and to punish firms deviating from agreed upon competitive practices. Collusion may take the form of firms agreeing to follow simple guidelines such as

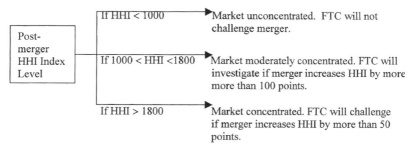

FIGURE 2-1. Federal Trade Commission (FTC) actions at various concentration levels. HHI, Herfinahl-Hirschman Index. (From FTC, 1999).

maintaining common prices, fixed price differentials, stable market shares, or customer or territorial restrictions.

Where detection and punishment is likely to be easy, individual firms have few incentives to deviate from coordinated practices. Consequently, regulators are interested in understanding the extent to which key information, such as output levels, individual transactions, and selling prices for individual firms, is readily available to other competitors. If such information is not readily available, it may be difficult to detect deviations from collusive practices allowing "cheating" to continue. Under this scenario, regulators are likely to be less concerned about the potential for collusion resulting from a merger or acquisition.

Differentiated Products

In some markets the products are differentiated in the eyes of the consumer. Consequently, products sold by different firms in the market are not good substitutes for one another. A merger between firms in a market for differentiated products may diminish competition by enabling the merged firms to profit by raising the price of one or both products above premerger levels.

Similarity of Substitutes

Market concentration may be increased if the merger of two firms whose products are viewed by customers as equally desirable merge. In this instance, market share may understate the anticompetitive impact of the merger if the products of the merging firms are more similar in their various attributes to one another than to other products in the relevant market. In contrast, market share may overstate the perceived undesirable competitive effects when the relevant products are less similar in their attributes to one another than to other products in the relevant market.

Step 3: Entry Analysis

The ease of entry into the market by new competitors is considered a very important factor in determining if a proposed business combination is anticompetitive. Ease of entry is defined as entry that would be timely, likely to occur, and sufficient to counter the competitive effects of a combination of firms that temporarily increases market concentration.

Barriers to entry such as proprietary technology or knowledge, patents, government regulations, exclusive ownership of natural resources or huge investment requirements can serve to limit the number of new competitors and the pace at which they enter a market. In such instances, a regulatory agency may rule that a proposed transaction will reduce competitiveness. In contrast, an acquisition may not be considered anticompetitive if new firms can enter relatively easily in response to higher product or service prices. Ease of entry appears to have been a factor in the DoJ's assessment of Microsoft's proposal to acquire Intuit (see Case Study 2-4).

CASE STUDY 2-4. JUSTICE DEPARTMENT BLOCKS MICROSOFT'S ACQUISITION OF INTUIT

In 1994, Bill Gates saw dominance of the personal financial software market as a means of becoming a central player in the global financial system. Critics argued that by dominating the point of access (the individual personal computer) to online banking, Microsoft believed that it may be possible to receive a small share of the value of each of the billions of future personal banking transactions once online banking became the norm (Radigan: 1994).

With a similar goal in mind, Intuit was trying to have its widely used financial software package, Quicken, incorporated into the financial standards of the global banking system. In 1994, Intuit had acquired the National Payment Clearinghouse Inc., an electronic bill payments system integrator, to help them develop a sophisticated payments system. By 1995, Intuit had sold more than 7 million copies of Quicken and had about 300,000 bank customers using Quicken to pay bills electronically.

Current efforts by Microsoft to penetrate the personal financial software market with its own product, Money, were lagging badly. Intuit's product, Quicken, had a commanding market share of 70% compared to Microsoft's 30%. Intuit's success reflected both a product that was easier to use and a series of alliances with financial services firms.

In 1994, Microsoft made a $1.5 billion offer for Intuit. Eventually, it would increase its offer to $2 billion. To appease its critics, it offered to sell its Money product to Novell Corporation. Almost immediately, the DoJ challenged the merger, citing its concern about the anticompetitive effects on the personal financial software market. Specifically, the DoJ argued that, if consummated, the proposed transaction would add to the dominance of the number one product Quicken, weaken the number two product (Money), and substantially increase concentration and reduce competition in the personal finance/checkbook software market (Talmor: 1995). Moreover, the DoJ argued that there would be few new entrants, because competition with the new Quicken would be even more difficult and expensive. The DoJ also noted that H&R Block had decided to exit the market because of the planned merger of Microsoft and Intuit by selling its finance software subsidiary, Meca Software, to Bank of America and NationsBank in May 1995.

Critics saw the sale of Microsoft's Money software to Novell as a ploy to distract the regulatory authorities. Further fueling the critics' ire were Microsoft's plans to introduce its new Microsoft Network (MSN). Critics believed that Microsoft's control over the personal computer desktop would be strengthened if Quicken were integrated into the Windows 95 software and the new online MSN service. This integration would provide consumers with a gateway to a host of financial and nonfinancial services (Bers: 1995).

Microsoft and its supporters argued that government interference would cripple Microsoft's ability to innovate and limit its role in promoting standards that advance the whole software industry. Only a Microsoft-Intuit merger could create the critical mass needed to advance home banking (Sraeel: 1995).

On May 20, 1995, Microsoft announced that it was discontinuing efforts to acquire Intuit. It said it wanted to avoid a protracted and expensive court battle with the DoJ.

Step 4: Efficiencies

Increases in efficiency that result from a merger or acquisition can enhance the combined firms' ability to compete and result in lower prices, improved quality, better service, or new products. However, efficiencies are difficult to measure and to verify since they will be realized only after the merger has taken place. Efficiencies are most likely to make a difference in the FTC's decision to challenge when the likely effects of market concentration are not considered significant. An example of verifiable efficiency improvements would be a reduction in the average fixed cost of production due to economies of scale.

Step 5: Alternative to Imminent Failure

Regulators also take into account the likelihood that a firm would fail and exit a market if it is not allowed to merge with another firm. The regulators must weigh the potential cost of the failing firm, such as a loss of jobs, against any potential increase in market power that might result from the merger of the two firms. The potentially failing firm must be able to demonstrate that it is unable to meet its financial obligations, that it would be unable to successfully reorganize under Chapter 11 of the United States Bankruptcy Code, and that it has been unsuccessful in its good faith efforts to find other potential merger partners.

ANTITRUST GUIDELINES FOR VERTICAL MERGERS

The guidelines described for horizontal mergers also apply to vertical mergers between customers and suppliers. Vertical mergers may become a concern if an acquisition by a supplier of a customer prevents the supplier's competitors from having access to the customer. Regulators are not likely to challenge this type of merger unless the relevant market has few customers and as such is highly concentrated (i.e., an HHI score in excess of 1800). Alternatively, the acquisition by a customer of a supplier could become a concern if it prevents the customer's competitors from having access to the supplier. The concern is greatest if the supplier's products or services are critical to the competitor's operations.

ANTITRUST GUIDELINES FOR
COLLABORATIVE EFFORTS

The formation of alliances or joint ventures (JVs) will generally not need approval of antitrust regulatory authorities in the United States, if the combined strength of the partners does not infringe on a significant share of the global market for a specific product or service. Smaller companies not holding dominant shares will have little to be concerned about. Any efforts by alliance or JV partners to fix prices or geographically allocate customers or markets are likely to be considered illegal. Moreover, alliances cannot be used to deprive competitors of vital resources (Lynch: 1993).

The Role of Collaborative Arrangements in the U.S. Economy

The DoJ believes that alliances play a vital role in the growth of the U.S. economy. Consequently, the DoJ has been systematically removing regulatory obstacles. Such endeavors as collaborative research, even among major industry players, are being encouraged when the research is shared among all participants in the JV. The DoJ tends to favor project-oriented alliances. Even in very concentrated markets, the DoJ may be receptive to alliances, if the partners in a horizontal alliance can show efficiency gains or that collaboration will result in new technologies. Purchaser–supplier alliances are treated in much the same way as vertical mergers and are not considered serious competitive threats.

Although the regulatory authorities have often viewed properly constructed alliances in a positive light during most of the 1980s and 1990s, they have been challenged a number of times as anticompetitive. These challenges arose when the alliances allegedly attempted to impose rules or standards in the marketplace that clearly tended to favor a single or a small number of competitors.

In 1992, the DoJ challenged Primestar, a JV consisting of cable companies intending to enter the direct broadcast satellite (DBS) industry. The JV included Time Warner, TCI, and other smaller cable companies. The DoJ claimed that the JV sought to delay the development of DBS by imposing rules on its members that discouraged them from providing programming to competing DBS companies. The case was settled with the elimination of the rules (*United States v. Primestar:* 1993).

In the mid-1980s, similar concerns were raised when Visa and Mastercard created a single JV, known as Entree, to issue debit cards. A group of 13 state attorneys general challenged the formation of the JV, alleging that Visa and Mastercard intended to retard the development of an online debit payment system, which they feared would erode the profitability of credit cards. In 1990, Visa and Mastercard agreed to abandon the Entrée JV. They have since created their own online debit card systems (*New York State v. Visa USA, Inc.,* 1990).

On October 1, 1999, the DoJ and the FTC circulated new guidelines to be applied to collaborative efforts among competitors such as JVs. JVs are unlikely to be challenged if they comprise less than 20% of the market in which they compete.

Moreover, if the participants in the JV have incentives to compete against the JV, the JV will probably not be challenged.

The Limitations of Antitrust Laws

Efforts to measure market share or concentration must inevitably take into account the explosion of international trade during the last 20 years. Actions by a single domestic firm to restrict its output in order to raise its selling price may be thwarted by a surge in imports of similar products. Moreover, the pace of technological change is creating many new substitute products and services, which may make a firm's dominant position in a rapidly changing market indefensible almost overnight.

The Electronic Commerce Marketplace

The rapid growth of electronic commerce as a marketplace without geographic boundaries has tended to reduce the usefulness of conventional measures of market share and market concentration. What constitutes a market on the Internet is largely undefined. Marketers routinely refer to market segments on the Internet as "spaces" with largely undefined competitive characteristics. These ambiguities lead to challenges for regulators. Do anticompetitive practices arise when a single vendor such as Microsoft tends to dominate the PC desktop or when the preponderance of users enter the Internet through the same "portal" or access point such as American Online or Yahoo? When does control of electronic access to the home constitute a monopolistic practice?

Open-Access Issues

The FTC has expressed concern about the potential for anticompetitive practices on the Internet (Balto: 1999). While medium-to-large-sized businesses have many ways to access the Internet, consumers are largely dependent on connecting to Internet service providers (ISPs). Because the technology is changing so rapidly, the Federal Communications Commission (FCC) has chosen not to require owners of broadband systems to open access to everyone, preferring to let cable and telephone companies fight it out in the marketplace. The FCC has taken the position that high-speed cable access to the home does not constitute a monopoly, because it competes with telephone companies' digital subscriber line (DSL) services as well as satellite delivery systems. On November 18, 1999, the FCC ruled that telephone companies must share their telephone lines into the home with DSL providers. This ruling should make DSL services more cost competitive with cable services.

On December 7, 1999, AT&T, after months of resisting the notion of providing access to competing ISPs over its cable lines, took steps to make "open access" a part of its company policy. AT&T signed a deal with MindSpring to give its customers a choice between AT&T and MindSpring as their internet service provider. The policy will take effect in 2002 when AT&T's exclusive contract with *Excite@Home* expires.

ISPs are undergoing substantial consolidation. In the merger of MCI and WorldCom, the DoJ, FCC, and the European Union alleged harm to competition. The consent decree settling the case required the divestiture of MCI's backbone infrastructure (WorldCom: 1998). The potential for increased concentration grew in late 1999 with MCI WorldCom's announcement of a merger with Sprint. In disallowing this merger in 2000, regulators at the FCC and DoJ were simply not convinced that the salutary effects of improved efficiency would lead to lower prices and more innovative products and offset the potentially anticompetitive effects of increasing concentration in the telecommunications industry (Case Study 2-5).

CASE STUDY 2-5. MCI WORLDCOM TO ACQUIRE SPRINT

On October 6, 1999, MCI WorldCom proposed to acquire Sprint in a stock-for-stock transaction valued at $115 billion, $129 billion including the assumption of debt. At this price, the merger would constitute the third largest transaction in history, behind Vodafone's acquisition of Mannesman and AOL's takeover of TimeWarner, and provide Sprint's shareholders with a 50% premium over the market value of Sprint and its Sprint PCS business. Sprint's operations are divided into two separately traded stocks, one representing its long-distance network and the other its wireless operation. MCI increased the premium significantly from its first offer as a result of a series of competing bids for Sprint made by BellSouth.

The new company would have had more than 40 million business and residential customers and 142,000 employees, as well as operations in 65 countries. The new company would have had revenue of $54 billion as compared to AT&T's $64 billion.

Within one day of the announcement, William Kennard, the Chairman of the FCC, asked, "how this merger could be good for consumers." He also said that the second and third largest long-distance telephone companies "will bear a heavy burden to show how consumers would be better off." The FCC was particularly concerned about the increased concentration in the long-distance market and in the Internet backbone.

With the loss of Sprint as a competitor, just two companies, AT&T and MCI WorldCom, would control 85% of the U.S. long-distance market. Qwest Communications, the third largest competitor, would control only 2% of the market. Together, Sprint and MCI WorldCom currently control 43% of the access points to the Internet in the United States.

The companies argued that the economics of the combination would be particularly compelling. Economies of scale and greater access to the capital markets were expected to play a major role in reducing the combined firms' operating expenses. Operating synergies, primarily from consolidations, were expected to reach $9.7 billion. In addition, capital expenditures were expected to be reduced by $5.2 billion. It was argued that the combined companies would have the capital, marketing strength, and state-of-the-art networks to compete more effectively against both domestic and foreign carriers. The combined companies would also have controlled about one-third of the U.S. long-distance market and offer wireless phone and paging services as well as access to the Internet.

The new company's strategy was to provide customers, especially businesses, with the full range of telecommunication services, including voice and data transmission, Internet access, as well as wireless and international calling. Not only would the new company have access to more customers in more countries, but also Sprint's wireless business would have filled a hole in MCI WorldCom's strategy of offering its customers a full array of telecommunication services.

Given its size, company officials believed that it will be able to more effectively compete against AT&T, which currently controls about 45% of the long-distance market in the United States. Moreover, it was argued that the new company would be in a better position to serve a larger market for its wireless and Internet products by bundling these services with its long-distance service. In the final analysis, the regulators simply did not agree.

Source: Bloomberg.com, 1999a; *Business Week*, 1999b.

Promoting Innovation: The Microsoft Antitrust Case

The government's 1998 suit against Microsoft was based on its anticompetitive practices defined under the Sherman Antitrust Act of 1890. The suit was largely an effort to protect consumers by keeping prices down and promoting choice. By late 1999, Microsoft had been found guilty of anticompetitive practices. On April 28, 2000, the government submitted its proposed remedy to the federal courts. The proposal consisted of splitting the firm into operating systems and applications software companies in an effort to promote innovation as well as to encourage price competition and consumer choice.

The proposed remedy did not deal directly with Microsoft's dominance of the PC operating system market, since the PC market does not represent the future of the computing industry. Rather, the proposed remedy may reflect an effort to limit Microsoft's ability to dominate the server market, high-powered computers that run networks. Currently, Microsoft Exchange, the most popular e-mail program around, runs only on servers using Windows NT or its successors. Therefore, companies must buy Windows server software if they want to deploy Exchange. Moreover, a number of features in the PC desktop version of Windows 2000 (e.g., automated back-ups) work only with servers operating on Windows

NT. If Microsoft is split into two companies, the software applications business is assumed to have sufficient incentive to develop versions of Exchange and other Microsoft applications that will run on Linux, Sun Solaris, and IBM's Unix operating systems that directly compete with Windows NT.

But the proposal seems to be based more on intuition than on empirical studies. According to the growth theories propounded by Paul Romer of Stanford University, a contributing author to the briefs supporting the government's case, innovation is the most important factor determining the well-being of consumers and that the pace of innovation is highly responsive to incentives. Such incentives are much stronger in an economy characterized by competition than by monopoly. Small firms are more likely to innovate without fear of being overwhelmed by larger firms that choose to embrace and extend the smaller firms' new technological innovations. The presumed result is that consumers would receive new types of software more rapidly (*Business Week,* 2000). The implications of the increasing importance of innovation in antitrust enforcement are discussed in Case Study 2-6.

STATE REGULATIONS AFFECTING MERGERS AND ACQUISITIONS

Numerous regulations affecting takeovers exist at the state level. The regulations often differ from one state to another, making compliance with all applicable regulations a challenge. State regulations often are a result of special interests that appeal to state legislators to establish a particular type of antitakeover statute to make it more difficult to ward off unfriendly takeover attempts. Such appeals are usually made in the context of an attempt to save jobs in the state.

STATE ANTITAKEOVER LAWS

States regulate corporate charters. Charters define the powers of the firm and the rights and responsibilities of its shareholders, boards of directors, and managers. However, states are not allowed to pass any laws that impose restrictions on interstate commerce or that conflict in any way with federal laws regulating interstate commerce.

First-Generation Laws

First-generation antitakeover laws tended to apply to all firms no matter how little business they did within the boundaries of a state. These early state antitakeover laws were overturned in a Supreme Court ruling in 1982, which found that an Illinois law violated interstate commerce and therefore was unconstitutional (*Edgar v. MITE Corporation:* 1982). Furthermore, the Supreme Court ruled that the Williams Act preempted state antitakeover laws, thus striking down the first-generation laws in 37 states.

> ### CASE STUDY 2-6. HOW THE MICROSOFT CASE COULD DEFINE ANTITRUST LAW IN THE "NEW ECONOMY"
>
> Even if the proposed remedy does not stand on appeal, the Microsoft case has precedent value due to the perceived importance of innovation in the information-based, technology-driven "new economy." The case may suggest that trust busters are trying to turn innovation into the central issue in enforcement policy. Regulators may seek to determine whether proposed business combinations either promote or impede innovation.
>
> Due to the accelerating pace of new technology, government is less likely to want to be involved in imposing remedies that seek to limit anticompetitive behaviors by requiring the government to continuously monitor a firm's performance to a consent decree. In fact, the government's frustration with the ineffectiveness of sanctions imposed on Microsoft in the early 1990s may have been a contributing factor in their proposal to divide the firm. The break-up of a dominant firm within an industry may be viewed as less intrusive than alternative measures and could become an important enforcement tool.
>
> Antitrust watchdogs are likely to pay more attention to the impact of proposed mergers or acquisitions on start-ups, which are viewed as major contributors to innovation. In some instances, business combinations among competitors may be disallowed if they are believed to be simply an effort to slow the rate of innovation. The challenge for regulators will be to recognize when cooperation or mergers among competitors may provide additional incentives for innovation through a sharing of risk and resources. However, until the effects on innovation of a firm's actions or a proposed merger can be more readily measured, decisions by regulators may appear to be more arbitrary than well reasoned.
>
> The economics of innovation are at best ill defined. Innovation cycles are difficult to determine and may run as long as several decades between the gestation of an idea and its actual implementation. Consequently, if it is to foster innovation, antitrust policy will have to attempt to anticipate technologies, markets, and competitors that do not currently exist in order to determine which proposed business combinations should be allowed and which firms with substantial market positions should be broken up.

Second-Generation Laws

Second-generation laws tended to apply only to corporations that were incorporated in the state or that conducted a substantial amount of their business within the state. These laws typically contained *fair price provisions* requiring that all

target shareholders of a successful tender offer receive the same price as those who actually tendered their shares. In a specific attempt to prevent highly leveraged transactions such as leveraged buyouts, some state laws include *business combination provisions,* which may specifically rule out the sale of the target's assets for a specific period of time. Because the sale of target assets is frequently a means of reducing indebtedness in highly leveraged transactions, these provisions would effectively preclude such transactions.

Other common characteristics of second-generation statutes include *cash-out and control share provisions.* Cash-out provisions require a bidder, whose purchases exceed a stipulated amount, to buy the remainder of the target stock on the same terms granted to those shareholders whose stock was purchased at an earlier date. By forcing the acquiring firm to purchase 100% of the stock, potential bidders lacking substantial financial resources are effectively eliminated from bidding on the target company. Control share provisions require that a bidder obtain prior approval from stockholders holding large blocks of target stock once the bidder's purchases of stock exceeds some threshold level. The latter provision can be particularly troublesome to an acquiring company when the holders of the large blocks of stock tend to support target management.

STATE ANTITRUST LAWS

As part of the Hart–Scott–Rodino Act of 1976, the states were granted increased antitrust power. The state laws are often very similar to federal laws. Under federal law, states have the right to sue to block mergers they believe are anticompetitive even if the DoJ or FTC does not challenge them.

REGULATED INDUSTRIES

In addition to the DoJ and the FTC, a variety of other agencies monitor activities in certain industries, such as commercial banking, railroads, defense, and cable TV. In each industry, the agency is typically responsible for both the approvals of M&As and subsequent oversight. Mergers in these industries often take much longer to complete due to the additional filing requirements.

BANKING

According to the Bank Merger Act of 1966, any bank merger not challenged by the attorney general within 30 days of its approval by the pertinent regulatory agency could not be challenged under the Clayton Antitrust Act. Moreover, the Bank Merger Act stated that anticompetitive effects could be offset by a finding that the deal meets the "convenience and needs" of the communities served by the bank.

Currently, three different agencies review banking mergers. Which agency has authority depends on the parties involved in the transaction. The comptroller of the currency has responsibility for transactions in which the acquirer is a national bank. The Federal Deposit Insurance Corporation oversees mergers where the acquiring or resulting bank will be a federally insured state-chartered bank that operates outside of the Federal Reserve System. The third agency is the Board of Governors of the Federal Reserve System. It has the authority to regulate mergers in which the acquirer or the resulting bank will be a state bank, which is also a member of the Federal Reserve System.

Although all three agencies conduct their own review, they consider reviews undertaken by the DoJ. Using a modified version of the HHI, the DoJ will generally not challenge a bank merger unless its HHI score exceeds 1800 and increases the index by more than 200 points.

COMMUNICATIONS

The federal agency charged with oversight, the FCC, has deferred to the DoJ and the FTC for antitrust enforcement. The FCC is an independent U.S. government agency directly responsible to Congress. Established by the 1934 Communications Act, the FCC is charged with regulating interstate and international communication by radio, television, wire, satellite, and cable. Headed by five commissioners appointed by the president and approved by Congress, it has seven operating bureaus including Cable Services, Common Carrier, Consumer Information, Enforcement, International Mass Media, and Wireless. These bureaus are responsible for developing and implementing regulatory programs, processing applications for licenses, analyzing complaints, and conducting investigations. The FCC is responsible for the enforcement of such legislation as the Telecommunications Act of 1996. This act is intended to promote competition and reduce regulation while promoting lower prices and higher quality services. (See Federal Communications Commission, WWW.fcc.gov).

The FCC employed an innovative solution to perceived competitive issues in the 1999 merger of Ameritech and SBC Communications (see Case Study 2-7). A tight timetable coupled with substantial fines if certain conditions are not satisfied is intended to accelerate the achievement of the objectives of the 1996 Telecommunications Act.

RAILROADS

The Surface Transportation Board (STB), the successor to the Interstate Commerce Commission, governs mergers of railroads. Under the ICC Termination Act of 1995, the STB employs five criteria to determine if a merger should be approved. These criteria include the impact of the proposed transaction on the adequacy of public transportation, the impact on the areas currently served by the carriers involved in the proposed transaction, and the burden of the total fixed charges resulting from completing the transaction. In addition, the interest of

---

CASE STUDY 2-7. FCC USES ITS POWER TO STIMULATE COMPETITION IN THE TELECOMMUNICATIONS MARKET

Having received approval from the DoJ and the FTC, Ameritech and SBC Communications received permission from the FCC to combine to form the nation's largest local telephone company in 1999. The FCC gave its approval of the $74 billion transaction subject to conditions requiring that the companies open their markets to rivals and enter new markets to compete with established local phone companies.

SBC, which operates under Southwestern Bell, Pacific Bell, SNET, Nevada Bell, and Cellular One brands, has 52 million phone lines in its territory. It also has 8.3 million wireless customers across the United States. Ameritech, which serves Illinois, Indiana, Michigan, Ohio, and Wisconsin, has more than 12 million phone customers. It also provides wireless service to 3.2 million individuals and businesses.

The combined business would control about one-third of the nation's local phone lines in 13 states. The FCC adopted 30 conditions to ensure that the deal would serve the public interest. The new SBC must enter 30 new markets within 30 months to compete with established local phone companies. In the new markets, it would face fierce competition from Bell Atlantic, BellSouth, and U.S. West. The company is required to provide deep discounts on key pieces of their networks to rivals who want to lease them.

The merged companies must also establish a separate subsidiary to provide advanced telecommunications services such as high-speed Internet access. At least 10% of its upgraded services would go toward low-income groups.

The conditions include stiff fines. The companies could face up to $1.2 billion in penalties for failing to meet the new market deadline and could pay another $1.1 billion for not meeting performance standards related to opening up their markets.

Source: Bloomberg.com, 1999b.

---

railroad employees is considered, as well as whether the transaction would have an adverse impact on competition among rail carriers in regions affected by the merger.

DEFENSE

During the 1990s, the defense industry in the United States has undergone substantial consolidation. The consolidation that has swept the defense industry is consistent with the Department of Defense's (DoD) philosophy that it is preferable to have three or four highly viable defense contractors that could more effectively compete than a dozen weaker contractors. Examples of transactions include the merger of Lockheed and Martin Marietta, Boeing's acquisition of Rockwell's defense and aerospace business, Raytheon's acquisition of the assets of defense-related product lines of Hughes Electronics, and Boeing's acquisition of Hughes space and communication business. However, regulators did prevent the proposed acquisition by Lockheed Martin of Northrop Grumman.

Although defense industry mergers are technically subject to current antitrust regulations, the DoJ and FTC have assumed a secondary role to the DoD. The DoD has a formal process of coordinating with the DoJ and the FTC. This involves the DoD making assessments of a proposed transaction on the defense industrial base of the country and then making a recommendation to the DoJ and FTC based on their findings.

OTHER REGULATED INDUSTRIES

Insurance

The insurance industry is regulated largely at the state level. Acquiring an insurance company normally requires the approval of state government and is subject to substantial financial disclosure by the acquiring company.

Public Utilities

Public utilities are highly regulated at the state level. Like insurance companies, their acquisition requires state government approval.

Airlines

The acquisition of more than 10% of a domestic airline's shares outstanding is subject to approval of the Federal Aviation Administration (FAA).

ENVIRONMENTAL LAWS

Environmental laws create numerous reporting requirements for both acquirers and target firms. Failure to adequately comply with these laws can result in enormous potential liabilities to all parties involved in a transaction. These laws require full disclosure of the existence of hazardous materials and the extent to which they are being released into the environment. Such laws include the Clean Water Act (CWA: 1974), the Toxic Substances Control Act (TSCA: 1978), the Resource Conservation and Recovery Act (RCRA: 1976), and the Comprehensive Environmental Response, Compensation, and Liability Act (CERCLA or Superfund: 1980). These laws require the notification of government authorities in case of spills of hazardous materials and related emergencies. Moreover, the TSCA and related regulations require producers of chemicals to report on the existence and use of hazardous materials on their premises.

Additional reporting requirements were imposed in 1986 with the passage of the Emergency Planning and Community Right to Know Act (EPCRA). This act requires that businesses provide detailed information about the presence of extremely hazardous materials in order to facilitate state and local emergency response planning. The act also requires companies to immediately contact local authorities in the event such materials are released into the environment. Unlike other federal environmental laws, much of the information that is required by EPCRA is available to the public. In addition to EPCRA, several states have also passed "right-to-know" laws, such as California's Proposition 65. Because EPCRA is largely implemented at the state level, the role of state reporting laws has diminished.

LABOR AND BENEFIT LAWS

A diligent buyer must also ensure that the target company is in compliance with the labyrinth of labor and benefit laws. These laws govern such areas as employment discrimination, immigration law, sexual harassment, age discrimination, and drug testing, as well as wage and hour laws. Labor and benefit laws also include the Medical Leave Act (FMLA), the Americans with Disabilities Act (ADA), and the Worker Adjustment and Retraining Notification Act (WARN), which governs notification prior to plant closings and retraining requirements.

BENEFIT PLAN LIABILITIES

Employee benefit plans frequently represent one of the biggest areas of liability to a buyer. The greatest potential liabilities are often found in defined pension benefit plans, postretirement medical, life insurance benefits, and deferred compensation plans. Such liabilities arise when the reserve shown on the seller's balance sheet does not accurately indicate the true extent of the liability.

The potential liability from improperly structured benefit plans grows with each new round of legislation starting with the passage of the Employee Retirement Income and Security Act of 1974 (ERISA). This act was followed by the Multiemployer Pension Plan Amendments Act of 1980 (MEPPAA), the Retirement Equity Act of 1984 (REA), the Single Employer Pension Plan Amendments Act of 1986 (SEPPAA), the Tax Reform Act of 1986 (TRA 1986), and the Omnibus Budget Reconciliation Acts (OBRA) of 1987, 1989, and 1990, and 1993. Buyers and sellers must also be aware of the Unemployment Compensation Act of 1992 (UCA), the Retirement Protection Act of 1994 (RPA), and Statements 87, 88, and 106 of the Financial Accounting Standards Board (Sherman, 1998).

THINGS TO REMEMBER

The Securities Acts of 1933 and 1934 established the SEC and require that all securities offered to the public must be registered with the government. The registration process requires the description of the company's properties and business, a description of the securities, information about management, and financial statements certified by public accountants.

Passed in 1968, the Williams Act consists of a series of amendments to the 1934 Securities Exchange Act, which were intended to provide target firm shareholders with sufficient information and time to adequately assess the value of an acquirer's offer. Any person or firm acquiring 5% or more of the stock of a public corporation must file a Schedule 13D with the SEC within 10 days of reaching that percentage ownership threshold. The disclosure is necessary even if the accumulation of the stock is not followed by a tender offer. Under Section 14(d) of the Williams Act, acquiring firms that initiate tender offers must disclose their intentions and business plans, as well as any agreements between the acquirer and the target firm, in a Schedule 14D-1.

Federal antitrust laws exist to prevent individual corporations from assuming too much market power such that they can raise prices without concern for any significant competitor reaction. Passed in 1890, the Sherman Act makes illegal such practices as agreements to fix prices and allocate customers among competitors, as well as attempts to monopolize any part of interstate commerce. In an attempt to strengthen the Sherman Act, the Clayton Act was passed in 1914 to make illegal the purchase the stock of another company if their combination results in reduced competition within the industry.

Current antitrust law requires prenotification of mergers or acquisitions involving companies of a certain size to allow the FTC and the DoJ to have sufficient time to challenge business combinations believed to be anticompetitive before they are completed. Bidding firms must execute a Hart–Scott–Rodino filing at the same time as it makes an offer to a target firm. The target firm is also required to file within 15 days following the bidder's filing. Before the takeover can be completed, a 30-day waiting period for transactions involving securities and 15 days for cash tender offers is required. Either the FTC or the DoJ may request a 20-day extension of the waiting period for transactions involving securities and 10 days for cash tender offers.

Antitrust regulators, in determining which business combinations to challenge, analyze market concentration, the potential for such anticompetitive practices as price fixing, ease of new competitors entering the market, efficiencies that may result from the business combination, the likelihood that a firm will fail if it is not acquired, and the impact on innovation. A decision by the federal antitrust regulatory authorities may be appealed in the federal circuit courts. As an alternative to what is likely to be very expensive litigation, a company may seek to negotiate a voluntary settlement of its differences with the FTC. Such settlements are usually negotiated during the review process and are called consent decrees.

There are numerous state regulations impacting M&As such as state antitakeover and antitrust laws. A number of industries are also subject to regulatory approval at the federal and state level. Examples include banking, insurance, telecommunications defense, public utilities, railroads, and airlines. Considerable effort must also be made to ensure that a transaction is in full compliance with applicable environmental and employee benefit laws. The resulting penalties for failure to do so can be litigation and fines that could seriously erode the profitability of the combined firms or result in bankruptcy.

CHAPTER DISCUSSION QUESTIONS

2-1. What was the motivation for the Federal Securities Acts of 1933 and 1934?

2-2. What was the rationale for the Williams Act?

2-3. What factors do U.S. antitrust regulators consider before challenging a merger or acquisition?

2-4. What are the obligations of the acquirer and target firms according to Section 14(d) of the Williams Act?

2-5. Discuss the pros and cons of federal antitrust laws.

2-6. Why is pre-merger notification (HSR filing) required by U.S. antitrust regulatory authorities?

2-7. When is a person or firm required to submit a Schedule 13D to the SEC? What is the purpose of such a filing?

2-8. What is the rationale behind state antitakeover legislation?

2-9. Give examples of the types of actions that may be required by the parties to a proposed merger subject to a FTC consent decree?

2-10. How might the growth of electronic commerce affect the application of current antitrust laws?

CHAPTER BUSINESS CASE

CASE STUDY 2-8. EXXON AND MOBIL MERGER

From the moment the proposed $81 billion merger was announced in December 1998, officials at the Federal Trade Commission promised a rigorous regulatory review. Following that review, they decided to challenge the Exxon-Mobil transaction on anticompetitive grounds. This paved the way for either a vigorous court challenge by the merger partners of the FTC's rulings, a negotiated settlement, or a withdrawal of merger plans.

Prior to the merger, Exxon was the largest oil producer in the United States and Mobil was the number two company. The combined companies would create the world's biggest oil company in terms of revenues. Top executives from Exxon Corporation and Mobil Corporation argued that they needed to implement their proposed merger due to the increasingly competitive world oil market. Falling oil prices during much of the late 1990s put a squeeze on oil industry profits. Moreover, giant state-owned oil companies are also posing a competitive threat due to their access to huge amounts of capital.

To offset these factors, Exxon and Mobil argued that they had to combine to achieve substantial cost savings. By combining their exploration and production activities, the two companies expected to save $2 billion annually in operating expenses. Analysts estimated that job cuts for the combined companies could reach as high as 20,000, about 16% of the combined companies' workforce.

After a yearlong review, antitrust officials at the FTC approved the Exxon–Mobil merger after the companies agreed to the largest divestiture in the history of the FTC. The divestiture involved the sale of 15% of their service station network, amounting to 2400 stations. This included about 1,220 Mobil stations from Virginia to New Jersey and about 300 in Texas. In addition, about 520 Exxon stations from New York to Maine and about 360 in California were divested. Exxon has also agreed to the divestiture of an Exxon refinery in Benecia, California.

The FTC had continuously expressed its concern about the potentially anti-competitive effects of the deal. However, they have noted that there is considerably greater competition worldwide. This is particularly true in the market for exploration of new reserves. The greatest threat to competition seems to be in the refining and distribution of gasoline. (Sources: CNNfn.com, March 11, 1999 and Bloomberg.com, September 12 and November 27, 1999.

Case Study Discussion Questions

1. How does the FTC define market share?
2. Why might it be important to distinguish between a global and a regional oil and gas market?
3. Why are the Exxon and Mobil executives emphasizing efficiencies as a justification for this merger?
4. Should the size of the combined companies be an important consideration in the regulators' analysis of the proposed merger?
5. How do the divestitures address perceived anticompetitive problems?

Solutions to these case study questions are found in the Appendix at the back of the book.

REFERENCES

Balto, David A., "Emerging Antitrust Issues in Electronic Commerce," Office of Policy and Evaluation, Bureau of Competition, Federal Trade Commission, November 2, 1999.

Bers, Joanna Smith, "Microsoft-DoJ suit exposes the pitfalls of electronic commerce." *Bank Systems & Technology,* vol. 32, n6, (June 1995), pp. 6–8.

Bloomberg.com, "Increasing Concentration in Telecommunications," October 17, 1999a.

Bloomberg.com, "Ameritech and SBC Receive FCC Approval to Merge," October 7, 1999b.

Bloomberg.com, "Arco-Amoco Merger Rejected," February 3, 2000a.

Bloomberg.com, "FTC Deepens Its Scrutiny of Mergers," February 18, 2000b.

Business Week, "Antitrust for the Digital Age," May 15, 2000, pp. 46–48.

Business Week, "MCI WorldCom and Spring to Merge," October 18, 1999, pp. 35–37

CNNfn, "FTC Intervenes in Staples Proposal to Buy Office Depot," December 20, 1996. www
.CNNfn.com.

Department of Justice, www.doj.gov.

Edgar v. MITE Corporation, 102 S. Ct. 2629 (1982).

Federal Communications Commission, Press release, November 8, 1999, www.fcc.gov.

Federal Trade Commission, *Merger quidelines,* 1999, www.ftc.com.

Gaughan, Patrick A., *Mergers, Acquisitions, and Corporate Restructurings,* 2 nd ed., John Wiley &
Sons, 1999, pp. 61–114.

Gilson, Ronald J. and Bernard S. Black, *The Law and Finance of Corporate Acquisitions,* 2 nd ed.,
Westbury, NY: The Foundation Press, Inc. 1995.

Loss, Louis and Joel Seligman, *Fundamental of Securities Regulation,* 3 rd ed., Boston: Little, Brown,
1995.

Lynch, Robert Porter, *Business Alliances Guide, The Hidden Competitive Weapon,* John Wiley &
Sons, Inc., 1993, pp. 257–258.

New York State v. Visa USA, Inc., 1990–1, Trade Case (CCH), 69016, SDNY: 1990.

Federal Trade Commission, Bureau of Competition, "A Study of the Commission's Divestiture Process," 1999.

The Motley Fool Lunchtime News, September 4, 1996. www.sur.be.fool.com/lunchnews/1996.

Radigan, Joseph, "Look out home banking, here comes William the Conqueror," *United States
Banker,* vol. 104, n12, December 1994, pp. 22–26.

Securities and Exchange Commission, www.sec.gov.

Sherman, Andrew J., *Mergers and Acquisitions from A to Z, Strategic and Practical Guidance for
Small and Middle Market Buyers and Sellers,* AMACOM, 1998, pp. 78–94.

Sraeel, Holly. Microsoft-DoJ appeal rejection of proposed antitrust settlement. *Bank Systems & Technology,* 32 (4), April 1995, pp. 6–8.

Talmor, Sharona, "Trials of the Game," *Banker,* 145, (832), June 1995, pp. 76–77.

Ton, Willard K., and Abbott B. Lipsky, Jr., *Antitrust Law Developments,* 3 rd ed., Volume I, American
Bar Association, 1992.

United States Department of Justice, Antitrust Division, www.usdoj.gov, 1999.

United States v. Primestar, L.P., 58 Fed Reg, 33944, June 22, 1993, (Proposed Final Judgment and
Competitive Impact Study).

Wasserstein, Bruce, *Big Deal: The Battle for Control of America's Leading Corporations,* New York:
Warner Books, 1998.

WorldCom, Inc., 13, FCC Ruling 18025, 1998.

3

COMMON TAKEOVER
TACTICS AND DEFENSES

There is no job so simple that it cannot be done wrong.
—Anonymous

As she is in the habit of doing eight or ten times a day, the CEO glances at a flickering monitor on a credenza behind her mahogany desk to review the price movement in her company's stock. Her eyes widen in amazement at the sharp jump in share price in the last hour. She knows that unexpectedly large movements are frequently a result of institutional trades of large blocks of stock to cover a short position or simply an overreaction to rumors on "the street." But this time, something is different. The stock price has run up more than eight points in the last week, accompanied by an unusually large number of block trades for such a short period of time. In the last hour, the stock has surged upward by more than two points. Her heart pounds as she pushes away from her desk, unable to concentrate on the contents of her in-box, and zaps an e-mail to her chief financial officer, corporate attorney, and head of public affairs setting up a meeting later in the morning. She can't get back to her daily routine until she knows what's going on. She has gone through this drill before in response to what appeared to be credible rumors. In all cases, they turned out to be all smoke and no fire. But maybe, just maybe, this time, it's for real.

OVERVIEW

The corporate takeover has been dramatized in Hollywood as motivated by excessive greed, reviled in the press as a destroyer of jobs and of local communities, sanctified on Wall Street as a means of dislodging incompetent management, and often heralded by shareholders as a source of windfall gains. The reality is that corporate takeovers may be a little of all of these things.

The purpose of this chapter is to discuss the commonly used tactics to acquire a company in a hostile takeover attempt and to evaluate the effectiveness of various takeover defenses. The chapter is divided into two major sections: alternative takeover tactics and alternative takeover defenses. Alternative takeover tactics are further subdivided into friendly and aggressive tactics. Aggressive tactics include the bear hug, proxy contests, open-market operations, and tender offers. Alternative takeover defenses are viewed in terms of two stages: prebid, those in place before a bid is made; and postbid, those put in place in response to a bid. The impact on shareholder returns of the various types of takeover defenses is also discussed. Finally, the case at the end of the chapter, entitled "Tyco Saves AMP from AlliedSignal," provides an excellent illustration of how takeover tactics are employed in a hostile takeover to penetrate a target firm's defenses and common reactions by target firms to such tactics.

ALTERNATIVE TAKEOVER TACTICS

Takeovers may be classified as friendly or hostile. Friendly takeovers are negotiated settlements that are often characterized by bargaining, which remains undisclosed until the agreement of purchase and sale has been signed. An example of a friendly takeover is a company desirous of being acquired soliciting another company to assess their interest in combining the two firms. A hostile takeover is generally considered an unsolicited offer made by a potential acquirer that is resisted by the target firm's management. Hostile transactions are normally disclosed in the press. Although it would seem easy to distinguish between friendly and hostile takeovers, the distinctions are sometimes more perceived than real.

An aggressive public rejection of an offer is often the first step in the process leading to a negotiated settlement. Public announcements are frequently part of a negotiating strategy. Sometimes firms engage in confidential negotiations before there is a public announcement of a bid or a completed transaction. In this instance, the transaction might be viewed as friendly. In other instances, the negotiations may start on a friendly basis but later become vitriolic. Bidders may choose to announce the negotiations publicly, if they feel that this would put pressure on the board and management of the target firm to accede to their terms. Similarly, the target's management may reveal the existence of the negotiations to elicit alternative bidders.

Friendly takeovers may be viewed as ones in which a negotiated settlement is possible without the acquirer resorting to such aggressive tactics as the bear hug, proxy contest, or tender offer. A *bear hug* involves the mailing of a letter containing an acquisition proposal to the board of directors of a target company without prior warning and demanding a rapid decision. A *proxy contest* is an attempt by a group of dissident shareholders to obtain representation on the board of directors or to change a firm's bylaws. A *tender offer* is a takeover tactic in which the acquirer bypasses the target's board and management and goes directly to the target's shareholders with an offer to purchase their shares.

Two theories have been proposed to explain the motives of target company management when approached by a potential acquirer. According to the *management entrenchment theory,* corporate managers take actions using various types of takeover defenses that are designed to ensure their longevity with the firm. Shareholders lose when the value of their shares declines in response to management's actions. In contrast, the *shareholder interests theory* argues that shareholders gain when management resists takeover attempts. Such resistance is viewed to be in the best interests of the shareholders, if it is undertaken to hold out for a higher offer either from the initial bidder or from competing bidders. Although there is evidence to support both theories, there appears to be more empirical evidence that management resists takeover attempts to maximize shareholder value (Schwert: 1999).

THE FRIENDLY APPROACH:
"SWEET-TALKING THE TARGET"

Friendly takeovers involve the initiation by the potential acquirer of an informal dialogue with the target's top management. In a friendly takeover, the acquirer and target agree early in the process on the combined businesses' long-term strategy, how the combined businesses will be operated in the short-term, and who will be in key management positions. A *standstill agreement* is often negotiated, in which the acquirer agrees not to make any further investments in the target's stock for a stipulated period of time. This compels the acquirer to pursue the acquisition only on friendly terms, at least for the time period covered by the agreement. It also permits negotiations to proceed without the threat of more aggressive tactics, such as a tender offer or proxy contest. From the target's perspective, the standstill agreement is an indication of the acquirer's true intentions.

According to Thompson Financial Securities Data Corporation (2000), about four out of five transactions were classified as friendly during the 1990s. However, this was not always the case. The 1970s and early 1980s were characterized by blitzkrieg-style takeovers. The CEO of a target firm could wake up to a full-page ad in the *Wall Street Journal* announcing a cash offer for the business. The federal prenotification regulations have slowed the process dramatically (see Chapter 2, this volume). Federal antitrust laws require a minimum 15-day waiting period. Federal securities laws require that a tender offer stay open for at least 20 days. A number of states also require shareholder approval for certain types of offers. Moreover, most large companies have antitakeover defenses in place, such as poison pills. Hostile takeovers are now more likely to last for months.

Although hostile takeovers today are certainly more challenging than in the past, they continue to have certain advantages over the friendly approach. In taking the friendly approach, the acquirer is surrendering the element of surprise. Even a warning of a few days gives the target's management time to take defensive action to impede the actions of the suitor. Negotiation also raises the likelihood of a leak and a spike in the price of the target's stock as arbitrageurs (arbs) seek to profit from the spread between the acquirer's and the target's stock prices. The speculative rise in the target's share price can dramatically add to the cost of the transaction as the initial offer by the bidder generally includes a premium over the target's current share price. Because a premium is usually expressed as a percentage of the target's share price, a speculative increase in the target firm's current share price will add to the overall purchase price paid by the acquiring firm. For these reasons, a potential bidder may opt for a more hostile approach.

THE AGGRESSIVE APPROACH

Successful hostile takeovers depend on the premium offered to the target's current share price, the composition of the board, the composition and sentiment of the target's current shareholders, the provisions of the target's bylaws, and the potential for the target to put in place additional takeover defenses.

Premium

The target's board will find it more difficult to reject offers exhibiting substantial premiums to the target's current stock price. Concern about their fiduciary responsibility and about stockholder lawsuits puts pressure on the target's board to accept the offer.

Board Composition

Despite the pressure of an attractive premium, the composition of the target's board greatly influences what the board does and the timing of its decisions. A board dominated by independent directors, nonemployees, or family members is more likely to resist offers in an effort to induce the bidder to raise the offer price or to gain time to solicit competing bids than to protect itself and current management. Shivdasani (1993) in an analysis of 169 tender offers from 1989 through 1992, concluded that the shareholder gain from the inception of the offer to its resolution is 62.3% for targets with an independent board, as compared to 40.9% for targets without an independent board.

Stock Ownership

The final outcome of a hostile takeover is also heavily dependent on the composition of the target's stock ownership and how stockholders feel about management's performance. To assess these factors, an acquirer must compile lists of stock ownership by category: management, officers, employee stock ownership plans (ESOPs), employees, and institutions such as pension and mutual funds. Sometimes the acquirer has to sue the company for shareholder lists. Once these categories are defined, an effort is made to determine the length of time that each group has held their stock. Such information can be used to estimate the target's "stock float." *Float* represents the amount of stock that can be most easily purchased by the acquirer. The float is likely to be largest for those companies that have been underperforming and where stockholders are disappointed with incumbent management. For this reason, tender offers are often made for the stock of firms whose performance has been lackluster.

Bylaws

The target's bylaws may provide numerous hurdles, which add to the cost of a takeover. Such provisions could include a staggered board, the inability to remove directors without cause, or supermajority voting requirements for approval of mergers. (These takeover defenses will be discussed in more detail later in this chapter.)

Potential Takeover Defenses

An astute bidder will always analyze the target's possible defenses, including golden parachutes for key employees, poison pills, or an authorization for a large number of shares that have not yet been issued. (These and other measures will also be discussed later in this chapter.)

THE BEAR HUG: LIMITING THE TARGET'S OPTIONS

If the friendly approach is considered inappropriate or is unsuccessful, the acquiring company may attempt to limit the options of the target's senior management by making a formal acquisition proposal, usually involving a public announcement, to the board of directors of the target. The intent is to move the board to a negotiated settlement. The board may be motivated to do so because of its fiduciary responsibility to the target's shareholders. Directors who vote against the proposal may be subject to lawsuits from target stockholders. This is especially true if the offer is at a substantial premium to the target's current stock price. Once the bid is made public, the company is effectively "put into play." Institutional investors and arbitragems add to the pressure by lobbying the board to accept the offer. Empirical data suggests significant abnormal returns associated with institutional activism (Bruner: 1999). Arbs are likely to acquire the target's stock and to sell the bidder's stock short (see Chapter 1, this volume). The accumulation of stock by arbs makes purchases of blocks of stock by the bidder easier. The public announcement may also attract other bidders for the target company.

The target company's board is unlikely to reject the bid without obtaining a "fairness" opinion from an investment banker stating that the offer is inadequate. The fairness opinion may be used to defend the board if lawsuits are filed by target shareholders.

The acquisition of Reynolds Aluminum by Alcoa in 1999 is a classic case in which the combination of poor profitability, weak takeover defenses, and limited shareholder support enabled Alcoa to purchase the company at a very modest premium simply by threatening more aggressive actions if Reynolds' management did not capitulate (Case Study 3-1).

CASE STUDY 3-1. ALCOA ACQUIRES REYNOLDS

Alcoa reacted quickly to a three-way intercontinental combination of aluminum companies aimed at challenging its dominance of the Western world aluminum market by disclosing an unsolicited takeover bid for Reynolds Metals in early August 1999. The offer consisted of $4.3 billion, or $66.44 a share, plus the assumption of $1.5 billion in Reynolds' outstanding debt. Reynolds appeared to be particularly vulnerable, because other logical suitors or potential white knights such as Canada's Alcan Aluminium, France's Pechiney SA, and Switzerland's Alusuisse Lonza Group AG were already involved in a three-way merger.

Alcoa's bear hug letter from its chief executive indicated that it wanted to pursue a friendly deal but suggested that it may pursue a full-blown hostile bid if the two sides could not begin discussions within a week. Reynolds appeared to be highly vulnerable because of its poor financial performance amid falling worldwide aluminum prices and because of its weak takeover defenses. It appeared that a hostile bidder could initiate a mail-in solicitation for shareholder consent at any time. Moreover, major Reynolds' shareholders began to pressure the board. Its largest single shareholder, Highfields Capital Management, a holder of more than four million shares, demanded that the board create a special committee of independent directors with its own counsel and instruct Merrill Lynch to open an auction for Reynolds.

Despite pressure, the Reynolds' board rejected Alcoa's bid as inadequate. Alcoa's response was to say that it would initiate an all-cash tender offer for all of Reynolds' stock and simultaneously solicit shareholder support through a proxy contest for replacing the Reynolds' board and dismantling Reynolds' takeover defenses. Notwithstanding the public posturing by both sides, Reynolds capitulated on August 19, slightly more than 2 weeks from receipt of the initial solicitation, and agreed to be acquired by Alcoa. The agreement contained a 30-day window during which Reynolds could entertain other bids. However, if Reynolds should choose to go with another offer, it would have to pay Alcoa a $100 million break-up fee.

Under the agreement, which was approved by both boards, each share of Reynolds was exchanged for 1.06 shares of Alcoa stock. When announced, the transaction was worth $4.46 billion and valued each Reynolds share at $70.88, based on an Alcoa closing price of $66.875 on August 19, 1999. The $70.88 price per share of Reynolds suggested a puny 3.9% premium to Reynolds' closing price of $68.25 as of the close of August 19.

> The combined annual revenues of the two companies will total $20.5 billion and account for about 21.5% of the Western world market for aluminum. To receive antitrust approval, the combined companies will have to divest selected operations.
>
> Source: Bloomberg.com, 1999.

PROXY CONTESTS IN SUPPORT OF A TAKEOVER

The two primary forms of proxy contests are those for seats on the board of directors and those concerning management proposals. Proxy fights are sometimes initiated if management opposes a takeover attempt. They may be used to replace specific board members or management with those more willing to vote for the merger. By replacing board members, proxy contests can be an effective means of gaining control without owning 51% of the voting stock, or they can be used to eliminate takeover defenses, such as poison pills, as a precursor of a tender offer.

A proxy fight may be costly. Substantial fees must be paid to hire proxy solicitors, investment bankers, and attorneys. Other expenses include printing, mailing, and advertising expenses. Litigation expenses may also be substantial. The cost of litigation can easily become the largest single expense item in highly contentious proxy contests. Nonetheless, a successful proxy fight represents a far less expensive means of gaining control over a target than a tender offer, which may require purchasing at a substantial premium a controlling interest in the target company.

Implementing a Proxy Contest

The proxy process may begin with the bidder, who is also a stockholder in the target company, attempting to call a special stockholders' meeting or placing a proposal to replace the board or management at a regularly scheduled stockholders' meeting. Prior to the meeting, the bidder may undertake an aggressive public relations campaign consisting of direct solicitations sent to shareholders and full-page advertisements in the press in an attempt to convince shareholders to support their proposals. The target corporation will undertake a similar campaign, but it will have a distinct advantage in being able to deal directly with its own shareholders. The bidder may have to sue the target corporation to get a list of its shareholder's names and addresses. Often such shares are held in the name of banks or brokerage houses under a "street name," and these depositories generally do not have the authority to vote such shares. Once the proxies are received by shareholders, shareholders may then sign and send their proxies directly to a designated collection point such as a brokerage house or bank. The votes are then counted, often under the strict supervision of voting inspectors to ensure accuracy.

Both the target firm and the bidder generally have their own proxy solicitors present during the tabulation process.

Legal Filings in Undertaking Proxy Contests

Securities Exchange Commission (SEC) regulations cover the solicitation of the target's shareholders for their proxy or right to vote their shares on an issue that is being contested. All materials distributed to shareholders must be submitted to the SEC for review 10 days before they are distributed. Proxy solicitations are regulated by Section 14(a) of the Securities Exchange Act of 1934. The party attempting to solicit proxies from the target's shareholders must file a proxy statement and Schedule 14A with the SEC and mail it to the target's shareholders.

The Impact of Proxy Contests on Shareholder Value

Despite a low success rate, there is some empirical evidence that proxy fights result in abnormal returns to shareholders of the target company regardless of the outcome. The gain in share prices occurred despite only one-fifth to one-third of all proxy fights actually resulting in a change in board control. In studies covering proxy battles during the 1980s through the mid-1990s, abnormal returns ranged from 6% to 19%, even if the dissident shareholders were unsuccessful in the proxy contest (Dodd and Warner: 1983; DeAngelo and DeAngelo: 1989; and Mulherin and Poulsen: 1998). Reasons for the gains of this magnitude may include the eventual change in management at most firms embroiled in proxy fights, the tendency for new management to restructure the firm, and investor expectations of a future change in control due to merger and acquisition activity. These conclusions were contradicted by Ikenberry and Lakonishok (1993), who found that proxy contests appear to be a result of the poor performance of firms and that firms experienced predominately negative returns during periods associated with proxy contests.

Pfizer's successful acquisition of Warner Lambert in early 2000 illustrates a highly contentious and highly visible hostile takeover involving three parties. The transaction illustrates the use of such tactics as proxy contests, litigation, and shareholder activists to wear down a target's defenses (Case Study 3-2).

CASE STUDY 3-2. PFIZER ACQUIRES WARNER-LAMBERT

After three stormy months, Warner Lambert agreed on February 8, 2000, to be acquired by Pfizer for $92.5 billion, forming the world's second largest pharmaceutical firm. The combined companies will be called Pfizer and have total sales of more than $29 billion, after-tax profits of $4.9 billion, and a research and development (R&D) budget of $4.7 billion. Although the new company will have slightly less than 7% of the world market for prescription drugs, it will be able to more effectively develop new medicines and cut overhead expenses. Pfizer has been among the best performing drug companies during the 1990s, but its growth was expected to slow without the acquisition because of too few new "blockbuster" drugs in its R&D pipeline. Moreover, patents on a number of drugs that had been key to its growth were set to expire by 2005. Pfizer was anxious to acquire the rights to Lipitor, the best-selling cholesterol reduction drug, and other drugs in development within Warner Lambert.

The takeover battle for Warner Lambert began in November 1999 when Warner Lambert announced a $58.3 billion merger with American Home Products (AHP). Pfizer followed with a hostile bid almost immediately. Warner Lambert rejected Pfizers's bid and threatened to cancel the companies' partnership to market Lipitor. Pfizer responded by exploiting a weakness in the Warner Lambert takeover defenses by utilizing a consent solicitation process that allows shareholders to change the board without waiting months for a stockholders' meeting. Pfizer also challenged in court two provisions in the contract with AHP on the grounds that they were not in the best interests of the Warner Lambert shareholders, because they would discourage other bidders. These provisions included a $1.8 billion break-up fee and an option for AHP to buy almost 15% of Warner Lambert's stock for $83.81 per share. Pfizer's earlier offers for Warner Lambert were contingent on the removal of these provisions. Pfizer was unsuccessful in eliminating the break-up fee and will have to pay AHP the largest such fee in history.

Initially, Warner Lambert refused to talk to Pfizer. However, it was forced to enter into discussions as a result of stockholder pressure. The pressure came from some of the firm's largest shareholders including the California Public Employees Retirement System and the New York City Retirement Fund.

The announced acquisition of Warner Lambert by Pfizer ended one of the most contentious corporate takeover battles in recent memory. The pending challenge for both companies is to put aside their nasty accusations and lawsuits and to integrate their respective research, sales, and manufacturing operations to make the combined companies successful. Pfizer's first step with Warner Lambert will be to identify an estimated $1.6 billion in cost savings to be achieved by 2002. The bulk of such savings are expected to come from layoffs. The track record for merged drug companies in recent years has been disappointing. Barrie G. James, president of Pharma Strategy Consulting, found that drug companies formed as a result of deals tended to lose market share in the years following the transaction when compared to those drug companies that had remained independent.

Source: *Business Week*, 1999; Bloomberg.com, 2000a.

PRE-TENDER OFFER TACTICS:
PURCHASING TARGET STOCK IN THE OPEN MARKET

Potential bidders often purchase stock in a target prior to a formal bid to accumulate stock at a price lower than the eventual offer price. Such purchases are normally kept secret in order not to drive up the price and increase the average price paid for such shares. The primary advantage accruing to the bidder of accumulating target stock before an offer is the potential leverage achieved with the voting rights associated with the stock it has purchased. This voting power is important in a proxy contest to remove takeover defenses, to win shareholder approval under state takeover statues, or for the election of members of the target's board. In addition, the target stock accumulated prior to the acquisition can be later sold, possibly at a gain, by the bidder in the event the bidder is unsuccessful in acquiring the target firm. This enables the losing bidder to recover some of the legal and investment banking expenses that it has incurred.

Street Sweep

Open-market purchases do not always lead to a tender offer. The bidder may conclude the stock is too closely held, that current shareholders are long-term investors, or that a tender offer is unlikely to garner as much stock as the bidder would like. In this circumstance, the bidder may choose to adopt a street sweep strategy of purchasing as much stock as possible as quickly as possible to gain control. This involves seeking out owners of large blocks of target stock, such as arbs. Such purchases may be made clandestinely before prenotification ownership percentages are reached through the bidder's affiliates, partnerships, or the bidder's investment bank.

Special Meetings

Once the bidder has established a toehold ownership position in the voting stock of the target company through open-market purchases, the bidder may attempt to call a special stockholders' meeting. The purpose of such a meeting may be to call for a replacement of the board of directors or for the removal of takeover defenses. The conditions under which such a meeting can be called are determined by the firm's articles of incorporation governed by the laws of the state in which the firm is incorporated. Generally, such meetings can be called if a certain number of stockholders call for the meeting.

Limitations to Open-Market Purchases

Federal and state antitrust and securities prenotification laws make it extremely difficult for a bidder to acquire a controlling interest in a target without such actions becoming public knowledge (see Chapter 2). Under federal antitrust law, a Hart–Scott Rodino filing must be made to the Department of Justice (DoJ) and Federal Trade Commission (FTC) if one of the firms has assets or sales of $100 million or more, and the other firm has $10 million *and* ownership of target stock or assets is $15 million or more. The transaction cannot be completed until a mandated 30-day waiting period (15 days for an all-cash transaction) has elapsed.

Once a purchaser's intentions are made public, the target's stock price will often soar in anticipation of an offer for the company. This will dash any hope the buyer may have of obtaining control at a lower average price than the eventual offer price. For this reason, the bidder may time the announcement of a tender offer to coincide with the first disclosure of its target stock holdings and intentions to achieve a controlling interest in the target.

TENDER OFFERS

During the early 1980s, tender offers appeared to be virtually unstoppable. With the tender offer, the takeover battle is taken directly to the shareholders rather than to the board of the target company. Although the bidder may seek to work with the board and management of the target company, the tender offer is a deliberate effort to circumvent the target's board and management. Acquirers often resort to tender offers whenever a friendly negotiated settlement is not possible.

The early successes of the tender offer generated new, more effective defenses, such as the poison pill, designed to raise the cost of a takeover to the potential acquirer. As a result of new defenses, discussed later in this chapter, tender offers rarely force a target to rapidly capitulate to the bidder. Takeover tactics had to adapt to the proliferation of more formidable takeover defenses. For example, during the 1990s, tender offers were used to go directly to shareholders in combination with proxy contests to overcome takeover defenses.

Implementing a Tender Offer

Tender offers can be for cash or for securities. If they are for securities, they are referred to as an exchange offer. In either case, the proposal is made directly to the shareholders of the target. The offer is extended for a specific period of time and may be unrestricted (any-or-all offer) or restricted to a certain percentage or number of the target's share. Restricted tender offers may be oversubscribed. When this occurs, the bidder may choose to purchase all of the target stock that is tendered or purchase only a portion of the tendered stock. For example, if the bidder has extended a tender offer for 70% of the target's outstanding shares and 90% of the target's stock is actually offered, the bidder may choose to prorate the purchase of stock by buying only 78% (70/90) from each shareholder owning the stock tendered to the bidder.

If the bidder chooses to revise the tender offer, the waiting period is automatically extended. If another bid is made to the target shareholders, the waiting period must also be extended by another 10 days to give them adequate time to consider the new bid. If securities are part of the tender offer, they must be registered with the SEC according to the Securities Act of 1933 as well as under the "Blue Sky Laws" of the states whose jurisdiction is applicable.

Once a tender offer is initiated, it is likely that the target will be eventually acquired, although not necessarily by the original bidder. Not surprisingly, uncontested tender offers result in the target being taken over more than 90% of the time. However, for contested tender offers, the target is eventually acquired about one-half of the time (Gaughan: 1999, p. 250).

Legal Filings in Undertaking Tender Offers

Federal securities laws impose a number of reporting, disclosure, and antifraud requirements on acquirers initiating tender offers. Once the tender offer has been made the acquirer cannot acquire any shares in the target other than the number specified in the tender offer. Thus, what actions constitute a tender offer are of great interest to the potential acquirer.

Defining a Tender Offer for Regulatory Purposes: The Eight-Factor Test

The SEC has taken the position that the term *tender offer* applies to actions in addition to a public announcement and direct mailing of an offer to acquire stock held by the target company's shareholders. Privately negotiated and open-market purchases by the acquirer may be considered tender offers. The SEC has devised an eight-factor test to determine what constitutes a tender offer (Exhibit 3-1).

EXHIBIT 3-1. THE EIGHT-FACTOR TEST
TO DETERMINE WHAT CONSTITUTES
A TENDER OFFER [1]

Actions taken by a bidder may be considered a tender offer if they involve the following:

1. Active and widespread solicitation of public shareholders;
2. Solicitation of a substantial percentage of the issuer's stock;
3. The offer price provides a premium to the current market price;
4. The terms of the offer are firm rather than negotiated;
5. The offer is contingent on the tender of a fixed number of shares;
6. The offer is open for a limited time;
7. Shareholders are pressured to sell the stock; and
8. Public announcement of a plan to purchase shares precedes or accompanies rapid accumulation.

[1] The courts have ruled that not all of the factors must be present for an open-market purchase to be declared a tender offer.

Although there has been much litigation on what constitutes a tender offer, no court has ruled that open-market purchases by themselves constitute a tender offer. Even purchases of large blocks of the target's stock or so-called "street sweeps" in the open-market in a short period of time have not been classified by the courts as tender offers. The courts have consistently ruled that the purchase of stock from institutional investors is not subject to the Williams Act (*Stromfeld v. Great Atlantic & Pacific Tea Company: 1980; Kennecott Cooper Corp. v. Curtiss Wright Corp.: 1978*).

The courts have also identified open-market purchases combined with privately negotiated purchases as tender offers. Such tactics were generally found to be tender offers whenever shareholders were under pressure to sell their stock. Shareholders were said to be subject to pressure created by a public announcement of the acquirer's intent to purchase the target's stock prior to a rapid purchase of stock by the acquirer (Wasserstein: 1998, pp. 622–623). Privately negotiated transactions have generally not been found to be tender offers by the courts. The key test seems to be the extent to which a privately negotiated transaction interferes with the stockholder's ability to consider the transaction in an unhurried manner.

Federal Securities Laws: Williams Act 14(d) Reporting Requirements

As noted in Chapter 2 (this volume), Section 14(d) of the Williams Act covers tender offers and requires that any individual or entity making a tender offer resulting in owning more than 5% of any class of equity must file a Schedule 14D-1 and all solicitation material with the SEC. In addition to the SEC, copies of the 14D-1 must be sent to the executive offices of the target company and to each of the public exchanges on which the target's stock is traded. The tender offer begins on the day when it is publicly announced, advertised, or submitted to the target firm. Once the tender offer begins, the bidder has 5 business days to disseminate all materials relating to the tender offer. The target company must respond to the tender offer by filing a Schedule 14D-9 within 10 days of the tender offer's commencement date with the SEC and with each exchange on which its stock is traded. The target must indicate whether it recommends acceptance or rejection of the tender offer to its shareholders.

The Williams Act also requires that a tender offer be held open for at least 20 days, that the bidder accept all shares that are tendered or at least on a pro rata basis, and that the bidder cannot buy any shares tendered until the end of the 20-day period. The bidder may extend the tender offer period, if it believes that it can get the shares it is seeking by doing so, or the bidder may discontinue the tender offer, if it does not receive the total number of shares requested under the terms of the tender offer.

In what has become the largest takeover in history, Klaus Esser, CEO of Mannesmann, the German cellular phone giant, managed to squeeze nearly twice as much money as first proposed out of Vodafone, the British cellular phone powerhouse. This transaction illustrates the intricacies of international transactions in countries in which hostile takeovers are viewed negatively and antitakeover laws generally favor target companies (see Case Study 3-3). The purchase price for Mannesmann is almost 20% higher than the second largest transaction in history, AOL's acquisition of Time Warner.

CASE STUDY 3-3. VODAFONE ACQUIRES MANNESMANN

On February 8, 2000, Vodafone AirTouch Plc, the world's largest wireless communications company, agreed to buy Mannesmann AG in a $183.0 billion stock swap. This agreement ended a 3-month struggle by Vodafone's CEO, Chris Gent, to gain control of Germany's largest cellular phone company. The merger forms a global colossus in wireless communication with 42 million customers worldwide. The newly formed company has a substantial U.S. presence through a new alliance between its AirTouch unit and Bell Atlantic's mobile operations. However, the combined firm's major concentration of customers is in Europe with 29 million in 11 countries. The new company is seeking to establish a single standard format enabling mobile customers to use the same phone wherever they travel. This is in marked contrast to current mobile phone systems around the world, which are largely incompatible with one another.

Gent's initial offer, valued at about $107 billion, was rebuffed by Klaus Esser, Mannesmann's CEO, who argued that the Mannesmann strategy of combining traditional and cellular services would provide greater value for the company's shareholders than Vodafone's narrower focus on mobile services. Following Esser's refusal to accept his offer, Gent threatened to initiate a tender offer for controlling interest in Mannesmann. However, German law requires that 75% of outstanding shares be tendered before control is transferred. In addition, the law allows individual shareholders to block deals with court challenges that can drag on for years. In a country where hostile takeovers are rare, public opinion was squarely behind management. Even German Chancellor Gerhard Schroeder came out strongly against hostile bids. In the end, Gent agreed to up the ante if Esser would back the deal.

Source: Bloomberg.com, 2000b.

THE TAKEOVER DECISION TREE

The various tactics that may be employed in the takeover process should not be viewed as discrete, independent events, but rather as a reasonably structured series of decision points, with options usually well defined and understood before a takeover attempt is initiated (see Table 3-2). Careful planning precedes the selection of which tactic or set of tactics to employ. Following a conscientious review of the target's current defenses, an assessment of the defenses that could be put in place by the target after an offer is made, and the size of the float associated with the target's stock, the bidder may choose the "friendly" approach.

The friendly approach has the advantage of generally being less costly than more aggressive tactics and minimizes the loss of key personnel during the fight for control of the target. Friendly takeovers avoid an auction environment, which generally raises the purchase price for the target company. Moreover, as noted in Chapter 6 (this volume), friendly acquisitions facilitate premerger integration planning and increase the likelihood that the combined businesses will be quickly and effectively integrated following closing. The primary risk of this approach is the loss of surprise. If the target is unwilling to reach a negotiated settlement, the acquirer is faced with the choice of abandoning the effort or resorting to more aggressive tactics. Such tactics are likely to be less effective due to the extra time afforded the target company's management to put additional takeover defenses in place.

In reality, the risk of loss of surprise may not be very great because of the prenotification requirements of the Williams and the Hart-Scott-Rodino Acts. As noted earlier, these requirements make it very difficult if not impossible to prevent the bidder's intentions from becoming public knowledge.

Reading Figure 3-1 from left to right, the bidder's options under the friendly

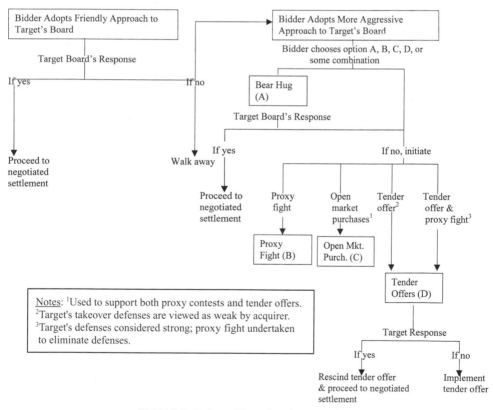

FIGURE 3-1.   Alternative takeover tactics.

approach are to either walk away or to adopt more aggressive tactics, if the target's management and board spurn the bidder's initial offer. If the choice is to become more aggressive, the bidder may undertake a simple bear hug to nudge the target toward a negotiated settlement. The fiduciary responsibilities of the directors require that they consider all reasonable offers. The bear hug tactic presumes that large institutional shareholders and arbs will pressure the Board into agreement with the bidder.

If the bear hug fails to convince the target's management to negotiate, the bidder may choose to buy a sizable block of stock in the open-market. This may enable the bidder to accumulate a sufficient number of voting rights to call a special stockholders' meeting, if a proxy fight is deemed necessary to change management, board members, or to dismember the target's defenses. If the target's defenses are viewed as relatively weak, the bidder may forego a proxy contest and initiate a tender offer for the target's stock. In contrast, if the target's defenses appear formidable, the bidder may implement concurrently a proxy contest and a tender offer.

ALTERNATIVE TAKEOVER DEFENSES:
PRE- AND POSTBID

Alternative takeover defenses can be grouped into two categories: those put in place prior to receiving a bid and those implemented following receipt of a bid. Pre-bid defenses are employed to prevent a sudden, unexpected hostile bid from gaining control of the company before management has time to properly assess their options. If the prebid defenses are sufficient to delay a change in control, the target firm has time to erect additional defenses after an unsolicited bid is received. Pre-bid defenses may also be referred to as preventive and postbid as active defenses. Table 3-1 identifies the most commonly used defenses. These defenses are discussed in more detail during the balance of this chapter.

PREDICTING THE LIKELIHOOD
OF BEING ACQUIRED

Many attempts have been made to determine conditions under which firms would be more prone to being acquired. In numerous empirical studies of predictors of hostile takeovers, only the size of the firm consistently proved to be a major deterrent to takeovers (Comment and Schwert, 1995). Larger firms are simply less likely to be acquired than smaller ones. However, mega-mergers of recent years, such as Citicorp and Travelers and Exxon and Mobil Oil, clearly illustrate that no company is immune from takeover. Table 3-2 summarizes the results of six empirical studies.

TABLE 3-1.   Alternative Pre- and Postbid Takeover Defenses

Pre-bid (preventive) defenses	Postbid (active) defenses

Poison Pills
  First-generation (preferred stock plans)
  Second-generation (flip-over rights
    plans)
  Third-generation (flip-in rights plans)
  Back-end plans
  Poison puts
	Greenmail (Bidder's investment purchased at
	  a premium to cost basis as inducement to
	  refrain from any further activity)

Shark repellants (implemented by changing
    by-laws or charter)
  Strengthening the board's defenses
    Staggered or classified board elections
    Cumulative voting rights
    "For cause" provisions
  Limiting shareholder actions
    Calling special meetings
    Consent solicitations
    Advance notice provisions
    Super majority rules
  Anti greenmail provisions (discourages
  target's use of greemail as a takeover
  tactic)
  Fair price provisions
  Super voting stock
  Reincorporation
	Standstill Agreements (often used in con-
	  junction with an agreement to buy bidder's
	  investment in the target company)

Golden and silver parachutes	Pac Man defense White knights and white squires Employee stock ownership plans Recapitalization Share repurchase plans Corporate restructuring Litigation "Just say no" defense

THE ROLE OF PLANNING

Because there appear to be relatively few factors that suggest the likelihood of being taken over, the best defense against unwanted suitors may be advance planning and preparation. Large public companies routinely review their takeover defenses. Many companies have "stock watch" programs in place that are intended to identify stock accumulations or stock price movements that reflect an impending takeover attempt. Such a program tracks trading patterns in a company's stock. Companies' require their stock transfer agent to provide up-to-date and accurate stock transfer sheets and to report any unusual movements in stock transfer

TABLE 3-2.   Predictors of the Likelihood of Being Acquired

Study	Good predictor	Poor predictor
Comment and Schwert (1995)	Size	
Shivadasani (1993)	Size, managerial holdings, and affiliate firm cross-holdings	Earnings growth and board composition (independent vs. employee or family members)
Mikkeleson and Partch (1989)	Size and affiliate firm cross-holdings	Leverage and managerial stockholdings
Morck, Schlieffer, and Vishny (1988)	Size and market/book value (applies to both hostile and friendly takeovers)	
Palepu (1986)	Size, sales growth, and leverage	
Hasbrouck (1985)	Size and market/book value	Liquidity and leverage

activity. For example, a large number of blocks of stock traded in the *street name* of brokerage houses may indicate that a potential suitor is accumulating stock. Street name refers to the name of the brokerage firm and not to the actual owner of the stock.

Stock watch programs routinely review SEC records for any Schedule 13D filings. Stock watch programs may also query specialists about large block trades in their stocks. Specialists are members of an exchange charged with maintaining an orderly market in a stock by buying and selling stock for its own account, whenever there is an imbalance in the demand and supply of a stock. Market makers perform a similar function for the over-the-counter (OTC) market.

Even though a takeover attempt may be detectable before it is made public, the rapidity of subsequent events may make an effective defense impossible unless certain defenses are already in place. A preventive strategy involves building defenses that are adequate to the task of slowing down a bidder to give the target company's management and board time to assess the situation and to decide on an appropriate response to an offer. A company's strategy should never be to try to build insurmountable defenses. Courts will disallow defenses, which appear to be designed only to entrench the firm's management.

The "Casual Pass"

A takeover attempt often starts with a "casual pass" in the form of a call to a board member or executive of the target company. Frequently, the individual contacted at the target firm is caught off guard and is ill prepared to respond. Ambiguous responses can be interpreted by the suitor as an expression of interest and invite an unwanted bid. The best response is a strong reaction intended to discourage any would-be suitor. Board members, the CEO, and other key members of management should be instructed to respond in this manner.

When Is Silence Appropriate?

Once a bid has been received, most companies choose never to comment on merger discussions until an agreement has been signed. Companies are understandably reluctant to disclose the receipt of an offer for fear of putting themselves in play. When such an event must be disclosed depends on how far along discussions are with the bidder. The U.S. Supreme Court has said that a company has an obligation to make accurate and nonmisleading statements once it has commented on a situation (see Wasserstein: 1998, p. 689). The Supreme Court has also said that a company's statement of "no comment" will be taken as silence and therefore not be considered as misleading.

PREBID OR PREVENTIVE DEFENSES

Prebid or preventive defenses generally fall into three categories: poison pills, shark repellants, and golden parachutes. The prevalence and sophistication of such measures has increased dramatically since 1980 in lockstep with the proliferation and effectiveness of takeover tactics. The objective of these defensive measures is to slow the pace of the takeover attempt and to make it more costly for the bidder.

Poison Pills

Poison pills represent a new class of securities issued by a company to its shareholders, which has no value unless an investor acquires a specific percentage of the firm's voting stock. If this threshold percentage is exceeded, the poison pill securities are activated in such a way so as to dilute the value of the investor's stake in the company. Poison pills have evolved through three generations, as new versions were introduced to solve problems existing with earlier versions (see Table 3-3). The "dead hand" poison pill has special characteristics, which prevent the board of directors from taking action to redeem or rescind the pill, unless the directors were the same directors who adopted the pill.

First-Generation Poison Pills

The brainchild of Marty Lipton, the famous Wall Street attorney, the first-generation poison pill was developed in 1982 and involved issuing preferred stock in the form of a dividend to shareholders convertible into the *common stock of the acquiring company* following a takeover. If a target company were acquired and merged into the acquirer, target company shareholders owning the special preferred stock could convert the preferred stock into multiple shares of the acquirer's stock. This would immediately dilute the acquirer's ownership interest in the earnings of the combined companies.

Second-Generation Poison Pills

The second-generation poison pill included a rights plan or *flip-over pill*. The flip-over pill involved the issuance of rights to the firm's shareholders to buy *a*

TABLE 3-3. Advantages and Disadvantages of Prebid or Preventive Takeover Defenses—Poison Pills

Type of poison pill	Advantages for target firm	Disadvantages for target firm
First-generation (preferred stock plans convertible into stock of the acquirer) Activated following completion of takeover	1. Dilutes ownership position of the acquirer 2. Studies show significant positive abnormal returns to target shareholders.	1. Activated following completion of merger 2. Issuer may redeem only after an extended time period (sometimes 10 years); limits target's flexibility if it is later decided to pursue a merger. 3. Increases leverage as preferred stock is often counted as debt by credit rating agencies
Second-generation (flip-over rights to buy stock in the acquirer) Countdown to expiration begins whenever a specific event occurs such as a hostile tender for 40% of a firm's stock. Exercisable after acquirer purchases 100% of target's stock	1. No impact on leverage 2. Simpler to implement since does not require issuance of preferred stock with attendant SEC filing requirements 3. Rights redeemable by buying them back from shareholders at nominal price 4. Studies show positive returns to target shareholders	1. Ineffective in preventing acquisition of less than 100% of target. Hostile bidders could buy controlling interest only and buy the remainder after rights expire. 2. Subject to hostile tender contingent on target board's redemption of the pill 3. Makes issuer less attractive to White Knights
Third-generation (flip-in rights to buy stock in target) Activated by an event such as a less than 100% change in ownership	1. Effective in dealing with bidders buying less than 100% of target. Dilutes target stock regardless of amount of stock purchased by acquirer 2. Flip-in rights are discriminatory (i.e., not given to investor who activated the rights) 3. Rights are redeemable at any point prior to the triggering event 4. Positive returns to target shareholders	1. May not be permissible in certain states due to their discriminatory nature 2. No poison pill provides any protection against proxy contests
Back-end plans	1. Back-end price set above market price, effectively setting a minimum price for a takeover. Deals effectively with two-tiered tender offer	1. Target's board put in position of effectively setting a sale price, while saying publicly that the company is not for sale
Poison puts	1. Places large cash demands on the combined firms	1. Rendered ineffective if acquirer can convince put holders not to exercise their options. Particularly true if bond's coupon rate exceeds market rates of interest

specific amount of stock in the acquiring company at a particular price for a specified time period. If the company were involved in a takeover, the rights entitled shareholders to buy stock in the surviving company at a substantial discount. The target company's shareholders were said to flip over and become acquirer shareholders. Once again, the ownership position of the acquiring company would be diluted.

Third-Generation Poison Pills

The third-generation pill was referred to as the *"flip-in, flip-over"* pill. Under this arrangement, shareholders receive a special dividend of one stock purchase right for each share they own. The rights are activated whenever an investor acquires a certain percentage of the stock of the company issuing the rights, without prior board approval. When the rights are activated, holders of the rights are *allowed to buy stock in the issuing company* at a substantial discount. This is referred to as a *flip-in*. In certain circumstances, the rights enable the holder to buy stock in the stock of the bidding company at a discount. This is the more traditional flip-over effect. It is the type most commonly used today.

Back-End Plans and Poison Puts

Other types of poison pills include back-end plans and poison puts. With *back-end plans,* shareholders receive a dividend of rights, which gives them the option of exchanging the rights along with a share of target stock for cash or senior debt securities for a specific price set by the target's board. The price is usually set above the current market price of the target company's shares. This effectively communicates to potential acquirers the asking price for the company as determined by the target's board. With *poison puts,* the target issues bonds containing put options exercisable, if and only if an unfriendly takeover occurs. This enables holders of these puts to cash in their bonds, thereby placing substantial cash demands on the acquiring company.

Poison Pills Effectively Slow but Rarely Prevent Takeovers

Although the pill has proven to be an effective means of delaying a takeover and of increasing the overall expense to the acquiring company, pill defenses rarely prevent a firm from being acquired, although not necessarily by the initial bidder (Georgeson & Company: 1997a). Most pills are put in place with the caveat or *escape clause* that the board of the issuing company can redeem the pill through a nominal payment to the shareholders. This is necessary to avoid dilution of the bidder's ownership position in the event the acquiring company is considered friendly. In addition, the Delaware Supreme Court, in approving the poison pill as a defensive measure and as a means of enabling the target to secure higher bids, made its approval largely conditional on the existence of a redemption feature or escape clause.

However, the existence of this redemption feature has made pill defenses vulnerable. For example, a tender offer may be made conditional on the board's redemption of the pill. The target's board will be under substantial pressure from institutions and arbs to redeem the pill, if the bidder has offered a significant premium over the current price of the target's stock. Alternatively, such takeover defenses could be dismantled through a proxy fight.

SHARK REPELLANTS

Shark repellants are specific types of takeover defenses that can be adopted by amending either a corporate charter or its bylaws. The charter gives the corporation its legal existence. The *corporate charter* consists of the *articles of incorporation,* a document filed with a state government by the founders of a corporation, and a *certificate of incorporation,* a document received from the state once the articles have been approved. The charter contains the corporation's name, purpose, amount of authorized shares, and number and identity of directors. The corporation's powers thus derive from the laws of the state and from the provisions of the charter. Rules governing the internal management of the corporation are described in the *corporation's bylaws,* which are determined by the corporation's founders.

Shark repellants are put in place largely to reinforce the ability of a firm's board of directors to retain control. Although shark repellants predate poison pills, their success in slowing down and making takeovers more expensive has been mixed. These developments have given rise to more creative defenses such as the poison pill. Today, shark repellants are intended largely as supplements to the poison pill defenses. Their role is primarily to make gaining control of the board through a proxy fight at an annual or special meeting more difficult.

In conjunction with the firm's charter and bylaws, the laws of the state in which the firm is incorporated determine what may be enacted as a bylaw without shareholder approval. In practice, most shark repellants require amendments to the firm's charter, which necessitate a shareholder vote. Although there are many variations of shark repellants, the most typical include staggered board elections, restrictions on shareholder actions, antigreenmail provisions, supervoting, and debt-based defenses. Table 3-4 summarizes the primary advantages and disadvantages of each type of shark repellant defense.

Strengthening the Board's Defenses

Poison pill defenses provide little protection for the board of directors of the target company from a proxy contest. Dissident shareholders may try to take control of a company by taking control of its board. Consequently, strengthening the board's defenses is an important consideration in preventing or slowing down a hostile takeover of a company. Common protections afforded the board include staggered elections of board members, limitations on shareholder actions, and defining the conditions under which board members may be removed.

Staggered or Classified Board Elections

Following an amendment to the firm's charter, the firm's directors are divided into a number of different classes. Only one class is up for reelection each year.

TABLE 3-4. Advantages and Disadvantages of Prebid or Preventive Takeover Defenses—Shark Repellents and Golden Parachutes

Type of defense	Advantages for target firm	Disadvantages for target firm
Shark repellents: Strengthening the board's defenses		
Staggered or classified boards	Delays assumption of control by a majority shareholder	May be circumvented by increasing size of board
Cumulative voting	Delays assumption of control by a majority shareholder	Gives dissident shareholder a board seat and access to confidential information
Limitations on when can remove directors	"For cause" provisions narrow range of reasons for removal	Can be circumvented unless supported by supermajority requirement for repeal
Shark repellents: limiting shareholder actions		
Limitations on calling special meetings	Limits ability to use special meetings to add board seats, remove or elect new members	States may require a special meeting if a certain percentage of shareholders request a meeting.
Limiting consent solicitations	Limits ability of dissident shareholders to expedite a proxy contest process	May be subject to court challenge
Advance notice provisions	Gives board time to select its own slate of candidates and to decide an appropriate response	May be subject to court challenge
Supermajority provisions	May be applied selectively to events such as hostile takeovers	Can be circumvented unless a supermajority of shareholders are required to change the provision
Other shark repellents		
Antigreenmail provision	Eliminates profit opportunity for raiders	Eliminates greenmail as a takeover defense
Fair price provisions	Increases the cost of a two-tiered tender offer	Raises the cost to a White Knight, unless waived by typically 95% of shareholders
Super voting stock	Gives "friendly" shareholders more voting power than others	Difficult to implement because requires shareholder approval; only useful when voting power can be given to pro-management shareholders; and only available to firms with such shares outstanding as of July 1988
Reincorporation	Takes advantage of most favorable state anti-takeover statutes	Requires shareholder approval; time consuming to implement unless subsidiary established prior to takeover solicitation
Defenses not requiring shareholder approval		
Golden parachutes	Emboldens target management to negotiate for a higher premium; provides modest abnormal returns to target shareholders; and raises the cost of a takeover to the hostile bidder	Negative public perception. Makes termination of top management expensive.

For example, for a board consisting of twelve members, the directors may be divided into four classes with each director elected for a 4-year period. In the first year, the three directors designated as class 1 directors are up for reelection, in the second year class 2 directors are up for election, and so on. Consequently, an insurgent stockholder who may hold the majority of the stock would still have to wait for three elections to gain control of the board. The size of the board is also limited to preclude the insurgent stockholder from simply adding board seats to take control of the board.

From a practical standpoint, the board may have to accede to the demands of the majority stockholder as a result of litigation initiated by dissident shareholder groups. The likelihood of litigation is highest and pressure on the board is greatest whenever the offer price for the target company is at a substantial price to the target firm's current share price.

Cumulative Voting Rights

Some firms have common stock carrying cumulative voting rights to maximize minority representation. Using the preceding example of a twelve member board, a shareholder, who has 100 shares of stock, has 300 votes for three open seats for class 1 directors. The shareholder may cumulate her votes and cast them for a single candidate. An insurgent stockholder may choose this approach to obtain a single seat on the board to gain access to useful information that is not otherwise readily available. However, cumulative voting rights may also backfire against the dissident shareholder. Cumulative voting may be used to counter the ability of the insurgent to gain control of the board by cumulating the votes of opposing shareholders and casting them for candidates who would vigorously represent the board's positions. Only about one-fifth of large companies have cumulative voting stock (see Bhagat and Brickley: 1984).

"For Cause" Provisions

Such provisions specify the conditions for removing a member of the board of directors. This narrows the range of reasons for removal and limits the flexibility of dissident shareholders in contesting board seats.

Limiting Shareholder Actions

Other means of reinforcing the board's ability to retain control include limiting the ability of shareholders to gain control of the firm by bypassing the board altogether. These include limiting their ability to call special meetings, to engage in consent solicitations, and the use of supermajority rules.

Calling Special Meetings

Many states require a firm to call a special meeting of the shareholders, if it is requested by a certain percentage of its shareholders. If a special meeting is called by the shareholders, the board is confronted with several challenges. The first challenge arises when special meetings are used as a forum for an insurgent shareholder or corporate raider to take control by replacing current directors with those who are likely to be more cooperative or by increasing the number of board seats. To limit this type of action, firms frequently include in their bylaws a provision that directors can be removed "for cause" defined in the charter or bylaws and a limitation on the number of board of directors seats. The second major challenge occurs when shareholders engage in a nonbinding vote to remove certain types of defenses such as a poison pill. The board must then decide to ignore the will of the shareholders or to remove the defenses.

Consent Solicitations

In some states, shareholders may take action to add to the number of seats on the board, to remove specific board members, or to elect new members without a special meeting. All that is required is the written consent of shareholders. Although the consent solicitation must abide by the disclosure requirements applicable to proxy contests, dissident stockholders may use this process to expedite their efforts to seize control or to remove defenses. This process circumvents the time delays inherent in setting up a meeting to conduct a stockholder vote. Companies have attempted to limit shareholders' ability to use this procedure by amending their charters or by revising their bylaws. The latter may not require shareholder approval, however, the courts have frequently frowned upon these types of actions, which restrict shareholder rights without shareholder approval.

Advance Notice Provisions

Some corporate bylaws require the announcement of shareholder proposals and board nominations well in advance of an actual vote. Some bylaws require advance notice of as long as 2 months. Such provisions buy significant time for the target's board to determine an appropriate response to an unsolicited offer.

Supermajority Rules

These rules require that a higher level of approval is required for amending the charter or for certain types of transactions such as a merger or acquisition. These supermajority rules are triggered if an "interested party" acquires a specific percentage of the ownership shares (e.g., 5–10%). Supermajority rules may require that as much as 80% of the shareholders must approve a proposed merger or a simple majority of all shareholders except the "interested party." Supermajority rules often include escape clauses, which allow the board to waive the requirement. For example, supermajority rules may not apply to mergers approved by the board.

Antigreenmail Provisions

During the 1980s, many raiders profited by taking an equity position in a target firm, threatening takeover, and subsequently selling their ownership position back to the target firm at a premium over what they paid for the target's shares. Many believed that the payment of greenmail only encouraged this type of behavior. Many corporations adopted charter amendments restricting the firm's ability to repurchase shares at a premium. By removing the incentive for greenmail, companies believed they were making themselves less attractive as potential takeover targets. As such, antigreenmail provisions may be viewed as an antitakeover tactic.

Fair-Price Provisions

A corporation may choose to call for a shareholder vote to amend its charter to require that any acquirer pay minority shareholders at least a fair market price for their stock. The fair market price may be expressed as some historical multiple of the company's earnings or as a specific price equal to the maximum price paid by the buyer when he acquired shares in the company. Fair-price provisions are most effective when the target firm is subject to a two-tiered tender offer. The fair-price provision forces the bidder to pay target shareholders, who tender their stock in the second tier, the same terms offered to those tendering their stock in the first tier.

Supervoting Stock

Companies may have more than one class of stock for many reasons; for example, to separate the performance of individual operating subsidiaries to compensating the subsidiary's operating management and to prevent hostile takeovers. As a takeover defense, a firm may issue several classes of stock having different voting rights. The objective is to concentrate stock with the greatest voting rights in the hands of those who are most likely to support management.

One class of stock may have 10 to 100 times the voting rights of another class of stock. Such stock is said to have "supervoting" rights. This stock is issued to all shareholders along with the right to exchange it for ordinary stock. Most shareholders are likely to exchange it for ordinary stock, because the stock with the multiple voting rights usually has a limited resale market and pays a lower dividend than other types of voting stock issued by the corporation. Management will usually retain the special stock. This effectively increases the voting control of the corporation in the hands of management.

Today, the creation of a new class of stock with supervoting privileges is generally not allowed under the voting rights policies of the SEC, the New York Stock Exchange (NYSE), American Exchange, and the National Association of Securities Dealers. However, companies that issued such stock prior to July 1988, when such issues were allowed, are permitted to continue to issue such stock.

Reincorporation

A potential target firm may choose to change its state of incorporation to one in which the laws are more favorable for implementing takeover defenses. Several factors need to be considered in selecting a state for possible reincorporation, including how the state's courts have ruled in lawsuits alleging breach of corporate director fiduciary responsibility in takeover situations, and the state's statutes pertaining to the treatment of poison pills, staggered boards, and hostile tender offers. Reincorporation involves the creation of a subsidiary in the new state. The parent is then merged into the subsidiary at a later date. Shareholders must normally approve such a move because a merger of the parent is involved.

GOLDEN, SILVER, AND TIN PARACHUTES

Golden parachutes are employee severance arrangements, which are triggered whenever a change in control takes place. Such a plan usually covers only a few dozen employees and obligates the company to make a lump-sum payment to employees covered under the plan, who are terminated following a change in control. A change in control is usually defined to occur whenever an investor accumulates more than a fixed percentage of a corporation's voting stock. Occasionally, changes in control due to friendly acquisitions may be exempted from triggering the plans. However, this obviates the stated purpose of the plans, which is generally to retain key employees who may feel threatened by a pending change in control. *Silver parachutes* are severance agreements that cover far more employees and are also triggered in the same manner as golden parachutes. Although golden parachute payments may equal several years of an employee's pay, silver parachute payments are usually much less, consisting of 6 months to 1 year of severance for all affected employees. In some instances, *tin parachute* plans cover virtually all employees and consist of very modest severance payments. When triggered, payments under such parachute plans make the takeover much more expensive for the acquiring company.

The board of directors can generally implement golden, silver, and tin parachutes without stockholder approval. Plans put in place prior to a specific takeover threat are generally protected by *the business judgment rule,* which states that management's actions are appropriate if they are implemented while management is acting in the stockholders' best interests (see *Buckhorn Inc. v. Ropak Corp.:* 1987).

According to the courts, boards putting plans in place prior to a specific takeover threat must be able to demonstrate that the company conducted a reasonable, good faith investigation of the perceived takeover threat and that the plan constituted a reasonable response (see Wasserstein: 1998, p. 711). Public criticism of such plans has caused many corporations to create compensation committees consisting of outside directors to review all compensation and benefit plans before they are implemented.

The 1986 Tax Act imposed stiff penalties on these types of plans if they create what is deemed an excess parachute payment. Such payments are defined as those exceeding three times the employee's average compensation over the last 5 years. Such payments are not tax deductible by the paying corporation. The employee receiving the parachute payment must also pay a 20% surcharge in addition to the normal tax due on the parachute payment.

DEFENSES UNDERTAKEN IN RESPONSE TO A BID
(POSTBID OR ACTIVE DEFENSES)

Once an unwanted suitor has approached a firm there are a variety of additional defenses that can be introduced, including greenmail to dissuade the bidder from continuing the pursuit; defenses designed to make the target less attractive, such as restructuring and recapitalization strategies; and efforts to place an increasing share of the company's ownership in friendly hands by establishing ESOPs and seeking white knights and squires. Table 3-5 summarizes the primary advantages and disadvantages of such postbid or active takeover defenses.

Greenmail

Greenmail is the practice of paying a potential acquirer to leave you alone. It usually consists of a payment to buyback shares at a premium price in exchange for the acquirer's agreement to not undertake a hostile takeover. In exchange for the payment, the potential acquirer is required to sign a standstill agreement, which typically specifies the amount of stock, if any, that the investor can own, the circumstances under which the raider can sell stock currently owned, and the term of the agreement. Despite their discriminatory nature, courts in certain states such as Delaware have found greenmail an appropriate response as long as it is made for valid business reasons. However, courts in other states, such as California, have favored shareholder lawsuits, based on the contention that greenmail constituted a breach of fiduciary responsibility (Wasserstein: 1998, pp. 719–720).

The importance of greenmail as a takeover defense has diminished since the late 1980s. Greenmail is arguably counterproductive, because once such a payment becomes public others may feign a takeover attempt to receive similar payments. In addition, the federal tax code was changed in 1987 to impose a 50% tax on any gains associated with the payment of greenmail. To be subject to the tax, the payment must have been made to acquire stock from a shareholder making or threatening to make a tender offer for the paying company's stock and who has held the stock for less than 2 years. Finally, in response to public criticism, some firms have amended their charters with antigreenmail provisions requiring management to obtain approval of the majority or the supermajority of nonparticipating shareholders prior to repurchasing a specific investor's stock at a premium.

Pac Man Defense

A rarely used, but highly aggressive, defense is for the target to make a hostile tender offer for the bidder. Such a defense is only effective if the target company has the financial resources to make a legitimate bid for the bidder. Such a scenario may be mutually destructive, as both companies may be left extremely highly leveraged in the wake of their attempts to implement hostile tenders for each other.

White Knights and White Squires

A target company seeking to avoid being taken over by a specific bidder may try to be acquired by another firm, a *white knight,* which is viewed as a more

TABLE 3-5. Advantages and Disadvantages of Postbid (Active) Takeover Defenses

Type of defense	Advantages for target firm	Disadvantages for target firm
Greenmail	Encourages raider to go away (Usually accompanied by a standstill agreement)	Reduces risk to raider of losing money on a takeover attempt; unfairly discriminates against non-participating shareholders; often generates litigation; and triggers unfavorable tax consequences
Standstill agreement	Prevents raider from returning for a specific period of time	Exacerbates negative returns to target shareholders and increases amount of greenmail paid to get raider to sign standstill
Pac-Man defense	Sends message that target will defend itself at all costs	Requires that target can fund such a strategy and may emasculate both the target and the bidder
White knights/white squires	May be a preferable alternative to the hostile bidder	Necessarily involves loss of target's independence
ESOPs	Alternative to white knight and highly effective if used in conjunction with certain states' anti-takeover laws	Support of employees is not guaranteed. Target must be careful ESOP does not overpay for stock. Transaction could be disallowed by federal employee benefit laws.
Recapitalizations	Makes target less attractive to bidder and may increase target shareholder value if incumbent management motivated to improve performance	As a takeover defense, it may generate substantial negative impact on returns to target shareholders and increased leverage reduces target's debt capacity
Share repurchase plans	Reduces number of target shares available for purchase by bidder, arbs, and others who may sell to bidder	Federal securities laws limit ability to self-tender without filing with SEC once hostile tender underway. A reduction in the shares outstanding may facilitate bidder's gaining control.
Corporate restructuring	Going private may be attractive alternative to bidder's offer for target shareholders and for incumbent management	Going private, sale of attractive assets, making defensive acquisitions, or liquidation may substantially reduce target's shareholder value vs. bidder's offer
Litigation	May buy time for target to build defenses and increases takeover cost to the bidder	Negative impact on target shareholder returns
"Just say know"	Buys time to build defenses and determine appropriate response	Must satisfy conditions established by the courts

appropriate suitor. To complete such a transaction, the white knight must be willing to acquire the target company on more favorable terms than those of the original bidder. The motivation for the white knight is generally more mercenary than chivalrous. Fearing that a bidding war might ensue, the white knight often demands some protection in the form of a *lock-up* in an agreement of purchase and sale eventually signed with the target. The lock-up may involve giving the white knight options to buy stock in the target that has not yet been issued at a fixed price or to acquire at a fair price target assets that are viewed as strategic by the white knight. Such lock-ups usually have the effect of making the target less attractive to the original bidder. In the event a bidding war ensues, the knight may exercise the stock options and sell the shares at a profit to the acquiring company.

White squires are firms that agree to purchase a large block of the target's stock. Such stock is often convertible preferred, which may have already been approved but has not yet been issued by the target company. If the target's stock trades on the NYSE, the target will still have to receive shareholder approval to sell such stock to a white squire. The NYSE requires shareholder approval if such shares are issued to officers or directors or if the number issued equals 20% of the target's outstanding shares. Warren Buffet is probably the most famous white squire following his investments in such companies as Gillette, Coca-Cola, U.S. Air, and Salomon Brothers.

Employee Stock Ownership Plans

ESOPs are trusts that hold a firm's stock as an investment for their employees' retirement program. ESOPs may be viewed as an alternative to a White Knight or White Squire defense. They can be established quickly with the company either issuing shares directly to the ESOP or having an ESOP purchase shares on the open-market. Any impact on earnings per share of issuing the stock to the ESOP can be offset by the firm repurchasing shares on the open-market. The stock held by ESOPs is likely to be voted in support of management in the event of a hostile takeover attempt. However, this support is not guaranteed, because according to federal benefits and tax laws, employees must be given the freedom to control how their stock held by the ESOP is voted.

Recapitalization

To recapitalize, a company may need shareholder approval depending on the company's charter and the laws of the state in which it is incorporated. A company may recapitalize by assuming substantial amounts of new debt, which is used to either buy back stock or finance a dividend to shareholders. In doing so, the target becomes less attractive to a bidder, because the additional debt reduces its borrowing capacity, which may have been used by the bidder to help finance the takeover of the target. Moreover, the payment of a dividend or a stock buyback may persuade shareholders to support the target's management in a proxy contest or hostile tender offer. The target firm is left in a highly leveraged position. Such practices are thought by some to be equivalent to scorched earth policies. However, in practice, they may significantly add to shareholder value.

Whether the recapitalization actually weakens the target firm in the long-term depends on its impact on the target firm's shareholder value. Shareholders will benefit from the receipt of a dividend or from capital gains resulting from a stock repurchase. Furthermore, the increased debt service requirements of the additional debt will shelter a substantial amount of the firm's taxable income and may encourage management to be more conscientious about improving the firm's performance. Thus, the combination of these factors may result in current shareholders benefiting more from this takeover defense than from a hostile takeover of the firm.

As an alternative to taking on more debt, the target firm may issue additional shares to make it more difficult for a bidder to gain a controlling interest. The increase in the number of shares will dilute earnings per share and reduce the target's share price.

Share Repurchase or Buyback Plans

Share repurchase or buyback plans are intended to reduce the number of shares that could be purchased by the potential acquirer or by those such as arbitrageurs who will sell to the highest bidder. However, by reducing the number of shares on the open-market, it may be easier for the buyer to gain control, because fewer shares have to be purchased in order to achieve 51% of the target's outstanding voting shares. A share buyback may work well in combination with a white squire strategy in which the target can place stock in friendly hands.

A share buyback can be implemented by purchasing shares on the open-market regardless of ownership by targeting specific shareholders who may sell to the hostile bidder, and through a self-tender offer in which the target buys its own stock. Self-tenders are regulated by Section 13e of the Securities and Exchange Act of 1934. Federal securities law prohibits purchase by an issuer of its own shares during a tender offer for its shares, unless it files a statement with the SEC disclosing the identity of the purchaser, stock exchanges that will be used for the purchase, the intent of the purchase, and the intended disposition of the shares.

Restructuring

Restructuring may involve taking the company private, the sale of attractive assets, undertaking a major acquisition, or even liquidating the company. "Going private" typically involves the management team's purchase of the bulk of a firm's shares. This may create a win–win situation for shareholders that receive a premium for their stock and management who retain control. To avoid lawsuits, the price paid for the stock must represent a substantial premium to the current market price. Alternatively, the target company may make itself less attractive by divesting assets the bidder wants. The cash proceeds of the sale could fund other defenses such as share buybacks or payment of a special stockholder dividend.

A target company may also undertake a so-called defensive acquisition to draw down any excess cash balances and to exhaust its current borrowing capacity. Liquidation represents the most drastic alternative. A firm may choose to liquidate the company, pay off outstanding obligations to creditors, and distribute the remaining proceeds to shareholders as a liquidating dividend. This option makes sense only if the liquidating dividend exceeds what the shareholders would have received from the bidder (see Chapter 13, this volume).

Litigation

Takeover litigation often includes antitrust concerns, alleged violations of federal securities laws, inadequate disclosure by the bidder as required by the Williams Act, and alleged fraudulent behavior. Targets often try to get a court injunction temporarily stopping the takeover attempt until the court has decided that the target's allegations are groundless. By preventing the potential acquirer from buying more stock, the target firm is buying time to erect additional takeover defenses. Litigation occurs in about one-third of takeover attempts (Jarrell: 1985b).

"Just Say No" Defense

A target board may attempt to buy time when faced with a hostile takeover attempt by simply refusing to accede to the bidder's demands. However, the refusal cannot be arbitrary. The board cannot refuse to withdraw certain defenses or decline the bid without being able to satisfy two conditions (*Unocal v. Mesa:* 1985). The first condition is that the board must establish that it has well-founded grounds that the bid is inadequate and that it threatens existing corporate strategy. The second condition requires that actions taken to defend against a hostile takeover attempt be in proportion to the size of the threat. Despite a resolute response, this defense will crumble due to shareholder pressure in the face of a highly attractive offer price.

Impact on Shareholder Value of Takeover Defenses: Empirical Evidence

The results of 24 empirical studies are summarized on Table 3-6. Those studies showing a negative return to shareholders support the argument that incumbent management acts in its own self-interest, the management entrenchment hypothesis; studies showing a positive shareholder return support the argument that incumbent management acts in the best interests of shareholders—the shareholder interests hypothesis.

With the exception of poison pills, it is difficult to draw compelling conclusions about the impact of takeover defenses on shareholder wealth from the available evidence. For many takeover defenses, empirical results cannot be confirmed by multiple studies, the available evidence is largely contradictory, or the findings are statistically insignificant, perhaps due to chance. Nonetheless, the empirical evidence does suggest that poison pills have the greatest positive impact on shareholder wealth, although most other defenses have either have a substantially negative impact or no measurable impact at all.

TABLE 3-6. Impact of Takeover Defenses on Target Shareholder Value—Empirical Evidence

Takeover defense	Study	Returns to target shareholders
Prebid (preventive) defenses		
Poison pills		
First-generation (preferred stock plans)	Georgeson & Company (1997b)	8 percentage points higher than firms without pills
Second-generation (flip-over plans)	Comment and Schwert (1995);	11–13 percentage points higher than firms without pills
Third-generation (flip-in rights plans)	Bradley, Desai, and Kim (1988);	
Back-end plans	Huang and Walking (1987)	
Poison puts	Malesta and Walking (1988); Ryngaert (1988)	Negative <1% returns to firms using pill defenses
Shark repellants (implemented by amending by-laws or charter)		
Staggering terms of board of directors	DeAngelo and Rice (1983); Ruback (1987)	Negative but statistically insignificant
Supermajority provisions	Jarrell and Poulsen (1986)	Negative 5% return
Fair price provisions	DeAngelo and Rice (1983); Linn and McConnell (1983)	No impact
Dual capitalization	Jarrell and Poulsen (1987)	Negative but statistically insignificant
	Partch (1987)	No impact
	Jarrell and Poulsen (1987)	Negative <1% return
Reincorporation	Netter and Poulsen (1989)	No impact
Golden parachutes	Lamber and Larker (1985)	Positive 3% return
	Machlin, Hyuk, & Miles (1993)	Small positive impact
Postbid (active) defenses		
Greenmail	Bradley and Wakeman (1983); Dann and DeAngelo (1983)	Modest negative returns to nonparticipating shareholders
	Mikkelson and Ruback (1986)	Positive 17%
Recapitalization	Dann and DeAngelo (1983)	Negative 22%
Litigation	Jarrell (1985b)	No impact

The major findings are summarized as follows:

1. The preponderance of evidence shows that shareholders of firms with poison pill defenses in place are likely to experience substantially greater returns in the event of a takeover as a result of receiving much larger premiums than firms without such defenses. The existence of poison pills often requires the bidder to raise its bid or to change the composition of its bid to an all-cash offer to put the target's board under pressure to dismantle its pill defenses. Moreover, according to a study by Georgeson & Company (1997a), there is no evidence that the presence of poison pills increases the likelihood that a friendly takeover bid will be withdrawn or that a hostile bid will be defeated. The study also concludes that there is no indication that poison pills reduce the chance that a company will become a takeover target.

2. Shark repellents including staggered boards, supermajority provisions, fair price provisions, reincorporation, and dual capitalization have no impact or a slightly negative impact on shareholder value.

3. Golden parachutes have a slightly positive impact. Jensen (1994) argues that properly constructed parachutes provide incumbent management with sufficient incentive to negotiate higher takeover premiums for shareholders.

4. The impact of greenmail is inconclusive. The negative effects of greenmail tend to be greater when targeted stock repurchases are coupled with standstill agreements (Mikkelson and Ruback: 1986).

5. Recapitalization resulting in substantial increases in leverage appears to result in large negative returns for target shareholders. It is unclear if the reduction in shareholder wealth is sustained.

6. There is no evidence that litigation initiated by the target company against the bidder has any significant impact on its share price. Target share prices tend to drop when litigation is initiated, with the decline occurring for both firms that were eventually acquired, 21%, and for those that remain totally independent, 23%. However, when an auction for the target firm develops following the initiation of litigation, the offer price for the target firm is about 17% higher than when there is no auction (Jarrell: 1985b). In this instance, litigation may provide sufficient time for other bidders to enter the fray.

THINGS TO REMEMBER

Takeovers are often divided into friendly and hostile categories. Friendly takeovers include those that reach a negotiated settlement without experiencing contentious proxy contests, tender offers, or litigation. A hostile takeover is generally considered an unsolicited offer made by a potential acquirer that is resisted by the target's management. The shareholder interests hypothesis suggests that target managers resist hostile offers to improve the terms of a takeover offer. The management entrenchment hypothesis suggests that target managers resist hostile offers to avoid being taken over. Although empirical evidence supports both hypotheses, the evidence seems to favor the belief that directors and managers resist hostile takeover bids to improve takeover premiums.

If the friendly approach is considered inappropriate or is unsuccessful, the acquiring company may attempt to limit the options of the target's senior management by making a formal acquisition proposal, usually involving a public announcement, to the board of directors of the target. This tactic is called a bear hug and is an attempt to pressure the target's board into making a rapid decision. Alternatively, the bidder may undertake a proxy contest. The two primary forms of proxy contests are those for seats on the board of directors and those concerning management proposals. By replacing board members, proxy contests can be an effective means of gaining control without owning 51% of the voting stock, or they can be used to eliminate takeover defenses, such as poison pills, as a precursor to a tender offer. In a tender offer, the bidding company goes directly to the shareholders of the target company with an offer to buy their stock. The tender offer is a deliberate effort to circumvent the target's board and management.

In the 1970s, target firms were often caught completely off guard by the speed with which a hostile takeover could be consummated. However, federal and state regulations have slowed the process dramatically by requiring waiting periods. A number of states also require shareholder approval for certain types of offers. Most large companies have takeover defenses in place such as poison pills. Hostile takeovers are now more likely to last for months.

Alternative takeover defenses can be grouped as prebid or preventive defenses and postbid or active defenses. The prevalence and sophistication of such measures has increased dramatically since 1980 in lockstep with the proliferation of new and more effective takeover tactics. Takeover defenses are designed to raise the overall cost of the takeover attempt and to provide the target firm with more time to install additional takeover defenses. Prebid or preventive defenses generally fall into three categories: poison pills, shark repellants, and golden parachutes.

Poison pills represent a new class of securities issued by a company to its shareholders, which have no value unless an investor acquires a specific percentage of the firm's voting stock. Takeover defenses that can be included in either a corporate charter or bylaws are often referred to as shark repellants or active defenses. These defenses are put in place largely to reinforce the ability of a firm's board of directors to retain control. Today, shark repellants are intended largely as supplements to the poison pill defenses. Golden parachutes are large severance packages granted senior management, which are activated if an individual or a single entity purchases a specific percentage of the target's outstanding voting stock.

Postbid or active defenses are those undertaken in response to a bid. Examples include greenmail, which is the practice of paying a potential acquirer to leave you alone. A target company seeking to avoid being taken over by a specific bidder may try to be acquired by another firm, a white knight, which is viewed as a more appropriate suitor. Takeover litigation is often initiated under the guise of antitrust concerns, alleged violations of federal securities laws, inadequate disclosure by the bidder as required by the Williams Act, and alleged fraudulent behavior. Targets often try to get a court injunction temporarily stopping the takeover attempt until the court has decided that the target's allegations are groundless. Empirical evidence suggests that poison pills have the greatest positive impact on shareholder wealth, whereas most other defenses have either no measurable impact or a negative one.

CHAPTER DISCUSSION QUESTIONS

3-1.   What are the management entrenchment and shareholder interests hypotheses? Which seems more realistic?

3-2.   What are the advantages and disadvantages of the friendly versus hostile approaches to a corporate takeover?

3-3.   What are proxy contests and how are they used?

3-4.   What is a tender offer? How do they differ from open-market purchases of stock?

3-5.   How are target shareholders affected by a hostile takeover attempt?

3-6.   How are the bidder's shareholders affected by a hostile takeover attempt?

3-7.   What are the primary advantages and disadvantages of commonly used takeover defenses?

3-8.   Of the most commonly used takeover defenses, which seem to have the most favorable impact on target shareholders?

3-9.   How may golden parachutes for senior management help a target firm's shareholders?

3-10. How might recapitalization as a takeover defense help or hurt a target firm's shareholders?

CHAPTER BUSINESS CASE

CASE STUDY 3-4. TYCO RESCUES AMP FROM ALLIEDSIGNAL

Background

In late November 1998, Tyco International Ltd., a diversified manufacturing and service company, agreed to acquire AMP Inc. for $11.3 billion, thereby successfully fending off a protracted takeover attempt by AlliedSignal Inc. Tyco agreed to exchange .7839 shares of its stock for each AMP share outstanding, as long as Tyco's share price traded between $60 and $67 during the 10-day period prior to closing. The share exchange ratio was set to change if Tyco shares fluctuated outside the range, but the exchange would not exceed a value of $55.95 per AMP share. AMP shareholders could expect to receive a purchase price per share within a range of $47.03 ($60 × .7839) to $52.52 ($67 × .7839). However, if Tyco's stock rose above the range, AMP's shareholders could receive as much as $55.95 ($71.37 × .7839) at the time of closing. As part of the merger agreement with Tyco, AMP rescinded its $165 million share buyback offer and its plan to issue an additional 25 million shares to fund its defense efforts. Tyco, the world's largest electronics connector company, saw the combination with AMP as a means of becoming the lowest cost producer in the industry.

An electrical components supplier, AMP had been attempting to fend off an unwanted bid from AlliedSignal for four months until a court decision gave AlliedSignal permission to proceed with a $10 billion consent solicitation bid. As of February 1999, AlliedSignal owned 200 million AMP shares, or 9.1% of the total outstanding. It had purchased these shares before making its $10 billion bid. After the Third U.S. Circuit Court of Appeals reversed a ruling from a lower court, AlliedSignal was poised to vote on the Tyco proposal to buy the Pennsylvania-based AMP. The law said that purchasers of more than 20% of a company's stock cannot vote the stock without first getting the approval of the other shareholders. Even though AlliedSignal had purchased less than 20%, the lower court ruled that the shares were "control shares" because they were purchased with the intent to acquire AMP. The appeals court ruled that the law requires the actual accumulation of at least 20% of the outstanding shares.

AlliedSignal Fires an Opening Salvo

Lawrence Bossidy, CEO of AlliedSignal, telephoned a AMP director in mid-1998 to inquire about AMP's interest in a possible combination of their two companies. The inquiry was referred to the finance committee of the AMP Board for consideration. The committee concluded that such a combination did not offer any benefits to AMP's businesses and that there was no interest in pursuing a combination with AlliedSignal.

By early August, AlliedSignal announced its intention to initiate an unsolicited tender offer to acquire all of the outstanding shares of AMP common stock for $44.50 per share to be paid in cash. The following week AlliedSignal initiated such an offer and sent a letter to William J. Hudson, then CEO of AMP, requesting a meeting to discuss a possible business combination. Mr. Bossidy also advised AMP of AlliedSignal's intention to file materials shortly with the SEC as required by federal law to solicit consents from AMP's shareholders. The consent solicitation materials were to include proposals to increase the size of AMP's Board of Directors from 11 to 28 members and to add 17 AlliedSignal nominees, all of whom were directors or executive officers of AlliedSignal. Within a few days, Mr. Hudson indicated in writing to Mr. Bossidy that it was premature for such a meeting, since the board had not yet reviewed AlliedSignal's proposal.

AMP Rejects AlliedSignal's Offer

The AMP board decided to continue to aggressively pursue its current strategic initiatives and business plans, because the AlliedSignal offer did not fully reflect the values inherent in AMP businesses. In addition, the AMP board also replaced Mr. Hudson with Robert Ripp as chairman and chief executive officer of AMP.

AMP Pressures Shareholders to Vote against AlliedSignal's Proposals

The AMP board also authorized an amendment to the AMP rights agreement dated October 25, 1989. The amendment provided that the rights could not be redeemed if there were a change in the composition of the AMP board following the announcement of an unsolicited acquisition proposal such that the current directors no longer comprised a majority of the board. An unsolicited acquisition proposal was defined as a transaction not approved by AMP's board and involving the acquisition by a person or entity of 20% or more of AMP's common stock.

AlliedSignal Amends Its Offer

By early September, AlliedSignal amended its tender offer to reduce the number of shares of AMP common stock it was seeking to purchase to 40,000,000 shares. AlliedSignal also stated that it would undertake another offer to acquire the remaining shares of AMP common stock at a price of $44.50 in cash following consummation of its offer to purchase up to 40,000,000 shares. In concert with its tender offer, AlliedSignal also announced its intention to solicit consents for a proposal to amend AMP's bylaws. The proposed amendment would strip the AMP board of all authority over the AMP rights agreement and any similar agreements and to vest such authority in three individuals selected by AlliedSignal.

In response, the AMP board unanimously determined that the amended offer from AlliedSignal was not in the best interests of AMP shareholders. The AMP board also approved another amendment to the AMP rights agreement, lowering the threshold that would make the rights nonredeemable from 20 to 10% of AMP's shares outstanding. AlliedSignal immediately modified its tender offer by reducing the number of shares it wanted to purchase from 40,000,000 to 20,000,000 shares at $44.50 per share to be paid in cash.

AMP Builds Additional Defenses

AMP announced a self-tender offer to purchase up to 30,000,000 shares of AMP common stock at a price of $55 per share in cash. The AMP self-tender offer was intended to provide AMP shareholders with an opportunity to sell a portion of their shares of common stock at a price in excess of AlliedSignal's $44.50 per share offer. Also on September 28, 1998, AMP stated its intention to create a new ESOP that would hold 25 million shares of AMP common stock to fund future AMP benefit and compensation requirements.

In early October, AlliedSignal announced that it had purchased 20,000,000 shares of AMP common stock, at a price of $44.50 per share. Following the commencement of the AMP self-tender offer, AlliedSignal indicated that if the AMP self-tender offer were consummated, it would reduce the consideration to be paid in any further offer undertaken by AlliedSignal to $42.64 per share. AlliedSignal indicated that the price could even be lower to take into account expenses incurred by AMP in connection with the AMP self-tender offer.

AMP Seeks a White Knight

Credit Suisse, AMP's investment banker, approached a number of firms, including Tyco, concerning their possible interest in acquiring AMP. In early November, Tyco stepped forward as a possible white knight. Based on limited information, Mr. Kozlowski, Tyco's CEO, set the preliminary valuation of AMP at $50.00 per share. This value assumed a transaction in which AMP shares would be exchanged for Tyco shares, accounted for as a pooling of interests, and was subject to the completion of appropriate due diligence and agreement on other transaction terms satisfactory to Tyco.

AlliedSignal Blinks?

In mid-November, Mr. Ripp and Mr. Bossidy met at Bossidy's request. Mr. Bossidy indicated that AlliedSignal would be prepared to increase its proposed acquisition price for AMP by a modest amount and to include an equity component for a limited portion of the total purchase price. The revised offer would also include a minimum share exchange ratio for the equity portion of the purchase price along with an opportunity for AMP shareholders to participate in any increase in AlliedSignal's stock before the closing. The purpose of including equity as a portion of the purchase price was to address the needs of certain AMP shareholders, who had a low tax basis in the stock and who wanted a tax-free exchange. Mr. Ripp indicated that the AMP board expected a valuation above $50.00 per share. Mr. Bossidy indicated that AlliedSignal would not go that high. After conferring with his board, Mr. Ripp told Mr. Bossidy that the AlliedSignal offer was inadequate.

Tyco Ups Its Offer

Tyco indicated a willingness to increase its offer to at least $51.00 worth of Tyco common shares for each share of AMP common stock. The offer would also include protections similar to those offered in AlliedSignal's most recent proposal. On November 20, 1998, the AMP board of directors voted unanimously to approve the merger agreement and to recommend approval of the merger to AMP's shareholders. They also voted to terminate the AMP self-tender offer, to terminate the ESOP, to terminate AMP's share repurchase plan, and to amend the AMP rights agreement so that it would not apply to the merger with Tyco.

Following the announcement of the Tyco transaction, AlliedSignal publicly announced that the price being paid by Tyco exceeded the value AlliedSignal had placed on AMP. AlliedSignal also stated that it would defer its consent solicitation pending clarification of certain legal issues with respect to AlliedSignal's efforts to gain control of AMP and pending verification that AMP shareholders will receive the value that had been announced.

AlliedSignal and Dissident AMP Shareholders Sue AMP

In early August, AlliedSignal filed a complaint against AMP in the United States District Court against the provisions of the AMP rights agreement. The complaint also questioned the constitutionality of certain antitakeover provisions of Pennsylvania state statutes. Concurrently, AMP shareholders filed four shareholder class action lawsuits against AMP and its board of directors. The suits alleged that AMP and its directors improperly refused to consider the original AlliedSignal offer and wrongfully relied upon the provisions of the AMP rights agreement and Pennsylvania law to block the original AlliedSignal offer.

AMP Countersues

In late August, AMP filed a complaint in the United States District court against AlliedSignal seeking an injunction to prevent AlliedSignal from attempting to pack the AMP board of directors with AlliedSignal executive officers and directors. The complaint also alleged that the Schedule 14D-1 filed by Allied-Signal with the SEC was false and misleading. The complaint alleged that the filing failed to disclose that some of AlliedSignal's proposed directors had conflicts of interest and that the packing of the board would prevent current board members from executing their fiduciary responsibilities to AMP shareholders.

The Court Agrees with AMP

In early October, the court agreed with AMP and enjoined AlliedSignal's board-packing consent proposals until it stated unequivocally that its director nominees have a fiduciary duty solely to AMP under Pennsylvania law. The court also denied AlliedSignal's request to deactivate antitakeover provisions in the AMP rights agreement. In addition, the court declared that AlliedSignal's consent proposal to amend AMP's bylaws. The court further held that shareholders might not sue the board for rejecting the AlliedSignal proposal.

AlliedSignal Appeals the Lower Court Ruling

AlliedSignal immediately filed in the United States Court of Appeals for the Third Circuit. The court ordered that although AlliedSignal could proceed with the consent solicitation, its representatives could not assume positions on the AMP board until the court of appeals completed its deliberations. The district court ruled that the shares of AMP common stock acquired by AlliedSignal are "control shares" under Pennsylvania law. As a result, the court issued an order enjoining AlliedSignal from voting any shares of AMP's common stock owned by Allied-Signal unless AlliedSignal's voting rights are restored under Pennsylvania law. AlliedSignal was able to overturn the lower court ruling on appeal.

Case Study Discussion Questions

1. What types of takeover tactics did AlliedSignal employ?
2. What steps did AlliedSignal take to satisfy federal securities laws?

3. What antitakeover defenses were in place at AMP prior to AlliedSignal's offer?
4. How did the AMP board use the AMP rights agreement to encourage AMP shareholders to vote against AlliedSignal's proposals?
5. What options did AlliedSignal have to neutralize or circumvent AMP's use of the rights agreement?
6. After announcing it had purchased 20 million AMP shares at $44.50, why did AlliedSignal indicate that it would reduce the price paid in any further offers it might make?
7. What other takeover defenses did AMP employ in its attempt to thwart AlliedSignal?
8. How did both AMP and AlliedSignal use litigation in this takeover battle?
9. Should state laws be used to protect companies from hostile takeovers?
10. Was AMP's board and management acting to protect their own positions (i.e., the management entrenchment hypothesis) or in the best interests of the shareholders (i.e., the shareholder interests hypothesis)?

Solutions to these questions are found in the Appendix at the back of this book.

REFERENCES

Bhagat, Sanjai, Andrei Shleiffer, and Robert Vishny, "Hostile Takeovers in the 1980's: The Return to Corporate Specialization," *Brookings Papers on Economic Activity,* 1990, pp. 1–72.

Bhagat, S., and J. A. Brickley, "Cumulative Voting: The Value of Minority Shareholders Rights," *Journal of Law and Economics,* 27, October 1984, pp. 339–366.

Bloomberg.com, "Reynolds Agrees to Be Acquired by Alcoa," August 19, 1999.

Bloomberg.com, "Pfizer's Stormy Courtship Ends," February 8, 2000a.

Bloomberg.com, "Vodafone to Buy Mannesmann," February 8, 2000b.

Bradley, Michael, Anand Desai, and E. Han Kim, "Synergystic Gains from Corporate Acquisitions and Their Division Between Stockholders of Target and Acquiring Firms," *Journal of Financial Economics,* 21, 1988, pp. 3–40.

Bradley, Michael, and I. MacDonald Wakeman, "The Wealth Effects of Targeted Share Repurchases," *Journal of Financial Economics, 11,* April 1983, pp. 301–328.

Bruner, Robert F., "An Analysis of Value Destruction and Recovery in the Alliance and Proposed Merger of Volvo and Renault," *Journal of Financial Economics, 51* (1), January 1999, pp. 125–166.

Buckhorn Inc. v. Ropak Corp., 656 F, Supp. 209 (S.D. Ohio) affected by summary order 815 F.2d 76 (6ᵗʰ Cir., 1987).

Business Week, "Addicted to Mergers," December 6, 1999, pp. 84–88.

Comment, Robert, and G. William Schwert, "Poison or Placebo: Evidence on the Deterrence and Wealth Effects of Modern Anti-takeover Measures," *Journal of Financial Economics,* 39, 1995, pp. 3–43.

Dann, Larry, and Harry DeAngelo, "Standstill Agreements, Privately Negotiated Stock Repurchases, and the Market for Corporate Control," *Journal of Financial Economics, 11* (1–4), April 1983, pp. 275–300.

DeAngelo, Harry, and Linda DeAngelo, "Proxy Contests and the Governance of Publicly Held Corporations," *Journal of Financial Economics, 23,* 1989, pp. 29–60.

DeAngelo, Harry, and Eugene Rice, "Anti-takeover charter Amendments and Stockholder Wealth," *Journal of Financial Economics 11* (1983), pp. 329–360.

Dodd, Peter, and Jerrold Warner, "On Corporate Government: A Study of Proxy Contests," *Journal of Financial Economics 11* (1–4), April 1983, pp. 401–438.

Gaughan, Patrick A., *Mergers, Acquisitions, and Corporate Restructurings* (2nd ed.) New York: John Wiley & Sons, Inc., 1999, pp. 243–288.

Georgeson & Company, "Poison Pills and Shareholder Value: 1992–1996," 1997a, www.georgeson.com/pubs.

Georgeson & Company, "Institutional Voting on Poison Pill Rescission," 1997b, www.georgeson.com/pubs.

Hasbrouck, Joel, "The Characteristics of Takeover Targets," *Journal of Banking and Finance,* 9, 1985, pp. 351–362.

Huang, Yen-Sheng, and Ralph A. Walking, "Target Abnormal Returns Associated with Acquisition Announcements: Payment, Acquisition Form, and Managerial Resistance," *Journal of Financial Economics, 19,* December 1987, pp. 329–349.

Ikenberry, David, and Josef Lakonishok, "Corporate Governance Through the Proxy Contest: Evidence and Implications," *Journal of Business,* 66, July 1993, pp. 405–435.

Jarrell, Gregg, "Wealth Effects of Litigating by Targets: Do Interests Diverge in a Merger?" *Journal of Law and Economics, 28,* April 1985a, pp. 151–177.

Jarrell, Gregg, "Wealth Effects of Litigating by Targets: Do Interests Diverge in a Merger?" *Journal of Law and Economics, 28,* April 1985b, pp. 151–177.

Jarrell, Gregg, and Annette B. Poulsen, "Shark repellents and Stock Prices: The Effects of Antitakeover Amendments Since 1980," *Journal of Financial Economics, 19* (1), September 1987, pp. 127–168.

Jensen, Michael, "Takeovers, Causes, and Consequences," in Patrick A. Gaughan, ed., *Readings in Mergers and Acquisitions,* Oxford: Basil Blackwell, 1994, pp. 15–43.

Kennecott Cooper Corp. v. Curtiss Wright Corp., 584 F. 2d 1195 (2nd Cir. 1978).

Lambert, Richard A., and David F. Larker, "Golden Parachutes, Executive Decision Making and Shareholder Wealth," *Journal of Accounting Economics,* 7, 1985, pp. 179–203.

Linn, Scott C., and John J. McConnell, "An Empirical Investigation of the Impact of Anti-takeover Amendments on Common Stock Prices," *Journal of Financial Economics, 11* (1–4), April 1983, pp. 361–399.

Machlin, Judith, Hyuk Choe, and James Miles, "The Effects of Golden Parachutes on Takeover Activity," *Journal of Law and Economics, 36* (2), 1993, pp. 861–876.

Malatesta, Paul H., and Ralph A. Walking, "Poison Pills Securities: Stockholder Wealth, Profitability and Ownership Structure," *Journal of Financial Economics, 20* (1.2), January/March 1988, pp. 347–376.

Manne, Henry G., "Mergers and the Market for Corporate Control," *Journal of Political Economy, 73,* 1965, pp. 110–120.

Mikkelson, Wayne H., and M. Megan Partch, "Managers' Voting Rights and Corporate Control, *Journal of Financial Economics, 25,* 1989, pp. 263–290.

Mikkelson, Wayne, and Richard Ruback, "Targeted Share Repurchases and Common Stock Returns," Working Paper No. 1707–86, Massachusetts Institute of Technology, Sloan School of Management, June 1986.

Morck, Randall, Andrei Schleiffer, and Robert W. Vishny, Characteristics of Targets of Hostile and Friendly Takeovers," In Alan J. Auerbach, (Ed.), *Corporate Takeovers: Causes and Consequences,* National Bureau of Economic Research: Chicago, Illinois, 1988, pp. 101–129.

Mulherin, J. Harold, and Annette B. Poulsen," Proxy Contests and Corporate Change: Implications for Shareholder Wealth," *Journal of Financial Economics, 47,* 1998, pp. 279–313.

Netter, Jeffrey, and Annette Poulsen, "State Corporation Laws and Shareholders: The Recent Experience," *Financial Management, 18* (3), Autumn 1989, pp. 29–40.

Palepu, Krishna G., "Predicitng Takeover Targets: A Methodological and Empirical Analysis," *Journal of Accounting and Economics, 8,* 1986, pp. 3–35.

Partch, Megan, "The Creation of a Class of Limited Voting Common Stock and Shareholder Wealth," *Journal of Financial Economics, 18* (2), June 1987, p. 313.

Ryngaert, Michael, "The Effects of Poison Pill Securities on Stockholder Wealth," *Journal of Financial Economics, 20,* January/March 1988, pp. 377–417.

Schwert, G. William, "Hostility in Takeovers: In the Eyes of the Bidder?" University of Rochester and National Bureau of Economic Research, Working Paper, Second Draft, April, 1999, http://schwert.ssb.rochester.edu/host.htm.

Shivdasani, Anil, "Board Composition, Ownership Structure, and Hostile Takeovers," *Journal of Accounting and Economics, 16,* 1993, pp. 167–198.

Stromfeld v. Great Atlantic & Pacific Tea Company, 484F. Supp. 1264 (S.D.N.Y. 1980), aff'd 6464 F. 2d 563 (2nd Cir. 1980)

Thompson Financial Securities Data Corporation, "The World is Not Enough . . . To Merge," Press release, January 5, 2000.

Unocal v. Mesa, 493 A.2d 949, (Del 1985).

Wasserstein, Bruce, *Big Deal: The Battle for Control of America's Leading Corporations,* New York: Warner Books, 1998, pp. 601–644.

PART

II

THE MERGERS
AND ACQUISITIONS
PROCESS

PHASES 1–10

4

PLANNING

DEVELOPING BUSINESS AND ACQUISITION PLANS— PHASES 1 AND 2 OF THE ACQUISITION PROCESS

If you don't know where you are going, any road will get you there.

—Alice in Wonderland

Lee had a reputation throughout the industry and within his company as a "big picture" guy, a visionary who seemed to see things that others couldn't. His detractors often quipped that he made so many predictions that some would have to be true . . . they just didn't know which ones or when. They were convinced that he did not know either.

He had come up through the ranks in his company during the 1990s when management agility and nimbleness in decision making were often viewed on Wall Street as signs of strong management. The virtues of "first mover advantage" were often used to justify deals that, had they been made in a less heady time, would have been viewed as reckless. Be first and fast. Build a brand name and market share to erect barriers to others who may choose to follow. After all, this was the age of accelerating change. This was the age of electronic commerce and the new economy.

Lee bought into this philosophy. After all, he was a visionary. Although his view of the future was understandably somewhat fuzzy, he reasoned that he did not have the time to consider his options. He had to act quickly or miss the opportunity. He had confidence in his instincts. He was a manager for the next millenium! But he had forgotten what his driving instructor had told him when he was first learning to drive. "Sometimes," he admonished, "speed kills."

OVERVIEW

A poorly designed or inappropriate business strategy is among the most frequently cited reasons for the failure of mergers and acquisitions (M&As) to satisfy expectations. Surprisingly, many textbooks on the subject of M&As fail to adequately address the overarching role that planning should take in conceptualizing and implementing business combinations.

The purpose of this chapter is to introduce a planning-based approach to mergers and acquisitions, which discusses M&A activity in the context of an integrated process consisting of 10 interrelated phases. This chapter focuses on the first two phases of the process, building the business and acquisition plans, and on tools commonly used to evaluate, display, and communicate information to key constituencies both inside (e.g., board of directors and management) and outside (e.g., lenders and stockholders) of the corporation. Phases 3–10 are discussed in Chapter 5 (this volume).

The literature on strategic planning that has emerged over the years runs the gamut from a focus on a more prescriptive and static approach involving the use of specific tools and checklists to more eclectic theories, which view planning as largely a dynamic and evolving process. Stryker (1986), Porter (1985), and Almaney (1992) make effective use of checklists to ensure that all key issues about a firm's internal and external operating environments are addressed. Other writers on the subject of strategic planning argue that planning is largely an iterative process in which the firm must continuously make "midcourse" corrections to its strategy as it adapts to changes in its operating environment. These writers view planning more as a way of thinking about the future (James, Mintzberg, and Quinn: 1988). However, such approaches, although conceptually appealing, are often difficult to apply in practice. Other approaches focus on the role of flexibility and nimbleness in implementing corporate strategies (Waterman: 1987). These approaches provide little guidance or discipline in their application. Still others advocate a rule-based approach to planning in which expert systems are developed to provide more disciplined guidance to the process (Chung and Davidson: 1987).

The planning tools described in this chapter are largely prescriptive in nature in that they recommend certain strategies based on the results generated by applying specific tools (e.g., experience curve) and answering checklists of relevant questions. Although these tools introduce some degree of rigor to strategic planning, their application should not be viewed as a completion of the planning process. Business plans must be updated frequently to account for changes in the firm's operating environment and its competitive position within that environment. Indeed, business planning is not an event but rather an evolving process.

There are few unambiguous answers. More often than not the planning process provides direction that is supported more by intuition than empirical evidence. This is particularly true in the current environment, which seems to be changing at an accelerating pace. In this volatile environment, planning is even more important. The ultimate value of a well-designed planning process is that it forces management to be introspective. The planning process should compel management to specify clearly all key assumptions underlying their chosen strategies and to reassess these strategies as changes in the environment render important assumptions obsolete.

A PLANNING-BASED APPROACH TO MERGERS AND ACQUISITIONS

The acquisition process envisioned in this chapter can be separated into a planning and an implementation stage. The planning stage consists of the development of the business and the acquisition plans. The implementation stage includes the search, screening, contacting the target, negotiation, integration planning, closing, integration, and evaluation activities. To understand the role of planning in the M&A process, it is necessary to understand the purpose of the acquiring firm's mission, strategy, and tactics.

MISSION, STRATEGY, AND TACTICS

A planning-based acquisition process consists of both a business plan and an acquisition plan, which drive all subsequent phases of the acquisition process. The *business plan* articulates a mission or vision for the firm and a strategy for realizing that mission. The business strategy is long-term oriented and usually cuts across organizational lines to impact many different functional areas. It is often broadly defined and provides relatively little detail.

In contrast, tactical plans, also known as implementation, action, or operational plans, include the detailed specification of how the business strategy will be executed. The *acquisition plan* is a tactical plan focused on supporting a specific element of the business plan. Tactical plans are focused on short-term results and are generally developed by functional areas. Tactical plans tend to be very detailed and highly structured. Tactical plans will result in a series of concrete actions for each function or business group, depending on the company's organization. It is common to see separate plans for such functions as marketing, manufacturing, research and development (R&D), engineering, and financial and human resources. These separate plans define how each functional area will support the implementation of the overall business strategy or a specific component of that strategy. Tactical plans should include clearly defined actions, timetables for achieving those actions, resources required, and the individual responsible for ensuring that the actions are completed on time and within budget.

Specific tactics could read as follows:

Set up a product distribution network in the northeastern United States capable of handling a minimum of one million units of product annually by 12/31/??
(Individual responsible: Truong Nuygen, estimated budget $2 million.)

Develop and execute an advertising campaign to support the sales effort in the northeastern United States by 10/31/?? (Individual responsible: Maria Gomez; estimated budget $.5 million.)

Hire a logistics manager to administer the distribution network by 9/15/?? (Individual responsible: Patrick Petty, estimated budget $100,000.)

Acquire a manufacturing company with sufficient capacity to meet the projected demand for the next 3 years by 6/30/?? at a purchase price not to exceed $100 million (Individual responsible: Chang Lee).

The relationship between mission, strategy, and tactics can be illustrated by an application software company, which is targeting the credit card industry.

Mission: To become recognized by its customers as the leader in providing accurate high-speed, high-volume transactional software for processing credit card remittances by 20??.

Strategy: Upgrade the firm's current software by adding the necessary features and functions to satisfy projected customer requirements through 20??.

Tactics: Purchase a software company at a price not to exceed $400 million capable of developing "state of the art" remittance processing software by 12/21/?? (Individual responsible: Donald Stuckee). Note that this assumes that the firm has completed an analysis of available options including internal development, partnering, licensing, or acquisition.

THE ACQUISITION PROCESS

It is sometimes convenient to think of an acquisition process as a series of largely independent events culminating in the transfer of ownership from the seller to the buyer. In theory, thinking of the process as discrete events facilitates the communication and understanding of the numerous activities that are required to complete the transaction. In practice, the steps involved in the process are frequently highly interrelated, do not necessarily follow a logical order, and involve, as new information becomes available, reiteration of steps in the process thought to have been completed.

Some individuals tend to shudder at the thought of following a structured process because of perceived delays in responding to both anticipated and unanticipated opportunities. Anticipated opportunities are those identified as a result of the business planning process. This process consists of understanding the firm's external operating environment, assessing internal resources, reviewing a range of reasonable options, and articulating a clear vision of the future of the business and a realistic strategy for achieving that vision (see Hill and Jones: 2001). Unanticipated or unforeseen opportunities result from new information becoming available. Rather than delaying the pursuit of an opportunity, the presence of a well-designed business plan provides for a rapid yet substantive evaluation of the perceived opportunity based on work completed while having developed the business plan. Decisions made in the context of a business plan are made with the confidence that comes from having already asked and answered the difficult questions.

Figure 4-1 illustrates the ten phases of the acquisition process described in this chapter and in Chapter 5. These phases fall into two distinct sets of activities (i.e., pre- and postpurchase decision activities). The crucial phase of the acquisition process is the negotiation phase. Negotiation consists of four largely concurrent and interrelated activities. The decision to purchase or walk away is determined as a result of continuous iteration through the four activities comprising the negotiation phase. Assuming the transaction is ultimately completed, the price paid for the target company is actually determined during the negotiation phase. The phases of the acquisition process are summarized below:

Phase 1: Develop a strategic plan for the entire business (Business Plan).
Phase 2: Develop the acquisition plan related to the strategic plan (Acquisition Plan).

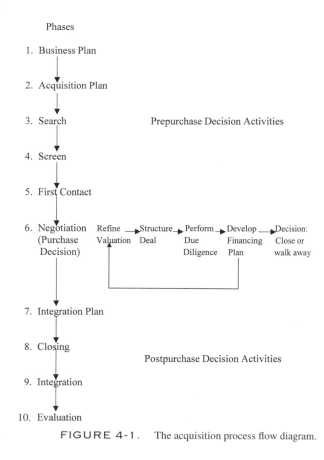

FIGURE 4-1.   The acquisition process flow diagram.

Phase 3: Actively search for acquisition candidates (Search).

Phase 4: Screen and prioritize potential candidates (Screen).

Phase 5: Initiate contact with the target (First Contact).

Phase 6: Refine valuation, structure deal, perform due diligence, and develop financing plan (Negotiation).

Phase 7: Develop plan for integrating the acquired business (Integration Plan).

Phase 8: Obtain all necessary approvals, resolve postclosing issues, and implement closing (Closing).

Phase 9: Implement postclosing integration (Integration).

Phase 10: Conduct postclosing evaluation of acquisition (Evaluation).

PHASE 1: BUILDING THE BUSINESS PLAN

KEY ACTIVITIES

A well-designed business plan consists of the following activities:

1. Determining where to compete (i.e., the industry or market in which the firm has chosen to compete)
2. Determining how to compete (i.e., conducting an external industry or market evaluation to determine how the firm can most effectively compete in its chosen market[s])
3. Self-assessment (i.e., conducting an internal analysis of the firm's strengths and weaknesses relative to the competition)
4. Defining a mission statement (i.e., summarizing where and how the firm has chosen to compete and the basic operating beliefs of management)
5. Setting objectives (i.e., developing quantitative measures of performance)
6. Strategy selection (i.e., selecting the strategy most likely to achieve the objectives in an acceptable time period subject to constraints identified in the self-assessment)

Each of these six activities is discussed during the balance of this section. In practice, the process of actually developing a business plan can be greatly facilitated by addressing a number of detailed questions corresponding to each activity listed above. Although literally hundreds of checklists are available (Porter: 1985; Stryker: 1986), the appendix to this chapter contains an abbreviated checklist of questions that should be addressed for each activity involved in the development of an appropriate business plan.

DETERMINING WHERE TO COMPETE

Determining where a firm should compete starts with deciding who are the firm's current or potential customers and what are their needs. This is the single most important activity in building a business plan and is based on the process of market segmentation.

Market Segmentation

Market segmentation involves identifying customers with common characteristics and needs. Collections of customers, whether individual consumers or other firms, comprise markets. A collection of markets is said to comprise an industry. In manufacturing, examples include the automotive industry, which could be defined to consist of the new and used car markets as well as the after-market for replacement parts. Markets may be further subdivided by examining cars by makes and model years. The automotive market could also be defined regionally (e.g., North America) or by country. Each subdivision, whether by product or geographic area, defines a new market within the automotive industry.

Identifying Market Segments

The process for identifying a target market involves a three-step procedure. The first step involves establishing evaluation criteria used to distinguish the market to be targeted by the firm from other potential target markets. This requires the management of the firm conducting the market segmentation to determine what factors are likely to affect a firm's overall attractiveness. The evaluation criteria may include market size and growth rate, profitability, cyclicality, the price sensitivity of customers, amount of regulation, degree of unionization, as well as entry and exit barriers. Larger firms are more likely to establish minimum size requirements for selecting target markets. In the mid-1980s, IBM announced that it would not pursue markets that could not generate at least $1 billion in total annual sales. Other firms may choose to avoid markets with extremely high growth rates because of the substantial investment levels required to sustain these high rates of growth.

The second step entails continuously subdividing industries and the markets within these industries and analyzing the overall attractiveness of these markets in terms of the evaluation criteria. For each market, the evaluation criteria are given a numerical weight reflecting the firm's perception of the relative importance of each criterion applied to that market to determine overall attractiveness. Higher numbers imply greater perceived significance. Note that some criteria may be given a zero weight. The evaluation criteria are then ranked from 1 to 5, with 5 indicating that the firm finds a market to be highly favorable in terms of a specific evaluation criterion.

In the third step, a weighted average score is calculated for each market and the markets are ranked according to their respective scores. The market with the highest score is considered to be the most attractive. How laborious the process becomes is largely dependent on management's willingness to narrow at the outset of the process the number of industries and markets to be analyzed. Some managers will require that a large number of industries be analyzed before selecting the target market. The intuitive appeal of this approach is that management is less likely to miss highly attractive markets. The practical risk to this approach is that it is likely to be much more time consuming, and it tends to defer making the difficult decisions. The process of "thinking broadly" tends to contribute to "analysis paralysis." This three-step procedure is illustrated in Table 4-1. Such a matrix is constructed for each market evaluated.

Segmenting Markets When Available Data Are Limited

Although it is generally possible to collect a sufficient amount of data for established industries to develop selection criteria, reasonably accurate data are of-

TABLE 4-1.   Industry–Market Attractiveness Matrix

Industry or market evaluation criteria	Weight (relative importance of criteria)[a]	Ranking (5 = highly favorable and 1 = highly unfavorable)[b]	Weighted score (Weight × Ranking)
Market size: Is it large or small? Global, national, or regional?	.10	4	.40
Growth rate: Is it slowing, declining, or accelerating?	.20	5	1.00
Profitability: Is it currently profitable? Expected to remain so?	.20	4	.80
Cyclicality: Is profitability volatile?	.05	2	.10
Seasonality: Is profitability seasonal?	.00	3	.00
Customers: Are the number, average size, and needs changing?	.05	4	.20
Competitors: Is it currently highly competitive? Will competition intensify?	.10	4	.40
Suppliers: Are they reliable?	.00	3	.00
Culture: What are the emerging trends?	.00	4	.00
Regulation: Is the industry heavily regulated?	.06	4	.24
Politics: Is the political climate stable?	.05	3	.15
Labor unions: Is it heavily unionized? Are unions cooperative or militant?	.05	4	.20
Technology: What are the emerging technological trends?	.10	5	.50
Entry and exit barriers: Is difficult to enter or leave?	.04	3	.12
Total	1.00		4.11

[a] Some of the criteria are viewed as insignificant when applied to this industry or market and are given a zero weight.

[b] The ranking is the extent to which each criterion is viewed as favorable by the firm.

ten not available for new or evolving industries. Despite the absence of good data, the market segmentation process can still be helpful in determining where the firm should compete.

For example, electronic commerce is commonly associated with the buying and selling of information, products, and services via computer networks. In broader terms, electronic commerce addresses the needs of organizations, merchants, and consumers to reduce costs, while improving the speed with which transactions can be consummated. Increasing interest in electronic commerce has spawned a headlong rush by both existing companies and start-ups to target products and services either for supporting the infrastructure requirements needed to support exploding usage (i.e., infrastructure providers) or for sale via the Internet (i.e., content providers). During the 1990s, companies that generated revenue by selling on the Internet or selling products and services that were used by companies during business on the Internet were often referred to simply as Internet companies. This lack of distinction among companies resulted in many companies exhibiting a high price-to-earnings (P/E) ratio simply because their business was somehow related to the Internet.

Despite a lack of reliable data to measure the size and growth rate of segments, market segmentation techniques can still provide helpful insights by creating a simplistic framework for characterizing the industry. Market segmentation forces the analyst to group firms having common characteristics. Instead of labeling all firms with "dot com" in their names as Internet companies, functionally similar firms are compared. Earthlink is clearly more closely related to other Internet service providers (ISPs) than with American Online (AOL), even though AOL also provides Internet access. In other instances, the distinction may be less clear. Should Amazon.com be compared to other online booksellers or to other retailers offering a broader product offering?

Infrastructure activities consist of network, equipment, software, and systems integration expertise. The network backbone underlying the Internet is managed by the major telecommunications carriers. Access to the network is gained through regional carriers, which in turn sell access to consumers and small businesses through ISPs. Equipment suppliers provide modems, routers, and servers to support access, communication, and processing of information. All of these activities rely on sophisticated client and server software applications supplied by software vendors. System integrators must meld complex systems using disparate software and hardware vendors. Content providers are dependent on vendors providing such enabling services as payments processing, security, advertising, web design, and search or directory services. Table 4-2 illustrates how this simple framework can be used to create discrete industry and market segments.

DETERMINING HOW TO COMPETE

Determining how to compete involves a clear understanding of the factors critical for successful competition in the targeted market. This outward-looking anal-

TABLE 4-2.   Internet-Focused Industries and Markets

Industry segment	Market segments (representative companies)				
Network providers	Internet backbone provider (MCI Worldcom)	Fiber-optic network provider (QWEST)	Regional backbone access provider (PSINET)	Internet access providers (Earthlink)	Wireless technology (Vodafone AirTouch)
Equipment	Access (3 COM)	Backbone (Cisco)	Servers (Sun Microsystems)	Data Networking (Lucent)	Transmission Gear (Ascend)
Software	Client (Oracle)	Server (Sun)	Development tools (Oracle)	Security (Raptor)	Personalized transactions (Broadvision)
Expertise	Creative (Earthweb)	Systems integration (Andersen)	Re-Engineering (CSC)	Advertising services (Doubleclick)	Domain names (Network Solutions)
Enabling services	Directories and portals (Yahoo)	Security (Verisign)	Payment systems (First Data)	Rating services (I/Pro)	Web-site hosting (GTE)
Content	Entertainment (Sportsline)	Financial (Bloomberg)	Retailers (Amazon.com)	News Feeds (Dow Jones)	Publishers (D&B)

ysis applies to the factors governing the environment external to the firm. Understanding market dynamics and knowing in what areas the firm must excel when compared to the competition is crucial if the firm is to compete effectively in its chosen market.

Profiling the Targeted Markets

Market profiling entails collecting sufficient data to accurately assess and characterize a firm's competitive environment within its chosen markets. Using Michael Porter's (1985) Five Forces framework, the competitive environment can be described in terms of the firm's customers, suppliers (including suppliers of capital), current competitors, potential competitors, and product or service substitutes. This framework may be modified to include other factors, such as the degree of unionization, the severity of governmental regulation, and the impact of global influences (e.g., fluctuations in exchange rates) (see Figure 4-2).

The required data include the following: (1) types of products and services, (2) market share in terms of dollars and units, (3) pricing, (4) selling and distribution channels and associated costs, (5) type, location, and age of production facilities, (6) product quality metrics, (7) customer service metrics, (8) compensation by major labor category, (9) R&D expenditures, (10) supplier performance metrics, and (11) financial performance in terms of growth and profitability. This

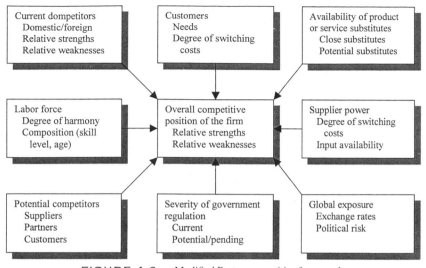

FIGURE 4-2.   Modified Porter competitive framework.

data must be collected on all significant competitors in the firm's chosen markets (see the appendix to this chapter for more detail on data requirements).

Customers

The firm must understand the key reasons its customers make buying decisions and rank order them from the most to the least important. Key reasons could include price, quality, service, convenience, or some combination. Market surveys can be conducted to determine how sensitive customers are to changes in these factors. Failure to understand even subtle differences in customer motivations can lead to a significant loss of business in highly competitive markets. For example, companies lending to consumers and businesses rely heavily on information supplied by the major credit reporting companies such as Experian, Equifax, Trans-Union, and Dun & Bradstreet for information to make credit-granting decisions. Although lenders require accurate, complete, and timely data, small differences in price will cause lenders to switch suppliers or renegotiate contracts with existing suppliers as soon as the current contracts expire.

Suppliers

The firm needs to determine the number and reputation for quality and reliability of critical suppliers. A single or a small number of relatively low-quality or unreliable suppliers may pose a significant threat to a firm attempting to expand its market share. Moreover, reliance on a single or a small number of suppliers shifts pricing power from the buyer to the seller. Examples include Intel's global dominance of the microchip market and Microsoft's worldwide supremacy in the market for personal computer operating systems. Suppliers can also make the products and services provided by former customers obsolete, as evidenced by Dell Computer's strategy of selling directly to customers (see Case Study 4-1).

Current Competitors

An analysis of competitors, both domestic and foreign, should reveal the factors contributing to their success, where revenue and earnings growth and overall profit margins could measure success. These "success factors" include such considerations as product line breadth, consistent quality, efficient product distribution, low cost production, or key patents. In the late 1960s and through most of the 1970s, it was widely believed that mini-mills (i.e., nonintegrated steel mills), which did not own their own coal and iron ore supplies, could not compete in the flat-rolled steel markets due to the limitations of their technology. However, by the late 1970s, such companies as Nucor Steel and Florida Steel were able to achieve major cost advantages by adopting continuous casting technologies, which enabled them to make significant inroads into the lucrative flat-rolled steel markets.

There are numerous tools, techniques, and sources of information that are readily available for evaluating the competitive position of one firm relative to its primary competitors (Murland, Sammon, and Spitnalic: 1984). Although the effort to amass a database on competitors is very time-consuming, it is generally easily updated and serves as a highly useful means of establishing performance benchmarks. Such benchmarks enable the firm to measure its progress in improving its overall competitive position relative to its primary competitors.

Potential Competitors

These include firms (both domestic and foreign) in the current market, those in related markets, current customers, and current suppliers. Amazon.com is attempting to expand well beyond its original product offering of books and has moved into the sale of CDs and pharmaceuticals as well as providing online auction services. Its stated goal is to become the Walmart of the Internet.

Product or Service Substitutes

What we don't know can hurt us. Examples include the shift of many products formerly ordered through traditional brick and mortar retail outlets to the Internet such as books, compact discs, and airline tickets; e-mail and faxes as substitutes for letters; and the replacement of the electric typewriter by the word processor.

Labor Force

Work stoppages create opportunities for competitors to gain market share. Customers are forced to satisfy their product and service needs elsewhere. While in some cases, the loss of customers may be temporary, it may be permanent if the customer finds that another firm's product or service is equal to or superior than what it had been purchasing. Frequent work stoppages may also have long-term impacts on productivity and production costs as a result of a less motivated labor force and increased labor turnover. High turnover can be particularly insidious as firms incur substantial search and retraining expenses to fill positions.

Government Regulation

Estimates of the total cost of complying with U.S. federal government regulations vary from about $200 to $700 billion annually (Hopkins: 1996). State and local regulations would add to this cost considerably. Regulations create both barriers to entering an industry as well as exiting an industry. Companies wishing to enter the pharmaceutical industry must have the capabilities to produce and test new drugs to the satisfaction of the Food and Drug Administration. Companies with large unfunded or underfunded pension liabilities may find exiting an industry impossible until they have met their pension obligations to the satisfaction of the U.S. Pension Benefit Guaranty Corporation.

Global Exposure

Global exposure refers to the extent to which participation in an industry necessitates having a multinational presence. For example, the automotive industry is widely viewed as a global industry in which participation requires having assembly plants and distribution networks in major markets throughout the world. As the major auto assemblers move abroad, they are also requiring their parts suppliers to build nearby facilities to ensure "just-in-time" delivery of parts. Global exposure introduces the firm to significant currency risk as well as political risk that could result in the confiscation of the firm's properties.

CASE STUDY 4-1. DELL COMPUTER'S DRIVE TO ELIMINATE THE MIDDLEMAN

Historically, personal computers (PCs) were sold either through a direct sales force to businesses (e.g., IBM), through company-owned stores (e.g., Gateway), or through independent retail outlets and distributors to both businesses and consumers (e.g., CompUSA). Retail chains and distributors constituted a large percentage of the customer base of other PC manufacturers such as Compaq and Gateway. Consequently, most PC manufacturers were saddled with the large overhead expense associated with a direct sales force, a chain of company-owned stores, a demanding and complex distribution chain contributing a substantial percentage of revenue, or some combination of all three.

Michael Dell, the founder of Dell Computer, saw an opportunity to take cost out of the distribution of PCs by circumventing the distributors and selling directly to the end user. Dell Computer introduced a dramatically new business model for selling PCs. By starting with this model when the firm was formed, Dell did not have to worry about being in direct competition with its distribution chain. Historically, this concern has limited the extent to which other major PC manufacturers, such as Compaq and Hewlett-Packard, felt they could sell directly to end users.

Dell has also changed the basis of competition in the PC industry by shifting much of its direct-order business to the Internet and by introducing made-to-order PCs. Businesses and consumers can specify the features and functions of a PC online and pay by credit card. The PC is assembled by Dell only after the order is processed and the customer's credit card has been validated. This has the effect of increasing both customer choice and convenience as well as dramatically reducing Dell's costs of carrying inventory. Moreover, Dell has developed 22,000 "Premier Pages" or web sites that allow businesses to conveniently order computers directly from the company.

The success of Michael Dell's business model is evident as Dell's U.S. PC market share increased from 4.2% in 1994 to 14.3% in 1999, placing it just behind industry leader, Compaq Computer's 15.7% market share. Dell currently sells about $18 million a day in computers on the Internet. This amounts to about 30% of its annual revenue. Competitors are trying to imitate the Dell model but continue to move slowly for fear of alienating their wholesale and retail customers. In contrast to Dell, Hewlett-Packard currently has only 800 specialized web sites for their customers to order directly from the company. IBM plans to have 1000 in place by the end of 1999.

Source: Dell Computer, 10K, Securities and Exchange Commission, 2000, www.sec.gov/edgarhp.htm

SELF-ASSESSMENT

What are the firm's critical strengths and weaknesses as compared to the competition? Can the firm's critical strengths be easily duplicated and surpassed by the competition? Can these critical strengths be used to gain strategic advantage in the firm's chosen market? Can the firm's key weaknesses be exploited by the competition? These questions must be answered as objectively as possible for the information to be useful in formulating a viable business strategy. Management may benefit by utilizing consultants knowledgeable in the target market to assist in developing credible answers. The objectivity of existing management may be clouded. Current managers may be comfortable with the way they have been doing things in the past, defensive about a loss of market share, or possess limited understanding of developments in markets related to the target market.

Business Attractiveness Matrix

Conducting a self-assessment consists of identifying those strengths or competencies necessary to compete successfully in the firm's chosen market. These strengths are often referred to as success factors. Examples of success factors could include the following: high market share compared to the competition; product line breadth; cost-effective sales distribution channels; age and geographic location of production facilities; relative product quality; price competitiveness; R&D effectiveness; customer service effectiveness; corporate culture; and profitability.

Once identified for the firm's target market, success factors are weighted to reflect their relative importance in determining the firm's probable degree of success in its target market. When success factors do not apply or are relatively insignificant in a specific market, they should be given a zero weight. The firm's competitive position with respect to each success factor is ranked relative to its primary competitors. A 5 ranking means that the firm is highly competitive with respect to a specific success factor when compared to the competition. A ranking of 1 indicates a very poor competitive position. The Business Attractiveness Matrix, Table 4-3, illustrates how the firm's overall attractiveness in its chosen market may be determined.

The weighted average score of 3.00 out of a possible score of 5.00 suggests that the firm's overall competitive position is somewhat favorable when compared to its primary competitor. This same matrix can be constructed for other competitors to compile a subjectively determined assessment of the firm's competitive position against other major competitors.

Core Competencies

Gary Hamel and C. K. Prahalad (1994) argue that a firm's strategy should be based on core competencies, which represent bundles of skills that can be applied to extend a firm's product offering in new areas. For example, Honda Motor Corporation has traditionally had a reputation for being able to manufacture highly efficient internal combustion engines. In addition to cars, these skills have been applied to lawnmowers and snowblowers. The expansion into these product areas has met with considerable success. Similarly, Hewlett-Packard was able to utilize its skills in producing highly precise measurement instruments to successfully move into calculators and later into PCs.

In identifying core competencies, management should take great care in how they are defined. If they are defined too broadly, they provide little practical guidance in formulating business strategy; if they are too narrowly defined, significant opportunities may be overlooked. Honda could have viewed its core competency as the ability to provide efficient transportation, which is so broad as to be functionally meaningless, or so narrowly (e.g., applied to specific functions of the internal combustion engine) as to exclude logical extensions of its product line based on its core skills.

TABLE 4-3.   Business Attractiveness Matrix

| Success factor | Weight | Compared to primary competitor | |
		Ranking (5 = highly favorable; 1 = highly unfavorable)	Weighted score
Market share: Firm's current market share?	.20	3	.60
Product line breadth: Does firm offer a broad or limited product line?	0.0	3	.00
Sales distribution: Are firm's distribution channels cost effective?	.15	4	.60
Price competitiveness: Are firm's prices high or low compared to the competition?	.10	2	.20
Age and location of facilities: Are firm's facilities properly located and new?	.05	2	.10
Production capacity: Can customer demand be served?	.05	3	.15
Relative product quality: How does the firm's product quality compare with the competition?	.15	4	.60
R&D: Is the firm a product innovator or follower?	.10	3	.30
Customer service: How does it compare with the competition?	.03	3	.09
Corporate culture: Is the firm's culture suitable for the industry?	.02	3	.06
Profitability: Can the firm attract capital financing needed for investments?	.15	2	.30
Total	1.00		3.00

Can these core competencies be used to gain and sustain strategic advantage in the firm's chosen market? This question really addresses the extent to which the firm's core competencies enable it to provide a product or service that is highly valued in the marketplace better than the competition. For example, an ability to mass produce analog cellular phones more efficiently than the competition will provide little advantage to the firm if its customers are shifting to digital cellular phones. Moreover, if a company is able to achieve a competitive edge by leveraging its core competencies, it may be able to sustain this advantage only through continuous innovation (see Case Study 4-2).

CASE STUDY 4-2. IS SUSTAINABLE COMPETITIVE ADVANTAGE POSSIBLE?

Can the firm's core competencies be easily duplicated and surpassed by the competition? In the early 1980s, Apple Computer introduced an icon-based screen for its Macintosh operating system, which allowed them to sell Macintoshes at a premium price. However, with the introduction of Microsoft's Windows operating system, the perceived advantage in terms of ease of use of the Macintosh system diminished. There were such great similarities that Apple sued Microsoft for its alleged plagiarism of the Mac's "look and feel" but lost in court. Similarly, Apple Computer sued a competitor for allegedly stealing the design of its enormously popular, highly stylish iMac computer. The Netscape browser software improved substantially earlier versions of the software, which enables users to access information in a multimedia environment on the World Wide Web, only to be surpassed by Microsoft's Internet Explorer browser. The direct competition between the two companies resulted in a dramatic compression of the software product development cycle from what had been as long as several years to as little as 4–6 months for new versions of the browser.

DEFINING A MISSION STATEMENT

At a minimum, a corporate mission statement seeks to describe the corporation's purpose for being. The mission statement should not be so general as to provide little practical direction. A good mission statement should include references to such areas as the firm's targeted markets, product or service offering, distribution channels, and management beliefs with respect to the firm's primary stakeholders. Stakeholders could include customers, employees, stockholders, suppliers, communities in which the firm has production facilities, and regulatory agencies.

Ultimately, the market targeted by the firm should reflect the fit between the corporation's primary strengths and competencies and its ability to satisfy customer needs better than the competition. The product and service offering should be relatively broadly defined so as to allow for the introduction of new products, which can be derived from the firm's core competencies. Distribution channels address how the firm chooses to distribute its products (e.g., through a direct sales force, agents, distributors, resellers, online, or through some combination of all of these methods). Customers are those targeted by the firm's products and services. Management beliefs establish the underpinnings of how the firm intends to behave with respect to its stakeholders.

SETTING STRATEGIC OR LONG-TERM
CORPORATE OBJECTIVES

Corporate objectives are defined as what is to be accomplished within a specific period of time. A good objective is both measurable and has a time frame in which it is to be realized. Typical corporate objectives include revenue growth rates, minimum acceptable financial returns, and market share. A good objective might state that the firm seeks to increase revenue from $1 billion currently to $5 billion by the year 20??. A poorly written objective would be that the firm seeks to increase revenue substantially.

Common Business Objectives

Return: The firm seeks to achieve a rate of return that will equal or exceed the return required by its shareholders (cost of equity), lenders (cost of debt), or the combination of the two (cost of capital).

Size: The firm seeks to achieve the critical mass defined in terms of sales volume to realize economies of scale.

Growth:
   a. Accounting objectives: The firm seeks to grow earnings per share (EPS), revenue, or assets at a specific rate of growth per year.
   b. Valuation objectives: Such objectives may be expressed in terms of the firm's common stock price to earnings per share, book value, cash flow, or revenue.

Diversification: The firm desires to sell current products in new markets or new products in current markets.

Flexibility: The firm desires to possess production facilities and distribution capabilities that can be shifted rapidly to exploit new opportunities as they arise. This has become increasingly important in the highly global economy. The major automotive companies have moved toward standardizing parts and car and truck platforms. This reduces the time required to introduce new products and facilitates the companies' ability to shift production from one region to another.

Technology: The firm desires to possess capabilities in core or rapidly advancing technologies. Firms desirous of staying on or ahead of the rapidly changing technology curve frequently place a high priority on owning or having access to the latest technologies. Microchip and software manufacturers, as well as defense contractors, are good examples of industries in which staying abreast of new technologies is a prerequisite for survival.

STRATEGY SELECTION

A firm should choose that strategy from among the range of reasonable alternatives that enables it to achieve its stated objectives in an acceptable time period subject to resource constraints. Resource constraints include limitations on both the availability of management talent and funds. Gaining access to highly competent management talent is frequently the more difficult of the two to overcome. Strategies can be reduced to one of four basic categories: (1) price or cost leadership, (2) product differentiation, (3) focus or niche strategies, and (4) hybrid strategies.

Price or Cost Leadership

This strategy reflects the influence of a series of tools introduced and popularized by the Boston Consulting Group (BCG). These tools include the experience curve, the product life cycle, and portfolio balancing techniques (Boston Consulting: 1985). Cost leadership is designed to make a firm the cost leader in its market by constructing efficient production facilities, tightly controlling overhead expense, and eliminating marginally profitable customer accounts. The experience curve postulates that as the cumulative historical volume of a firm's output increases, cost per unit of output decreases geometrically as the firm becomes more efficient in producing that product (Conley: 1978). Therefore, the firm with the largest historical output should also be the lowest cost producer. The implied strategy for this firm should be to enter markets as early as possible and to reduce product prices aggressively to maximize market share (Marrus: 1984).

Experience Curve

The applicability of the experience curve varies across industries. It seems to work best for largely commodity-type industries in which scale economies can lead to substantial reductions in per unit production costs. Examples include the manufacturing of PCs or cell phone handsets. The strategy of continuously driving down production costs may make most sense for the existing market share leader in an industry. If the leader already has a cost advantage over its competitors due to its significantly larger market share compared to its competitors, it may be able to improve its cost advantage by more aggressively pursuing market share through price cutting.

This strategy may be highly destructive if pursued concurrently by a number of firms with approximately the same market share. Customers are likely to purchase equally from all the firms, as price cutting by one firm is matched by others and customers do not see any significant product quality or customer service advantages in buying from any specific firm. Under such circumstances, repetitive price cutting by firms within the industry is likely to drive down profitability for all firms in the industry. Industry profitability can continue to fall precipitously for many years as the least profitable firms cannot exit the industry as a result of high fixed obligations in the form of long-term leases, leverage, or worker pension and health insurance obligations. Exhibit 4-1 illustrates how the experience curve can be estimated.

EXHIBIT 4-1. APPLYING THE
EXPERIENCE CURVE

In its simplest form, the experience curve (EC) represents the relationship between cost and volume when accumulated volume has doubled. The slope of the EC when accumulated volume has doubled equals 2^{α}. This formula implies that, each time the accumulated volume in units of the product doubles, costs drop by $1-2^{\alpha}$.

$EC = 1 - 2^{\alpha}$, where $\alpha = (\log C_2 - \text{Log } C_1)/(\log AV_2 - \log AV_1)$

Where C_1 = Total costs less raw material costs per unit of output in real dollars in period 1

C_2 = Total costs less raw material cost per unit of output in real dollars in period 2

AV_1 = Accumulated volume in period 1

AV_2 = Accumulated volume in period 2

Converting nominal or current dollars to real dollars:

Real dollars = (Nominal Dollars / Price Deflator) $\times$ 100

Calculating accumulated volumes: Add annual volume and take a cumulative total each year

Year	Annual data	Accumulated data
1996	12	12
1997	14	26
1998	10	36
1999	15	51
2000	20	71

Example: Computer Corporation of America produced .1 million units in 1990, its first year of production. Its accumulated annual production since 1990 reached 10 million units in 1999 (i.e., the sum of annual production since 1990). Its value-added costs (i.e., total costs less raw material costs) were $2,500 per PC in 1990 and $300 per PC in 1999 in constant 1990 dollars. The firm's selling price of a PC in 1990 was $3000 and $400 in 1999 in constant 1990 dollars. Estimate the firm's experience curves based on costs and prices.

$$EC_{cost} = 1 - 2^{\{(\log \$300 - \log \$2,500)/(\log 10,000,000 - \log 100,000)\}}$$

$$= 1 - 2^{\{(2.4771 - 3.3979)/(7.000 - 5.000)\}} = 1 - 2^{-.4604}$$

$$= -.3759$$

(Whenever output doubles, costs per unit of production fall by 37.59%)

$$EC_{price} = 1 - 2^{\{(\log\ \$400\ -\ \log\$3000)/(\log\ 10,000,000\ -\ \log100,000)\}}$$
$$= 1 - 2^{\{2.6021\ -\ 3.4771)/2.000\}} = 1 - 2^{-.4375}$$
$$= -.3543$$

(Whenever output doubles, constant dollar prices fall by 35.43%.)

Implication: These curves are useful for projecting both costs and selling prices for commodity-type industries in which economies of scale are important.[1]

[1] Real dollar costs and prices are calculated by dividing the actual dollar figures by a price index for that year, such as the implicit price deflator for gross domestic product. To convert the $400 selling price expressed in constant 1990 dollars to 1999 dollars, multiply $400 by the 1999 implicit price deflator.

Product Life Cycle

BCG's second major contribution is the product life cycle, which characterizes a product's evolution in four stages: embryonic, growth, maturity, and decline (see Figure 4-3). Strong sales growth and low barriers to entry characterize the first two stages. However, over time entry becomes more costly as early entrants into the market accumulate market share and experience lower per unit production costs as a result of the effects of the experience curve. New entrants have substantially poorer cost positions as a result of their small market shares when compared to earlier entrants and cannot catch up to the market leaders as overall market growth slows. During the later phases characterized by slow market growth, falling product prices push marginal firms and unprofitable firms out of the market or to consolidate with other firms.

A great deal of insight can be gained by identifying the industry's current phase of the product life cycle. During the high growth phase, firms in the industry

FIGURE 4-3.   Product life cycle.

normally have high investment requirements associated with capacity expansion and increasing working capital needs. Operating cash flow is normally negative. During the mature and declining growth phases, investment requirements are lower and cash flow becomes positive. Although the phase of the product life cycle provides insights into current and future cash requirements for both the acquiring and target companies, determining the approximate length of each phase can be challenging. In addition, the introduction of significant product enhancements can reinvigorate industry growth and extend the length of the current growth phase. This is particularly true in high-tech industries (see Moore: 1991).

The microchip industry is an excellent example of an industry in which innovation (e.g., Pentiums I, II, and III) continually extends the product life cycle of operating system microchips by increasing their processing speed. Reflecting both economies of scale and more effective production techniques learned through accumulated experience (the experience curve effect), the cost of improved processing speed continues to decline when measured in terms of real dollars per megahertz. Other industries that have pursued price or cost leadership strategies include the PC and the cellular phone manufacturers.

Share-Growth Matrix

The final BCG innovation, *portfolio balance theory,* reflects the movements of products and firms through the product life cycle. Portfolio balance theory dictates that companies should fund high-growth, cash-poor businesses with cash-generated from the more mature cash-generating businesses. Businesses in the growth phase of the product life cycle have low market share but substantial cash needs, and those in the mature or declining growth phase have higher market share.

Businesses in a firm's portfolio having high market share and high growth rates relative to the industry's growth rate and excellent profit potential are referred to as *stars.* The high growth potential of the stars means they also have high reinvestment requirements. As the industry moves through its product life cycle and reaches the maturity stage, the stars begin to generate cash flow well in excess of their reinvestment requirements. As their potential growth rate slows, they may be reclassified by the company's management as cash cows. This excess cash flow generated by these *cash cows* can be used by the firm to fund other stars within the firm's portfolio or to acquire new or related businesses that appear to have the potential to become stars. Businesses that have low growth and market share are deemed to be either *question marks* or *dogs* and are frequently candidates for divestiture. High-growth, low-market-share question marks may be the next stars or dogs. Question marks use up more cash than they generate and may become liabilities if they cannot transform themselves into market leaders. Most companies cannot afford to fund all of their stars and question marks; consequently, some are likely to be divested, spun off to shareholders, or combined with other businesses in a joint venture operation.

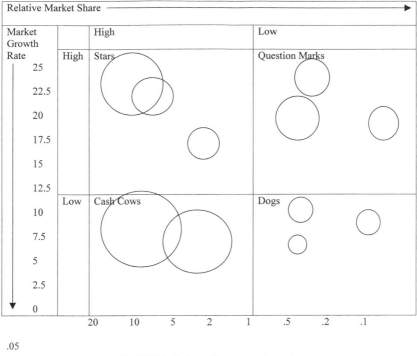

FIGURE 4-4.   Share-growth matrix.

Figure 4-4 illustrates the portfolio of a company with lines of business (LOBs) in all four quadrants. The circles represent each business and are drawn in proportion to the annual sales volume of the largest LOB in the firm. For example, if the annual sales of the second largest LOB are one-half of the largest LOB, the circle for the second largest LOB will be one-half of the size of the circle for the largest LOB.

The position of each circle in the quadrants reflects their growth rate and relative market share (RMS). The growth rate is the compound annual average growth rate of the market in which the business or product line competes. RMS is the business' or product line's market share divided by that of its next largest competitor. If an LOB in the firm is the market share leader in its market with a 30% share, and the next largest competitor has a 20% share, the relative market share of the market leader can be represented as follows:

$$RMS_{market\ leader} = \text{Market Leader Share/Second Largest Company's Share}$$
$$= .30/.20$$
$$= 1.5$$

For all other LOBs in the firm's portfolio, RMS is calculated as follows:

$$RMS_{\text{other LOB share}} = \text{Other LOB Share} / \text{Market Leader Share}$$

Product Differentiation

Differentiation represents a range of strategies in which the product or service offered is perceived to be slightly different by customers from other product or service offerings in the marketplace. Differentiation can be accomplished through brand image, technology features, or through alternative distribution channels, such as the ability to download products via the Internet. Examples of product differentiation strategies abound. Some firms attempt to compete by offering customers a range of features or functions. For example, many banks issue credit cards such as MasterCard or Visa. Each bank tries to differentiate its card by offering a higher credit line, a lower interest rate or annual fee, or by providing prizes. Software companies justify charging for upgrades based on additional features to word-processing or spreadsheet programs, which are not found on competing software packages. Other firms compete on the basis of consistent product quality by providing excellent service. Today, Dell Computer is perceived to be a strong competitor by providing both excellent quality and service, which seems to allow the firm to charge a slightly higher price for its PCs. Other firms attempt to compete by offering their customers excellent convenience. Amazon.com falls in this category by offering consumers the opportunity to buy books whenever and from wherever they choose.

Focus or Niche Strategies

Firms adopting these types of strategies tend to concentrate their efforts by selling a few products or services to a single market and compete primarily on the basis of understanding their customers' needs better than the competition. In this strategy, the firm seeks to carve a specific niche with respect to a certain group of customers, a narrow geographic area, or a particular use of a product. Examples include the major airlines, airplane manufacturers (e.g., Boeing), and major defense contractors (e.g., Lockheed-Martin). Many companies that start with a single focus later diversify to broaden their revenue base. Recent examples include Yahoo and AOL which started as an Internet search engine and a consumer Internet access and content provider, respectively. Currently, they are widely viewed as emerging multimedia or network companies.

Hybrid Strategies

These strategies involve some combination of the above strategies (see Table 4-4). For example, Coca-Cola pursues both a differentiated and highly market-focused strategy. Coca-Cola derives the bulk of its revenues by focusing on the worldwide soft drink market. Its product is differentiated in that consumers perceive it to have a distinctly refreshing taste. Moreover, consumers can expect the taste to be consistently the same. Other companies that pursue focused yet differ-

TABLE 4-4.   Hybrid Strategies

	Cost leadership	Product differentiation
Niche focus approach	Cisco Systems WD-40	Coca-Cola McDonald's
Multimarket approach	Wal-Mart Oracle	America Online Microsoft

entiated strategies include fast-food industry giant McDonald's, which competes on the basis of providing fast food of a consistent quality in a clean, comfortable environment.

As is always true, there are examples of highly successful companies that simply do not fit neatly into any model. These are the result of creative people daring to think the unthinkable. The Williams Companies, a large oil and gas transmission pipeline company, conceived of the idea of running fiber-optic cable through their extensive natural gas pipeline network. In doing so, they did not have to devote considerable sums of money to acquiring the right of way through extensive geographic areas. Wiltel, the subsidiary of The Williams Companies responsible for this fiber-optic network, was later sold and eventually became the telecommunications powerhouse WorldCom.

Business-Market Attractiveness Matrix

The business-market attractiveness matrix matches the attractiveness of markets with a firm's capabilities (see Table 4-5). McKinsey & Company and General Electric Corporation introduced this analytical tool, which incorporates the results of self-assessment with the results of the firm's evaluation of its chosen market, as a means of summarizing the competitive position of all of a firm's lines of business. This matrix can be constructed from information obtained from the Industry/Market Attractiveness Matrix (Table 4-1) and the Business Attractiveness Matrix

TABLE 4-5.   Business–Market Attractiveness Matrix

Business strengths	Market attractiveness		
	High	Average	Low
High	Invest or acquire		
Average			
Low			Divest or manage for cash

(Table 4-3) *for each line of business* in the firm's business portfolio. Each LOB is positioned in the Business-Market Attractiveness Matrix by using as coordinates the weighted average numerical scores from its Industry/Market Attractiveness and Business Attractiveness Matrices.

The Business-Market Attractiveness matrix displays what the firm believes to be those LOBs that are most attractive in terms of the firm's strengths and in terms of the characteristics of the marketplace. The strategic implications of this planning tool are that a firm should invest or acquire in that market which has favorable growth and profit potential and in which the firm is likely to satisfy customer needs better than other competitors in the market. The firm should divest those LOBs in those markets that are viewed as unattractive and in which the firm has a weak overall competitive position. As noted earlier, market attractiveness may be defined in terms of such factors as size, growth rate, price sensitivity of customers, degree of regulation, global exposure, and degree of unionization. Business strengths, relative to the competition, could include market share or cost, quality (real or perceived), and customer service advantages. Those LOBs with the highest scores fall in the upper left-hand quadrant (high market attractiveness and business strengths) and those with the lowest fall in the lower right-hand quadrant.

STRATEGY IMPLEMENTATION

Once a firm has determined the appropriate business strategy (i.e., price–cost leadership, differentiation, focus or niche, or a hybrid strategy), attention must be turned to deciding the best means of implementing the desired strategy. Implementation involves selecting the right option from the range of reasonable options. Generally, a firm has five choices: (1) build (i.e., implement the strategy based solely on internal resources), (2) partner, (3) invest, (4) acquire, or (5) swap assets. Each option has significantly different implications. Table 4-6 provides a comparison of the different options in terms of their advantages and disadvantages.

In theory, the decision to choose among alternative options should be made based upon the discounting of the cash flow stream to the firm resulting from each option. In practice, there are many other considerations at work.

The Role of Intangible Factors

Although financial analyses are conducted to evaluate the various options, the option chosen may ultimately depend on such nonquantifiable factors as the senior manager's risk profile, patience, and ego. The degree of control offered by the various alternatives displayed in Table 4-6 is often the central issue confronted by senior management in choosing among the various options. Although the building or acquisition options offer the highest degree of control, they are often among the most expensive but for very different reasons. Typically, a build strategy will take considerably longer to realize key strategic objectives, and it may, depending upon the magnitude and timing of cash flows generated from investments, have a significantly lower net present value than the alternatives. In contrast, gaining con-

TABLE 4-6. Strategy Implementation: Build, Partner, Invest, Acquire, or Swap

Basic options	Advantages	Disadvantages
Build (organic growth)	• Control	• Capital/expense requirements • Speed
Partner • Marketing/distribution alliance • Joint venture • License • Franchise	• Limits capital and expense investment requirements • May be precursor to acquisition	• Lack of or limited control • Potential for diverging objectives • Potential for creating a competitor
Invest (e.g., minority investments in other firms)	• Limits initial capital/expense requirements	• High risk of failure • Lack of control • Time
Acquire	• Speed • Control	• Capital/expense requirements • Potential earnings dilution
Swap assets	• Limits use of cash • No earnings dilution • Limits tax liability if neither party's tax basis in the assets swapped changes	• Finding willing parties • Reaching agreement on assets to be exchanged

trol through acquisition can also be very expensive because of the substantial premium the acquirer normally has to pay to gain a controlling interest in another company.

The joint venture may represent a practical alternative to either a build or acquire strategy by giving a firm access to such factors as skills, product distribution channels, proprietary processes, and patents at a lower initial expense than might be involved otherwise. The joint venture is frequently a precursor to an acquisition, because it gives both parties time to determine if their respective corporate cultures and strategic objectives are compatible.

Asset swaps may represent an attractive alternative to the other options, but they are generally very difficult to establish in most industries unless the assets involved are substantially similar in terms of physical characteristics and use. The best example of an industry in which this practice is relatively common is in commercial and industrial real estate. The cable industry is another example of how asset swaps can be used to achieve strategic objectives. In recent years, the cable industry has been swapping customers in different geographic areas in order to allow a single company to dominate a specific geographic area and to realize the full benefits of economies of scale. An interesting recent asset swap involved Cox

Communications Inc. and AT&T, in which Cox swapped its 1.4% stake in AT&T, valued at $2.8 billion, for 495,000 AT&T cable TV customers and $750 million in cash. Cox's objective was to strengthen its cable customer base in such areas as Oklahoma, Arkansas, Louisiana, Texas, and New Mexico. Following the transaction, Cox will serve about 5.5 million customers nationwide.

Accounting Considerations

Table 4-6 distinguishes between capital investment and expense investment. Although both types of investment have an immediate impact on actual cash flow, they have substantially different effects on accounting or reported profits. The impact of capital spending impacts reported profits by adding to depreciation expense. This effect is spread over the accounting life of the investment. In contrast, expense investment refers to expenditures made on such things as application software development or database construction. Although it may be possible to capitalize and to amortize some portion of these investments over several years, they are usually expensed in the year in which the monies are spent.

Firms with publicly traded stocks may base strategic investment decisions on accounting considerations (e.g., the preservation of earnings per share) rather than on purely economic considerations. Consequently, a publicly traded company may be inclined to purchase a very expensive piece of depreciable equipment rather than to develop a potentially superior piece of equipment internally through R&D expenditures, which may have to be expensed. As discussed in detail in Chapter 10 (this volume), accounting considerations can also play a major role in M&A decisions.

Analyzing Assumptions

To assist in the selection of the appropriate option, it is crucial to clearly state explicit and implicit assumptions. Assumptions will fall into two categories: those that are common to each option considered and those that are unique to a specific option. Assumptions common to all strategic options (i.e., build, partner, invest, acquire, or swap) include market assumptions such as the market's rate of growth, customer needs, and factors affecting customer buying decisions. Assumptions that will vary from one option to another include the amount and timing of investments and financing requirements. Competitors may also react quite differently depending upon which option the firm selects. An acquisition strategy may be viewed by the competition as very aggressive; consequently, such a strategy may elicit a far more aggressive response from competitors than a more benign approach involving making minority investments in a number of different firms. Therefore, assumptions made with respect to competitors may also vary depending upon the option selected.

With the assumptions displayed, the reasonableness of the various options can be more readily compared. The option with the highest net present value is not necessarily the preferred strategy if the assumptions underlying the analysis strain credulity. Understanding clearly stated assumptions underlying the chosen strategy and those underlying alternative strategies forces senior management to make choices based on a discussion of the reasonableness of the assumptions associated with each option. This is preferable to placing a disproportionately high level of confidence in the numerical output of computer models.

The Upside and Downside of Models

Computer-generated projections can sometimes have a substantial impact on decision making because they have the appearance of precision and internal consistency. All too often this is a case of seductive appearance without real substance. The proper role of computer models should be to facilitate decision making more through their ability to rapidly generate and assess alternative scenarios than on their accuracy. As is often the case, the accuracy of a model's projection is largely dependent on the accuracy of the inputs into the model.

PHASE 2: BUILDING THE ACQUISITION PLAN

If it is determined following an analysis of available options that an acquisition is necessary to implement the business strategy, an acquisition plan is required. The acquisition plan focuses on tactical rather than strategic issues. It is similar in structure to any other tactical plan. It consists of management objectives, a resource assessment, a market analysis, clearly specified tactics or actions, a timetable for completing the acquisition, and the name of the individual responsible for making it all happen.

The acquisition plan communicates to those charged with acquiring a company the preferences of senior management. These are expressed in terms of management objectives and tactics defined in the plan. The objectives specify management's expectations for the acquisition, and the tactics provide guidance on how the acquisition process should be managed. This guidance could include the specification of the criteria for selecting potential acquisition targets and willingness to engage in a hostile takeover. Moreover, tactics could also indicate management's choice of the form of payment (stock, cash, or debt), willingness to accept earnings per share dilution, preference for a stock or asset purchase, and limitations on contacting competitors.

MANAGEMENT OBJECTIVES

The acquisition plan's stated objectives and tactics should be completely consistent with the firm's strategic objectives. Objectives include both financial and nonfinancial considerations.

Financial Objectives

Financial objectives in the acquisition plan could include a minimum rate of return or operating profit, revenue and cash flow targets to be achieved within a specified time period. Minimum or required rates of return targets may be substantially higher than those specified in the business plan, which relates to the required return to shareholders or to total capital. The required return for the acquisition may reflect a substantially higher level of risk as a result of the perceived variability of the amount and timing of the expected cash flows resulting from the acquisition.

Basic financial theory teaches that the goal of the managers of the firm should be to maximize the wealth of the owners of the firm (i.e., the shareholders) (Gitman: 1998). The presumption is that managers should accept only those investments contributing to shareholder wealth. Although shareholder wealth maximization is widely viewed as the primary goal, many firms have added to this overarching objective the desire to meet the needs of other stakeholders. In addition to shareholders, stakeholder groups include employees, customers, suppliers, creditors, communities, and regulatory agencies.

Recognizing the needs of the other stakeholders while diligently pursuing the goal of maximizing shareholder wealth makes good business sense. Failure to make good-faith efforts to meet the reasonable needs of the other stakeholders may seriously impede the firm's ability to satisfy its shareholders. Examples of failures to satisfy reasonable stakeholder demands include plant closures due to protracted strikes and increasing government-imposed rules such as health, safety, and environmental regulations.

Nonfinancial Objectives

Nonfinancial objectives address the motivations for making the acquisition that support the achievement of the financial returns stipulated in the business plan. In many instances, such objectives provide substantially more guidance for those responsible for managing the acquisition process than financial targets. Nonfinancial objectives in the acquisition plan could include the following:

1. Obtain rights to products, patents, copyrights or brand names.
2. Provide growth opportunities in the same or related markets.
3. Develop new distribution channels in the same or related markets.
4. Obtain additional production capacity in strategically located facilities.
5. Add R&D capabilities.
6. Obtain access to proprietary technologies, processes, and skills.

MARKET ANALYSIS

Assuming the proposed acquisition is in the firm's target market, there is no need to conduct a separate external or internal assessment, which was completed as part of the business plan. If the market to be entered is new to the firm, a complete market assessment is required. Market assessments were discussed earlier in this chapter under the Modified Porter Competitive Framework (see Figure 4-2).

RESOURCE AVAILABILITY

Early in the acquisition process, it is important to determine the maximum amount of the firm's available resources that senior management will commit to a merger or acquisition. This information is used when the firm develops target selection criteria prior to undertaking a search for potential target firms. Financial resources that are *potentially* available to the acquirer include those provided by internally generated cash flow in excess of normal operating requirements plus funds from the equity and debt markets. If the target firm is known, the potential pool of funds includes funds provided by the internal cash flow of the combined companies in excess of normal operating requirements, as well as the capacity of the combined firms to issue equity or increase leverage.

Financial theory suggests that a firm will always be able to attract sufficient funding for an acquisition if the acquiring firm can demonstrate that it can earn its cost of capital. In practice, senior management's risk tolerance plays an important role in determining what the acquirer believes it can afford to spend on a merger or acquisition. Consequently, risk-adverse management may be inclined to commit only a small portion of the total financial resources potentially available to the firm.

Determining Affordability

Three basic types of risk confront senior management considering making an acquisition. These risks affect how they feel about the affordability of an acquisition opportunity. These include operating risk, financial risk, and overpayment risk. How managers perceive these risks will determine how much of their potential available resources they will be willing to commit to making an acquisition.

Operating Risk

Operating risk addresses the ability of the buyer to manage the acquired company. It is generally perceived to be higher for M&As in markets that are unrelated to the acquirer's core business. The limited understanding of managers in the acquiring company of the competitive dynamics of the new market and the inner workings of the target firm may negatively impact the postmerger integration effort as well as the ongoing management of the combined companies. As noted in Chapter 1 (this volume), this perception is supported by empirical studies.

Financial Risk

Financial risk refers to the buyer's willingness and ability to leverage a transaction as well as the willingness of shareholders to accept near-term earnings per share dilution. Management's tolerance of financial risk can be measured in part by the credit rating the acquiring firm attempts to maintain. To retain a specific credit rating, the acquiring company must maintain certain levels of financial ratios such as debt to equity and interest coverage. A firm's incremental debt capacity can be approximated by comparing the relevant financial ratios to those of comparably rated firms in the same industry. The difference represents the amount they could theoretically borrow without jeopardizing their current credit rating. Senior management could also gain insight into how much EPS dilution equity investors may be willing to tolerate through informal discussions with Wall Street analysts and an examination of recent comparable transactions financed by issuing stock.

Overpayment Risk

Overpayment risk involves the dilution of earnings per share (EPS) or a reduction in its growth rate resulting from paying significantly more than the economic value of the acquired company. The effects of overpayment on earnings dilution can last for years. To illustrate the effects of overpayment risk, assume the acquiring company's shareholders' are satisfied with the company's projected annual average increase in EPS of 20% annually for the next 5 years. The company announces that it will be acquiring another company and that a series of "restructuring" expenses will slow EPS growth in the coming year to 10%. However, management argues that the savings resulting from combining the two companies will ultimately raise the combined companies' EPS growth rate to 30% in the second through fifth year of the forecast. The risk is that the savings cannot be realized in the timeframe assumed by management and the slowdown in earnings extends well beyond the first year. Failure to achieve the EPS growth rates promised investors is likely to result in a substantial deterioration in the firm's share price.

TACTICS

Acquisition tactics should reflect senior management's preferences for conducting the acquisition process. To ensure that the process is managed in a manner consistent with management's risk tolerance and biases, management must set the general direction in the following areas:

1. Determining the criteria used to evaluate prospective candidates (e.g., size, price range, current profitability, growth rate, or geographic location)
2. Specifying methods for finding candidates (e.g., soliciting board members; analyzing competitors; contacting brokers, investment bankers, lenders, law firms, and the trade press)
3. Establishing roles and responsibilities of the acquisition team, including the use of outside consultants and defining the team's budget
4. Identifying acceptable sources of financing (e.g., equity issues, bank loans, unsecured bonds, seller financing, or asset sales)
5. Preferences for an asset or stock purchase and form of payment (cash, stock, or debt)
6. Tolerance for goodwill
7. Openness to partial rather than full ownership

8. Willingness to launch an unfriendly takeover
9. Setting affordability limits. Such limits can be expressed as a maximum price to earnings, book, earnings before interest and taxes; or cash flow multiple or a maximum dollar figure
10. Desire for related or unrelated acquisitions.

Substantial upfront participation by management will dramatically aid in the successful implementation of the acquisition process. Unfortunately, senior management frequently avoids providing significant input early in the process, despite recognizing the value of communication. Management's reticence to get involved early in the process may reflect a very demanding schedule or uneasiness with the proceedings. In either case, limited participation by management inevitably leads to miscommunication, confusion, and poor execution later in the process by those charged with making it happen.

SCHEDULE

The final component of a properly constructed acquisition plan is a schedule that recognizes all of the key events that must take place throughout the acquisition process. Each event should be characterized by beginning and ending milestones or dates as well as the name of the individual responsible for ensuring that each milestone is achieved. The timetable of events should be aggressive but realistic. The timetable should be sufficiently aggressive to motivate all participants in the process to work as expeditiously as possible to meet the management objectives established in the acquisition plan. However, an overly optimistic timetable may prove to be demotivating to those involved, as uncontrollable or unforeseen circumstances delay reaching certain milestones.

THINGS TO REMEMBER

The success of an acquisition is frequently dependent on the focus, understanding, and discipline inherent in a thorough business plan. There are four overarching questions that must be addressed in developing a viable business plan. These include the following:

1. Where should the firm compete?
2. How should the firm compete?
3. How can the firm satisfy customer needs better than the competition?
4. Why is the chosen strategy preferable to other reasonable options?

To answer these questions, the business planning process should consist of a thorough analysis of customers and their needs; a thorough analysis of the firm's strengths and weaknesses compared to the competition; and a clearly articulated mission and quantified objectives with associated timeframes. Using this information, a strategy is selected from a range of reasonable options. The assumptions underlying the strategy and supporting financial statements should be clearly identified. This last step is crucial because the reasonableness of any business strategy is solely dependent of the credibility of its underlying assumptions.

An acquisition is only one of many options available for implementing a business strategy. The decision to pursue an acquisition often rests on the desire to achieve control and a perception that the acquisition will result in achieving the desired objectives more rapidly than other options. Firms all too often pay far too much for control. Alternative options may prove to be less risky. A firm may choose to implement what amounts to a phased acquisition by first entering into a joint venture with another company before acquiring it at a later date.

Once a firm has decided that an acquisition is key to realizing the strategic direction defined in the business plan, an acquisition plan should be developed. The acquisition plan should be viewed as a tactical plan supporting the implementation of the firm's business strategy. The acquisition plan defines the specific objectives management hopes to achieve by completing an acquisition, addresses issues of resource availability, and identifies the specific tactics management chooses to employ to complete a transaction. The acquisition plan also establishes a schedule of milestones to keep the process on track and clearly defines the authority and responsibilities of the individual charged with managing the acquisition process.

CHAPTER DISCUSSION QUESTIONS

4-1.   Why is it important to think of an acquisition or merger in the context of a process rather than as a series of semirelated, discrete events?

4-2.   How does planning facilitate the acquisition process?

4-3.   What are the major activities that should be undertaken in building a business plan?

4-4.   What is market segmentation and why is it important?

4-5.   What are the basic types of strategies that companies commonly pursue and how are they different?

4-6.   What is the difference between a business plan and an acquisition plan?

4-7.   What are the advantages and disadvantages of using an acquisition to implement a business strategy as compared to a joint venture?

4-8.   Why is it important to understand the assumptions underlying a business plan or an acquisition plan?

4-9.   Why is it important to get senior management heavily involved early in the acquisition process?

4-10. In your judgment, which of the acquisition plan tactics discussed in this chapter are the most important and why?

CHAPTER BUSINESS CASE

CASE STUDY 4-3. CONSOLIDATION IN THE GLOBAL PHARMACEUTICAL INDUSTRY CONTINUES: THE GLAXO WELLCOME AND SMITHKLINE BEECHAM EXAMPLE

Background

During the 1970s and 1980s, pharmaceuticals were sold largely through massive sales and marketing forces who made "detailing" calls on as many points of contact as possible. These points of contact included physicians' offices, hospitals, and pharmacies. During these sales calls, the company representatives would explain new drugs that have been developed to treat specific conditions. Once a drug became popular, drug development costs would often escalate as companies introduced "me-too" drugs.

Changing Market Dynamics

By the mid-1980s, demands from both business and government were forcing pharmaceutical companies to change the way they did business. Increased government intervention, lower selling prices, increased competition from generic drugs, and growing pressure for discounting from managed care organizations such as health maintenance and preferred provider organizations began to squeeze drug company profit margins. The number of contact points between the sales force and the customer shrank dramatically as more drugs were being purchased through managed-care organizations and pharmacy benefit managers. Drugs were commonly sold in large volumes and often at heavily discounted levels as a result of discussions between senior managers of the buying and selling companies.

The demand for generic drugs was also declining. The use of formularies, drug lists from which managed care doctors are required to prescribe, gave doctors less choice and made them less responsive to direct calls from the sales force. The situation was further compounded by the ongoing consolidation in the hospital industry. Hospitals began centralizing purchasing and using stricter formularies allowing physicians virtually no leeway to prescribe unlisted drugs. The growing use of formularies resulted in buyers needing fewer drugs and sharply reduced the need for multiple similar drugs.

The First Merger Wave among Pharmaceutical Firms

The industry's first major wave of consolidations took place in the late 1980s, with such mergers as SmithKline and Beecham and Bristol Myers and Squibb. This wave of consolidation was driven by increased scale and scope economies largely realized through the combination of sales and marketing staffs.

Horizontal consolidation represented a considerable value creation opportunity for those companies able to realize cost synergies. In analyzing the total costs of pharmaceutical companies, William Pursche (1996) argued that the range of actual savings that could be achieved based on the mergers of the late 1980s is 15–25% of total R&D spending, 5–20% of total manufacturing costs, 15–50% of marketing and sales expenses, and 20–50% of overhead costs.

Continued consolidation seemed likely, enabling further cuts in sales and marketing. Formulary driven purchasing and declining overall drug margins spurred pharmaceutical companies to take action to increase the return on their R&D investments. Because development costs are not significantly lower for generic drugs, it became increasingly difficult to generate positive financial returns from marginal products. Duplicate overhead offered another opportunity for cost savings through consolidation, as combining companies could eliminate redundant personnel in such support areas as quality assurance, manufacturing management, information services, legal services, accounting, and human resources.

The Second Merger Wave

The second merger wave began in the late 1990s. The sheer magnitude and pace of activity is striking. Of the top 20 companies in terms of global pharmaceutical sales in 1998, one-half have either merged or announced plans to do so (see Table 4-7). More are expected as drug patents expire for a number of companies during the next several years and the cost of discovering and commercializing new drugs continues to escalate.

The current round of consolidation is tied to the great strides that have been made by modern science in unlocking the secrets of the human genome. These genetic discoveries have yielded more than 10,000 viable biological targets around which to develop new medicines, but it will take billions of dollars to convert these new discoveries into new drugs. The consolidation that is underway in the industry will enable companies to more readily pay for the expensive clinical trials that are necessary to exploit the countless opportunities emerging from gene sequencing. Consolidation will also enable companies to utilize new technologies such as bio-informatics, which uses new computer software to find similarities among gene sequences.

A New Industry Leader Emerges

On January 17, 2000, British pharmaceutical giants Glaxo Wellcome PLC and SmithKline Beecham PLC agreed to merge to form the world's largest drug company. The merger is valued at $76 billion. The resulting company will be called Glaxo SmithKline and have annual revenue of $25 billion and a market value of $184 billion. The combined companies will also have a total R&D budget of $4 billion and a global sales force of 40,000. Total employees will number 105,000 worldwide.

While stressed as a merger of equals, Glaxo shareholders will own about 59% of the shares of the two companies. The combined companies would have a market share of 7.5% of the global pharmaceutical market. The companies expect annual pretax cost savings of about $1.76 billion after 3 years. The cost savings

TABLE 4-7. Pharmaceutical Company Mergers[a]

Rank	Company	1998 Revenue ($ billions)	Merger status
1	Novartis	10.6	
2	Merck & Co.	10.6	
3	Glaxo Wellcome	10.5	Acquired SmithKline Beecham
4	Pfizer	9.9	Acquired Warner-Lambert
5	Bristol-Meyers Squibb	9.8	
6	Johnson & Johnson	9.0	
7	American Home Products	7.8	Lost out in bid to acquire Warner-Lambert
8	Roche	7.6	
9	Lilly	7.4	
10	SmithKline Beecham	7.3	Acquired by Glaxo
11	Astra	6.9	Merged with Zeneca
12	Abbott	6.4	
13	Hoechst Marion Roussel	6.2	Merged with Rhone
14	Schering-Plough	6.2	
15	Warner-Lambert	6.0	Acquired by Pfizer
16	Bayer	5.2	
17	Rhone Poulenc Rorer	4.6	Merged with Hoechst
18	Pharmacia & Upjohn	4.5	Merged with Monsanto
19	Zeneca	3.7	Merged with Astra
20	Boehringer Ingelheim	3.6	

[a] From: "Pharmaceutical Company Mergers," *Orange County Register,* data from IMS Health, Inc., February 14, 2000.

will come primarily from job cuts among middle management and administration over the next 3 years. (Source: *Business Week,* 2000; Bloomberg.com, 2000; Pursche: 1996.)

Case Study Discussion Questions

1. What drove change in the pharmaceutical industry in the late 1990s?
2. In your judgment, what are the likely strategic business plan objectives of the major pharmaceutical companies and why are they important?
3. What are the alternatives to mergers available to the major pharmaceutical companies? What are the advantages and disadvantages of each alternative?
4. How would you classify the typical drug company's strategy in the 1970s

and 1980s: cost leadership, differentiation, focus, or hybrid? Explain your answer. How have their strategies changed in recent years?

5. What do you think was the major motivating factor behind the Glaxo Smith-Kline merger and why was it so important?

Solutions to these questions are found in the Appendix at the end of this book.

APPENDIX A: BUSINESS PLAN CHECKLIST

For our purposes, a checklist is a questionnaire consisting of a succinct set of questions designed to focus management attention on what really matters in the process of formulating a business strategy. The following list is arranged by the major components of a well-designed business plan as discussed in this chapter. This checklist attempts to focus only on key strategic issues rather than the accumulation of reams of data, which may cloud the identification, understanding, and resolution of the truly critical issues. The checklist should be used in conjunction with some of the strategic planning tools discussed in this chapter.

1. Determining where to compete (i.e., the industry or market in which the firm has chosen to compete)
   a. What are the key selection criteria? Consider growth rate, absolute size in terms of both units and dollars, degree of unionization, degree of regulation, exposure to foreign competition, the current basis of competition (i.e., price, quality, service, etc.), capital requirements, the pace of technological change, industry or market structure (i.e., the number of firms currently competing), and the degree of fit with the firm's perceived core competencies.
   b. How would you rank order the criteria from most to the least important? It is sometimes helpful to assign numerical scores to these criteria in order to calculate a total score for each industry or market segment examined. The market ultimately selected is the one with the highest numerical score.
   c. What industries (collections of markets) rank the highest in terms of the selection criteria?
   d. What markets within the industries analyzed rank the highest in terms of the selection criteria?
2. Profiling the target market. This activity involves characterizing the market in terms of key functional areas.
   a. Products and services
      1. What products and services are offered by firms currently serving the targeted market?
      2. What is the size of the market by major product or service category in terms of units and dollars?
      3. What is the trend of revenue by product or service category? Why?

  b. Market share
  1. What is the market share of each current competitor?
  2. What is the trend in market share for each competitor? Why?
  c. Pricing
  1. How is pricing determined? Cost-plus, value-based, other?
  2. What has been trend in product and services prices? Why?
  d. Selling and distribution
  1. Is the distribution of products or services local, regional, national, or international in its coverage? Why?
  2. Are products generally distributed through a direct sales force or indirectly through distributors, licensees, agents or resellers? Why?
  e. Production facilities
  1. Where are production facilities located? Are they centrally located or geographically dispersed? Why?
  2. Are production facilities located near raw materials, labor, suppliers, and customers? Why?
  3. What is the capacity and age of the facilities?
  4. What is the general layout of the production process?
  f. Product quality
  1. What are standard measures of quality (e.g., defect rates per thousand units)?
  2. What are current quality levels as measured by these standards?
  g. Service
  1. What are standard measures of service (e.g., response time to remedy complaints)?
  2. What are current service levels as measured by these standards?
  h. Human resources
  1. What are prevailing wage and benefit levels by major job categories?
  2. What is the trend? Why?
  3. What is the average level of spending on training as a percent of revenue for all competitors in this market? What is it for each competitor?
  4. What is the trend in (3)? Why?
  i. Research and development
  1. What is the average level of spending as a percent of revenue for the firms in the market? What is it for each competitor?
  2. How has the level of R&D spending affected the rate of new product introduction?
  j. Suppliers
  1. How many suppliers of the most critical inputs into your production process are there?
  2. How would you assess the quality of their products and the timeliness of their deliveries?

    k. Financial

        1. What are the key industry-average financial ratios? What are these key ratios for each major competitor? Note: Key financial ratios include the following: liquidity (current and quick ratios), activity ratios (average collection period, average payment period, and inventory turnover), debt ratios (debt/equity, long-term debt/total assets, times interest earned); profitability ratios (operating margin, net margin, return on equity, return on investment); and market ratios (price/earnings, cash flow/earnings and dividend yield)

        2. What has been the trend in these ratios? Why?

3. Determining how to compete (i.e., conducting an external industry or market evaluation to determine how the firm can most effectively compete). The input for the following questions comes largely from the market profiling completed in Section 2 of this checklist.

    a. Customers and products

        1. What are the customers' most important needs?

        2. How well are they currently being satisfied?

        3. How might they change in the future?

        4. Are the firm's product and service prices higher or lower than those of its competitors? Why?

    b. Suppliers

        1. Are suppliers of critical materials powerful enough to set prices?

        2. Are current suppliers showing signs of moving beyond their current product and service offering and into the sale of their customers' products (i.e., forward integration)?

        3. Will the quality and reliability of current suppliers limit your firm's expansion efforts?

        4. Under what circumstances would it make sense to produce internally items currently purchased from others?

    c. Current competitors

        1. How many competitors (both foreign and domestic) currently serve the market?

        2. What are their key strengths and weaknesses?

        3. What are the factors that are critical to their success?

        4. Do they compete on the basis of price, quality, service, etc.?

        5. How rapidly and in what manner do they react to changes in the competitive strategies of other competitors?

        6. Do current competitors have the financial and managerial resources to react in a significant way to an aggressive change in your strategy?

        7. What is your firm's market share relative to key competitors? (Calculate the ratio of your firm's market share to the market leader's market share or the average of the top two or three firm's market shares. If your firm is the market share leader, your relative market share is 1.)

8. How do your firm's financial performance ratios compare to key competitors?

9. How does your firm's spending on employee training, R&D, capital spending, and advertising as a percent of revenue compare to key competitors?

10. What differences are there, if any, in how your firm distributes its products as compared to key competitors? Why?

d. Potential competitors

1. Are there other firms in the private sector that could become a competitor in the foreseeable future? Consider suppliers, customers, and partners (e.g., distributors, licensees, and joint venture participants) within the industry or market segment as well as those in related industries.

2. Is it likely that a government or quasi-government agency will become a competitor? For example, the United States Post Office's Overnite Express delivery service directly competes with Federal Express in the overnight package delivery market.

e. Product or service substitutes

1. What products or services not currently being sold in this market have the potential for displacing products and services currently being sold in this market?

2. What key developments would have to occur for these potential substitutes to be introduced into the market? For example, if the price of oil reaches $x per barrel, users of oil may shift to using natural gas or synthetic fuels. Moreover, increasing congestion on the Internet may move users from conventional dial-up services to digital subscriber line (DSL), satellite, or cable modem-based services.

f. Degree of unionization

1. Do unions currently exist? Are they likely to emerge in the foreseeable future?

2. If so, to what extent do they affect work practices and overall production costs?

3. Are unions a stabilizing or de-stabilizing influence in the marketplace? Unions are frequently thought of only in terms of work stoppages. However, a good working relationship with a union may result in higher worker morale, reduced labor turnover, and higher labor productivity.

g. Degree of regulation

1. What current federal, state, and local regulations apply?

2. What new, if any, regulations might apply in the future?

h. Exchange rate risk

1. To what extent do exchange rate fluctuations affect competition in this industry or market?

4. Self-assessment (i.e., conducting an internal analysis of the firm)
   a. What are the firm's core competencies? Focus only on those that are at least equal to or preferably exceed those of your competitors and which enable your firm to provide a product or service that will be valued by customers in the firm's chosen market. Consider the following areas:
      1. Research and development (e.g., patents)
      2. Production (e.g., proprietary process)
      3. Marketing (e.g., trademarks) and distribution
      4. Customer service (e.g., proprietary process)
   b. Can the identified competencies be used to gain strategic advantage in the firm's targeted market?
      1. What opportunities can be pursued as a result of these competencies?
      2. What additional complementary competencies would the firm need to pursue selected opportunities?
   c. Can the identified competencies be easily duplicated or surpassed by the competition?
      1. If yes, what must the firm do to maintain its superior position in its core competencies?
5. Defining a mission statement (i.e., summarizing where and how the firm has chosen to compete)
   a. Does the mission statement define the firm's targeted market, product or service offering, distribution channels, customers, and management's beliefs and values?
   b. Is the mission statement succinct, clear, and inspirational?
6. Setting objectives (i.e., establishing quantitative measures of performance)
   a. Are the objectives measurable?
   b. Do they have a specific time horizon?
7. Strategy selection (i.e., selecting the strategy most likely to achieve the objectives in an acceptable time period subject to constraints identified in the self-assessment)
   a. Does the firm have sufficient resources to implement the strategy?
   b. Have all reasonable alternatives available for implementing the strategy been evaluated?
   c. What are the key assumptions underlying the various strategic options under consideration?
   d. Why was the chosen strategy selected from among the range of reasonable alternative strategies?

REFERENCES

Almaney, A. J., *Strategic Management: A Framework for Decision Making and Problem Solving,* Shelfield Publishing Company, 1992.

Bloomberg.com, "Glaxo, SmithKline Agree to Merge," January 18, 2000.

Boston Consulting Group, *The Strategy Development Process,* Boston: The Boston Consulting Group, 1985.

Business Week, "Burying the Hatchet Buys a Lot of Drug Research," January 31, 2000.

Chung, Mary, and Alistair Davidson, "Business Experts," *PC AI,* Summer 1987, pp. 16–21.

Gitman, Lawrence J., *Principles of Managerial Finance,* Brief Edition, New York: Addison-Wesley, 1998, p. 22.

Hamel, Gary C., and C. K. Prahalad, *Competing for the Future,* Cambridge, MA: Harvard Business School Press, 1994.

Hill, Charles W. L., and Gareth R. Jones, *Strategic Management: An Integrated Approach* (5th ed.), Boston: Houghton-Mifflin, 2001, pp. 158–233.

Hopkins, Thomas D., "Regulatory Costs in Profile," Center for the Study of American Business, Washington University, 1996.

James, Robert M., Henry Mintzberg, and James Brian Quinn, *The Strategy Process,* Englewood Cliffs, New Jersey: Prentice-Hall, 1988.

Marrus, Stephanie K., *Building the Strategic Plan: Find, Analyze and Present the Right Information,* New York: John Wiley & Sons, 1984, pp. 23–28.

Moore, Geoffrey A., *Crossing the Chasm,* Harper Business, 1991.

Murland, Mark A., William L. Sammon, & Robert Spitalnic, *Business Competitor Intelligence: Methods for Collecting, Organizing and Using Information,* New York: John Wiley & Sons, 1984.

Porter, Michael E., *Competitive Advantage,* New York: The Free Press, 1985.

Pursche, William A., "Pharmaceuticals—The Consolidation Isn't Over," *The McKinsey Quarterly* (2), 1996, pp. 110–119.

Stryker, Steven C., *Plan to Succeed: A Guide to Strategic Planning,* Princeton, NJ: Petrocelli Books, 1986.

Waterman, Robert H. Jr., *The Renewal Factor,* New York: Bantam Books, 1987.

5

IMPLEMENTATION:

SEARCH THROUGH CLOSING—
PHASES 3 TO 10

Say no, then negotiate.

—Anonymous

"Well, do we have a deal or not?" the lead negotiator for Timco demanded. Her patience strained by the seemingly endless negotiations that had been underway for more than 2 months, LeAnn leaned forward in her chair as if to underscore that she was no longer willing to accept the buyer's tendency to focus on details while avoiding the big issues. Delay was no longer acceptable. She wanted a straight answer and she wanted it now.

As part of their initial agreement they had set a time limit of 90 days in which the buyer was to complete their review of Timco's plants and decide if they would close the deal. But they seem to have spent countless hours discussing the condition of the firm's warehouses in Memphis, the increase in employee turnover at a plant in Baton Rouge, and the age of high-speed extrusion machines at the firm's facility in Dallas. After all this time, she realized that they had not yet put a firm offer on the table. They seemed to be accumulating reasons for lowering their initial offer.

As the "drop dead" date approached, she felt increasingly uneasy. It seemed that this is precisely what they were about to do. Timco had a lot at stake. Word had leaked to their employees, customers, and suppliers that they were for sale. Their customers were calling almost daily now for a reassurance that there would be no disruption in shipments. Employees grumbled that they were being kept in the dark. Suppliers were concerned that any change in ownership could imperil their position with Timco. A lot was on the line, and the buyer knew it.

Carla had represented the buyer in these types of negotiations many times in recent years. She knew that stall tactics would no longer work. She also knew that Timco wanted to sell. She braced herself in her chair as she prepared to respond. "Yes," Carla said slowly, "but only if certain changes in the initial terms and conditions are made." "These include . . ."

OVERVIEW

The firm's business plan sets the overall direction for the business. It defines where the firm has chosen to compete (i.e., target market) and how the firm has chosen to compete (i.e., through price–cost leadership, differentiation, or a focused strategy). An acquisition plan is required if the firm decides that an acquisition is needed to implement the firm's business strategy. The acquisition plan delineates key management objectives for the takeover that support specific strategic objectives in the business plan, resource constraints, and appropriate tactics for implementing the proposed transaction. An acquisition plan furnishes the appropriate guidance to those charged with successfully completely the transaction by providing critical input into all subsequent phases of the acquisition process.

The acquisition plan communicates to those charged with acquiring a company the preferences of senior management. It ensures that the acquisition team conducts itself in a manner consistent with management's risk tolerance. The acquisition plan defines the criteria, such as size, profitability, industry, and growth rate, used to select potential acquisition candidates. It may specify the degree of relatedness to the acquiring firm's current businesses and define the types of firms that should not be considered (e.g., current competitors). The plan also stipulates the roles and responsibilities of team members, including outside consultants, and sets the team's budget. Moreover, the plan indicates management's preference for the form of payment (stock, cash, or debt), acquiring stock or assets, and for partial or full ownership. It may preclude any hostile takeover attempts or indicate a desire to limit goodwill. It may also specify management's desire to minimize the impact of the acquisition on the earnings per share (EPS) of the combined companies immediately following closing. Finally, the acquisition plan may establish limits on what the acquiring firm is willing to pay for any acquisition by setting a ceiling on the purchase price in terms of a maximum price-to-earnings (P/E) multiple or multiple of some other measure of value.

This chapter starts with the presumption that a firm has developed a viable business plan that requires an acquisition to realize the firm's strategic direction. While Chapter 4 (this volume) addressed the creation of business and acquisition plans (Phases 1 and 2), this chapter focuses on Phases 3–10 of the acquisition process, including search, screen, first contact, negotiation, integration planning, closing, integration implementation, and evaluation. The negotiation phase is the most complex aspect of the acquisition process involving refining the preliminary valuation, deal structuring, due diligence, and developing a financing plan. It is in the negotiation phase that all elements of the purchase price are actually determined.

PHASE 3: THE SEARCH PROCESS

INITIATING THE SEARCH

Initiating the search for potential acquisition candidates involves a two-step procedure. The first step is to establish the primary screening or selection criteria. At this stage of the search process it is best to use a relatively small number of criteria. The primary criteria should include the industry and size of the transaction. It may also be appropriate to add a geographic restriction. The size of the transaction is best defined in terms of the maximum purchase price a firm is willing to pay. This can be expressed as a maximum price to earnings, book, cash flow, or revenue ratio or a maximum purchase price stated in terms of dollars.

For example, an acute-care private hospital holding company wants to buy a skilled nursing facility within a range of 50 miles of its largest acute-care hospital in Allegheny County, Pennsylvania. Management believes that it cannot afford to pay more than $25 million for the facility. Its primary selection criteria could include the following: an industry (skilled nursing), location (Allegheny County), and maximum price (five times cash flow not to exceed $25 million). Similarly, a Texas-based manufacturer of patio furniture with manufacturing operations in the Southwestern United States is seeking to expand its sales in California by purchasing a patio furniture manufacturer in the far western United States for an amount not to exceed $100 million. Its primary selection criteria could include an industry (outdoor furniture), a location (California, Arizona, and Nevada), and a maximum purchase price (15 times after-tax earnings not to exceed $100 million).

The second step is to develop a search strategy. Such strategies normally entail using computerized databases and directory services such as Disclosure, Dun & Bradstreet, Standard & Poors' *Corporate Register,* or Thomas' *Register* and *Million Dollar Directories* to identify qualified candidates. Firms may also query their law, banking, and accounting firms to identify other candidates. Investment banks, brokers, and leveraged buyout firms are also fertile sources of candidates, although they are likely to require an advisory or finder's fee.

The Internet makes research much easier than in the past. Today, the analyst has much more information at their fingertips. Such services as Yahoo! Finance, Hoover's, or EDGAR Online enable researchers to quickly gather data about competitors and customers. These sites provide easy access to a variety of public documents filed with the Securities and Exchange Commission (SEC) (Exhibit 5-1).

EXHIBIT 5-1. SEC FILINGS
AT YOUR FINGERTIPS

10-K: Provides detailed information on a company's annual operations, business conditions, competitors, market conditions, legal proceedings, risk factors in holding the stock, and other related information.

10-Q: Updates investors about the company's operations each quarter.

S-1: Filed when a company wants to register new stock. Can contain information about the company's operating history and business risks.

S-2: Filed when a company is completing a material transaction such as a merger or acquisition. Provides substantial detail underlying the terms and conditions of the transaction, the events leading up to completing the transaction, and justification for the merger or acquisition.

8-K: Filed when a company faces a "material event" such as a merger.

Schedule 14A: A proxy statement. Gives details about the annual meeting and biographies of company officials and directors including stock ownership and pay.

Web sites:

www.sec.gov
www.edgar-online.com
www.freedgar.com
www.quicken.com
www.hooveronline.com
www.aol.com
www.yahoo.finance.com

If confidentiality is not an issue, a firm may seek to advertise its interest in acquiring a particular type of firm in the *Wall Street Journal* or the trade press. Although this is likely to generate substantial interest, it is less likely to generate high-quality prospects. Considerable time is wasted sorting through responses from those interested in getting a free estimate of their own company to those responses from brokers claiming their clients fit the buyer's criteria as a ruse to convince the buyer that they need the broker's services.

PHASE 4: THE SCREENING PROCESS

The screening process is a refinement of the search process. It starts with a pruning of the initial list of potential candidates created by applying such primary criteria as the type of industry and the maximum size of the transaction. Because relatively few primary criteria are used, the initial list of potential acquisition candidates may be lengthy. Additional or secondary selection criteria may be employed to shorten the list.

Care should be taken to limit the number of secondary criteria used. An excessively long list of selection criteria will severely limit the number of candidates that will pass the screening process. Whenever possible, the selection criteria should be quantified. In addition to the maximum purchase price, industry, or geographic location criteria employed to develop the initial list, secondary selection criteria may include a specific market segment within the industry or a specific product line within a market segment. Other measures often include the firm's profitability, degree of leverage, and market share.

MARKET SEGMENT

The search process involved the specification of the target industry. It is now necessary to identify the target segment in the industry. For example, a steel fabrication company may decide to diversify by acquiring a manufacturer of aluminum flat-rolled products. A primary search criterion would include only firms in the aluminum flat-rolled products industry. Subsequent searches may involve a further segmenting of the market to identify only those companies that manufacture aluminum tubular products.

PRODUCT LINE

This criterion identifies the target product line within the target market segment. The steel fabrication company in the previous example may decide to focus its search on companies manufacturing aluminum tubular products used in the manufacturing of lawn and patio furniture.

PROFITABILITY

This criterion should be defined in terms of the percent return on sales, assets, or total investment. This enables a more accurate comparison among candidates of different sizes. A firm with after-tax earnings of $5 million on sales of $100 million may be less attractive than a firm with earnings of $3 million and sales of $50 million, because the latter firm may be more efficient.

DEGREE OF LEVERAGE

Debt to equity or debt to total capital ratios are often used to measure the level of indebtedness. The acquiring company may not want to purchase a company whose heavy debt burden may cause the acquiring company's leverage ratios to exceed targeted levels and jeopardize the acquirer's credit rating.

MARKET SHARE

The acquiring firm may only be interested in firms that are number one or number two in market share in the targeted industry or in firms whose market share is some multiple (e.g., $2\times$ of the next largest competitor). Firms having substantially greater market share than their competitors are often able to achieve lower cost positions than their competitors because of economies of scale.

PHASE 5: FIRST CONTACT

ALTERNATIVE APPROACH STRATEGIES

The approach suggested for initiating contact with a target company depends on the size of the company and if it is publicly or privately held.

Small Companies

For small companies ($<$$25 million in sales) in which the buyer has no direct contacts, a vaguely worded letter expressing interest in a joint venture or marketing alliance and indicating that you will follow-up with a telephone call is often all that is necessary. During the follow-up call, be prepared to discuss a range of options with the seller including the possibility of acquisition.

Preparation before the first telephone contact is essential. If possible, script your comments. Get to the point quickly but indirectly. Identify yourself, your company, and its strengths. Demonstrate your understanding of the contact's business and how a loose, perhaps noncontractual partnership could make sense. Be able to quickly and succinctly explain the benefits of your proposal to the contact. If the opportunity arises, propose a range of options including an acquisition. Listen carefully to the contact's reaction. If the contact is willing to entertain the notion of an acquisition, request a face-to-face meeting.

Medium-Sized Companies

For medium-sized companies (between $25 and $100 million) or a division of a larger company, make contact through an intermediary. Intermediaries can be less intimidating than a direct approach from the potential suitor. Intermediaries could include members of the acquirer's board of directors or the firm's outside legal counsel, accounting firm, lender, or investment banker.

Large Companies

For large, publicly traded companies, contact should also be made through an intermediary, but in this instance, it is critical to make contact at the highest level possible. Discretion is extremely important due to the target's concern about being "put into play." Even rumors of acquisition can have substantial, adverse consequences for the target. Current or potential customers may express concern about the uncertainty associated with a change of ownership. A change in ownership could imply changes in product or service quality, reliability, and the level of service provided under product warranty or maintenance contracts. Suppliers worry about possible disruptions in their production schedules as the transition to the new owner takes place. Employees worry about possible layoffs or changes in compensation.

Competitors will do what they can to fan these concerns to persuade current customers to switch and potential customers to defer buying decisions; key employees will be encouraged to defect to the competition. Shareholders may experience a dizzying ride as arbitrageurs buying on the rumor bid up the price of the stock only to bail out if denial of the rumor appears credible.

Companies have a fiduciary responsibility to their shareholders to consider all legitimate offers. Even though a large percentage of expressions of interest are rejected, the investment community may now be on notice that someone finds something attractive about the target. Therefore, a company that had previously been ignored may now be the target of both strategic buyers and investor groups. The diversion of management time to deal with these distractions can negatively affect continuing operations.

DISCUSSING VALUE

Getting the contact at the target company's to provide a value for their business can be a daunting task. Neither the buyer nor seller has an incentive to be the first to provide an estimate of value. Getting a range may be the best you can do. This may be done by discussing values for recent acquisitions of similar businesses. Listen carefully to the contact's reasons for wanting to sell so that any proposal made can be structured to satisfy as many of the seller's primary needs as possible. With the agreement of the seller, establish a timeline consisting of next steps to be taken and stick to it.

PRELIMINARY LEGAL DOCUMENTS

Although a common first step in a transaction is to negotiate a bilateral confidentiality agreement and letter of intent, the acquirer has an incentive to avoid signing a letter of intent, which could result in some legal risk to the buyer if the deal is not consummated. The letter of intent may create legal liabilities if one of the parties is later accused of not negotiating the definitive agreement in "good faith." In contrast, the seller is often unwilling to proceed without a written offer.

Confidentiality Agreement

In the bilateral confidentiality agreement, the buyer requests as much audited historical data and collateral information as the seller is willing to provide. The prudent seller requests similar information about the buyer to assess the buyer's financial credibility. It is very important for the seller to determine the buyer's credibility early in the process in order not to waste time with a potential buyer incapable of raising the financing to complete the transaction. The agreement should be mutually binding, cover only information that is not publicly available, and have a reasonable expiration date.

Letter of Intent

The letter of intent lays out the principal areas of agreement between the two parties. It is often useful in identifying early in the process areas of agreement and disagreement; however, it may delay the signing of a definitive agreement of purchase and sale or, in the case of a public company, necessitate a public announcement to be in compliance with securities laws if it is likely to have a "material" impact on the buyer or seller. Depending upon how it is written, it may or may not be legally binding.

The letter of intent formally stipulates the reason for the agreement, major terms and conditions, the responsibilities of both parties while the agreement is in force, a reasonable expiration date, and how all fees associated with the transaction will be paid. Major terms and conditions include a brief outline of the structure of the transaction, which may entail the payment of cash or stock for certain assets and the assumption of certain liabilities of the target company. The letter may also specify certain conditions such as an agreement that selected personnel of the target company will not compete with the combined companies for some period of time if they should leave. Another condition may indicate that a certain portion of the purchase price will be allocated to the *noncompete agreement.* Such an allocation of the purchase price is in the interests of the buyer because the amount of the allocation can be amortized over the life of the agreement and taken as a tax-deductible expense, but it may constitute taxable income for the seller. The agreement may also indicate a desire to place a portion of the purchase price in escrow.

The proposed purchase price may be expressed as a specific dollar figure, as a range, or as a multiple of some measure of value such as operating earnings or cash flow. The letter of intent also specifies the types of data to be exchanged and the duration and extent of the initial due diligence. The letter of intent will usually terminate if the buyer and the seller do not reach agreement by a certain date. The buyer usually demands a *no-shop provision* preventing the seller from sharing the terms of the buyer's proposal with other potential buyers with the hope of instigating an auction environment. Legal, consulting, and deed transfer fees may be paid for by the buyer, seller, or shared.

A well-written letter of intent usually contains language that limits the extent to which the agreement binds the two parties. Price or other provisions are generally subject to *closing conditions,* such as the buyer having full access to all of the seller's books and records and having completed due diligence, the ability of the buyer to obtain financing, and approvals including both boards of directors, stockholders, and regulatory bodies. Other standard conditions include the requirement for signed employment contracts for key executives of the selling company and the completion of all necessary merger and acquisition documents. Failure to satisfy any of these conditions will invalidate the agreement.

PHASE 6: NEGOTIATION

Phases 1–5 of the acquisition process could be viewed as discrete activities or events. Unlike the previous phases, the negotiation phase is an interactive, iterative process with many activities conducted concurrently by various members of the acquisition team. The actual purchase price paid for the acquired business is determined during this phase and will frequently be considerably different from the preliminary valuation of the target company made prior to due diligence and based on sketchy publicly available information.

DEFINING THE PURCHASE PRICE

There are three commonly used definitions of purchase price. These include the total consideration, the total purchase price or enterprise value, and the net purchase price. Each definition serves a different purpose.

Total Consideration

In the agreement of purchase and sale, the *total consideration* consists of cash (C), stock (S), new debt issues (D), or some combination of all three. It is a term commonly employed in legal documents to reflect the different types of remuneration received by the target company shareholders. Note that the remuneration can include both financial and nonfinancial assets such as real estate. Nonfinancial compensation is sometimes referred to as *payment-in-kind.*

The debt counted in the total consideration is what the target company shareholder receives as payment for their stock, along with any cash or acquiring company stock. Each component of the total consideration may be viewed in present value terms; therefore, the total consideration is itself expressed in present value terms (PV_{TC}). The present value of cash is its face value. The stock component of the total consideration would be the current value (PV_S) of future dividends or net cash flows, or the acquiring firm's stock price per share times the number of shares to be exchanged for each outstanding share of the seller's stock. New debt issued by the acquiring company as part of the compensation paid to shareholders can be expressed as the present value (PV_{ND}) of the cumulative interest payments plus principal discounted at some appropriate market rate of interest.

Total Purchase Price (Enterprise Value)

The *total purchase price* or *enterprise value* (PV_{TPP}) of the target firm consists of the total consideration (PV_{TC}) plus the market value of the target firm's debt (PV_{AD}) assumed by the acquiring company. The enterprise value of the firm is often quoted in the financial press and other media as the purchase price, because it is most visible to those not familiar with the details to the transaction. It is important to analysts and shareholders alike because it approximates the total investment made by the acquiring firm to purchase the target firm. It is an approximation because it does not necessarily measure liabilities the acquirer is assuming that are not visible on the target firm's balance sheet. Nor does it reflect the potential for recovering a portion of the total consideration paid to target company shareholders by selling undervalued or redundant assets.

Net Purchase Price

The *net purchase price* (PV_{NPP}) is the total purchase price plus other assumed liabilities (PV_{OAL}) less the proceeds from the sale of discretionary or redundant target assets (PV_{DA}) on or off the balance sheet. PV_{OAL} are those assumed liabilities not fully reflected on the target firm's balance sheet or accounted for in estimating the economic value of the target firm. Other assumed liabilities and discretionary assets will be explained in more detail later.

The net purchase price is the most comprehensive measure of the actual price paid for the target firm. It includes all known cash obligations assumed by the acquirer as well as any portion of the purchase price that is recovered through the sale of assets. It may be larger or smaller than the total purchase price. The various definitions of price can be summarized as follows:

$$\text{Total Consideration: } PV_{TC} = C + PV_S + PV_{ND}$$

$$\text{Total Purchase Price/Enterprise Value: } PV_{TPP} = TC_{TC} + PV_{AD}$$

$$\text{Net Purchase Price: } PV_{NPP} = PV_{TPP} + PV_{OAL} - PV_{DA}$$
$$= (C + PV_S + PV_{ND} + PV_{AD}) + PV_{OAL} - PV_{DA}$$

Although the total consideration is most important to the target company's shareholders as a measure of what they receive in exchange for their stock, the acquirer's shareholders tend to focus on the total purchase price or enterprise value as the actual amount paid for the target firm. The total purchase price tends to be most visible to the acquirer's shareholders. However, the total purchase price tends to ignore other adjustments that should be made to determine actual or pending "out-of-pocket" cash spent by the acquirer. The net purchase price reflects the relevant adjustments to the total purchase price and is a much better indicator of whether the acquirer overpaid (i.e., paid more than its economic value including estimated synergy) for the target firm. The application of the various definitions of the purchase price is addressed in more detail in Chapter 8 (this volume).

Other Assumed Liabilities

The adjustment to the total purchase price referred to as other assumed liabilities consists of items that are not adequately accounted for on the target's balance sheet. If all of the target firm's balance sheet reserves reflected accurately all known future obligations, and if there were no significant potential off-balance sheet liabilities, there would be no need to adjust the purchase price for assumed liabilities other than for short- and long-term debt assumed by the acquiring company. Earnings and book value per share would accurately reflect the expected impact of known liabilities. Operating cash flows, which reflect both earnings and changes in items on the balance sheet, would also accurately reflect future liabilities. Therefore, valuations based on a multiple of earnings, book value, or discounted cash flow would accurately reflect the fair market value of the business.

In practice, this is rarely the case. Reserves are often inadequate to satisfy pending claims. This is particularly true if the selling company attempts to improve current earnings performance by understating reserves. Common examples include underfunded or underreserved employee and health-care obligations, uncollectable receivables, underaccrued vacation and holidays, accrued bonuses, and deferred compensation, such as employee stock options. Other examples include product warranties, environmental liabilities, pending lawsuits, severance expenses, and maintenance and service agreements, and any other obligations of the selling company accepted by the buyer at closing.

To the extent that such factors represent a future use of cash, the present value of their future impact, to the extent possible, should be estimated. Case Study 5-1 illustrates how these liabilities can substantially add to the actual out-of-pocket cost of an acquisition.

CASE STUDY 5-1. THE CASH IMPACT OF PRODUCT WARRANTIES

Reliable Appliances, a leading manufacturer of washing machines and dryers, acquired a marginal competitor, Quality-Built, which had been losing money during the last several years. To help stanch losses, Quality-Built reduced its quality-control expenditures and began to purchase cheaper parts. Quality-Built knew that this would hurt business in the long run, but it was more focused on improving its current financial performance to increase the firm's prospects for eventual sale. Reliable Appliances saw an acquisition of the competitor as a way of obtaining market share quickly at a time when Quality-Built's market value was the lowest in 3 years. The sale was completed quickly at a very small premium to the current market price.

Quality-Built had been selling its appliances with a standard industry 3-year warranty. Claims for the types of appliances sold tended to increase gradually as the appliance aged. Quality-Built's warranty claims' history was in line with the industry experience and did not appear to be a cause for alarm. Not surprisingly, in view of the Quality-Built's cutback in quality-control practices and downgrading of purchased parts, warranty claims began to escalate sharply within 12 months of Reliable Appliance's acquisition of Quality-Built. Over the next several years, Reliable Appliance paid out $15 million in warranty claims. The intangible damage may have been much higher as Reliable Appliance's reputation had been damaged in the marketplace.

Discretionary Assets

Discretionary assets are undervalued or redundant assets not required to run the acquired business and which can be used by the buyer to recover some portion of the purchase price. Such assets include land valued at its historical cost on the balance sheet, inventory and equipment whose resale value exceeds its fully depreciated value, cash balances in excess of normal working capital needs, and product lines or operating units considered nonstrategic by the buyer. The sale of discretionary assets are not considered in the calculation of the economic value of the target firm, because economic value is determined by future operating cash flows before consideration is given to how the transaction will be financed.

CONCURRENT ACTIVITIES

The negotiation phase consists of four concurrent activities: (a) refining valuation, (b) deal structuring, (c) due diligence, and (d) developing a financing plan. Refining the preliminary valuation based on new information uncovered during due diligence provides the starting point for negotiating the agreement of purchase and sale. Deal structuring involves meeting the needs of both parties by addressing issues of risk and reward by constructing an appropriate set of compensation, legal, tax, and accounting structures. Due diligence provides additional information enabling the buyer to better understand the nature of the liabilities the buyer is being asked to assume and to confirm perceived sources of value. Finally, the financing plan provides a reality check on the buyer because it defines the maximum amount the buyer can reasonably expect to finance and in turn pay for the target company.

Refining Valuation

The first activity within the negotiation phase of the acquisition process deals with updating the preliminary valuation of the target company based on new information. At this stage, the buyer requests and reviews at least 5 years of historical financial data. Although it is highly desirable to examine data that has been audited in accordance with Generally Accepted Accounting Principals (GAAP), such data may not be available for small, privately owned companies. In fact, small companies rarely hire outside accounting firms to conduct expensive audits unless they are required to do so as part of a loan agreement.

The 5 years of historical data should be *normalized* or adjusted for nonrecurring gains, losses, or expenses. Nonrecurring gains or losses can result from the sale of land, equipment, product lines, patents, software, or copyrights. Nonrecurring expenses include severance, employee signing bonuses, and settlement of litigation. These adjustments are necessary to allow the buyer to smooth out or "normalize" irregularities in the historical information and to better understand the underlying dynamics of the business.

Once the data have been normalized, each major expense category should be expressed as a percent of revenue. By observing year-to-year changes in these ratios, sustainable trends in the data are more discernable. For example, it is commonplace for sellers to temporarily improve operating profits by postponing normal maintenance expenses. A decline in the ratio of capital spending, research and development, training, and advertising expenditures to sales from their historical average may indicate deliberate underinvestment in the business. An increase in the average time to collect receivables may suggest growing financial problems among the seller's customers. If the number of times inventory is being replaced each year is declining (i.e., slowing inventory turnover), the seller may be facing decelerating sales due to a loss of market share or simply capacity constraints, which limit the firm's ability to build inventory.

The normalized historical data will help the buyer project a minimum of 5 years of cash flows and adjust the projected cash flows for the amount and timing of anticipated synergy. The assumptions underlying the projections should be clearly stated. The buyer should heavily discount any projections provided by the seller. Chapter 8 (this volume) describes the process of refining valuations in more detail using standard financial modeling techniques.

Deal Structuring

In purely financial terms, deal structuring involves the allocation of cash flow streams (with respect to amount and timing), the allocation of risk, and, therefore, the allocation of value between different parties to the transaction. In terms of the personalities of the parties involved, deal structuring entails much more. It is the process of identifying and satisfying as many of the highest priority objectives of the parties involved in the transaction subject to their tolerance for risk.

In practice, deal structuring is about understanding the potential sources of disagreement from a simple argument over basic facts to substantially more complex issues, such as the form of payment, legal, accounting, and tax structures. It also requires understanding the potential conflicts of interest that can influence the outcome of the discussions. For example, when a portion of the purchase price depends on the long-term performance of the acquired business, the management of the business, often the former owner, may not behave in a manner that is in the best interests of the acquirer. The deal-structuring process also embodies feedback effects in which one element of the process such as the nature of payment, including the amount, timing, and risk, may impact tax and accounting treatments.

Moreover, decisions made throughout the deal-structuring process influence various attributes of the deal. These attributes include, but are not limited to, how ownership is determined, how assets are transferred, how ownership interests are protected (governance), and how risk is apportioned among parties to the transaction. Other attributes include the type, number, and complexity of the documents required for closing, the types of approvals required, and the time needed to complete the transaction. These decisions will also influence how the combined companies will be managed, the amount and timing of resources committed, the magnitude and timing of current and future tax liabilities, and the method of accounting for the transaction structure (McCarthy: 1998; Tillinghast: 1998).

Reflecting this complexity, the deal-structuring process should be viewed as consisting of a number of interdependent components. At a minimum, these include the acquisition vehicle, the postclosing organization, the form of payment, the form of accounting, the form of acquisition, and tax structure. The process starts with the determination by each party of their initial negotiating positions, potential risks, options for managing risk, levels of tolerance for risk, and conditions under which either party will "walk away" from the negotiations. The acquisition vehicle refers to the legal structure (e.g., corporate or partnership) used to acquire the target company. The postclosing organization is the organizational and legal framework used to manage the combined businesses following the completion of the transaction. The form of payment may consist of cash, common stock, debt, or some combination of all three. Some portion of the payment may be deferred or dependent on the future performance of the acquired entity. The form of acquisition reflects both what is being acquired (e.g., stock or assets) and the form of payment. Consequently, the form of acquisition largely determines accounting and tax structures. How and why these things happen are discussed in substantial detail in Chapter 10 (this volume).

EXHIBIT 5-2. CHARACTERISTICS OF SUCCESSFUL DEALS

According to a Harvard University study, business deals, including mergers, acquisitions, joint ventures, and alliances, that have proved successful over a long period of time tend to have the following characteristics:

1. They are simple.
2. They do not fall apart when there are minor deviations from projections.
3. They may be changed.
4. They consider the incentives of each party to the deal under a variety of circumstances.
5. They provide mechanisms for communication and interpretation.
6. They are based primarily on trust rather than contract law.
7. They are not patently unfair to any party.
8. They do not make it too difficult to raise additional capital.
9. They match the needs of the parties involved.
10. They reveal information about each party (e.g., their faith in their ability to deliver on promises).
11. They allow for new information before financing is required.
12. They rely on incentives to ensure that the objectives of owners and managers are consistent.
13. They take into account the time required to raise additional capital.
14. They improve the chances for success for the venture.

Source: Harvard Business School, 1989.

Conducting Due Diligence

The parties to any transaction should always conduct their own due diligence to obtain the most accurate assessment of potential risks and rewards. Although some degree of protection is achieved through a well-written contract, legal agreements should never be viewed as a substitute for conducting formal due diligence.

Buyer Due Diligence

Buyer due diligence is the process of validating assumptions underlying valuation. The primary objectives are to identify and to confirm "sources of value" and to mitigate real or potential liability by looking for fatal flaws that reduce value. Due diligence involves three primary reviews: (1) a strategic/operational/marketing review conducted by senior operations and marketing management; (2) a financial review directed by financial and accounting personnel; and (3) and a legal review conducted by the buyer's legal counsel.

A rigorous due diligence requires the creation of comprehensive checklists. The strategic and operational review questions focus on the seller's management team, operations, as well as sales and marketing strategies. The financial review questions focus on the accuracy, timeliness, and completeness of the seller's financial statements. Finally, legal questions deal with corporate records, financial matters, management and employee issues, tangible and intangible assets of the seller, as well as material contracts and obligations of the seller such as litigation and claims. Interviews with key management provide invaluable sources of information (see Krallinger: 1997).

The importance of performing a thorough due diligence cannot be overstated. Case Study 5-2 illustrates one of the more egregious examples of fraudulent accounting practices experienced in recent years. Note how swiftly shareholders abandoned the company, resulting in a dramatic loss of shareholder value.

CASE STUDY 5-2. MCKESSON HBOC RESTATES REVENUE

McKesson Corporation, the nation's largest drug wholesaler, acquired medical software provider HBO & Co. in a $14.1 billion stock deal in early 1999. The transaction was touted as having created the country's largest comprehensive health care services company. McKesson had annual sales of $18.1 billion in fiscal year 1998, and HBO & Co. had fiscal 1998 revenue of $1.2 billion. HBO & Co. makes information systems that include clinical, financial, billing, physician practice, and medical records software. Charles W. McCall, the chairman, president, and chief executive of HBO & Co., was named the new chairman of McKesson HBOC.

HBO was the leader in selling hospitals and doctors software to track financial and clinical data. As one of the decade's hottest stocks, it had soared 38-fold since early 1992. McKesson's first attempt to acquire HBO in mid-1998 collapsed following a news leak. However, McKesson's persistence culminated in a completed transaction in January 1999. In its haste, McKesson closed the deal even before an in-depth audit of HBO's books had been completed. In fact, the audit did not begin until after the close of the 1999 fiscal year. McKesson was so confident that its auditing firm, Deloitte-Touche, would not find anything that it released unaudited results that included the impact of HBO shortly after the close of the 1999 fiscal year on March 31, 1999. Within days, indications that contracts had been backdated began to surface.

By May, McKesson hired forensic accountants skilled at reconstructing computer records. By early June, the accountants were able to reconstruct deleted computer files, which revealed a list of improperly recorded contracts. This evidence underscored HBO's efforts to deliberately accelerate revenues by backdating contracts that weren't final. Moreover, HBO shipped customers software they had not ordered, while knowing that it would be returned. In doing so, they were able to boost reported earnings, the company's share price, and ultimately the purchase price paid by McKesson.

In mid-July, McKesson announced that it would have to reduce revenue by $327 million and net income by $191.5 million for the past 3 fiscal years to correct for accounting irregularities. The company's stock had fallen by 48% since late April when it first announced that it would have to restate earnings.

McKesson's senior management had to contend with rebuilding McKesson's reputation, resolving more than 50 lawsuits, and attempting to recover $9.5 billion in market value lost since the need to restate earnings was first announced. When asked how such a thing could happen, McKesson spokespeople said they were intentionally kept from the due-diligence process before the transaction closed. Despite not having adequate access to HBO's records, McKesson decided to close the transaction anyway.

Source: Edgar-Online, 1998; Bloomberg.com, 1999.

Selecting the Due Diligence Team

One of the most important aspects of performing due diligence is knowing the right questions to ask. This comes with experience in having performed due diligence numerous times and from having in-depth knowledge of the industry and the operations to be reviewed. Teams should include those with the required specialized expertise to address environmental, legal, and technical issues. This often necessitates the use of consultants. Selecting the right advisors has become more challenging in recent years.

The advent of mergers among the major accounting firms and the tendency to bundle auditing and consulting services has increased the potential for conflict of interest. During the past decade, the "Big 8" accounting firms have been reduced to five. These include Price Waterhouse Coopers, KPMG Peat Marwick, Arthur Andersen, Ernst & Young, and Deloitte Touche Tohmatsu. Moreover, the larger accounting firms are rapidly acquiring the smaller regional firms. The larger firms are also interested in leveraging their client relationships on the accounting side of their business with other types of consulting services such as strategic planning, systems integration, pension planning, software development, benefits management, and legal services.

Imagine a situation in which the legal division in a consulting firm is asked to give a legal opinion on an audit performed by the accounting division of the same firm, if partners in both divisions are paid from the same profit pool. Some consulting firms attempt to minimize potential conflicts by erecting "Chinese walls" among the various divisions that may participate in a merger or acquisition. Despite such efforts, the potential for breaching these walls exists. To minimize potential conflicts of interest, it may be appropriate to avoid "one-stop shopping" and to purchase the necessary advisory services from different firms (Nanus: 1998).

Limiting Due Diligence

Due diligence is an expensive and exhausting process. The buyer will frequently want as much time as necessary to complete due diligence. In contrast, the seller will frequently want to limit the length and scope as much as possible. By its nature, due diligence is highly intrusive and places substantial demands on managers' time and attention.

Due diligence rarely works to the advantage of the seller, since a long and detailed due diligence is likely to uncover items that the buyer will use as an excuse to lower the purchase price. Consequently, sellers may seek to terminate due diligence before the buyer feels it is appropriate. In the interests of maintaining a cooperative relationship during negotiations, it is almost always in the best interests of the buyer to conduct a thorough due diligence in the shortest period of time possible so as not to disrupt the business and alienate the seller.

In some instances, buyers and sellers may agree to an abbreviated due diligence period. The theory is that the buyer can be protected in a well-written agreement of purchase and sale. In the agreement, the seller is required to make certain representations and warrant that they are true. Such "reps and warranties" could include the seller's acknowledgement that they own all assets listed in the agreement free and clear of any liens or attachments. If the representation is breached (found not to be true), the agreement will generally include a mechanism for compensating the buyer for any material loss. What constitutes material loss is defined in the contract. Relying on "reps and warranties as a substitute for a thorough due diligence is rarely a good idea (see Case Study 5-3).

CASE STUDY 5-3. WHEN "REPS AND
WARRANTIES" DON'T PROVIDE
ADEQUATE PROTECTION

A large financial services firm in the mid-1990s acquired a small database company, which provided data supporting the lending process. The
seller signed a contract with all the necessary reps and warranties that all
their computer systems were fully operational and in compliance with prevailing laws. The buyer also withheld about 20% of the purchase price in
the event that the operational effectiveness of the systems was not at the
level specified in the contract. It became apparent almost immediately following closing that the seller had dramatically misstated the viability of his
business. The buyer had to eventually shut down the business and write off
the full extent of the purchase price. The buyer also had to submit to binding
arbitration in order to recover that portion of the purchase price that had
been placed in escrow. The buyer had virtually no recourse to the seller who
had few assets in his own name and who may have moved the bulk of the
cash received for his stock to banks that were beyond the jurisdiction of the
U.S. legal system.

A data room is another method commonly used by sellers to limit due diligence. This amounts to the seller sequestering the buying company's team in a
single room to complete due diligence. Typically, the data room consists of a
conference room filled with file cabinets and boxes of documents requested by the
buyer's due-diligence team. Formal presentations by the seller's key managers are
given in the often-cramped conditions of the data room. Not surprisingly, the data
room is rarely an adequate substitute for a tour of the seller's facilities.

Seller's Due Diligence

Although the bulk of due diligence is performed by the buyer on the seller, the
prudent seller should also perform due diligence on the buyer. In doing so, the
seller can determine if the buyer has the financial wherewithal to finance the purchase price. In addition, a seller, as part of its own due-diligence process, will
frequently require all of its managers to sign documents stating that to the "best
of their knowledge" what is being represented in the contract that pertains to their
area of responsibility is indeed true. By conducting an internal investigation of
their own operations, the seller hopes to mitigate liability stemming from inaccuracies in the seller's representations and warranties made in the agreement of purchase and sale.

Developing the Financing Plan

The final activity of the negotiation phase is to develop balance sheet, income, and cash-flow statements for the combined firms, in accordance with GAAP. Unlike the financial projections of cash flow made to value the target company, these statements should include the expected cost of financing the transaction.

This activity is a key input into the determination of the purchasing price, as it places a practical limitation on the amount of the purchase price the buyer can offer the seller. According to capital budgeting theory, an investment should be funded as long as its net present value NPV is greater than or equal to zero. Applying the same concept to an acquisition, the buyer should be able to finance a purchase price (P_{TPP}) equal to the present value of the target company as an independent entity (PV_I) plus synergy (PV_S) created by combining the acquiring and target companies discounted at the acquirer's cost of capital.

$$NPV = PV_I + PV_S - P_{TPP} \geq 0$$

The financing plan is appended to the acquirer's business and acquisition plan and used to obtain financing for the transaction. No matter what size the transaction, lenders and investors will want to see a coherent analysis explaining why the proposed transaction is a good investment opportunity for them. For large transactions, the financing plan is often taken on the road, as part of a glitzy, multimedia presentation, to visit a number of different lenders or potential investors. No matter whom the intended audience, the financing plan is largely used as a marketing or sales document to negotiate the best possible terms for financing the proposed transaction.

Obtaining Bridge or Interim Financing

For an all-cash transaction, the buyer will go to the traditional sources of financing. These include banks, insurance companies, investment bankers and underwriters, venture capitalists and leveraged buyout funds, and the seller. Banks are commonly used to provide temporary or *bridge* financing to pay all or a portion of the purchase price and meet possible working capital requirements until permanent financing is found. Bank lending is normally asset based, for which the collateral may consist of such tangible assets as accounts receivable, inventory, land, or fixed equipment.

Buyers usually seek more long-term sources of financing to replace bank debt because of the onerous covenants that restrict how the buyer may operate the combined firms. Covenants are promises made by the borrower that certain acts will be performed and others will be avoided. Covenants are designed to protect the lender's interests and cover such matters as working capital, debt-to-equity ratios, and corporate dividend policies.

The nominal or stated rate on bank loans is generally significantly less than unsecured bond financing, reflecting differences in maturity and the underlying collateral. However, the actual cost of the bank loan is much higher than the stated rate, because banks usually require the borrower to maintain large, low-yielding "compensating balances" with the bank. In addition, banks frequently demand warrants or rights to buy equity in the combined companies at some specified future date and price. When these warrants are exercised, there may be significant erosion of shareholder value, as new shares are issued at a price less than the prevailing share price.

Case 5-4 describes how acquiring companies arrange interim financing to meet immediate cash requirements at closing. These cash requirements consist of the need to pay target company shareholders the cash portion of the total consideration as well as the payment of cash for fractional shares. For large transactions, banking syndicates will include many banks to spread the risk of the transaction. These bank loans are usually short-term in nature and are either "rolled over" at the prevailing rate of interest or refinanced using long-term debt.

CASE 5-4. VODAFONE FINANCES ACQUISITION OF AIRTOUCH

In April, 1999, Vodafone Group Plc reached an agreement with 11 banks to underwrite and arrange the "facility" for financing the merger with Air-Touch Communications, Inc. Under the terms of the transaction, AirTouch common shareholders will receive five Vodafone AirTouch ADSs (equivalent to five Vodafone AirTouch ordinary shares) plus $9 in cash. The transaction closed in July 1999 and was valued at $55 billion.

The banking syndicate consisted of Bank of America, Barclay's, Banque Nationale de Paris, Citibank, Deutsche Bank, Goldman Sachs, HSBC, ING Barings, National Australia Bank, NatWest, and WestLB. The total facility was set at between $10 and $13 billion. The actual amount required could not be determined until the closing, when a more precise estimate of cash requirements could be determined.

The term of the major part of the facility is for 364 days, with the remaining balance multiyear. The initial borrowing rate is to be 60–70 basis points above the London Interbank Overnight Rate (LIBOR). The actual spread will vary with the tranche (term) selected, utilization level (amount borrowed), and guarantee structure (the credit-worthiness of those banks issuing letters of credit).

Following completion of the merger, a substantial part of the facility will be refinanced in the bond and commercial paper markets through the banks, which have arranged the facility. The long-term financing consisted of a medium-term Euro note and U.S. commercial paper. These programs were not activated until after the merger was completed.

Source: Bloomberg.com, 1999b.

Mezzanine Financing

Such financing refers to capital that in liquidation has a priority between senior debt and common stock. While mezzanine financing may take the form of redeemable preferred stock, it is generally subordinated debt, with warrants convertible into common stock. It is generally unsecured, with a fixed coupon rate, and a maturity of 5–10 years.

Mezzanine investors usually look for firms with revenues in excess of $10 million. Such investors focus on a broad spectrum of businesses rather than on a single industry such as high-tech firms. Specialty retailing, broadcasting, communications, environmental services, distributors, and consumer or business service industries have tended to be more attractive to mezzanine investors (Remey: 1993).

Permanent Financing

"Permanent" financing usually consists of long-term unsecured debt. Such debt is generally not rated by the major credit-rating agencies, such as Standard & Poor's and Moody's services, and may be referred to as junk bond financing. Such financing may be obtained by investment bankers or underwriters raising funds by a "private placement" of all or a portion of the bond issue with investors willing to hold the bonds for long periods of time. These investors include insurance companies and pension funds, which are interested in matching their investment income stream with their obligations to policyholders and pensioners. Such debt is usually subordinate to bank debt if the firm is forced into bankruptcy. Junk bonds may also be sold to mutual funds or directly to the public. If a significant percentage of the debt is to be sold to the public, raising permanent financing will require many months in order to satisfy SEC requirements for full disclosure of risks associated with the bond issue.

Venture Capital Firms

Venture capitalists (VCs) are also a significant source of funds for financing both start-ups and acquisitions. VC firms identify and screen opportunities, transact and close deals, monitor and add value, and raise additional capital. General partners receive a 2–3% fee and 15–25% of capital gains from initial public offerings (IPO) and mergers. The remaining 75–85% of capital gains plus a return of principal goes back to investors in the VC fund (Bygrave and Timmons: 1992). Only 2–4% of the firms contacting VC firms actually receives funding (Vachon: 1993; Wetzel: 1984).

VCs are sometimes willing to lend when the more traditional sources, such as banks, insurance companies, and pension funds, are not. VCs usually demand a large equity position in the firm for a relatively low price per share. Consequently, the firm's owners are ceding a significant percentage of their ownership position for what could appear to be very high-cost financing in the future if the firm is successful in ultimately enhancing its market value. VC firms generally require a 60–70% return on their investments.

Seller Financing

Seller financing represents a highly important source of financing for buyers. Seller financing is a euphemism for the seller's willingness to defer receiving a portion of the purchase price until some future date. The advantages to the buyer include a lower overall risk of the transaction because of the need to provide less capital at the time of closing and the shifting of operational risk to the seller if the buyer ultimately defaults on the loan to the seller.

The "Road Show"

To arrange both bridge and permanent financing, the buyer will develop elaborate presentations to take on a "road show" to convince potential lenders of the attractiveness of the debt. It is referred to as a "road show" for good reason, as immaculately dressed borrowers passionately display confidence in their business plan through carefully rehearsed and choreographed presentations in stuffy conference rooms throughout the country. It represents an opportunity for potential lenders to see management and to ask the "tough questions." If the "road show" is successful, at least several lenders will compete for all or a portion of the bond issue. Lender competition will not only mean lower stated rates on the loans but less onerous loan covenants.

As a cautionary note, taking management on the road to convince lenders that they should lend money is a very exhausting exercise and represents a major distraction from day-to-day operations. It is common for the short-term performance of the target and the buyer companies to suffer as they spend more and more of their time dealing with due diligence and financing activities. Highly acquisitive companies run the risk of exhausting operating management through frequent presentations to external groups.

Technology may be making the "road show" more palatable. Network Appliances Inc., seeking to raise $140 million in a stock offering in early 1999, shifted its efforts from the road to the Internet. Its investment banker, Lehman Brothers, set up a "virtual road show." Investors, who had been issued passwords by Lehman, accessed videotaped presentations by Network's management via the Internet. Investors could later telephone the firm with specific questions. Increasingly, investment bankers are routinely scheduling Internet presentations in lieu of, or to augment, personal visits to investors.

Prospectuses are now available on such Internet sites as theiposite.com, IPO maven.com, and IPO.com. In 1998, Web-based companies such as NetRoadshow created 132 productions or "virtual road shows" for clients. In 1999, that figure doubled. Now owned by Yahoo, NetRoadshow's growth could accelerate.

Selecting Alternative Financial Structures

The various methods of financing the transaction include cash, cash and notes, stock, and all debt. The latter option usually requires the presence of substantial amounts of unencumbered assets and a consistently strong operating cash flow. In practice, the total consideration paid to the seller is often financed using some combination of these alternative sources of funds. Table 5-1 summarizes the various types and sources of financing.

Computer models, which simulate the financial impact of various financial structures on the combined firms, are excellent tools for determining the appropriate capital structure. Although leverage raises the potential rate of return to equity investors, it also adds to risk. Increasing credit obligations to lenders implies increasing fixed interest expense, which raises the point at which the firm's revenue covers its costs. An unanticipated downturn in the economy or aggressive pricing actions by competitors can erode cash flow and the firm's ability to meet its interest expense. This could ultimately lead to bankruptcy. This risk can be measured by creating various scenarios each representing a different capital structure and determining the impact of lower than expected sales growth.

Financing Contingencies

Most well-written agreements of purchase and sale contain a financing contingency. The buyer is not subject to the terms of the contract if the buyer cannot obtain adequate funding to complete the transaction. Shrewd sellers often negotiate a break-up clause requiring the buyer to pay the seller an amount at least equal to the seller's cost associated with the ill-fated transaction. These *break-up fees* are often so large as to discourage the buyer from breaking off the engagement except under the most exceptional circumstances.

TABLE 5-1.   Financing Mergers and Acquisitions

	Debt	Equity
Alternative types		
Asset-based lending	Tangible assets	
	Accounts receivable	
	Revolving credit lines	
	Term loans	
	Sale/Lease-back	
Cash flow-based lending	Projected cash flow	
Seller financing	Deferred payments	Common stock
	Earn-outs	Preferred stock
	Installment sales	
Public offering and	Senior	Common stock
private placements	Convertible	Preferred stock
	Subordinated	
Alternative sources	Commercial banks	Buyout funds
	Insurance companies	Venture capital
	Pension funds	Strategic investors
	Investment/merchant banks	Individual investors ("Angels")

In 2000, Pfizer was successful in acquiring Warner Lambert, which had previously agreed to merge with American Home Products. To avoid a lawsuit, Pfizer agreed to pay American Home Products the $2 billion break-up fee it had negotiated as part of its earlier agreement with Warner Lambert. Apparently, Pfizer simply viewed the break-up fee as part of the purchase price required to buy Warner Lambert.

PHASE 7: DEVELOPING THE INTEGRATION PLAN

The euphoria that surrounds the successful completion of a transaction erodes quickly once the challenges of making the combined firms perform in line with the predictions laid out in the business and acquisition plans become apparent. It is surprising how little effort goes into planning for these inevitable challenges before the agreement of purchase and sale is signed. Once the documents are signed the buyer has lost most, if not all, leverage over the seller.

EARNING TRUST

Decisions made prior to closing affect postclosing integration activity. Benefits packages, employment contracts, and bonuses to retain key employees (i.e., retention bonuses) are normally negotiated before closing. Contractual covenants and conditions also impact integration. Earn-outs, payments to the seller based on future performance, and deferred purchase price mechanisms, involving the placement of some portion of the purchase price in escrow until certain contractual conditions have been realized, can limit the buyer's ability to effectively integrate the target into the acquirer's operations. Successfully integrating firms requires getting employees in both firms to work toward achieving common objectives. This comes about through building credibility and trust, not through superficial slogans, pep talks, and empty promises. Trust comes from people cooperating and experiencing mutual success.

EARN-OUTS

Earn-outs are generally very poor ways to create trust and often represent major impediments to the integration process. The two firms are generally kept physically separate. Accounting and management reporting systems are not merged immediately, data centers remain separate, and sales forces remain largely independent. The buyer's concern is that efforts to integrate the firms as soon as possible after closing will make tracking the financial progress of the acquired company toward meeting its earn-out goals difficult. Moreover, the merging of facilities and sales forces could create a highly contentious situation once the earn-out period has elapsed if the acquired company did not meet the earn-out goals.

Employees covered by the earn-out could plead in court that they were prevented from doing so by not being allowed by the buyer to implement the business plan on which the earn-out was based. The hazards of earn-outs are illustrated in Case Study 5-5.

CASE STUDY 5-5. THE DOWNSIDE OF EARN-OUTS

In the mid-1980s, a well-known aerospace conglomerate acquired a high-growth systems integration company by paying a huge multiple of earnings. The purchase price could ultimately become much larger if certain earn-out objectives were achieved during the 4 years following closing. However, the buyer's business plan assumed close cooperation between the two firms, despite holding the system integrator as a wholly owned but largely autonomous subsidiary. The dramatic differences in the cultures of the two firms constituted a major impediment to building trust and achieving the cooperation necessary to make the acquisition successful. Years of squabbling over policies and practices tended to delay the development and implementation of new systems. The absence of new systems made it difficult to gain market share.

Moreover, because the earn-out objectives were partially defined in terms of revenue growth, many of the new customer contracts added substantial amounts of revenue but could not be completed profitably under the terms of these contracts. The buyer was slow to introduce new management into its wholly owned subsidiary for fear of violating the earn-out agreement. Finally, market conditions changed, and what had been the acquired company's unique set of skills became commonplace. The aerospace company ultimately wrote off most of the purchase price and merged the remaining assets of the acquired company into one of its other product lines after the earn-out agreement had expired.

CHOOSING THE INTEGRATION MANAGER

Great care should be taken prior to closing in the selection of the integration manager. This person should have excellent interpersonal and project management skills. During the integration phase, the skills of being able to get along with others are frequently more important than one's professional and technical skills. The buyer must determine what is critical for continuation of the acquired company's success during the first 12–24 months following closing. Critical activities include the identification of key managers, vendors, and customers and what is needed to retain these valued assets.

The preclosing integration planning activity should also include the determination of operating norms or standards required for continued operation of the businesses. These include executive compensation, labor contracts, billing procedures, product delivery times, and quality metrics. Finally, a communication plan must be designed for all stakeholders to be implemented immediately following closing (Porter and Wood: 1998). Preclosing planning and postclosing integration are discussed in considerable detail in Chapter 6 (this volume).

PHASE 8: CLOSING

This phase of the acquisition process consists of obtaining all necessary shareholder, regulatory, and third party consents (e.g., customer and vendor contracts). Like all other phases, this activity requires significant upfront planning if it is to go smoothly. Unfortunately, this is frequently impractical in view of all the activities that are underway during the acquisition process. All such activities tend to converge on the closing date.

Even when it appears that both parties have reached agreement on the major issues, what were previously minor issues seem to resurface on a grander, more complex scale. Sometimes this happens because the parties did not realize the significance of an item until the last minute; other times, one party intentionally takes a hard line on an issue as the closing date approaches in the hope of gaining a negotiating advantage. This strategy is frequently ill advised. The resulting confrontation and dissolution of trust that had been built up during the acquisition process may ultimately force one party to walk away from the transaction. This strategy amounts to playing Russian Roulette and is ethically questionable.

ASSIGNING CUSTOMER AND VENDOR CONTRACTS

Aside from errors of omission or last-minute changes in negotiating strategy, there are many daunting logistical challenges that must be overcome before closing can take place. In a purchase of assets, many customer and vendor contracts cannot be assigned to the buyer without receiving written approval from the other parties. Although this may be a largely mechanical process, both vendors and customers may view this as an opportunity to attempt to negotiate more favorable terms. Licenses must also receive approval from the licensor, and they can also be a major impediment to a timely closing if not properly planned for well in advance. In one instance, a major software vendor demanded a substantial increase in royalty payments before they would transfer the license to the buyer. The vendor knew that the software was critical for the ongoing operation of the business' data center. The exorbitant increase in the fee had a significant adverse impact on the economics of the transaction from the buyer's viewpoint and almost caused the deal to collapse.

A number of transitional issues must also be addressed prior to closing. These may include continued payroll processing support by the seller on behalf of the buyer until the buyer is able to assume this function and the return of checks received by the seller from customers continuing to send checks to the seller's checking accounts after closing. Similarly, the buyer will want to be reimbursed by the seller for payments made by the buyer to vendors for materials supplied or services provided before closing but not paid until after closing.

GAINING THE NECESSARY APPROVALS

The buyer's legal counsel labors endlessly to ensure that the transaction is in full compliance with securities laws, antitrust laws, and state corporation laws. Significant planning before closing is again crucial to minimizing roadblocks that a target company may place before the buyer. As noted in Chapter 3 (this volume), target companies can be highly skilled at using prevailing laws as antitakeover measures.

Great care must be exercised to ensure that all of the filings required by law have been made with the Federal Trade Commission (FTC) and the Department of Justice (DoJ). Noncompliance can delay or prevent a merger or acquisition (see Chapter 2, this volume). Finally, many transactions require approval by the shareholders of both the acquiring and target companies before ownership can be legally transferred.

COMPLETING THE DEFINITIVE AGREEMENT

The cornerstone of the closing documents is the definitive agreement of purchase and sale, which indicates all of the rights and obligations of the parties both before and after closing. The length of the definitive agreement depends upon the complexity of the transaction. The major segments of an asset purchase agreement are outlined below (Sherman: 1998).

Purpose of Acquisition

In an asset sale, this section of the agreement specifies the specific assets or the shares to be acquired. It also stipulates the assets to be excluded from the transaction.

Price

The purchase price or total consideration may be fixed at the time of closing, subject to future adjustment, or be contingent on future performance. The purchase price may be initially fixed based on the seller's representations of the firm's total assets, total book value, tangible book value, or some other measure of value. However, the agreed-upon price may be adjusted following a postclosing audit. An independent auditing firm typically does such audits. In asset transactions, cash on the target's balance sheet is frequently excluded from the transaction; the price paid for noncurrent assets such as plant and intangible assets will be fixed, but the price for current assets will depend on their levels at closing. Contingent purchase prices or "earn-outs" may be employed if the seller does not have any current earnings or if the seller represents the accuracy of its forecasted cash flows.

Allocation of Price

Both parties should agree on how the purchase price should be allocated to the various assets acquired in an asset transaction. This eliminates the chance that the parties involved will take different positions for tax purposes. The buyer typically has an incentive to allocate as much of the purchase price to depreciable assets such as fixed assets, customer lists, and noncompete agreements, which will shelter future income. In contrast, the seller may wish not to allocate any portion of the purchase price to noncompete agreements, which would constitute taxable income. Despite agreement between the parties, the Internal Revenue Service may challenge any positions taken.

Payment Mechanism

Payment may be made at closing by wire transfer or cashier's check. The buyer may defer the payment of a portion of the purchase price by issuing a promissory note to the seller. The buyer and seller may also agree to put the unpaid portion of the purchase price in escrow. This will facilitate the settlement of claims that might be made in the future.

Assumption of Liabilities

The assets to be accepted by the buyer are identified in considerable detail in an asset deal. The seller retains those liabilities not assumed by the buyer. In instances such as environmental liabilities, the courts may go after the buyer and seller. In a purchase of shares transaction or a merger, the buyer assumes all known and unknown liabilities.

Representations and Warranties

"Reps and warranties" are intended to provide for full disclosure of all information germane to the transaction. They typically cover the areas of greatest concern to both parties.

Covenants

Covenants cover the obligations of both parties between the signing of the definitive agreement and closing. A prime example is the requirement that the seller continues to conduct business in the usual and customary manner. The seller will often be required to seek approval for all expenditures that may be considered out of the ordinary.

Conditions for Closing

The transaction cannot be closed until certain preconditions set forth in the definitive agreement have been met. Common preconditions include the presumption of the continued accuracy of the seller's representations and warranties and the extent to which the seller is living up to their obligations under the covenants. Other examples include the completion of legal opinions, the execution of other agreements such as promissory notes, and the absence of any "material adverse change" in the target company.

Indemnification

The definitive agreement will require the seller to indemnify or absolve the buyer of liability in the event of misrepresentations or breaches of warranties or covenants. Similarly, the buyer usually agrees to indemnify the seller. Both parties generally want to limit the survival period of indemnity clauses. At least 1 full year of operation and a full audit is necessary to identify claims. Some claims such as environmental claims extend beyond the survival period of the indemnity clause. Usually, neither party can submit claims to the other until some minimum threshold has been exceeded.

Merger Agreements

A merger is structurally simpler than an asset agreement, because it does not require the stipulation of assets being transferred to the buyer and liabilities assumed by the buyer. Although it may take less time to negotiate and draft than an asset agreement, it may take longer to complete. A merger with a public company requires approval of the target companies' shareholders and must comply with prevailing securities laws. Public shareholder approval must be obtained through proxy solicitation. As prescribed by law, such proxies contain information such as financial data on the merger partner as well as the partner's intent in proposing the merger (see Chapter 2, this volume).

OTHER CLOSING DOCUMENTS

In addition to resolving the issues outlined above, closing is complicated by the number and complexity of the documents required to complete the transaction. In addition to the agreement of purchase and sale, the more important documents could include the following:

a. Patents, licenses, royalty agreements, trade names, and trademarks
b. Labor and employment agreements
c. Leases
d. Mortgages, loan agreements, and lines of credit
e. Stock and bond commitments and details
f. Supplier and customer contracts
g. Distributor and sales representative agreements
h. Stock option and employee incentive programs
i. Health and social benefit plans (must be in place at closing to eliminate lapsed coverage)
j. Complete description of all foreign patents, facilities, and investments
k. Intermediary fee arrangements
l. Insurance policies, coverage, and claims pending

m. Litigation pending for and against each party

n. Environmental compliance issues resolved or on track to be resolved

o. Seller's corporate minutes of the board of directors and any other significant committee information

p. Articles of incorporation, bylaws, stock certificates, and corporate seals

IS CLOSING EVER SIMPLE?

The closing experience runs the gamut from mind-numbing routine to bombastic confrontation. How smoothly the process goes depends upon its overall complexity and the level of trust among the parties involved. The size of the transaction is not a good indicator of complexity. Small transactions in terms of revenue or purchase price can be horrifically complicated where multiple parties are involved or multiple levels of regulatory approval are required.

For small, uncomplicated transactions, the closing can consist of a simple faxing back and forth of documents between the buyer and seller to ensure that there is complete agreement on the closing documents. Signature pages are then signed by one party and sent via overnight mail to the other party for their signature. However, the situations are not always that mechanical. In one instance, with both parties seated around a conference room table reviewing the final closing documents, the buyer began to raise issues that were either new or thought to have been resolved much earlier in the process. The seller was able to get the closing back on track only by threatening to walk away from the transaction. Case Study 5-6 illustrates the circus-like atmosphere that characterizes some closings.

CASE STUDY 5-6. SLEEPLESS IN PHILADELPHIA

Closings can also take on a somewhat surreal atmosphere. In one transaction valued at $20 million, the buyer intended to finance the transaction with $10 million in secured bank loans, a $5 million loan from the seller, and $5 million in equity. However, the equity was to be provided by wealthy individual investors in individual amounts of $100,000. The closing took place in Philadelphia around a long conference room table in the law offices of the firm hired by the buyer, with lawyers and business people representing the buyer, the seller, and the several banks reviewing the final documents. Throughout the day and late into the evening, the wealthy investors (some in chauffeur-driven limousines) and their attorneys would stop by to provide cashiers' checks, mostly in $100,000 amounts, and to sign the appropriate legal documents. The sheer number of people involved created an almost circus-like environment. The next morning a briefcase full of cashiers' checks was taken to the local bank.

PHASE 9: IMPLEMENTING
POSTCLOSING INTEGRATION

The postclosing integration activity is widely viewed as among the most important phase of the acquisition process. Postclosing integration will be discussed in considerable detail in Chapter 6 (this volume). What follows is a discussion of those activities required immediately following closing. Such activities fall into four categories: (1) implementation of a communication plan; (2) retaining key managers; (3) identifying immediate operating cash flow requirements; and (4) employing the best practices of both companies.

COMMUNICATION PLANS

Implementing a communication plan immediately following closing is crucial for purposes of retaining employees of the acquired firm and maintaining morale and productivity. The plan should address employee, customer, and vendor concerns. Employees need to understand how their compensation, including benefits, might change under new ownership. Employees may find a loss of specific benefits palatable if they are perceived as offset by improvements in other benefits or working conditions. Customers will want reassurance that there will not be any deterioration in product or service quality or delivery time during the transition from old to new ownership. Vendors will also be very interested in understanding how the change in ownership will affect their sales to the new firm.

Whenever possible, communication is best done on a face-to-face basis. Senior officers of the acquiring company can be sent to address employee groups, if possible on site. Senior officers should also contact key customers preferably in person or at least by telephone to provide the needed reassurances. Meeting these reasonable requests for information from employees, customers, and vendors immediately following closing with complete candor will contribute greatly to the sense of trust among stakeholders that is necessary for the ultimate success of the acquisition.

EMPLOYEE RETENTION

Retaining middle-level managers should also be a top priority during this phase of the acquisition process. Frequently, senior managers of the target company that the buyer chooses to retain are asked to sign employment agreements as a condition of closing. Without these signed agreements, the buyer would not have completed the transaction. Although senior managers provide overall direction for the firm, middle-level managers execute the day-to-day operations of the firm. Plans should be in place to minimize the loss of such people, many of whom are likely to be receiving offers of employment from competitors once the transaction has been publicly announced. Bonuses, stock options, and enhanced sales commission schedules are commonly put in place to keep such managers.

SATISFYING CASH FLOW REQUIREMENTS

Invariably, operating cash flow requirements are higher than expected, despite having completed a thorough due diligence prior to closing. Conversations with middle-level managers following closing will reveal areas in which maintenance expenditures have been deferred. Customer disputes may result in invoices going unpaid for long periods of time. Receivables previously thought to be collectable may have to be written off. Production may be disrupted as employees of the acquired firm find it difficult to adapt to new practices introduced by the acquiring company's management or if inventory levels are inadequate to maintain desired customer delivery times. More customers than had been anticipated are lost to competitors, which use the change in ownership as an opportunity to woo them away with various types of incentives.

EMPLOYING BEST PRACTICES

An important motivation for takeovers is to realize specific operating synergies, which result in improved operating efficiency, product quality, customer service, and on-time delivery. Both parties in a transaction are likely to excel in different areas. An excellent way for the combined companies to take advantage of the strengths of both companies is to employ the "best practices" of both. However, in some areas, neither company may be employing what its customers believe to be the best practices in the industry. In these circumstances, management should look beyond its own operations to accept the practices of other companies that customers find preferable to what either company had been doing prior to the takeover.

Integrating the new practices throughout the organization can be accomplished by transferring those most familiar with the practice elsewhere in the combined companies, using teams consisting of employees from both companies, and cross-training workers in both organizations. This will result in employees from the acquiring firm and from the target working together and building trust and confidence in each other. The new practices can be widely communicated by developing quantitative performance measures, which are used to monitor the implementation of the new practices. These performance measures should consist of factors that are important to customers. Depending upon the type of business, they could include the number of billing errors per billing cycle, on-time delivery performance, and the length of time a customer must wait on hold for a customer service representative.

CULTURAL ISSUES

Corporate cultures reflect the set of beliefs and behaviors of the management and employees of a corporation. In some instances, these belief systems and desired behaviors are codified in the firm's mission statement. Beliefs and desired behaviors may include acting with integrity, being nimble with respect to decision making, a strong customer service orientation, and understanding customer needs. Many behaviors may be implicit. Some corporations are very paternalistic and others very "bottom-line" oriented. Some empower employees, whereas others believe in highly centralized control. Some promote problem solving by applying employee teams; others promote individual performance.

Inevitably different corporate cultures will impede postacquisition integration efforts. The key to success is to be sensitive to these differences and to take the time to explain to all employees of the new firm what is expected and why these beliefs and behaviors are desired in the new company. Once again, communication of desired beliefs and consistent practice of these beliefs from senior management on down the organization chart is necessary to overcome the stickiest of challenges.

PHASE 10: CONDUCTING POSTCLOSING EVALUATION

The primary reasons for conducting a postclosing evaluation of all acquisitions are to determine if the acquisition is meeting expectations, to determine corrective actions if necessary, and to identify what was done well and what should be done better in future acquisitions.

DON'T CHANGE PERFORMANCE BENCHMARKS

Once the acquisition appears to be operating normally, evaluate the actual performance to the performance projected in the acquisition plan. This is an important step in measuring success. Success should be defined in terms of actual performance to planned performance. All too often, management simply ignores the performance targets stipulated in the acquisition plan and accepts less than plan performance in order to justify the acquisition. In some instances, this may be appropriate if circumstances beyond the firm's control cause a change in the operating environment. Examples include a recession, which slows the growth in revenue, or changing regulations, which preclude the introduction of a new product.

ASK THE DIFFICULT QUESTIONS

An introspective analysis of an acquisition should address as objectively as possible a series of targeted questions. The types of questions asked should vary depending upon the elapsed time since closing. After 6 months, what has the buyer learned about the business? Were the original valuation assumptions reasonable? If not, what did the buyer not understand about the target company and why? What did the buyer do well? What should have been done differently? What can be done to ensure that the same mistakes are not made in future acquisitions? After 12 months, is the business meeting expectations? If not, what can be done to put the business back on track? Is the cost of fixing the business offset by expected returns? Are the right people in place to manage the business for the long-term? After 24 months, does the acquired business still appear attractive? If not, should it be divested? If yes, when and to whom?

LEARN FROM MISTAKES

While sometimes embarrassing, it always pays to take the time to identify lessons learned from each transaction. This is often a neglected exercise and results in firms repeating the same mistakes. This occurs even in the most highly acquisitive firms, since those involved in the acquisition process may change from one acquisition to another. Lessons learned in an acquisition completed by the management of one of the firm's product lines may not be readily communicated to those about to undertake acquisitions in other parts of the company. Highly acquisitive companies can benefit greatly by dedicating certain legal, human resource, marketing, financial, and business development resources to support acquisitions made throughout the company. In doing so, the company minimizes the chance that the same mistakes will be made twice.

THINGS TO REMEMBER

The first two phases of the acquisition process, the business plan and the acquisition plan, define the overall strategic direction for the business, key objectives, and available resources and tactics for completing an acquisition. The next phase consists of the search for appropriate acquisition candidates. To initiate this phase, selection criteria need to be developed. At this stage, selection criteria should be relatively few in number and, whenever possible, should be quantified. At a minimum, criteria should include the industry and size (e.g., maximum price or revenue). The screening phase is a refinement of the search phase and entails applying more criteria to reduce the list of candidates surfaced during search process. Key criteria in this phase may include profitability, market segment, product line, degree of leverage, and market share.

How the potential acquirer initiates first contact depends on the size of the target and the availability of intermediaries with highly placed contacts within the target firm. If the target is interested in proceeding, a letter of intent formally defining the reasons for the agreement, responsibilities of the two parties while the agreement is in force, and the expiration date is negotiated. Confidentiality agreements covering both parties should also be negotiated. If the target rebuffs overtures from the suitor, a tender offer may ensue to circumvent management and go straight to the target's shareholders.

The negotiation phase is an interactive, iterative process with many activities conducted concurrently. Such activities include refining valuation, deal structuring, conducting due diligence, and developing a financing plan. The actual amount and composition of the purchase price is determined during this phase.

The total purchase price or enterprise value of the target company consists of the total consideration (cash, stock, debt, or some combination) plus assumed debt currently on the target's books. The net purchase price includes the total purchase price plus other assumed liabilities that were not completely taken into account in estimating the economic value of the target's future cash flows less the proceeds from the sale of discretionary assets.

There is no substitute for performing a complete due diligence on the target company. Many activities underway during the negotiation phase are affected by the findings of due diligence. Refining valuation based on new information uncovered during due diligence affects the determination of the total consideration to be paid to the seller. New information will also impact how risks and liabilities are shared between the buyer and seller during the deal-structuring process. The financing plan may be affected by the discovery during due diligence of assets that can be sold to pay off debt accumulated to finance the transaction. Due diligence is not limited to the buyer. The seller should perform due diligence on the buyer to ensure that it will be able to finance the purchase price. Moreover, the seller should also perform due diligence on its own operations to ensure that its representations and warranties in the definitive agreement are accurate.

Integration planning is a highly important aspect of the acquisition process that must be done before closing. Once closing occurs, the acquiring company loses much of the leverage it may have had before the transaction was completed. Without adequate planning, integration is unlikely to provide the synergies anticipated by, at the cost included in, and on the timetable provided in the acquisition plan. Successful integration ultimately arises from building trust among all parties involved, which comes from people working cooperatively and experiencing mutual success.

The closing phase goes well beyond organizing, finalizing, and signing all the necessary legal documents. It includes wading through the logistical quagmire of getting all the necessary third-party consents and regulatory and shareholder approvals. The postclosing integration phase consists of effective communication to all stakeholders, retaining key employees, and identifying and resolving immediate cash flow needs. The postclosing evaluation phase is the most commonly overlooked phase. Although many acquiring companies do closely monitor the performance of the acquisition to plan, many stop short of formally questioning how effective they were in managing the acquisition process. Such lessons can sometimes be embarrassing but they are always instructive. Unfortunately, without identifying and communicating lessons learned to those involved in making future acquisitions, we are likely to relive our past mistakes.

CHAPTER DISCUSSION QUESTIONS

5-1.   What resources are commonly used to conduct a search for potential acquisition targets?

5-2.   Identify at least three criteria that might be used to select a manufacturing firm as a potential acquisition candidate. A financial services firm? A high technology firm?

5-3.   Identify alternative ways to make "first contact" with a potential acquisition target. Why is confidentiality important? Under what circumstances might a potential acquirer make its intentions public?

5-4.   What are the advantages and disadvantages of a letter of intent?

5-5.   How do the various activities that are undertaken concurrently as part of the negotiation phase affect the determination of the purchase price?

5-6.   What are the differences between total consideration, total purchase price/enterprise value, and net purchase price? How are these different concepts used?

5-7.   What is the purpose of the buyer and seller performing due diligence?

5-8.   What is the purpose of a financing plan?

5-9.   Why is preclosing integration planning important?

5-10. What are the key activities that comprise a typical closing?

CHAPTER BUSINESS CASE

CASE STUDY 5-7. MATTEL ACQUIRES THE LEARNING COMPANY

Background

Mattel, Inc., is the world's largest designer, manufacturer, and marketer of a broad variety of children's products selling directly to retailers and to consumers. Most people recognize Mattel as the maker of the famous Barbie Doll, the best-selling fashion doll in the world, generating sales of $1.7 billion annually. The company also manufactures a variety of other well-known toys and owns the primary toy license for the most popular kids educational program "Sesame Street." In 1988, Mattel revived its previous association with The Walt Disney Company and signed a multiyear deal with them for the worldwide toy rights for all of Disney's television and film properties. Under this agreement, Mattel has the right to Disney's characters including the following: Mickey and Minnie Mouse, Goofy, Donald Duck, and Winnie the Pooh. Mattel also has the rights to film characters from such popular movies as The Lion King, Beauty and the Beast, A Bug's Life, Alladin, and Mulan.

Business Plan

Mission Statement and Strategy

Mattel's mission is to maintain its position in the toy market as the largest and most profitable family products marketer and manufacturer in the world. Mattel will continue to create new products and innovate in their existing toy lines to satisfy the constant changes of the family-products market. Its business strategy is to diversify Mattel beyond the market for traditional toys at a time when the toy industry is rapidly changing. This will be achieved by pursuing the high-growth and highly profitable children's technology market, while continuing to enhance Mattel's popular toys in order to gain both market share and increase earnings in the toy market.

Mattel believes that its current software division, Mattel Interactive, lacks the technical expertise and resources to penetrate the software market as quickly as Mattel desires. Consequently, Mattel seeks to acquire a software business that will be able to manufacture and market children's software that Mattel will distribute through its existing channels and through Mattel's web site (Mattel.com). The software division will allow Mattel to combine their strong brand names with the trend toward software-based toys. For example, the new division will develop Barbie, Hot Wheels, and Sesame Street software for the children's market.

Defining the Marketplace

The toy market is a major segment within the leisure time industry. Included in this segment are many diverse companies, ranging from amusement parks to yacht manufacturers. Mattel is one of the largest manufacturers within the toy segment of the leisure time industry. Other leading toy companies are Hasbro, Nintendo, and Lego. Annual toy industry sales in recent years have exceeded $21 billion. Approximately one-half of all sales are made in the fourth quarter, reflecting the Christmas holiday.

Customers   Mattel's major customers are the large retail and e-commerce stores that distribute their products. These retailers and e-commerce stores include Toys "R" Us Inc., Wal-Mart Stores Inc., Kmart Corp., Target, Consolidated Stores Corp., E-toys, ToyTime.com, Toysmart.com, and Toystore.com. The retailers are Mattel's direct customers; however, the ultimate buyers are the parents, grandparents, and children who purchase the toys from these retailers.

Competitors   The two largest toy manufacturers are Mattel and Hasbro, which together account for almost one-half of industry sales. In the past few years, Hasbro has acquired several companies whose primary products include electronic or interactive toys and games. On December 8, 1999, Hasbro announced a major restructuring in which it will cut 2,200 jobs, close two plants, and shift its focus to software and other electronic toys. Traditional games, such as Monopoly, will be converted into software. The distinction between customers and competitors is becoming increasingly blurred. Internet retailer, eToys, which purchases many of its toys from Mattel, captured more than 50% of the $50 million online toy market in 1999 and competes directly with Mattel.com.

Potential Entrants   Potential entrants face substantial barriers to entry in the toy business. Current competitors, such as Mattel and Hasbro, have already secured distribution channels for their products based on long-standing relationships with key customers such as Wal-Mart Stores and Toys "R" US Inc. It would be costly for new entrants to replicate these relationships. Moreover, brand recognition of such toys as Barbie, Nintendo, and Legos makes it difficult for new entrants to penetrate certain product segments within the toy market. Proprietary knowledge and patent protection provide additional barriers to entering these product lines. The large toy makers have licensing agreements that grant them the right to market toys based on the products of the major entertainment companies. For example, Mattel's licensing agreement with Disney guarantees access to a continuous flow of new product lines based on Disney's animated feature films and television programs.

Product Substitutes   One of the major substitutes for traditional toys such as dolls and cars are video games and computer software. In 1997, video games saw an increase of 45% in dollar sales and 62% in unit sales. Consumer demand continued strong for both the Nintendo 64 and Sony Playstation video game systems. Even traditional toy product lines such as Mattel's famous Barbie doll have taken on electronic elements. CD-ROM titles for Barbie have been released that allow children to style Barbie's hair on screen. Other product substitutes include virtually all kinds of entertainment including books, athletic wear, tapes, and TV. However, these entertainment products are less of a concern for toy companies than the Internet or electronic games because they are not direct substitutes for traditional toys.

Suppliers   Today an estimated 80% of toy production is manufactured abroad. Both Mattel and Hasbro own factories in the Far East and Mexico to take advantage of low labor costs. Parts, such as software and microchips, are often outsourced to nonMattel manufacturing plants in other countries and then imported for the assembly of such products as Barbie within Mattel-owned factories. Although outsourcing has resulted in labor cost savings, it has also resulted in inconsistent quality. Frequently, toys or parts imported from other countries must be reworked to comply with U.S. safety regulations.

Opportunities and Threats

Opportunities

New distribution channels: Mattel.com represents 80 separate toy and software offerings. Mattel hopes to spin this operation off as a separate company when it becomes profitable. Mattel.com lost about $70 million in 1999. The other new channel for distributing toys is directly to consumers through catalogs. The so-called direct channels offered by the Internet and catalogue sales help Mattel reduce its dependence on a few mass retailers.

Aging population: Grandparents accounted for 14% of U.S. toy purchases in

1999. The number of grandparents is expected to grow from 58 million in 1999 to 76 million in 2005.

Interactive Media: As children have increasing access to computers, the demand for interactive computer games is expected to accelerate. The "high-tech" toy market segment is growing 20% annually compared to the modest 5% growth in the traditional toy business.

International growth: In 1999, 44% of Mattel's sales came from its international operations. Mattel has already redesigned its Barbie doll for the Asian and the South American market by changing Barbie's face and clothes.

Threats

Decreasing demand for traditional toys: Children's tastes are changing. Popular items are now more likely to include athletic clothes and children's software and video games rather than more traditional items such as dolls and stuffed animals.

Distributor returns: Toys found to be unsafe or unpopular may be returned by distributors. A quality problem with the Cabbage Patch Doll could cost Mattel more than $10 million in both returns and in settling lawsuits.

Shrinking target market: Historically, the toy industry has considered their prime market to be children from birth to age 14. Today, the top toy-purchasing years for a child range from birth to age ten.

Just-in-time inventory management: Changing customer inventory practices make it difficult to accurately forecast reorders, which has resulted in lost sales as unanticipated increases in orders could not be filled from current manufacturer inventories.

Internal Assessment

Strengths

Mattel's key strengths lie in its relatively low manufacturing cost position, with 85% of its toys manufactured in low labor cost countries like China and Indonesia, and its established distribution channels. Moreover, licensing agreements with Disney enable Mattel to add popular new characters to its product lines. These factors are believed to give Mattel a significant competitive edge over many of its smaller competitors.

Weaknesses

Mattel's Barbie and Hot Wheels product lines are mature, but the company has been slow to reposition these core brands. The lack of technical expertise to create and to innovate software-based products limits Mattel's ability to exploit the shift away from traditional toys to video or interactive games. In addition, Mattel's board of directors has lost confidence in senior management because of their inability to achieve financial targets communicated to the investment community during the last 2 years.

Acquisition Plan

Objectives

Mattel's corporate strategy is to diversify Mattel beyond the mature traditional toys segment into high-growth segments. Mattel believed that it had to acquire a recognized brand identity in the children's software and entertainment segment of the toy industry, sometimes called the "edutainment" segment, to participate in the rapid shift to interactive, software-based toys that are both entertaining and educational. Mattel believed that such an acquisition would remove some of the seasonality from sales and broaden their global revenue base. Key acquisition objectives included building a global brand strategy, doubling international sales, and creating a $1 billion software business by January 2001.

Definition of the Target's Industry

The "edutainment" segment has been experiencing strong growth predominantly in the entertainment segment. Parents are seeing the importance of technology in the workforce and want to familiarize their children with the technology as early as possible. In 1998, more than 40% of households had computers and, of those households with children, 70% had educational software. One-fourth of preschool and kindergarten classrooms are equipped with two-to-four personal computers loaded with children's software programs. As the number of homes with PCs continues to increase worldwide and with the proliferation of video games, the demand for educational and entertainment software is expected to accelerate.

Tactics

Mattel was looking for an independent children's software company with a strong brand identity and over $400 million in annual sales. Mattel preferred not to acquire a business that was part of another competitor (e.g., Hasbro Interactive). Mattel's management stated that the target company must have brands that complement Mattel's business strategy and the technology to support their existing brands as well as to develop new brands for Mattel. Mattel preferred to engage in a stock-for-stock exchange in any transaction in order to maintain manageable debt levels and to ensure that it preserved the rights to all software patents and licenses. Moreover, Mattel reasoned that such a transaction would be more attractive to potential targets, as it would enable target shareholders to defer the payment of taxes.

Potential Targets

Mattel selected Goldman Sachs to undertake a target search and initiate contact. Game and edutainment development divisions are often part of software conglomerates, such as Cendant, Electronic Arts, and GT Interactive, which produce software for diverse markets including games, systems platforms, business management, home improvement, and pure educational applications. Other firms may be subsidiaries of large book, CD-ROM, or game publishers. The parent firms showed little inclination to sell these businesses at what Mattel believed were reasonable prices. Therefore, Mattel focused on five publicly traded firms: Acclaim Entertainment, Inc., Activision, Inc., Interplay Entertainment Corp, The Learning Company, Inc., and Take-Two Interactive Software. Of these, only Acclaim, Activision, and The Learning Company had their own established brands in the games and edutainment sectors and the size sufficient to meet Mattel's revenue criterion.

Acclaim Entertainment   Acclaim had annual revenue over $400 million and an expected annual growth rate of 20% during the next 5 years. Although Acclaim had a gross profit margin somewhat in excess of the industry average of 55%, it had difficulty in funding its rapid growth rate. Moreover, this company is more focused on the children's video game segment than the children's software market.

Activision, Inc.   Although it satisfied the revenue criterion, Activision's gross profit margin, 37%, was relatively unattractive. Of greater concern, they did not appear to have enough product lines or the technical expertise to launch Mattel into the software industry at a pace necessary for Mattel to reach its revenue target of $1 billion by January 2001.

The Learning Company   In 1999, The Learning Company (TLC) was the second largest consumer software company in the world, behind Microsoft. TLC was the leader in educational software with a 42% market share and in-home productivity software (i.e., home improvement software) with a 44% market share. The company has been following an aggressive expansion strategy, having completed 14 acquisitions since 1994. At 68%, TLC also had the highest gross profit margin of the target companies reviewed. TLC owns the most recognized titles and has the management and technical skills in place to handle the kind of volume that Mattel desires. Their sales are almost $1 billion, which would enable Mattel to achieve its objective in this "high-tech" market. Thus, TLC seemed the best suited to satisfy Mattel's acquisition objectives.

Completing the Acquisition

Despite disturbing discoveries during due diligence, Mattel acquired TLC in a stock-for-stock transaction valued at $3.8 billion on May 13, 1999. Mattel had determined that TLC's receivables were overstated because product returns from distributors were not deducted from receivables and its allowance for bad debt was inadequate. A $50 billion licensing deal had also been prematurely put on the balance sheet. Finally, TLC's brands were becoming outdated. TLC had substantially exaggerated the amount of money put into research and development for new software products. Nevertheless, driven by the appeal of rapidly becoming a big player in the children's software market, Mattel closed on the transaction aware that TLC's cash flows were overstated.

Epilogue

Mattel's profits during the third quarter of 1999, the first full quarter following consolidation of TLC with Mattel, fell $50 million short of expectations due to asset write-offs and questionable accounting practices. Consolidated net income for the third quarter was $135.3 million as compared to $168.7 million during the same period in 1998. Profits were negatively impacted by TLC distributor and retailer returns and an increase in bad debt reserves of $56 million, of which $35 million related to one of TLC's major distributors. Mattel also decided not to complete a significant TLC licensing agreement, which was expected to generate approximately $60 million in pretax earnings. For all of 1999, TLC represented a pretax loss of $206 million. After restructuring charges, Mattel's consolidated 1999 net loss was $82.4 million on sales of $5.5 billion.

TLC's top executives left Mattel and sold their Mattel shares in August, just before the third quarter's financial performance was released. Mattel's stock fell by more than 35% during 1999 to end the year at about $14 per share. On February 3, 2000, Mattel announced that its CEO, Jill Barrad, was leaving the company.

(Sources: 1998 Annual Reports and 10Ks for Mattel, The Learning Company, Activision, and Acclaim Entertainment, www.sec.gov/edgarhp.htm and www.reportgallery.com; available CNNfn.com, December 8, 1999; Mattel press release, February 3, 2000, www.mattel.com)

Case Study Discussion Questions

1. Why was Mattel interested in diversification?
2. What alternatives to acquisition could Mattel have considered? Discuss the pros and cons of each alternative.
3. How might the Internet affect the toy industry? What potential conflicts with customers might be created?
4. What are the primary barriers to entering the toy industry?
5. What could Mattel have done to protect itself against risks uncovered during due diligence?

Solutions to this case study are provided in the Appendix at the back of the book.

REFERENCES

Bloomberg.com, "McKesson Revises Earnings," July 17, 1999a.

Bloomberg.com, "Vodafone Secures Financing for Air Touch Merger," May 14, 1999b.

Bygrave, William D., and Jeffrey A. Timmons, *Venture Capital at the Crossroads,* Boston: Harvard Business School Press, 1992.

Edgar-online, HBO 1998 101C, Securities and Exchange Commission, available at www.edgar-on line.com.

Harvard Business School, "Notes on Financial Contracting: Deals," *Cases and Reviews,* 9-288-014, June 22, 1989, p. 34.

Krallinger, Joseph, *Mergers & Acquisitions: Managing the Transaction,* New York: McGraw-Hill, 1997, pp. 94–116.

McCarthy, Paul, "Legal Aspects of Acquiring U.S. Enterprises," In David J. BenDaniel and Arthur H. Rosenbloom, (Eds.), *International M&A, Joint Ventures & Beyond: Doing the Deal,* Wiley & Sons, 1998, pp. 27–57.

Nanus, Michael R., "Accounting Aspects of International Mergers and Acquisitions," In David J. BenDaniel and Arthur H. Rosenbloom, (Eds.), *International M&A, Joint Ventures & Beyond: Doing the Deal,* Wiley & Sons, 1998, pp. 95–133.

Porter, Richard, and Cynthia N. Wood, "Postmerger Integration," In David J. BenDaniel and Arthur H. Rosenbloom, (Eds.), *International M&A, Joint Ventures & Beyond: Doing the Deal,* Wiley & Sons, 1998, pp. 459–457.

Remey, Donald P., "Mezzanine Financing: A Flexible Source of Growth Capital," In D. Schutt, (Ed.), *Pratt's Guide to Venture Capital Sources,* New York: Venture Economics Publishing, 1993, pp. 84–86.

Sherman, Andrew, *Mergers and Acquisitions From A to Z: Strategic and Practical Guidance for Small- and Middle-Market Buyers and Sellers,* New York: AMACOM, 1998, pp. 171–218.

Tillinghast, David R., "Tax Aspects of Inbound Merger and Acquisition and Joint Venture Transactions," In David J. BenDaniel and Arthur H. Rosenbloom, (Eds.), *International M&A, Joint Ventures & Beyond: Doing the Deal,* New York: Wiley & Sons, 1998, pp. 151–172.

Vachon, Michael, "Venture Capital Reborn," *Venture Capital Journal,* January 1993, p. 32.

Wetzel, William H., Jr., "Angels and Risk Capital," *Sloan Management Review, 24,* (4), Summer 1984, pp. 23–34.

6

INTEGRATION:

MERGERS, ACQUISITIONS, AND
BUSINESS ALLIANCES

What could be worse than being without sight?
Being born with sight and no vision.

—*Helen Keller*

Unlike most gossip around the water cooler, the conversation appeared to be unusually urgent between an engineer and draftsman employed by an engineering services company, which had recently been taken over by its competitor. "Do you think there will be substantial layoffs?" one worried engineer asked, shaking his head in dismay. The draftsman nodded somberly noting that not only had terminations been announced immediately following the last two acquisitions in the industry but also that there had been some loss of employer paid benefits for most of the workforce. Concern seemed to turn to anger as they discussed the windfall that some senior managers were likely to receive when they exercised their stock options. "I think its obscene that some of the brass is already out buying new cars . . . you would think they could just wait until, well, until the other shoe dropped."

The intensity of their conversation caught the attention of others in nearby cubicles, who set aside their work to join in the conversation. Normally conscientious employees were increasingly oblivious to project deadlines when their only source of information seemed to come from the "gossip mill." No one really knew if the rumors that circulated were accurate, but the more often they were repeated the more they were believed. A tide of paranoia swept throughout the office engulfing all but a few at the top who actually knew what was going to happen.

OVERVIEW

Motives for purchasing a company vary widely. Acquirers tend to fall into two broad categories: strategic buyers and financial buyers. Financial buyers are typically those who buy a business for eventual resale. They do not intend to integrate the acquired business into another entity. Moreover, instead of managing the business, they tend to monitor the effectiveness of current management. In contrast, strategic buyers are interested in making a profit by managing a business for an extended period of time. The strategic buyer may choose to manage the acquisition as a separate subsidiary in a holding company environment or merge it into another business.

This chapter assumes that integration is the goal of the acquirer immediately after the transaction closes. The chapter begins by stressing the importance of the integration phase of the acquisition process in contributing to the eventual success of the merger or acquisition. As noted in Chapter 1, ineffective integration is the second most commonly cited factor contributing to the failure of mergers and acquisitions to meet or exceed expectations.

If done correctly, the integration process can help to mitigate the loss of key talent or managers and the potential deterioration in employee morale and productivity. The potential loss of this "human capital" is perhaps one of the greatest risks associated with mergers and acquisitions (M&As). Although key talent and managers do not represent the only value in most acquisitions, it is widely recognized as among the most important. In a recent survey of 190 CEOs and CFOs from companies with M&A experience, more than three-fourths of the respondents cited the retention of key talent and managers as critical to the eventual success of a merger or acquisition (Watson Wyatt Worldwide, 1999).

The factors critical to the success of any integration activity are addressed in this chapter. These include careful premerger planning, candid and continuous communication, the pace at which the businesses are combined, the appointment of an integration manager and team with clearly defined lines of authority, and making the difficult decisions early in the process. This chapter views integration as a process consisting of six activities: planning, developing communication plans, creating a new organization, developing staffing plans, functional integration, and integrating corporate cultures. This chapter concludes with a discussion of how to overcome some of the unique obstacles encountered in integrating business alliances.

THE ROLE OF INTEGRATION IN SUCCESSFUL MERGERS AND ACQUISITIONS

In a global study of 100 acquisitions, each of which is valued at more than $500 million, Andersen Consulting (1999) concluded that integration is the most important stage of the mergers and acquisitions process. The Andersen survey results indicate that merging companies must be done quickly to achieve proper staffing requirements, eliminate redundant assets, and to generate the financial returns expected by shareholders and Wall Street analysts. If done well, most post-merger activities are completed within 6 months to 1 year. Case Study 6-1 illustrates the extent to which an effective integration process can reap rewards for the combined companies' shareholders.

CASE STUDY 6-1. THE PHARMACEUTICAL INDUSTRY—REALIZING COST SAVINGS THROUGH HORIZONTAL MERGERS

For some companies, horizontal acquisitions (i.e., mergers between competitors), may be the best source of creating shareholder wealth in the short-run. In an assessment of the pharmaceutical industry, one study found that the range of actual cost savings achieved has been 15–25% on research and development, 5–20% on manufacturing, 15–20% on marketing and sales, and 20–50% on administration. The savings vary according to differences in the extent of geographic, product, and R&D overlap. In the aggregate, these savings can amount to 30–40% of the acquired company's total cost base.

Source: Pursche, 1996.

THE IMPORTANCE OF RAPID INTEGRATION

For our purposes, the term *rapid* is defined as relative to the pace of normal operations for a firm. The importance of rapid integration can be demonstrated using a simple numerical example. Suppose a firm has a current market value of $100 million and that this value accurately reflects the firm's future cash flows discounted at its appropriate cost of capital. Assume an acquirer is willing to pay a $25 million control premium for this firm, believing that it can recover the control premium by realizing cost savings resulting from integrating the two firms. The amount of cash the acquirer will have to generate to recover the premium will increase the longer it takes to integrate the target company. If the cost of capital is 10% and integration is completed by the end of the first year, the acquirer will have to earn $27.5 million by the end of the first year to recover the control premium plus its cost of capital (i.e., $25 + $25 × .10). If integration is not completed until the end of the second year, the acquirer will have to earn incremental cash flow of $30.25 million (i.e., $27.5 + $27.5 × .10).

Numerous studies also support the conclusion that rapid integration efforts are more likely to result in mergers that achieve the acquirer's expectations (see McKinsey Company: 1987; *Business Week:* 1995; Marks: 1996; and Coopers & Lybrand: 1996). However, the pace of integration, although among the most commonly cited factors, is certainly not the only factor contributing to the success or failure of mergers and acquisitions. Overly optimistic assessments of potential synergies and poor strategy are also among the most common explanations for the failure of M&As.

THE IMPACT OF EMPLOYEE TURNOVER

Although it is not true that firms necessarily experience an actual reduction in their total workforce following an acquisition, the volatility of total employment does tend to be higher. A comprehensive 1996 study by David Birch of Cognetics found that, for public companies acquired between 1992 and 1995, 24% experienced declines in employment, 36% showed gains, and 40% showed no significant change in the 3 years following their having been acquired. However, during the same period, 80% of the companies that remained independent showed no significant change in employment.

While the Cognetics' study shows only that the volatility of total employment tends to increase after acquisitions, other studies show that management turnover does increase after a corporate takeover (see Hayes: 1979; Walsh: 1989; Walsh and Ellwood: 1991; and Shivdasani: 1993). Some loss of managers is intentional as part of an effort to eliminate redundancies and overlapping positions, while others quit during the turmoil of integration. Flanagan and O'Shaughnessy (1998) found that layoffs were announced about the same time as mergers about 50% of the time.

What is difficult to measure in any of these studies is whether the employees that leave represent a significant "brain drain" or loss of key managers. For many acquisitions, talent and management skill represents the primary value of the target company to the acquirer. This is especially true in high-technology and service companies for which assets are largely the embodied knowledge of their employees. Consequently, the loss of key employees rapidly degrades the value of the target company, thereby making earning back any premium paid to target shareholders increasingly difficult for the buyer.

The cost of employee turnover does not stop with the loss of key employees. The loss of any significant number of employees can be very costly. Current employees have already been recruited and trained. Firms will incur both recruitment and training costs again when equally qualified employees are hired to replace those lost. Moreover, the loss of employees is likely to reduce the morale of those who remain and add to benefit claims. Studies by the American Management Association and CIGNA Corporation show that employees, whether they leave or stay with the new firm, file more disability claims for longer periods of time after downsizing (*Wall Street Journal,* November 21, 1996).

INTEGRATION OFTEN MISMANAGED

Companies involved in integrating acquisitions frequently botch "people" issues. In a survey of 179 mergers since 1995, Right Management Consultants (1999) found that only 30% of the executives surveyed said they had successfully integrated the workforces and combined the cultures of the two companies. These results are particularly startling when we take into account that more than four-fifths of the survey responses came from companies at least 1 year after the acquisition. With respect to integrating the workforces, just 33% said they had effectively redeployed management talent, and only 34% reported good employee morale through the transition period. In terms of success in combining cultures, only one-fifth of the executives surveyed said that the career objectives of the employees of the acquired company were in synch with the combined companies' goals.

KEY FACTORS CONTRIBUTING TO SUCCESSFUL INTEGRATION

Perhaps the best way to retain employees is for the acquiring company to maintain a reputation as a good place to work. This reputation must be maintained in all future acquisitions. The new owner must demonstrate to employees at all levels that the future is bright. Through clear and constant communication, the acquirer must provide answers to questions that are on employees' minds, the so-called "me-issues." These include questions about pay, benefits, job security, relocation, corporate direction, and their future role in the combined company.

Despite immediate and compelling communication, employees of both the acquiring and target companies are likely to resist change in the wake of a corporate takeover. Differences in the way the management of the acquiring and target companies make decisions, the pace of decision making, perceived values, as well as the frequency and content of communication can result in major differences in corporate cultures. These differences can be overcome by applying time and transaction-tested techniques for integrating businesses (see Exhibit 6-1).

EXHIBIT 6-1. INTEGRATION SUCCESS FACTORS

1. Plan carefully, act quickly. Fast change limits uncertainty and deteriorating productivity. Before closing the transaction, make sure that someone is in charge of the integration activity and that lines of authority have been clearly delineated.
2. Introduce project management. Integration should be managed as a fully coordinated project with clearly communicated objectives, sup-

porting timetables, and individuals responsible for achieving each
objective.
3. Communicate from the top of the organization. Tell people as much
   as you can as soon as you can. Address the "me-issues."
4. Provide clear leadership. Define and communicate the future direction of the combined companies. Do not exaggerate or overcommit.
   Make sure that you meet or exceed all your commitments.
5. Focus on customers. Mergers can result in lost sales and deteriorating customer service. Actions to boost sales and service must be
   carefully planned but executed quickly.
6. Make the tough decisions as soon as possible. Decide on the organizational structure, reporting relationships, spans of control, people
   selection, roles and responsibilities, and workforce reductions as
   early as possible during the integration phase.
7. Focus on the highest leverage issues. Prioritize objectives carefully
   and concentrate resources on achieving those offering the greatest
   payoff first.

Source: Adapted from Marks, 1998.

VIEWING INTEGRATION AS A PROCESS

The activities involved in integrating an acquired business into the acquirer's
business do not fall neatly into a well-defined process. Some activities fall into
a logical sequence, while others are continuous and in some respects unending.
The major activities fall loosely into the following sequence: premerger planning, addressing communication issues, defining the new organization, developing staffing plans, functional and departmental integration, and building a new
corporate culture. In practice, communication with all major stakeholder groups
and developing a new corporate culture are largely continuous activities, running
throughout the integration period and beyond. Each of these six activities will be
discussed in the coming sections of this chapter in the sequence outlined in Figure 6-1.

INTEGRATION PLANNING

Thinking about how the postmerger integration may be implemented should
begin before the deal is completed. However, assumptions made before the closing based on information accumulated during due diligence must be re-examined
once the transaction is consummated to ensure their validity. For an excellent discussion of postmerger integration challenges, see Reed-Lajoux, (1998).

Integration Planning	Developing Communication Plans	Creating a New Organization	Developing Staffing Plans	Functional Integration	Integrating Corporate Cultures
Premerger planning: -Refine valuation -Resolve transition issues -Negotiate contract assurances	Stakeholders: -Employees -Customers -Suppliers -Investors -Communities (including regulators)	Learn from the past	Determine personnel requirements for the new organization	Revalidate due diligence data	Identify cultural issues through profiling
		Business needs drive organizational structure	Determine resource availability	Conduct performance benchmarking	Integrate through shared: -Goals -Standards -Services -Space
		Integrate corporate structures	Establish staffing plans & timetables	Integrate functions: -Operations -Information technology -Finance -Sales -Marketing -Purchasing -R&D -Human resources	
			Develop compensation strategy		
			Create supporting information systems		

FIGURE 6-1. The mergers and acquisition process.

Premerger Integration Planning

Initiating the integration planning prior to closing is intended to accomplish a number of important objectives. The process enables the acquiring company to refine further its original estimate of the value of the target company and to deal with transition issues in the context of the agreement of purchase and sale. Furthermore, the buyer has an opportunity to insert into the agreement the appropriate representations (claims) and warranties (promises), as well as conditions of closing that facilitate the postmerger integration process. Finally, the planning process creates a postmerger integration organization to expedite the integration process following closing.

Refining Valuation

Part of the integration planning process involves the preclosing due diligence activity. One responsibility of the due diligence team is to identify ways in which assets, processes, and other resources can be combined in order to realize cost savings, productivity improvements, or other perceived synergies. This information is also essential for refining the valuation process by enabling planners to better understand the necessary sequencing of events and the resulting pace at which the expected synergies may be realized. Consequently, understanding how and over what time period the integration will be implemented is important in determining the magnitude and timing of the cash flows of the combined companies used in making the final assessment of value.

Contract-Related Transition Issues

Integration planning also involves addressing human resource, customer, and supplier issues that overlap the change of ownership. These issues should be resolved as part of the agreement of purchase and sale. For example, the agreement may stipulate how target company employees will be paid and how their benefit claims will be processed.

Payroll systems must be in place to ensure that employees of the acquired company continue to be paid without disruption. For a small number of employees this may be easily accommodated by loading the acquirer's payroll computer system with a computer tape containing the necessary salary and personal information prior to closing or by having a third-party payroll processor perform these services. For larger operations or where employees are geographically dispersed, the target's employees may continue to be paid using the target's existing payroll system.

Employee health care or disability claims tend to escalate just before a transaction closes. This is especially true if the target's employees believe that the benefits to be provided by the acquirer are likely to be less attractive than their current benefit coverage. The sharp increase in such expenses can pose an unexpected burden for the acquirer if the responsibility for payment of such claims has not been addressed in the merger agreement. For example, the agreement may read that all claims incurred within a specific number of days prior to closing, but not submitted by employees for processing until after closing, will be reimbursed by the seller after the closing. Alternatively, such claims may be paid from an escrow account containing a portion of the purchase price set aside to cover these types of expenses.

Similar timing issues exist for target company customers and suppliers. For example, the merger agreement should specify how the seller should be reimbursed for products shipped or services provided by the seller prior to closing but not paid for by the customer until after closing. A prudent buyer would typically be the recipient of such payments, because the seller's previous lockboxes (i.e., checking accounts) would have been closed and replaced by the buyer's.

Likewise, the buyer will want to be reimbursed by the seller for monies owed to suppliers for products or services provided to the seller prior to closing but not billed until after closing. The merger agreement may indicate that both parties will keep track of customer and supplier invoices paid during the 60 to 90 days following closing and will submit them for reimbursement to the other party at the end of that period.

Contract Assurances

At a minimum, the agreement of purchase and sale will contain basic assurances that the seller is what it claims to be and that the seller has a right to sell the business. Similar assurances will apply to the acquiring company. For example, the buyer must assert that it has the right and the financial capacity to buy the target firm. A comprehensive set of "reps and warranties" may be viewed as a due diligence checklist for the buyer. The "reps and warranties" provide the buyer with recourse to the seller if any of these claims or promises are not true.

A prudent buyer will want to include certain assurances in the agreement of purchase and sale to limit its postclosing risk. Most seller representations and warranties made to the buyer refer to the past and present condition of the seller's business. Such "reps and warranties" usually pertain to such items as the ownership of securities; real and intellectual property; current levels of receivables, inventory and debt; and pending lawsuits, worker disability, and customer warranty claims. Although "reps and warranties" apply primarily to the past and current state of the seller's business, they do have ramifications for the future. For example, if a seller claims that there are no lawsuits pending and a lawsuit is filed shortly after closing, the buyer may seek to recover damages from the seller.

Moreover, sellers commonly provide potential acquirers with financial projections. The seller may have an incentive to provide an overly optimistic forecast to inflate the purchase price. To minimize this possibility, the prudent buyer will demand that the seller represent the reasonableness of the assumptions underlying the forecast and the accuracy of the data used in making the projections. If the acquired company's financial performance deteriorates following closing, the acquirer may be able to recover damages by claiming breach of contract. For this reason, sellers normally vigorously oppose providing any warranty for financial projections.

The buyer may also insist that certain conditions must be satisfied before closing can take place. Common conditions include employment contracts, agreements not to compete, financing, as well as regulatory and shareholder approval. The buyer will usually insist that key target company employees sign contracts obligating them to remain with the newly formed company for a specific period of time. The former owners, managers, and other key employees are also asked to sign agreements precluding them from going into any business that would directly compete with the new company during the duration of the noncompete agreement. Financial buyers in particular will usually require that they have firm commitments from lenders before completing the transaction. Finally, the buyer will want to make the final closing contingent on receiving approval from the appropriate regulatory agencies and shareholders of both companies before any money changes hands.

Postmerger Integration Organization

A postmerger integration organization with clearly defined goals and responsibilities should be in place prior to closing. For friendly mergers, the organization, including supporting work teams, should consist of individuals from both the acquiring and target companies, who have a vested interest in the newly formed company. The extent to which such an organization can be assembled during a hostile takeover is problematic given the lack of trust that may exist between the parties to the transaction. In such circumstances, the acquiring company is likely to find it difficult to gain access to the necessary information and to get the involvement of the target company's management in the planning process before the transaction actually closes.

Postmerger Integration Organization: Composition and Responsibilities

The postmerger integration organization should consist of both a management integration team (MIT) and a series of integration work teams. Each work team is focused on implementing a specific portion of the integration plan (see Figure 6-2).

Management Integration Team

The MIT consists of senior managers from the two merged organizations and is charged with delivering on sales and operating synergies identified during the preclosing due diligence. The composition of the work teams should also reflect employees from both the acquiring and target companies. Other team members might include outside advisors, such as investment bankers, accountants, attor-

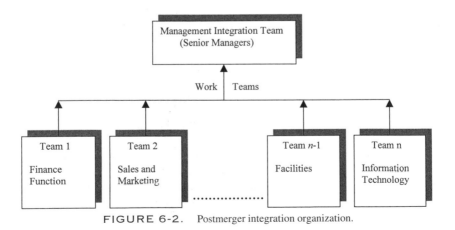

FIGURE 6-2.   Postmerger integration organization.

neys, and consultants. The MIT's emphasis during the integration period should be on those activities creating the greatest value for shareholders. The team should not get bogged down in details. The MIT's primary responsibility is to focus on key concerns such as long-term profit, performance targets, and cost management, as well as product and customer strategies. Exhibit 6-2 summarizes the key tasks that should be performed by the MIT to realize anticipated synergies.

EXHIBIT 6-2. KEY MANAGEMENT INTEGRATION TEAM RESPONSIBILITIES

1. Build a master schedule of what should be done by whom and by what date.
2. Determine the required economic performance for the combined entity.
3. Establish work teams to determine how each function and business unit will be combined (e.g., structure, job design, and staffing levels).
4. Focus the organization on meeting ongoing business commitments and operational performance targets throughout the integration process.
5. Create an early warning system consisting of performance indicators to ensure that both the integration effort and the business stay on plan.
6. Monitor and expedite key decisions.
7. Establish a rigorous communication campaign to aggressively and repeatedly support the integration plan, addressing both internal (e.g., employees) and external (e.g., customers, suppliers, and regulatory authorities) constituencies.

Integration Work Teams

Although the MIT cannot do everything, it is responsible for making sure that everything gets done. Dedicated integration work teams perform the detailed integration work. In addition to driving the integration effort, the MIT ensures that the managers not involved in the integration effort remain focused on running the business. The MIT allocates dedicated resources to the integration effort and clarifies nonteam membership roles and enables day-to-day operations to continue at premerger levels.

The management integration team should be careful to give the work teams not only the responsibility to do certain tasks but also the authority to get the job done.

The teams should be encouraged to inject ideas into the process to foster creativity by encouraging solutions rather than by dictating processes and procedures. To be effective, the work teams must have access to accurate, timely information as well as receive candid, timely feedback. The teams should also be given adequate resources to do the task they have been asked to do and be kept informed of the broader perspective of the overall integration effort so that they will not become too narrowly focused.

Institutionalizing the Integration Process

In recognition of the importance of integration, firms that frequently acquire companies in the same industry often find it useful to develop full-time staffs to manage this process. The presumption is that integration is likely to proceed more smoothly and rapidly if those guiding the process have substantial experience in integrating certain types of businesses. This may explain the apparent success some companies such as Cisco Systems have had in acquiring companies during the 1990s (see Case Study 6.2).

CASE STUDY 6-2. CISCO INTEGRATION TEAM

Cisco Systems, the Internet infrastructure behemoth, provides the hardware and software to support efficient traffic flow over the Internet. Between 1993 and 1999, Cisco spent $19 billion on 42 acquisitions using its high-flying stock as its acquisition currency. With engineering talent in short supply and a dramatic compression in product life cycles, Cisco turned to acquisitions to expand existing product lines and to enter new businesses.

The firm's track record in acquiring and absorbing these acquisitions has been impressive. In fiscal year 1999, Cisco acquired 10 companies. During the same period, its sales and operating profits soared by 44% and 55%, respectively. In view of its pledge not to layoff any employees of the target companies, its turnover rate among employees acquired through acquisition is 2.1% versus an average of 20% for other software and hardware companies.

Cisco's strategy for acquiring companies is to evaluate its targets' technologies, financial performance, and its management talent with a focus on ease of integrating the target into Cisco's operations. Cisco tends to target small companies having a viable commercial product or technology. Cisco believes that larger, more mature companies tend to be more difficult to integrate, because they have entrenched beliefs about technologies, hardware and software solutions, and product development processes. Cisco often acquires a minority ownership position before attempting to takeover a firm.

The frequency with which Cisco makes acquisitions has caused the firm to "institutionalize" the way in which it integrates acquired companies. The integration process is tailored for each acquired company and is implemented by an integration team of twelve professionals. Newly acquired employees receive an information packet including descriptions of Cisco's business strategy, organizational structure, benefits, a contact sheet if further information is required, and an explanation of the strategic importance of the acquired firm to Cisco. On the day the acquisition is announced, teams of Cisco human resources people travel to the acquired firm's headquarters and meet with small groups of employees to answer questions.

Working with the newly acquired firm's management, integration team members help place newly acquired employees within Cisco's workforce. Generally, product, engineering, and marketing groups are kept independent, whereas sales and manufacturing functions are merged into existing Cisco departments. Cisco payroll and benefits systems are updated to reflect information about the new employees, who are quickly given access to Cisco's online employee information systems. Cisco also offers customized orientation programs intended to educate managers about Cisco's hiring practices; sales people about Cisco's products; and engineers about the firm's development process. The entire integration process is generally completed in 4–6 weeks. This lightning-fast pace is largely due to Cisco's tendency to purchase small, highly complementary companies, to leave much of the acquired firm's infrastructure in place, and to dedicate a staff of human resource and business development people to facilitate the process.

Source: Goldblatt, 1999, pp. 177–180; Cisco Systems, 1999.

DEVELOPING COMMUNICATION PLANS

Before there is any public announcement of an acquisition, the acquiring company should have prepared a communication plan. The plan should be developed jointly by the management integration team and the public relations department or outside PR consultant. It should contain key messages as well as specify target stakeholders and appropriate media for conveying the messages to each group. The major stakeholder groups should include employees, customers, suppliers, investors, and communities. Regulatory agencies often become key stakeholders in highly regulated industries or whenever a pending transaction is viewed as potentially anticompetitive (see Chapter 2, this volume).

A consistent theme throughout all messages should be the intent of the new organization to live up to commitments made to its major stakeholders. This is the first step in building trust between the management of the new company and its stakeholders. This does not mean that the new firm has to continue all practices in place under the previous management of the acquired firm. It simply underscores the need for the new management's actions to be consistent with promises made to stakeholders in the new company. In all cases, the new organization should be prepared to honor both the letter and the spirit of all prior contractual commitments. In some instances, the management of the new company would also be well advised to honor certain unwritten or implicit commitments made to stakeholders by prior management.

Employees

As noted earlier, target company employees typically represent a substantial portion of the value of the acquired business. This is particularly true for technology and service-related businesses having few tangible assets. These types of businesses comprise an increasingly larger share of the number of transactions consummated each year. Therefore, to preserve the value of the acquisition, companies must be highly sensitive to when and how something is communicated to employees, as well as to the accuracy of its content.

When to Communicate

Communication, particularly during crisis periods, should be as frequent as possible. A report of "nothing to report" can be comforting. It is better to report that there is no change than to remain silent. Silence breeds uncertainty, which adds to stress associated with what constitutes a major life change for most people. Stress engendered by transition from one corporate parent to another can undermine employee morale and endanger productivity. Deteriorating job performance, absences from work, fatigue, anxiety, and depression are clear signs of workforce stress.

How to Communicate

The CEO should lead the effort to communicate to employees at all levels through employee meetings on site or via teleconferencing. Many companies find it useful to create a single source of information accessible to all employees. This may be an individual whose job it is to answer questions or a menu-driven automated phone system programmed to respond to commonly asked questions.

The best forum for communication in a crisis is through regularly scheduled employee meetings. All external communication in the form of press releases should be coordinated with the public relations department to ensure that the same information is concurrently released to employees. This minimizes the likelihood that employees will learn about important developments second hand. Internal e-mail systems, voicemail, or intranets may be used to facilitate employee communications. In addition, personal letters, question-and-answer sessions, newsletters, or videotapes are highly effective ways of delivering the desired messages.

What to Communicate

Employees are highly interested in any information pertaining to the merger and more importantly how it will affect them. They will want to know how changes will affect the overall strategy, business operations, job security, working conditions, and total compensation. The human resources (HR) staff plays an important role in communicating to employees. HR representatives must learn what employees know and want to know, what the prevailing rumors are, and what employees find most disconcerting. This can be achieved through surveys, interviews, focus groups, or employee meetings.

Changes in work practices and compensation may be viewed as reneging on commitments made by prior management. This may accelerate the loss of key employees. To minimize this potential, changes must be explained honestly and at a level of detail necessary to explain why they are being made. Employees can more readily understand change if it is to ward off the eventual loss of jobs or even bankruptcy. Change will be perceived as fair and more readily accepted if it impacts everyone.

Customers

The firm must continuously communicate to customers the benefits of the merger. From the customer's perspective, the merger can increase the range of products or services offered or provide lower selling prices as a result of economies of scale and new applications of technology. However, the firm's actions must support its talk. To minimize customer attrition, the newly merged firm must strive to maintain or improve product quality, on-time delivery, and customer service. Despite these efforts some attrition related to the acquisition is inevitable.

Acquisition-Related Customer Attrition

During normal operations, businesses can expect a certain level of churn in their customer list. Depending upon the industry, normal churn due to competitive conditions can be anywhere from 20–40%. A newly merged company will experience a loss of another 5–10% of its existing customers as a direct result of the merger (Down, 1995). The loss of customers may reflect uncertainty about on-time delivery and product quality as well as more aggressive pricing by competitors. It is common for competitors following an acquisition to spread rumors about production delays occurring at the newly merged firms. Competitors may also use the postacquisition period to gain market share by offering more attractive contract terms to the new firm's customers while they are spreading rumors about production and quality problems.

Meeting Commitments to Current Customers

The buyer should always be aware of the set of explicit (contractual) or implicit (handshake) agreements that the target company has made to its customers. To fulfill commitments to wholesalers and distributors buying directly or in bulk, the integration team needs to review all of the legal agreements the new company has inherited from the target company. These commitments include the volume, price, and payment terms the target company has agreed to for each of its customers having a written contract as well as for those without a written agreement but who have been receiving specific terms for an extended period of time. In fulfilling commitments to retail customers buying indirectly or in small quantities, the new company must be aware of promises, such as slogans used in advertising or product warranties, the target company has made publicly.

Fulfilling these commitments is of utmost importance. Current customers are often worth more than new ones, because the cost of maintaining an existing relationship is usually less expensive than acquiring a new one. This is recognized in the process of allocating purchase price to customer lists. Customers with a known value and life, usually those with contracts, receive a much larger allocation than the assignment of value to future customer relationships. Appraisers use the income approach to value customer contracts, since they can identify income directly attributable to these customers. When they cannot identify a specific income stream, appraisers use a replacement cost approach by assuming that the amount of money a business is willing to spend on attracting a new customer equals the value of an existing customer without a contract.

Suppliers

Long-term contracts with current suppliers cannot be broken without redress. Moreover, just as a current customer is often worth more than a new one, a current supplier with a proven track record may also be worth more than a new one. It is a buyer's market following an acquisition, so the new company should approach its suppliers carefully. Although substantial cost savings are possible by "managing" suppliers, the new company should be seeking a long-term relationship rather than simply a way to reduce costs. Suppliers should be viewed as partners rather than adversaries. Aggressive negotiation can get high-quality products and services at lower prices in the short-run, but it may be transitory if the new company is a large customer of the supplier and if the supplier's margins are continuously squeezed. The supplier's product or service quality will suffer, and the supplier may eventually exit the business. Ways to effectively manage the supply chain following an acquisition will be discussed later in this chapter.

Investors

The new firm must be able to present a compelling vision of the future to investors. The vision should be appealing to the existing investors of both companies. Regular press releases and briefings are critical for providing information to the investment community.

There are compelling economic motivations for appealing to current investors of both the acquirer and target companies in a share-for-share exchange, as target shareholders will become shareholders in the newly formed company. Retaining current shareholders is simply less expensive than a highly aggressive campaign to acquire new ones. Loyal shareholders tend to provide for more stable ownership, reduce share price volatility, and in doing so may contribute to increased shareholder value. Recognizing that maintaining existing relationships is easier than developing new ones, investor relations departments in acquiring companies devote a large part of their time after a merger or acquisition to informing their current shareholders rather than trying to attract new ones.

Maintaining current shareholder loyalty is often easier when acquiring a firm in the same industry. The challenge is substantially greater if the acquisition is of a firm in a significantly different industry. All firms attract particular types of investors. Companies such as public utilities that have paid high dividends consistently attract investors interested in earning a steady and predictable level of income. Investors willing to accept more risk in exchange for potential capital gains are attracted to growth-oriented firms.

Even the more aggressive investors will display clear preferences for certain types of companies. This was amply illustrated in the acquisition of Time Warner by American Online in January 2000. The combined market value of the two firms lost 11% in the 4 days following the announcement, as investors puzzled over what had been created. The selling frenzy following the announcement may have involved different groups of investors who bought Time Warner for its rich and diverse content and American Online for its meteoric growth rate of 70% per annum. The new company may not have met the expectations of either group.

Communities

Companies are an integral part of the communities in which they are located. Companies should communicate plans to build or keep plants, stores, or office buildings in a community as soon as they can be confident that these actions will be implemented. These pronouncements translate readily into new jobs and increased taxes. Good working relations with surrounding communities are simply good public relations. A community, which views a firm as a partner, is more prone to making changes in zoning restrictions and in offering tax incentives. However, the company must be prepared to satisfy commitments to invest in the community. It is both ethically correct and ensures that the company will not be subject to lawsuits by communities seeking to recover any expenses they incurred in demolishing and clearing sites on behalf of the firm. Firms having contracts with the community may also be subject to nonperformance penalties.

CREATING A NEW ORGANIZATION

Organization or structure is traditionally defined in terms of titles and reporting relationships. For the purpose of this chapter, we will follow this definition. A properly structured organization should support not retard the acceptance of a culture in the new company that is desired by top management. An effective starting point in setting up a structure is to learn from the past and to recognize that the needs of the business drive structure and not the other way around.

Learn from the Past

Building new reporting structures for combining companies requires a knowledge of the target company's prior organization, some sense as to the effectiveness of this organization in the decision-making process, and the future business needs of the newly combined companies. Therefore, in creating the new organization, it is necessary to start with previous organization charts. They provide insights into how individuals from both the target and acquiring companies will interact within the new company, because they reveal the past experience and also future expectations of individuals with regard to reporting relationships.

Business Needs Drive Structure

The next step is to move beyond the past and into the future by creating a structure that focuses on meeting the business needs of the combined companies rather than attempting to make everyone happy. All corporations require some degree of structure to facilitate decision making, provide internal controls, and to promote behaviors consistent with the mission and principles of the new company. Often acquiring companies simply impose their reporting structures on the target company. This is particularly true if the acquirer is much larger than the target. By ignoring the target's existing organizational structure, the acquiring company is in effect ignoring the expectations of the target's employees. Unfulfilled expectations will lead to disappointment and demotivate target company employees. No structure guarantees behavior; it only makes it easier or more difficult to get things accomplished (Lajoux, 1998, pp. 175–214).

Basic Organizational Structures

There are three basic types of structures: functional, product or service, and divisional. The functional tends to be the most centralized and the divisional the most decentralized.

In a functional organization, people are assigned to specific groups or departments such as accounting, engineering, marketing, sales, distribution, customer service, manufacturing, or maintenance. This type of structure tends to be highly centralized and is becoming less common. According to A. T. Kearney Inc. (1998), the number of companies organized in this manner dropped from 39% in 1990 to 15% in 1995 and to an estimated 12% in 1998.

In a product or service organization, functional specialists are grouped by product line or service offering. Each product line or service offering has its own accounting, human resources, sales, marketing, customer service, and product development staffs. These types of organizations tend to be somewhat decentralized. Individuals in these types of organizations often have multiple reporting relationships. For example, a product line finance manager may report to both the product line manager and to the manager of a centralized financial organization. A. T. Kearney (1998) indicates that the number of such organizations has grown from 13% in 1990 to 18% in 1995 and an estimated 20% in 1998.

Divisional organizations continue to be the dominant form of organizational structure in which groups of products are combined into independent divisions or "strategic business units." Such organizations have their own management teams and tend to be highly decentralized. Divisional structures may be the most complex of the various types of structures, with product–service line or functional organizational structures often existing within each division. Divisional structures are often used in this manner, because each division can stand alone while containing other types of organizational structures.

According to A. T. Kearney (1998), the divisional organizational structure accounted for about 68% of all organizational structures in 1998, as compared to 58% in 1995 and 48% in 1990.

Decentralized vs. Centralized Structures

The popularity of decentralized versus centralized management structures tends to vary with the state of the economy. During recessions when top management is under great pressure to cut costs, companies often tend to move toward centralized management structures, only to decentralize when the economy recovers. Highly decentralized authority can retard the pace of integration, as there is no single authority to resolve issues or determine policies. In contrast, a centralized structure may make postmerger integration much easier. Senior management can dictate policies governing all aspects of the combined companies, centralize all types of functions providing support to operating units, and resolve issues among the various units.

Although centralized control does provide significant advantages during postmerger integration, it can also be highly detrimental if the policies imposed by the central headquarters are simply not appropriate for the operating units. Highly centralized parent company management may destroy value by imposing too many rigid controls, by focusing on the wrong issues, by hiring or promoting the wrong managers, or by monitoring the wrong performance measures. Moreover, highly centralized parent companies often have multiple layers of management to link multiple operating units and centralized functions providing services to the operating units. The parent companies pass the costs of centralized management and support services on to the operating units. There are a number of studies that suggest that the costs of this type of structure outweigh the benefits (Chakrabarti: 1990; Alexander, Campbell, and Gould: 1995; Campbell, Sadtler, and Koch: 1997).

The right structure may well be an evolving one. The substantial benefits of a well-managed, rapid integration of the two businesses suggests a centralized management structure initially with relatively few layers of management. This does not mean that all integration activities should be driven from the top without any input from middle managers and supervisors of both companies. It does mean taking decisive and timely action based on the best information available. Once the integration is viewed as relatively complete, the new company should move to a more decentralized structure in view of the well-documented explicit and implicit costs of centralized corporate organizations.

Integrating Corporate Structures

A corporate hierarchy is often associated with slow decision making and unfair pay scales. During the 1990s, companies have modified corporate hierarchies to reflect different levels of business rather than management. At the corporate level, managers set strategy and determine corporate policies; managers at the business unit level focus on strategy execution. Finally, within each business unit, work teams focus on improving efficiency, product quality, and customer service.

Merging Corporate Boards

Mergers can have significant impacts on the boards of the two companies. What happens depends largely on the type of transaction. In a merger of companies of comparable size, the members of both boards are merged into the board of the newly formed company. Downsizing the board comes through attrition, retirement policies, and director term limits. In some cases, a planned reduction in the size of the board of the combined company is made part of the merger agreement. In a merger in which the participants are markedly different in terms of size, the smaller company's board will generally not be included in the new company's board if the acquired company is to be fully integrated into the acquirer. However, if the acquired company is to be operated as a subsidiary of the parent, its board may remain in place.

Maintaining continuity of board membership is often important in meeting the long-term objectives of the combined companies. The boards of the two companies may work together to determine the size and type (i.e., skills and experience) of board the new company will require. The board must then determine if the current size and composition of the board is appropriate. Incumbent board members may be encouraged to leave to achieve an appropriate size or to make room for new directors with the desired skills and experience.

A poll of 99 representatives from the largest pension funds and money managers in the United States determined that the attributes of an effective corporate board included quality, independence, and accountability (*Business Week,* 2000). Respondents indicated that the quality of a board should be measured by the extent to which board meetings included open discussion among members who truly understood the issues being addressed. Independence was measured by a virtual absence of members who were close associates of the CEO. Respondents indicated that key committees, such as audit and compensation, should include only "outside directors." Finally, accountability reflected the extent to which board members held significant equity positions in the company and were willing to challenge the CEO about the company's underperformance.

Integrating Senior Management

A review of the historical performance of both companies and their respective organizations by the management integration team will provide crucial insight into the selection of the best candidates for senior management positions in the new company. An external facilitator may be used to break deadlocks. The team should agree on the new strategy for the combined companies and subsequently select people who are best suited to implement this strategy.

Integrating Middle Management

Once senior managers have been selected, they should be given full responsibility for selecting their direct reports. As is true for senior managers, jobs for middle-level and supervisory positions should go to those with the superior integration skills.

DEVELOPING STAFFING PLANS

Staffing plans should be formulated as soon as possible in the integration process. For friendly acquisitions, the process should begin prior to closing. The early development of such plans provides an opportunity to include the key personnel from both firms in the integration effort. Other benefits from early planning include the increased likelihood of retaining those with key skills and talents, maintaining corporate continuity, and team building. Figure 6-3 describes the logical sequencing of staffing plans and the major issues addressed in each segment.

Personnel Requirements

The appropriate organizational structure is one able to meet the current functional requirements or needs of the business and flexible enough to be expanded to satisfy future business requirements. The process for creating such a structure should involve input from all levels of management, be consistent with the combined firm's business strategy, and reflect expected sales growth.

Functional Requirements

Before establishing the organizational structure, the integration team should agree on what specific functions are needed to run the combined businesses. These discussions should reflect a clear understanding of the specific roles and responsibilities of each function.

Organizational Structure

Once the necessary functions have been identified, the effort to project personnel requirements by function should start with each functional department describing the ideal structure to meet the roles and responsibilities assigned by senior management. By asking for department input, department personnel are involved in the process, can communicate useful insights, and can contribute to the creation of a consensus for changing the organization.

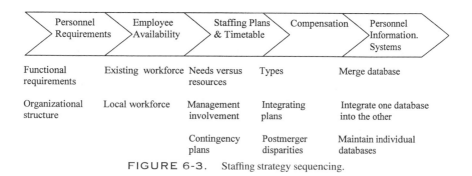

FIGURE 6-3.   Staffing strategy sequencing.

Employee Availability

Availability refers to the number of each type of employee required by the new organization that can be identified in the new company's existing workforce and in the local communities in which the new company has operations. The skills of the existing workforce should be documented and compared to the current and future functional requirements of the new company. An examination of the current workforce should also involve a demographic profile in terms of sex and ethnic makeup to ensure that the new organization is in compliance with prevailing regulations. The local labor pool can be used to augment the existing workforce. These workers represent potential new hires for the combined firms. Data should be collected on the educational levels, skills, and demographic composition of the local workforce, as well as prevailing wage rates by skill category.

Staffing Plans and Timetable

Following the determination of the appropriate organizational structure and the pool of current and potential employees available to staff the new organization, a detailed staffing plan can be developed.

Staffing Needs versus Employee Availability

By matching the number of workers and skills required to support current and future business requirements with the current workforce, gaps in the firm's workforce needing to be filled from recruiting outside the company can be readily identified. The effort to externally recruit should be tempered by its potentially adverse impact on current employee morale. The filling of gaps should be prioritized and phased in over time in recognition of the time required to fill certain types of positions and the impact of major hiring programs on local wage rates in communities with relatively small labor pools.

Management Involvement

Once management positions have been filled, the managers should be enlisted to interview, evaluate, and select new employees to fill job openings in their departments and operations. Senior management should stress that filling job openings should be given top priority, particularly when the skills required are crucial to successfully completing the integration of the acquired business. During the integration period, managers are under the enormous stress of having to continue to conduct normal business operations as well as to integrate portions of the acquired business. In view of the increased workload, it is common for managers to defer the time-consuming hiring process by assuming multiple responsibilities. This hurts both the manager's morale and health as well as the completion of the integration process, as many of these managers are insufficiently trained to handle many of these assumed responsibilities.

Contingency Plans

As noted previously, key employees will inevitably be lost to the new company. Other employees should be trained to fill positions considered critical to the long-term viability of the organization. This can be accomplished by developing job descriptions that clearly identify the skills required to fill the position and then by cross-training other workers in the position.

Compensation

Merging compensation plans can be one of the most challenging activities of the integration process. Such activities must be conducted in compliance with prevailing regulations and with a high degree of sensitivity.

Types of Compensation

Total compensation consists of base pay, bonuses or incentive plans, benefits, and special contractual agreements. Bonus or incentive pay is compensation designed to encourage employees to meet predetermined performance targets. Bonuses may take the form of a lump sum of cash or stock paid to an employee for meeting or exceeding these targets.

Special contractual agreements may consist of noncompete agreements in which key employees sign agreements in exchange for an agreed upon amount of compensation not to compete against the newly formed company if they should leave. Special agreements may also take the form of golden parachutes for senior management the new firm wishes to retain and severance agreements to compensate employees in the event of job loss. Finally, retention bonuses are often given to employees if they agree to stay with the new company for a specific period of time.

Integrating Compensation Plans

The extent to which compensation plans are integrated depends on whether the two companies are going to be managed separately or integrated. Financial acquirers may be intent on reselling the acquired business in a few years; as such, they may choose to keep compensation plans separate. The strategic acquirer may also keep the plans separate especially if it is moving into an industry in which compensation differs from that prevailing in its current industry. In instances in which the parent chooses to combine plans, the design of the new plan is generally done in consultation with the acquired unit's management. The parent will set guidelines, such as how much stock senior executives should own (e.g., a percent of base pay), and how managers will receive the stock (e.g., whether they will be awarded stock or will have to buy it at a discount from its current market price). The parent will also set guidelines for base pay. For example, the parent may decide that base pay will be at market, below market, or above market adjusted for regional differences in the cost of living. Moreover, the parent may also decide on how bonuses will be paid, while the operating unit will determine who receives them. Finally, the parent will determine the benefits policy and plans. Such plans normally require specialized expertise to administer and must be in compliance with the prevailing regulations.

Postmerger Disparities

Base pay for employees may differ by geographic area and industry for similar jobs. Bonuses may differ widely for firms acquired in different industries. In recent years, commercial banks have acquired investment banks and brokerage firms where bonuses may be four or five times base salary levels. Bonuses may also be linked to different performance measures, such as sales and market share for high-growth subsidiaries, and to operating profit or cash flow for mature businesses. Benefits may also differ for acquired firms in different industries to reflect the incentives required to attract and to retain employees in that industry.

Personnel Information Systems

The acquiring company may choose to merge all personnel data into a new database, to merge one corporate database into another, or to maintain the individual businesses' personnel databases. A single database enables authorized users to more readily access employee data, to more efficiently plan for future staffing requirements, and to conduct analyses and print reports. Maintenance expense associated with a single database may also be lower. The decision to keep personnel databases separate may reflect plans to divest the unit at some time in the future.

FUNCTIONAL INTEGRATION

Previous activities within the integration process dealt primarily with planning for the actual integration of the acquired business into the acquirer's business. Functional integration refers to the actual execution of the plans.

The first consideration of the MIT is to determine the extent to which the two companies' operations and support staffs are to be centralized or decentralized. The main areas of focus should be information technology, manufacturing operations, sales, marketing, finance, purchasing, research and development, and the requirements to staff these functions. However, before any actual integration takes place, it is crucial to revalidate data collected during due diligence and to benchmark all operations by comparing them to industry standards, whenever available.

Due-Diligence Data Revalidation

Data collected during due diligence should be revalidated immediately following closing. In theory, this should not be necessary if a thorough due diligence is conducted. In practice, it is highly unlikely that the necessary in-depth analyses were actually completed. The pressure exerted by both the buyer and the seller to complete the transaction often results in a haphazard preclosing review. For example, in an effort to compress the time devoted to due diligence, sellers often allow buyers access to senior managers only. Middle level managers, supervisory personnel, and equipment operators are often excluded from the interview process. For similar reasons, site visits by the buyer are often limited to only those with the largest concentrations of employees, thus ignoring the risks and opportunities that might exist at sites not visited.

The buyer's legal and financial reviews are normally conducted only on the largest customer and supplier contracts, promissory notes, and operating and capital leases. Receivables are evaluated and physical inventory counted using sampling techniques. The effort to determine if intellectual property has been properly protected, with key trademarks or service marks properly registered and copyrights and patents filed, is often spotty.

Although some of these exposures can be limited by including the appropriate "reps and warranties" in the agreement of purchase and sale, buyer efforts to recover damages due to breaches of contract may require extended and expensive legal battles. Moreover, an abbreviated due diligence also limits the opportunity to understand the potential synergies between the two businesses and the actual cost of integrating the acquired business.

Exxon's merger with Mobil demonstrates how revalidation of earlier due diligence findings resulted in an approximate 26% upward revision in expected pretax cost savings due to personnel reductions (Case Study 6-3). In contrast, Albertson's acquisition of American Stores shows the downside of inadequate due diligence (Case Study 6-4). Substantial upward revisions in postclosing estimates of the actual cost of integrating the two businesses contributed to a more than 50% reduction in Albertson's stock price during 1999.

CASE STUDY 6-3. EXXON-MOBIL:
A STUDY IN COST CUTTING

Having obtained access to more detailed information following consummation of the merger, Exxon-Mobil announced dramatic revisions in its estimates of cost savings. The world's largest publicly owned oil company will cut almost 16,000 jobs by the end of 2002. This is an increase from the 9,000 cuts estimated when the merger was first announced in December 1998. Of the total, 6,000 will come from early retirement. Estimated annual savings are expected to reach $3.8 billion, up by more than $1 billion from when the merger was originally announced. The combined companies are expected to earn $1 billion more in net income in 2001 and $2.5 billion by 2003.

Source: Bloomberg.com, 1999a.

CASE STUDY 6-4. ALBERTSON'S ACQUIRES
AMERICAN STORES—UNDERESTIMATING
THE COSTS OF INTEGRATION

In 1999, Albertson's acquired American Stores for $12.5 billion, making it the nation's second largest supermarket chain with over 1000 stores. The corporate marriage stumbled almost immediately. Escalating integration costs resulted in a sharp downward revision of its fiscal year 2000 profits. In the quarter ended October 28, 1999, operating profits fell 15% to $185 million, despite an increase in sales of 1.6% to $8.98 billion. Albertson proceeded to update the Lucky supermarket stores that it had acquired in California and to combine the distribution operations of the two supermarket chains. It appears that Albertson's substantially underestimated the complexity of integrating an acquisition of this magnitude. Albertson's spent about $90 million before taxes to convert more than 400 stores to its information and distribution systems as well as to change the name to Albertson's. Albertson's share price fell 11% following the announcement of the lower earnings outlook, its biggest one-day drop in more than 3 years. By the end of 1999, Albertson's stock had lost more than one-half of its value.

Source: Bloomberg.com, 1999b.

Performance Benchmarking

Benchmarking important functions such as the acquirer's and the target's manufacturing and information technology operations and processes is a useful starting point for determining how to integrate these activities. Standard benchmarks include the International Standards Organization's (ISO) 9001 Quality Systems-Model for Quality Assurance in Design, Development, Production, Installation, and Servicing. The ISO is a worldwide standard-setting organization that has achieved global acceptance in a variety of industries. Other benchmarks that can be used include the Federal Drug Administration's (FDA) Good Manufacturing Practices and the Department of Commerce's Malcolm Baldridge Award. Sanderson and Uzumeri (1997, p. 135) provide a comprehensive list of standards-setting organizations.

Manufacturing and Operations

The data revalidation process for integrating and rationalizing facilities and operations requires in-depth discussions with key target company personnel and on-site visits to all facilities. The objective should be to reevaluate overall capacity, the potential for future cost reductions, the age and condition of facilities, adequacy of maintenance budgets, and compliance with environmental laws. Careful consideration should be given to manufacturing capabilities that duplicate those of the acquirer. The integration team needs to also determine if the duplicate facilities are potentially more efficient than those of the buyer. As part of the benchmarking process, the operations of both the acquirer and the target company should be compared to industry standards to properly evaluate their efficiency.

Manufacturing Processes

The quality of the processes associated with an operation are often an accurate indicator of overall operational efficiency (Porter and Wood: 1999). The four processes that should be examined include planning, materials ordering, order entry, and quality control. For example, production planning is often a very inaccurate exercise, particularly when the operations are relatively inflexible and require long-term forecasts of sales. The production planning and materials ordering functions need to work closely together, because the quantity and composition of the materials ordered depends on the accuracy of sales projections. Inaccurate projections result in shortages or costly excess inventory accumulation.

The order entry activity may offer significant opportunities for cost savings. Companies building to stock and subsequently satisfying orders from finished product inventories frequently have huge working capital requirements. For this reason, companies such as personal computer manufacturers are building inventory according to orders received to minimize finished product inventories. A key indicator of the effectiveness of quality control is the percentage of products that go through the manufacturing process without being inspected. Companies whose "first run yield" is in the 70–80% range may have serious quality problems.

Facility Consolidation

Plant consolidation starts with the adoption of a common set of systems and standards for all manufacturing activities. Such standards include cycle time between production runs, cost per unit of output, first-run yield, and scrap rates. Links between the different facilities are then created by sharing information management and processing systems, inventory control, supplier relationships, and transportation links. Vertical integration can be achieved by focusing on different stages of production. Different facilities specialize in the production of selected components, which are then shipped to other facilities to assemble the finished product. Finally, a company may close certain facilities whenever there is excess capacity.

Information Technology

Information technology (IT) spending constitutes an ever-increasing share of most businesses' budgets. In view of this trend, it is crucial that IT operations be monitored not only by technical people but also by general managers. Studies have shown that about 80% of software projects have failed to meet their performance expectations or deadlines (*Financial Times,* 1996). Almost one-half are scrapped before they are completed; and about one-half cost two or three times their original budgets and take three times as long as expected to complete (*Wall Street Journal*, 1996). Studies conclude that managers tend to focus too much on technology and not enough on the people and processes that will use it.

If the buyer intends to operate the target company independently, the information systems of the two companies may be kept separate as long as communications links between the two companies' systems can be established. However, if the buyer intends to integrate the target, the process can be daunting. To implement full integration, the new IT systems must usually be combined into a new operation. Studies show that nearly 70% of buyers choose to combine their information systems immediately after closing. Almost 90% of acquirers eventually combine these operations (Cossey: 1991).

Following the determination of the extent to which the information systems should be combined, the integration team must revalidate the quality and effectiveness of each company's system. This process should focus on hardware, software, communications capabilities, technical support, and compatibility of existing systems (Porter and Wood: 1998).

Hardware and Software Systems

Hardware and software systems should be catalogued by type, how they are used, whether they are owned or leased, where they are located, and their age and reliability. All communications technology and networks should also be examined to determine the types of voice and data communications equipment used, whether there are local area or wide area networks, and the number and locations of all terminals and personal computers that might have access to the network. The integration team should also analyze the types of technical support available, technical documentation, and vendor agreements including training and maintenance. Once the inventory of existing systems and support services has been completed, the integration team needs to define the systems required by the new company and to develop a systems integration plan.

Are newer systems necessarily better than older systems? It is often a mistake to assume that newer technology will improve productivity more than the older, legacy systems of the target company. For example, legacy systems have been tested and in use for an extended time period and have demonstrated that they can meet current production requirements. Moreover, the legacy systems have evolved over time and often represent a collection of disparate hardware platforms containing many different types of technologies. Examples include businesses having mainframe, client/server, and networked systems running at the same time. The acquiring company has the option of continuing to use the legacy systems exclusively, to phase in new technology while continuing to use the legacy systems, or to replace the old systems with new technologies.

IT Integration

Back office operations, such as order entry and billing, of many companies often consist of software that runs on one technical platform but will not run on another. New programming languages, such as Sun Microsystem's JAVA, help to resolve these cross-platform problems. Moreover, new solutions to bridging, routing, and switching are emerging. However, software problems that arise during integration are often unusual and do not lend themselves to "off-the-shelf" solutions. Solving these problems may be further compounded by the continuing shift from mainframe systems to client–server to networked computers.

Finance

Some target companies will be operated as stand-alone operations, while others will be completely merged with the acquirer's existing business. Many international acquisitions involve companies in areas that are geographically remote from the parent company and operate largely independently from the parent. Such situations require a great deal of effort to ensure that the buyer can monitor the financial results of the new business' operations from a distance, even if the parent has its representative permanently on site. This monitoring requires reliable financial reporting.

Implementing Internal Controls and Financial Reporting

The acquirer should establish a budgeting process and signature approval levels to control spending. Signing authority levels refer to levels of expenditures that must be approved in writing by a designated manager. The magnitude of approval levels will vary by the size of firm. At a minimum, the budget should require projections of monthly cash inflows and outflows for the coming year. The budget projection will be used to monitor the firm's actual progress against forecast.

Implementing External Financial Reporting

In the United States, certain companies must file annual and quarterly reports with the SEC (see Chapter 2, this volume). These reports include balance sheets as of the end of the most recent and prior fiscal years. Comparative income statements and statements of cash flows must be included for the most recent and preceding 2 fiscal years. Notes to the financial statements are required for the most recent 2 fiscal years. Although annual financial statements must be audited, quarterly statements need not be. Returns must be filed annually with the Internal Revenue Services and in compliance with the rules and regulations included in the Internal Revenue Code.

Integrating Financial Functions

If the objective of the new company is to provide these types of support services at the lowest possible cost, the firm may choose to centralize and standardize many finance-related activities. Under this arrangement, decision making would be highly centralized. In contrast, if the intent is to increase focus on the customer, the new company may choose to place as many key functions as close to the customer as possible. This implies that the finance and accounting functions should be decentralized and moved to the operating units. In either case, several operational imperatives must be followed. There can be no disruption of the flow of accurate financial information during the integration process. Information systems put in place must be sufficiently flexible to grow with the new organization and to accommodate future acquisitions. Finally, substantial effort should be devoted to ensuring that billing errors are kept to a minimum. Customer surveys consistently show that billing errors are among the greatest areas of concern. The potential for escalating errors is highest during integration because of the sheer magnitude of the task at hand.

Sales

The extent to which the sales forces of the two firms are combined depends on the their relative size, the nature of their products and markets, and their geographic location. Based on these considerations, the sales forces may be wholly integrated or operated separately. A relatively small sales force may be readily combined with the larger sales force if the products they sell and the markets they serve are sufficiently similar. In contrast, the sales forces may be kept separate if the products they sell require in-depth understanding of the customers' needs and a detailed knowledge of the product. For example, firms using the "consultative selling" approach employ highly trained specialists to advise current or potential customers on how the firm's product and service offering can be used to solve particular customer problems. Consequently, a firm may have a separate sales force for each product or service sold to specific markets. Sales forces in globally dispersed businesses are often kept separate to reflect the uniqueness of their markets except for certain support activities such as training or technical support. These activities are often centralized and used to support sales forces in several different countries. Geographically dispersed sales forces may be linked by reporting relationships to regional or other centralized sales management structures.

The benefits of integrating sales forces include significant cost savings by eliminating duplicate sales representatives and related support expenses such as travel and entertainment expenses and training. A single sales force may also minimize potential confusion by enabling customers to deal with a single sales representative in the purchase of multiple products and services. Moreover, an integrated sales force may facilitate product cross-selling (i.e., the sale of one firm's products to the other firm's customers).

Marketing

Often the greatest challenges facing the integration of the marketing function center on ensuring that the customer sees a consistent image in advertising and promotional campaigns. For example, the acquired company may be offering an explicit or implied warranty that the acquirer finds unacceptable. However, ensuring consistency should not result in confusing the customer by radically changing a product's image or how it is sold. Other challenges include the extent to which some portion of the marketing services can be provided by outside vendors.

The location and degree of integration of the marketing function depends on the global nature of the business, the diversity or uniqueness of product lines, and the pace of change in the marketplace. A business with operations worldwide is often inclined to decentralize marketing to the local countries to increase awareness of local laws and cultural patterns. Companies with a large number of product lines, which can be grouped into logical categories or which require extensive product knowledge, may also opt to disperse the marketing function to the various operating units. Finally, if the market for a product or set of products is changing rapidly, it is crucial that the marketing function be kept as close to the customer as possible. This expedites the inclusion of changing customer requirements into product development cycles and changes in the advertising and promotional campaigns needed to support the sale of these products.

Purchasing and Supply Chain Management

According to an analysis of 50 M&As, managing the merged firm's purchasing function and supply chain efficiently can reduce the total cost of goods and services purchased by merged companies by 10–15%. Companies in this sample have been able to recover at least half of the premium paid for the target company by moving aggressively to manage their purchasing activities (Chapman, Dempsey, Ramsdell, and Bell: 1998). For firms in this sample, purchased goods and services, including office furniture, raw materials, and outside contractors, constituted up to 75% of the firms' total spending.

The opportunity to reap substantial savings from suppliers comes immediately following closing of the transaction. A merger creates uncertainty among both companies' suppliers, particularly if they might have to compete against each other for business with the combined firms. Many will offer cost savings as well as new partnership arrangements, given the merged organization's greater bargaining power to renegotiate contracts.

The newly combined company may choose to realize savings by reducing the number of their suppliers. The first step is for both the acquirer and the acquired company to identify their critical suppliers. This should have been done as part of the premerger due diligence. The list should be kept relatively short. The focus should be on those accounting for the largest share of purchased materials expenses. These suppliers should be subject to a certification program which companies use to approve suppliers. Such programs tend to be common for manufacturing but not for service companies.

Research and Development

The role of R&D is an extremely important source of value in many mergers and acquisitions. Often the buyer's and seller's organizations are either working on duplicate projects or projects not germane to the buyer's long-term strategy. Consequently, such activities need to be rationalized. The integration team responsible for managing the integration of R&D activities needs to define future areas of R&D collaboration and to set priorities for future R&D research subject to senior management approval.

Barriers to R&D integration include the differing research time frames of different projects and of the personnel involved in conducting research. For example, some scientists and engineers may feel that their current projects require at least 10 years of continuing research, whereas others are looking for results in a much shorter time frame. Another obstacle is that some personnel stand to lose in terms of titles, prestige, and power if they collaborate. Finally, the acquirer's and the target's R&D financial return expectations may be different. The acquirer may wish to give R&D a higher or lower priority in the combined operation of the two companies.

A starting point for integrating R&D is to have researchers from both companies make presentations of their work to each other, meet with each other, and to co-locate. Work teams can also follow a balanced scorecard approach for obtaining funding for their projects. In this process, R&D projects are scored according to their impact on key stakeholders, such as shareholders and customers. Those projects receiving the highest scores are funded while others are deferred or eliminated.

Human Resources

Traditionally, human resource (HR) departments have been highly centralized and have been responsible for conducting opinion surveys, assessing managerial effectiveness, developing hiring and staffing plans, and providing training. HR departments are often instrumental in conducting strategic reviews of the strengths and weaknesses of potential target companies, in the integration of the acquirer's and target's management teams, in recommending and implementing pay and benefit plans, and in the dissemination of information about acquisitions. More recently, the trend has been to disperse the human resources function to the operating unit. Highly centralized HR functions have been found to be very expensive and not responsive to the local needs of the operating units. Hiring and training can often be more effectively done at the operating unit level. Most of the traditional HR activities are conducted at the operating units with the exception of the administration of benefit plans, management of HR information systems, and in some cases organizational development (see Porter & Wood: 1998).

INTEGRATING CORPORATE CULTURES

Culture refers to a common set of values, traditions, and beliefs that influence behavior. Large, diverse businesses have an overarching culture and a series of subcultures that reflect local conditions. When two companies with different cultures merge, the newly formed company will take on a new culture that may be quite different from either the acquirer's or the target's culture. Cultural differences are not inherently bad or good. They can instill creativity in the new company or create a contentious environment.

Cultural Issues

Cultural issues can run the gamut from dress codes to compensation. They differ by size and maturity of the company, by industry, and by geographic location. Maturity is defined by the number of years in business.

Company Size and Maturity

Start-up companies are usually highly unstructured and informal in terms of dress and decision making. Compensation may consist largely of stock options and other forms of deferred income. Benefits, beyond those required by state and federal law, and other "perks," such as company cars, are largely nonexistent. Company policies are frequently either nonexistent, not in writing, or made up as needed. Internal controls covering items such as employee expense accounts are often minimal. In contrast, larger, mature companies are frequently more highly structured with well-defined internal controls, compensation structures, benefit packages, and employment policies. Such firms have grown too large and complex to function in an orderly manner without some structure in the form of internal policies and controls. Employees usually have clearly defined job descriptions and career paths. Decision making can be either decentralized at the operating unit level or centralized within a corporate office. In either case, the process for decision making is often well defined. Decision making may be rapid or ponderous, requiring consensus within a large management bureaucracy.

Industry Differences

Industry and geographic differences create another set of challenges. High-technology companies, no matter what the size, are often far more informal in terms of dress codes and working hours. In contrast, companies dealing directly with the public, such as banks and retailers, often have formal dress codes and require a high level of decorum to instill a sense of confidence and trust in the public.

International Considerations

Language barriers and different customs, working conditions, work ethics, and legal structures create an entirely new set of challenges in integrating cross-border transactions. If cultures are extremely different, integration may be inappropriate. For this reason, acquiring and acquired companies in international transactions frequently maintain separate corporate headquarters, stock listings, and CEOs for an extended period of time (*Wall Street Journal,* 1996).

In choosing how to manage the new acquisition, a manager with an in-depth knowledge of the acquirer's priorities, decision-making processes, and operations is appropriate in entering a new country where the acquirer expects to make very large new investments. However, when the acquirer already has existing operations within the country, a manager with substantial industry experience in the country is generally preferable because of their cultural sensitivity and knowledge of local laws and regulations. Local managers are especially helpful when foreign customer requirements are substantially different from domestic customers or when all production is done within the foreign country.

Case Study 6-5 illustrates how the acquirer's sensitivity to potential cultural conflicts helps maintain the value of the target company. Note how Allianz AG attempted to minimize cultural conflict by keeping Pimco's operations largely intact and allowing a high level of local autonomy. Allianz recognized that the real value in this acquisition is in the expertise and reputation of Pimco's money managers. To retain key personnel, Allianz offered operational independence, employment contracts, and very lucrative deferred compensation packages. Allianz also recognized that the highly successful portfolio management techniques used by Pimco's money managers could best be applied to managing customer accounts in Europe by transferring selected Pimco personnel to their European operations.

CASE STUDY 6-5. OVERCOMING CULTURE CLASH: ALLIANZ AG BUYS PIMCO ADVISORS LP

On November 7, 1999, Allianz AG, the leading German insurance conglomerate, acquired Pimco Advisors LP for $3.3 billion. The Pimco acquisition boosts assets under management at Allianz from $400 billion to $650 billion, making it the sixth largest money manager in the world. The acquisition gives the firm the critical mass to compete against Citigroup, Axa, and other financial service giants. The transaction also gives Allianz a foothold in the U.S. money management business to help offset fluctuations in Allianz's income generated in other geographic areas.

The cultural divide separating the two firms represented a potentially daunting challenge. Allianz's management was well aware that firms distracted by culture clashes and the morale problems and mistrust they breed are less likely to realize the synergies and savings that caused them to acquire the company in the first place. Allianz was acutely aware of the potential problems as a result of difficulties they had experienced following the acquisition of Firemen's Fund, a major U.S.-based property–casualty company. A major motivation for the merger acquisition was to obtain the well-known skills of the elite Pimco money managers to broaden Allianz's financial services product offering.

Although retention bonuses can buy loyalty in the short run, employees of the acquired firm need much more than money in the long term. Pimco's money managers have stated publicly that they want Allianz to let them operate independently, the way Pimco existed under their former parent, Pacific Mutual Life Insurance Company. Allianz has decided not only to run Pimco as an independent subsidiary but also to move $100 billion of Allianz's assets to Pimco. Bill Gross, Pimco's legendary bond trader, and other top Pimco money managers are collecting about one-fourth of their compensation in the form of Allianz stock. Moreover, most of the top managers are being asked to sign long-term employment contracts and have received retention bonuses.

Historically, Pimco's bond fund managers have outperformed their counterparts both in the United States and Europe. Allianz wanted to spread these skills throughout the Allianz organization. To achieve this objective, several top investment managers at Pimco are being transferred from Orange County, California, to Germany to teach Allianz their money-management techniques.

Joachim Faber, chief of money management at Allianz, played an essential role in smoothing over cultural differences. Led by Faber, top Allianz executives had been visiting Pimco for months and having quiet dinners with top Pimco fixed income investment officials and their families. The intent of these intimate meetings was to reassure these officials that their operation would remain independent under Allianz's ownership. The perceived value in this merger is clearly the acquisition of investment talent. Faber noted that "There's not one penny of savings from synergies in this deal."

Source: Lansner, 1999.

Characteristics of the New Corporate Culture

When two separate corporate cultures combine, it is crucial to realize from the outset that the combined companies will create a new culture that in some respects may be distinctly different from the two previous cultures. Moreover, it may be impossible to predict the distinguishing features of the new culture. In general, cultural issues are going to be less in mergers taking place between companies in the same industry (except perhaps for firms which had been virulent competitors) and of comparable size than in cross-industry or cross-border transactions or those involving companies substantially different in size and maturity.

Because a company's culture is something that evolves over a long period of time, it is doubtful that changing the culture can be carefully managed. A more realistic expectation is that employees in the new company can be encouraged to take on a shared vision, set of core values, and behaviors deemed important by senior management. However, getting to the point at which employees wholly embrace management's desired culture may take years and may be unachievable in practice. What follows is a process intended to expedite the acceptance of the desired vision, values, and behaviors by the new corporate culture.

Cultural Profiling

The first step in integrating cultures is to develop a cultural profile of both the acquirer and the acquired companies. The information may be obtained from employee surveys, interviews, and by observing management styles and practices in both companies. The information is then used to show how the two cultures are alike or different and what are the comparative strengths and weaknesses of each culture. Common differences may include having one culture value individualism while the other values teamwork. Following a review of this information, senior management must decide those characteristics of both cultures that should be emphasized in the new business' culture.

Techniques for Integrating Corporate Cultures

Sharing common goals, standards, services, and space can be highly effective and practical ways to integrate disparate cultures (Malekzadeh and Nahavandi: 1990, pp. 55–57; Lajoux: 1998, pp. 187–191).

Shared Goals

Common goals serve to drive different units to cooperate. For example, at the functional level, setting exact timetables and procedures for new product development can drive the different units of the organization to work together as project teams to launch the product by the target date. At the corporate level, a multiyear plan to improve the stock price can drive collective performance for the duration of the plan. Although it is helpful in the integration process to have shared or common goals, individuals must still have specific goals to minimize the tendency of some to underperform while benefiting from the collective labors of others.

Shared Standards

Shared standards or practices enable the adoption of the "best practices" found in one unit or function by another entity. Standards include operating procedures, technological specifications, ethical values, internal controls, employee performance measures, and comparable reward systems throughout the combined companies.

Shared Services

Some functional services can be logically centralized. The centralized functions then provide services to the operating units. Commonly centralized services include accounting, legal, public relations, internal audit, and information processing. The most common way to share services is to use a common staff. Alternatively, a firm can create a support services unit and allow operating units to purchase services from it or to buy similar services outside the company.

Shared Space

Isolating target company employees in a separate building or even a floor of the same building will impair the integration process. Mixing offices or even locating acquired company employees in space adjacent to the parent's offices is a highly desirable way to improve communication and idea sharing. Sharing laboratories, computer rooms, or libraries can also facilitate communication and cooperation.

TRAVELERS AND CITICORP MERGER

The merger of Travelers and Citicorp (Case Study 6-6) illustrates many of the problems encountered during the integration period. At $73 billion, the merger between Travelers and Citicorp was the second largest merger in 1998 and is an excellent example of how integrating two businesses can be far more daunting than consummating the transaction.

Their experience demonstrates how everything can be going smoothly in most of the businesses being integrated, except for one, and how this single business can sop up all of management's time and attention to correct its problems. In some respects, it highlights the ultimate challenge of every major integration effort: getting people to work together, despite coming from distinctly different corporate cultures. It also spotlights the complexity of managing large, intricate businesses when authority at the top is divided among several managers. Citicorp was widely regarded as a very strong marketing and planning organization, but it was viewed as weak operationally and on execution of business plans.

CASE STUDY 6-6. TRAVELERS AND CITICORP MERGE

The strategic rationale for the merger relied heavily on cross-selling the financial services products of both corporations to the other's customers. The combination would create a financial services giant capable of making loans, accepting deposits, selling mutual funds, underwriting securities, selling insurance, and dispensing financial planning advice. Citicorp had relationships with thousands of companies around the world. In contrast, Travelers' Salomon Smith Barney unit dealt with relatively few companies. It was believed that Salomon could expand its underwriting and investment banking business dramatically by having access to the much larger Citicorp commercial customer base. Moreover, Citicorp lending officers, who frequently had access only to midlevel corporate executives at companies within their customer base, would have access to more senior executives as a result of Salomon's investment banking relationships.

At the time, Citicorp-Travelers was faced with the challenge of either changing current law or selling off large portions of Travelers' insurance business. Under new financial service legislation, such combinations are now legal. Although the characteristics of the two businesses seemed to be conceptually complementary, motivating all parties to cooperate proved a major challenge. Due to the combined firm's Co-CEO arrangement, the lack of clearly delineated authority exhausted management time and attention without resolving major integration issues. This was particularly true in the Global Corporate Business product area.

Some decisions proved to be relatively easy. Others were not. Citicorp, in stark contrast to Travelers, was known for being highly bureaucratic with marketing, credit, and finance departments at the global, North American, and business unit levels. North American departments were quickly eliminated. Salomon was highly regarded in the fixed income security area, so Citicorp's fixed income operations were folded into Salomon. Citicorp received Salomon's foreign exchange trading operations due to their pre-merger reputation in this business. However, both the Salomon and Citicorp derivatives' business tended to overlap and compete for the same customers. Each business unit within Travelers and Citicorp had a tendency to believe they "owned" the relationship with their customers and were hesitant to introduce others that might ultimately assume control over this relationship. Pay constituted a very thorny issue. Investment banker salaries in Salomon Smith Barney tended to dwarf those of Citicorp middle-level managers. When it came time to cut costs, issues arose around who would be terminated.

Citicorp was organized along three major product areas: global corporate business, global consumer business, and asset management. The merged companies' management structure consisted of three executives in the global corporate business area, and two in each of the other major product areas. Each area contained senior managers from both companies. Moreover, each area reported to the Co-Chairmen and CEOs John Reed and Sanford Weill, former CEOs of Citicorp and Travelers, respectively. Of the three major product areas, the integration of two was progressing well, reflecting the collegial atmosphere of the top managers in both areas. However, the global business area was well behind schedule, beset by major riffs among the three top managers. Travelers' corporate culture was characterized as strongly focused on the bottom line, with a lean corporate overhead structure and a strong predisposition to impose its style on the Citicorp culture. In contrast, Citicorp, under John Reed, tended to be more focused on the strategic vision of the new company rather than on day-to-day operations.

During 1998, Travelers was subject to sizable fixed-income trading losses at its Salomon Smith Barney operations; both Citicorp and Travelers sustained huge losses when Russia defaulted on its debt. Although these problems occurred independently of the merger, they compounded efforts to support the stock price while the two businesses were being integrated. The organizational structure coupled with personal differences among certain key managers ultimately resulted in the termination of James Dimon, who had been a star as President of Travelers before the merger, leaving each major product area co-CEOs.

On July 28, 1999, the co-chairman arrangement was dissolved. Sanford Weill assumed responsibility for the firm's operating businesses and financial function, while John Reed became the focal point for the company's Internet, advanced development, technology, human resources, and legal functions. This change in organizational structure was intended to help clarify lines of authority and to overcome some of the obstacles in managing a large and complex set of businesses that result from split decision-making authority. On Februray 28, 2000, John Reed formally retired.

Source: *Fortune,* 1999; *Business Week,* 1999; Bloomberg.com, 1999c.

INTEGRATING BUSINESS ALLIANCES

Business alliances, particularly those created to consolidate resources such as manufacturing facilities or sales forces, must also pay close attention to integration activities. Unlike M&As, alliances usually involve shared control. Successful implementation requires maintaining a good working relationship between venture partners. When partners cannot maintain a good working relationship, the alliance is destined to fail. The breakdown in the working relationship is often a result of an inadequate integration (see Lynch: 1993, pp. 189–205).

INTEGRATING MECHANISMS

Robert Porter Lynch suggests six integration mechanisms to apply to business alliances: (1) leadership, (2) teamwork and role clarification, (3) control by coordination, (4) policies and values, (5) consensus decision making, and (6) resource commitments.

Leadership

Although the terms *leadership* and *management* are often used interchangeably, there are critical differences. A leader sets direction and makes things happen, while a manager follows through and ensures that things continue to happen. Leadership involves vision, drive, enthusiasm, and strong selling skills; management involves communication, planning, delegating, coordinating, problem solving, making choices, and clarifying lines of responsibility. Successful alliances require the proper mix of both sets of skills. The leader must provide clear direction, values, and behaviors to create a culture that focuses on the alliance's strategic objectives as its top priority. Managers foster teamwork and promote long-term stability in the shared control environment of the business alliance.

In most U.S. alliances, there is only one leader, with other participants willing to follow. If the other partners agree to be followers, there is not any problem. However, in many international alliances involving large firms from industrialized nations, partners are often unwilling to assume a subordinate role. The emphasis will be on shared control or equality.

Teamwork and Role Clarification

Teamwork is the underpinning that makes alliances work. Teamwork comes from trust, fairness, and discipline. Teams reach across functional lines and often consist of diverse experts or lower level managers with critical problem-solving skills. The team provides functional managers with the broader, flexible staffing to augment their own specialized staff. Teams tend to create better coordination and communication at lower levels of the alliance, as well as between partners in the venture. Because teams represent individuals with varied backgrounds and possibly conflicting agendas, they can be a forum for fostering rather than resolving conflict. The alliance manager must be diligent in clarifying what types of behaviors will not be tolerated. Problems must be confronted openly and resolved amicably, even if it involves changing the composition of the team.

Coordination

In contrast to an acquisition, no one company is in charge. Alliances do not lend themselves to control through mandate; rather in the alliance, control is best exerted through coordination. The best alliance managers are those who coordinate activities through effective communication. When problems arise, the manager's role is to manage the decision-making process, not necessarily to make the decision. Decisions are made by bringing together the relevant parties to create a consensus.

Policies and Values

Alliance employees need to understand how decisions are made, what the priorities are, who will be held accountable, and how rewards will be determined. When people know where they stand and what to expect, they are better able to deal with ambiguity and uncertainty. This level of clarity can be communicated through a distinct set of policies and procedures that are well understood by employees throughout the joint venture or partnership. The extent to which the partners can agree on policies depends to a great extent on the degree of trust between partners. Formal policies serve as a substitute for the traditional corporate hierarchy.

Consensus Decision Making

Consensus decision making does not mean that decisions are based on unanimity. Rather, decisions are based on the premise that all participants have had an opportunity to express their opinions and that they are willing to accept the final decision even though they may not be in complete agreement. Like any other business, operating decisions must be made within a reasonable period of time. The formal decision-making structure will vary with the type of legal structure. Joint ventures often have a board of directors and a management committee, which meet quarterly and monthly, respectively. Projects are normally governed by steering committees.

Boards, management committees, and steering committees consist of representatives from all alliance participants. These groups must clearly define roles and operational reporting relationships at the outset. The level of operational autonomy for the alliance manager needs to be clearly spelled out. When conflicts do arise, the responsibility for resolving these issues must be given to a predetermined level within the organization.

Resource Commitments

Many alliances are started to take advantage of complementary skills or resources available from alliance participants. The alliance can achieve its strategic objective only if all parties to the alliance live up to the resources they agreed to commit. The failure of one party to meet its commitments will erode trust, undermine teamwork, and limit the alliance's ability to meet its objectives. Meeting resource commitments also means contributing high-quality resources, such as a partner's best managers or most highly skilled employees. Personnel contributed to the alliance by a partner should be those whose goals and skills match the needs of the venture. Unfortunately, all too often alliances become "dumping grounds" for second-rate managers and employees who could not work well in the alliance's parent organizations.

THE PACE OF INTEGRATION FOR BUSINESS ALLIANCES

Although M&As focus on speed, most business alliances tend to phase their integration efforts over time. A period of rapid consolidation of facilities and staff takes place at the outset of the alliance formation. However, subsequent integration activity tends to slow dramatically. Once the business alliance has been formed, the pace and extent of integration is largely determined by the relative bargaining power of the parents. Many business alliances require resource contributions from their parents throughout the life of the venture. Efforts to integrate additional resources are often slowed by the parents' efforts to understand the impact their own contributions can have on their potential bargaining power within the alliance (Andersen Consulting: 1999). Resource contributions, which augment a parent's bargaining power the most, are those which are integral to the success of the alliance and are easy for the contributor to withdraw.

THINGS TO REMEMBER

Postclosing integration is a critical phase of the M&A process. Integration can itself be viewed in terms of a process consisting of six activities: integration planning, developing communication plans, creating a new organization, developing staffing plans, functional integration, and integrating corporate cultures. Both communication and cultural integration extend beyond what is normally considered the conclusion of the integration period.

Combining companies must be done quickly (i.e., 6 to 12 months) to achieve proper staffing levels, eliminate redundant assets, and generate the financial returns expected by shareholders. Delay contributes to employee anxiety and accelerates the loss of key talent and managers, as well as to the deterioration of employee morale among those that remain. The loss of key talent and managers is often viewed as the greatest risk associated with the integration phase. This is especially true for high-technology and services companies with few tangible assets.

Successfully integrated M&As are those that demonstrate leadership in candidly and continuously communicating a clear vision, a set of values, and unambiguous priorities to all employees. Successful integration efforts are those that are well planned, that appoint an integration manager and team with clearly defined lines of authority, and that make the tough decisions early in the process. These decisions include organizational structure, reporting relationships, spans of control, people selection, roles and responsibilities, and workforce reduction. Throughout the integration process, all effort is focussed on those issues having the greatest near-term impact.

Unlike mergers and acquisitions, the integration of business alliances tends to be phased. Resources are contributed at the outset to enable the formation of the alliance. Subsequent resource contributions are subject to a lengthy negotiation process in which the partners are trying to get the most favorable terms. Since alliances involve shared control, the integration process requires good working relationships with the other participants. Successful integration also requires leadership capable of defining a clear sense of direction and well-defined priorities and managers who accomplish their objectives as much by coordinating activities through effective communication as by unilateral decision making. Like M&As, cross-functional teams are widely used to achieve integration. Finally, the successful integration of business alliances, as well as M&As, demands that the necessary resources, in terms of the best people, the appropriate skills, and sufficient capital, be committed to the process.

CHAPTER DISCUSSION QUESTIONS

6-1.   Why is the integration phase of the acquisition process considered so important?

6-2.   Why should acquired companies be integrated quickly?

6-3.   Why might the time required to integrate acquisitions vary by industry?

6-4.   What are the costs of employee turnover?

6-5.   Why is candid and continuous communication so important during the integration phase?

6-6.   What are the messages that might be communicated to the various audiences or stakeholders of the new company?

6-7.   What are examples of difficult decisions that should be made early in the integration process?

6-8.   What are some of the contract-related "transition issues" that should be resolved before closing?

6-9.   How does the process for integrating business alliances differ from that of integrating an acquisition? How are they similar?

CHAPTER BUSINESS CASE

CASE STUDY 6-7. DAIMLER ACQUIRES CHRYSLER—
ANATOMY OF A CROSS-BORDER TRANSACTION

The combination of Chrysler and Daimler created the third largest auto manufacturer in the world, with more than 428,000 employees worldwide. Conceptually, the strategic fit seemed obvious. German engineering in the automotive industry was highly regarded and could be used to help Chrysler upgrade both its product quality and production process. In contrast, Chrysler had a much better track record than Daimler in getting products to market rapidly. Daimler's distribution network in Europe would give Chrysler products better access to European markets; Chrysler could provide parts and service support for Mercedes-Benz in the United States. With greater financial strength, the combined companies would be better able to make inroads into Asian and South American markets.

Daimler's product markets were viewed as mature, and Chrysler was being pressured by escalating R&D costs and retooling demands in the wake of rapidly changing technology. Both companies watched with concern the growing excess capacity of the worldwide automotive manufacturing industry. Daimler and Chrysler had been in discussions about doing something together for some time. They initiated discussions about creating a joint venture to expand into Asian and South American markets, where both companies had a limited presence. Despite the termination of these discussions as a result of disagreement over responsibilities, talks were renewed in early 1998. Both companies shared the same sense of urgency about their vulnerability to companies such as Toyota and Volkswagen.

The limitations of cultural differences became apparent during efforts to integrate the two companies. Daimler had been run as a conglomerate, in contrast to Chrysler's highly centralized operations. Daimler managers were accustomed to lengthy reports and meetings to review the reports. Under the direction of Jurgen Schrempp, the Daimler CEO, many top management positions in Chrysler went to Germans. Only a few former Chrysler executives reported directly to Schrempp. Made rich by the merger, the potential for a loss of American managers within Chrysler was high. Chrysler managers were accustomed to a higher degree of independence than their German counterparts. Mercedes dealers in the United States balked at the thought of Chryslers' trucks still sporting the old Mopar logo delivering parts to their dealerships. All the trucks had to be repainted.

Charged with the task of finding cost savings, the integration team identified a list of hundreds of opportunities, offering billions of dollars in savings. For example, Mercedes dropped its plans to develop a battery-powered car in favor of Chrysler's electric minivan. The finance and purchasing departments were combined worldwide. This would enable the combined company to take advantage of savings on bulk purchases of commodity products such as steel, aluminum, and glass. In addition, inventories could be managed more efficiently, as surplus components purchased in one area could be shipped to other facilities in need of such parts. Long-term supply contracts and the dispersal of much of the purchasing operations to the plant level meant that it could take as long as 5 years to fully integrate the purchasing department.

The time required to integrate the manufacturing operations could be significantly longer, since both Daimler and Chrysler had designed their operations differently and are subject to different union work rules. Changing manufacturing processes will require re-negotiating union agreements as the multiyear contracts expire. All of this must take place without causing product quality to suffer. To facilitate this process, Mercedes has issued very specific guidelines for each car brand pertaining to R&D, purchasing, manufacturing, and marketing. Source: Daimler-Chrysler: 1998; Freepress.com: 1998; Shilling: 1999; *BBC News:* 1998.

Case Study Discussion Questions

1. Identify ways in which the merger combined companies with complementary skills and resources.
2. What are the major cultural differences between Daimler and Chrysler?
3. What were the principal risks to the merger?
4. Why might it take so long to integrate manufacturing operations and certain functions such as purchasing?

Solutions to these questions are found in the Appendix at the back of this book.

REFERENCES

Alexander, Marcus, Andrew Campbell, and Michael Gould, "Parenting Advantage," *Prism,* Arthur D. Little, Incorporated, Second Quarter 1995, pp. 23–33.

Altier, William J., "A Method for Unearthing Likely Post-Deal Synergies," *Mergers and Acquisitions,* January/February 1997, pp. 33–35.

Anderson Consulting, *Global Survey Acquisition and Alliance Integration,* 1999. Available: www.ac .com/overview

BBC News, "Daimler, Chrysler Confirm Merger," May 7, 1998. Available: http://news1.thisbbc.co.uk

Bloomberg.com, "Profit Improvement at Exxon-Mobil," December 16, 1999a.

Bloomberg.com, "Albertsons and American Stores: A Marriage in Trouble," November 1, 1999b.

Bloomberg.com, "Citicorp-Travelers Merger," February 20, 1999c.

Burke, Warner, and Peter Jackson, "Making the SmithKline Beecham Merger Work," *Human Resources Management,* 30, no. 1, Spring 1991, pp. 69–87.

Business Week, "This Case against Mergers," October 31, 1995, pp. 122–125.

Business Week, "Citigroup: So Much for 50–50," August 16, 1999, p. 80.

Business Week, "Making Corporate Boards Effective," January 24, 2000, pp. 142–152.

Campbell, Andrew, David Sadtler, and Richard Koch, *Breakup! When Companies are Worth More Dead than Alive,* Oxford: Capstone, 1997.

Cartwright, Sue, *Mergers and Acquisitions: The Human Factor,* Boston: Butterworth and Heinemann, 1998, pp. 56–65.

Chakrabarti, Alok, "Organizational Factors in Post-Acquisition Performance," *IEEE Transactions in Engineering Management,* 37 (4), November 1990, pp. 259–266.

Chapman, Timothy L., Jack J. Dempsey, Glenn Ramsdell, and Trudy E. Bell, "Purchasing's Big Moment—After a Merger," *The McKinsey Quarterly,* 1, 1998, pp. 56–65.

Cisco Systems, "Annual Report, 1999." Available: www.reportgallery.com

Clemente, Mark N. and David S. Greenspan, *Empowering Human Resources in the Mergers and Acquisitions Process,* Clemente, Greenspan & Company, 1999.

Copeland, Tom, Tim Koller, and Jack Murrin, *Valuation: Measuring and Managing the Value of Companies,* John Wiley & Sons, 1990.

Coopers & Lybrand, "Most Acquisitions Fail, C&L Study Says," *Mergers & Acquisitions Report 7,* no. 47, November 18, 1996, pp. 2–4.

Cossey, Bernard, "Systems Assessment in Acquired Subsidiaries," *Accountancy,* January 1991, pp. 98–99.

Daimler-Chrysler, "Daimler Buys Chrysler," [Press Release], July 2, 1998.

Down, James W., "The M&A Game is Often Won or Lost after the Deal," *Management Review Executive Forum,* November 1995, p. 10.

Financial Times, "Bugged by Failures," November 29, 1996, p. 8.

Flannagan, David J., and K. C. O'Shaughanessy, "Determinants of Layoff Announcements Following Mergers and Acquisitions: An Empirical Investigation," *Strategic Management Journal,* 19 (10), October 1998, pp. 989–999.

Freepress.com, "Automakers to Announce Changes Together," October 17, 1998. Available: www .freep.com

Fortune, "Citigroup: Scenes from a Merger," January 11, 1999, pp. 76–96.

Goldblatt, Henry, "Merging at Internet Speed," *Fortune,* November 8, 1999, pp. 164–165.

Hayes, Robert H., "The Human Side of Acquisitions," *Management Review,* November 1979, p. 41.

Kearney Inc., A.T., *Shaping the Organizational Future,* Special Report Series, No. 45, 1998.

Lajoux, Alexandra Reed, *The Art of M&A Integration,* New York: McGraw-Hill, 1998.

Lansner, Jonathan, "Common Ground Was Key," *Orange County Register,* November 1, 1999, p. 4.

Lynch, Robert P., *Business Alliances Guide: The Hidden Competitive Weapon,* John Wiley & Sons, 1993.

Malekzadeh, Ali R. and Nahavandi, Afsaneh, "Making Mergers Work by Managing Cultures," *Journal of Business Strategy,* vol. 11, no. 3, May/June 1990, pp. 55–57.

Marks, Mitchell, L., *From Turmoil to Triumph: New Life after Mergers, Acquisitions, and Downsizing,* Lexington Books, 1996

Marks, Mitchell L., *Joining Forces: Making One Plus One Equal Three in Mergers, Acquisitions and Alliances,* Jossey-Bass, 1998.

McKinsey & Company, "Creating Shareholder Value through Merger and / or Acquisition: A McKinsey & Company Perspective, April 1987, cited in Tom Copeland, Tim Koller, and Jack Murrin, (Eds.), *Valuation: Measuring and Managing the Value of Companies,* New York: John Wiley & Sons, 1990, p. 321.

Porter, Richard, and Cynthia N. Wood, "Post-Merger Integration," in David J. BenDaniel and Arthur H. Rosenbloom (Eds.), *International M&A: Joint Ventures and Beyond,* New York: John Wiley & Sons, 1998, pp. 459–497.

Pursche, William R., "Pharmaceuticals—The Consolidation Isn't Over," *The McKinsey Quarterly,* (2), 1996, pp. 110–119.

Reed-Lajoux, Alexandra, *The Art of M&A Integration: A Guide to Merging Resources, Processes, and Responsibilities,* New York: McGraw-Hill, 1998.

Right Management Consultants, *Lessons Learned From Mergers & Acquisitions: Best Practices in Workforce Integration,* 1999. Available: www. right.com

Sanderson, Susan and Mustafa Uzumeri, *The Innovative Imperative: Strategies for Managing Products, Models, and Families,* Burr Ridge, Il: Irwin Professional, Publishing, 1997.

Shilling, A. Gary, "The Acquire and Fire Economy," *Forbes,* January 25, 1999.

Shivdasani, Anil, " Board Composition, Ownership Structure, and Hostile Takeovers," *Journal of Accounting and Economics,* 16, 1993, pp. 167–198.

Wall Street Journal, "When Things Go Wrong," November 18, 1996, p. R-25.

Shaping the Organizational Future, no. 45, Chicago, A.T. Kearney, Inc., 1998.

Wall Street Journal, "Disability Claims Mirror Rising Job Cuts," November 21, 1996, p. A-2.

Wall Street Journal, "Together but Equal," September 26, 1996, p. R-20.

Walsh, James P., "Doing a Deal: Merger and Acquisition Negotiations and Their Impact Upon Target Company Top Management Turnover," *Strategic Management Journal,* 10 (4), July/August 1989, pp. 307–322.

Walsh, James P., and John W. Ellwood, "Mergers, Acquisitions, and the Pruning of Managerial Deadwood," *Strategic Management Journal,* 12 (3), March 1991, pp. 201–217.

Watson Wyatt Worldwide, *Assessing and Managing Human Capital—A Key to Maximizing the M&A Deal,* 1998/99 Mergers and Acquisitions Survey, December 1999. Available: www .watsonwyatt.com

PART

III

MERGER AND ACQUISITION TOOLS AND CONCEPTS

7

A PRIMER ON MERGER
AND ACQUISITION
VALUATION

Happiness is positive cash flow.

—*Fred Adler*

As the chief financial officer for her firm, Sara Bertram poured over reams of computer printouts provided by her subordinates. Clearly, considerable effort had been expended to develop a preliminary estimate of the value of a potential acquisition target. As a publicly traded company, considerable financial detail on the target was available. Four financial analysts had labored feverishly through the weekend to collect the data necessary to project cash flows. These cash flows, along with other measures of value, were used to determine the "economic value" of the target firm. By all accounts, the analysis seemed rigorous and complete. Yet something was lacking.

Sara was having considerable difficulty in understanding why projected revenue for the target firm was expected to grow at more than twice the pace of working capital. Similarly, forecasts of capital spending seemed to lag the expected robust growth of the potential acquisition target. Moreover, operating margins were growing throughout the forecast period. The combination of these factors caused the target's projected cash flow to escalate at an unprecedented rate. Were sales growing because of an anticipated improvement in market share? Perhaps improved inventory controls were contributing to a reduction in working capital per dollar of sales during the forecast period. It wasn't clear why capital spending should not at least grow at its historical rate. Could expected improvements in productivity account for the improvement in operating profit margins? Frustrated, Sara summoned the financial analysts to a meeting to explain the assumptions they made in generating the forecast. While expressing appreciation for their substantial effort, she admonished them to be more careful in clearly stating their assumptions. "After all," she said, "the credibility of any forecast is solely dependent on the reasonableness of its underlying assumptions."

OVERVIEW

The purpose of this chapter is to provide an overview of the basics of valuing mergers and acquisitions (M&As). The chapter assumes the reader has a working knowledge of elementary finance and begins with a brief review of rudimentary finance concepts including measuring risk and return, the capital asset pricing model (CAPM), the effects of leverage on risk and return, and calculating present and future values of cash flow.

The cash flow definitions, free cash flow to equity and to the firm, discussed in this chapter will be used in valuation problems in subsequent chapters. The distinction between these cash flow definitions will be particularly relevant for the discussion of leveraged buy-outs in Chapter 11. Five basic methods of valuation are addressed including the income or discounted cash flow, market-based, asset-oriented, cost, and weighted-average methods. The chapter concludes with a discussion of the valuation of intangible assets in recognition of the increasingly important role of technology, knowledge-based, and service-oriented businesses in the global economy.

REQUIRED RETURNS

Investors require a minimum rate of return on an investment to compensate them for the perceived level of risk associated with that investment. The required rate of return must be at least equal to what the investor can receive on alternative investments exhibiting a comparable level of perceived risk. For an excellent discussion of basic concepts of finance, see Laurence Gitman (1997) or Lasher (2000); and Moyer, Mcguigan, and Kretlow (1998).

COST OF EQUITY

The cost of equity (k_e) is the rate of return required to induce investors to purchase a firm's equity. The cost of equity can also be viewed as an opportunity cost because it represents the rate of return investors could earn by investing in equities of comparable risk. The cost of equity can be estimated by using the CAPM, which measures the relationship between expected risk and expected return. It postulates that investors require higher rates of return for accepting higher levels of risk. It also states that the investor's required return is equal to the risk-free rate of return, such as the interest rate on 10-year U.S. Treasury securities, plus a risk premium. Treasury securities are used to approximate the risk-free rate because of the excellent credit worthiness of the U.S. government. The risk premium refers to the additional rate of return in excess of the risk-free rate of return that investors require to purchase a firm's equity. Of the various Treasury debt issues, the 10-year bond rate is often used as a proxy for the risk-free rate, because it is commonly used as a benchmark for pricing other securities, among the most highly liquid debt markets, and less volatile than Treasury issues of a shorter maturity.

$$\text{CAPM: } k_e = R_f + \beta (R_m - R_f),$$

where R_f = risk free rate of return

β = beta

R_m = the expected rate of return on equities

$R_m - R_f$ = 5.5% (i.e., its historical average since 1963, Ibbotson: 1999)

PRETAX COST OF DEBT

The cost of debt represents the cost to the firm of borrowed funds. It reflects the current level of interest rates and the level of default risk as perceived by investors. Interest paid on debt is tax deductible by the firm. In bankruptcy, bondholders are paid before shareholders as the firm's assets are liquidated. Default risk can be measured by the firm's credit rating. However, many smaller firms are not rated.

To approximate the pretax cost of debt for firms that have not been rated by the major credit rating agencies such as Standard and Poor's, compare standard measures of a firm's leverage and ability to satisfy interest expense and principal repayments with those of similar firms that have been rated. Such standard measures include debt-to-equity or total capital ratios, interest coverage ratios, and operating margins. Alternatively, use the firm's interest rate paid on recently borrowed funds. Much of this information can be found in local libraries in such publications as Moody's *Company Data;* Standard & Poor's Corporation's *Descriptions, The Outlook,* and *Bond Guide;* and Value Line's *Investment Survey.*

COST OF CAPITAL

The weighted average cost of capital (WACC) is a broader measure than the cost of equity and represents the return that a firm must earn in order to induce investors to buy its stock and bonds. The WACC is calculated using a weighted average of the firm's cost of equity and cost of debt.

$$\text{WACC} = k_e \times \frac{E}{D + E} + i (1 - t) \times \frac{D}{D + E}$$

where   E = the market value of equity,

                                D = the market value of debt,

                                i = the interest rate on debt,

                                t = the firm's marginal tax rate.

A portion of interest paid on borrowed funds is recoverable by the firm because of the tax deductibility of interest. Therefore, the actual cost of borrowed funds to the firm is estimated by multiplying the pretax interest rate, i, by $(1 - t)$. Furthermore, note that $[E/(D + E)]$ and $[D/(D + E)]$, the weights associated with the cost of equity and debt, reflect the firm's *target* capital structure or capitalization. It is important to remember that these are targets and not the current actual values. The actual market value of equity and debt as a percent of total capitalization may differ from the targets.

Market values rather than book values are used because WACC measures the cost of issuing debt and equity securities. Such securities are issued at market and not book value. The cost of capital formula can be generalized to include other sources of funds available to firms such as preferred stock.

COST OF PREFERRED STOCK

Preferred stock exhibits some of the characteristics of long-term debt in that its dividend is generally constant over time, and it is paid out in the event of bankruptcy before dividends to common shareholders. Unlike interest payments on debt, preferred dividends are not tax deductible. Since preferred stock is riskier than debt but less risky than common stock in bankruptcy, the cost to the company to issue preferred stock should be less than the cost of equity but greater than the cost of debt. Viewing preferred dividends as paid in perpetuity, the cost of preferred stock can be calculated as dividends per share of preferred stock divided by the market value of the preferred stock.

ANALYZING RISK

Risk is the degree of uncertainty associated with the outcome of an investment. It takes into consideration the probability of a loss as well as a gain on an investment. Risk consists of a diversifiable component, such as strikes, defaulting on debt repayments, and lawsuits, and a nondiversifiable component, which affects all firms such as inflation and war.

A *beta coefficient* (β) is a measure of nondiversifiable risk or the extent to which a firm's (or asset's) return changes due to a change in the market's return. It is a measure of the risk of a stock's financial returns, as compared to the risk of the financial returns to the general stock market. $\beta > 1$ means that the stock is more risky than the general market; $\beta < 1$ means the stock is less risky, whereas $\beta = 1$ means that the stock is as risky as the overall stock market.

β may be estimated by applying linear regression analysis to explain the relationship between the dependent variable, stock returns (R_j), and the independent variable, market returns (R_m). The intercept or constant term (α) of the regression equation provides a measure of R_j's performance as compared to the general market during the regression period. The following equations express R_j as defined by the linear regression model and R_j as defined by the CAPM.

$$R_j = \alpha + \beta R_m \text{ (regression equation formulation)}$$

$$R_j = R_f + \beta(R_m - R_f)$$
$$= R_f + \beta R_m - \beta R_f$$
$$= R_f(1 - \beta) + \beta R_m \text{ (CAPM formulation)}$$

If α is greater than $R_f(1 - \beta)$, this particular stock's rate of return, R_j, performed better than would have been expected using the CAPM during the same time period. The cumulative daily difference between α and $R_f(1 - \beta)$ is a measure of "abnormal return" for a specified number of days often used in empirical studies assessing the impact of acquisitions on the shareholder value of both acquiring and target companies (see Exhibit 7-1).

EXHIBIT 7-1. ESTIMATING β FOR PUBLICLY TRADED COMPANIES

Calculate the return to the jth company's shareholders as capital gains (or losses) plus dividends paid during the period adjusted for stock splits that take place in the current period. Regress this adjusted return against a similarly defined return for a broadly defined market index.

$$\frac{SP \times P_{jt} - P_{jt-1} + SP \times \text{Dividends}}{P_{jt-1}}$$

$$= \alpha + \beta \frac{(S\&P500_t - S\&P500_{t-1} + \text{Dividends})}{S\&P500_{t-1}}$$

1. SP is equal to 2 for a two-for-one stock split, 1.5 for a three-for-two split, and 1.33 for a four-for-three split. If we do not adjust for stock splits that may take place in the current period, the stock price will drop resulting in a negative return.
2. Betas for public companies can be obtained from estimation services such as Value Line, Standard & Poor's, Ibbotson, Bloomberg, and Barra.
3. Betas for private companies can be obtained by substituting a beta for comparable publicly traded companies.

EFFECTS OF LEVERAGE ON BETA

The presence of debt magnifies financial returns to shareholders. A firm whose total capital consists of $1 million in equity generates a return to shareholders of 10% if its after-tax profits are $100,000. A firm, whose total capital is $1 million consisting of $500,000 in equity and $500,000 in debt, will achieve a 20% return ($200,000/$500,000) to the shareholder on the same level of after-tax profits.

In the absence of debt, β measures the volatility of a firm's financial return to changes in the general market's overall financial return. Such a measure of volatility or risk is called an *unlevered* β and is denoted as β_u. Increasing leverage will raise the level of uncertainty of shareholder returns and increase the value of β. However, this will be offset to some extent by the tax deductibility of interest, which reduces shareholder risk by increasing after-tax cash flow available for shareholders. A beta reflecting the effects of both the increased volatility of earnings and the tax-shelter effects of leverage is called a leveraged β and is denoted as β_l.

These relationships can be expressed as follows:

$$\beta_l = \beta_u(1 + (1 - t)(D/E)) \text{ and}$$
$$\beta_u = \beta_l/(1 + (1-t)D/E))$$

EXHIBIT 7-2. CALCULATING A LEVERED β

Company X has no debt, a tax rate of .4, and an unlevered beta of 1.2. It is considering borrowing up to 50% of its equity value in 2000 and up to 75% in 2003. What would be the impact on its unlevered beta of this decision?

$$\beta_{l,2000} = \beta_u(1 + (1 - t)(D/E)_{2000}) = 1.2(1 + (1 - .4)(.5)) =$$
$$1.2(1.3) = 1.56$$

$$\beta_{l,2003} = \beta_u(1 + (1 - t)(D/E)_{2003}) = 1.2(1 + (1 - .4)(.75)) = 1.74$$

CALCULATING FREE CASH FLOWS

An increase in the amount of cash flow tends to raise the value of an asset, unless offset by increasing risk and an increasing discount rate associated with that cash flow. Conversely, decreases in cash flow tend to reduce the value of the asset, for a given level of risk and discount rate. Generally speaking, the cash flow of a firm is equal to the difference between cash earnings and cash investments (see

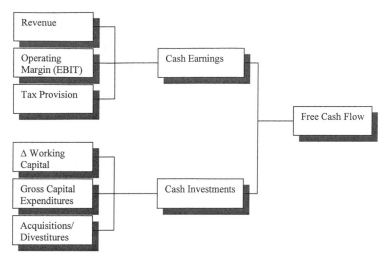

FIGURE 7-1.   Major sources and uses of free cash flow to the firm. EBIT, earnings before interest and taxes.

Figure 7-1). Cash earnings include after-tax income plus such noncash charges as depreciation expenses. The major components of cash investments include changes in working capital, gross capital expenditures, and acquisitions and divestitures. For an excellent discussion of cash flow concepts, see Damodaran (1997).

For our purposes, firms have three major sources of funds: common equity, preferred stock, and debt. The following definitions of free cash flow can be generalized to include any number of alternative sources of funds. Much of the data required to construct cash flow can be found from sources available on the Internet (e.g., reportgallery.com and edgar.com).

FREE CASH FLOW TO EQUITY INVESTORS

Free cash flow to equity investors (FCFE) is the cash flow remaining for paying dividends to common equity investors after the firm satisfies all obligations (Damodaran: 1997). These obligations include debt payments, capital expenditures, changes in net working capital, and preferred dividend payments.

Income and cash flow statements differ in terms of how they treat depreciation. The income statement amortizes the cost of capital equipment over its depreciable accounting life and deducts depreciation expense from revenue. Depreciation is an expense item that does not actually involve an outlay of cash by the firm. Although depreciation reduces income, it does not reduce cash flow. In calculating FCFE, depreciation is added back to net income. Net income plus depreciation is often referred to as a measure of the firm's ability to generate funds from internal operations. FCFE can be defined as follows:

$$\text{FCFE} = \text{Net Income} + \text{Depreciation} - \text{Gross Capital Expenditures}$$
$$- \Delta \text{ Net Working Capital} + \text{New Debt Issues}$$
$$- \text{Principal Repayments} - \text{Preferred Dividends}$$

$$= \text{Net Income} - (\text{Gross Capital Expenditures} - \text{Depreciation})$$
$$- \Delta \text{ Net Working Capital} + \text{New Debt Issues}$$
$$- \text{Principal Repayments} - \text{Preferred Dividends}$$

Gross capital expenditures less depreciation represents that portion of capital spending that cannot be financed from internal cash flow. Other expense items that do not involve an actual expenditure of cash that should be added back to net income in the calculation of free cash flow include the amortization expense associated with such items as goodwill or capitalized software.

FREE CASH FLOW TO THE FIRM

Free cash flow to the firm (FCFF) represents cash available to satisfy all investors holding claims against the firm's resources. These claim holders include common stockholders, lenders, and preferred stockholders. FCFF can be calculated in two ways: First, by adding up cash flows to all of a firm's claim holders,

$$\text{FCFF} = \text{FCFE} + \text{Interest Expense } (1 - \text{Tax Rate}) + \text{Principal Repayments}$$
$$- \text{New Debt Issues} + \text{Preferred Dividends}$$

Second, by adjusting operating earnings before interest and taxes (EBIT),

$$\text{FCFF} = \text{EBIT } (1 - \text{Tax Rate}) - (\text{Gross Capital Expenditures} - \text{Depreciation})$$
$$- \Delta \text{ Net Working Capital}$$

In the FCFF formulation, there is no effort to adjust for payments of interest or preferred dividends, because this measure of cash flow is calculated before any consideration is given to how expenditures will be financed. The tax rate refers to the firm's marginal tax rate.

Differences between FCFE and FCFF are due to debt-related cash flow plus nonequity claims. Interest expense is multiplied by $(1 - \text{tax rate})$ to adjust FCFF for that portion of interest paid to bondholders that is not recoverable by shareholders as a result of the tax deductibility of interest. The effects of this tax savings are already included in net income.

Note that the calculation of FCFF based on adjusting EBIT is frequently the preferred methodology for valuation purposes, because it does not require an analyst to estimate future debt repayment schedules in order to project principal repayments. This methodology is most helpful when a firm's level of future borrowing is expected to change substantially during the forecast period, thereby making the estimation of debt repayment schedules very difficult. However, the estimation of FCFF starting with EBIT does require assumptions about the acquiring firm's target debt-to-equity ratio to calculate the firm's weighted average cost of capital.

EXHIBIT 7-3. CALCULATING
FREE CASH FLOWS

The market served by Cash Cow Corporation (CCC) has matured. CCC has the dominant market share in the industry and is the recognized leader in product quality. The company is spending very little to modernize or expand its production capacity or on research and development. Efficient inventory control and cash management systems have helped to minimize working capital requirements. High barriers to entry limit the number of direct competitors. Gross capital expenditures in 1999 are $600 million, slightly above their year-earlier level. The firm's 1999 principal repayment is $75 million on $1.2 billion in short- and long-term debt, and the firm's combined federal, state, and local tax rate is .40. The firm also issued $50 million in subordinated debt in 1999. Annual dividends on preferred stock total $10 million. Total working capital is $95 million and $115 million in 1998 and 1999, respectively. What is CCC's FCFF and FCFE in 1999?

	1998	1999
Revenue	$4,200	$4,400
Less operating expenses	2,730	2,900
Less depreciation	500	505
Equal EBIT	970	995
Less interest expense	100	102
Less taxes	348	357
Equal net income	522	536

FCFE = $536 + $505 − $600 − $20 + $50 − $75 − $10 = $386.
FCFF = $995(1 − .4) − $600 + $505 − $20 = $482.

TIME VALUE OF MONEY

This concept rests on the basic premise that money received today is worth more than the same sum received tomorrow, because it can be invested at the current rate of interest. Moreover, the growth in the money received today and reinvested will be equal to the amount of interest income earned on the initial investment plus the interest earned on that interest income.

FUTURE VALUE

Future value compounding (FV) refers to the value of an initial investment, after a specified period of time, at a specific rate of interest. This can be expressed as follows:

FV of \$1 invested at interest rate (i) for 1 year = \$1 $\times$ (1 + i)

FV of \$1 invested at interest rate (i) for 2 years = \$1 $\times$ (1 + i) $\times$ (1 + i)

$$\vdots$$

FV of \$1 invested at interest rate (i) for n years = \$1 $\times$ (1 + i)^n

This formula can be generalized for an amount A invested for n periods and written as follows:

$$FV = A \times (1 + i)^n$$

EXHIBIT 7-4. FUTURE VALUE COMPOUNDING

What is the future value of \$100 deposited for 2 years earning 10%/year?

$$FV = \$100(1.10)(1.10) = \$100(1.10)^2$$
$$= \$100(FVIF_{2,10}) \quad = \$100(1.21)$$
$$= \$121$$

where $FVIF_{2,10}$ is the future value interest factor for 2 years at 10% annually. $FVIF_{2,10}$ may be found on a future value interest table.

What is the future value of \$100 deposited for 3 years at 10% for the first 2 years and 5% for the third year?

$$FV = \$100(1.10)(1.10)(1.05) = \$127$$

Note: This is sometimes referred to as cumulative compounding when the interest rate differs from one period to the next.

Continuous compounding represents an extreme case in which interest is compounding over all time periods, no matter how small. In this instance, the equation for future value compounding would approach infinity. The future value equation can be rewritten as follows:

$FV = A \times e^{ixn}$, where e is the exponential function whose value is 2.7183.

PRESENT VALUE

PV of future returns refers to the cash value, today, of future returns after adjustments are made for the time value of money.

$$PV = \frac{FV}{(1 + i)^n}$$

EXHIBIT 7-5. PRESENT VALUE
OF FUTURE RETURNS

What is the PV of $121 received 2 years from now discounted at 10%?

$$PV = \$121/(1 + .10)^2$$
$$= \$121(.826)$$
$$= \$99.95$$

Note that the present value of an amount invested using continuous compounding is the reciprocal of the FV calculation and can be written as follows:

$PV = A \times e^{-ixn}$, where e is the exponential function whose value is 2.7183.

ANNUITIES

An annuity is a series of equal payments, or receipts, made at any regular interval of time.

Future Value of an Annuity

The FV of an annuity (FVA) for equal payments, A, made at n regular intervals, and invested at an interest rate, i, can be written as follows:

$$FVA = A \times \frac{(1 + i)^n - 1}{i}$$

EXHIBIT 7-6. FUTURE VALUE OF ANNUITIES

Find the total FV of payments for a $100 annuity payment made once a year over a period of 4 years. Assume a 10% compound rate of interest.

$$FVA = \$100 \times \frac{(1 + .10)^4 - 1}{.10}$$
$$= \$100(4.641)$$
$$= \$464.10$$

Present Value of an Annuity

The present value of an annuity (PVA) can be calculated by discounting each cash flow to the present and then adding up the discounted values. Alternatively,

PVA for equal payments, A, made for n time periods, at an interest rate (i) can be written as follows:

$$PVA = A \left[\frac{1 - (1/(1 + i)^n)}{i} \right]$$

EXHIBIT 7-7. PRESENT VALUE OF ANNUITIES

Find the PV of a stock, which will return $100 annually for 4 years. Assume a 10% discount rate.

$$PVA = \$100 \left[\frac{(1 - (1/(1 + .10)^4)}{.10} \right]$$
$$= \$100(3.169)$$
$$= \$316.90$$

ALTERNATIVE APPROACHES TO VALUATION

There are a variety of ways that are commonly used to value firms. These include the income or discounted cash flow, market-based, asset-oriented, cost, and weighted-average valuation methods. These methods provide estimates of the economic value of a company, which do not need to be adjusted if the intent is to acquire a small portion of the company. However, if the intention is to obtain a controlling interest in the firm, a control premium must be added to the estimated economic value of the firm to determine the purchase price.

INCOME OR DISCOUNTED CASH FLOW METHOD

The income method focuses on some measure of cash flow or income. Valuation may be based on historical or projected data. Cash flow can be defined as FCFE or FCFF and income may be defined as after-tax (NI), operating earnings or earnings before interest and taxes (EBIT), or earnings before interest, taxes, depreciation and amortization (EBITDA).

Two commonly used techniques to value a company's cash flow or income stream include the *discounted cash flow* (DCF) *method* and the *capitalization* of income or cash flow method. The DCF approach involves forecasting year-by-year results and then converting these annual projections into their current value or PV by dividing each annual figure by a discount rate. The discount rate reflects the investor's required return to purchase an asset exhibiting a specific level of risk. At the end of the forecast period, a final estimation is made to determine the *terminal value*, which represents the estimated value of future cash flows or income at that point in time. The terminal value is then discounted to the present and added to the sum of the discounted values of the annual cash flow or income projections. The PV of the firm calculated in this manner is sometimes referred to as the intrinsic value of the firm. As will be discussed later in this chapter, the DCF model may be adjusted to account for variable or supernormal growth rates.

Industry practitioners frequently refer to two special cases of the DCF model as the capitalization method. These special cases include zero or constant growth of cash flow or income. The capitalization method is a simplification of the DCF method in which a single-year's cash flow or earnings of a firm is divided by a capitalization rate to determine the PV of the firm.

MARKET-BASED OR RELATIVE VALUE METHOD

This method assumes that markets are efficient in that the current values of businesses determined in the marketplace embody all the information currently available about the business. Current values represent what a willing buyer and seller, having access to the same information, would pay for the business. Using this approach, value is determined by multiplying market-determined value measures, such as price-to-earnings, price-to-book, or price-to-sales ratios, of other firms in the same industry, comparable industries, or comparable recent sales of similar firms by the earnings, book value, or sales of the firm to be valued. The resulting calculation provides an estimate of the PV or current value of the firm.

ASSET-ORIENTED METHODS

Asset-oriented approaches, such as tangible book, liquidation, and breakup values, are useful in highly specialized situations. The calculation of tangible book value per share, book value less goodwill, may be very useful in valuing financial services and distribution companies because highly liquid assets often comprise a large percentage of the total assets of such firms. The liquidation value of a firm is the current market value of the firm's assets as if it is going out of business less the cash value of its liabilities and costs incurred to liquidate the firm. Alternatively, a diversified firm consisting of multiple operating units or product lines can be valued by summing the PVs of each operating unit or product line, as if they are operated independently. In a manner similar to calculating liquidation value, the breakup value of the firm is determined by estimating the after-tax proceeds from the sale of the firm's operating units and deducting the PV of the firm's liabilities and costs incurred in selling the company in pieces. Asset-oriented approaches ignore potential synergies that might exist.

COST METHOD

The cost approach estimates what it would cost to replace the target firm's assets at current market prices using professional appraisers less the PV of the firm's liabilities. The difference provides an estimate of the market value of equity. This approach does not take into account the *going concern value* of the company, which reflects how effectively the assets are being used in combination (i.e., synergies) to generate profits and cash flow. Valuing the assets separately in terms of what it would cost to replace them may seriously understate the firm's true going concern value. This approach may also be inappropriate if the firm has a significant amount of intangible assets on its books due to the difficulty in valuing such assets. For these reasons, the discussion in this chapter will focus on the income, market, and asset-oriented approaches.

EXHIBIT 7-8. SUMMARIZING COMMONLY USED METHODS TO VALUE FIRMS

1. Income or DCF Method
   a. Capitalization Method
      1. Zero-growth model
      2. Constant-growth model
   b. Variable-growth model
   c. Supernormal "high-flyer" growth model
2. Market-based methods
   a. Comparable companies
   b. Comparable transactions
   c. Same industry or comparable industry
3. Asset-oriented methods
   a. Tangible book value
   b. Liquidation value
   c. Break-up value
4. Cost method (Cost to replace the target firm's assets)
5. Weighted average method (Uses an average of alternative valuation methods adjusted to reflect the analyst's confidence in the relative importance of each method)

INCOME OR DISCOUNTED CASH FLOW METHOD

The various DCF models employed to value acquisitions are special cases of the conventional capital budgeting process. Capital budgeting is the process for evaluating and comparing alternative investment opportunities in order to ensure the best long-term financial return for the firm.

In the capital budgeting process, cash flows are projected over the expected life of the project and discounted to the present at the firm's cost of capital. The resultant PV is then subtracted from the initial investment required to generate the cash flow stream in order to calculate net PV (NPV) for the project. In this manner, NPV of each alternative project is calculated and ranked from the highest to the lowest in terms of dollar value. The firm can then maximize the value of the firm by first undertaking the project with the highest NPV, then the project with the second highest NPV, and so forth, until the firm has exhausted its available financial resources. M&As can be viewed as one of the alternative investment opportunities available to the firm.

CAPITALIZATION METHOD

The capitalization method is applied when projected cash flow or income is not expected to grow or is expected to grow at a constant rate.

Zero-Growth Valuation Model

This model assumes that free cash flow is constant in perpetuity. The value of the firm at time zero (P_0) is the discounted or capitalized value of its annual cash flow. In this instance, the discount rate and the capitalization rate are the same. The subscript FCFF or FCFE refers to the definition of cash flow used in the valuation.

$P_{0,FCFF}$ = FCFF$_0$/WACC, where FCFF$_0$ is free cash flow to the firm at time 0 and WACC is the cost of capital.

$P_{0,FCFE}$ = FCFE$_0$/k_e, where FCFE$_0$ is free cash flow to equity investors at time 0 and k_e is the cost of equity.

EXHIBIT 7-9. ZERO GROWTH VALUATION MODEL

1. What is the value of a firm, whose annual FCFF$_0$ of $1 million is expected to remain constant in perpetuity and whose cost of capital is 12%?

$$P_{0,FCFF} = \$1/.12 = \$8.3 \text{ million}$$

2. Calculate the cost of capital and the value of a firm whose capital structure consists only of common equity and debt. The firm desires to limit its leverage to 30% of total capital. The firm's marginal tax rate is .4 and its beta is 1.5. The corporate bond rate is 8% and the ten year U.S. Treasury bond rate is 5%. The expected annual return

on stocks is 10%. Annual FCFF is expected to remain at $4 million indefinitely.

$$k_e = .05 + 1.5(.10 - .05) = .125 \times 100 = 12.5\%$$

$$\text{WACC} = .125 \times .7 + .08 \times (1 - .4) \times .3 = .088 + .014$$
$$= .102 \times 100 = 10.2\%$$

$$P_{0,\text{FCFF}} = \$4/.102$$
$$= \$39.2 \text{ million}$$

Constant Growth Valuation Model

The constant growth model is applicable for firms in mature markets, characterized by a moderate and somewhat predictable rate of growth. Examples of such industries include beverage, cosmetics, prepared foods, and cleaning products. Growth rates can be projected by simply extrapolating the industry's growth rate over the past 5–10 years.

The constant growth model is frequently referred to as the Gordon model (Gordon: 1962). In this model, next year's cash flow to the firm (FCFF_1) or the first year of the forecast period is expected to grow at a constant rate of growth (g). Therefore, $\text{FCFF}_1 = \text{FCFF}_0(1 + g)$.

$$P_{0,\text{FCFF}} = \text{FCFF}_1/(\text{WACC} - g), \text{ where } g \text{ is the expected}$$
$$\text{rate of growth of FCFF}_1.$$

$$P_{0,\text{FCFE}} = \text{FCFE}_1/(k_e - g), \text{ where } \text{FCFE}_1 = \text{FCFE}_0(1 + g)$$

In this instance, the capitalization rate (CR) is equal to the difference between the cost of capital (WACC) or equity (k_e) and the expected growth rate g.

EXHIBIT 7-10. CONSTANT GROWTH MODEL

1. The value of a firm whose projected free cash flow to the firm next year is $1 million, WACC is 12%, and expected annual cash flow growth rate is 6% is

$$P_{0,\text{FCFF}} = \$1/(.12 - .06) = \$16.7 \text{ million}$$

2. Estimate the value of a firm (P_0) whose cost of equity is 15% and whose earnings are projected to grow 10% per year. The current year's free cash flow to equity holders is $2 million.

$$P_{0,\text{FFCF}} = (2.0 \times 1.1)/(.15 - .10) = \$44.0 \text{ million}$$

VARIABLE GROWTH VALUATION MODEL

Many firms experience periods of high growth followed by a period of slower, more stable growth. Examples of such industries include cellular phones, personal computers, and cable TV. Firms within such industries routinely experience double-digit growth rates for periods of 5–10 years because of low penetration of these markets in the early years of the product's life cycle. As the market becomes more saturated, growth inevitably slows to a rate more in line with the overall growth of the economy or the general population. The PV of such firms is equal to the sum of the PV of the discounted cash flows during the high-growth period plus the discounted value of the cash flows generated during the stable growth period. In capital budgeting terms, the discounted value of the cash flows generated during the stable growth period is called the terminal value.

The terminal value may be estimated using the Gordon growth model. Free cash flow during the first year beyond the n year forecast period, $FFCF_{n+1}$, is divided by the difference between the assumed cost of capital and the cash flow growth rate beyond the forecast period. The use of the Gordon model provides a convenient and theoretically sound means of estimating the value of the firm created beyond the end of the forecast period. However, the selection of the earnings growth rate and cost of capital must be done very carefully. Small changes in assumptions can result in dramatic swings in the terminal value and, therefore, in the valuation of the firm. Table 7-1 illustrates the sensitivity of a terminal value of $1 million to different spreads between the cost of capital and the stable growth rate.

There are numerous other ways terminal values can be estimated. The price-to-earnings, price-to-cash flow, or price-to-book techniques value the target as if it is sold at the end of a specific number of years. At the end of the forecast period, the terminal year's earnings, cash flow, or book value is projected and multiplied by a price-to-earnings, cash flow, or book value believed to be appropriate for that year. The terminal value may also be estimated by assuming the firm's cash flow

TABLE 7-1.   Impact of Changes in Assumptions
on a Terminal Value of $1 Million

Difference between cost of capital and cash flow growth rate	Terminal value ($ millions)
3%	33.3
4%	25.0
5%	20.0
6%	16.7
7%	14.3

or earnings in the last year of the forecast period will continue in perpetuity. This is equivalent to the zero-growth valuation model discussed previously.

Using the definition of free cash flow to the firm, P_0 can be estimated using the variable growth model as follows (see Exhibit 7-11):

$$P_{0,\text{FCFF}} = \sum_{t=1}^{n} \frac{\text{FCFF}_0 \times (1 + g_t)^t}{(1 + \text{WACC})^t} + \frac{P_n}{(1 + \text{WACC})^n},$$

where

$$P_n = \frac{\text{FCFF}_n \times (1 + g_m)}{(\text{WACC}_m - g_m)}$$

FCFF_0 = FCFF in year 0

WACC = Weighted average cost of capital through year n

WACC_m = Cost of capital assumed beyond year n

p_n = Value of the firm at the end of year n (terminal value)

g_t = Growth rate through year n

g_m = Stabilized or long-term growth rate beyond year n

After having determined the value of the firm using free cash flow to the firm, the value of the firm to equity investors can be estimated in either of two ways.

$$P_{0,\text{FCFE}} = \sum_{t=1}^{n} \frac{\text{FCFE}_0 \times (1 + g_t)^t}{(1 + k_e)^t} + \frac{P_n}{(1 + k_e)^n},$$

where

$$P_n = \frac{\text{FCFE}_n \times (1 + g_m)}{(k_{em} - g_m)}$$

FCFE_0 = FCFE in year 0

k_e = Cost of equity through year n

k_{em} = Cost of equity used to determine terminal value

Alternatively, the value of the firm to equity investors can be estimated by deducting the market value of the firm's debt, MV_0, from the value of the firm estimated using free cash flow to the firm. Therefore, $P_{0,\text{FCFE}} = P_{0,\text{FCFF}} - MV_0$ (see Exhibit 7-12).

EXHIBIT 7-11. VARIABLE GROWTH VALUATION MODEL

Estimate the value of a firm (P_0) whose free cash flow is projected to grow at a compound annual average rate of 35% for the next 5 years. Growth is then expected to slow to a more normal 5% annual growth rate. The current year's cash flow to the firm is $4.00 million. The firm's cost of capital during the high-growth period is 18% and 12% beyond the fifth year, as growth stabilizes.

Present value of cash flows during the forecast period:

$$\text{PV}_{1-5} = \frac{4.00 \times 1.35}{(1.18)} + \frac{4.00 \times (1.35)^2}{(1.18)^2} + \frac{4.00 \times (1.35)^3}{(1.18)^3}$$

$$+ \frac{4.00 \times 1.35^4}{(1.18)^4} + \frac{4.00 \times 1.35^5}{(1.18)^5}$$

$$= 5.40/1.18 + 7.29/1.18^2 + 9.84/1.18^3$$

$$+ 13.29/1.18^4 + 17.93/1.18^5$$

$$= 4.58 + 5.24 + 5.99 + 6.85 + 7.84 = 30.50$$

Calculation of terminal value:

$$\text{PV}_5 = \frac{((4.00 \times (1.35)^5 \times 1.05))/(.12 - .05)}{(1.18)^5}$$

$$= \frac{18.83/.07}{2.29}$$

$$= 117.65$$

$$P_{0,\text{FCFF}} = \text{PV}_{1-5} + \text{PV}_5 = 30.50 + 117.65 = 148.15$$

EXHIBIT 7-12. ESTIMATING EQUITY VALUE BY DEDUCTING THE MARKET VALUE OF DEBT FROM FIRM VALUE

The value of a firm using the free cash flow to the firm valuation method is estimated to be $1,500,000. The book value of the firm's debt is $1 million, with annual interest expense of $80,000 and term to maturity of 4 years. The debt is an "interest only" note with a repayment of principal at maturity. The firm's current cost of debt is 10%. What is the value of the firm to equity investors?

$$\text{MV}_0 = \$80,000 \times \left[\frac{1 - (1/1.10)^4}{.10}\right] + \frac{\$1,000'000}{1.10^4}$$

$$= \$80,000(\text{PVIFA}_{4,10}) + \$1,000,000(\text{PVIF}_{4.10})$$

$$= \$80,000(3.17) + \$1,000,000(.683)$$

$$= \$253,600 + \$683,000$$

$$= \$933,600$$

$$P_{0,\text{FCFE}} = \$1,500,000 - \$933,600$$

$$= \$566,400.$$

Notes:

1. The formula for the PVA is used to calculate the market value of debt because of the four equal interest payments made during the remaining term to maturity. PVIFA is the present value interest factor associated with a 4-year annuity at a 10% interest rate.
2. The firm's current cost of debt of 10% is higher than the implied interest rate of 8% ($80,000/$1,000,000) on the loan currently on the firm's books. This suggests that the market rate of interest has increased since the firm borrowed the $1 million "interest-only" note.
3. Alternatively, MV_0 could be approximated by calculating the weighted-average interest expense for all of the firm's outstanding debt and dividing it by its current cost of debt.

SUPERNORMAL "HIGH-FLYER" GROWTH VALUATION MODEL

Some companies display initial periods of what could be described as hyper-growth, followed by an extended period of rapid growth, before stabilizing at a more normal and sustainable growth rate. Initial public offerings and start-up companies may follow this model. This pattern reflects growth over their initially small revenue base, the introduction of a new product, or the sale of an existing product to a new or underserved customer group. The growth rate of many Internet-related companies would seem to place them in the "high-flyer" category. All companies that fall into this category are not small. Microsoft, Cisco, and American Online, after years of growing at more than 50% per year, continue to grow at rates well above 20% annually.

The following illustration assumes that a firm is expected to grow for two consecutive periods, each of which is 5 years in length, before assuming a more normal long-term growth rate. Because the cost of capital in each 5-year period is different reflecting the growth rate of cash flow in that period, each year's cash flows must be discounted by the cumulative cost of capital from prior years.

$$P_0 = \sum_{t=1}^{5} \frac{FCFF_t \times (1 + g_{1-5})^t}{(1 + WACC_{1-5})^t} + \sum_{t=6}^{10} \frac{(FCFF_t \times (1 + g_{6-10})^t}{(1 + WACC_{1-5})^5 (1 + WACC_{6-10})^t}$$
$$+ \frac{FCFF_{10}(1 + g_{11})/(WACC_{11} - g_{11})}{(1 + WACC_{1-5})^5 (1 + WACC_{6-10})^5},$$

where

$$FCFF_t = \text{Free cash flow to the firm at time } t$$
$$FCFF_1 = FCFF_0 \times (1 + g_{1-5})$$
$$FCFF_6 = FCFF_5 \times (1 + g_{6-10})$$

$$g_{1-5} = \text{Growth rate during years 1 to 5}$$
$$g_{6-10} = \text{Growth rate during years 6 to 10}$$
$$g_{11} = \text{Sustainable growth rate}$$
$$g_{1-5} > g_{6-10} > g_{11}$$
$$\text{WACC}_{1-5} = \text{Cost of capital during years 1 to 5}$$
$$\text{WACC}_{6-10} = \text{Cost of capital during years 6 to 10}$$
$$\text{WACC}_{11} = \text{Sustainable growth period cost of capital}$$
$$\text{WACC}_{1-5} > \text{WACC}_{6-10} > \text{WACC}_{11}$$

EXHIBIT 7-13. SUPERNORMAL "HIGH-FLYER" VALUATION MODEL

In the year prior to going public, a firm has revenues of $20 million and an EBIT of $4 million. The firm has no debt and revenue is expected to grow at 50% for the next 5 years, 30% annually during the following 5 years, and 6% annually thereafter. Operating margins are expected to remain constant throughout. Capital expenditures are expected to grow in line with depreciation, and working capital requirements are minimal. The average β of a publicly traded company in this industry is 1.50 and the average debt/equity ratio is 20%. The firm does not intend to borrow during the next 5 years and then expects to move to the industry average debt/equity ratio thereafter. The pretax cost of debt is 7%, the 10-year Treasury bond rate is 6% and the tax rate is 40%. The normal spread between the return on stocks and the risk-free rate of return is believed to be 5.5%. Estimate the value of the firm's equity.

a. β_u for comparable firms $= \left(\dfrac{\beta_1}{1 + (1 - t)(D/E)} \right)$

$$= \frac{1.5}{(1 + .2 \times .6)}$$

$$= \frac{1.5}{1.12}$$

$$= 1.34$$

b. $k_{e1-5} = R_f + \beta_u (R_m - R_f) = .06 + 1.34\,(.055) = 13.4\%$

c. $\text{WACC}_{1-5} = k_{e1-5} = 13.4\%$ (as the firm does not plan to borrow during this period)

d. $k_{e6-10} = .06 + 1.5(.055) = 14.3\%$

e. $WACC_{6-10} = .143 \times .8 + .07(1 - .4) \times .2 = .114 + .008 = 12.2\%$

f. Projected free cash flows to the firm during the two consecutive 5-year periods:

					($Millions)						Terminal
Year	1	2	3	4	5	6	7	8	9	10	Year
	3.6	5.4	8.1	12.2	18.3	23.8	30.9	40.2	52.3	68.0	72.0

g. Terminal value $= \$72.0/(.122 - .06) = \$1,161.29$

PV (using 13.4% for the first 5 years and 12.2% thereafter) is calculated as follows:

$$= \frac{\$3.6}{(1.134)} + \frac{\$5.4}{(1.134)^2} + \frac{\$8.1}{(1.134)^3} + \frac{12.2}{(1.134)^4} + \frac{18.3}{(1.134)^5}$$

$$+ \frac{23.8}{(1.134)^5(1.122)} + \frac{\$30.9}{(1.134)^5(1.122)^2} + \frac{\$40.2}{(1.134)^5(1.122)^3}$$

$$+ \frac{\$52.3}{(1.134)^5(1.122)^4} + \frac{\$68.0}{(1.134)^5(1.122)^5} + \frac{\$1,161.29}{(1.134)^5(1.122)^5}$$

$$= \$456.09$$

Notes:

1. In (a), β_u must be calculated because the firm to be valued is debt-free, and its β is to be estimated from the β's of public companies in an industry whose debt averages 20% of equity. Therefore, the average industry β reflects the effects of this leverage.
2. In (d), the public companies' β of 1.5 is used as the firm will be borrowing up to the industry average debt-to-equity ratio.
3. In (f) FCFF $=$ EBIT$(1 - t)$ since capital expenditures are assumed to be fully offset by depreciation and the change in working capital is assumed to be minimal.
4. In (f), FCFF in year 1 $= \$4 \times 1.5 \times .6 = 3.6$; FCFF in year 2 $= 3.6 \times 1.5 = 5.4$, etc.

DETERMINING GROWTH RATES

The key premise of discounted cash flow analysis is that the value of the firm can be represented by the sum of the high-growth period(s) plus a stable growth period extending indefinitely into the future. A key risk is the sensitivity of the terminal values to the choice of assumptions about the stable growth period, such as the cash flow growth rate and the discount rate associated with that period.

The stable growth rate is generally going to be less than or equal to the overall growth rate of the industry in which the firm competes or the general economy. Stable growth rates in excess of these levels implicitly assume that the firm's output will eventually exceed that of its industry or the general economy. Similarly, for multinational firms, the stable growth rate should not exceed the projected growth rate for the world economy or for a particular region of the world.

Growth rates can be readily calculated based on the historical experience of the firm or industry. The average annual growth rate (g) for a time series extending from t_1 to t_n can be calculated by solving the following equation:

$$g = (t_n/t_1)^{1/n} - 1$$

Care should be taken to discard aberrant data points resulting from infrequent or nonrecurring events such as labor stoppages and droughts. Such data points will result in a distortion of the growth rate.

Determining the appropriate length of time for the high-growth period can also be elusive. There are no compelling rules. However, intuition suggests that the length of the high-growth period should be longer the greater is the current growth rate of a firm's cash flow when compared to the stable growth rate. This is particularly true when the high-growth firm has a relatively small market share and there is little reason to believe that its growth rate will slow in the foreseeable future. For example, if the industry is expected to grow at 5% annually and the target firm, which has only a negligible market share, is growing at three times that rate, it may be appropriate to assume a high-growth period of 5–10 years. Moreover, if the terminal value comprises a substantial percentage (e.g., three-fourths) of total PV, the forecast period should be extended beyond the customary 5 years to at least 10 years. The extension of the time period reduces the impact of the terminal value in determining the market value of the firm.

High-growth rates are usually associated with increased levels of uncertainty. In applying discounted cash flow methodology, risk is incorporated into the discount rate. Consequently, the discount rate during the high-growth (less predictable) period or periods should generally be higher than during the stable growth period.

MARKET-BASED METHODS

Market-based methods estimate how much investors are willing to pay for a share of a firm by multiplying some measure of value, such as the firm's earnings, cash flow, sales, and book value by price-to-earnings, cash flow, sales, and book ratios for comparable companies, comparable transactions, or the same or comparable industry averages. Because of the requirement for positive current or near-term earnings or cash flow, market-based methods are meaningful only for companies with a stable earnings or cash flow record.

For highly capital-intensive industries characterized by high levels of depreciation, broader measures of earnings should be used. The commonly used measure is the EBITDA multiple. EBITDA refers to earnings before interest, taxes, depreciation, and amortization. Examples of industries where EBITDA may be appropriate include steel, airlines, real estate, and equipment leasing.

COMPARABLE COMPANIES' METHOD

Applying this approach requires that the analyst identify companies that are substantially similar to the target firm (see Table 7-2). The primary advantage of this approach is that it employs market-based values rather than assumption-driven discounted cash flow-based valuations. For this reason, this approach is widely used in so-called "fairness opinions," which investment bankers are frequently asked to give prior to a request for shareholder approval of an acquisition. Because it is frequently viewed as more objective than alternative approaches, the comparable companies' method also enjoys widespread use in legal cases.

The principal limitations to this approach include the difficulty in obtaining truly comparable companies and the potential for widely divergent ratios and values. In practice, it is frequently difficult to find companies that are substantially similar to the target company in terms of markets served, product offering, degree of leverage, and size. Even when companies appear to be substantially similar, there are likely to be significant differences in these ratios at any one moment in time. These differences may result from investor overreaction to one-time events, which quickly abate with the passage of time. Consequently, comparisons made at different times can provide distinctly different results. By taking an average of multiples over 6 months or 1 year, these differences may be minimized. Finally, the best comparisons may be with privately held companies or with subsidiaries or product lines of public companies for which no data are available.

COMPARABLE TRANSACTIONS' METHOD

This approach is conceptually similar to the comparable companies' approach. Multiples used to estimate the value of the target company are based on purchase prices of comparable companies that were recently acquired. Price-to-earnings, sales, cash flow and book value are calculated using the purchase price for the recent transaction. Earnings, sales, cash flow, and book value for the target company are subsequently multiplied by these ratios to obtain an estimate of the market value of the target company (see Table 7-3). The obvious limitation to the approach is the difficulty in finding truly comparable, recent transactions.

TABLE 7-2.   Valuing a Target Company Using Comparable Companies

| Value indicator | Market value of equity times indicator | | | $ Millions | |
	Comparable company 1	Comparable company 2	Comparable company average	Target company projections	Estimated value of target
Revenue	1.2×	1.4×	1.3×	$150	$195
Net income	18×	22×	20×	$15	$300

TABLE 7-3. Valuing a Target Company Using Comparable Transactions

	Transaction purchase price times indicator			$ Millions	
Value indicator	Comparable transaction 1	Comparable transaction 2	Average comparable transaction	Target company projections	Estimated value of target
Revenue	1.4×	2.0×	1.7×	$200	$340
Net income	24×	30×	27×	$20	$540

SAME OR COMPARABLE INDUSTRY METHOD

In this instance, the analyst multiplies the target company's earnings, revenue, cash flow, and book value by the ratio of the market value of shareholders' equity to earnings, revenue, cash flow, and book value for the average company in the target firm's industry or for a comparable industry (see Exhibit 7-14). Such information can be obtained from Standard & Poor's, Value Line, Moody's, Dun & Bradstreet, and from Wall Street analysts. The primary advantage of this technique is the ease of use. Disadvantages include the presumption that industry multiples are actually comparable and that analysts' projections are unbiased.

EXHIBIT 7-14. VALUING A TARGET COMPANY USING THE SAME OR COMPARABLE INDUSTRIES

A firm's earnings per share (E/S) for the coming year is estimated by industry analysts to be $3.00. The firm has one million shares of common stock outstanding. The industry in which the firm competes currently has an average price-to-earnings ratio (P/E) of 20. What is the firm's estimated price per share (P/S) and market value (MV).

$$P/S = (E/S) \times (P/E) = \$3.00 \times 20 = \$60$$

$$MV = \$60 \times 1,000,000 = \$60,000,000$$

VALUE DRIVER-BASED VALUATION

In the absence of earnings, other factors that drive the creation of value for a firm may be used for valuation purposes. Such factors are commonly used to value start-up companies and initial public offerings, which often have little or no earnings performance records. Measures of profitability and cash flow are simply manifestations or measures of value. These measures are dependent on factors both external and internal to the firm. Value drivers exist for each major functional category of the firm including sales, marketing and distribution; customer service; operations and manufacturing, and purchasing.

There are both micro- and macro value drivers. Micro value drivers are those that directly influence specific functional aspects of the firm. Micro value drivers for sales, marketing, and distribution could include product quality measures such as part defects per 100,000 units sold, on-time delivery, the number of multiyear subscribers, and the ratio of product price to some measure of perceived quality. Customer service drivers could include average waiting time on the telephone, the number of billing errors, and the time required to correct such errors. Operational value drivers include average collection period, inventory turnover, and the number of units produced per manufacturing employee hour. Purchasing value drivers include average payment period, on-time vendor delivery, and the quality of purchased materials and services.

Macro value drivers are more encompassing than micro value drivers in that they may impact all aspects of the firm. Examples of macro value drivers include market share, overall customer satisfaction measured by survey results, total asset turns, and revenue per employee.

Using value drivers to value businesses is straightforward. First, the analyst needs to determine the key determinants of value or value drivers for the target company. Second, the market value for comparable companies is divided by the value driver selected for the target company in order to calculate the dollars of market value per unit of value driver. Third, multiply this figure by the same indicator or value driver for the target company.

For example, if the market leader in an industry has a $300 million market value and a 30% market share, the market is valuing each percentage point of market share at $10 million. If the target company in the same industry has a 20% market share, the market value of the target company is $200 million (20 points of market share × $10 million per market share point).

Similarly, the market value of comparable companies could be divided by other known value drivers, such as the number of visitors or page views per month for an Internet content provider; the number of subscribers of a magazine; and the number of households with TVs in a specific geographic area for a cable TV company. Using this method, AT&T's acquisitions of the cable companies TCI and Media One in the late 1990s would appear to be a "bargain" in that it spent an average of $5,000 per household (the price paid for each company divided by the number of customer households acquired) in acquiring these companies' customers. In contrast, Deutsche Telekom and Mannesmann spent $6000 and $7000 per customer, respectively, in buying mobile phone companies One 2 One and Orange Plc (*Business Week:* February 21, 2000, p. 60).

The major advantage of this approach is its simplicity. Its major disadvantages include the assumption that a single value driver or factor is representative of the total value of the business.

CASE STUDY 7-1. VALUING INTERNET SERVICE PROVIDER EARTHLINK USING VALUE DRIVERS

An analyst reasons that the number of new subscribers to Earthlink is a primary source of revenue and determinant of future profitability in this industry. A growing subscriber base represents an increasing source of revenue not only from monthly connect fees but also from advertising revenues. More advertisers will be induced to buy space as the number of possible viewers of their content increases.

The analyst seeks another company that is comparable to calculate how investors value each additional subscriber. The analyst's objective is to estimate the price investors would pay for each additional subscriber. She selects America Online (AOL), because it is the largest Internet service provider (ISP) that is publicly traded. She realizes that some adjustments will be required, because AOL is also a major content provider. Consequently, the motivation to subscribe to AOL is much broader than for subscribing to Earthlink, which is primarily an ISP.

The analyst adopts the following methodology:

Price per subscriber =

$$\frac{\text{Market value of equity (MV)} + \text{Debt (D)} - \text{Excess cash (C)}}{\text{Number of subscribers}},$$

where $D - C = \text{Net Debt}$[1]

1. Develop benchmark by determining what investors have been willing to pay per subscriber for comparable companies (e.g., AOL)

   AOL market value of the firm per subscriber: MV_{AOL} + $(D_{AOL} - Cash_{AOL})/1998$ AOL subscribers = \$67.6 billion/ 16.5 million = \$4,097

2. Adjust what investors would be willing to pay per subscriber for Earthlink subscribers to reflect its less liquid stock, less well-known brand name, and limited content offering:

   Assumption: \$3,500 per subscriber (approximate 15% discount from AOL's figure)

3. Calculate Earthlink's (EL) market-based equity value:

   MV_{EL} + $(Debt_{EL} - Cash_{EL})/1998$ EL subscribers = \$3,500
   Multiplying through by the number of EL subscribers and solving for MV_{EL}, MV_{EL} = (\$3,500 × 1 million subscribers) − $Debt_{EL}$ + $Cash_{EL}$ = \$3.85 billion

4. Price per share =$3.85 billion / 41 million (including convertible
preferred shares)
=$94 (vs. actual closing price on 3/12/99 of $63.06)

Based on this methodology, the analyst concludes that Earthlink is currently undervalued when compared to similar companies.

[1] *Net debt* represents the firm's fixed obligations that cannot be met by using cash balances in excess of normal operating balances.

ASSET-ORIENTED METHODS

TANGIBLE BOOK VALUE OR EQUITY PER SHARE METHOD

Book value is a much-maligned indicator of value, because book asset values rarely reflect actual market values. They may over or understate market value. For example, the value of land is frequently understated on the balance sheet, whereas inventory is often overstated if it is old or obsolete. The applicability of this approach varies by industry. Although book values generally do not mirror actual market values for manufacturing companies, they may be more accurate for distribution companies with high inventory turnover rates. Examples of such companies include pharmaceutical distributor Bergen Brunswick and personal computer distributor Ingram Micro. Book value is also widely used for valuing financial services companies, where tangible book value is primarily cash or liquid assets. Tangible book value is book value less goodwill.

EXHIBIT 7-15. VALUING COMPANIES USING BOOK VALUE

Target Company has total assets (TA) of $15 million, of which goodwill (GW) accounts for $2 million. Total liabilities (TL) are $9 million. Total shares outstanding (S) are 2 million. Estimate tangible book value per share (BVS)

$$BVS = (TA - TL - GW)/S = (\$15 - \$9 - \$2)/2 = \$2$$

Another firm in the same industry as Target Company and of approximately the same size, customer base, and profitability was recently sold at a price that equated to five times its book value per share. Estimate the implied market value of Target Company using BVS as a measure of value.

$$\text{Market Value Per Share} = 5 \times \$2 = \$10$$

LIQUIDATION OR BREAKUP VALUE

The terms *liquidation* and *breakup value* are often used interchangeably. However, there are subtle distinctions. Liquidation or breakup value is the projected price of the firm's assets sold separately less its liabilities. Liquidation may be involuntary as a result of bankruptcy or voluntary if a firm is viewed by its owners as worth more in liquidation than as a going concern. The going concern value of a company may be defined as the value of the firm in excess of the sum of the value of its parts. The breakup value of the firm is synonymous with its voluntary liquidation value. Liquidation and breakup strategies will be explored in more detail in Chapter 13.

During the late 1970s and throughout most of the 1980s, highly diversified companies were routinely valued by investors in terms of their value if broken up and sold as discrete operations as well as their going concern value as a consolidated operation. Companies lacking real synergy among their operating units or sitting on highly appreciated assets were often viewed as more valuable when broken up.

For example, natural resource companies such as Weyerhauser, a leading forest products company and owner of enormous tracts of timberland, or Mobil Oil, a global energy giant possessing vast amounts of oil and gas reserves, were often valued in terms of their book value per share because of the escalating value of their tangible assets. If the tangible book value per share exceeded their current market value per share for any significant period of time, they could become acquisition candidates and subsequently be dismembered for sale in discrete pieces. FEDCO, the creator of the large warehouse-discount-store concept, determined in 1999 that its shareholders would be better served if the board of directors liquidated the firm rather than spent the money necessary to refurbish the firm's stores. The value of the firm's real estate exceeded the value that could be created by continuing to operate the firm.

In practice, the calculation of liquidation value, voluntary or otherwise, requires a concerted effort by appraisers, who are intimately familiar with the operations to be liquidated. In some instances, the expenses incurred in terms of legal, appraisal, and consulting fees may constitute a larger percentage of the dollar proceeds of the sale of the firm's assets. Guidelines do exist for the probable liquidation value of various types of assets. However, they will differ dramatically from one industry to another. They also depend on the condition of the economy and on whether the assets must be liquidated in a hurry to satisfy creditors.

Analysts frequently estimate the liquidation value of a target company to determine the minimum value of the company in the worst-case scenario of bankruptcy. They make a simplifying assumption that the assets can be sold in an orderly fashion, which is defined as a reasonable amount of time to solicit bids from qualified buyers. "Orderly fashion" is normally defined as 9 to 12 months. Under these circumstances, high-quality receivables typically can be sold for 80–90% of book value. Inventories might realize 80–90% of book value depending upon the condition and the degree of obsolescence. More rapid liquidations might reduce the value of inventories to 60–65% of book value. The liquidation value of equipment will vary widely depending upon the age and condition.

Inventories need to be reviewed in terms of obsolescence, receivables in terms of collectability, equipment in terms of age and effectiveness, and real estate in terms of true market value. Equipment such as lathes and computers with a zero book value may have a significant economic market value. Land can be a hidden source of value, as it is frequently undervalued on generally accepted accounting principles (GAAP) balance sheets. Prepaid assets such as insurance premiums can sometimes be liquidated with a portion of the premium recovered. The liquidation value will be dramatically reduced if the assets have to be liquidated in "fire sale" conditions under which assets are sold to the first rather than the highest bidder (see Table 7-4).

VALUING THE FIRM USING THE
WEIGHTED AVERAGE METHOD

Weights reflect the analyst's relative confidence in the various methodologies. Valuations of multiples based on recent comparable transactions are frequently given the greatest weight, followed by discounted cash flow calculations. Liquidation values are generally given the smallest weight as they generally represent the worst-case scenario (see Exhibit 7-16).

TABLE 7-4.   Calculating Liquidation Value[a]

Balance sheet item	Book value ($000)	Orderly sale value ($000)
Cash	100	100
Receivables	500	450
Inventory	800	720
Equipment (after depreciation)	200	60
Land	200	300
Total assets	1,800	1,630
Total liabilities	1,600	1,600
Shareholders' equity	200	30

[a] Titanic Corporation has declared bankruptcy and the trustee has been asked by its creditors to estimate its liquidation value assuming orderly sale conditions. This example does not take into account legal fees, taxes, management fees, and contractually required employee severance expenses. In certain cases, these expenses can comprise a substantial percentage of the proceeds from liquidation.

EXHIBIT 7-16. WEIGHTED AVERAGE VALUATION OF ALTERNATIVE METHODOLOGIES

An analyst has estimated the value of a company using multiple valuation methodologies. The discounted cash flow value is $220 million, comparable transactions' value is $234 million, the P/E-based value is $224 million, and the liquidation value is $150 million. The analyst has greater confidence in certain methodologies than others. Estimate the weighted average value of the firm using all valuation methodologies and the weights or relative importance the analyst gives to each methodology.

Estimated value ($millions)	Relative weight	Weighted average ($millions)
220	.30	66.0
234	.40	93.6
224	.20	44.8
150	.10	15.0
	1.00	219.4

RELATING DISCOUNTED CASH FLOW TO MARKET-BASED VALUATION METHODS

Market-based valuation methods using multiples such as P/E ratios can be related to variables that drive valuation, such as the earnings growth rate, dividend payout rate, and the firm's cost of equity (Damodaran: 1997, p. 649). This relationship is useful, because it enables the analyst to determine the effects of changes in the firm's dividend policy or cost of equity on its P/E multiple. It also illustrates why increases in a firm's P/E ratio reduce its required return on acquisitions financed by issuing stock.

If we use the Gordon Constant Growth Model but substitute the firm's dividend payments for cash flow, we can write the following expression:

$$\frac{P_0}{S_0} = \frac{d_0/S_0 \times (1 + g)}{(k_e - g)},$$

where

P_0/S_0 = current price per share

d_0/S_0 = current dividend per share

g = expected earnings growth rate

k_e = cost of equity

Dividing both sides by current earnings per share (E_0/S_0),

$$\frac{P_0/E_0}{E_0/S_0} = \frac{d_0/S_0 \times (1 + g)/(k_e - g)}{E_0/S_0}$$

$$P_0/S_0 = \frac{d_0/S_0 \times (1 + g) \times S_0/E_0}{(k_e - g)}$$

$$P_0/E_0 = \frac{d_0/E_0 \times (1 + g)}{(k_e - g)}$$

$$= \frac{d_1/E_0}{(k_e - g)}$$

Solving this equation for k_e provides the following expression:

$$k_e = d_1/P_0 + g \quad \text{or} \quad (d_1 + gP_0)/P_0$$

This expression suggests that increases in a firm's share price relative to earnings (i.e., increases in its P/E ratio) lowers the firm's required return on acquisitions financed by issuing stock. This explains why high levels of M&A activity frequently coincide with booming stock markets. For example, if d_1 is $1, g is 10%, and $P_0 = \$10$, k_e is 20%. However, if P_0 increases to $20 and g and d_1 remain the same, k_e declines to 15%. Note that an increase in P_0 without an increase in earnings growth (g) implies a higher P/E ratio for the firm.

VALUING INTANGIBLE ASSETS

Intangible assets may represent significant sources of value on a target firm's balance sheet. However, they tend to be difficult to value. AOL's primary asset is its subscriber base, yet its value is not fully reflected on its balance sheet. Similarly, the true value of Coca Cola's brand name and its highly effective distribution system are not carried as specific assets on the balance sheet. The balance sheets of Microsoft and Dell are also understated to the extent that they do not reflect their brand images, the knowledge of their workers, and the presence of online ordering and customer service systems.

There are few satisfactory solutions to revaluing the balance sheet to reflect these factors. One alternative is to capitalize R&D, marketing and advertising, franchise systems, employee training, and the noncapital portions of customer service systems. These capitalized values are subsequently amortized over what is believed to be their useful lives. Although this alternative may seem theoretically appealing, the determination of what portion of such expenses to capitalize and over how many years to spread the cost are highly subjective. GAAP accounting strives to relate revenue recorded in a specific accounting period with actual expenses incurred to generate those revenues. Because adjustments to the balance sheet are often highly subjective, they may simply distort reported earnings.

If the markets are truly efficient, investors should be able to understand the impact of these intangible factors in generating future earnings and build these factors into the price of the stock. A study by Chan, Lakonishok, and Sougainnis (1999) provides evidence that the value of intangible spending such as R&D expenditures are indeed factored into a firm's current share price.

CLASSIFYING INTANGIBLE ASSETS

Intangible assets can be classified into three categories: operational intangibles, production or product intangibles, and marketing intangibles (see Table 7-5). Operational intangibles have been defined as the ability of a business to continue to function and generate income without interruption as a consequence of a change in ownership (*VGS Corp v. Commissioner:* 1977). Production or product intangibles are values placed on the accumulated intellectual capital resulting from the production and product design experience of the combined entity. This experience gives the combined firm an ability to create a product or service, which has a competitive advantage to other similar products or services. Marketing intangibles are those factors that help a firm to sell a product or service. For tax and financial reporting purposes, goodwill is a residual item equal to the difference between the purchase price for the target company and the fair market value of tangible and intangible assets, including operational, production, and marketing intangible assets.

TABLE 7-5. Alternative Intangible Categories

Intangible asset category	Examples
Operating intangibles	Assembled and trained workforce Operating and administrative systems Corporate culture
Production or product intangibles	Patents Technological know-how Production standards Copyrights Software Favorable leases and licenses
Marketing intangibles	Customer lists and relationships Price lists and pricing strategies Marketing strategies, studies and concepts Advertising and promotional materials Trademarks and service marks Trade names Covenants not to compete Franchises

In most cases, intangible assets, like tangible assets, have separately determinable values, with limited useful lives. In certain cases, the useful lives are defined by the legal protection afforded by the agency issuing the protection, such as the U.S. Patent Office. In contrast, the useful life of such intangible assets as customer lists is more difficult to define.

Examples of how some of these intangible items could be valued are described in the following sections. The concepts and methodologies discussed previously may be applied to many of the different types of intangible assets.

Patents

A patent is a grant of some privilege by the government to someone to exclude others from making, selling, or using one's invention and includes the right to license others to make, use, or sell the invention. At the time of an acquisition, the value of the patent is generally based on some measure of the future after-tax cash flows that can reasonably be expected to result from the use or licensing of the patent. In the absence of a predictable cash flow stream, the cost of developing a comparable invention or technology may be used to estimate the value of a patent.

Patents without Applications

Many firms have patents for which no current application within the firm has yet been identified. However, the patent may have value to an external party. Prior to closing, the buyer and seller may negotiate a value for a patent that has not yet been licensed to a third party based on the cash flows that can reasonably be expected to be generated over its future life. In cases where the patent has been licensed to third parties, the valuation is based on the expected future royalties that are to be received from licensing the patent over its remaining life.

Patents Linked to Existing Products or Services

When a product is used internally to produce a product, it is normally valued based on the "avoided cost" method. This method uses market-based royalty rates (RR) paid on comparable patents multiplied by the projected future stream of revenue (REV) from the products whose production depends on the patent discounted to its present value. The present value of the patent, the tax rate, and the cost of capital are PV_{pat}, t, and WACC, respectively.

$$PV_{pat} = \sum_{i=1}^{n} \frac{REV_i \times RR(1 - t)}{(1 + WACC)^n}$$

Note that patents may still have value even after their protection expires. This occurs when the presence of the patent creates a continuing business opportunity beyond the life of the patent protection. Even though the cash flow generated by the patent or products based on the patent may decline as competitors copy the patent, additional patents may emerge that relate to the original product and extend the original life of the invention far beyond its inception.

Patent License Agreements

A firm may receive an exclusive right to an invention in return for helping the inventor develop the invention, developing and marketing products based on the invention, and paying the inventor a royalty on future sales. The patent license agreement is valued as if the licensee owns the patent. Cash flows generated, as a result of the patent, are reduced by any lump-sum or royalty payments made under the license agreement.

Patent Portfolios

Products and services often depend upon a number of patents. This makes it exceedingly difficult to determine the amount of the cash flow generated by the sale of the products or services to be allocated to each patent. In this case, the patents are grouped together as a single portfolio and valued as a group using a single royalty rate applied to a declining percentage of the company's future revenue and then discounting this cash flow stream to its present value. Using a declining percentage of revenue reflects the probable diminishing value of the patents with the passage of time.

Customer Lists

Projections of free cash flow to the firm make a number of simplifying, albeit often heroic, assumptions about growth rates of the various components of cash flow. For example, revenue projections can be determined either by assuming a continuation of the historical growth rate or by building up revenue projections based on the known characteristics of the customer base. The latter approach is generally preferred if the analyst has access to reasonably reliable data.

How reliable such projections are depends to a certain extent on assumptions about normal customer attrition rates, the number of new customers by major product category that are expected to be added, and the size and length of customer contracts. Multiyear customer contracts, which are noncancelable due to a change in the ownership of the business, are particularly valuable. Such contracts provide a highly reliable estimate of future revenues while they are in force.

In situations where there are hundreds of contracts or possibly thousands, as is true for magazine subscriptions, the value of a customer list may be approximated by calculating the present value of the average cash flows generated by these customers during the average life of the current contracts. If you assume that the list does not deteriorate over time, but rather it is self-generating through renewals, a terminal value may be calculated.

Leases

Leases are generally viewed only as a debt obligation, but in some instances, they represent an opportunity to reduce operating expenses by "buying out" the remainder of a lease contract if the space is viewed by the buyer as redundant. However, leases should also be considered as a potential source of value to the acquiring firm. If long-term leases were signed in years past when lease rates were lower than they are currently, the assumption of these leases by the buyer can provide a source of competitive advantage. This is particularly true for businesses such as banks having large branch networks and retailers with multiple locations.

Operating leases have a life span of no more than 5 years. Maintenance and repairs are the responsibility of the lessor; leases can be cancelled at the option of the lessee. At the end of the lease, the lessee returns the asset to the lessor. Operating leases do not have to be included on the balance sheet because the lessee does not assume the risk of ownership, although they are normally recorded in a footnote. At the end of the year, total lease payments are deducted from revenues. Capital leases are long-term contracts between the lessee and the lessor and cannot be canceled; the asset is usually fully amortized and maintenance and repairs are the responsibility of the lessee.

The value to the acquiring company of below-market lease rates can be approximated by estimating the present value of the difference between the lease rates paid on space currently leased by the target company and the current lease rate if the acquirer had to lease comparable space. The discount rate should be the acquiring firm's current pretax cost of unsecured debt, which represents the cost of borrowing funds to buy the piece of equipment or space that is being leased.

Trademarks and Service Marks

A trademark is the right to use a name associated with a company, product, or concept; a service mark is the right to use an image associated with a company, product, or concept. Trademarks and service marks have recognition value. Examples include Bayer Aspirin, Kellogg's Corn Flakes, or Compaq Computer. For these firms and others like them, name recognition reflects the firm's longevity, cumulative advertising expenditures, the overall effectiveness of their marketing programs, and the consistency of perceived product quality. Although we know there is value in the trademark or service mark, the challenge is to estimate it in terms of dollars. There are five commonly used methods for doing so: cost avoidance, comparable firms, recent transactions, focus groups, and surveys.

Cost-Avoidance Approach

The underlying assumption in applying this approach to the valuation of trademarks and service marks is that cumulative advertising and promotion campaigns build brand recognition and association with certain desirable characteristics such as consistent quality or value (i.e., high quality at a reasonable price). The initial outlays for promotional campaigns are the largest and tend to decline as a percentage of sales over time as the brand becomes more recognizable. Consequently, the valuation of a trademark associated with a specific product or business involves multiplying projected revenues by a declining percentage to reflect the reduced level of spending, as a percentage of sales, that is required to maintain brand recognition. These projected expenditures are then adjusted for taxes, since marketing expenses are tax deductible, and discounted to the present at the acquiring firm's cost of capital.

Comparable Firm Approach

Assume that we have two firms, F1 and F2, which have similar cost structures. However, F1 is able to command significantly higher product selling prices than F2 due to its greater brand recognition. As such, F1 will also have significantly higher operating margins than F2. If the firms are growing at approximately the same rate and have similar risk characteristics, F1 should have a significantly higher market value than F2. The difference between the market value of the two firms reflects the dollar value of the brand recognition. However, such situations are relatively hard to find in practice.

Recent Transactions

Companies may license the right to use a trademark or service mark. The acquiring company may apply the license rate required to obtain the rights to comparable trademarks and service marks and apply it as a percentage of the cash flows that can reasonably be expected to be generated by selling the products or services under the licensed trademark or service mark during the remaining term of the license. The resulting cash flows are then discounted to the present using the acquiring company's cost of capital.

Alternatively, a value may be determined by examining recent outright purchases of comparable trademarks or, in the case of the Internet, web addresses or domain names. For example, in early 2000, Bank of America revealed that it had purchased the rights to the Loans.com web address for $3 million in an online auction. The largest payment for a domain name occurred in 1999 when eCompanies, a venture capital firm, purchased the www.business.com address for $7.5 million (*Orange County Register:* 2000).

Focus Groups and Surveys

Estimating the value of such an intangible asset may be accomplished indirectly through such techniques as customer surveys or an analysis of product selling prices. The key question is how much more would consumers be willing to pay for a widely recognized brand name product than for a generic product. Focus groups may be used to determine how a representative sample of the consumers of a specific product would respond to this question. Alternatively, the percentage difference between the selling prices of branded products and generic products may serve as a reasonable proxy for the value of the brand name to the firm selling the branded products. For example, if these surveys and analyses of selling prices reveal that consumers are willing to pay 20% more for the branded product, an analyst may attribute 20% of the firm's market value to its brand recognition. Similarly, an acquiring company may believe that 20% of its proposed purchase price for this same firm is attributable to the firm's brand name.

USING REAL OPTIONS TO VALUE
INTANGIBLE ASSETS

An option is the exclusive right, but not the obligation, to buy, sell, or utilize property for a specific period of time in exchange for an agreed upon sum of money. Options that are traded on financial exchanges, such as puts and calls, are called financial options. Options that are not publicly traded, such as licenses, copyrights, trademarks, and patents, are called real options. Other examples of real options include the right to buy land, commercial property, and equipment.

Patents and licenses owned by a target company may appear to have little value, particularly if they have never been used. As noted earlier in this chapter, they can be valued and added to the total present value of the target company by applying conventional capital budgeting techniques. This involves the discounting of projected cash flows generated from products based on the patent and deducting the resulting present value from the cost of developing the technology, process, or product.

Even if the NPV is negative, the patent or license owned by the target company may still have significant value. The acquiring company will ordinarily gain access to the patents and licenses owned by the target company. The acquirer may choose to provide whatever funds are necessary to exploit the patents or licenses. Alternatively, the acquiring company may choose to transfer ownership by selling the patent or license to another party, who may choose to fund implementation of the patent or license. If we think of the ownership rights to the unused or underutilized patent or license as essentially an unexploited opportunity, such ownership rights can be viewed as call options. The owner of the call option has the right to exercise the option at a predetermined price. The right expires at a specific time in the future, when the patent or license expires.

Options to assets whose cash flows have large variances and that have a long time before they expire are typically more valuable than those with smaller variances and less time remaining. The greater variance and time to expiration increases the chance that the factors affecting cash flows will change a project from one with a negative NPV to one with a positive NPV.

Option pricing theory that has traditionally been applied to valuing financial options can also be applied to value real options. The Black and Scholes Option Pricing Model (OPM) is the most well-known methodology for pricing financial options (Black and Scholes: 1989). If we know the values of five variables, we can use OPM to establish a theoretical price for an option. The Black-Scholes' formula for valuing a call option is given as follows (Kolb: 1993):

$$C = SN(d_1) - Ee_f^{-R,xt}N(d_2),$$

where C = Theoretical call option value

$$d_1 = \frac{\ln(S/E) + [R_f + (1/2)\sigma^2]t}{\sigma\sqrt{t}}$$

$$d_2 = d_1 - \sigma \sqrt{t}$$

S = Stock price or underlying asset price

E = Exercise price

R_f = The risk-free rate of interest

σ^2 = Variance of the stock's or underlying asset's returns

t = Time to expiration of the option

$N(d_1)$ and $N(d_2)$ = Cumulative normal probability values of d_1 and d_2

Of these five variables, the risk associated with the projected cash flows of the project is probably the most difficult to estimate. Risk can be estimated based on past experience with similar projects by calculating the average percentage difference between projected and actual cash flows for these projects. Alternatively, probabilities or risks can be assigned to optimistic, pessimistic, and most likely scenarios. The average of the probabilities in the three cases can be used to estimate the risk factor to be used in the Black-Scholes formula.

The term $Ee_f^{-R,xt}$ is the present value of the exercise price when continuous discounting is used. The terms $N(d_1)$ and $N(d_2)$, which involve the cumulative probability function, are the terms that take risk into account. These two values are Z-scores from the normal probability function, and they can be found in cumulative distribution function tables for the standard normal random variable. Exhibit 7-17 illustrates how a license could be valued as a call option and sold to a third party.

EXHIBIT 7-17. VALUING REAL OPTIONS

Assume that a company has a 10-year license to produce and market a product in a designated geographic area to a specific set of customers. The cost of retooling the firm's manufacturing operations, training and equipping the sales force, promotional literature, advertising, and license fees requires an initial investment of $100 million. The present value of projected cash flows from utilizing the license is $80 million. Although the product is currently expensive to produce in small quantities, the cost of production is expected to fall as larger volumes are sold. Furthermore, improvements in production technology are expected to lower production costs. Lower production costs will enable a reduction in the price of the product. It is uncertain by how much sales of the product will increase due to the declining price. An analysis of similar projects in the past suggests that the variance of the projected cash flows is 3%. The current 10-year Treasury bond rate is 6%.

Even though the project has a negative net present value of $20 million,

estimate the value of the license as a call option, which could be sold to another party.
   Solution:

Value of the asset (PV of projected cash flows from utilizing the license)   = $80 million

Exercise price (PV of the cost of developing and marketing the product)   = $100 million

Variance of the cash flows   = .03

Time to expiration   = 10 years

Risk-free interest rate   = .06

$$d_1 = \frac{\ln(\$80/\$100) + [.06 + (1/2).03]10}{\sqrt{.03}\sqrt{10}}$$

$$= \frac{-.2231 + .7500}{.1732 \times 3.1623}$$

$$= \frac{.5269}{.5477}$$

$$= .9620$$

$$d_2 = .9620 - .5477$$

$$= .4143$$

$$C = \$80(.8531) - \$100(2.7183)^{-.06 \times 10}(.6736)$$

$$= \$68.25 - \$36.97$$

$$= \$31.28 \text{ (value of the call option)}$$

If this company were being valued for possible acquisition, the acquirer may choose to add $31.28 million to the total valuation for this firm.

Notes:
1. Z scores: The probability of drawing a value from the distribution of possible outcomes associated with this investment opportunity that is less than or equal to $d_1 = 1.1501$ is .8944 and of $d_2 = .6024$ is .7422.
2. The Z scores were calculated at the 5% significance level.

THINGS TO REMEMBER

   The CAPM is widely used to estimate the cost of equity. The cost of equity can also be estimated from the firm's dividend yield plus its earnings growth rate. The pretax cost of debt for nonrated firms can best be approximated by comparison with similar firms, whose debt is rated by the major credit-rating agencies or by looking at interest rates on debt currently on the firm's books. Weights for the firm's cost of capital should reflect the acquiring firm's target capital structure.

FCFF is widely used as a measure of cash flow for valuing an acquisition target, since it does not require an estimate of the firm's debt-repayment schedule during the forecast period. FCFF is generally defined for valuation purposes as follows:

$$FCFF = EBIT \, (1 - tax \ rate) - (Gross \ Cap. \ Exp. - Depreciation) - \Delta \, WC$$

FCFE is used primarily when the proposed transaction does not entail debt.

Discounted cash flow valuation is far more an art than a science. It is highly sensitive to the choice of the discount rate as well as the magnitude and timing of future cash flows. Despite its shortcomings, it is essential to determining a preliminary or baseline valuation. Other valuation techniques should be employed to provide additional credibility for the estimate provided by the discounted cash flow method.

In the constant growth model, free cash flow to the firm is expected to grow at a constant rate. This model is commonly used in the calculation of terminal values.

$$P_0 = FCFF_1 / (WACC - g), \text{ where } FCFF_1 = FCFF_0 \, (1 + g).$$

In the variable growth model, cash flow exhibits both a high and a stable growth period. Total PV in this case represents the sum of the discounted value of the cash flows over both periods.

$$FCFF: P_0 = \sum_{t=1}^{n} \frac{FCFF_0 \times (1 + g_t)^t}{(1 + WACC)^t} + \frac{P_n}{(1 + WACC)^n},$$

where

$$P_n = \frac{FCFF_n \times (1 + g_m)}{(WACC_m - g_m)}$$

The cost of capital during the stable growth period should be lower than during the high-growth period to reflect the reduced rate of uncertainty associated with the slower rate of growth of cash flow. The terminal value frequently accounts for most of the total PV calculation and is highly sensitive to the choice of the growth rate of free cash flow and discount rate during the stable growth period. If the terminal value accounts for a large percentage of the total PV (e.g., more than three-fourths), the conventional 5-year projection of future cash flows should be extended to at least 10 years. In any valuation exercise, assumptions should always be clearly stated. The credibility of any valuation is ultimately dependent on the credibility of its underlying assumptions.

Market-based valuation techniques offer a variety of alternatives to discounted cash flow estimates. The comparable companies' approach entails the multiplication of certain measures of value for the target such as earnings by the appropriate valuation multiple for comparable companies. Similarly, the comparable transactions' method involves the multiplication of the target's earnings by the same valuation multiple for recent, similar transactions. If available, similar transactions are generally the most reliable of these market-based valuation methods. The comparable industry approach applies industry average multiples to earnings, cash flow, book value, or sales. Asset-oriented methods, such as tangible book value, are very useful for valuing financial services companies and distribution companies. Liquidation or breakup value is the projected price of the firm's assets sold separately less its liabilities. Liquidation may be involuntary as a result of bankruptcy or voluntary if a firm is viewed by its owners as worth more in liquidation than as a going concern.

CHAPTER DISCUSSION QUESTIONS

7-1. What is the significance of the weighted average cost of capital? How is it calculated? Do the weights reflect the firm's actual or target debt to total capital ratio? Why?

7-2. What does a firm's β measure? What is the difference between an unlevered and levered β? Why is this distinction significant?

7-3. What are the primary differences between FCFE and FCFF?

7-4. Explain the primary differences between the income (discounted cash flow), market-based, and asset-oriented valuation methods?

7-5. Which discounted cash flow valuation methods require the estimation of a terminal value? Why?

7-6. Do small changes in the assumptions pertaining to the estimation of the terminal value have a significant impact on the calculation of the total value of the target firm? If so, why?

7-7. In your judgment, does valuing a firm using the weighted average valuation method make sense? If yes, why? If no, why not?

7-8. Why do increasing P/E ratios increase the attractiveness of stock for stock exchanges for acquiring companies?

7-9. How is the liquidation value of the firm calculated? Why is the assumption of orderly liquidation important?

7-10. Explain how you would value a patent under the following situations: a patent without any current application, a patent linked to an existing product, and a patent portfolio.

CHAPTER BUSINESS CASE

CASE STUDY 7-2. @HOME AND EXCITE FORM
EXCITE@HOME

Background Information

@Home Network announced its merger with Excite Inc. in January 1999 for $6.7 billion. Prior to the announcement, Excite's market value was about $3.5

billion. The transaction closed in May 1999. The announced purpose of the transaction was to create a new media company capable of providing home and business customers high speed, 24-hour access to personalized services from their PCs, pagers, cellular phones, and television sets. The new company combines the search engine capabilities of one of the best known brands on the Internet, Excite, with @Home's agreements with 21 cable companies worldwide. @Home gains access to the nearly 17 million households that are regular users of Excite.

At the time, this transaction constituted the largest merger of Internet companies ever. As of July 1999, Excite @Home displayed a P/E ratio in excess of 260 based on the consensus estimates for the year 2000 of $.21 per share. The firm's market value was $18.8 billion, 270 times sales. Investors really had great expectations for the future performance of the combined firms, despite their lackluster profit performance since their inception.

Founded in 1995, @Home provided interactive services to home and business users over its proprietary network, telephone company circuits, and through the cable companies' infrastructure. Cable connections provide connections at more than 100 times the speed of dial-up services. @Home also provides branded content in this broadband environment. Subscribers pay $39.95 per month for the service.

Assumptions

- Excite is properly valued immediately prior to announcement of the transaction.
- Annual customer service costs equal $50 per customer.
- Annual customer revenue in the form of @Home access charges and ancillary services equals $500 per customer. This assumes that declining access charges in this highly competitive environment will be offset by increases in revenue from the sale of ancillary services.
- None of the current Excite user households are current @Home customers.
- New @Home customers acquired through Excite remain @Home customers in perpetuity.
- @Home converts immediately 2% or 340,000 of the current 17 million Excite user households. A 2% response rate is typical of both online and direct mail solicitations.
- @Home's cost of capital is 20% during the growth period and drops to 10% during the slower, sustainable growth period; its combined federal and state tax rate is 40%.
- Capital spending equals depreciation; current assets equal current liabilities.
- FCFF from synergy increases by 15% annually for the next 10 years and 5% thereafter. Its cost of capital after the high-growth period drops to 10%.
- The maximum purchase price @Home should pay for Excite equals Excite's current market price plus the synergy that results from the merger of the two businesses.

Case Study Discussion Questions

1. Did @Home overpay for Excite?
2. What other assumptions might you consider?
3. What are the limitations of the valuation method employed in this case?
4. What alternative valuation techniques could you utilize?

Solutions to these questions are found in the Appendix at the back of this book.

REFERENCES

Black, Fischer, and Myron Scholes, "The Pricing of Options and Corporate Liabilities," *Journal of Applied Corporate Finance, 1*(4), Winter 1989, pp. 67–73.

Business Week, "What's a Cell-Phone User Worth?" February 21, 2000, p. 60.

Chan, Louis K. C., Josef Lakonishok, and Theordore Sougiannis, "Investing in High R&D Stocks," *BusinessWeek,* October 11, 1999, p. 28.

Damodaran, Aswath, *Corporate Finance: Theory and Practice,* New York: John Wiley & Sons, 1997, pp. 160–193.

Gitman, Lawrence J., *Principles of Managerial Finance,* 8th ed., New York: Addison-Wesley, 1997.

Gordon, Myron, *The Investment, Financing, and Valuation of the Modern Corporation,* Homewood, IL: Irwin, 1962.

Ibbotson, Roger, *Stocks, Bonds, Bills, and Inflation Yearbook,* Chicago: Ibbotson Associates, 1999, www.ibbotson.com.

Kolb, Robert W. *Financial Derivatives,* Englewood Cliffs, NJ: The New York Institute of Finance, 1993, pp. 76–125.

Lasher, William R., *Practical Financial Management,* 2nd ed., Cincinnati: Southwestern College Publishing, 2000.

Moyer, R. Charles, James R. Mcguigan, and William J. Kretlow, *Contemporary Financial Management,* 7th ed., Cincinnati: Southwestern College Publishing, 1998.

Orange County Register, "B of A Buys Loans.com Domain Name," February 7, 2000, Business Section, p. 2.

VGS Corp v. Commissioner (1977), 68 TC 563, 591–2.

8

APPLYING FINANCIAL MODELING TECHNIQUES TO VALUE AND STRUCTURE MERGERS AND ACQUISITIONS

If you don't agree with me, it means you haven't been listening.

—Sam Markewich

It was crunch time. Both parties to the negotiation were in heated discussions to resolve several key sticking points. The seller was insisting on a higher price for certain assets that the buyer simply could not justify paying. Nonetheless, the buyer was a seasoned veteran and realized that as long as both parties were motivated a deal was still possible. To bridge the gap between what the seller was demanding and what the buyer was willing to pay, the buyer would have to be creative to meet the seller's needs. However, the proposed changes to the terms of the transaction would clearly have implications for the combined companies' taxes, leverage, compliance with loan covenants, and earnings per share.

The buyer turned to a financial model he had constructed of the combined firms to assess the impact of various changes in the terms of the transaction. After changing certain assumptions that had been used to generate the initial offer, the buyer was able to estimate the potential risk to the combined companies if the buyer made the changes demanded by the seller. The model's results were pleasantly surprising to the buyer. The impact of the changes on variables the buyer considered critical was much less than had been imagined. Armed with this information, the buyer returned to the negotiating table optimistic that an agreement could be reached.

OVERVIEW

Financial modeling refers to the application of spreadsheet software to define simple arithmetic relationships among variables within the firm's income, balance sheet, and cash flow statements, as well as the interrelationships among the various financial statements. Examples of simple relationships within individual financial statements include the effects of price, quantity, and product mix on revenue and profitability on the income statement and the relationship between shareholders' equity and total assets and liabilities on the balance sheet. Common interrelationships among the financial statements include the link between net income less dividends and the change in retained earnings as well as between net income and the change in cash flow.

The application of financial modeling to mergers and acquisitions (M&As) typically involves developing spreadsheets for the acquiring firm, the target firm, and the combined firms. Models are used to value the acquiring firm in the absence of any acquisitions. Models are then used to value a prospective target acquisition and the potential synergy with the acquiring firm. The two models can then be consolidated to estimate the combined value of the acquirer and target firms.

The primary objective in applying financial modeling techniques is to create a computer-based model, which facilitates the acquirer's understanding of the impact of changes in certain operating variables on the firm's overall performance and valuation. Examples include the effects of product selling prices and volume levels on the firm's break-even point and increasing leverage on the firm's financial returns. Once in place, these models can be used to simulate alternative scenarios to determine which one enables the acquirer to achieve its objectives without violating identifiable and measurable constraints. Financial objectives could include earnings per share for publicly traded firms, return on total capital for privately held firms, or return on equity for leveraged buyout firms. Typical constraints include Wall Street analysts' expectations for the firm's earnings per share (EPS), the acquirer's leverage compared to other firms in the same industry, and loan covenants limiting how the firm uses its available cash flow and currently unencumbered assets as collateral for new borrowing. Another important constraint is the risk tolerance of the acquiring company, which could be measured by the acquirer's target debt to equity ratio.

The models can be used to answer several different sets of questions. The first set pertains to valuation. How much is the target company worth without the effects of synergy? What is the value of expected synergy? What is the maximum price that the acquiring company should pay for the target company? The second set of questions pertains to financing. Can the maximum price be financed? What combination of potential sources of funds, both internally generated and external sources, provides the lowest cost of funds for the acquirer, subject to known constraints? The final set of questions pertains to deal structuring. What is the impact on the acquirer's financial performance if the deal is structured as a taxable rather than a nontaxable transaction? What is the impact on financial performance and valuation if the acquirer is willing to assume certain target company liabilities? Deal structuring considerations are discussed in more detail in Chapter 10 (this volume).

The objectives of this chapter are to emphasize the limitations of financial data used in the valuation process and to provide a simple procedure for building a financial model in the context of a merger or acquisition. The procedure allows the analyst to determine the minimum and maximum prices for a target firm. The chapter contains examples of how these techniques may be applied. Finally, simple formulae for calculating share exchange ratios and assessing the impact on postmerger earnings per share are provided. These can be included in models used to evaluate the impact of various scenarios on earnings per share.

THE LIMITATIONS OF FINANCIAL DATA

There are several major sources of error in any valuation methodology. These include the conceptual limitations of the valuation methodology described in Chapter 7 (this volume), the difficulty in predicting either the magnitude and the timing of projected earnings or cash flows, and the inaccuracies inherent in the published data used to apply the various valuation tools. Limitations of the data can result in severe distortions in any of the valuation techniques employed.

MANAGING EARNINGS

Daily gyrations in the stock prices of publicly traded companies underscore the importance of meeting or exceeding investor expectations. Acutely aware of the potentially catastrophic consequences of disappointing investors, corporate managers have for many years attempted to smooth earnings fluctuations and hopefully fluctuations in the share price of their corporation. The effort to "manage earnings" has in some cases required the use of certain accounting artifices. These include the alleged misuse of restructuring charges, acquisition accounting, reserves, and revenue recognition.

THE IMPORTANCE OF GENERALLY ACCEPTED ACCOUNTING PRINCIPLES

Generally accepted accounting principles (GAAP) provide specific guidelines as to how to account for specific events, although some require judgment calls. Few would argue that GAAP ensures that all transactions are accurately recorded; nonetheless, the scrupulous application of GAAP does ensure consistency in comparing one firm's financial performance to another. It is customary for definitive agreements of purchase and sale to require that a target company represent that its financial books are kept in accordance with GAAP. Consequently, the acquiring company at least understands how the financial numbers were assembled. During due diligence, the acquirer can look for discrepancies between the target's reported numbers and GAAP practices. Such discrepancies are often indications of potential problems. It is comforting to know that the target firm's financial statements used for a preliminary valuation of the business were compiled in accordance with GAAP. Unfortunately, this may provide a false sense of security.

THE FINDINGS OF SECURITY EXCHANGE
COMMISSION INVESTIGATIONS

In late 1998, Arthur Levitt, Chairman of the Securities and Exchange Commission (SEC), committed his agency to a high-priority attack on earnings management. "What's at stake," he said, "is nothing less than the credibility of the U.S. financial-reporting system" (Loomis: 1999, p. 75). Without credible data, the range of potential error in efforts to value target companies expands considerably. Hence, the analyst should never become so preoccupied with the choice and application of the valuation methodology that he or she overlooks the need to understand the limitations of the data.

Revenue Recognition

The most widespread abuse of GAAP occurs when the decision is made to count a sale to a customer as revenue. In a recent study, improper revenue recognition was found to be the most common form of financial reporting fraud. The Committee on Sponsoring Organizations of the Treadway Commission (COSO), an association of accounting and financial industry trade associations and regulatory bodies, reported that approximately one of every two cases of alleged fraud studied in a sample of 200 firms for the 11-year period ending in 1997 had stated revenue incorrectly (COSO: 1998).

GAAP is very specific about when a sale should be counted as revenue. Revenue can be recognized when the product or service provided by the firm has been received by the customer or performed in full and the firm providing the product or service has either received cash or a receivable that is both observable and measurable. Expenses that are directly tied to the generation of that revenue must be recognized in the same period in which the revenue is recognized. For long-term contracts spanning multiple accounting periods, revenue is recognized on the basis of the percentage of the contract completed. When there is considerable uncertainty about the customer's ability to pay, the firm may recognize revenue only when it receives portions of what it is owed on an installment basis.

Well-publicized abuses of revenue recognition include Al Dunlap, the former CEO of Sunbeam, who allegedly recorded the sale of goods, despite having not yet shipped them to customers. In other instances, firms have been caught creating false invoices or holding the accounting period open beyond the end of the quarter in order to boost revenue.

Restructuring Reserves

Firms sometimes set up reserves in order to smooth fluctuations in earnings. According to GAAP, firms intending to undertake a restructuring of their operations are required to estimate the costs they will eventually incur, such as severance expenses, and to charge them against current earnings. A reserve liability is set up on the balance sheet to reflect these anticipated expenses. The actual cash outlay may not occur for several years or perhaps not at all. Firms may reverse or eliminate the reserve at a later time. This has the effect of increasing earnings at the time the reserve is reversed. Some firms build reserves when taxable income is high and later reverse those reserves when income is less robust. Examples of expenses that should not be included in the estimate of reserves include legal and accounting fees, investment banking fees, special bonuses, and training expenses.

In 1999, the SEC required that Rite Aid Pharmacies, which took a restructuring charge in the fiscal year ending in February 1999 in anticipation of closing 379 stores, to reduce the size of its restructuring charge from $290 million to $233 million. In addition, the SEC required Rite Aid to add certain expenses to its operating costs and to restate profits from the unaudited $158 million that it had reported in March 1999 to $144 million. Reflecting the substantial disappointment of investors, Rite Aid lost more than $7 billion in market value during the first half of 1999.

Other abuses of reserves include the so-called "cookie jar" reserves. Such reserves represent earnings held back from the period in which they should have been recognized only to be used later during lackluster earnings periods. GAAP states that reserves cannot be established for contingencies because such costs cannot be predicted. Contingent events should impact the income statement in the period in which they occur.

In Process Research and Development Expenditures

Merger accounting has also been a source of abuse in those industries that rely heavily on research and development (R&D) to introduce new products. An acquiring company must assign values to all the assets it has purchased, record them on the balance sheet, and write them off in future years. In-process R&D can be written off immediately, as GAAP states that in-process R&D expenditures refer to spending on largely untested rather than proven technology. Acquiring companies have an incentive to assign a high value to R&D assets and then to write them off immediately to avoid charges against future earnings.

Because accounting abuses can go on for years before they are discovered, the SEC requires a restatement of earnings going back several years. This is what happened to W. R. Grace, Cendant, and McKesson-HBOC. Although it is unclear if these cases will encourage firms to comply more diligently with GAAP, they clearly underscore the need for the valuation analyst to be circumspect in their use of data. This is true even if financial data are represented in the agreement of purchase and sale to have been compiled in accordance with GAAP.

THE MODEL-BUILDING PROCESS

The M&A model-building process can be thought of as a series of discrete steps beginning with a thorough analysis of the dynamics of the industry in which the target company competes, and its overall competitive position within that industry. Using this knowledge, detailed financial statements can be constructed and cash flows for the target can be projected over some appropriate time frame. If the target is part of a larger firm, the projected cash flows must be adjusted to reflect all costs and revenue associated with the target operation. Factors contributing to, as well as detracting from, economic value are then estimated and used to construct an appropriate price range for the target firm. Finally, the target and acquiring firm's financial statements are consolidated, adjusted to reflect the net effects of synergy, and run through a series of iterations until a financial structure satisfying certain criteria can be identified (see Figure 8-1).

STEP 1: UNDERSTANDING INDUSTRY AND COMPANY COMPETITIVE DYNAMICS

The accuracy of any valuation is heavily dependent on understanding the historical competitive dynamics of the industry, the historical performance of the company within the industry, and the reliability of the data used in the valuation. A careful examination of historical information can provide insights into key relationships among various operating variables and represents the first step in the process for modeling both the acquirer and the target companies. Examples of relevant historical relationships include seasonal or cyclical movements in the data, the relationship between fixed and variable expenses, and the impact on revenue of changes in product prices and unit sales. If these relationships can reasonably be expected to continue through the forecast period, they can be used to project the earnings and cash flows that will be used in the valuation process.

Normalizing Historical Data

To ensure that these historical relationships can be accurately defined, it is necessary to cleanse the data of anomalies, nonrecurring changes, and questionable

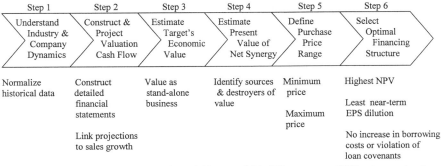

FIGURE 8-1. The mergers and acquisitions model-building process. NPV, net present value; EPS, earnings per share.

accounting practices. For example, cash flow may be adjusted by adding back unusually large increases in reserves or by deducting large decreases in reserves from free cash flow to the firm. Similar adjustments can be made for significant nonrecurring gains or losses on the sale of assets or for nonrecurring expenses such as those associated with the settlement of a lawsuit or warranty claim. Monthly revenue data may be aggregated into quarterly or even annual information to minimize period-to-period distortions in earnings or cash flow due to inappropriate accounting practices. Ideally, at least 3–5 years of historical data should be normalized.

Common-Size Financial Statements

Common-size financial statements are among the most frequently used tools to uncover data irregularities. These statements may be constructed by calculating the percentage each line item of the income statement, balance sheet, and cash flow statement is of annual sales for each quarter or year for which historical data are available.

Common-size financial statements are useful for comparing businesses of different sizes in the same industry at a specific moment in time. Such analyses are called *cross-sectional comparisons.* By expressing the target's line-item data as a percent of sales, it is possible to compare the target company with other companies' line item data expressed in terms of sales to highlight significant differences. For example, a cross-sectional comparison may indicate important differences in the ratio of capital spending to sales between the target firm and other firms in the industry. This discrepancy may simply reflect "catch-up" spending underway at the target's competitors, or it may suggest a more troubling development in which the target is deferring necessary plant and equipment spending.

To determine which is the case, it is necessary to calculate common-size financial statements for the target firm and its primary competitors over a number of consecutive periods. This type of analysis is called a *multiperiod comparison.* Comparing companies in this manner will help to confirm whether the target has simply completed a large portion of capital spending that others in the industry are currently undertaking or whether the target is woefully behind in making necessary expenditures.

Even if it is not possible to collect sufficient data to undertake cross-sectional and multiperiod comparisons of both the target firm and its direct competitors, constructing common-size statements for the target firm only will provide useful insights. Abnormally large increases or decreases in these ratios from one quarter or one year to the next highlight the need for further examination to explain why these fluctuations occurred. If it is determined that they are likely to be one-time events, these fluctuations may be eliminated by averaging the data immediately preceding and following the period in which these anomalies occurred. The anomalous data are then replaced by the data created through this averaging process. Alternatively, anomalous data can be completely excluded from the analysis of historical data. In general, nonrecurring events impacting more than 10% of the net income or cash flow for a specific period should be "smoothed" or discarded from the data to allow for a clearer picture of trends and relationships in the firm's historical financial data.

STEP 2: PROJECT VALUATION CASH FLOW

Valuation cash flow is a generic term used to include the various definitions of cash flow that may be used to value companies. Valuation cash flow for the target company can be estimated by projecting each of its components directly or by calculating each component's percentage of sales and then applying these historical percentages to projections of sales. The latter approach is strongly recommended. This method is intuitively appealing, because sales are normally the principal determinant of changes in cash flow over long periods of time. This method is also simple to apply, because only one variable—sales—must be projected. Of course, the implicit assumptions are that all components of cash flow grow at the same rate as sales over time and that the historical relationship between the various components of cash flow and sales will continue to apply to the forecast period.

If the historical ratio between each major component of cash flow and sales is known, each major line item of the income statement, balance sheet, and cash flow statements can be determined by multiplying the historical ratios by sales projections. In the most basic models, items such as sales, general and administrative expenses (SG&A), cost of sales (COS), depreciation, capital expenditures, current assets, and current liabilities may be expressed as a percentage of sales to estimate the primary components of valuation cash flow. However, all financial variables need not or conceptually should not be expressed as a function of sales. These include the following:

1. Interest expense = cost of borrowed funds $\times$ amount of debt outstanding
2. Long-term debt = amount outstanding $-$ annual principal repayment
3. Income taxes = .40 $\times$ earnings before taxes (EBT), where .40 represents the combined state, local, and federal tax rate
4. Earnings per share = (net income $-$ preferred dividends) / total shares outstanding
5. Working capital = current assets $-$ current liabilities
6. Shareholders' equity = total assets $-$ current liabilities—long-term debt
7. Valuation cash flow or free cash flow to the firm (FCFF) = EBIT $(1 - t)$ + depreciation $-$ capital expenditures $-$ Δ working capital (Note: Valuation cash flow may be defined as free cash flow to the firm or to equity investors.)

Table 8-1 illustrates a more sophisticated way of modeling principal repayments. It provides an example of how to amortize a $1 million loan at an interest rate of 12% over a 3-year period, assuming a level annual loan payment. The

TABLE 8-1.   Calculating Level Loan Payments[a]

Year	Level loan payment[b]	Interest = .12 × unpaid balance	Principal = payment − interest	Balance = loan − principal repayment
1	$416,349	$120,000	$296,349	$703,651
2	$416,349	$84,438	$331,911	$371,740
3	$416,349	$44,609	$371,740	0

[a] $1,000,000 Loan, @ 12% for 3 years.
[b] Present value of annuity (PVA) = Payment (PMT) × Present value interest factor (PVIFA) and PMT = PVA / PVIFA = $1,000,000 / 2.402 = $416,349.

annual level payment (PMT) is calculated utilizing the formula for the present value of an annuity (PVA) and applying the present value interest factor (PVIFA) for 3 years at 12% per year. A more detailed example is provided in Chapter 11 (this volume).

STEP 3: ESTIMATE THE ECONOMIC VALUE OF THE ACQUISITION TARGET

Calculate the economic value of the target company, as if it were a stand-alone business, using income, market-based, and asset-oriented valuation techniques. The estimates resulting from the various techniques can then be averaged to arrive at a single valuation. The stand-alone economic value is the value of the business when all the costs of running the business and all the revenues associated with the business have been included in the valuation. This is especially important whenever the target is part of a larger company.

Accounting for Administrative Expenses

As an operating unit within a larger company, administrative costs such as legal, tax, audit, benefits, and treasury may be heavily subsidized or even provided without charge to the subsidiary. Alternatively, these services may be charged to the subsidiary as part of an allocation equal to a specific percentage of the subsidiary's sales or cost of sales. If these expenses are accounted for as part of an allocation methodology, they may substantially overstate the actual cost of purchasing these services from outside parties. Such allocations are often ways for the parent to account for expenses incurred at the level of the corporate headquarters but that have little to do with the actual operation of the subsidiary. Such activities may include the expense associated with maintaining the corporation's headquarters building and airplanes.

If the cost of administrative support services are provided free or are heavily subsidized by the parent, the subsidiary's reported profits should be reduced by the actual cost of providing these services. If the cost of such services is measured by using some allocation methodology, the subsidiary's reported profits may be increased by the difference between the allocated expense and the actual cost of providing the services.

Accounting for Intercompany Revenue

When the target company is an operating unit of another firm, it is common for its reported revenue to reflect sales to other operating units of the parent firm. Unless the parent firm contractually commits as part of the divestiture process to continue to buy from the divested operation, such revenue may evaporate as the parent firm satisfies its requirements from other suppliers. Moreover, intercompany revenue may be overstated, because the prices paid for the target's output reflect artificially high internal transfer prices rather than market prices. The parent firm may not be willing to continue to pay the inflated transfer prices following the divestiture.

The Importance of Stating Assumptions

The credibility of any valuation ultimately depends on the validity of its underlying assumptions. Valuation-related assumptions tend to fall into five major categories: (1) market, (2) income statement, (3) balance sheet, (4) synergy, and (5) valuation. Note that implicit assumptions about cash flow are already included in assumptions made about the income statement and changes in the balance sheet, which together drive changes in cash flow.

Market assumptions are generally those that relate to the growth rate of unit volume and product price per unit. Income statement assumptions include the projected growth in revenue, the implied market share, and the growth in the major components of cost in relation to sales. Balance sheet assumptions may include the growth in the primary components of working capital and fixed assets in relation to the projected growth in sales. Assumptions about synergy relate to the amount and timing associated with each type of anticipated synergy, including cost savings from workforce reductions, productivity improvements due to the introduction of new technologies or processes, and revenue growth as a result of increased market penetration. Finally, examples of important valuation assumptions include the acquiring firm's target debt to equity ratio used in calculating the cost of capital, the discount rate used during the forecast and stable growth periods, and the growth assumptions used in determining the terminal value.

A clear statement of all relevant assumptions forces the analyst to display their biases and to be prepared to defend their assumptions to others. The discipline imposed by this process may result in refinements to the assumptions that enhance the overall accuracy of the valuation estimate. Another advantage of making as many assumptions as possible is the potential for offsetting errors. Although some assumptions may be overly optimistic, they are likely to be offset by others that are too pessimistic. In this manner, the potential for offsetting errors may increase the chance that the estimated value of the target company will approximate its true economic value.

STEP 4: CALCULATE PRESENT VALUE OF NET SYNERGY

Synergy is generally considered to consist only of those factors or sources of value adding to the economic value of the combined firms. However, factors that destroy value should also be considered in the estimation of the economic value of the combined firms. Net synergy is the difference between estimated sources of value and destroyers of value.

Sources of Value

Look for quantifiable sources of value and destroyers of value while conducting due diligence. The most common include the potential for cost savings resulting from shared overhead, duplicate facilities, and overlapping distribution channels. Potential sources of value also include assets not recorded on the balance sheet at fair value and off-balance sheet items. Common examples include land, "obsolete" inventory and equipment, patents, licenses, and copyrights. Underutilized borrowing capacity can also make an acquisition target more attractive. The addition of the acquired company's assets, low level of indebtedness, and strong cash flow from operations could enable the buyer to increase substantially the borrowing levels of the combined companies. Other sources of value could include access to new customers; intellectual property such as patents, trade names, and rights to royalty streams; and new technologies and processes. Income tax loss carry forwards and tax credits may also represent an important source of value for an acquirer seeking to shelter significant amounts of pretax income.

Sometimes even popular expressions are viewed as potentially having value by particular firms or individuals. When America Online subscribers receive e-mail, they hear "you've got mail" and the message "you have mail" appears on their computer screen. AOL saw substantial brand recognition value in these expressions and, in 1999, filed suit against AT&T, which started using the expression on its AT&T Worldnet service, claiming that it had exclusive rights to use the expression. The court ruled in AT&T's favor, arguing that these expressions are commonly used English phrases.

Destroyers of Value

Factors that can destroy value include poor product quality, wage and benefit levels above comparable industry levels, and high employee turnover. A lack of customer contracts or poorly written contracts frequently result in customer disputes about the terms and conditions of a contract and what amounts are actually owed. Verbal agreements made by the seller's sales representatives with customers may also become obligations for the buyer. These are particularly onerous, because commissioned sales forces frequently make agreements that are not profitable for their employer. Nonexistent or poorly written contracts are commonplace among large as well as small companies.

Environmental issues, product liabilities, unresolved lawsuits, and other current or pending liabilities are also major potential destroyers of value for the buyer. These also serve as ticking time bombs, because the actual liability may not be apparent for years following the acquisition. Moreover, the magnitude of the liability may actually force a company into bankruptcy. In the 1980s, a major producer of asbestos, Johns Manville Corporation, was forced into bankruptcy because of the discovery that certain types of asbestos, used for decades for insulating buildings, could be toxic.

Net Synergy

To the extent possible, known sources and destroyers of value should be quantified in terms of their cash inflows or outflows. Careful consideration should be given to the timing of such cash flows. This information should then be used to estimate the present value of sources of and destroyers of value. The present value of net synergy is equal to the difference between the present values of the sources and destroyers of value.

Implementation Costs

In calculating net synergy, it is important to include the costs associated with recruitment and training, realizing cost savings, achieving productivity improvements, and exploiting revenue opportunities. No matter how much care is taken to minimize employee attrition following closing, some employees will be lost. Often these are the most skilled. Once a merger or acquisition is announced, target company employees start to circulate their résumés. The best employees start to receive job solicitations from competitors or executive search firms. Consequently, the costs associated with replacing employees who leave following closing can escalate sharply. Not only will the firm incur recruitment costs but also the cost of training the new hires. Moreover, the new hires are not likely to reach the productivity levels of those they are replacing for some period of time.

Cost savings are likely to be greatest when firms with similar operations are consolidated, and redundant or overlapping positions are eliminated. Many analysts take great pain to estimate savings in terms of wages, salaries, benefits, and associated overhead, such as support staff and travel expense without accurately accounting for severance expenses associated with layoffs. How a company treats its employees during layoffs will have a significant impact on the morale of those that remain. Consequently, severance packages should be constructed as fairly as possible.

Realizing productivity improvements will frequently require additional spending in new structures and equipment, retraining employees that remain with the combined companies, or redesigning workflow. Such spending may be sizable. Similarly, exploiting revenue-raising opportunities may require substantial training of the sales force of the combined firms in selling each firm's products or services and additional advertising expenditures to inform current or potential customers of what has taken place.

STEP 5: DEFINE THE MINIMUM AND
MAXIMUM PURCHASE PRICE RANGE

The minimum offer price may be defined as the target's stand-alone or present value (PV_T) or its current market value (MV_T) (i.e., the target's current stock price times its shares outstanding). The maximum price is the sum of the minimum price plus the present value of net synergy (PV_{NS}). Note that the maximum price may be overstated if the current market value of the target firm reflects investor expectations of an impending takeover. As such, the current market value may reflect some portion of future synergies. Consequently, simply adding the present value of net synergy to the current market value of the target firm can result in double counting some portion of future synergy.

The final negotiated price (P_F) is the sum of both the minimum purchase price and some percentage between 0 and 1 of the PV of net synergy. In theory, the final negotiated purchase price should lie somewhere between the minimum and maximum purchase price for the target company. These relationships can be expressed as follows:

Minimum purchase price: $PV_{MIN} = (PV_T$ or $MV_T)$

Maximum purchase price: $PV_{MAX} = PV_{MIN} + PV_{NS}$

Final or negotiated purchase price: $P_F = PV_{MIN} + \alpha\, PV_{NS}$, where $0 \leq \alpha \leq 1$.

Purchase price range: $(PV_T$ or $MV_T) < P_F < (PV_T$ or $MV_T) + PV_{NS}$

Exhibit 8-1 illustrates the calculation of the purchase price range. It is logical that the purchase price should fall between the minimum and maximum prices for two reasons. First, it is unlikely that the target company can be purchased at the minimum price, as the acquiring company normally will have to pay a premium to the current market value to induce target shareholders to sell their stock. Second, at the maximum end of the range, the acquiring company would be ceding all of the net synergy value created by the combination of the two companies to the target company's shareholders. Moreover, it is prudent to pay significantly less than the maximum price, as the amount of synergy actually realized tends to be less than the amount anticipated.

In practice, the final or negotiated purchase price depends on the bargaining strength of the target firm relative to the acquiring firm. The acquirer's offer will generally be at the lowest point in the range between the minimum and maximum prices consistent with the acquirer's perception of what constitutes an acceptable price to the target firm. If the target's financial performance is remarkable, the target firm will command a high premium and the final purchase price will be close to the maximum price. Moreover, the acquirer may make a bid close to the maximum price to preempt other potential acquirers from having sufficient time to submit competing offers. However, hubris on the part of the acquirer's management or an auction environment may push the final negotiated purchase price to or even above the maximum economic value of the firm.

EXHIBIT 8-1. ESTIMATING THE PURCHASE PRICE RANGE

Acquiring Company is considering buying Target Company. Target Company is a small biotechnology firm that develops products that are licensed to major pharmaceutical firms. Development costs are expected to generate negative cash flows during the first 2 years of the forecast period of $(10) and $(5) million, respectively. Licensing fees are expected to generate positive cash flows during years 3–5 of the forecast period of $5, $10, and $15 million, respectively. Due to the emergence of competitive products, cash flow is expected to grow at a modest 5% annually after the fifth year. The discount rate for the first 5 years is estimated to be 20% and then to drop to 10% beyond the fifth year. Also, the PV of the estimated synergy by combining Acquiring and Target companies is $30 million. Calculate the minimum and maximum purchase prices for Target Company.

Solution:

Year	Cash flow ($)	Discount rate (%)	Present value ($)
1	(10)	$1.20^1 = 1.2000$	(8.33)
2	(5)	$1.20^2 = 1.4400$	(3.47)
3	5	$1.20^3 = 1.7280$	2.89
4	10	$1.20^4 = 2.0736$	4.82
5	15	$1.20^5 = 2.4883$	6.03
			Sum = 1.94

$$\text{Terminal Value} = \frac{(\$15 \times 1.05)/(.10 - .05)}{2.4883}$$

$$= \frac{\$15.75/.05}{2.4883} = \frac{\$315}{2.4883} = \$126.59$$

Minimum Price: PV = $1.94 + $126.59 = $128.53

Maximum Price: $128.53 + $30.00 = $158.53

Relating Economic Value to Other Definitions of Purchase Price

In this chapter, purchase price is defined as the economic value of the target firm defined as a stand-alone business. In Chapter 5 (this volume), purchase price was defined in a different context as total consideration, total purchase price or enterprise value, and net purchase price. These definitions were provided with the implicit assumption that the acquiring company had determined the economic value of the firm on a stand-alone basis and the value of net synergy. Economic value is determined before any consideration is given to how the transaction will be financed. As explained in Chapter 5, each of these alternative definitions has a different application.

Total consideration is the remuneration paid to target shareholders consisting of cash, stock, debt, or some combination of all three. It reflects how the purchase price will be financed. Therefore, it is set subsequent to the determination of the economic value of the target firm. This is the definition of greatest interest to target shareholders. The total purchase price or enterprise value includes the total consideration plus the market value of any debt on the books of the target assumed by the acquiring firm. For publicly traded companies, this is the price most visible to the public and is, therefore, most commonly quoted by the news media. Net purchase price includes the total consideration plus other assumed liabilities not adequately accounted for in the determination of the stand-alone value of the target firm less the proceeds from the sale of nonstrategic target assets. Net purchase price represents the PV of actual cash paid for the target company. Exhibit 8-2 illustrates the linkages between the various definitions of purchase price discussed in this book.

EXHIBIT 8-2. DEFINING THE PURCHASE PRICE

Minimum economic value (PV_{MIN}):[1] $PV_{MIN} = (PV_T \text{ or } MV_T)$, whichever is greater,

where PV_T = Present value of the target as a stand-alone business

           MV_T = Market value of the target's equity

Maximum economic value (PV_{MAX}): $PV_{MAX} = PV_{MIN} + PV_{NS}$,

where PV_{NS} = Present value of net synergy (i.e., the difference between sources and destroyers of value)

Final or negotiated purchase price (P_F): $P_F = PV_{MIN} + \alpha\, PV_{NS}$, where $0 \leq \alpha \leq 1$.

Purchase price range: $(PV_T \text{ or } MV_T) < P_F < (PV_T \text{ or } MV_T) + PV_{NS}$

Total consideration (PV_{TC}): $PV_{TC} = C + PV_S + PV_{ND} = P_F$,

where   C   = Cash paid to target shareholders

         PV_S = Present value of stock paid to target shareholders

         PV_{ND} = New debt issued to target shareholders as part of the purchase price

Total purchase price or enterprise value (PV_{TPP}): $PV_{TPP} = PV_{TC} + PV_{AD}$,

where PV_{AD} = Debt currently on the target's books assumed by the acquirer

Net purchase price (PV_{NPP}): $PV_{NPP} = PV_{TPP} + PV_{OAL} - PV_{DA}$

$$= C + PV_S + PV_{ND} + PV_{AD}$$
$$+ PV_{OAL} - PV_{DA},$$

where　　PV_{OAL} = Other target liabilities assumed by the acquirer

　　　　　PV_{DA} = Present value of the proceeds from the sale of discretionary assets

[1] PV_T is the present value of the firm's common equity. If FCFF (i.e., both common equity and debt holders) is used to determine stand-alone value, PV_T can be estimated by subtracting the market value of the target's debt from the PV estimated using FCFF. For example, $PV_{FCFF} = PV_{FCFE} + PV_{AD}$ or $PV_{FCFE} = PV_{FCFF} - PV_{AD}$.

An Alternative Estimation of the Minimum and Maximum Purchase Price Range

The purchase price range may also be calculated as the difference between the PV of the target as a stand-alone business (or its market value) and the PV of the target as a stand-alone business including the effects of synergy. Previously, the PV of net synergy was estimated independently and added to the stand-alone value of the target business to calculate the maximum purchase price. An alternative methodology is to calculate the maximum purchase price as the present value of the target including the anticipated impact of synergy. Using this approach, the dollar value of sources and destroyers of value are estimated annually for each year during the forecast period. The cost of sales for the target firm is adjusted for cost savings resulting from such factors as the elimination of redundant jobs, bulk purchases of raw materials, and closure of overlapping sales offices and territories. The adjusted cost of sales is then used to calculate free cash flow, including the effects of anticipated synergy (see Table 8-2).

STEP 6: SELECT THE OPTIMAL FINANCING OR CAPITAL STRUCTURE

In most transactions, the agreement of purchase and sale includes a closing condition related to the ability of the buyer to finance the negotiated purchase price. If the buyer cannot obtain adequate financing within the period of time stipulated in the contract, the deal would not be consummated. Such a closing condition might be omitted from the merger agreement if the buyer's known financial resources are so large relative to the proposed purchase price that their ability to finance the purchase price is not in question.

As previously noted, the purchase price paid to the target company could consist of the acquirer's stock, debt, cash, or some combination of all three. The actual composition of the purchase price depends on what is acceptable to the target

TABLE 8-2. Adjusting Target Company Projections for the Estimated Value of Synergy

	Forecast period ($ Millions)				
	Year 1	Year 2	Year 3	Year 4	Year 5
Net sales[a]	200	220	242	266	293
Cost of sales[b]	160	176	194	213	234
Anticipated cost savings					
Labor					
Direct	2	4	6	8	8
Indirect	1	2	4	4	4
Purchased materials	2	3	5	5	5
Selling expenses	1	3	5	5	5
Total	6	12	20	23	23
Cost of sales (including synergy)	154	164	174	190	211
Cost of sales / net sales	77.0%	74.6%	71.9%	71.4%	72.0%

[a] Net sales are projected to grow at an annual rate of 10% during the forecast period.
[b] Cost of sales before synergy is assumed to comprise 80% of net revenue during the forecast period.

company and what the financial structure of the combined companies can support. Consequently, the acquirer needs to determine the optimal capital structure of the combined companies, including debt, common equity, and preferred equity. An optimal capital structure is defined as that capital structure enabling the following criteria to be satisfied:

1. The acquirer is able to achieve its financial return objectives for the combined companies.
2. The target firm's shareholders receive what they believe is an appropriate purchase price.
3. Financial constraints, such as loan covenants or debt service ratios that are standard for the industry in which the combined companies compete, are not violated.

For publicly traded companies, financial return objectives are often couched in terms readily understood by investors, such as earnings per share. Acquiring companies must be able to convince investors that any EPS dilution is temporary and that the long-term EPS growth of the combined companies will exceed what the acquirer could have achieved without the acquisition. Financial returns for both public and private companies may also be described as the firm's estimated cost of capital or in terms of the return on total capital, assets, or equity. Moreover, the combined companies' cash flow must be sufficient to meet any incremental interest and principal repayments resulting from borrowing undertaken to finance all or some portion of the purchase price without violating existing loan covenants or deviating from debt service ratios typical for the industry. If loan covenants are violated, lenders may require the combined companies to take immediate remedial action or be declared in technical default and forced to repay promptly the outstanding loans. Moreover, if the combined firms' interest coverage or debt to equity ratios deviate significantly from what is considered appropriate for similar firms in the same industry, borrowing costs may escalate sharply.

To determine the optimal capital structure, the target and acquiring firms' financial statements are consolidated. The consolidated statements are then adjusted to reflect the net effects of synergy and run through a series of scenarios until a financial structure satisfying the above criteria is identified. For example, each scenario could represent different amounts of leverage as measured by the debt-to-equity ratio. For a public company, the optimal capital structure would be that scenario whose debt-to-equity ratio results in the highest net PV for cash flows generated by the combined businesses, the least near-term EPS dilution, no violation of loan covenants, and no significant increase in borrowing costs. Excluding EPS considerations, private companies could determine the optimal capital structure in the same manner.

ESTIMATING POSTMERGER SHARE PRICE

The stock market is often viewed as an efficient mechanism for determining whether an acquiring company has overpaid for an acquisition. Frequently, the price of both the acquirer's and the target's stock will adjust immediately following the announcement of a pending acquisition. The target's current stock will increase by somewhat less than the announced purchase price as arbitrageurs buy the target's stock in anticipation of a completed transaction. The difference between what they pay and the announced purchase price is their potential profit. The current stock price of the acquiring company may decline, reflecting a potential dilution of its EPS or a growth in EPS of the combined companies that is somewhat slower than the growth rate investors had anticipated for the acquiring company without the acquisition. For these reasons, immediately following the acquisition announcement, investors may place a somewhat lower price-to-earnings (P/E) ratio on the acquiring company's EPS and later on the combined companies' EPS than had prevailed for the acquiring company prior to the announcement of the acquisition.

SHARE-EXCHANGE RATIOS

For public companies, the exchange of the acquirer's shares for the target's shares requires the calculation of the appropriate exchange ratio. The share-exchange ratio (SER) indicates the number of shares of the acquirer's stock to be exchanged for each share of the target's stock. SER is equal to the ratio of the target's stock price (P_T), including any premium, to the acquirer's stock price (P_A). The SER is calculated by the following equation:

$$SER = P_T / P_A$$

The SER can be less than, equal to, or greater than one, depending upon the value of the target's shares relative to the acquirer's shares on the date set during the negotiation for valuing the transaction. Exhibit 8-3 illustrates how the SER is calculated.

EXHIBIT 8-3. CALCULATING SERs

The price offered and accepted by the target company is $40 per share, and the acquiring company's share price is $60. What is the SER?

$$SER = \$40 / \$60 = .6667$$

Implication: To complete the merger, the acquiring company will give .6667 shares of its own stock for each share of the target company.

POSTMERGER EARNINGS PER SHARE

The critical "go, no go" decision variable for senior management of many publicly traded acquiring companies is the impact of the acquisition on EPS following the acquisition. This measure is perhaps the simplest summary measure available of the economic impact of an acquisition or merger on the acquiring company. As such, it is among the most widely followed indicators by market analysts and investors. Earnings dilution, even though temporary, can cause a dramatic loss of market value for the acquiring company.

As illustrated in Exhibit 8-4, the calculation of postmerger EPS reflects the EPS of the combined companies, the price of the acquirer's stock, the price of the target's stock, and the number of shares of acquirer and target stock outstanding (Moyer, McGuigan, and Kertlow: 1998).

$$\text{Postmerger EPS} = \frac{E_{T\&A}}{N_A + N_T \times (P_T/P_A)}$$

E_{T+A} = the sum of the current earnings of the target and acquiring companies plus any increase in earnings due to synergy

N_A = the acquiring company's outstanding shares

P_T = price offered for the target company

N_T = number of target company's outstanding shares

P_A = current price of the acquiring company's stock

EXHIBIT 8-4. CALCULATING POSTMERGER EPS

The acquiring company's share price is $40 and the price offered to the target, including an appropriate premium, is $20. The combined earnings of the two companies including estimated synergies are $1,000,000. If the acquiring company has 200,000 shares outstanding and the target company has 100,000 shares outstanding, what is the postmerger EPS for the combined companies?

$$\text{Postmerger EPS} = \frac{\$1,000,000}{200,000 + 100.000 \times (\$20/\$40)}$$

$$= \frac{\$1,000,000}{250,000}$$

$$= \$4.00$$

POSTMERGER SHARE PRICE

The share price of the acquiring company following an acquisition reflects both anticipated EPS and the P/E ratio investors are willing to pay for the anticipated per-share earnings. Exhibit 8-5 provides an example of how this process works for a share-for-share exchange and for an all-cash purchase.

EXHIBIT 8-5. CALCULATING THE POSTMERGER SHARE PRICE

Share-for-Share Exchange

Acquiring Company is considering the acquisition of Target Company in a stock-for-stock transaction in which Target Company would receive $84.30 for each share of its common stock. The acquiring company does not expect any change in its price/earnings multiple after the merger and chooses to value the target company conservatively by assuming no earnings growth due to synergy. We have the following data on the companies:

	Acquiring Company	Target Company
Earnings available for common stock	$281,500	$62,500
Number of shares of common outstanding	112,000	18,750
Market price per share	$56.25	$62.50

1. Purchase price premium = Offer price for Target Company stock/
   Target Company market price per share

$$= \$84.30 / \$62.50$$
$$= 1.35 \text{ or } 35\% \text{ (i.e., } 1.35 - 1.00)$$

2. Exchange ratio = Price per share offered for Target Company/Market price per share for the acquiring company

$$= \$84.30 / \$56.25$$
$$= 1.5 \text{ (i.e., Acquiring Company issues 1.5 shares of stock}$$
$$\text{for each share of Target Company's stock)}$$

3. New shares issued by Acquiring Company = 18,750 (shares of Target Company) × 1.5 (Exchange ratio) = 28,125
4. Total shares outstanding of the combined companies = 112,000 + 28,125 = 140,125
5. Postmerger EPS of the combined companies = ($281,500 + $62,500)/140,125

$$= \$344,000 / 140,125$$
$$= \$2.46$$

6. Premerger EPS of acquiring company = $281,500/112,000 = $2.51
7. Premerger P/E = Premerger price per share/premerger earnings per share =

$$= \$56.25 / \$2.51$$
$$= 22.4$$

8. Postmerger share price = Postmerger EPS × Premerger P/E

$$= \$2.46 \times 22.4$$
$$= \$55.10 \text{ (as compared to } \$56.25 \text{ premerger)}$$

9. Postmerger equity ownership distribution:

Target Company = 28,125/140,125 =   20.1%
Acquiring Company = 100 − 20.1 =   79.9
                                 100.0%

Implications: The acquisition results in an $1.15 reduction in the share price of the acquiring company due to a $.05 decline in the EPS of the combined companies. (Recall that Acquiring Company assumed no gains in earnings of the combined companies due to synergy.) Whether the acquisition is a poor decision depends upon what happens to the earnings of the combined companies over time. If the combined companies' earnings grow more rapidly than the acquiring company's earnings would have in the absence of the acquisition, the acquisition may contribute to the market value of the acquiring company.

All-Cash Purchase

Instead of a share-for-share exchange, Target Company agrees to an all-cash purchase of 100% of its outstanding stock for $84.30 for each of its 18,750 shares of common stock outstanding. When the transaction is closed, the 18,750 shares of Target Company's stock are retired. Acquiring Company believes that investors will apply its premerger P/E to determine the postmerger share price. Moreover, the acquiring company finances the purchase price by using cash balances on hand in excess of its normal cash requirements.

1. Postmerger EPS of the combined companies = ($281,500+$62,500)/ 112,000 = $3.07
2. Postmerger share price = Postmerger EPS × Premerger P/E

$$= \$3.07 \times 22.4$$

$$= \$68.77 \text{ (as compared to \$56.25 premerger)}$$

Implications: The all-cash acquisition results in a $12.52 increase in the share price of the combined companies. This is a result of a $.56 improvement in the EPS of the combined companies as compared to the $2.51 premerger EPS of Acquiring Company. In practice, the improvement in EPS would not have been as dramatic, if the earnings of the combined companies had been reduced by accrued interest on the excess cash balances of the acquirer or by interest expense if the acquirer had chosen to finance the transaction using debt.

MAINTAINING SHAREHOLDER VALUE IN A STOCK-FOR-STOCK EXCHANGE

A *fixed SER* is one in which the number of acquirer's shares exchanged for each target share does not change between the agreement date, when the SER is agreed upon, and the actual closing date. However, the value of the shares of the acquiring and target companies may in fact change between the agreement and closing dates. This problem may be remedied if the SER is allowed to float until a specific point in time, which may be at closing or a day just prior to closing. Such an arrangement is called a *floating SER*. The actual exchange ratio at that time is then used to calculate the number of acquirer's shares that will be exchanged for each target share outstanding. The risk of a completely floating SER is that the actual purchase price for the target company cannot be determined at the time shareholders are asked to approve a proposed merger. Consequently, transactions involving fully floating SERs may be unattractive to shareholders, particularly if the time between the agreement date and closing is lengthy due to the requirement for regulatory approvals.

Share-exchange transactions can be made more attractive to shareholders by limiting the extent of the fluctuation in the actual SER before the agreed upon ratio is adjusted. One commonly used method of preserving value is to employ a *collar agreement.* A typical agreement states that, if the actual SER calculated from the share prices of the two stocks on the closing date goes above or below a specific value, there will be an adjustment of the previously agreed upon SER. The agreement protects the acquiring firm from "overpaying" in the event that its share price is higher or the target firm's share price is lower on the closing date than it was on the day the actual agreement on the SER was finalized. Similarly, the target shareholders are protected from receiving less than the originally agreed upon purchase price if the acquirer's stock declines in value by the closing date. In essence, a collar agreement involves the preservation of a fixed price for the target stock (see Exhibit 8-6).

EXHIBIT 8-6. ALTERNATIVE SHARE EXCHANGE RATIO STRATEGIES

	At point of agreement		At closing		
	Number of acquirer's shares exchanged for each target share (target's shares/ acquirer's shares)	Offer price/ acquirer's share price	Number of acquirer's shares exchanged for each target share	Offer price/ acquirer's actual share price	Actual value received by target shareholders
Fixed[a]	1 / 1 = 1	$50 / $50	1 / 1	Varies	Varies
Floating[b]	1 / 1 = 1	$50 / $50	1 / 1.250	$50 / $40	$50 (1.250 × $40)
Fixed with collar[c]	1 / 1 = 1	$50 / $50	1 / 1.250 or 1 / .833	$50 / $40 or $50 / $60	$50 (1.250 × $40 or .833 × $60)

[a] The target agrees to exchange one share of its stock for each share of the acquirer's stock. The acquirer's stock on the day of the agreement is valued at $50 per share. The implied offer price for each target share is $50.

[b] The target agrees to exchange each share of its stock for $50 worth of the acquirer's stock. By the closing date, the market value of the acquirer's stock has dropped to $40 per share. The acquirer changes the share exchange ratio by whatever amount is necessary to ensure that the target firm's shareholders receive the equivalent of $50 per share of its stock at closing.

[c] The target agrees to exchange each share of its stock for the equivalent of $50 worth of the acquirer's stock. The acquirer agrees to adjust the share exchange ratio by as much as plus or minus 20 percent, if its share price changes between the agreement and closing dates.

Failure to preserve the value of the originally agreed upon SER can cause a deal to unravel if the values of the shares of the companies involved change significantly before closing. Case Study 8-1 illustrates the implications of such a situation.

CASE STUDY 8-1. QWEST COMMUNICATIONS STUMBLES IN ITS EFFORTS TO BUY U.S. WEST AND FRONTIER CORPORATION

Largely on the strength of a high-flying stock price, Qwest Communications International Inc. was able to complete a number of acquisitions that helped to make Qwest the country's fourth largest long-distance carrier. But in a hostile bid for both U.S. West and Frontier Corp. in June 1999, Qwest's management made a tactical mistake. In attempting to outbid rival Global Crossing Ltd., Qwest offered a fixed number of its shares for the two companies. This meant that the value of its bid would rise and fall with Qwest's stock price.

On the first day of trading after the offer for the two companies was made public, Qwest's stock dropped 24%. At the lower level, Qwest's offer for U.S. West was about the same as that offered by Global Crossing and was actually less for Frontier. Qwest could have prevented this embarrassment by having offered U.S. West and Frontier shareholders a fixed dollar price, with the understanding that the SER would be changed to preserve the fixed price in the event that Qwest's stock fluctuated widely.

The situation appeared to have been resolved by late August when Qwest agreed to increase the number of its shares exchanged for each share of U.S. West to complete this $45.2 billion acquisition and withdrew its offer for Frontier. Frontier was to merge with Global Crossing. However, on March 1, 2000, Qwest's shares jumped 27% on speculation of a possible takeover bid from Deutsche Telekom. U.S. West has threatened to sue Qwest if it tried to back out of its agreement to acquire U.S. West without paying an $800 million breakup fee.

Source: *Top Financial News:* 2000.

BUSINESS CASE: FORD ACQUIRES VOLVO

The purpose of this business case is to illustrate how Ford may have looked at Volvo in the context of the approach to financial modeling outlined in this chapter. The case illustrates how the dynamically changing worldwide automotive market is spurring a move toward consolidation among automotive manufacturers. Table 8-3 uses both historical and projected data for Volvo to illustrate the first three steps of the financial modeling procedure outlined earlier in this chapter. Tables 8-4 through 8-6 illustrate the final three steps of the process, including accounting for the impact of synergy, defining the purchase price range, determining the appropriate financial structure, and specifying key assumptions underlying the valuation process.

The Volvo financials used in the valuation are for illustration only, as they include revenue and costs for all of the firm's product lines. For purposes of exposition, we shall assume that Ford's acquisition strategy with respect to Volvo was to acquire all of Volvo's operations and later divest all but the passenger car and possibly the truck operations.

BACKGROUND

By the late 1990s, excess global automotive production capacity totaled 20 million vehicles, and three-fourths of the auto manufacturers worldwide were losing money. Consumers continued to demand more technological innovations, while expecting to pay lower prices. Continuing mandates from regulators for new, cleaner engines and more safety measures added to manufacturing costs. With the cost of designing a new car estimated at $1.5 billion to $3 billion, companies were finding mergers and joint ventures an attractive means to distribute risk and maintain market share in this highly competitive environment (Welch and Howes: 1999).

FORD'S MERGER STRATEGY

By acquiring Volvo, Ford hoped to expand its 10% worldwide market share with a broader line of near-luxury Volvo sedans and station wagons as well as to strengthen its presence in Europe. Ford saw Volvo as a means of improving its product weaknesses, expanding distribution channels, entering new markets, reducing development and vehicle production costs, and capturing premiums from niche markets. Volvo Cars is now part of Ford's Premier Automotive Group, which also includes Aston Martin, Jaguar, and Lincoln.

FORD MOTOR COMPANY PROFILE

The Ford Motor Company is the second largest automobile manufacturer in the world. It offers a highly diverse and extensive line of vehicles under six major brands. These include the Aston Martin, Ford, Jaguar, Lincoln, Mazda, and Mercury. Each of these brands has been defined to appeal to a specific market segment to minimize market overlap.

Ford of Europe is very strong in the small-to-medium-sized European car market. The Ford product line consists of small-to-medium-sized cars, the Ford Explorer SUV, and a minivan. Ford has had difficulty moving into the luxury car market, because it is not perceived as a luxury brand. The other Ford brands sold in Europe include Aston Martin, Jaguar, and Mazda. Aston Martin and Jaguar have the same product line worldwide. Mazda offers a competitive small car line in Europe.

Strengths

Ford's strength is its dominant position in the booming U.S. truck market. Each of Ford's truck products is a leader in its class. The popularity of Ford's trucks has also proven to be very profitable. For example, Ford makes $15,000 per Lincoln SUV sold. Currently, Ford is aggressively trying to expand its success in trucks, by launching larger SUV's with pickup beds. Other areas of strength include customer loyalty and satisfaction, global brand leverage, and relatively low total production costs. Ford's dominance of the highly profitable light truck market has provided the company with significant cash reserves at a time when many auto manufacturers are struggling to survive. A strong and diverse line of products and brands and effective distribution channels allow Ford to compete in most market segments. Ford's management has been able to create an organization that has learned how to streamline new product development, share components and platforms between models and brands, and that has reduced cost by pushing more parts manufacturing to outside suppliers (Ford Motor Company, 1999).

Weaknesses

Although Ford has been riding high on the success of its truck business, its domestic passenger car line has experienced product and positioning difficulties, which have led to disappointing sales. For example, the Ford Taurus was the best-selling car in the U.S. in 1997 and 1998. However, Ford lost its top spot when it introduced a more futuristic design that did not appeal to customers. Regaining its position as a leader in passenger car sales is one of the highest priorities for Ford executives.

VOLVO COMPANY PROFILE

Between 1987 and 1998, Volvo posted operating profits amounting to 3.7% of sales. Excluding the passenger car group, operating margins would have been 5.3%. In order to stay competitive, Volvo would have to introduce a variety of new passenger cars over the next decade. Volvo viewed the capital expenditures required to develop new cars as overwhelming for a company the size of Volvo.

Historically, Volvo has filled a small niche in the marketplace by appealing to safety-conscious family-oriented buyers who can afford a European-made automobile. Unfortunately, Volvo does not have the necessary sales volume to support the enormous cost of developing new cars. The company made it clear that they were interested in a buyer in an effort to keep the company viable over the long-run. (Volvo: 1999).

Volvo has a relatively limited product line that includes a sporty coupe, mid-sized sedans, and station wagons that compete in the luxury segment of the market. Volvo's major source of value is its brand name and close association with producing safe, reliable passenger cars. Volvos are priced from $28,000 to $44,000. Volvo's customers tend to be equally divided between men and women and range in age from 34–53 years old.

HISTORICAL AND PROJECTED DATA

The initial review of Volvo's historical data suggests that cash flow is highly volatile. However, by removing nonrecurring events, it is apparent that Volvo's cash flow is steadily trending downward from its high in 1997. Table 8-3 displays a common-sized, normalized income statement, balance sheet, and cash flow statement for Volvo including both the historical period from 1993 through 1999 and a forecast period from 2000 through 2004. Although Volvo has managed to stabilize its cost of goods sold as a percent of net sales, operating expenses as a percent of net revenue have escalated in recent years. Operating margins have been declining since 1996. To regain market share in the passenger car market, Volvo would have to increase substantially its capital outlays. The primary reason valuation cash flow turns negative by 2004 is the sharp increase in capital outlays during the forecast period.

POTENTIAL SYNERGY

Ford's acquisition of Volvo will enable volume discounts from vendors, reduced development costs due to platform sharing, access to wider distribution networks, and increased penetration in selected market niches due to the Volvo brand name. Savings from synergies are phased in slowly over time and not fully realized until 2004. There is no attempt to quantify the increased cash flow that might result from increased market penetration.

Volume Purchase Discounts from Common Vendors

Although Volvos and Fords have been designed by different organizations, the cars share many common parts. Purchasing standard parts for both companies will allow for greater volume discounts from common vendors. For example, both Ford and Volvo currently purchase fuel injection and antilock brake components from Bosch of Germany. By combining the two companies' purchases, Volvo will experience a reduction in part costs just by tapping into Ford's giant volume discounts.

Platform Sharing and Reduced Development Costs

Ford has demonstrated with its acquisition of Jaguar that it can purchase a car company and not damage the image or personality of the brand name. Ford's effort to maintain Jaguar's high level of quality and distinct design is evident in their decision to allow the vehicles to continue to be designed and manufactured in England. Ford's commitment to Jaguar is one of the strongest reasons why Volvo believes that Ford is a good acquisition fit.

As Volvo becomes more integrated with Ford, these two companies can reduce development costs by beginning to share platforms. Utilizing common parts and configurations at the platform level could have significant economic benefits without compromising consumers' perception of Volvo as a passenger car offering safety, quality, and European styling. Maintaining this perception is important for preserving the brand identities and to avoid having the various Ford product lines compete against each other. Adopting the best practices of each company in designing and commercializing new products can also reduce development costs.

Distribution

Ford estimates that the cost of distribution is anywhere from 18–25% of the sticker price. In order to address these costs and increase customer satisfaction, Ford has started a strategy called the Ford Retail Network (FRN). The strategy is basically to sell all of Ford's brands under a single roof. Reduced costs come from economies of scale at large regional dealerships, reduced commissions with salaried sales people, and lower transaction costs with no haggle pricing/internet purchasing. Promotion costs are also expected to be significantly lower as a result of FRN advertising as compared to the five individual brand dealers advertising on their own. Ford initiated the FRN strategy in late 1999, with two test FRN dealerships in place. As Ford continues to roll out the FRN concept across the country, these new dealerships can be built to accommodate the Volvo brand.

Brand Name

Volvo and Ford will jointly own the Volvo brand name. Ford will have the right to use it for passenger cars, minivans, sport utility vehicles, and light trucks. Volvo will use the brand name for commercial trucks and other products.

DETERMINING THE INITIAL OFFER PRICE

Tables 8-4 and 8-5 provide the data and the underlying assumptions used in estimating Volvo's value on a stand-alone basis at $15 billion. The present value of anticipated synergy is $1.1 billion. This suggests that the purchase price for Volvo should lie within a range of $15 to about $16 billion. Although the potential synergies appear to be substantial, savings due to synergies are phased in gradually between 2000 and 2004.

In 1998, Volvo had rejected an approximate $7 billion bid by Renault for the car and truck operations. By late 1998, there were no other immediate bidders for Volvo. The absence of other current bidders for the entire company and the apparent urgency on the part of Volvo to find a partner to help fund its future capital expenditures in the passenger car business suggest that the initial offer price can be set at the lower end of the range. Consequently, the initial offer price could be conservatively set at about $15.25 billion, reflecting only about one-fourth of the total potential synergy resulting from combining the two businesses.

Assuming the offer is made to Volvo at the end of January 1999, other valuation methodologies tend to confirm this purchase price estimate. The market value of Volvo was $11.9 billion on January 29, 1999. To gain a controlling interest, Ford had to pay a premium to the market value on January 29, 1999. Applying the 26% premium Ford paid for Jaguar, the estimated purchase price including the premium is $15 billion, or $34 per share. This compares to $34.50 per share

TABLE 8-3. Volvo Common-Size Normalized Income Statement, Balance Sheet, and Cash Flow Statement (Percent of Net Sales)[a]

	1993	1994	1995	1996	1997	1998	1999	2000	2001	2002	2003	2004
Income statement												
Net sales	1.000	1.000	1.000	1.000	1.000	1.000	1.000	1.000	1.000	1.000	1.000	1.000
Cost of goods sold	.772	.738	.749	.777	.757	.757	.757	.757	.757	.757	.757	.757
Operation expense	.167	.101	.120	.077	.119	.133	.132	.131	.129	.128	.127	.126
Depreciation	.034	.033	.033	.034	.029	.038	.038	.039	.040	.040	.041	.042
EBIT	.027	.128	.098	.112	.088	.073	.073	.074	.074	.074	.075	.075
Interest on debt	.050	.023	.022	.021	.015	.023	.023	.022	.021	.021	.020	.020
Earnings before taxes	.024	.017	.076	.091	.072	.049	.051	.052	.053	.054	.055	.056
Income taxes	.004	.018	.022	.012	.015	.014	.014	.015	.015	.015	.015	.016
Net income	.028	.087	.054	.079	.057	.035	.036	.037	.038	.039	.040	.040
Balance sheet												
Current assets	.632	.503	.444	.524	.497	.500	.500	.500	.500	.500	.500	.500
Current liabilities	.596	.400	.283	.298	.304	.350	.350	.350	.350	.350	.350	.350
Working capital	.036	.103	.161	.226	.192	.150	.150	.150	.150	.150	.150	.150
Total assets	1.210	.889	.809	.905	.889	.906	.880	.858	.839	.822	.808	.795
Long-term debt	.371	.211	.227	.236	.256	.234	.215	.196	.180	.165	.151	.307
Equity	.244	.278	.299	.371	.329	.321	.316	.312	.309	.308	.307	.307
Selected valuation cash flow items												
EBIT (1 – T)	.022	.150	.126	.126	.105	.093	.094	.094	.095	.095	.096	.096
Capital expenditures	.031	.027	.033	.053	.054	.061	.069	.078	.088	.099	.112	.126
Δ Working capital	.025	.077	.068	.049	.000	.017	.020	.020	.020	.020	.020	.020
FCFF	.047	.079	.053	.059	.088	.087	.044	.036	.027	.017	.005	(.008)

[a] EBIT, earnings before interest and taxes; EBIT, (1 - T) EBIT after taxes; FCFF, free cash flow to the firm.

TABLE 8-4. Volvo Normalized Income, Balance Sheet and Cash Flow Statement, Valuation, and Purchase Price Range Determination[a]

	1993	1994	1995	1996	1997	1998	1999	2000	2001	2002	2003	2004
Income statement ($ millions)												
Net sales	76,659	107,494	118,283	107,628	126,638	145,634	167,479	192,600	221,491	254,714	292,921	336,859
Cost of goods sold	(59,200)	(79,374)	(88,641)	(83,620)	(95,855)	(110,233)	(126,768)	(145,784)	(167,651)	(192,799)	(221,719)	(254,977)
Operation expense	(12,814)	(10,814)	(14,156)	(8,266)	(15,114)	(19,352)	(22,061)	(25,150)	(28,671)	(32,685)	(37,261)	(42,477)
Depreciation	(2,605)	(3,522)	(3,901)	(3,690)	(4,687)	(5,484)	(6,416)	(7,507)	(8,783)	(10,276)	(12,023)	(14,067)
EBIT	2,039	13,783	11,586	12,051	10,982	10,564	12,233	14,160	16,386	18,955	21,919	25,339
Interest on debt	(3,861)	(2,488)	(2,591)	(2,256)	(1,895)	(3,404)	(3,782)	(4,210)	(4,694)	(5,244)	(5,868)	(6,577)
Earning before taxes	(1,822)	11,295	8,995	9,795	9,087	7,161	8,451	9,950	11,691	13,710	16,051	18,762
Income taxes	(323)	(1,919)	(2,580)	(1,259)	(1,866)	(2,045)	(2,366)	(2,786)	(3,274)	(3,839)	(4,494)	(5,253)
Net income	(2,145)	9,376	6,415	8,537	7,221	5,116	6,085	7,164	8,418	9,872	11,557	13,509
Balance sheet ($ millions)												
Current assets	48,452	54,051	52,511	56,406	62,890	72,817	83,739	96,300	110,745	127,357	146,461	168,430
Current liabilities	45,666	43,038	33,460	32,036	38,536	50,972	58,618	67,410	77,522	89,150	102,522	117,901
Working capital	2,787	11,013	19,051	24,370	24,354	21,845	25,122	28,890	33,224	38,207	43,938	50,529
Total assets	92,770	95,574	95,654	97,351	112,617	131,900	147,439	165,300	185,835	209,446	236,599	267,827
Long-term debt	28,423	22,652	26,884	25,401	32,405	34,122	35,931	37,835	39,840	41,952	44,175	46,517
Equity	18,681	29,884	35,310	39,914	41,690	46,806	52,891	60,055	68,473	78,344	89,901	103,410
Shares	78	444	464	464	442	442	442	442	442	442	442	442
Valuation cash flow ($ millions)												
EBIT (1 – T)	1,678	16,126	14,909	13,600	13,237	13,581	15,658	18,125	20,974	24,262	28,056	32,434
Depreciation	2,605	3,522	3,901	3,690	4,687	5,484	6,416	7,507	8,783	10,276	12,023	14,067
Capital expenditures	(2,390)	(2,948)	(4,477)	(5,655)	(6,802)	(8,843)	(11,495)	(14,944)	(19,427)	(25,256)	(32,832)	(42,682)
Change in working capital	1,930	(8,226)	(8,038)	(5,319)	16	2,509	(3,277)	(3,768)	(4,334)	(4,984)	(5,731)	(6,591)
Valuation cash flow	3,824	8,474	6,296	6,316	11,137	12,731	7,302	6,919	5,995	4,298	1,516	(2,772)
NPV (WACC = 11.54%)-												
1999~2004	18,644											
Terminal value (2004~)	(3,652)											
Total NPV	14,992											
Purchase price range ($ millions)												
Lower range	14,992											
Lower range + 25% of Synergy	15,273											
Lower range + Synergy	16,117											

[a]EBIT, earnings before interest and taxes; EBIT, (1 - T) EBIT after taxes; NPV, net present value; WACC, weighted average cost of capital.

TABLE 8-5. Assumptions for Tables 8-3 and 8-4

1. Net sales, cost of goods and services, and depreciation grow 15% annually, in line with historical average annual growth rate for these line items

2. Average interest rate on debt 4% (according to the historical average interest rate of debt)

3. Swedish corporate income tax rate is 28%

4. Current assets would be roughly 50% of net sales, after removal of the excess cash flow. (According to the average ratio of current asset to net sales in the past)

5. Current liabilities would be roughly 35% of net sales. (According to the average ratio of current liabilities to net sales in the past)

6. Long-term debt growth rate is 5.3%. (According to the average growth of the past trend in the growth of long term debt)

7. Capital expenditure growth rate is 30%. (According to the average growth of the past trend in capital spending)

8. Cost of equity is 8.19% (k_e = 0.05 + 0.58 * 0.055)
   Treasury note rate = 5%. Beta = 0.58. Risk Premium = 5.5% (Beta obtained from Yahoo's Market Guide)

9. Cost of debt during forecast period is 6% (Average of short term and long term debt)

10. The exchange rate used to convert to dollars is 1 SEK/$1.45 for the calculations.

11. For NPV calculation, Ford's WACC is estimated to be 11.54%.

12. The growth rate for cash flow used in calculating the terminal value is −20%.

13. Note that the Volvo financials are presented for illustration only and include all revenue from Volvo's nonpassenger car product lines.

---

estimated by dividing the initial offer price of $15.25 billion by Volvo's total common shares outstanding of $442 million. Thus, the initial offer price can be reasonably set at between $34.00 and $34.50 per share.

DETERMINING THE OPTIMAL FINANCING STRUCTURE

Ford had $23 billion in cash and marketable securities on hand at the end of 1998 (Naughton: 1999). This amount of cash is well in excess of its normal cash operating requirements. The opportunity cost associated with this excess cash is equal to Ford's cost of capital, which is estimated to be 11.5%, about three times the prevailing interest on short-term marketable securities at that time. By reinvesting some portion of these excess balances to acquire Volvo, Ford would be adding to shareholder value because the expected return, including the effects of synergy, exceeds the cost of capital. Moreover, by using this excess cash, Ford is also making itself less attractive as a potential acquisition target. Excess cash balances were often used in the 1980s by corporate raiders to help finance a takeover.

The acquisition is expected to increase Ford's EPS. The loss of interest earnings on the excess cash balances would be more than offset by the addition of Volvo's pretax earnings. Furthermore, severance expenses and one-time write-offs at closing are expected to be modest.

TABLE 8-6. Ford and Volvo with Synergy: All Cash Purchase ($ Millions)[a]

	1993	1994	1995	1996	1997	1998	1999	2000	2001	2002	2003	2004
Income statement ($ millions)												
Net sales	185,180	235,933	255,420	254,619	280,265	313,404	350,695	392,685	439,996	493,336	553,512	621,442
Cost of goods sold	(150,962)	(182,284)	(199,236)	(202,206)	(214,474)	(239,773)	(268,234)	(300,274)	(336,364)	(377,045)	(422,927)	(474,710)
Operation expense	(17,295)	(17,497)	(21,652)	(16,392)	(24,812)	(28,956)	(32,971)	(37,544)	(42,750)	(48,679)	(55,430)	(63,118)
Depreciation	(10,073)	(12,858)	(15,620)	(16,481)	(18,270)	(21,304)	(24,841)	(28,967)	(33,777)	(39,387)	(45,928)	(53,556)
Synergy							—	3	10	19	34	47
EBIT	6,849	23,293	18,913	19,539	22,709	23,372	24,648	25,904	27,114	28,245	29,261	30,107
Interest on debt	(4,668)	(3,209)	(3,213)	(2,951)	(2,683)	(4,264)	(4,722)	(5,236)	(5,815)	(6,468)	(7,205)	(8,037)
Earning before taxes	2,181	20,084	15,700	16,588	20,026	19,107	19,926	20,668	21,299	21,777	22,056	22,070
Income taxes	(1,673)	(5,248)	(4,959)	(3,425)	(5,607)	(6,226)	(6,974)	(7,234)	(7,455)	(7,622)	(7,720)	(7,724)
Net income	384	14,684	10,554	12,983	14,141	12,881	12,952	13,434	13,844	14,155	14,336	14,345
Balance sheet ($ millions)												
Current assets	172,090	181,164	193,447	212,998	230,261	251,069	278,403	308,885	342,902	380,888	423,333	470,792
Current liabilities	126,259	136,479	140,770	149,465	163,239	180,601	200,181	222,007	246,351	273,523	303,870	337,785
Working capital	45,832	44,685	52,677	63,533	67,022	70,469	78,222	86,879	96,551	107,365	119,463	133,007
Total assets	291,708	315,196	338,937	360,218	391,714	435,694	478,115	525,236	577,620	635,900	700,788	773,091
Long-term debt	83,407	87,859	100,618	102,537	112,650	122,455	133,166	144,870	157,663	171,649	186,944	203,674
Equity	34,255	51,542	59,857	66,676	72,424	85,305	99,871	116,296	134,828	155,746	179,366	206,049
Valuation cash flow ($ millions)												
EBIT	6,849	23,293	18,913	19,539	22,709	23,372	24,648	25,904	27,114	28,245	29,261	30,107
EBIT (1 − T)	4,452	15,141	12,294	12,700	14,761	15,191	16,021	16,838	17,624	18,359	19,020	19,569
Depreciation	10,073	12,858	15,620	16,481	18,270	21,304	24,841	28,967	33,777	39,387	45,928	53,556
Capital expenditures	(9,204)	(11,494)	(13,474)	(14,306)	(15,519)	(18,161)	(21,457)	(25,593)	(30,811)	(37,425)	(45,841)	(56,588)
Change in working capital	1,276	1,147	(7,992)	(10,856)	(3,489)	(3,447)	(7,753)	(8,657)	(9,672)	(10,814)	(12,098)	(13,544)
Valuation cash flow	13,447	40,945	25,361	23,559	36,732	38,259	36,301	37,458	38,032	37,752	36,269	33,099
Synergy calculation ($ millions)												
NPV (1999~2004)	66											
Terminal Value (2004~)	1,058											
Total NPV	1,125											

[a] The combined tax rate used is the U.S. tax rate of 35%; Synergy—the first year is 0, second year 0.001% of COGS, 3rd year 0.003%, 4th yr. 0.005%, 5th yr. 0.008%, 6th yr. 0.01%; Terminal value calculated using a growth rate of 9.4% (the average growth rate from 1993~1997 of COGS).

EPILOGUE

Seven months after the megamerger between Chrysler and Daimler-Benz in 1998, Ford Motor Company announced that it was acquiring only Volvo's passenger-car operations. Ford acquired Volvo's passenger car operations on March 29, 1999, for $6.45 billion. At $16,000 per production unit, Ford's offer price is considered generous when compared to the $13,400 per vehicle that Daimler-Benz AG paid for Chrysler Corporation in 1998. The sale of the passenger car business allows Volvo to concentrate fully on its truck, bus, construction equipment, marine engine, and aerospace equipment businesses.

THINGS TO REMEMBER

Financial modeling in the context of M&As facilitates the process of valuation, deal structuring, and selection of the optimal financing plan. The process entails six steps:

1. Understand industry and company competitive dynamics. This requires normalizing the components of historical valuation cash flow. Aberrations in the data should be omitted. Common-size financial statements applied at a point in time, over a number of periods, and compared with other companies in the same industry provide useful insights into how to properly value the target firm. This normalized information can be used to understand both industry and company competitive dynamics.
2. Project valuation cash flow. This can be accomplished by linking all key financial variables to a common variable such as net sales. Although simplistic, this modeling approach ensures consistency of growth rates among the variables that must be projected to obtain an estimate of cash flow and facilitates scenario planning based on alternative revenue growth rates.
3. Estimate the economic value of the acquisition target. The target should be valued as a stand-alone business, properly accounting for all costs and revenues associated with the business. All key assumptions should be clearly stated to provide credibility for the valuation and to inject a high degree of discipline into the valuation process.
4. Calculate the PV of net synergy. Estimate PV of net synergy (PV_{NS}) by deducting the PV of destroyers of value from the PV of sources of value. Ensure that all costs that are likely to be incurred in realizing synergy are included in the calculation of net synergy.
5. Define the minimum and maximum purchase price range.

$$(PV_T \text{ or } MV_T) < P_F < (PV_T \text{ or } MV_T) + PV_{NS}$$

Where PV_T and MV_T are the economic value of the target as a stand-alone company and the market value of the target, respectively. P_F is the final negotiated purchase price.

6. Determine the optimal financing or capital structure. The optimal capital structure of the combined businesses is that which enables the acquirer to meet or exceed its required financial returns, satisfies the seller's price expectations, and does not violate any significant financial constraints such as loan covenants and prevailing industry average debt service ratios. The optimal capital structure for the combined companies can be determined by iterating the consolidated financial statements through various scenarios reflecting different debt to equity ratios. The optimal capital structure would be that scenario whose debt to equity ratio provides the highest net present value and the least immediate EPS dilution, without violating any loan covenants or increasing borrowing costs.

CHAPTER DISCUSSION QUESTIONS

8-1. Why are financial modeling techniques used in analyzing M&As.

8-2. Give examples of the limitations of financial data used in the valuation process.

8-3. Why is it important to analyze historical data on the target company as part of the valuation process?

8-4. Explain the process of normalizing historical data and why it should be done before undertaking the valuation process.

8-5. What are common-size financial statements and how might they be used to analyze a target firm?

8-6. Why should a target company be valued as a stand-alone business? Give examples of the types of adjustments that might have to be made if the target company is part of a larger company?

8-7. Define the minimum and maximum purchase price range for a target company.

8-8. What are the differences between the final negotiated price, total consideration, total purchase price, and net purchase price?

8-9. Can the final negotiated purchase price ever exceed the maximum purchase price? If yes, why? If no, why not?

8-10. Why is it important to clearly state assumptions underlying a valuation?

CHAPTER BUSINESS CASE

CASE STUDY 8-2. MAINTAINING SHAREHOLDER VALUE IN A STOCK-FOR-STOCK EXCHANGE

Company A offers to acquire 100% of Company B's stock for $50 a share (a $10 premium to the current price). Company A's stock is currently selling for $100 per share. Company B has one million shares of common stock outstanding.

1. What is the SER of Company B's stock in terms of Company A's stock?
2. What is the dollar value of A's shares exchanged for 100 shares of B's stock?

Suppose Company A's share price falls to $75 before the transaction is consummated. B's shareholders are protected if Company B has negotiated a floating exchange ratio of Company B's stock in terms of Company A's stock.

3. What is the new SER?
4. What is the dollar value of A's shares received by a holder of 100 shares of B's stock?

Solutions to these questions are found in the Appendix at the back of this book.

REFERENCES

Committee of Sponsoring Organizations of the Treadway Commission, 1998. Cited in Loomis, C. J., "Lies, Damned Lies, and Managed Earnings," *Fortune, 140*(3), 1999, p. 75.

Ford Motor Company, "Ford Completes Acquisition of Volvo Cars," [Press Release], March 31, 1999.

Loomis, Carol J., "Lies, Damned Lies, and Managed Earnings," *Fortune, 140*(3), 1999, pp. 74–79.

Moyer, Charles R., James R. McGuigan, and William J. Kretlow, *Contemporary Financial Management,* Cincinnati: South Western College Publishing, 1998, pp. 810–811.

Naughton, Keith, "The Global Six," *Business Week,* January 25, 1999, pp. 68–72.

Top Financial News, "U.S. West Threatens to Sue if Quest Fails to Follow through on Acquisition," March 3, 2000.

Volvo, "Volvo Enters into Agreement with Ford to Sell Volvo Cars and Concentrate on Commercial Products," [Press Release], January 23, 1999.

Welch, David, and Daniel Howes, "Ford Buyout will Save Volvo, Shareholders Told," *Detroit News,* February 24, 1999.

9

ANALYSIS AND VALUATION

OF PRIVATELY HELD

COMPANIES

*Maier's Law: If the facts do not conform to the theory,
they must be disposed of.*

Things just didn't seem to add up. Alan had led due diligence teams for his firm before. He was well aware that the reliability of the financial data provided by the 30-year-old family-owned microfiche company, Imaging Services, was not completely consistent with generally accepted accounting standards and that some of the firm's practices would have to change if the company were acquired. While impressed with some of the family members on the payroll, he wasn't yet convinced that they were all contributing as much as they could to the overall operation of the firm. The "handshake agreements" the owners had with several large customers reflected the informal practices of many small companies. The absence of detailed travel expense accounts was also troubling.

Despite these observations, a restatement of the firm's historic profitability to eliminate certain anomalies indicated that the firm had clearly been consistently profitable for the last 5 years. Moreover, the firm's cash flow had shown a strong upward trend during this period. A survey of customers indicated substantial satisfaction with product quality and turnaround time, factors that were highly valued by the firm's clientele. Because of these considerations, customers were willing to pay a premium to have their paper records converted to microfilm by Imaging Services.

Alan was puzzled by the relatively small expense entry recorded for disposal of silver nitrate, a highly toxic chemical that is used in the conversion of paper to microfilm. The owners assured him that such chemicals had been properly disposed of and that they had negotiated favorable terms with a local waste disposal company. Alan decided to crosscheck this explanation by interviewing several employees, who had been with the firm for a number of years and who were not family members or shareholders. During these interviews, Alan learned that chemicals were often dumped down the drain rather than into barrels that were to be emptied by the local disposal company. The drain emptied into a grassy area behind the building. An environmental consultant was hired to evaluate the toxicity of the property and confirmed Alan's worst fears. It would cost at least $500,000 to make the property compliant with both state and federal standards.

Alan confronted the owners with an ultimatum. Accept a reduction in the purchase price or he would recommend that his firm not complete the acquisition. The owners relented. Imaging Services was acquired but at a much lower price.

OVERVIEW

If you own an interest in a privately held business, you cannot simply look in the *Wall Street Journal* to see what your investment is worth. This is the situation with the vast majority of the nation's businesses. Publicly traded businesses comprise a miniscule .003 of 1% of all businesses that file tax returns with the Internal Revenue Service. The absence of an easy and accurate method of valuing your investment can create significant financial burdens for both investors and business owners alike.

Investors and business owners may need a valuation as part of a merger or acquisition, for settling an estate, or because employees wish to exercise their stock options. Employee stock ownership plans (ESOPs) may also require periodic valuations. In other instances, shareholder disputes, court cases, divorce, or the payment of gift or estate taxes may necessitate a valuation of the business.

In addition to the absence of a public market, there are other significant differences between publicly traded versus privately held companies. The availability and reliability of data for public companies tends to be much greater than for small private firms. Moreover, in large publicly traded corporations and large privately held companies, managers are often well versed in contemporary management practices, accounting, and financial valuation techniques. This is frequently not the case for small privately owned businesses. Finally, managers in large public companies are less likely to have the same level of emotional attachment to the business than is frequently found in family-owned businesses.

The intent of this chapter is to discuss how the analyst deals with these problems. Issues concerning making initial contact and negotiating with the owners of privately held businesses were addressed in Chapter 5 (this volume). Consequently, this chapter will focus on the challenges of valuing private or closely held businesses. Specifically, this chapter begins with a detailed discussion of the hazards of dealing with both limited and often unreliable data associated with privately held firms. The chapter then focuses on how to properly adjust questionable data as well as how to select the appropriate valuation methodology and discount or capitalization rate. The chapter also includes a discussion of how corporate shells, created through reverse mergers, and leveraged ESOPs are used to acquire privately owned companies.

The information in this chapter is decidedly practical, based more on actual experience than theoretical concepts. Unfortunately, the amount of empirical research in applying valuation techniques to privately held firms is highly limited due to the paucity of reliable data. Although the same tools and techniques discussed in earlier chapters still apply, their reliability is likely to be less as a result of the limited, inconsistent, and possibly erroneous information that the analyst must use to analyze privately owned businesses.

Investment bankers and business brokers have long recognized these limitations and have introduced numerous clever adjustments that allegedly make the valuations more accurate. Adjustments to data, like medieval efforts to convert base metals into gold, do not necessarily make it more valuable. A propensity to overadjust data may change the fundamental nature of the data and further reduce its reliability. In this regard, the valuation of privately held firms becomes far more an art than a science.

CHALLENGES OF VALUING PRIVATELY HELD COMPANIES

Because of the need to satisfy both the demands of stockholders and regulatory agencies, public companies need to balance the desire to minimize taxes with the goal of achieving quarterly earnings levels consistent with investor expectations. Failure to do so frequently results in an immediate loss in the firm's market value. The presence of such regulatory agencies as the Securities and Exchange Commission (SEC) limits the ability of public companies to manipulate financial information. In contrast, private companies have much more opportunity to do so, particularly when they are not widely followed by investment analysts or subject to ongoing regulation and periodic review. The anonymity of many privately held firms, the potential for manipulation of information, problems specific to small firms, and the tendency of owners of private firms to manage in a way to minimize tax liabilities creates a number of significant valuation risks. These issues are addressed in the next sections of this chapter.

LACK OF EXTERNALLY GENERATED INFORMATION

There is generally a lack of analyses of private firms generated by sources outside of the company. There is little incentive for outside analysts to cover these firms due to the absence of a public market for their securities; consequently, there are few forecasts of their performance other than those provided by the firm's management. Press coverage is usually quite limited, and what is available is again often based on information provided by the firm's management. Even highly regarded companies purporting to offer demographic and financial information on small privately held firms use largely superficial and infrequent telephone interviews with the management of such firms as their primary source of such information.

LACK OF INTERNAL CONTROLS AND INADEQUATE REPORTING SYSTEMS

Private companies are generally not subject to the same level of rigorous controls and reporting systems as public companies. Public companies are required to prepare audited financial statements for their annual reports. The SEC enforces the accuracy of these statements under the authority provided by the Securities and Exchange Act of 1934. The use of audits is much more rigorous and thorough than other types of reports known as accounting reviews and compilations. Although accounting reviews are acceptable for quarterly 10Q reports, compilation reports are not acceptable for either 10Ks or 10Qs. The audit consists of a professional examination and verification of a company's accounting documents and supporting data for the purpose of rendering an opinion as to their fairness, consistency, and conformity with generally accepted accounting principles (GAAP).

Although reporting systems in small firms are generally poor or nonexistent, the lack of formal controls, such as systems to monitor how money is spent and an approval process to ensure that funds are spent appropriately, invites fraud and misuse of company resources. Documentation is another formidable problem. Intellectual property is a substantial portion of the value of many private firms. Examples include system software, chemical formulae, and recipes. Often only one or two individuals within the firm know how to reproduce these valuable intangible assets. The lack of documentation can destroy a firm if such an individual leaves or dies. Moreover, customer lists and the terms and conditions associated with key customer relationships may also be largely undocumented, creating the basis for customer disputes upon a change in ownership.

FIRM-SPECIFIC PROBLEMS

There are also a number of factors that may be unique to the private firm making valuation difficult. The company may lack product, industry, and geographic diversification. There may be insufficient management talent to allow the firm to develop new products for its current markets or to expand into new markets. The company may be highly sensitive to fluctuations in demand because of significant fixed expenses. Its small size may limit its influence with regulators and unions. The company's size may also limit its ability to gain access to efficient distribution channels and leverage with suppliers and customers. Finally, the company may have an excellent product but very little brand recognition. Such considerations normally tend to reduce the stand-alone value of the business because of the uncertainty associated with efforts to forecast future cash flows. However, these considerations also present an opportunity for a shrewd buyer to realize synergy by merging firms with complementary strengths.

FOCUS ON TAX MINIMIZATION

A privately held firm can lower taxable income in two ways: by lowering reported revenue or increasing reported costs. Businesses operating on a cash basis may opt to report less revenue because of the difficulty outside parties have in tracking transactions. Although illegal, it is a major factor in the growth of the so-called "underground economy." Owners of private businesses may overstate their contribution to the firm by giving themselves or family members' unusually high salaries, bonuses, and benefits. Because the vast majority of all businesses are family owned, this is a widespread practice.

COMMON FORMS OF MANIPULATING REPORTED INCOME

Overstating Revenue

Private business owners may be inclined to inflate revenue, if the firm is to be sold. Common examples include manufacturers, which rely on others to distribute their products. These manufacturers can inflate revenue in the current accounting period by booking as revenue products shipped to resellers without adequately adjusting for probable returns. Membership or subscription businesses, such as health clubs and magazine publishers, may inflate revenue by booking the full value of multiyear contracts in the current period rather than prorating the payment received at the beginning of the contract period over the life of the contract. This distortion results in a significant boost to current profitability because not all of the costs associated with multiyear contracts, such as customer service, are incurred in the period in which the full amount of revenue is booked.

If the buyer believes that revenue has been overstated in a specific accounting period by the seller, the buyer can reconstruct revenue by examining usage levels, in the same accounting period, of the key inputs required to produce the product or service. While not necessarily precise, examining activity or usage levels does tend to highlight discrepancies that might exist in the data provided by the seller. Case Study 9-1 illustrates how this might be done.

CASE STUDY 9-1. DUE DILIGENCE UNCOVERS MISSTATED REVENUE

The owner of a custom brass doorknob manufacturer states that one million doorknobs of a certain specification were produced during the last calendar year. During due diligence, the potential buyer learns that one skilled worker can produce 100 brass doorknobs in 1 hour. He also learns that there was no overtime last year and that that hourly workers were paid for a standard 2080 hours (52 weeks per year times 40 hours per week) each during the year and accrued 2 weeks of paid vacation and holiday time. In addition, he discovers that, since there was no reduction in finished goods inventories during the year, all products reported sold during the year must have been produced during that same year.

The prospective buyer reasons that one worker could produce in 1 year, assuming an average of 2 weeks of vacation time, 200,000 doorknobs (100 doorknobs per hour × 2000 hours). Since there were only four skilled workers employed during the year, annual production of this particular specification could not have exceeded 800,000 doorknobs. Therefore, the sales figures reported by the owner appear to be overstated by as much as 200,000 units. The owner needs to explain what appears to be a logical discrepancy between the reported number and the theoretically determined number of doorknobs produced.

Overstating Cost

The most common distortion of costs comes in the form of higher than normal salary and benefits provided to family members and key employees. Other examples of extraordinary expenses, which are really other forms of compensation for the owner, his family, and key employees, may include the rent on the owner's summer home or hunting lodge and salaries for the pilot and captain for the owner's airplane and yacht. Current customers or potential customers are sometimes allowed to use these assets. Owners frequently argue that these expenses are necessary to maintain customer relationships or to close large contracts and are therefore legitimate business expenses. One way to determine if these are appropriate business expenses is to ascertain how often these assets are used for the purpose the owner claims they were intended.

Other areas that are commonly abused include travel and entertainment, personal insurance, and excessive payments to vendors supplying services to the firm. Due diligence will frequently uncover situations in which the owner or a family member is either an investor in or an owner of the vendor supplying the products or services.

ADJUSTING THE INCOME STATEMENT

The purpose of adjusting the income statement is to provide an accurate estimate of the current year's operating income or earnings before interest and taxes (EBIT). In valuing private firms, it is likely that the historical financial information available to the buyer will be misstated. The common misconception is that the costs will be overstated. Although this is frequently the case, it is by no means always true. A cost item, such as key employee salaries, may reflect the true value of services received by the firm. An analyst can seriously overstate profitability by ignoring areas in which the target firm is underspending. Competitive pressures may cause a firm to cut back on advertising, employee training, and safety and environmental compliance.

The key point is that the analyst must always make adjustments based on the best information available. It is often appropriate to hire subject matter experts to assist in making sizable adjustments to important data items. Adjustments should never be made based on preconceptions, personal biases, or emotion.

MAKING INFORMED ADJUSTMENTS

Owner/Officer's Salaries

Before drawing any conclusions, the analyst should determine the actual work performed by all key employees and the compensation generally received for performing the same or a similar job in the same industry. Comparative salary information can be obtained by employing the services of a compensation consultant familiar with the industry or simply by scanning "employee wanted" advertisements in the industry trade press and magazines and the "help-wanted" pages of the local newspaper. Case Study 9-2 illustrates how the failure to complete this type of analysis can lead to a substantial disruption to the business following a change in ownership.

Benefits

Depending upon the industry, benefits can range from 14–30% of employee base salary. Certain employee benefits, such as Social Security and Medicare taxes, are mandated by law and, therefore, are an uncontrollable cost of doing business. Other types of benefits may be more controllable. These include items such as pension contributions and life insurance coverage, which are calculated as a percentage of base salary. Consequently, efforts by the buyer to trim salaries, which appear to be excessive, will also reduce these types of benefits. Efforts to reduce such benefits may also contribute to higher overall operating costs in the short-run. Operating costs may increase due to higher employee turnover and the need to retrain replacements as well as the potential negative impact on the productivity of those that remain.

Travel and Entertainment

Travel and entertainment (T&E) expenditures tend to be one of the first cost categories cut when a potential buyer attempts to value a target company. The initial reaction is almost always that actual spending in this area is far in excess of what it needs to be. However, what may look excessive to one relatively unfamiliar with the industry may in fact be necessary for retaining current and acquiring new customers. Establishing, building, and maintaining relationships is particularly important for personal and business services companies, such as consulting and law firms. Account management may require consultative selling at the customer's site. A complex product like software may require on-site training. Indiscriminant reduction in the T&E budget could lead to a serious loss of customers following a change in ownership.

Auto Expenses and Personal Life Insurance

Before assuming auto expenses and life insurance are excessive, ask if they represent a key component of the overall compensation required to attract and to retain key employees. This can be determined by comparing total compensation paid to employees of the target firm with compensation packages offered to employees in similar positions in the same industry. A similar review should be undertaken with respect to the composition of benefits packages.

Depending upon the demographics and special needs of the target firm's workforce, an acquirer may choose to alter the composition of the benefits package by substituting other types of benefits for those eliminated or reduced. By carefully substituting benefits that meet the specific needs of the workforce, such as on-site day-care services, the acquirer may be able to provide an overall benefits package that better satisfies the needs of the employees. Alternatively, the acquirer may find that administrative costs associated with reimbursable benefits such as car expenses may be reduced by simply offering a standard car allowance or by increasing the employees' salaries to compensate for anticipated car-related expenses.

Family Members

Similar questions need to be asked about family members on the payroll. Frequently, they do perform real services and tend to be highly motivated because of their close affinity with the business. If the business has been in existence for many years, the loss of key family members who have built up relationships with customers over the years may result in a subsequent loss of key accounts. Moreover, family members may be those who possess proprietary knowledge necessary for the ongoing operation of the business.

Rent or Lease Payments in Excess of Fair Market Value

Check who owns the buildings housing the business or equipment used by the business. This is a frequent method used by the owner to transfer company funds to the owner in excess of their stated salary and benefits. However, rents may not be too high if the building is a "special-purpose" structure retrofitted to serve the specific needs of the tenant.

Professional Services Fees

Professional services could include legal, accounting, personnel, and actuarial services. This is an area that is frequently subject to abuse. Once again check to see if there is any nonbusiness relationship between the business owner and the firm providing the service. Always consider any special circumstances that may justify unusually high fees. An industry that is subject to continuing regulation and review may incur what appear to be abnormally high legal and accounting expenses when compared to firms in other industries.

Depreciation Expense

Accelerated depreciation methodologies may make sense for tax purposes, but they may seriously understate current earnings. For financial reporting purposes, it may be appropriate to convert depreciation schedules from accelerated to straight-line depreciation, if this results in a better matching of when expenses are actually incurred and revenue is actually received.

Reserves

Current reserves may be inadequate to reflect future events. An increase in reserves lowers taxable income, while a decrease in reserves raises taxable income. Collection problems may be uncovered following an analysis of accounts receivable. It may be necessary to add to reserves for doubtful accounts. Similarly, the target firm may not have adequately reserved for future obligations to employees under existing pension and health-care plans. Reserves may also have to be increased to reflect known environmental and litigation exposures.

Accounting for Inventory

During periods of inflation, businesses frequently use the last-in, first out (LIFO) method to account for inventories. This approach results in an increase in the cost of sales that reflects the most recent and presumably highest cost inventory; and, therefore, reduces gross profit and taxable income. During periods of inflation, the use of LIFO also tends to lower the value of inventory on the balance sheet, because the items in inventory are valued at the lower cost of production associated with earlier time periods. In contrast, the use of first-in, first-out (FIFO) accounting for inventory assumes that inventory is sold in the chronological order in which it was purchased. During periods of inflation, the FIFO method produces a higher ending inventory, a lower cost of goods sold, and higher gross profit. Although it may make sense for tax purposes to use LIFO, the buyer's objective for valuation purposes should be to obtain as realistic an estimate of actual earnings as possible in the current period. FIFO accounting would appear to be most logical for products that are perishable or subject to rapid obsolescence and, therefore, are most likely to be sold in chronological order.

CASE STUDY 9-2. LOSS OF KEY EMPLOYEE CAUSES CARPET PADDING MANUFACTURER TO GO FLAT

A manufacturer of carpet padding in southern California had devised a unique chemical process for converting such materials as discarded bedding and rags to high-quality commercial carpet padding. Over a period of 10 years, the firm established itself as the regional leader in this niche market. With annual sales in excess of $10 million, the firm consistently earned pretax profits of 18–20% of sales.

The owner and founder of the company had been trained as a chemist and developed the formula for decomposing the necessary raw materials purchased from local junkyards into a mixture to produce the foam padding. In addition, the owner routinely calibrated all of the company's manufacturing equipment to ensure that the machines ran at peak efficiency, without any deterioration in product quality. Over the years, the owner also had developed relationships with a network of local junk dealers to acquire the necessary raw materials. The owner's reputation for honesty ensured very little customer turnover. The owner was also solely responsible for acquiring several large accounts, which consistently contributed about 30% of annual revenue.

When the firm was sold, the owner's salary and benefits of $200,000 per year were believed to be excessive by the buyer. Efforts to reduce his total compensation caused him to retire. The new owner was soon forced to hire several people to replace the former owner, who had been performing the role of chemist, maintenance engineer, and purchasing agent. These were functions that did not appear on any organization chart when the buyer performed due diligence. Consequently, the buyer did not increase the budget for salaries and benefits to provide personnel to perform these crucial functions. This tended to overstate profits and inflated the purchase price paid by the buyer.

Replacing the owner required hiring a chemist, a machinist, a purchasing agent, and a salesperson at an annual cost in salary and benefits of more than $300,000. Despite the additional personnel, the new owner also found it necessary to hire the former owner under a consulting contract valued at $25,000 per year. To add insult to injury, the firm lost several large customers, who accounted for $2,000,000 in annual sales, because of the change in ownership.

AREAS COMMONLY UNDERSTATED

Projected increases in sales normally require more aggressive marketing efforts, more effective customer service support, and enhanced employee training.

Nonetheless, it is common to see the ratio of annual advertising and training expenses to annual sales decline during the period of highest projected growth in forecasts developed by either the buyer or the seller. The seller has an incentive to hold costs down during the forecast period to provide the most sanguine outlook possible. The buyer may simply be overly optimistic about how much more effectively the business can be managed as a result of a change in ownership.

While understating these expenses may reduce the profitability of future revenues, overlooking or understating expenses associated with environmental clean-up, employee safety, and pending litigation can put the acquiring firm into bankruptcy. Even in an asset purchase, the buyer may still be liable for certain types of risks such as environmental problems and pension obligations. From a legal standpoint, both the buyer and the seller are often held responsible for these types of obligations.

AREAS COMMONLY OVERLOOKED

Understandably, buyers find the valuation of tangible assets easier than intangible assets. Unfortunately, in many cases, the value in the business is more in its intangible than tangible assets. The best examples include the high valuations placed on many Internet-related and biotechnology companies. The target's intangible assets may include customer lists, intellectual property, licenses, distributorship agreements, leases, regulatory approvals (e.g., Federal Drug Administration approval of a new drug), and employment contracts. An aggressive seller often attempts to "showcase" these items in an attempt to increase the buyer's perceived valuation of the firm. Intangibles are particularly tricky to value because of their highly subjective nature. The prudent buyer should pay a professional appraiser with specific subject matter expertise to evaluate these items.

Table 9-1 illustrates how a target firm's financial reporting statements could be restated to reflect what the buyer believes to be a more accurate characterization of costs. Note that although some cost items are reduced, others are increased. The implications for other cost categories of cost reductions in one area must be determined. For example, while rents are reduced by $100,000 as a result of the elimination of out-of-state sales offices, the sales and marketing-related portion of the T&E budget is increased by $50,000 to accommodate the increased travel that will be necessary to service out-of-state customer accounts once the regional offices are closed.

APPLYING VALUATION METHODOLOGIES TO PRIVATE COMPANIES

DEFINING VALUE

The most common generic definition of value used by valuation professionals is fair market value. Hypothetically, *fair market value* is the cash or

TABLE 9-1.   Adjusting the Target's Financial Statements[a]

| | ($ Thousands) | | | |
	Target's statements	Net adjustment	Adjusted statements	Explanation of adjustment
Revenue	8000		8000	
Less: COS, incl. all direct costs	5000	(400)	4600	LIFO COS higher than FIFO cost; adjustment converts to FIFO costs
Equals: Gross profit	3000		3400	
Less: depreciation	100	(40)	60	Convert depreciation to straight line from accelerated on book and tax returns
Less: Selling				
Salaries and benefits	1000	(100)	900	Eliminate part-time family members
Rent	200	(100)	100	Eliminate out-of-state sales offices
Insurance	20	(5)	15	Eliminate owner's life and car insurance
Advertising	20	10	30	Increase targeted advertising
Travel and entertainment	150	50	200	Increase to support out-of-state customer accounts
All other	100		100	
Total selling	1490	(145)	1345	
Less: Administration				
Salaries and benefits	600	(100)	500	Reduce owner's salary and benefits
Rent	150	(30)	120	Reduce office space
Insurance	50		50	
Travel and entertainment	150	(30)	120	
Director fees	30	(30)	0	Remove family members as directors
Professional fees	100	20	120	Increase training budget
All other	50		50	
Total admin	1130	(170)	960	
Equals: EBIT	280	(755)	1035	

[a] COS, cost of sales; LIFO, last-in, first-out; FIFO, first-in, first-out; EBIT, earnings before interest and taxes.

cash-equivalent price that a willing buyer would propose and a willing seller would accept for a business, if both parties have access to all relevant information. Furthermore, fair market value assumes that neither the seller nor the buyer is under any obligation to buy or sell. As described in Chapter 7 (this volume), the income or market valuation approaches are often used to determine fair market value.

It is easier to obtain the fair market value for a public company because of the existence of public markets in which stock in the company is actively traded. The concept may be applied to privately held firms, if similar publicly traded companies exist. However, because finding substantially similar companies is rare, valuation professionals have developed a related concept of fair value. *Fair value* is applied when no strong market exists for a business or it is not possible to identify the value of substantially similar firms. Fair value is by necessity more subjective, as it represents the dollar value of a business based upon an appraisal of the tangible and intangible assets of the business.

HIRING VALUATION PROFESSIONALS

The usefulness of valuation methodologies depends on the competence and experience of the analyst conducting the valuation. Thus, the two most important elements in selecting a valuation professional are experience and demonstrated ability in the industry in which the firm to be valued competes. In selecting valuation professionals, it is important to understand what the various certifications obtained by valuation professionals really mean. Historically, many individuals could enter the valuation field without much specialized or formal training. Consequently, the depth of experience and expertise varies widely.

The American Society of Appraisers (ASA) is one of the nation's oldest and most respected appraisal societies, and it is generally considered to be the leading accrediting body of business valuation professionals. The major business valuation firms require that their appraisers obtain an ASA certification. The requirements for the ASA's Accredited Senior Member certification include a minimum of 5 years of full-time business valuation experience and passing four courses in financial analysis and valuation techniques. Other certificates that are available include the Certified Business Appraiser (CBA), Certified Valuation Analyst (CVA), and Accredited in Business Valuation (ABV). Of these, only the ABV requires the candidate to have performed at least 10 valuations.

SELECTING THE APPROPRIATE
VALUATION METHODOLOGY

Valuing private or closely held businesses involves three important steps. The first step involves the adjustment of data so that they accurately reflect the true profitability and cash flow of the firm. This was discussed at length previously in this chapter. The second and third steps entail the determination of the appropriate methodology for valuing the firm and the selection of the proper discount or capitalization rate. These steps are discussed in detail during the balance of this chapter.

The terms *discount rate* and *capitalization rate* are often used interchangeably. Whenever the growth rate of a firm's cash flows are projected to vary over time, the term *discount rate* generally refers to the factor used to convert the projected cash flows to present values. In contrast, if the cash flows of the firm are not expected to grow or are expected to grow at a constant rate indefinitely, the discount rate employed by practitioners is often referred as the capitalization rate.

As noted in Chapter 7 (this volume), appraisers, brokers, and investment bankers generally classify valuation methodologies into four distinct approaches: income, market, replacement cost, and asset oriented. Table 9-2 summarizes the strengths and weaknesses of alternative valuation methodologies. Although the strengths noted for each valuation technique are also true when applied to publicly traded firms, the weaknesses tend to be most pronounced when applied to the valuation of private or closely held companies.

Income Approach

This method was discussed at length in Chapter 7 (this volume). It requires projected cash flows for a specific number of periods plus a terminal value to be discounted to the present using an appropriate discount rate. The method is heavily dependent on the particular definition of income or cash flow and selection of an appropriate discount rate.

Capitalization is also the conversion of a future income stream into a present value. It generally applies when future income or cash flows are not expected to grow or to grow at a constant rate. When no growth in future income or cash flows is expected, the capitalization rate is defined as the perpetuity growth model. When future cash flow or income is expected to grow at a constant rate, the capitalization rate is defined as the difference between the discount rate and the expected growth rate (i.e., the constant growth or Gordon model) (see Chapter 7, this volume).

TABLE 9-2.   Applying Alternative Valuation Methodologies to Privately Held Firms

	Strengths	Weaknesses
Income approach		
Discounted cash flow	• Considers differences in the magnitude and timing of cash flows • Adjusts for risk	• Requires forecasting of cash flows for each period, a terminal value, and discount or capitalization rate(s), using limited or unreliable data
Capitalization	• Simplicity: easily under-stood and communicated	• Highly sensitive to the accuracy of income or cash flow and capitalization rate estimates

TABLE 9-2.　*(continued)*

	Strengths	Weaknesses
Market-based approach		
Comparable companies	• Utilizes market-based price-to-earnings, sales, or book value for substantially similar companies	• Truly comparable public companies rarely exist • Valuations must be adjusted to reflect control premiums • Reflects accounting-based historical data
Comparable transactions	• Uses the most accurate market-based valuation at a point in time	• May be few in number or not current • Limited availability of specific transaction related data
Same or comparable industry	• Provides additional valuation for comparative purposes	• Assumes industry average valuation multiples are applicable to a specific company • Industry information often non-existent
Replacement cost approach		
Applied to tangible assets	• Applicable whenever the Discounted cash flow or market approaches are unsuitable because of limited information	• May be of limited use if the target firm is highly profitable • Requires use of appraisers with specialized knowledge • Ignores value created by operating the assets in combination as a going concern
Applied to intangible assets	• Simplicity: relies on cumulative investment required to create intangible asset	• Assumes historical investment in intangible asset proxy for future cost of replacement
Asset-oriented approach		
Tangible book value	• Useful for financial services and distribution companies where assets tend to be highly liquid	• Book value may not equate to market value • Limited availability of required data
Break-up value	• May unlock value in operating subsidiaries whose actual value cannot be easily determined by analysts outside the company	• Assumes that individual businesses can be sold quickly without any material loss of value • Available markets often highly illiquid
Liquidation Value	• Provides estimate of minimum value of a firm	• Frequently assumes that an "orderly" liquidation is possible • Available markets often highly illiquid

Several alternative definitions of income or cash flow can be used in either the discounting or capitalization process. These include free cash flow to equity holders or to the firm; earnings before interest, taxes, depreciation and amortization (EBITDA); EBIT, earnings before taxes (EBT), or earnings after taxes (EAT or NI). The present value or capitalized value may vary widely depending upon the definition of income or cash flow used.

Capitalized values and capitalization rates are often used in valuing small businesses because of their inherent simplicity. Many small business owners lack sophistication in financial matters. Consequently, a valuation concept, which is easy to calculate, understand, and communicate to the parties involved, may significantly facilitate completion of the transaction.

Market Approach

This approach is widely used in valuing private firms by business brokers or appraisers to establish a purchase price. The Internal Revenue Service (IRS) and the U.S. tax courts have encouraged the use of market-based valuation techniques. Therefore, in valuing private companies, it is always important to keep in mind what factors the IRS thinks are relevant to the process, because the IRS may contest any sale requiring the payment of estate, capital gain, or unearned income taxes. The IRS' positions on specific tax issues can be determined by reviewing revenue rulings.

Revenue Rulings

A revenue ruling is an official interpretation by the IRS of the Internal Revenue Code, related statutes, tax treaties, and regulations. These rulings represent the IRS' position on how the law is applied to a specific set of circumstances. Such rulings are published by the IRS in the Internal Revenue Bulletin to assist taxpayers, IRS personnel, and other concerned parties in interpreting the Internal Revenue Code.

Revenue Ruling 59–60

Issued in 1959, Revenue Ruling 59–60 describes the general factors that the IRS and tax courts consider relevant in valuing private businesses. These factors include general economic conditions, the specific conditions in the industry, the type of business, historical trends in the industry, the firm's performance, and the firm's book value. In addition, the IRS and tax courts consider the ability of the company to generate earnings and pay dividends, the amount of intangibles such as goodwill, recent sales of stock, and the stock prices of companies engaged in the "same or similar" line of business.

In deference to Revenue Ruling 59–60, tax courts have historically supported the use of the comparable company method of valuing private businesses. However, they have differed on their interpretation of the notion of "same or similar." In one case, appraisers used companies that had similar capital structures and financial ratios to the company that was being valued. The court rejected the valuation, because it argued that the companies selected were not in the same line of business as the company being valued (*Northern Trust Company v. Commissioner:* 1986). In contrast, the courts were willing to use companies in substantially different lines of business in settling an estate associated with Hallmark Cards. American Greeting was the only company found that was truly comparable to Hallmark. Appraisers were allowed to use other companies in very different lines of business, such as Coca-Cola, IBM, Anheuser Busch, McDonald's, and Avon, because they exhibited financial structures, brand recognition, and dominant market share comparable to Hallmark (*Estate of James C. Hall v. Commissioner:* 1989).

Replacement Cost Approach

This approach states that the assets of a business are worth what it would cost to replace them. The approach is most applicable to businesses that have substantial amounts of tangible assets for which the actual cost to replace them can be easily determined. In the case of a business whose primary assets consist of intellectual property, it may be very difficult to determine the actual cost of replacing the firm's intangible assets using this method. The accuracy of this approach is heavily dependent on the skill and specific industry knowledge of the appraisers employed to conduct the analyses.

Moreover, the replacement cost approach ignores the value created in excess of the cost of replacing each asset by operating the assets as a going concern. For example, an assembly line may consist of a number of different machines each performing a specific task in the production of certain products. The value of the total production coming off the assembly line over the useful lives of the individual machines is likely to far exceed the sum of the costs to replace each machine. Consequently, the business should be valued as a going concern rather than the sum of cost to replace its individual assets.

The replacement cost approach is sometimes used to value intangible assets by examining the amount of historical investment associated with the asset. For example, the cumulative historical advertising spending targeted at developing a particular product brand or image may be a reasonable proxy for the intangible value of the brand name or image. However, because consumer tastes tend to change over time, applying historical experience to the future may be highly misleading.

Asset-Oriented Approach

Like the replacement cost approach, the accuracy of asset-oriented approaches depends on the overall proficiency of the appraiser hired to establish value and the availability of adequate information.

Tangible Book Value

Book value is an accounting concept and is generally not considered a good measure of market value, because book values generally reflect historical rather than current market values. However, as noted in Chapter 7, tangible book value (i.e., book value less intangible assets) may be a good proxy for the current market value for both financial services and product distribution companies.

Breakup Value

Breakup value is an estimate of what the value of a business would be if each of its primary assets were sold independently. This approach may not be practical if there are few public markets for the firm's assets.

Liquidation Value

Liquidation value is a reflection of the firm under duress. A firm in liquidation must normally sell its assets within a specific period of time. Consequently, the cash value of the assets realized is likely to be much less than their actual replacement value or value if the firm were to continue as a viable operation. Liquidation value is thus a good proxy for the minimum value of the firm.

DEVELOPING CAPITALIZATION RATES

The discount or capitalization rate can be derived from the capital asset pricing model (CAPM), cost of capital, accounting based returns, price-to-earnings (P/E) ratio, or the buildup method. These five methods are explored below.

Capital Asset Pricing Model

The CAPM method provides an estimate of the acquiring firm's cost of equity, which may be used as the discount or capitalization rate when no debt is involved in the transaction. However, the cost of equity may have to be adjusted to reflect risk specific to the target company, when it is applied to valuing a private or closely held company.

The Nature of Specific Business Risk

The CAPM may significantly understate the specific business risk associated with acquiring a privately held firm, because it may not adequately reflect the risk associated with such firms. As noted earlier, private or closely held firms are often subject to risks not normally found with public firms. These include inconsistent or improperly stated financial information resulting in inaccurate financial statements, inadequate controls increasing the possibility of fraudulent activities, and potential "hidden" liabilities, such as noncompliance with Occupational Safety and Health Administration and Environmental Protection Agency regulations. Private or closely held firms may also be subject to significant commercial risk due to reliance on a few customers or suppliers or a narrow product offering. Consequently, it is appropriate to adjust the CAPM for the additional risks associated with private or closely held firms.

Adjusting the CAPM for Specific Business Risk

Recall that risk premiums for public companies are determined by examining the historical premiums earned by stocks over some measure of risk-free returns, such as 10-year treasury bonds. This same logic may be applied to calculating specific business risk premiums for small private firms. The specific business risk premium can be measured by the difference between the junk bond and risk-free rate or the return on comparable small stocks and the risk-free rate. Note that comparable companies are more likely to be found on the NASDAQ, OTC, or regional stock exchanges than on the New York Stock Exchange (NYSE).

For example, consider an acquiring firm that is attempting to value a small software company. If the risk-free return is 6%, the historical return on all stocks minus the risk-free return is 5.5%, and the historical return on OTC software stocks minus the risk-free return is 10%, the cost of equity (k_e) can be calculated as follows:

$$k_e = \text{Risk-Free Return} + \text{Market Risk Premium}$$
$$+ \text{ Specific Business Risk Premium}$$
$$= 6\% + 5.5\% + 10\% = 21.5\%$$

Cost of Capital

In the presence of debt, the cost of capital method should be used to estimate the discount or capitalization rate. This method involves the calculation of a weighted average of the cost of equity and the after-tax cost of debt. The weights reflect the market value of the acquirer's target debt to equity ratio.

Accounting-Based Returns

The return on equity (ROE) and the return on investment (ROI) are sometimes used as capitalization rates. ROE is the return to equity owners in the business. ROI measures the return on total capital, which includes both the debt and equity of the business. Although after-tax income is normally used to calculate these returns, pretax income should be used for private firms because of the unreliability of after-tax income for such companies.

EXHIBIT 9-1. ACCOUNTING-BASED CAPITALIZATION RATES

Doors Unlimited, Inc., has pretax earnings of $1 million, debt of $5 million, and equity of $15 million.

$$\text{ROE} = \$1/\$15 = 6.7\%$$

$$\text{ROI} = \$1/\$20 = 5.0\%$$

The capitalized value of the business using ROE is $1/.067 = $14.93 million.

The capitalized value of the business using ROI is $1/.05 = $20 million.

Price-to-Earnings Ratio

The capitalization rate can also be measured by calculating the reciprocal of the P/E ratio (i.e., E/P). The P/E ratio used for this purpose can be for the current, the most recent, or a projected year. The P/E used for valuing a private firm should be selected from among the P/Es of comparable public companies adjusted to reflect risks specific to the target firm. Ways of adjusting P/Es were discussed in detail in Chapter 7 (this volume).

The Buildup Method

This approach attempts to compensate for some of the shortcomings associated with applying CAPM to evaluating private or closely held businesses. The buildup method involves the adjustment of the underlying discount rate to reflect risks associated with such businesses. Using this method, the capitalization rate (R_{cr}) can be expressed as follows:

$$R_{cr} = R_f + \beta(R_m - R_f) + (R_j - R_f) + R_{ji},$$

where R_f = the risk-free rate of return

        R_m = the return on all stocks

        R_j = the return on the jth stock

        $(R_m - R_f)$ = the market risk premium

        $(R_j - R_f)$ = the specific business risk premium

        R_{ji} = the liquidity risk associated with jth stock

        β = the beta associated with the jth stock

The risk associated with an illiquid market for the specific stock (R_{ji}) is often referred to as the *marketability* or *liquidity* discount. Liquidity is the ease with which an investor can sell their stock without a serious loss of value. An investor in a small company may find it difficult to quickly sell their shares because of limited interest in the company. Consequently, the investor may find it necessary to sell their shares at a significant discount from what they paid for the shares.

R_f is free of default risk and is usually taken to be the rate on U.S. Treasury notes or bonds. The market risk premium, $R_m - R_f$, the difference between the return on stocks and the risk-free rate, has been averaging about 5.5% since 1960 (Ibbotson: 1999). The β for a private firm may be estimated by using the β for a comparable publicly traded firm or by using an industry-average β. The solution to the case study at the end of this chapter provides an example of how to approximate the β for a private firm, if comparable publicly traded firms are available. In the absence of comparable publicly traded firms, analysts often employ the buildup methodology by assuming a β of 1.

The specific business risk premium, $R_j - R_f$, the difference between the return on small company stocks and the risk-free rate, has been averaging about 9% since

1960. $R_j - R_f$ can also be measured using the difference between junk bond yields and the risk-free rate of return. Information on junk bonds and small stocks may be found in the financial press such as in the *Wall Street Journal.* Historical data are available through Ibbotson Associates (www.ibbotson.com).

Exhibit 9-2 summarizes the calculation of both the discount and capitalization rates using the buildup method. The risk-free return is assumed to be 6%, and the long-term rate of growth in earnings is estimated at 8.5%. For purposes of illustration, R_{ji}, the marketablity or illiquidity discount, is assumed to be 33%. (How this discount is determined is discussed in considerable detail in the next section.) For purposes of illustration, the specific business risk premium, $R_j - R_f$, is estimated to be 9% based on the historical difference between the return on small company stocks and the risk-free rate of return.

In practice, the magnitude of the business-specific risk premium can vary widely depending upon the perceived risk characteristics of the firm such as leverage, dependence on a single product, outstanding litigation, or environmental liabilities. For example, for a sample of 51 firms, Kaplan and Ruback (1995) estimated that the return required by investors to invest in highly leveraged transactions averages about 16–17%, almost twice the spread between the average return on small company stocks and the risk-free rate of return.

EXHIBIT 9-2. CALCULATING CAPITALIZATION RATES USING THE BUILDUP METHOD

Risk-Free Rate (R_f)	6.0
+ Market risk premium required to invest in stocks $(R_m - R_f)$[1]	5.5
+ Specific business risk premium $(R_j - R_f)$	9.0
+ Marketability discount (R_{ji})	33.0
= Discount rate (0 earnings growth model)	53.5
− Long-term earnings growth rate	8.5
= Capitalization rate (R_{cr}) (constant earnings growth model)	45.0

[1] The β in this example is assumed to be 1, because, in this illustration, it is assumed that there are no publicly traded comparable firms.

ESTIMATING THE MARKETABILITY OR LIQUIDITY DISCOUNT

Measuring the cost of illiquidity associated with stocks lacking a ready resale market is a challenge. This is especially true for closely held companies such as family-owned firms. There is generally only a limited market for such stocks. When such businesses are sold, it is common to follow the guidelines suggested in Revenue Ruling 59–60 and to use the comparable companies' method to estimate the value of the subject firm. Valuation professionals frequently use P/E multiples and other indicators of value associated with publicly traded companies. The stock of such companies usually trades in more liquid markets than closely held companies. Consequently, estimates of the value of closely held companies based on the comparable companies' approach are likely to be overstated, since they do not reflect the lower marketability of closely held shares. Numerous studies have been done to estimate the amount of the marketability discount. These include analyses of restricted stock, initial public offerings (IPOs), and option pricing.

Restricted Stock

Restricted stock, also called letter stock, is similar to other types of common stock except that its sale on the open market is prohibited for a period of time. Restricted stock is issued by a firm but not registered with the SEC. It can be sold through private placements to investors, but it cannot be resold to the public, except under provisions of the SEC's Rule 144, which allows limited amounts of the stock to be sold 2 years after the issuance date.

Differences between the value of restricted and unrestricted stock in the same firm are believed to be an accurate reflection of the marketability discount, because the only difference between the two is the waiting period before the restricted stock can be sold. A comprehensive study, undertaken by the SEC in 1971 examined restricted stock for 398 publicly traded companies, found that the average discount for trades involving the restricted stock was about 26% (*Institutional Investor Study Report:* 1971). An analysis completed by Gelman (1972) on a smaller sample of 146 publicly traded firms found that restricted shares sold at discounts averaging 33%. Other studies by Maher (1976) and Trout (1977) estimated the discount to be in the 33–35% range.

The results of these studies suggest that the average liquidity discount is about 33% for private or closely held firms. However, the size of the discount should be adjusted for the size of the firm, with a larger discount used for smaller firms.

Initial Public Offerings

An alternative to estimating marketability discounts is to compare the value of a company's stock that is sold before an IPO, largely through private placements, with the actual IPO offering price. Because the level of liquidity available to stockholders is substantially less before the IPO, the difference is believed to be an estimate of the marketability discount. In six separate studies of 173 companies over an 18-month period, Emory (1985) found an average discount of 47% between the pre-IPO transaction prices and the actual post-IPO prices.

Applying Marketability Discounts: Controlling versus Minority Interests

The bulk of the estimates of marketability discounts seem to lie within a range of 33–50%. Given the wide variability of estimates, it should be evident that marketability discounts must be applied with care. Circumstances specific to the company's situation must be taken into account when determining the appropriate size of the discount. These circumstances include differences in the size of the interests being valued, the timing of the sale, the attractiveness of the firm to potential investors, and the size of the market for stocks of companies most similar to the subject company. The implication is that there is no such thing as a standard marketability discount.

Despite the subjective nature of these adjustments, some analysts argue that additional adjustments are required to reflect the size of the investor position in the privately held firm (Pratt, Reilly, and Scheweihs: 1995 and Pratt: 1998). Intuitively, the size of the discount should vary with the size of the ownership position in the private firm. An investor holding a controlling interest in a company is better able to affect change in the company than a minority shareholder. Control can include the ability to select management, determine compensation, set policy and change the course of the business, acquire and liquidate assets, award contracts, make acquisitions, sell or recapitalize the company, and register the company's stock for a public offering. Control also involves the ability to declare and pay dividends, change the articles of incorporation or bylaws, or to block any of the aforementioned actions. Therefore, it may be argued that the marketability discount applied to the value of the stock for the investor with a controlling interest should be lower than that for the minority interest shareholder. The key question is how much higher.

A marketability discount in the range of 33–50% may be appropriate for many transactions, with the size of the discount varying with the size of the equity interest being valued. For example, the value of a 20% equity interest might be reduced by 50%, whereas the value of a 60% interest may be reduced by only 33%. In ether case, the investor should be wary, as the adjustment remains quite arbitrary.

CASE STUDY 9-1. PACIFIC WARDROBE ACQUIRES SURFERDUDE APPAREL

BUSINESS PLAN

Pacific Wardrobe (Pacific) is a privately owned California corporation that has annual sales of $20 million and pretax profits of $2 million. Its target market is the surfwear/sportswear segment of the apparel industry. The surfwear/sportswear market consists of two segments: cutting-edge and casual brands. The first segment includes high-margin apparel sold at higher-end retail establishments. The second segment consists of brands that sell for lower prices at retail stores such as Sears, Target, and J.C. Penny.

Pacific operates primarily as a United States importer/distributor of largely casual sportswear for young men and boys between 10–21 years of age. Pacific's strategic business objectives are to triple sales and pretax profits during the next 5 years. Pacific intends to achieve these objectives by moving away from the casual sportswear market segment and more into the high-growth, high-profit cutting-edge surfer segment. Because of the rapid rate at which trends change in the apparel industry, Pacific's management believes that it can take advantage of current trends only through a well-conceived acquisition strategy.

PACIFIC'S OPERATIONS AND COMPETITIVE ENVIRONMENT

Pacific imports all of its apparel from factories in Hong Kong, Taiwan, Nepal, and Indonesia. Its customers consist of major chains and specialty stores. Most customers are lower-end retail stores. Customers include J.C. Penney, Sears, Stein Mart, Kids 'R Us, and Target. No one customer accounts for more than 20% of Pacific's total revenue. The customers in the lower end market are extremely cost sensitive. Customers consist of those in the 10–21 years of age range, who want to wear cutting-edge surf and sport styles but who are not willing or able to pay high prices. Pacific offers an alternative to the expensive cutting-edge styles at affordable prices.

Pacific has found a niche in the young men's and teenage boy's sportswear market. Pacific offers similar styles as the top brand names in the surf and sport industry, such as Mossimo, Red Sand, Stussy, Quick Silver, and Gotcha, but at a lower price point. Pacific indirectly competes with these top brand names by attempting to appeal to the same customer base. There are few companies that compete with Pacific at their level—low cost production of "almost" cutting-edge styles. Furthermore, Pacific has access to resources that a new entrant would not. Potential entrants would include a company that has both the financial and production resources in place in order to be able to compete on quantity and price without sacrificing quality.

Pacific's Strengths and Weaknesses

Pacific's core strengths lie in their strong vendor support in terms of quantity, quality, service, delivery, and price/cost. Pacific's production is also scaleable and has the potential to produce at high volumes to meet peak demand periods. Additionally, Pacific also has strong financial support from local banks and a strong management team, with an excellent track record in successfully acquiring and integrating small acquisitions. Pacific also has a good reputation for high-quality products and customer service, as well as on-time delivery. Finally, Pacific has a low cost of goods sold when compared to the competition. Pacific's major weakness is that it does not possess any cutting-edge/trendy labels. Furthermore, their management team lacks the ability to develop trendy brands.

ACQUISITION PLAN

Objectives

Pacific's management objectives are to grow sales, improve profit margins, and to increase its brand life cycle by acquiring a cutting-edge surfware retailer with a trendy brand image. Pacific intends to improve its operating margins by increasing its sales of trendy clothes under the newly acquired brand name, while obtaining these clothes from its own low-cost production sources.

Tactics

Pacific would prefer to use its stock to complete an acquisition, because it is currently short of cash and wishes to use its borrowing capacity to fund future working capital requirements. Pacific's target debt-to-equity ratio is 3 to 1. Pacific desires a friendly takeover of an existing surfwear company in order to facilitate integration and avoid a potential "bidding war." The target will be evaluated on the basis of profitability, target markets, distribution channels, geographic markets, existing inventory, market brand recognition, price range and overall "fit" with Pacific. Pacific will locate this surfwear company by analyzing the surfwear industry, reviewing industry literature and making discrete inquiries relative to the availability of various firms to board members, law firms, and accounting firms. Pacific would prefer an asset purchase because of the potentially favorable impact on cash flow, and because it is concerned about unknown liabilities that might be assumed if it acquired the stock.

Pacific's screening criteria for identifying potential acquisition candidates include the following:

1. Industry: Garment industry targeting young men, teens, and boys
2. Product: Cutting-edge, trendy surfwear product line
3. Size: Revenue ranging from $5 to $10 million
4. Profit: Minimum of break-even on operating earnings for fiscal year 1999
5. Management: Company with management expertise in brand and image building
6. Leverage: Maximum debt-to-equity ratio of 3 to 1

After a review of fourteen companies, Pacific's management determined that SurferDude best satisfied their criteria. SurferDude is a widely recognized brand in the surfer sports apparel line, marginally profitable, sales of $7 million, and a debt-to-equity ratio of 3 to 1. SurferDude's current lackluster profitability reflects a significant advertising campaign undertaken during the last several years.

Based on financial information provided by SurferDude, industry averages, and comparable companies, the estimated purchase price ranges from $1.5 million to $15.0 million. The maximum price reflects the full impact of anticipated synergy. The price range was estimated using several valuation methods.

DISCOUNTED CASH FLOW

On a stand-alone basis, sales for both Pacific and SurferDude are projected to increase at a compound annual average rate of 20% during the next

5 years. SurferDude's sales growth assumes that its advertising expenditures in 1998 and 1999 have created a significant brand image, thus increasing future sales and gross profit margins. Pacific's sales growth rate reflects the recent licensing of several new apparel product lines. Consolidated sales of the combined companies are expected to grow at an annual growth rate of 25% due to the sales and distribution synergies created between the two companies.

The discount factor was derived using different methods, such as the buildup method or the CAPM. Because this was a private company, the buildup method was utilized and then supported by the CAPM. At 12%, the specific business risk premium is assumed to be somewhat higher than the 9% historical average difference between the return on small stocks and the risk-free return due to the capricious nature of the highly style-conscious surf-ware industry. The marketability discount is assumed to be a relatively modest 20%, because Pacific is acquiring a controlling interest in SurferDude. After growing at a compound annual average growth rate of 25% during the next 5 years, the sustainable long-term growth rate in SurferDude's stand-alone revenue is assumed to be 8%.

The buildup calculation included the following factors:

	%
Risk-free rate:	6.00
Market risk premium to invest in stocks:	5.50
Specific business risk premium:	12.00
Marketability discount:	20.00
Discount rate	43.5
Long-term growth rate	8.00
Capitalization rate	35.5

The CAPM method supported the buildup method. One comparable company, Apparel Tech, had a β estimated by Yahoo.Marketguide.com to be 4.74, which results in a k_e of 32.07 for this comparable company. The weighted average cost of capital using a target debt-to-equity ratio of 3–1 for the combined companies is estimated to be 26%.

The stand-alone values of SurferDude and Pacific assume that fixed expenses will decrease as a percentage of sales due to economies of scale. Pacific will outsource production through its parent's overseas facilities, thus significantly reducing the cost of goods sold. SurferDude's administrative expenses are expected to decrease from 25% of sales to 18% as only senior managers and the design staff are retained.

The sustainable growth rate for the terminal period for both the stand-alone and the consolidated models is a relatively modest 8%. Pacific believes this growth rate is reasonable considering the growth potential throughout the world. Although Pacific and SurferDude's current market concentration resides largely in the United States, it is forecasted that the combined companies will develop a global presence, with a particular emphasis in developing markets. The value of the combined companies including synergies equals $15.0 million, with the terminal value representing 71.2% of the total value of the company.

Developing an Initial Offer Price

Using price-to-cash flow multiples to develop an initial offer price, the target was valued on a stand-alone basis using an industry wide multiple of 16.42, and a multiple of 4.51 for a comparable publicly held company called Stage II Apparel Corp. Using these multiples, the stand-alone valuation of SurferDude ranges from $621,000 to $2,263,000, excluding synergies.

NEGOTIATING STRATEGY

Pacific expects to initially offer $2.25 million and close at $3.0 million. Pacific's management believes that SurferDude can be purchased at a modest price when compared to anticipated synergy, because an all-stock transaction would give SurferDude's management ownership of between 25 and 30% of the combined companies. All of SurferDude's management range in age between 35 and 40 years old and are expected to be attracted by the significant upside growth potential of the combined companies.

INTEGRATION

A transition team consisting of two Pacific and two SurferDude managers will be given full responsibility for consolidating the businesses following closing. A senior Pacific manager will direct the integration team. Once an agreement of purchase and sale has been signed, the team's initial responsibilities will be to first contact and inform employees and customers of SurferDude that operations will continue as normal until the close of the transaction. As an inducement to remain through closing, Pacific intends to offer severance packages for those SurferDude employees who will be terminated following the consolidation of the two businesses. The transition team's postacquisition responsibilities include communicating Pacific's plans to both their own and SurferDude's customers, as well as directing the elimination of duplicate administrative overhead.

Source: Adapted from Contino, Costa, Deyhimy, and Hu, 1999.

REVERSE MERGERS

Many small businesses fail each year. In a number of cases, all that remains is a business with no significant assets or operations. Such companies are referred to as shell corporations. Shell corporations may also be part of a deliberate business strategy in which a corporate legal structure is formed in anticipation of future financing, a merger, joint venture, or some other infusion of operating assets.

THE VALUE OF CORPORATE SHELLS

Is there any value in shells resulting from corporate failure or bankruptcy? The answer may seem surprising, but it is a resounding yes. Merging with an existing corporate shell of a formerly publicly traded company may be a reasonable alternative for a firm wanting to go public that is unable to provide the 2 years of audited financial statements required by the SEC or unwilling to incur the costs of going public. Thus, merging with a shell corporation may represent an effective alternative to an initial public offering for a small firm (see Exhibit 9-3).

EXHIBIT 9-3. GHS HELPS ITSELF BY AVOIDING AN IPO

In 1999, GHS, Inc., a little known supplier of medical devices, engineered a reverse merger to avoid the time-consuming, disclosure-intensive, and costly process of an initial public offering to launch its new Internet-based self-help web site. GHS spun off its medical operations as a separate company to its shareholders. The remaining shell is being used to launch a "self-help" web site, with self-help guru Anthony Robbins as its CEO. The shell corporation will be financed by $3 million it had on hand as GHS and will receive another $15 million from a private placement. With the inclusion of Anthony Robbins as the first among many brand names in the self-help industry that it hopes to feature on its site, its stock soared from $.75 per share to more than $12 between May and August 1999.

Robbins, who did not invest anything in the venture, has stock in the new company valued at $276 million. His contribution to the company is the exclusive online rights to his name, which it will use to develop Internet self-help seminars, chat rooms, and e-commerce sites.

Source: Bloomberg.com, 1999.

AVOIDING THE COSTS OF GOING PUBLIC

Direct issuance costs associated with going public include the underwriter spread (i.e., the selling price to the public less the proceeds to the company), as well as administrative and regulatory costs. The underwriter spread can range from less than 1% of gross proceeds for a high-quality company to more than 8% for lower quality companies. Administrative and regulatory fees consist of legal and accounting fees, taxes, and the cost of SEC registration. For offerings less than $10 million in size, total direct issuance costs may exceed 10% of gross proceeds. For equity issues between $20 and $50 million in size, these costs average less than 5% of gross proceeds and less than 3% for those issues larger than $200 million (Hansen: 1986).

Direct issuance costs are higher for common stock than for preferred stock issues, and direct costs of preferred issues are higher than those of debt issues. The difference in costs reflects the differences in risk to the underwriters. Investment bankers normally incur greater marketing expenses for common stock than for preferred stock or debt issues. Indirect costs include the cost of management time associated with new security offerings and the cost of underpricing a new equity issue below the current market value. The latter occurs because of the uncertainty surrounding its true value and the desire to ensure that the issue is a success. Underpricing results in significant amounts of money being "left on the table" (Ritter: 1987).

EXPLOITING INTANGIBLE VALUE

Shell corporations may also be attractive for investors interested in capitalizing on the intangible value associated with the existing corporate shell. This could include name recognition; licenses, patents, and other forms of intellectual properties; and underutilized assets such as warehouse space and fully depreciated equipment with some economic life remaining. Exhibit 9-4 illustrates one such instance.

EXHIBIT 9-4. THE SHELL GAME

ShellCo, a company widely known for providing security, cleaning, and office plant maintenance services to businesses, sold substantially all of its operating assets for cash at a significant gain for its shareholders. With few earnings-generating assets remaining, the company was essentially a corporate shell. Its primary assets following the sale include its reputation, a small office building that it owns free and clear of any liens, office furniture and equipment, several trucks, and all the state and local licenses necessary to do business in its municipality. The firm's monthly payments on a long-term lease negotiated some years earlier on prime commercial warehouse space are two-thirds of the currently prevailing lease terms for comparable space. The company name is widely recognized in the local business community and is synonymous with quality and reliability. The company has cash balances in excess of working capital requirements of $50,000.

The firm's dilemma is that without sufficient revenue it will have to liquidate its operations and force existing stockholders to incur additional tax

---

liabilities. As an alternative to liquidation, the firm hires a local business broker to solicit other companies, which may have an interest in the corporate shell.

The business broker is charged with the responsibility of finding potential buyers who see value in the firm's name and reputation, valuable lease terms, office building, furniture and fixtures, as well as licenses and regulatory approvals. The broker understands that in any likely transaction, the excess cash would be distributed to current shareholders and would therefore have no value to potential acquirers. The broker develops a list of local firms in the same or similar business as the shell corporation. The list includes other commercial security, cleaning, pest control operations, food, custodial, and temporary employment services, which might be interested in growing their existing businesses or expanding their service offering to their current customers or ShellCo's former customers.

The broker is optimistic that a suitable buyer can be found. The current ShellCo stockholders are very interested in minimizing tax liabilities and dispensing with the inconvenience and risk of liquidation, which would involve the sale of the building, subleasing of the leased commercial office space, and disposal of office furniture, fixtures, and other miscellaneous assets. Potential buyers will be interested in the opportunity to utilize ShellCo's brand name in the local community, to dispense with the expense and aggravation of obtaining licenses and other regulatory approvals, the favorable lease terms, and the office building. The broker begins to make initial contacts of the potential interested parties with these factors woven into a compelling sales pitch.

CALCULATING OWNERSHIP SHARE: THE VENTURE CAPITAL METHOD

Historically, venture capitalists (VCs) have been among the few willing to invest in firms that have no prospect of earnings for an extended period of time. The investment technique employed by VCs to determine their appropriate share of equity involves estimating net income in the year in which the investor plans to suspend investment and harvest the business. The VC calculates the terminal value at the "harvest" year by multiplying the projected net income for that year by the appropriate P/E, determined by studying current multiples of companies with similar characteristics. The terminal value is then discounted to the present using discounts rates of 35–80%. The investor's required ownership percentage (IOR) is based on the initial investment and is calculated by dividing the initial investment by the estimated present value (Sahlman, 1988). The IOR equation for a terminal value n periods in the future can be shown as follows:

$$\text{IOR} = \frac{I_R}{[(P/E)_{TV} \times NI_{TV}]/(1 + i)^n}$$

where

IOR = Investor's required ownership percentage

I_R = Required initial investment in dollars

$(P/E)_{TV}$ = Projected price/earnings ratio for terminal year

NI_{TV} = Terminal year's net income

i = Venture capitalist's cost of capital or hurdle rate

EXHIBIT 9-5. CALCULATING OWNERSHIP SHARE: THE VENTURE CAPITAL METHOD

Assume a start-up company is seeking $3 million in initial financing from a VC group. The VC requires a 50% compound annual average return, expects to hold the investment for 7 years, projects that the firm which is currently losing money, will earn $3 million in net income in the 7th year. After looking at current multiples of net income for comparable firms, the VC estimates the P/E in the seventh year to be 30. What is the ownership position (OP) required by the VC?

$$OP = \frac{\$3}{(3 \times 30)/(1 + .5)^7}$$

$$= \frac{\$3}{90/17.09}$$

$$= .57$$

Implication: The venture capitalist will demand a 57% share of equity in the start-up business in exchange for $3 million. Note that a higher discount rate would result in a larger share of owner's equity demanded by the VC.

USING LEVERAGED EMPLOYEE STOCK OWNERSHIP PLANS TO BUY PRIVATE COMPANIES

An ESOP is a means whereby a corporation can make tax-deductible contributions of cash or stock into a trust. The assets are allocated to employees and are not taxed until withdrawn by employees. ESOPs are generally required to invest at least 50% of their assets in employer stock. There are three types of ESOPs recognized by the 1974 Employee Retirement Income Security Act:

(1) leveraged (ESOP borrows to purchase qualified employer securities); (2) leverageable (ESOP is authorized but not required to borrow); and (3) nonleveraged (ESOP may not borrow funds).

FINANCIAL INCENTIVES

The incentives for firms, lenders, and employees to participate in ESOPs are substantial. Both the interest and principal of ESOP loans are tax deductible to the sponsoring firm. Dividends paid on stock contributed to ESOPs are also deductible, if they are used to repay ESOP debt. Effective in 1983, tax credits equal to .5 percent of covered payroll can be used by the sponsoring firm if contributions in that amount are made to the ESOP. Banks, insurance companies, and investment companies can reduce their taxable income by 50% of their income earned on loans to ESOPs that own more than 50% of the sponsoring firm's stock. Employees accumulate on a tax-deferred basis common equity in the sponsoring firm. This may be helpful in attracting, retaining, and motivating employees.

THE PROCESS

Employees commonly use leveraged ESOPs to buy out owners of private companies, who have most of their net worth in the firm. The firm establishes an ESOP. The owner sells at least 30% of his stock to the ESOP, which pays for the stock with borrowed funds. The owner may invest the proceeds and defer taxes if the investment is made within twelve months of the sale of the stock to the ESOP; the ESOP owns at least 30% of the firm; and neither the owner nor his family participates in the ESOP. The firm makes tax-deductible contributions to the ESOP in an amount sufficient to repay interest and principal. Shares held by the ESOP are distributed to employees as the loan is repaid. As the outstanding loan balance is reduced, the shares are allocated to employees who eventually own the firm.

ANALYZING PRIVATE
SHAREHOLDER RETURNS

In contrast to the mountain of empirical studies of the impact of M&A activity on public company shareholders, there are very few rigorous studies of privately held companies because of the limited availability of data. Chang (1998) in a study of the returns to public company shareholders when they acquire privately held firms found an average positive 2.6% abnormal return for shareholders of bidding firms for stock offers but not for cash transactions. Chang's sample consisted of 281 transactions, of which 131 were cash offers, 100 stock offers, and the remainder a combination of stock and cash, from 1981 to 1992.

The finding of positive abnormal returns earned by buyers using stock to acquire private companies is in sharp contrast with the negative abnormal returns earned by bidders using stock to acquire publicly traded companies (see Chapter 3, this volume). Chang (1998) notes that ownership of privately held companies tends to be highly concentrated, such that a stock exchange tends to create a few very large stockholders. Close monitoring of management and the acquired firm's performance may contribute to abnormal positive returns experienced by firms bidding for private firms. This conclusion is consistent with studies of returns to companies that issue stock and convertible debt in private placements (Hertzel and Smith: 1993; Wruck: 1989; and Fields and Mais: 1991). It is generally argued that in private placements large shareholders are effective monitors of managerial performance, thereby enhancing the prospects of the acquired firm (Demsetz and Lehn: 1996).

THINGS TO REMEMBER

Valuing private companies tends to be more challenging than efforts to value public companies. The current value of a private company can be very difficult to obtain because of the absence of published price information that is readily available for publicly traded companies. The problem is made more difficult because there is generally very little published information about the firm produced by sources external to the privately held firm. The data provided by sources within the firm are often confusing and distorted. Private firms tend to focus on minimizing taxes by understating reported income. Substantial effort is often required to restate the data to determine actual current profitability.

The data that are available are often inaccurate and out-of-date and presented in an inconsistent manner because of poor reporting systems within private companies. The absence of internal controls in many private firms means that fraud or waste may go largely undetected. Private firms often face problems that may be unique to their size and market position. These include inadequate management talent, lack of sophistication, limited access to capital and distribution channels, as well as a limited ability to influence customers, suppliers, unions, and regulators.

Owners considering the sale of their firms may overstate revenue by inadequately adjusting for product returns. Other ploys used to inflate revenue include booking as revenue products not yet shipped or received by the customer, as well as counting revenue as earned in the current accounting period that should have been spread over a number of periods. Costs may be overstated or understated. Common examples of overstatement include above-market salaries and benefits for family members and expenses paid by the firm for services largely enjoyed by the owner and his family. Areas that are frequently understated include employee training, advertising, safety, and environmental clean-up.

Although many small businesses have few hard assets, they may have substantial intangible value in areas that are commonly overlooked. These areas include the following: customer lists, intellectual property, licenses and regulatory approvals, distributor agreements, franchises, supply contracts, leases, and employment contracts.

In view of these considerations, it is crucial to restate the firm's financial reports to determine the current period's actual profitability. Once this has been achieved, comparisons with similar publicly traded firms or projections of cash flow to determine value will be more meaningful.

Revenue Ruling 59–60 describes factors the IRS and the tax courts think are relevant in valuing privately held companies. They should be viewed largely as guidelines, as they tend to be incomplete and in some instances of limited value. Nonetheless, in a court of law, the valuation professional may be called upon to address these issues. Historically, the tax courts have applauded the use of the comparable companies' approach to valuation of private companies, but their interpretation of what constitutes a truly comparable company has varied.

Fair market value is the cash value that a willing buyer or seller would accept for a business assuming they both have access to all necessary information and that neither party is under duress. Fair value is a term applied whenever public markets for purposes of valuing the firm simply do not exist and the value is estimated based on the informed judgment of appraisers.

The capitalization rate is equivalent to the discount rate when the firm's earnings or cash flows are not expected to grow. When earnings or cash flow are expected to grow at a constant rate, the capitalization rate equals the difference between the discount rate and the projected constant rate of growth. The capitalization rate may be estimated using the CAPM, cost of capital, accounting returns, P/E ratio, and the buildup method. The latter equals the sum of the risk-free rate, the premium required to induce investors to invest in equities, the premium required to induce investment in a specific stock, and the marketability discount.

Empirical evidence suggests that marketability discounts generally lie in a range of 33 to 50%, although factors specific to the firm could result in discounts outside of this range. Although largely subjective, the discounts are estimated by looking at the difference between the prices of restricted and nonrestricted stock for comparable companies or the spread between the price of sales of the stock that took place prior to an IPO and the actual IPO price. The size of the adjustment should reflect the degree of control the equity interest has in the firm. The value of a controlling interest should be discounted less than that of a minority interest.

CHAPTER DISCUSSION QUESTIONS

9-1. Why is it more difficult to value privately held companies than those that are publicly traded?

9-2. What factors should be considered in adjusting target company data?

9-3.   What is the capitalization rate and how does it relate to the discount rate?

9-4.   What are the common ways of estimating the capitalization rate?

9-5.   What is the marketability discount and what are common ways of estimating this discount?

9-6.   Give examples of private company costs that might be understated and explain why.

9-7.   How can an analyst determine if the target firm's costs and revenues are understated or overstated?

9-8.   What is the difference between the concept of fair market value and fair value?

9-9.   What is the importance of Revenue Ruling 59–60?

9-10. Why might shell corporations have value?

CHAPTER BUSINESS CASE

CASE STUDY 9-2. VALUING
A PRIVATELY HELD COMPANY

Background

BigCo is interested in acquiring PrivCo, whose owner desires to retire. The firm is 100% owned by the current owner. PrivCo has revenues of $10 million and an EBIT of $2 million in the preceding year. The market value of the firm's debt is $5 million; the book value of equity is $4 million. For publicly traded firms in the same industry, the average D/E ratio is .4 (based on the market value of debt and equity), and the marginal tax rate is 40%. Typically, the ratio of the market value of equity to book value for these firms is 2. The average β of publicly traded firms that are in the same business is 2.00.

Capital expenditures and depreciation amounted to $.3 million and $.2 million in the prior year. Both items are expected to grow at the same rate as revenues for the next 5 years. Capital expenditures and depreciation are expected to be equal beyond 5 years (i.e., capital spending will be internally funded). Due to excellent working capital management practices, the change in working capital is expected to be essentially zero throughout the forecast period and beyond. The revenues of this firm are expected to grow 15% annually for the next 5 years, and 5% per year after that. Net income is expected to increase 15% a year for the next 5 years and 5% thereafter. The 10-year treasury bond rate is 6%. The pretax cost of debt for a nonrated firm is 10%. No adjustment is made in the calculation of the cost of equity for a marketability discount.

Estimate the shareholder value of the firm.

A solution to this case is provided in the back of this book.

REFERENCES

Bloomberg.com, "Self-Help Goes on the Internet," August 14, 1999.

Chang, Saeyoung, "Takeovers of Privately Held Targets, Methods of Payment, and Bidder Returns," *Journal of Finance, 53*(3), June 1998.

Contino, Maria, Domenic Costa, Lauri Deyhimy, and Jenny Hu, Loyola Marymount University, MBAF 624, Los Angeles, CA, Fall 1999.

Demsetz, Harold, and Kenneth Lehn, "The Structure of Corporate Ownership: Causes and Consequences," *Journal of Political Economy, 93,* 1996, pp. 1155–1177.

Emory, John D., "The Value of Marketability as Illustrated in Initial Public Offerings of Common Stock," *Business Valuation News,* September 1985, pp. 21–24.

Estate of James C. Hall v. Commissioner, 92 T.C. 19 (1989).

Fields, L. Paige, and Eric L. Mais, "The Valuation Effects of Private Placements of Convertible Debt," *Journal of Finance, 46,* 1991, pp. 1925–1932.

Gelman, Martin, "An Economist-Financial Analyst's Approach to Valuing Stock of a Closely Held Company," *Journal of Taxation,* June 1972, pp. 46–53.

Hansen, Robert, "Evaluating the Costs of a new Equity Issue," *Midland Corporate Finance Journal,* Spring 1986, pp. 42–55.

Hertzel, Michael, and Richard L. Smith, "Market Discounts and Shareholder Gains for Placing Equity Privately," *Journal of Finance, 48,* 1993, pp. 459–485.

Ibbotson, Roger, *Stocks, Bonds, Bills, and Inflation: Classic Edition Yearbook,* Ibbotson Associates: Chicago, Illinois, 2000. Available: www.ibbotson.com

Institutional Investor Study Report, Securities and Exchange Commission (Washington, D.C.: U.S. Government Printing Office), Document No. 93–64, March 10, 1971.

Kaplan, Steven N., and Richard S. Ruback, "The Valuation of Cash Flow Forecasts," *Journal of Finance, 50*(4), September 1995, pp. 1059–1094.

Maher, J. Michael, "Discounts for Lack of Marketability for Closely Held Business Interests," *Taxes, 54*(9), September 1976, pp. 562–571.

Northern Trust Company v. Commissioner, 87 T.C. 349 (1986).

Pratt, Shannon P., Robert F. Reilly (Contributor), and Robert P. Scheweihs (Contributor), *Valuing a Business: The Analysis and Appraisal of Closely Held Companies* (3rd ed.), Toronto: Irwin Professional Publishers, October 1995.

Pratt, Shannon, *Cost of Capital: Estimation and Applications,* New York: John Wiley & Sons, 1998.

Ritter, J. B., "The Costs of Going Public," *Journal of Financial Economics,* December 1987, pp. 269–281.

Sahlman, A. L., "A Method for Valuing High Risk Long-Term Investments: The Venture Capital Method," Note 9-288-006, Harvard Business School, 1988, pp. 2–4.

Sherman, Andrew J., *Mergers and Acquisitions from A to Z, Strategic and Practical Guidance for Small- and Middle-Market Buyers and Sellers,* New York: AMACOM, 1998.

Trout, Robert R., "Estimation of the Discount Associated with the Transfer of Restricted Securities," *Taxes, 55,* June 1977, pp. 381–385.

Wruck, Karen H., "Equity Ownership Concentration and Firm Value: Evidence from Private Equity Financing," *Journal of Financial Economics, 23,* 1989, pp. 3–28.

10

STRUCTURING THE DEAL:

PAYMENT, LEGAL, TAX, AND
ACCOUNTING CONSIDERATIONS

"If you can't convince them, confuse them."
—*Harry S. Truman*

It was apparent that the fast-paced, highly informal, and entrepreneural environment of HiTech Corporation would not readily blend with the more structured and reserved environment of BigCo., Inc. Nonetheless, BigCo.'s senior management knew that they needed access to certain patents owned by HiTech to become more cost competitive in the firm's primary markets. Concerned about creating competitors, HiTech chose not to license its technologies to others. Consequently, BigCo. felt compelled to gain complete control of these patents and any further updates to this technology by acquiring HiTech.

As Chief Executive Officer of BigCo., Kristen Bailey and her staff studied the demographic profile of HiTech shareholders and employees. As a publicly traded company, considerable information was available through Securities Exchange Commission filings, newspaper articles, and presentations made by HiTech's senior managers at trade association meetings. She understood that almost one-half of the stock was held by the firm's founders, about one-fourth by employees whose average age was about 30, and the remainder by unaffiliated investors and institutions. At last year's stockholders' meeting, HiTech's management, while responding to questions from attendees, indicated that remaining independent would better serve the shareholders' interests at this stage of the firm's development. After all, the firm was less than 10 years old, and management believed they were on the verge of a technological breakthrough whose full commercial value could not yet be determined. Management did acknowledge that once the technology had been developed, they might consider being acquired or partnering with another firm which had excess manufacturing capacity and effective distribution channels that HiTech currently lacked.

Kristen believed that, once BigCo.'s bid for HiTech become public knowledge, BigCo.'s competitors' were likely to make offers for HiTech. To preempt its competitors, Kristen reasoned that BigCo.'s initial offer would have to be structured to meet as many of the primary needs of HiTech's shareholders, managers, and employees as possible. By satisfying the concerns of management, BigCo. was more likely to gain their support in obtaining approval by HiTech's shareholders. Moreover, by meeting the needs of employees, BigCo. was more likely to minimize attrition once the transaction was closed.

Kristen recommended to her board of directors that BigCo. acquire all of the stock of HiTech to ensure that it would own the rights to the firm's existing and future intellectual property. She suggested that the BigCo.'s stock be used as the primary form of payment. By combining BigCo.'s state-of-the-art manufacturing facilities, which were only 65% utilized, and highly effective sales force with HiTech's technology, she believed that HiTech's shareholders and senior managers could be persuaded that the combined companies would be able to grow more rapidly than if HiTech remained independent. Moreover, by accepting stock, HiTech shareholders could defer the payment of capital gains taxes. This would be highly attractive to the founders whose average cost in the stock was very low. Moreover, in view of the relative youthfulness of the workforce, HiTech employees might jump at the chance to own an interest in the combined companies. Finally, BigCo. would assure HiTech managers that HiTech would be operated as a wholly owned subsidiary with minimal interference in its daily operations from BigCo.'s management.

Kristen received approval to proceed. Contact was made through a BigCo. board member who had served on an industry trade association board with HiTech's CEO. HiTech's CEO said that he was flattered by the proposal and would like to confer with his board before making a formal response. Kristen waited impatiently for the drama to unfold.

OVERVIEW

The form or structure of a transaction follows the determination of why a merger or acquisition is preferable to other options for implementing a business strategy and how the target company "fits" with the business strategy. Once the strategic fit is well understood and the preliminary financial analysis is satisfactory, it is time to consider how to properly structure the transaction. The process of deal structuring involves identifying the primary goals of the parties involved, the risks associated with satisfying those goals, alternative ways to attain those goals, and how to share risks. The appropriate deal structure is that which satisfies, subject to an acceptable level of risk, as many of the primary objectives of the parties involved as necessary to reach overall agreement.

In this chapter, the deal-structuring process is conceptualized as consisting of six interdependent components. These include the acquisition vehicle, the post-closing organization, the form of payment, the form of accounting, the form of acquisition, and tax structure. This chapter will only briefly address the form of the acquisition vehicle and postclosing organization, as these are discussed in some detail elsewhere in this book. The focus will be on the form of payment, form of accounting, form of acquisition, and tax structure and strategy. The chapter will also address the interrelatedness of payment, legal, tax, and accounting forms by illustrating how decisions made in one area affect other aspects of the overall deal structure.

THE DEAL-STRUCTURING PROCESS

The deal-structuring process is fundamentally about satisfying as many of the primary objectives of the parties involved and determining how risk will be shared. Risk sharing refers to the extent to which the acquirer assumes all, some, or none of the liabilities, disclosed or otherwise, of the target. The process can become horrifically complex in large transactions involving multiple parties, approvals, forms of payment, and sources of financing. Decisions made in one area inevitably impact other areas of the overall deal structure. Containing risk associated with a complex deal is analogous to catching a water balloon. Squeezing one end of the balloon simply forces the contents to shift elsewhere.

KEY COMPONENTS

Figure 10-1 summarizes the deal-structuring process. The process begins with addressing a set of key questions, whose answers greatly influence the primary components of the entire structuring process. Answers to these questions help to define initial negotiating positions, potential risks, options for managing risk, levels of tolerance for risk, and conditions under which the buyer or seller will "walk away" from the negotiations.

The *acquisition vehicle* refers to the legal structure used to acquire the target company. The *postclosing organization* or structure is the organizational and legal framework used to manage the combined businesses following the consummation of the transaction. Commonly used structures for both the acquisition vehicle and postclosing organization include the corporate or divisional, holding company, joint venture (JV), partnership, limited liability company (LLC), and employee stock ownership plan (ESOP) structures.

Although the two structures are often the same before and after completion of the transaction, the postclosing organization may differ from the acquisition vehicle depending upon the acquirer's strategic objectives for the combined firms. An acquirer may choose a corporate or divisional structure to purchase the target

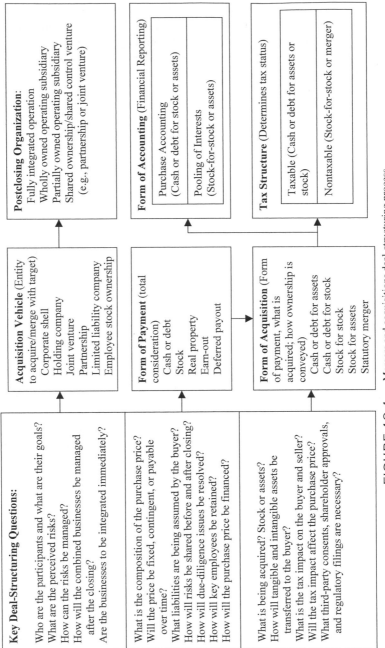

FIGURE 10-1. Mergers and acquisitions deal-structuring process.

firm and to rapidly integrate the acquired business to realize synergies. Alternatively, the acquirer may opt to undertake the transaction using a JV or partnership vehicle to share risk. Once the operation of the acquired entity is better understood, the acquirer may choose to buy out its partners and to operate within a corporate or divisional structure. Similarly, the acquirer may complete the transaction using a holding company legal structure. The acquirer may operate the acquired firm as a wholly owned subsidiary to preserve the attractive characteristics of its culture for an extended time period and later move to a more traditional corporate or divisional framework.

The *form of payment* or total consideration may consist of cash, common stock, debt, or a combination of all three types of payment. The payment may be fixed at a moment in time, contingent on the future performance of the acquired unit, or payable over time. The form of payment influences the selection of the appropriate form of acquisition. The *form of acquisition* reflects both what is being acquired (stock or assets) and the form of payment (cash, debt, or stock). As such, the form of acquisition largely determines the *form of accounting* (either pooling of interest or purchase) and the *tax structure* (taxable or nontaxable). In general, if the stock or assets of the target company are acquired with something other than the acquirer's stock, the purchase method of accounting must be used for financial reporting purposes. A transaction is usually taxable to the target firm's shareholders if the firm's assets or stock are purchased with some form of payment other than the acquirer's stock. The form of acquisition also defines how the ownership of assets will be conveyed from the seller to the buyer, either by rule of law as in a merger or through transfer and assignment as in a purchase of assets. These considerations are explored in considerably greater detail later in this chapter.

COMMON LINKAGES

For simplicity, many of the linkages or interactions, which reflect how decisions made in one area impact other aspects of deal, are not shown in Figure 10-1. Common linkages or interactions among various components of the deal structure are illustrated through examples described below.

Form of Payment Influences Choice of Acquisition Vehicle

If the buyer and seller agree on a price, the buyer may offer a purchase price that is contingent on the future performance of the target company. The buyer may choose to operate the acquired company as a wholly owned subsidiary within a holding company structure during the term of the "earn-out."

Form of Acquisition Impacts Acquisition Vehicle

If the form of acquisition is a statutory merger, all known and unknown or contingent liabilities are transferred to the buyer. Under these circumstances, the buyer may choose to change the form of the acquisition vehicle to one better able to protect the buyer from the liabilities of the target company, such as a holding company arrangement.

Tax Status Impacts Purchase Price

If the transaction is taxable to the target's shareholders, it is likely that the purchase price will be increased to compensate the target's shareholders for their tax liability. The increase in the purchase price may impact the form of payment. The acquirer may maintain the present value of the total cost of the acquisition by deferring some portion of the purchase price by altering the terms to include more debt or installment payments.

Form of Acquisition Impacts Purchase Price

The assumption of all seller liabilities through a merger may also induce the buyer to change the form of payment to lower the present value of the cost of the transaction. The buyer may also attempt to negotiate a lower overall purchase price.

Form of Accounting Impacts Form of Payment

To take advantage of the perceived benefits of a particular type of accounting treatment, such as the pooling of interests, the acquiring company may be willing to pay a higher premium for the target business. This may be necessary to induce the seller to agree to a stock-for-stock exchange, which is a key condition required to qualify for pooling of interests accounting.

FORM OF ACQUISITION VEHICLE

The acquisition vehicle is the legal entity used to acquire the target company and will generally continue to own and operate the acquired company after closing. Which form of legal entity is used has markedly different risk and tax implications for the acquirer. The various forms of potential acquisition vehicles are discussed in detail in Chapters 1 and 12. They include the corporate/divisional structure, LLCs, JV corporations, holding companies, general and limited liability partnerships (LLPs), and ESOPs.

CORPORATION (INCLUDING LLCs AND JVs)

The major advantage of the corporation structure is that the stockholders' liability is limited to the extent of their investment in corporation shares. The corporation is a more permanent form of legal organization than other types of legal entities, because the legal existence of the corporation is not affected by whether the stockholders sell their shares. The corporation also facilitates change of ownership, because the corporation continues to exist in its original form after shares are sold. Finally, the corporation is able to raise large amounts of capital, as a result of the limited liability of its shareholders. The major disadvantage of this structure is the potential for double taxation of dividends. The corporate structure or some variation is the most commonly used acquisition vehicle. In such an arrangement, the acquired company is generally integrated into an existing operating division within the corporation.

A limited liability corporation avoids double taxation and allows flexibility in allocating profits and losses. This type of legal framework is particularly attractive in situations such as JVs in which the target company is going to be owned by two or more unrelated parties. Used as an acquisition vehicle, the JV corporation offers a lower level of risk than a direct acquisition of the target firm by one of the JV corporate owners. By acquiring the target firm through the JV, the corporate investor limits the potential liability to the extent of their investment in the JV corporation.

HOLDING COMPANY

A holding company does not have to own the majority of the stock in another company to gain control. However, it must own at least 80% of the subsidiary's voting stock to receive dividends made to the parent tax-free and to be allowed to consolidate operating losses for tax purposes. Non-U.S. buyers intending to make additional acquisitions may prefer a holding company structure. The advantages of this structure over a corporate merger are the ability to control other companies by only owning a small portion of the company's voting stock and to gain this control without getting shareholder approval. The major disadvantages include multiple taxation whenever less than 80% of the subsidiary's stock is owned. Moreover, the holding company may become excessively leveraged due to the pyramiding effects of holding debt at various levels of the holding company.

PARTNERSHIPS

Partnerships spread the risk of an acquisition over a number of partners, avoid double taxation, and achieve flexibility in distributing profits and losses. However, they lack the continuity and financing flexibility of the corporate structure. Target firms may find partnership interests unattractive, because they are often illiquid.

EMPLOYEE STOCK OWNERSHIP PLANS

Sellers may create an ESOP to buy all or substantially all of the company. As noted in Chapter 1 (this volume), the leveraged ESOP uses borrowed funds either directly from the company or from a third-party lender based on a guarantee from the company, with the securities of the company used as collateral, to acquire the employer's securities. The loan is repaid by the ESOP from employer and employee contributions, as well as from any dividends paid on the employer's securities. A nonleveraged ESOP may consist of a stock bonus plan that purchases the employer's securities with funds the employer would have otherwise paid as some other form of compensation to employees (Sherman: 1998).

POSTCLOSING ORGANIZATION

What form the postclosing structure takes depends largely on the objectives of the acquiring company. If the acquirer is interested in integrating the target business immediately following closing, the corporate or divisional structure may be most desirable, because the acquirer is most likely to be able to gain the greatest control by using this structure. In other structures, such as JVs and partnerships, decision making may be slower or more contentious due to dispersed ownership. Decision making is more likely to depend on close cooperation and consensus building, which may slow efforts to rapidly integrate the acquired company (see Chapter 6, this volume).

In contrast, a holding company structure in which the acquired company is managed as a wholly owned subsidiary may be preferable when an earn-out is involved, the target is a foreign firm, or the acquirer is a financial investor. In an earn-out agreement, the acquired firm must be operated largely independently from other operations of the acquiring firm to minimize the potential for lawsuits. If the acquired firm fails to achieve the goals required to receive the earn-out payment, the acquirer may be sued for allegedly taking actions that prevented the acquired firm from reaching the necessary goals. When the target is a foreign firm, it is often appropriate to operate it separately from the rest of the acquirer's operations because of the potential disruption due to significant cultural differences. Prevailing laws in the foreign country may also impact the form of the organization. Finally, a financial buyer may use a holding company structure because they have no interest in operating the target firm for any length of time.

A partnership or JV structure may be appropriate if the risk associated with the target firm is believed to be high. Consequently, partners or JV owners can limit their financial exposure to the amount they have invested in the partnership or JV. The acquired firm may also benefit from being owned by a partnership or JV because of the expertise that may be provided by the different partners or owners. The availability of such expertise may actually reduce the overall risk of managing the business.

FORM OF PAYMENT
OR TOTAL CONSIDERATION

Determining the proper form of payment can be a surprisingly complicated exercise. Each form of payment can have significantly different implications for the parties involved in the transaction. The use of cash is the simplest and most commonly used means of payment for acquiring shares or assets. Although cash payments will generally result in an immediate tax liability for the target company's shareholders, there is no ambiguity about the value of the transaction as long as no portion of the payment is deferred.

NONCASH FORMS OF PAYMENT

The use of common equity may involve certain tax advantages for the parties involved. This is especially true for the selling company. However, the use of shares is much more complicated than cash, since it requires compliance with the prevailing security laws (see Chapter 2, this volume). Moreover, the acquirer's share price may suffer if investors believe that the newly issued shares will result in a long-term dilution in earnings per share (EPS) (i.e., a reduction in an individual shareholder's claim on future earnings).

The use of convertible preferred stock or debt can be attractive to both buyers and sellers. Convertible preferred provides some downside protection to sellers in the form of continuing dividends, while providing upside potential if the acquirer's common stock price increases above the conversion point. Acquirers find convertible debt attractive because of the tax deductibility of interest payments.

The major disadvantage in using securities of any type is that the seller may find them unattractive. Debt instruments may be unacceptable because of the perceived high risk of default associated with the issuer. When offered common equity, shareholders of the selling company may feel the growth prospects of the acquiring company's stock may be limited. Finally, debt or equity securities may be illiquid due to the small size of the resale market for these types of securities.

Other forms of payment include real property, rights to intellectual property, royalties, earn-outs, and contingent payments. Real property consists of such things as a parcel of real estate. So-called "like-kind" exchanges or swaps may have favorable tax consequences. Real property exchanges are most common in commercial real estate. Granting the seller access to valuable licenses or franchises limits the use of cash or securities at the time of closing; however, it does raise the possibility that the seller could become a future competitor. The use of debt or other types of deferred payments reduces the overall present value of the purchase price to the buyer by shifting some portion of the purchase price into the future.

CLOSING THE GAP ON PRICE

When buyers and sellers cannot reach agreement on purchase price, balance sheet adjustments, earn-outs, rights to intellectual property, licensing fees, and consulting agreements are commonly used.

Balance Sheet Adjustments

Balance sheet adjustments are most often used in purchases of assets when the elapsed time between the agreement on price and the actual closing date is lengthy.

This may be due to the need to obtain regulatory or shareholder approvals or a result of ongoing due diligence. During this period, balance sheet items, particularly those related to working capital, may change significantly. As indicated in Table 10-1, to protect the buyer or seller, the buyer reduces the total purchase price by an amount equal to the decrease in net working capital or shareholders' equity of the target company and increases the purchase price by any increase in these measures during this period. Buyers and sellers generally view purchase price adjustments as a form of insurance against any erosion or accretion in assets, such as receivables or inventories. Such adjustments protect the buyer from receiving a lower dollar value of assets than originally believed or the seller from transferring to the buyer more assets than expected. The actual payments are made between the buyer and seller after a comprehensive audit of the target's balance sheet by an independent auditor is completed sometime after closing.

Earn-Outs

Earn-outs are payments made subsequent to closing and are based upon the achievement of agreed-upon goals stipulated in the closing contract. Earn-outs are frequently employed whenever the buyer and seller cannot agree on the probable performance of the seller's business over some future period. The earn-out normally requires that the acquired business be operated as a wholly owned subsidiary of the acquiring company under the management of the former owners or key executives of the business. Both the buyer and seller are well advised to keep the calculation of such goals and resulting payments as simple as possible, as disputes frequently arise due to the difficulty in measuring actual performance to the goals.

Exhibit 10-1 illustrates how a simple earn-out formula could be constructed. The purchase price consists of two components. At closing, the seller receives a lump-sum payment of $100 million. The seller and the buyer agree to a baseline projection for a 3-year period and that the seller will receive a fixed multiple of the average annual performance of the acquired business in excess of the baseline projection. Thus, the earn-out provides an incentive for the seller to operate the business as effectively as possible. Normally, the baseline projection is what the buyer used to value the seller's business. Shareholder value for the buyer is created whenever the acquired business' actual performance exceeds the baseline projection and the multiple applied by investors at the end of the 3-year period exceeds

TABLE 10-1. Balance Sheet Adjustments

	Purchase price ($ Millions)			
	At time of negotiation	At closing	Purchase price reduction	Purchase price increase
If working capital equals	$110	$100	$10	
If working capital equals	$110	$125		$15

the multiple used to calculate the earn-out payment. This assumes that the baseline projection accurately values the business and that the buyer does not overpay. By multiplying the anticipated multiple investors will pay for operating cash flow at the end of the 3-year period by projected cash flow, it is possible to estimate the potential increase in shareholder value.

EXHIBIT 10-1: EARN-OUT AS PART OF THE PURCHASE PRICE

Purchase price

1. Lump sum payment at closing: The seller receives $100 million.
2. Earn-out payment: The seller receives four times the excess of the actual average annual net operating cash flow over the baseline projection at the end of 3 years.

Base year (First full year of ownership)	Year 1	Year 2	Year 3
Baseline projection (net cash flow)	$10	$12	$15
Actual performance (net cash flow)	$15	$20	$25

Earn-out at the end of 3 years[a]:

$$\frac{(\$15 - \$10) + (\$20 - \$12) + (\$25 - \$15)}{3} \times 4 = \$30.67$$

Potential increase in shareholder value[b]:

$$\left\{ \frac{(\$15 - \$10) + (\$20 - \$12) + (\$25 - \$15)}{3} \times 10 \right\} - \$30.67 = \$46$$

[a] The cash flow multiple of 4 applied to the earn-out is a result of negotiation prior to closing.

[b] The cash flow multiple of 10 applied to the potential increase in shareholder value for the buyer is the multiple the buyer anticipates that investors would apply to a 3 year average of actual operating cash flow at the end of the 3-year period.

Earn-outs tend to shift risk from the acquirer to the seller or acquired firm in that a higher price is paid only when the seller or acquired firm has met or exceeded certain performance criteria. However, earn-outs may also create some perverse results during implementation. Management motivation may be lost if the acquired firm does not perform well enough to achieve any payout under the earn-out formula or if the acquired firm substantially exceeds the performance targets, effectively guaranteeing the maximum payout under the plan.

Moreover, the management of the acquired firm may have an incentive to take actions not in the best interests of the acquirer. For example, management may cut back on certain expenses such as advertising and training to improve the operation's current cash flow performance. In addition, management may make only those investments that improve short-term profits at the expense of investments that may generate immediate losses but favorably impact profits in the long-term. As the end of the earn-out period approaches, management may postpone any investments at all in order to maximize their bonus under the earn-out plan.

Rights, Royalties, and Fees

Other forms of payment that can be used to close the gap between what the buyer is willing to offer and what the seller expects include such things as the rights to intellectual property, royalties from licenses, and fee-based consulting or employment agreements. Having the right to use a proprietary process or technology for free or at a below market rate may be of interest to the former owners who are considering pursuing business opportunities in which the process or technology would be useful. Note that such an arrangement, if priced at below market rates or if free to the seller, would represent taxable income to the seller. Obviously, such arrangements should be coupled with reasonable agreements not to compete in the same industry as their former firm.

Consulting or employment contracts are also widely used to provide ongoing or deferred payment to the former owners. Contracts may be extended to both the former owners and their family members. By spreading the payment of consulting fees or salary over a number of years, the seller may be able to reduce the income tax liability that might have resulted from receiving a larger lump-sum purchase price.

Table 10-2 summarizes the various forms of payment in terms of their advantages and disadvantages. Note the wide range of options available to satisfy the various needs of the parties to the transaction.

FORM OF ACQUISITION

The form of acquisition describes the mechanism for conveying ownership of assets or stock and associated liabilities from the target to the acquiring firm. Although the form of acquisition may vary widely, the most commonly used methods include the following: asset purchases, stock purchases, statutory mergers, stock-for-stock purchases, and stock-for-assets purchases (see Figure 10-2). Table 10-3 highlights the primary advantages and disadvantages of these alternative forms of acquisition.

TABLE 10-2. Form of Payment Risk Evaluation

Form of payment	Advantages[a]	Disadvantages[b]
Cash (including highly marketable securities)	*Buyer:* Simplicity. *Seller:* Ensures payment if acquirer's creditworthiness questionable.	*Buyer:* Must rely solely on protections afforded in contract to recover claims. *Seller:* Creates immediate tax liability.

Stock
  Common
  Preferred
  Convertible preferred
	Buyer: High P/E relative to seller's P/E increases value of combined businesses. *Seller:* Defers taxes and provides potential price increase. Retains interest in the business.	*Buyer:* Adds complexity; potential EPS dilution *Seller:* Potential decrease in purchase price if the value of equity received declines.

Debt
  Secured
  Unsecured
  Convertible
	Buyer: Interest expense tax deductible. *Seller:* Defers tax liability on principal.	*Buyer:* Adds complexity and increases leverage. *Seller:* Risk of default.

Performance-related earn-outs	*Buyer:* Shifts some portion of risk to seller. *Seller:* Potential for higher purchase price.	*Buyer:* May limit integration of businesses. *Seller:* Increases uncertainty of sales price.
Purchase price adjustments	*Buyer:* Protection from eroding values of working capital before closing. *Seller:* Protection from increasing values of working capital before closing.	*Buyer:* Audit expense. Buyer and seller often share audit costs. *Seller:* Audit expense.

Real property
  Real estate
  Plant and equipment
  Business or product line
	Buyer: Minimizes use of cash; potentially tax free, if exchange of substantially similar properties. *Seller:* May minimize tax liability.	*Buyer:* Opportunity cost. *Seller:* Real property may be illiquid.

Rights to intellectual property
  License
  Franchise
	Buyer: Minimizes cash use. *Seller:* Gains access to valuable rights and spreads taxable income over time.	*Buyer:* Potential for setting up new competitor. *Seller:* May be illiquid. Income taxed at ordinary rates.

Royalties from
  Licenses
  Franchises
	Buyer: Minimizes cash use. *Seller:* Spreads taxable income over time.	*Buyer:* Opportunity cost. *Seller:* Income taxed at ordinary rates.

Fee-based
  Consulting contract
  Employment agreement
	Buyer: Uses seller's expertise and removes seller as potential competitor for a limited time. *Seller:* Augments purchase price and allows seller to stay with the business.	*Buyer:* May involve de-motivated employees. *Seller:* Limits ability to compete in same line of business. Income taxed at ordinary rates.

[a] P/E, price-to-earnings ratio.
[b] EPS, earnings per share.

1. Asset Purchase: Acquirer buys all or a portion of the target's assets for cash, debt, or stock.

2. Stock Purchase: Target company shareholders sell their shares to the acquiring company for cash, debt, or stock and the target becomes a subsidiary of the acquirer.

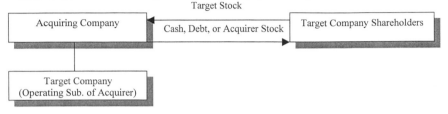

3. Statutory Merger: Acquirer exchanges stock, cash, or debt for the stock held by the target company's shareholders. Governed by state law.

4. Stock-for-Stock Purchase: Acquirer exchanges stock for target stock as an alternative to a merger.

5. Stock-for-Assets Purchase: Acquirer exchanges stock for all or substantially all of the assets of the target corporation. Target firm passes acquirer stock on to its shareholders.

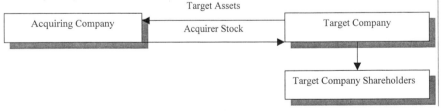

FIGURE 10-2.   Basic forms of acquisition.

Asset purchases involve the acquiring companys buying all or a portion of the target company's assets and assuming all, some, or none of the target's liabilities in exchange for cash or assets. Stock purchases involve the exchange of the

TABLE 10-3. Advantages and Disadvantages of Alternative Forms of Acquisition[a]

	Advantages	Disadvantages
Purchase of assets		
Buyer	• Allows targeted purchase of assets • Asset write-up • May renegotiate union and benefits agreements	• Lose NOLs and tax credits • Lose rights to intellectual property • May require consents to assignment of contracts
Seller	• Maintains corporate existence and ownership of unacquired assets • Retains NOLs and tax credits	• Potential double-taxation if shell liquidated • State transfer taxes • Necessity of disposing of unwanted residual assets
Purchase of stock		
Buyer	• Assets transfer automatically • May avoid need to get consents to assignment • Less documentation • NOLs and tax credits pass to buyer • No state transfer taxes	• Responsible for known and unknown liabilities • No asset write-up unless 338 election taken by buyer • Union and employee benefit agreements do not terminate • Potential for minority shareholders
Seller	• Favorable tax treatment for target shareholders if stock received • Liabilities generally pass to the buyer	• Loss of NOLs and tax credits • Favorable tax treatment lost if buyer adopts 338 election
Merger	• Stock and assets transfer automatically • No state transfer taxes • No minority shareholders	• May have to pay dissenting shareholders appraised value of stock • May be time consuming due to need for shareholder approvals
Stock-for-stock transaction	• May operate target company as a subsidiary	• May postpone realization of synergies
Stock-for-assets transaction	• Favorable tax treatment for target shareholders	• May dilute acquiring shareholders' ownership position
Staged transactions	• Provides greater strategic flexibility	• May postpone realization of synergies

[a] NOLs, net operating loss carryovers.

target's stock for either cash, debt, or the stock of the acquiring company. A statutory merger involves the exchange of shares, in which one firm ceases to exist. The statutes of the state or states, in which the parties to the transaction are located, govern such transactions. Stock-for-stock or stock-for-assets transactions represent alternatives to a merger.

PURCHASE OF ASSETS

Advantages: Buyer's Perspective

Buyers can be selective as to which assets of the target company will be purchased. The buyer is generally not responsible for the seller's liabilities, unless specifically assumed under the contract. However, the buyer can be held responsible for certain liabilities such as environmental claims, property taxes, and in some states substantial pension liabilities and product liability claims. To protect against such risks, buyers usually insist on seller indemnification (i.e., payment of damages resulting from such claims). Of course, such indemnification is worthwhile only as long as the seller remains solvent.

Acquired assets may be revalued to market value on the closing date under the purchase method of accounting. This increase or "step-up" in the tax basis of the acquired assets to fair market value provides for higher depreciation and amortization expense deductions for tax purposes. Such expense deductions are said to *shelter* pretax income from taxation. Buyers are generally free of any undisclosed or contingent liabilities. The asset purchase normally results in the termination of union agreements, thereby providing an opportunity to renegotiate agreements viewed as too restrictive. Benefit plans may be maintained or terminated at the discretion of the acquirer. The acquiring company will frequently terminate existing plans if it feels it can obtain comparable benefits from other providers on better terms. Failure by the acquiring company to provide comparable benefits can result in the loss of key employees.

Advantages: Seller's Perspective

Sellers are able to maintain their corporate existence and hence ownership of tangible assets not acquired by the buyer and of intangible assets such as licenses, franchises, and patents. The seller retains the right to use the corporate identity in subsequent marketing programs, unless ceded to the buyer as part of the transaction. The seller also retains the right to use all tax credits and accumulated net operating losses, which can be used to shelter future income from taxes.

Disadvantages: Buyer's Perspective

The buyer loses the seller's net operating losses and tax credits. Rights to assets such as licenses, franchises, and patents cannot be transferred to buyers. Such rights are viewed as belonging to the owners of the business (i.e., stockholders of the target company). These rights can sometimes be difficult to transfer because of the need to obtain consent from the agency (e.g., U.S. Patent Office) issuing the rights. The buyer must seek the consent of customers and vendors to transfer existing contracts to the buyer. The transaction is more complex and costly, as acquired assets must be listed on appendices to the definitive agreement and the sale of and titles to each asset transferred must be recorded. Moreover, a lender's consent may be required if the assets to be sold are being used as collateral for loans.

Disadvantages: Seller's Perspective

Taxes may also be a problem as the seller may be subject to double taxation. If the tax basis in the assets or stock is low, the seller may experience a sizable gain on the sale. In addition, if the corporation is subsequently liquidated, the seller may be responsible for the recapture of taxes deferred due to the use of accelerated rather than straight-line depreciation. If the number of assets transferred is large, the amount of state transfer taxes may become onerous. Whether the seller or the buyer actually pays the transfer taxes or they are shared is negotiable.

PURCHASE OF STOCK

Advantages: Buyer's Perspective

All assets are transferred with the target company's stock resulting in less need for documentation to complete the transaction. This sometimes enables the transaction to be completed more rapidly than a purchase of assets. State asset transfer taxes may be avoided with a purchase of shares. Net operating losses and tax credits pass to the buyer with the purchase of stock. The right of the buyer to use the target's name, licenses, franchises, patents, and permits is also preserved. Furthermore, the purchase of the seller's stock provides for the continuity of contracts and corporate identity. This obviates the need to renegotiate contracts and enables the acquirer to utilize the brand recognition that may be associated with the name of the target firm. However, some customer and vendor contracts, as well as permits, may stipulate that the buyer must gain consent before the contract is transferred.

Advantages: Seller's Perspective

The seller is able to defer paying taxes. If stock is received from the acquiring company, taxes are paid by the target's shareholders only when the stock is sold. All obligations, disclosed or otherwise, transfer to the buyer. This advantage for the seller is usually attenuated by the insistence by the buyer that the seller indemnify the buyer from damages resulting from any undisclosed liability. The applicable tax is the more favorable capital gains rate. Finally, the seller is not left with the problem of disposing of assets not purchased by the acquiring company, which the seller does not wish to retain.

Disadvantages: Buyer's Perspective

The buyer is liable for all unknown, undisclosed, or contingent liabilities. The seller's tax basis is carried over to the buyer at historical cost, unless the seller consents to take certain tax code elections. These elections can potentially create a tax liability for the seller and, therefore, they are rarely used. Consequently, there is no step-up in the cost basis of assets and no tax shelter is created. Dissenting shareholders have the right to have their shares appraised, with the option of being paid the appraised value of their shares or to remain as minority shareholders. The purchase of stock does not terminate existing union agreements or employee benefit plans.

Disadvantages: Seller's Perspective

The seller cannot pick and choose the assets to be retained and loses all net operating losses and tax credits.

MERGERS

With a merger, two corporations are combined and one disappears. Mergers require approval from the target's board of directors and shareholders and a public filing with the state in which the merger is to be consummated. The purchase price can consist of cash, stock, or debt, giving the acquiring company more latitude in how it will pay for the purchase of the target company's stock.

Advantages

The primary advantage is that the transfer of assets and the exchange of stock between the acquirer and the target happen automatically by "rule of law." Target company shareholders cannot retain their stock; however, as with the purchase of stock, dissenting shareholders have the right to have their shares appraised and to be paid the appraised value rather than what is being offered by the acquiring firm. Transfer taxes are not paid, because there are no asset transfer documents. However, contracts, licenses, patents, and permits do not automatically transfer. This transfer can be accomplished by merging a subsidiary set up by the buyer with the target corporation. The subsidiary can be merged with the parent immediately following closing.

Disadvantages

Mergers of public corporations can be costly and time consuming because of the need to obtain shareholder approval and to conform to proxy regulations (see Chapter 3, this volume). The resulting delay can open the door to other bidders, create an auction environment, and boost the final purchase price.

Statutory Mergers

Among the most common forms of acquisition, statutory mergers are governed by the statutory provisions of the state or states in which the parties to be merged are chartered. State statutes typically address considerations such as the percentage of the total voting stock that is required for approval of the transaction, who is entitled to vote, how the votes are counted, and the rights of the dissenting voters.

The Delaware statute is typical of state merger statutes. According to this statute, the boards of both companies must first approve the transaction. It is subsequently submitted for ratification to the shareholders of each corporation, which must be approved by a majority of those holding stock with voting rights. Once the appropriate documents are filed with the states in which the participating corporations are incorporated, the merger becomes legal. One corporation survives, while the other goes out of existence. The surviving corporation assumes the other corporation's assets, contract rights, and all disclosed and undisclosed liabilities, unless otherwise specified in the merger agreement.

Alternatives to Mergers

Stock-for-Stock Purchase

As an alternative to a merger, the acquiring company exchanges its voting stock for the stock of the target company. The target company is then managed as a wholly owned subsidiary of the acquirer. The acquirer may choose to merge the subsidiary into the parent at a later date. This is likely to be a nontaxable event for shareholders of the target company. The motivation for a subsidiary structure is explained in more detail under the discussion of "staged transactions." The major disadvantage of a subsidiary structure is the postponement of any significant effort to integrate rigorously the acquired company into the acquirer's operations to realize the benefits of synergy. The use of voting stock may also seriously erode the ownership position of acquiring company shareholders.

Stock for Assets

The acquiring company exchanges its voting stock for all or substantially all of the assets of the target corporation. While generally tax-free for the shareholders of the target company, this transaction may become taxable if the target is forced to liquidate. The use of voting stock may reduce the ownership position of the acquirer's shareholders.

Staged Transactions

There are a number of motivations for a staged or multistep transaction. Staged transactions may be used to structure an earn-out, to enable the target to complete the development of a technology or process, to await regulatory approval, to eliminate the need to obtain shareholder approval, and to minimize cultural conflicts with the target.

Supporting an Earn-Out Structure

As part of an earn-out agreement, the acquirer may agree to allow the target company to operate as a wholly owned but largely autonomous unit until the earn-out period expires. This suggests that there will be little attempt to integrate facilities, overhead operations, and distribution systems during the earn-out period.

Enable Completion of a Technology or Process

The value of the target may be greatly dependent on the target developing a key technology, production process, receiving approval from a regulatory authority such as the Federal Communications Commission, or signing a multiyear customer or vendor contract. The ability of the target to realize these objectives may be enhanced if it is aligned with a larger company or receives a cash infusion to fund the required research. A potential acquirer may assume a minority investment in the target with an option to acquire the company at a later date. Similarly, the potential acquirer may provide support to the target via a strategic alliance or licensing arrangement, which provides funding for the target, potential revenues for the acquirer, and an opportunity to merge at a later time.

Awaiting Regulatory Approval

The target company may also have reason to wait for certain events to occur before proceeding with a transaction. If the long-term value of the acquirer's stock offered to the target is dependent on the acquirer receiving approval from a regulatory agency, developing a new technology, or landing a key contract, the target may be well advised to wait. The two parties may enter into a letter of intent, with the option to exit the agreement without any liability to either party if certain key events are not realized within a stipulated period of time.

Eliminate Need for Shareholder Vote

Another motivation for staged transactions may be a desire to eliminate the need for a shareholder vote. This may be accomplished through a triangular merger. The acquiring company may create a special merger subsidiary. The subsidiary is subsequently funded by the consideration to be used in the merger and then the subsidiary and the target company merge. Because the acquirer is the sole shareholder in the operating subsidiary, the only approval required may be the board of directors of the subsidiary. This board may be essentially the same as that of the parent or acquiring company. However, this tactic may not work for stocks traded on some exchanges that may still require a shareholder vote.

Minimize Cultural Conflicts

Companies that acquire a foreign firm may choose to initially manage the acquired company as a subsidiary because of substantial cultural differences. Daimler-Benz managed Chrysler Corporation as a wholly owned subsidiary, even maintaining separately traded stocks, before merging the two corporations more than 1 year after closing.

FORM OF ACCOUNTING TREATMENT

The two principal forms of accounting for financial reporting purposes for mergers and acquisitions are purchase accounting and the pooling of interests. *Pur-*

chase accounting treatment is defined as one firm's acquisition of another that does not qualify as a pooling of interest. A *pooling of interests* is defined for financial reporting purposes as the representation of two formerly independent shareholder groups as a single group. A purchase implies a change in control resulting from the acquisition of one firm by another. In contrast, a pooling implies no change in control. Acquirer and target shareholders own the same percentage of the combined firms as they would have had the market values of the two firms been added together prior to the transaction. For an excellent discussion of M&A accounting issues, see Pahler and Mori (1997).

PURCHASE ACCOUNTING

When a company buys another company's stock for cash or some other non-equity form of payment, the total price paid is reflected on the books of the combined companies using the purchase method of accounting. The theory behind the purchase method of accounting is that the acquiring firm is much larger than the target, whose operations are absorbed into the acquirer's operations. With purchase accounting, analysts gain more insight into the premium paid for a company, because the purchase price is allocated to tangible assets and certain intangible assets such as customer lists, patents, franchises, and licenses. The balance is then entered as goodwill. All liabilities are transferred at the net present value of their future cash payments. Therefore, the difference in the shareholders' equity of the acquiring company before the transaction and the shareholders' equity of the combined companies immediately following the closing date equals the purchase price of the target company.

Under purchase accounting, the cost of the acquired entity becomes the new basis for recording the acquirer's investment in the assets of the target company. If part of the purchase price consists of something other than cash, the cost of the assets is determined using either the fair market value of the assets acquired or the fair market value of the noncash component of the purchase price plus the cash portion of the purchase price.

Balance Sheet Considerations

For financial reporting purposes, the purchase price (PP) paid for the target company consists of three components: the book value of equity (BVE) of the target company, goodwill (GW), and the portion of the PP allocated to revalued acquired assets (RVA). The excess of the PP paid over the BVE of the target company is assigned to either acquired tangible or intangible assets up to their fair market value or to GW. Thus, RVA equals the difference between the fair market value (FMV) and the book value of the acquired assets (BVA). RVA can either be positive (i.e., FMV > BVA) or negative (i.e., FMV < BVA).

These relationships can be summarized as follows:

$$PP = BVE + GW + RVA \text{ and}$$

$$GW = PP - (BVE + RVA)$$

Note that GW can be either positive [i.e., PP > (BVE + RVA)], or negative [i.e., PP < (BVE + RVA)]. Negative GW arises if the acquired assets are purchased at a discount to their FMV.

For financial reporting purposes, GW must be currently written off over a period not to exceed 40 years. Positive goodwill is a deduction from earnings and negative goodwill is an addition to earnings. The shareholders' equity accounts of the acquired company are eliminated to reflect the change in ownership. The total common stock account is calculated as the total number of shares multiplied by the par value per share. The total amount paid (total debit) less any additional credit to the common stock account is a balancing item credited to the paid-in capital account. Consolidated retained earnings is the amount of retained earnings of the acquiring firm only. The specific methodology for valuing each major balance sheet category is discussed in Exhibit 10-2.

EXHIBIT 10-2: VALUATION METHODOLOGY FOR PURCHASE ACCOUNTING

1. Cash and accounts receivable, reduced for bad debt and returns, are valued at their values on the books of the target company prior to the acquisition.
2. Marketable securities are valued at their realizable value after any transaction costs.
3. Inventories are broken into finished goods and raw materials. Finished goods are valued at their liquidation value; raw material inventories at their current replacement cost. Last-in, first-out (LIFO) inventory reserves maintained by the target before the acquisition are eliminated.
4. Property, plant, and equipment are valued at FMV.
5. Accounts payable and accrued expenses are valued at the levels stated on the target's books prior to the acquisition.
6. Notes payable and long-term debt are valued at their net present value of the future cash payments discounted at the current market rate of interest for similar securities.
7. Pension fund obligations are booked at the excess or deficiency of the present value of the projected benefit obligations over the present value of pension fund assets. This may result in an asset or liability being recorded by the consolidated firms.

8. All other liabilities are recorded at their net present value of future cash payments.
9. Intangible assets are booked at their appraised values.
10. Goodwill is the difference between the acquisition purchase price less the book value of the target's equity and revalued acquired tangible and intangible assets. Positive goodwill is recorded as an asset, whereas negative goodwill is allocated to all long-lived acquired assets other than marketable securities.

INCOME STATEMENT CONSIDERATIONS

For financial reporting purposes, an upward valuation of tangible and intangible assets raises depreciation and amortization expenses, which lowers operating and net income. For tax purposes, GW created after July 1993 may be amortized up to 15 years and is tax deductible. Goodwill booked before July 1993 is not tax deductible. Reported net income is lower than under pooling of interests accounting because of GW amortization and the revaluation of assets, whether tax deductible or nontax deductible.

CASH FLOW CONSIDERATIONS

Cash flow benefits from the tax deductibility of additional depreciation and amortization expenses that are written off over the useful lives of the assets. This assumes that the acquirer paid more than the net book value of the target's assets. Cash flow is higher than under pooling by the amount of the tax shelter provided by the depreciation of the step-up of depreciable tangible assets and amortization of intangible assets including goodwill created after 1993.

PURCHASE ACCOUNTING EXAMPLE

Exhibit 10-3 illustrates a simplified hypothetical purchase accounting transaction. See the notes to the exhibit for a detailed explanation. For current financial reporting purposes, any transaction that does not satisfy all of the 12 criteria required to qualify for a pooling of interests must be accounted for using the purchase method of accounting. The criteria to qualify for a pooling of interests are discussed in Exhibit 10-4.

Recall that a debit is an entry on the left-hand side of an account constituting an addition to an expense or asset account or a deduction from revenue, a net worth, or a liability account. A credit is an entry on the right-hand side of an account constituting an addition to revenue, net worth, or a liability account and a deduction from an expense or asset account. Accounts payable and accrued expenses are included on the books of the acquirer at their values stated on the target's books prior to the acquisition; notes payable and long-term debt are valued at their net present value.

EXHIBIT 10-3. EXAMPLE OF PURCHASE ACCOUNTING ($000)

	Acquiring firm	Target firm	Adjustments		Consolidated
			Debit	Credit	
Current assets	300	100			400
Land	200	100			300
Gross plant and equipment	500	200	1,000	50	1,650
Less: Depreciation	100	50	50		100
Net plant and equipment	400	150			1,550
Goodwill			750		750
Total assets	900	350			3,000
Current liabilities	200	60			260
Long-term debt	100	40			140
Total Liabilities	300	100			400
Common stock	150	50	50	150	300
Paid-in-surplus	250	150	150	1,850	2,100
Retained earnings	200	50	50		200
Shareholders Equity	600	250			2,600
Total liabilities + shareholders' equity	900	350	2,050	2,050	3,000

ASSUMPTIONS AND ACCOUNTING PROCEDURE

Assumptions

1. The acquirer paid $50 per share for 40,000 target shares or $2,000,000. This represents 100% of the target's shares.
2. The share exchange ratio is .75 shares of the acquirer's stock for each share of the target's stock.
3. The acquirer's shareholders' equity consists of 30,000 shares at a par value of $5 per share or $150,000 in common stock and paid-in-surplus and retained earnings are as shown. The acquirer issues another 30,000 shares at a par value of $5 per share to purchase the

target. The composition of the target's shareholders' equity is as shown.

4. As a result of an appraisal of the target's assets, 57.14% of the excess of the purchase price over the target's shareholders' equity is allocated to plant and equipment and the balance to goodwill.

Accounting Procedure

1. Calculate the excess of the purchase price over the target's shareholders' equity. The target's shareholders' equity is eliminated by subtracting the target's equity of $250,000 from the purchase price of $2,000,000. The difference of $1,750,000 is first allocated to fixed assets and then goodwill.

2. $1,000,000 (57.14%) of $1,750,000 is allocated (debited) to plant and equipment and the rest to goodwill in the "adjustments" column. Because the acquired assets are being revalued, the target's historical depreciation is eliminated with a debit and an offsetting credit of $50,000. Consolidated plant and equipment equals $500,000 + $200,000 + $1,000,000 − $50,000 = $1,650,000. The accumulated depreciation of $100,000 is the acquirer's depreciation. Therefore, net plant and equipment is $1,550,000. Goodwill is debited by $750,000 (i.e., $2,000,000 − $250,000 − $1,000,000 = $750,000).

3. The target company shareholders' equity accounts are eliminated by debiting the "adjustments" column by the amounts for the target's common stock, paid-in-surplus, and retained earnings.

4. Total debits are $2,050,000. A credit of $150,000 in the "adjustment's column" is made to common stock in an amount equal to the 30,000 new shares issued at a par value of $5. It is necessary to make an additional credit of $1,850,000 (i.e., $2.050,000 − $50 − $250) to paid-in-surplus to ensure that the total debits and credits balance.

POOLING-OF-INTERESTS ACCOUNTING

Assets and liabilities of both companies are added together. Companies are presumed to be about the same size and to continue to reflect the influence of both firms. To qualify for a pooling of interests, the transaction must satisfy all twelve of the conditions listed on Exhibit 10-4. The first two define the characteristics of the companies to be combined, the next seven describe the way in which the firms are to be combined, and the final three stipulate the absence of any planned transactions.

**EXHIBIT 10-4: REQUIREMENTS TO QUALIFY
FOR A POOLING OF INTERESTS**

1. Each of the parties to the transaction has not been a part of another business for at least 2 years before the start date of the proposed transaction. The start date is the earlier of the date when the stockholders of either party are informed of a tender offer or when significant transaction terms are presented to shareholders.
2. No more than 10% of the voting stock of the other party to the proposed transaction can be owned by either party prior to the start date.
3. The combination of the two parties may be completed as a single transaction or as a series of transactions completed within 1 year after the start date.
4. The combination must be completed by an exchange of common shares for at least 90% of the targets' shares.
5. The equity interest, excluding dividends, in the common shares of the combining entities is not changed in anticipation of the proposed transaction for at least 2 years prior to the start date or closing date.
6. Neither of the parties purchases their voting common stock for reasons related to the proposed transaction. Routine purchasing of common stock to satisfy employee stock option plans is excluded from this test.
7. The percentage interest of common shareholders in relation to other shareholders remains the same following the exchange of stock.
8. The voting rights represented by the shares of common stock owned by all of the combined stockholders are not restricted.
9. There are no contingent shares of stock to be issued subsequent to closing.
10. There are no agreements for the combined entity to retire or reacquire any of the shares of stock used to consummate the transaction.
11. No other financial arrangements can be made for the benefit of former shareholders of the combining entities.
12. There is no intent to sell a significant portion of the assets of the combining firms for at least 2 years after the closing date.

Pooling of Interests: Example

Exhibit 10-5 illustrates a simplified hypothetical example of a business combination that qualifies for a pooling of interests. See the assumptions and accounting procedures section of the exhibit for a detailed explanation of the example. Note that there is no goodwill or asset revaluation. Assets and liabilities of the

---

EXHIBIT 10-5: AN EXAMPLE OF POOLING OF INTERESTS ($000)

	Acquiring firm	Target firm	Adjustments		Consolidation
			Debits	Credits	
Current assets	300	100			400
Net fixed assets	600	250			850
Total assets	900	350			1,250
Current liabilities	200	60			260
Long-term debt	100	40			140
Total liabilities	300	100			400
Common stock	150	50		100	300
Paid-in-surplus	250	150	100		300
Retained earnings	200	50			250
Shareholders' equity	600	250			850
Shareholders' equity + total liabilities	900	350	100	100	1,250

ASSUMPTIONS AND ACCOUNTING PROCEDURES

Assumptions

1. The acquiring company issues 30,000 shares at a par value of $5 valued at $150,000.
2. The share exchange ratio is .75 acquirer shares for each of the target's 40,000 shares.

Accounting procedures

1. Balance sheet line items are added together.
2. The consolidated common stock account totals $300,000, consisting of the acquirer's original common stock account of $150,000, the target's common stock account of $50,000, and a credit to the common stock account of $100,000. The offsetting debit of $100,000 is to the paid-in-surplus account.
3. Consolidated retained earnings is the sum of the two companies' retained earnings; however, if the debit to paid-in-surplus exhausts the total paid-in-surplus account, any remaining debit would be made to the retained earnings account.

combining companies are added together at the values carried on the books of the two companies at the closing date. Stockholders' equity of the two firms is combined by adding together the retained earnings of the two companies.

Although the sum of the combined firm's equity will not change, their composition may change. Additional shares of common stock issued by the acquirer may result in the common stock account of the combined company exceeding the common stock account created by the sum of the two companies. Paid-in surplus is first reduced and then retained earnings until any excess has been eliminated.

Consolidated income statements represent the summation of the individual firm's income statements. Historical EPS for the combined firms is restated to reflect the new number of shares outstanding and the continuity of ownership interests in the combined companies.

COMPARATIVE IMPACTS OF PURCHASE VERSUS POOLING-OF-INTERESTS ACCOUNTING

The implications of the two methods of accounting for business combinations are quite different. The alternative accounting techniques affect key financial performance indicators, such as net income, cash flow, leverage, and EPS. Pooling-of-interests accounting has no impact on net income, cash flow, and leverage, but it may reduce EPS due to the increase in the number of shares of the combined companies. Whether there is any dilution depends largely on the extent of the increase in earnings due to potential synergy. In contrast, purchase accounting tends to reduce net income but increase cash flow when compared to pooling of interests accounting. The impact on leverage using the purchase method depends on what form of payment is used and the amount of debt assumed by the acquiring company in the transaction. If stock is used and the acquiring company is assuming relatively little debt, leverage could decline; however, leverage could increase if the acquiring company chooses to use debt or cash. These impacts are summarized in Table 10-4.

IMPACT OF THE FORM OF ACCOUNTING ON MERGERS AND ACQUISITION PREMIUMS

Mergers accounted for using the pooling-of-interests treatment have tended to have higher premiums than those accounted for using the purchase method. For a sample of 36 purchase and 59 pooling transactions for the 10 years ending in 1982, the average bid premium for pooling-type transactions was 64% as compared to 42% for purchase transactions (Robinson and Shane: 1990). Other studies have confirmed this finding. For a sample of 108 pooling of interest and 69 purchase transactions between 1971–1982, Davis determined that the average premium paid for acquirers employing pooling of interest was about three times that paid by firms employing purchase accounting (Davis: 1990). These higher premiums may represent what acquirers are willing to pay for the advantages of using

TABLE 10-4.   Purchase versus Pooling Accounting

	Purchase accounting	Pooling of interests
Net income	Lower than for pooling due to additional depreciation and amortization of tangible and intangible assets	No impact
Cash flow	Higher than for pooling by the dollar amount of the tax shelter	No impact
Leverage	Reduced when the purchase is made using stock and increased when the purchase is made from excess cash or using debt	No impact
Earnings per share	May be reduced by increased depreciation and amortization expense	May be reduced if the addition of the target's to the acquirer's earnings is offset by the increase in common stock issued

the pooling method of accounting. Despite the perceived benefits of pooling of interests by the acquirer's management, there is evidence that stock prices for acquiring firms using pooling of interests are lower than for those firms using the purchase method. This may occur because acquiring firms are more likely to pay an excessive premium to avoid using the purchase method (Davis: 1996).

Lys and Vincent (1995), in an analysis of AT&T's $7.5 billion acquisition of NCR, concluded that AT&T paid between $50 and $500 million to induce NCR to accept certain terms in the sales agreement needed to qualify the transaction as a pooling of interests. While this boosted EPS by as much as 17%, it left cash flows unchanged. The resulting acquisition reduced AT&T shareholder wealth by $3.9 to $6.5 billion and resulted in negative synergies of $1.3 to $3 billion. The negative synergy resulted from the restriction imposed by the use of pooling of interests accounting on selling any of the acquired assets for a period of 2 years following the closing date.

Although many companies with high multiples may be encouraged to use pooling-of-interests accounting to avoid GW, the use of this form of accounting does tend to limit the merged companies' postmerger flexibility. For example, America Online (AOL) chose to use purchase accounting in its 2000 takeover of Time Warner, despite the resulting $150 billion in GW that the company will have to write-off. This decision gives the new company, AOL Time Warner, the flexibility to make new acquisitions or to divest under-performing assets. Under pooling-of-interests accounting, the company would not have been able to sell more than 10% of its assets for more than 2 years.

The attraction of the pooling of interest accounting treatment is not limited to companies whose stocks are currently publicly traded. If they qualify, privately held firms acquiring a public company or another privately held company can elect to use the pooling-of-interests treatment. They may choose to avoid the creation of GW as a result of such transactions in anticipation of an initial public offering of their stock.

PENDING CHANGES TO ACCOUNTING
FOR BUSINESS COMBINATIONS

The Financial Accounting Standards Board (FASB) is an independent organization funded entirely by the private sector whose mission is to set accounting and reporting standards to protect users of financial information, particularly investors and creditors. The current accounting standards for business combinations were set in 1970. They require that mergers and acquisitions be reported using either the purchase method or the pooling-of-interests method. As noted, these two methods produce dramatically different results for purposes of financial reporting for essentially the same or similar economic transactions.

On September 8, 1999, the FASB proposed that all combinations would be accounted for under the purchase method and that the pooling-of-interest's method would be eliminated. The proposal is based on the following arguments:

1. The pooling method ignores the values exchanged in a business combination, whereas the purchase method reflects such values.
2. Under the pooling method, users of financial statements cannot tell how much was invested in the transaction, nor can they track the subsequent performance of that investment.
3. Having two different methods of accounting makes it difficult for investors to compare companies that have used different methods to account for their business combinations.
4. Because future cash flows are the same using either method, the boost in earnings under the pooling method reflects artificial accounting differences rather than real economic differences.
5. With the increasing number of cross-border mergers and acquisitions, there is a need for financial reporting to be comparable internationally. In most countries, the pooling method is either prohibited or used only on an exception basis.

At the time of this writing, FASB estimates that the public commentary process will be completed by the end of 2000 and that a final standard will be in place for all business combinations occurring after January 1, 2001 (Jenkins: 2000).

FASB is also reconsidering the treatment of GW. Before 1970, GW was carried as an asset on a corporation's books indefinitely. In 1970, the accounting policy board ruled that GW should be treated as any other asset whose value declines with time and ruled that GW had to be amortized over a period not to exceed 40 years. Current proposals state that the useful life of GW should be presumed to be 10 years or less unless sufficient evidence can be provided to support a longer life. The period of amortization should not exceed 20 years. Moreover, other intangible assets should be amortized over their useful lives, with the period not exceeding 20 years. The new rules would take effect on the same date as the elimination of the pooling-of-interests' method.

TAX STRUCTURES AND STRATEGIES

Taxes are an important consideration in almost any transaction. However, taxes are seldom the primary motivation for an acquisition. The fundamental economics of the transaction should always be the deciding factor. Tax benefits accruing to the buyer should simply reinforce a purchase decision. Transactions may be non-taxable or entirely or partially taxable. These alternative structures are discussed in detail next. See Table 10-5 for a summary of the primary characteristics of taxable and tax-free transactions. For a comprehensive discussion of these issues, see Scholes and Wolfson (1992) and Tillinghast (1998).

TAXABLE TRANSACTIONS

A transaction will generally be considered taxable if it involves the purchase of stock or assets for cash, notes, or some other nonequity consideration.

Taxable Purchase of Assets

If a transaction involves a purchase of assets, the target company's tax cost or basis in the acquired stock or assets is increased or "stepped up" to their FMV, which is equal to the purchase price paid by the acquirer. The resulting additional depreciation and amortization reduces the tax liability of the combined companies. To compensate the target company shareholders for any tax liability they may incur, the buyer will usually have to increase the purchase price. Buyers are willing to do this only if the present value of the tax savings resulting from the step-up of the target's assets is greater than the increase in the PP required to compensate the target's shareholders for the increase in their tax liability.

There is little empirical evidence that the tax shelter resulting from the ability of the acquiring firm to increase the value of acquired assets to their FMV is a highly important motivating factor for a takeover (Auerbach and Reishus: 1988, pp. 69–88). Nonetheless, tax considerations do provide some value to the acquiring company and are considered in undertaking transactions. Auerbach and Reishus found the gain from tax benefits averaged about 10.5% of the acquiring firm's FMV for a sample of 318 mergers and acquisitions between 1968 and 1983. The majority of the firms in the sample were in manufacturing and substantially larger than the target companies (Auerbach and Reishus: 1988, pp. 300–313). Taxable transactions have been made somewhat more attractive since 1993, when a change in the legislation allowed acquirers to amortize intangible assets, including GW, over 15 years for tax purposes.

Taxable Purchase of Stock

Taxable transactions usually involve the purchase of stock, because the purchase of assets will automatically trigger a taxable gain for the target company, if the FMV of the acquired assets exceeds the firm's tax basis in the assets. All stockholders are impacted equally in a taxable purchase of assets, because the target company is paying the taxes. In contrast, in a taxable stock purchase, the impact of the potential tax liability will vary depending on the individual shareholder's tax basis in the stock. If the transaction involves a purchase of stock, the assets will not be automatically stepped up to FMV unless the acquirer adopts a special election. This is found in Section 338 of the U.S. tax code.

Section 338 Election

According to Section 338 of the U.S. tax code, a purchaser of 80% or more of the stock of the target may elect to treat the acquisition as if it were an acquisition of the target's assets. This enables the acquiring corporation to avoid having to transfer assets and obtain consents to assignment of all contracts, while still benefiting from the write-up of assets, assuming the FMV exceeds the book value of the acquired assets.

TAX-FREE TRANSACTIONS

As a general rule, a transaction is taxable if the target company's shareholders receive something other than the acquirer's stock and nontaxable if they receive the acquirer's stock. Transactions may be partially taxable, if the shareholders of the target company receive some nonequity consideration, such as cash or debt, in addition to the acquirer's stock. This nonequity consideration or "boot" is taxable either as a dividend, if all shareholders receive it pro rata, and taxed as ordinary income or as a capital gain to the extent it does not exceed the shareholder's overall gain as a result of the transaction. If the transaction is tax-free, the acquiring company is able to transfer or carry over the target company's tax basis to its own financial statements. In the tax-free transaction, there is no increase or step-up in assets to FMV.

Continuity of Interests Requirement

Under the law, tax-free transactions contemplate substantial continuing involvement of the target company's shareholders. This continued involvement is intended to demonstrate a long-term or strategic commitment on the part of the acquiring company to the target company. Nontaxable transactions usually involve mergers, with the acquirer's stock exchanged for the target's stock or assets. Nontaxable transactions are also called *tax-free reorganizations.*

Avoiding the Loss of Tax-Free Status

Tax-free reorganizations generally require that all or substantially all of the target company's assets or shares be acquired. The divestiture of a significant portion of the acquired company immediately following closing could jeopardize the tax-free status of the transaction. Such an action would run counter to the IRS's notion that the acquirer is making a long-term strategic commitment to the entire business for the transaction to be tax-free. The loss of tax-free status can be avoided by spinning off the unwanted business to the shareholders of the target company in a tax-free exchange. The target company is then merged into a subsidiary of the acquirer in a tax-free statutory merger. See Table 10-5 for a comparison of taxable and tax-free transactions.

Tax-free reorganizations also require that substantially all of the consideration received by the target's shareholders be paid in common or preferred stock. However, if the preferred stock is redeemable or has a dividend that is indexed to interest rates, the Internal Revenue Service could disallow the tax-free status. In this instance, the preferred stock will be viewed as debt rather than equity.

Alternative Tax-Free Reorganizations

The eight principal forms of tax-free reorganizations are described in Section 368 of the Internal Revenue Code. Three are excluded from our discussion. These include Type D, transfers between related corporations; Type E, the restructuring of a firm's capital structure; and Type F, a reorganization in which the firm's name or location is changed.

TABLE 10-5.   Key Characteristics of Taxable versus Tax-Free Transactions

Taxable transactions[a]	Tax-free transactions[b]
Purchase of stock for cash, notes, or other non-equity consideration	Exchange of the acquirer's stock for the target's stock
Purchase of assets for cash, notes, or other non-equity consideration	Exchange of the acquirer's stock for substantially all of the target's assets
Acquiring firm: 1. Stepped up basis for acquired assets 2. Loss of net operating losses and tax credits Target firm: 1. Immediate recognition of gain by target shareholders 2. Recapture of tax credits and excess depreciation	Acquiring firm: 1. Net operating loss carryover 2. Tax credit carryover Target firm: 1. Deferred taxable gains for shareholders

[a] Taxable transactions are those in which the target shareholders have little continuing equity participation in the acquired firm.

[b] Tax-free transactions are those in which the target shareholders have a continuing direct or indirect interest in the acquired firm enabling deferral by target shareholders of any gain.

What follows is a discussion of the Type A statutory merger, Type B stock-for-stock merger, and Type C stock-for-assets merger and the two primary mechanisms used to implement tax-free reorganizations. These mechanisms include the forward and reverse triangular subsidiary mergers in which the acquiring company creates a shell subsidiary as an intermediary to complete the transaction. The forward triangular merger is commonly used in tax-free asset purchases; the reverse triangular merger is commonly used in tax-free stock purchases. The principal advantage of using a subsidiary in this manner is to enable the acquirer, as parent of the subsidiary, to assume control of the target without necessarily assuming responsibility for the debt of the target corporation. See Table 10-6 for a comparison of alternative tax-free structures.

Type A and B are the most common tax-free reorganizations. The IRS views both reorganizations as a continuation of interest in the original corporation in a reorganized form rather than as true sales. The IRS requires that shareholders of the target company must continue to hold a substantial equity interest in the acquiring company. As such, they may be wholly (all stock) or partially tax-free (stock and other nonequity consideration).

Type A Reorganization

Type A reorganizations are statutory mergers or consolidations governed by state law. To qualify for a Type A reorganization, the transaction must be either a merger or a consolidation. There are no limitations on the type of consideration involved. Target company shareholders may receive cash, voting or nonvoting common or preferred stock, notes, or real property. The acquirer may choose not to purchase all of the target's assets. At least 50% of the purchase price must be in the stock of the acquiring company to ensure that the IRS' continuity of interests requirement is satisfied.

For target company shareholders receiving acquiring company shares, no taxable gain or loss is recognized at the time of the transaction, and the basis in the target shares carries over to the shares received from the acquiring company. Any taxable gain is deferred until the acquiring firm's shares are sold. At that time, the taxable gain is equal to the difference between the value of the acquirer's shares received at the time of the transaction less the target shareholder's original basis in the target's stock. This gain is taxed at the capital-gains rate. Nonequity remuneration received by target shareholders is taxed as ordinary income.

Type A reorganizations are widely used because of their great flexibility. Because there is no requirement to use voting stock, acquiring firms enjoy more options. By issuing nonvoting stock, the acquiring corporation may acquire control over the target without diluting control over the combined or newly created company. Moreover, there is no stipulation as to the amount of target assets that must be acquired. Finally, there is no maximum amount of cash that may be used in the purchase price and the limitations articulated by both the IRS and the courts allow significantly more cash than Types B or C reorganizations.

Flexibility with respect to the amount of cash being used may be the most important consideration, because it enables the acquirer to better satisfy the disparate requirements of the target's shareholders. Some will want cash and some will want stock. The acquirer must be careful that not too large a proportion of the purchase price be composed of cash, because this might not meet the IRS' requirement for continuity of interests of the target shareholders and disqualify the transaction as a Type A reorganization.

The acquirer normally requests an advance ruling from the IRS to ensure that they are not violating the continuity-of-interests' requirement. The IRS takes the position on advance rulings that the continuity-of-interests' requirement is satisfied if at least 50% of the total consideration consists of the acquirer's stock. Transactions contemplating the use of more than 50% cash have had limited success in the courts.

Type B Stock-for-Stock Reorganizations

The acquisition must be consummated using only the acquirer's voting stock for at least 80% of voting stock of the target company and at least 80% of the target's nonvoting shares. Any cash or debt will disqualify the transaction as a Type B reorganization. However, cash may be used to purchase fractional shares.

Type B reorganizations are used as an alternative to a merger or consolidation. Following the merger, the target may be liquidated into the acquiring company or maintained as an independent operating subsidiary. The transaction may also be phased over a period of time. Stock in the target company may be purchased over 12 months or less as part of a formal acquisition plan. Only stock may be used to acquire the target, although the acquirer may have used cash to purchase some portion of the target's stock in the past as long as it was not part of the acquisition plan.

The Type B reorganization is rarely used because of the requirement to use only voting stock. Type B may be appropriate if the acquiring company wishes to conserve cash or its borrowing capacity.

Type C Reorganization

This is a stock-for-assets reorganization with the requirement that at least 80% of the FMV of the target's assets, as well as the assumption of certain specified liabilities, are acquired solely in exchange for voting stock. Cash may be used to purchase the remainder of the stock only if the assumed liabilities amount to less than 20% of the FMV of the acquired assets. As part of the plan of reorganization, the target subsequent to closing dissolves and distributes the acquirer's stock to the target's shareholders for the now-canceled target stock.

The Type C reorganization is used when it is essential for the acquirer not to assume any undisclosed liabilities. It is technically more difficult than a merger, because all of the acquired assets must be conveyed. In a merger, all assets (and liabilities) pass by operation of law. The requirement to use only voting stock is also a major deterrent to the use of this type of reorganization.

Forward Triangular Merger

This is the most commonly used form of reorganization for tax-free asset acquisitions. It involves three parties: the acquiring firm, the target firm, and a shell subsidiary of the acquiring firm (see Figure 10-3). The parent funds the shell corporation by buying stock issued by the shell with cash or the parent's own stock. The target is acquired by the subsidiary with cash or the stock of the parent. The target company is merged into the acquirer's subsidiary in a statutory merger under state law. The parent's stock may be voting or nonvoting, and the acquirer must purchase substantially all of the assets of the target company. The transaction qualifies as a Type A tax-free reorganization.

Reverse Triangular Merger

This structure is most commonly used to effect tax-free stock acquisitions (see Figure 10-4). The acquirer forms a new shell subsidiary, which is merged into the target company in a statutory merger governed by state law. The target company is the surviving entity. In the merger, the acquirer receives shares of the merged company, while the shareholders of the target company receive the acquirer's shares. The surviving company must end up with substantially all of the assets of both the target company and the shell subsidiary. At least 80% of the total purchase price must consist of the acquirer's voting shares. This transaction qualifies as a Type B tax-free reorganization.

Although the reverse triangular merger is similar to a Type B reorganization in which the acquiring company purchases the target's stock in exchange for its stock, it permits the acquirer to use up to 20% cash. This is something that could not be done in a pure Type B reorganization. A reverse merger is also advantageous in cases where the target is closely held by a few large shareholders owning more than 80% of the stock and who have a very low tax basis in the stock. They will want to receive stock from the buyer. Under these circumstances, the buyer

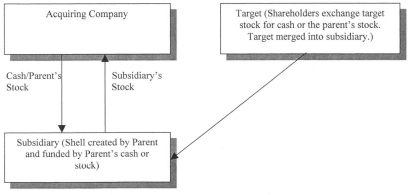

FIGURE 10-3.   Forward triangular merger.

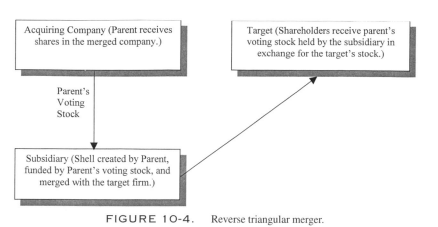

FIGURE 10-4. Reverse triangular merger.

knows that at least 80% of the stock will be tendered and the remaining 20% can be purchased with cash. The reverse merger is also highly attractive when the transfer of the target's properties through an asset purchase requires the inconvenience and expense of gaining consents to transfer contracts but would not be required if a merger were implemented.

TAX REFORM ACT OF 1986

Many aspects of the 1986 Tax Reform Act affected corporate restructuring activities. The most significant areas included the treatment of net operating losses, corporate capital gain taxes, the introduction of the alternative corporate minimum tax, the treatment of greenmail for tax purposes, and the repeal of the General Public Utilities Doctrine.

Net Operating Loss Carry Forwards

The Tax Act introduced an annual limit on the use of net operating loss carry forwards (NOLs). The limit is triggered if there is a greater than 50% change in ownership in a corporation generating cumulative losses within the 3-year period immediately preceding the change in ownership. Such corporations are referred to as *loss corporations*. The maximum amount of the NOL that can be used annually to offset earnings is limited to the value of the loss corporation at the date of the acquisition multiplied by the long-term tax-exempt bond rate. Furthermore, the loss corporation cannot use an NOL carry forward, unless it remains in essentially the same business for at least 2 years following the closing of the acquisition.

Corporate Capital Gains Taxes

Prior to the 1986 Tax Act, corporate capital gains had been taxed at 28%. Effective July 1, 1987, both short-term and long-term corporate capital gains are taxed as ordinary income and are subject to a maximum corporate tax rate of 34%.

TABLE 10-6. Summary of Alternative Tax-Free Structures

Type of reorganization	Maximum cash payment requirement	Requirement to purchase substantially all the assets	Type of stock	Commonly used when
A	50% under advance ruling from IRS	No	Voting or nonvoting	Substantial portion of purchase price is cash
B	0% for advance ruling	No	Voting only	Acquirer wants to limit use of cash or leverage
C	20% reduced by any target liabilities assumed by acquirer	Yes	Voting only	Acquirer wants to avoid undisclosed and contingent liabilities
Forward triangular merger	Same as Type A	Yes	Voting or nonvoting	Tax-free asset acquisitions
Reverse triangular merger	20%	Yes	Voting only	Tax-free stock acquisitions

This change in the law has increased the popularity of alternative legal structures having more favorable tax attributes, such as Master Limited Partnerships (MLP) and Subchapter S Corporations. Profits distributed directly to MLP partners or to Subchapter S Corporations shareholders are taxed at their personal tax rates.

Alternative Corporate Minimum Tax

Before 1986, corporations paid a minimum tax on specific tax preference items that was added on to its normal statutory tax rate. With the 1986 Tax Act, this minimum tax was replaced by an alternative minimum tax with a flat rate of 20%. The introduction of the alternative minimum tax has proven to be particularly burdensome for leveraged buyouts (LBOs), which are by intent highly leveraged and have little if any taxable income because of their high annual interest expense. Consequently, the imposition of the alternative minimum tax reduced the potential returns to equity investors that could be achieved as a result of highly leveraged transactions.

Greenmail Payments

Greenmail refers to payments made to "corporate raiders" to buy back positions they had taken in target companies (see Chapter 3, this volume). Greenmail was made more expensive for corporations to pay as a result of the 1986 Tax Act, which sharply reduced the amount of such payments that could be deducted from before tax profits.

General Public Utilities Doctrine

According to the General Public Utilities Doctrine, the sale of corporate assets and a liquidating distribution to shareholders were exempt from capital gains taxation. Acquirers could sell off assets of a target and distribute the proceeds as a liquidating dividend to shareholders without incurring a capital gains obligation. Any gain on the sale of assets was assumed to be offset by a corresponding reduction in the value of the target's stock. This was referred to as a "mirror transaction." This favorable tax treatment encouraged corporate raiders to pay a price for target companies that may have exceeded their economic value. Any excess price could be paid for by the exemption from taxes of any capital gains that resulted from the breakup of the target company and the subsequent sale in pieces. The 1986 Tax Act repealed the General Public Utilities Doctrine.

NET OPERATING LOSSES

NOL carry-forwards are provisions in the tax laws allowing firms to use NOLs generated in the past to offset future taxable income. Although the 1986 Tax Act reduced the attractiveness of NOLs to acquirers, they still represent a potentially significant source of value to acquirers that should be considered during the process of valuing an acquisition target. Exhibit 10-6 illustrates how the analyst might value NOLs on the books of a target corporation.

EXHIBIT 10-6: VALUING NOLs

Acquiring Company is contemplating buying Target Company, which has a tax loss carry-forward of $8,000. Acquiring Company has a 40% tax rate. Assume the tax-loss carry-forward is within the limits of the Tax Reform Act of 1986 and that the firm's cost of capital is 15%. The following information is given for the two firms:

Years remaining in loss carry-forward	Amount ($)	Years after acquisition	Earnings before tax ($)
1	2,000	1	1,800
2	2,000	2	2,000
3	800	3	1,000
4	1,200	4	1,000
5	800	5	2,000
Total	6,800	Total	7,800

Calculate Acquiring Company's tax payments without the acquisition.

Years	Tax Benefit
1	720
2	800
3	400
4	400
5	800

Calculate Acquiring Company's tax payment for each year with the proposed acquisition:

Years	Earnings before taxes ($)	Tax Loss ($)	Amount Carried Forward ($)	Use of Tax Loss ($)	Taxable Income ($)	Tax Payment ($)
1	1,800	2,000		1,800	0	0
2	2,000	2,000	200	2,000	0	0
3	1,000	800	0	1,000	0	0
4	1,000	1,200	200	1,000	0	0
5	2,000	800	0	1,000	1,000	400

What is the most Acquiring Company should pay for Target Company if its only value is its tax loss?

The Acquiring Company should not pay more than the present value of the net tax benefit: $720, $800, $400, $400, and $400. The present value of the cumulative tax benefits discounted at a 15% cost of capital is $1,921.58.

Notes:
1. Tax benefits are equal to earnings before tax times the 40% marginal tax rate of Acquiring Company. Therefore, the tax benefit in year 1 is $1,800 × .4 = $720.
2. The net tax benefit in the 5th year is equal to the $800 tax benefit less the $400 in tax payments required in the 5th year.

Although NOLs represent a potential source of value, their use must be carefully monitored in order to realize the full value resulting from the potential for deferring income taxes. An acquirer must be highly confident that expected future pretax income stream would be realized. Without the future income, the NOLs will expire worthless. Because the acquirer can never be certain that future income will be sufficient to fully realize the value of the NOLs, loss carry-forwards alone rarely justify an acquisition.

Studies show that it is easy to overstate the value of loss carry-forwards because of the potential for them to expire before they can be fully utilized. Empirical analyses indicate that the actual tax savings realized from loss carry-forwards tends to be about one-half of their expected value (Auerbach and Potrerba: 1987).

THINGS TO REMEMBER

The deal-structuring process addresses satisfying as many of the primary objectives of the parties involved and determining how risk will be shared. The process begins with addressing a set of key questions, whose answers help to define initial negotiating positions, potential risks, options for managing risk, levels of tolerance for risk, and conditions under which the buyer or seller will "walk away" from the negotiations. The deal-structuring process can be defined in terms of six major components. These components include the form of the acquisition vehicle, the postclosing organization, the form of payment, the form of acquisition, the form of accounting, and tax structure.

The form of the acquisition vehicle refers to the legal structure used to acquire the target company. The postclosing organization is the legal framework used to manage the combined businesses following the consummation of the transaction. The postclosing organization may differ from the acquisition vehicle depending upon the acquirer's strategic objectives for the combined firms. The form of payment or total consideration may consist of cash, common stock, debt, or some combination of all three. The form of acquisition reflects what is being acquired, the form of payment, and how the ownership of assets will be conveyed from the seller to the buyer. Finally, the form of acquisition drives the accounting treatment and the tax structure for the combined companies.

Commonly used structures for both the acquisition vehicle and the postclosing organization include the corporate, holding company, JV, partnership, LLC, and ESOP structures. The choice of the acquisition vehicle will largely depend on the strategic objectives of the acquiring company. A holding company framework may make more sense if the acquirer is a financial buyer seeking a short-term profit, concerned about unknown or contingent liabilities, attempting to preserve the unique corporate culture of the acquired company, or has negotiated an earn-out with the seller. In contrast, if it is important to rapidly realize synergy, the acquisition vehicle may be a corporate structure in which the acquired company is immediately consolidated with an existing division.

The simplest form of payment is cash. The form of payment may be modified to reflect the requirements of the target's shareholders to include common and preferred equity, conventional and convertible debt, and nonequity considerations such as real estate. When buyers and sellers are unable to agree on price, different forms of payment such as earn-outs, rights to intellectual property, license fees, employment agreements, and consulting contracts can be used to close the gap.

The form of acquisition describes the mechanism for conveying ownership of assets or stock and associated liabilities from the target to the acquiring firm. There are many different forms of acquisition. The most common include asset purchases, stock purchases, statutory mergers, stock-for-stock purchases, and stock-for-assets purchases. For stock purchases, the primary advantages to the buyer include the preservation of tax benefits and certain rights to use items such as patents and licenses. However, the buyer is also responsible for all unknown and contingent liabilities. From the seller's perspective, the advantages include the deferral of taxes and favorable treatment afforded by capital gains taxes; however, the seller loses NOLs and tax credits, which pass to the buyer. For asset purchases, buyers benefit from additional tax shelter due to the write-up of assets to FMV, as well as protection from liabilities not assumed in the contract and, in general, undisclosed, unknown, and contingent liabilities. However, tax benefits and rights that would automatically transfer with the stock are lost. Sellers retain tax benefits and rights associated with the stock, but they may be subject to double taxation if forced to liquidate the remaining corporate assets.

The form of acquisition reflects what is being acquired and the form of payment. The form of acquisition drives the tax structure and the form of accounting. Taxable transactions are those in which the target shareholders have little continuing equity participation in the acquired firm. Tax-free transactions are those in which the target shareholders have a continuing direct or indirect interest in the acquired firm, enabling deferral by target shareholders of any gain. Taxable transactions usually involve the purchase of stock or assets for cash, notes, or other nonequity consideration. Tax-free transactions entail the exchange of the acquirer's stock for the target stock or substantially all of the target's assets. The Type A tax-free reorganization is the most common form, because there is no requirement to buy all of the target's assets, restriction on the type of stock that may be used, and because a substantial portion of the purchase price may be in cash.

The form of acquisition also largely determines the form of accounting for financial reporting purposes. The two principal accounting treatments for financial reporting purposes for mergers and acquisitions are purchase accounting and the pooling of interests. A purchase is defined as one firm's acquisition of another that does not qualify as a pooling of interest. The purchase method of accounting is used when the buyer purchases the target's stock for cash. The excess of the purchase price over the target's book value of equity and restated values of acquired assets is treated as GW on the acquirer's balance sheet. GW is currently amortized over a period not to exceed forty years. However, this accounting treatment for GW is likely to change by 2001, when in most instances GW will be amortized over a period of not more than 20 years. Pooling-of-interest accounting can be employed when an exchange of stock takes place. Assets and liabilities of the acquirer and target are added together. However, as of the writing of this book, FASB has announced its intentions to require that acquisitions closed after January 1, 2001, must be accounted for using the purchase method.

CHAPTER DISCUSSION QUESTIONS

10-1. Describe the deal-structuring process.

10-2. Provide two examples of how decisions made in one area of the deal-structuring process are likely to impact other areas.

10-3.   What are some of the reasons acquirers may choose a particular form of acquisition vehicle?

10-4.   Describe techniques commonly used to "close the gap" when buyers and sellers cannot agree on price.

10-5.   How does the purchase method of accounting affect the income statement, balance sheet, and cash flow statements of the combined companies?

10-6.   What are the advantages and disadvantages of a purchase of assets from the perspective of the buyer and seller?

10-7.   What are the advantages and disadvantages of a purchase of stock from the perspective of the buyer and seller?

10-8.   What are the advantages and disadvantages of a statutory merger?

10-9.   What are the reasons some acquirers choose to undertake a staged or multistep takeover?

10-10. What are the primary conditions that must be satisfied for a transaction to be deemed nontaxable by the Internal Revenue Service?

CHAPTER BUSINESS CASE

CASE STUDY 10-1. VODAFONE ACQUIRES AIRTOUCH

The worldwide wireless telecommunications industry is experiencing explosive growth. The introduction of new cellular licenses all over the world has made it possible for people to have telephone service in areas previously inaccessible with standard landline phone service. Before 1997, there were essentially only two providers of personal communication services (PCS) in most areas of the United States. The number expanded to five PCS carriers with the auctioning off of licenses in 1997.

The increased competition is leading to new product enhancements, "creative pricing" options, and enhanced service delivery using new digital technologies. Digital communication technology provides the customer clearer, more fraud-resistant service as well as new features, such as caller ID and text message paging capabilities. Prepaid cellular, a pay-as-you-go wireless service, has exploded in Europe. This type of product is being targeted to customers with insufficient credit histories or who are infrequent users. This service is experiencing increasing success in the United States.

Deregulation of the telecommunications industry has led to many changes and potential mergers. In Europe, rising competition is the catalyst driving merger targets. In the United States, the break up of AT&T and the subsequent deregulation of the industry has led to key alliances, JVs, and mergers, which have created cellular powerhouses capable of providing nationwide coverage. Such coverage is being achieved by roaming agreements between carriers and acquisitions by other carriers.

Although competition has been heightened due to deregulation, the telecommunications industry continues to be characterized by substantial barriers to entry. These include the requirement to obtain licenses and the network infrastructure required to provide service. Wireless communications continue to grow largely at the expense of traditional landline services as cellular service pricing continues to decrease. Even though the market is likely to continue to grow rapidly, success is expected to go to those with the financial muscle to satisfy increasingly sophisticated customer demands.

What follows is a brief discussion of the motivations for the merger between Vodafone and AirTouch Communications, a chronology of events leading up to the merger, and a description of the key elements of the deal structure that made the Vodafone offer more attractive than a competing offer from Bell Atlantic.

VODAFONE

Company History

Vodafone is a wireless communications company based in the United Kingdom. The company is located in 13 countries in Europe, Africa, and Australia/New Zealand. Vodafone reaches over 9.5 million subscribers. It has been the market leader in the UK since 1986 and currently has over 5 million subscribers in the UK alone. The company has been very successful at marketing and selling the prepaid service in Europe. In Europe, if a landline customer calls a mobile telephone, the landline party pays for the cellular phone call. This has made the prepaid service enormously successful.

Vodafone is also involved in a venture called Globalstar, LP, a limited partnership with Loral Space and Communications and Qualcomm, a phone manufacturer. "Globalstar will construct and operate a worldwide, satellite-based communications system offering global mobile voice, fax, and data communications in over 115 countries, covering over 85% of the world's population" (Airtouch, *Annual Report:* 1997).

Strategic Intent

Vodafone's focus is on global expansion. They are expanding through partnerships and by purchasing licenses. Notably, Vodafone lacked a significant presence in the U.S., the largest mobile phone market in the world. For Vodafone to be considered a truly global company, the firm needs a presence in the Unites States.

Vodafone's success in the prepaid phone environment is leading to a further penetration of this type of billing option into other areas in which it competes. Minutes of usage are continuing to increase as well as revenue. Most companies, including Vodafone, believe that continuously increasing the number of minutes used by subscribers is the key to the future. Vodafone emphasizes customer service as a means of retaining its customers.

Vodafone's strategy is focused on maintaining high growth levels in its markets and increasing profitability, maintaining their current customer base, expanding into 3G technology (the next generation in digital technology), and increasing their global presence through acquisitions, partnerships, or purchases of new licenses. Vodafone's current strategy calls for it to merge with a company with substantial market share in America and Asia, which would fill several holes in Vodafone's current geographic coverage. Ideally, the target firm should have a low presence in Britain and Europe, because Vodafone has this geography covered. With more extensive geographic coverage, Vodafone could potentially offer services such as global roaming to their customers traveling throughout the world.

Company Structure

The company is very decentralized. The responsibilities of the corporate headquarters in the UK lie in developing corporate strategic direction, compiling financial information, reporting and developing relationships with the various stock markets, and evaluating new expansion opportunities. The management of operations is left to the countries' management, assuming business plans and financial measures are being met. They have a relatively flat management structure. All of their employees are shareowners in the company. They have record low levels of employee turnover, and the average age of the workforce is 33 years old.

AIRTOUCH

Company History

AirTouch Communications launched it first cellular service network in 1984 in Los Angeles during the opening ceremonies at the 1984 Olympics. The original company was run under the name PacTel Cellular, a subsidiary of Pacific Telesis. In 1994, PacTel Cellular spun off from Pacific Telesis and became AirTouch Communications, under the direction of Chairman and Chief Executive Officer, Sam Ginn. Ginn believed that the most exciting growth potential in telecommunications is in the wireless and not the landline services segment of the industry. In 1998, AirTouch operated in thirteen countries on three continents, serving more than 12 million customers, as a worldwide carrier of cellular, PCS, and paging services. Currently, AirTouch employs both digital and analog technology to serve their customers. They also hold a 5.7% interest in Globalstar, L.P. AirTouch has chosen to compete on a global front through various partnerships and JVs. Recognizing the massive growth potential outside the United States, AirTouch began their global strategy immediately after the spinoff.

Strategic Intent

AirTouch has chosen to differentiate itself in its domestic regions based on the concept of "Superior Service Delivery." The company's focus is on being available to its customers 24 hours a day, 7 days a week, and on delivering pricing options that meet the customer's needs. AirTouch allows customers to change pricing plans without penalty. The company also emphasizes call clarity and quality and extensive geographic coverage.

The key challenges AirTouch faces on a global front is in reducing churn (i.e., the percent of customers leaving), implementing improved digital technology, managing pressure on service pricing, and maintaining profit margins by focusing on cost reduction. Other challenges include creating a domestic national presence through acquisition or JV agreements and increasing penetration by pursuing profitable new global ventures.

Company Structure

AirTouch is decentralized. Regions have been developed in the U.S. market and are run autonomously with respect to pricing decisions, marketing campaigns, and customer care operations. Each region is run as a profit center. The various regions compete on the basis of service, coverage, features, or pricing, depending upon the requirements on the region's customers. Its European operations are also run independently from each other to be able to respond to the competitive issues unique to the specific countries. All employees are shareowners in the company and the average age of the workforce is in the low to mid-thirties. Both companies are comparable in terms of size and exhibit operating profit margins in the mid-to-high teens. AirTouch has substantially less leverage than Vodafone (see Table 10-7).

MERGER HIGHLIGHTS

Vodafone began exploratory talks with Airtouch as early as 1996 on a variety of options ranging from partnerships to a merger. Merger talks continued informally until late 1998 when they were formally broken off. Bell Atlantic, interested in expanding its own mobile phone business' geographic coverage, immediately jumped into the void by proposing to AirTouch that together they form a new

TABLE 10-7.   Comparative Financial Performance[a]

	Vodafone ($, year ended 3/31/98)	AirTouch ($, year ended 12/31/98)
Sales[b]	4,199.1	5,181.0
Operating profit (EBIT)	635.9	946.0
Earnings per share (fully diluted)	.20	1.30
Earnings per American depository share	2.07	Not applicable
Total assets	6,842.2	17,553.0
Total long-term debt	1,106.1	2,746.0

[a] Financials are based on U.S. generally accepted accounting principles.

[b] EBIT, earnings before interest and taxes.

wireless company. In early 1999, Vodafone once again entered the fray, sparking a sharp takeover battle for AirTouch. Vodafone emerged victorious by mid-1999. Table 10-8 summarizes the chronology of key events in this hotly contested merger.

TABLE 10-8. Merger Timeline

Date/event	Outcome
Exploratory talks begin on partnering opportunities in 1996 and 1997	Opportunities for joint ventures, controlled roaming purchasing arrangements, and merger were discussed at the conceptual level only.
Sept./early Oct. 1998 High-level meetings take place between Vodafone and AirTouch	Chris Gent, CEO of Vodafone, and Sam Ginn, CEO of AirTouch, met to engage in more formal merger discussions.
Oct. 21, 1998	Merger talks terminated.
Nov. 13, 1998 Bell Atlantic proposes merger	Bell Atlantic proposes formation of a new wireless company. The proposal contemplated that AirTouch would become part of the new company and that both Bell Atlantic and GTE, which had recently entered into a merger agreement with Bell Atlantic, would contribute their wireless assets to the new company in return for a controlling interest. The discussion evolved into merger talks.
Dec. 31, 1998 Merger discussions made public	AirTouch and Bell Atlantic issue a joint press release discussing exploratory talks on January 3, 1999.
Jan. 2, 1999 Vodafone makes formal merger proposal	Vodafone offers 5 of its shares, equivalent to .5 ADSs,[a] and $6 in cash for each share of AirTouch common. An exchange of stock and cash was undertaken to make the offer more attractive in light of potential offers from other suitors and to ensure tax-free treatment for AirTouch shareholders.
Jan. 7 and 10, 1999 Special board meetings are held	AirTouch Board holds a special meeting to review strategic options. AirTouch continues to negotiate with both Vodafone and Bell Atlantic.
Jan. 14, 1999 Vodafone ups the ante	Vodafone raises its offer to 5 of its common shares plus $9 for each share of AirTouch common.
Jan. 15, 1999 Board accepts Vodafone's proposal	AirTouch submits terms and conditions of both proposals to its Board. Board votes unanimously to accept the Vodafone proposal and both parties execute the merger agreement.
June 27, 1999 Vodafone and AirTouch merger completed	Transaction valued at about $55 billion.

[a] ADS is an American Depository Share representing 10 Vodafone ordinary shares. ADSs were created to allow U.S. shareholders to more easily hold and trade Vodafone AirTouch shares in U.S. markets after the merger.

MOTIVATION FOR THE MERGER

Shared Vision

The merger would create a more competitive, global wireless telecommunications company than either company could achieve separately. Moreover, both firms shared the same vision of the telecommunications industry. Mobile telecommunications is believed to be the among the fastest growing segment of the telecommunications industry and that over time mobile voice will replace large amounts of telecommunications traffic carried by fixed-line networks and will serve as a major platform for voice and data communication. Both companies believe that mobile penetration will reach 50% in developed countries by 2003, and 55% and 65% in the United States and developed European countries, respectively, by 2005 (AirTouch, *Proxy Statement:* 1999).

Complementary Assets

Scale, operating strength, and complementary assets were also given as compelling reasons for the merger. The combination of AirTouch and Vodafone would create the largest mobile telecommunication company at the time, with significant presence in the United Kingdom, United States, continental Europe, and Asian Pacific region. The scale and scope of the operations is expected to make the combined firms the vendor of choice for business travelers and international corporations. Interests in operations in many countries will make Vodafone AirTouch more attractive as a partner for other international fixed and mobile telecommunications providers. The combined scale of the companies is also expected to enhance its ability to develop existing networks and to be in the forefront of providing technologically advanced products and services.

Synergy

Anticipated synergies include after-tax cost savings of $340 million annually by the fiscal year ending March 31, 2002. The estimated net present value is $3.6 billion discounted at 9%. The cost savings arise from global purchasing and operating efficiencies, including volume discounts, infrastructure and other assets, lower leased line costs, more efficient voice and data networks, savings in development and purchase of third generation mobile handsets, infrastructure, and software. Revenues should be enhanced by providing more international coverage and through the bundling of services for corporate customers that operate as multinational businesses and business travelers.

AIRTOUCH'S BOARD ANALYZES OPTIONS

Morgan Stanley, AirTouch's investment banker, provided analyses of the current prices of both the Vodafone and Bell Atlantic stocks, their historical trading ranges, and the anticipated trading prices of both companies' stock upon completion of the merger and upon redistribution of the stock to the general public. Table 10-9 highlights the primary characteristics of the two competing offers.

TABLE 10-9.   Comparative Offers

Vodafone	Bell Atlantic[a]
Five shares of Vodafone common plus $9 for each share of AirTouch common	1.54 shares of Bell Atlantic for each share of Air-Touch common subject to the transaction being treated as a pooling of interest under U.S. GAAP.
	SER adjusted upward 9 months out to reflect the payment of dividends on the Bell Atlantic stock.
	An SER collar would be employed to ensure that AirTouch shareholders would receive shares valued at $80.08. If the average closing price of Bell stock were less than $48, the SER would be increased to 1.6683. If the price exceeded $52, the exchange rate would remain at 1.54.[b]

[a] GAAP, generally accepted accounting principles; SER, share exchange ratio.
[b] The collar guarantees the price of Bell Atlantic stock for the AirTouch shareholders, since $48 × 1.6683 and $52 × 1.54 both equal $80.08.

Morgan Stanley's primary conclusions were as follows:

1. Bell Atlantic had a current market value of $83 per share of AirTouch stock based on the $53.81 closing price of Bell Atlantic common stock on January 14, 1999. The collar would maintain the price at $80.08 per share if the price of Bell Atlantic stock during a specified period prior to closing were between $48 and $52 per share.
2. The Vodafone proposal had a current market value of $97 per share of AirTouch stock based on Vodafone's ordinary shares (i.e., common) on January 17, 1999.
3. Following the merger, the market value of the Vodafone ADSs to be received by AirTouch shareholders under the Vodafone proposal could decrease. However, as long as Vodafone's ADSs trade above $148, the market value of the Vodafone proposal would exceed the market value of Bell Atlantic's proposal. This assumed that Bell Atlantic's stock price did not change.
4. Following the merger, the market value of Bell Atlantic's stock could also decrease, particularly in light of the expectation that the proposed transaction would dilute Bell Atlantic's EPS by more than 10% through 2002.

In addition to Vodafone's higher value, the board tended to favor the Vodafone offer because it involved less regulatory uncertainty. As U.S. corporations, a merger between AirTouch and Bell Atlantic was likely to receive substantial scrutiny from the U.S. Justice Department, the Federal Trade Commission, and the Federal Communications Commission. Moreover, while both proposals could be completed tax free, except for the small cash component of the Vodafone offer, the Vodafone offer was not subject to achieving any specific accounting treatment such as pooling of interests under U.S. generally accepted accounting principles (GAAP).

Recognizing their fiduciary responsibility to review all legitimate offers in a balanced manner, the AirTouch Board also considered a number of factors that made the Vodafone proposal less attractive. The failure to do so would no doubt trigger shareholder lawsuits. The major factors that detracted from the Vodafone proposal included the following:

1. Combining with Vodafone, unlike combining with Bell Atlantic, would not address strategic issues facing AirTouch, such as gaining a national presence in the United States.
2. Joining with Vodafone may be subject to more market risk because it had a higher P/E ratio than companies in its peer group in the U.S. and since Vodafone's stock has been more volatile than Bell Atlantic's share price.
3. Vodafone will incur significant additional indebtedness to finance the cash portion of the purchase price.
4. Vodafone's and AirTouch's noncontrolling positions in certain key markets may limit the combined company's ability to achieve all of the potential synergies.

Despite these concerns, the higher offer price from Vodafone (i.e., $97 to $83) won the day. Following this transaction, the highly aggressive Vodafone went on to consummate the largest merger in history in 2000 by combining with Germany's telecommunications powerhouse, Mannesmann, for $183 billion (see Chapter 3, this volume).

Case Study Discussion Questions

1. Did the AirTouch board make the right decision? Why or why not?
2. How valid are the reasons for the proposed merger?
3. What are the potential risk factors related to the merger?
4. Why did the merger happen so quickly?
5. Why was Bell Atantic interested in a pooling-of-interest accounting treatment? Why was this a concern about Bell Atlantic's purchase price?
6. The Vodafone merger will be treated as a purchase of assets under GAAP and create $3.4 billion in annual GW expenses. Why might the merger have been accounted for financial reporting purposes using the purchase method of accounting?
7. Is this merger likely to be tax free, partially tax free, or taxable?
8. What are some of the challenges the two companies are likely to face while integrating the businesses?
9. How would the collar protect AirTouch shareholders from a decline in Bell Atlantic's stock?

Solutions to these questions appear at the back of this book.

REFERENCES

AirTouch Communications, *Annual Report,* 1997. Available: www.edgar.com

AirTouch Communications, *Stockholder Proxy Statement,* April 22, 1999, p. 32. Available: www.edgar.com

Auerbach, Alan J., and David Reishus, "Taxes and the Merger Decision." In John C. Coffee Jr., Louis Lowenstein, and Susan Rose Ackerman, (Eds.), *Knights, Raiders, and Targets,* New York: Oxford University Press, 1988, pp. 300–313.

Auerbach, Alan J., and James Poterba, "Tax Loss Carry Forwards and Corporate Tax Incentives." In Martin Feldstein (Eds.), *The Effect of Taxation on Capital Accumulation,* Chicago: University of Chicago Press, 1987.

Davis, Michael L., "Differential Market Reaction to Pooling and Purchase Methods," *The Accounting Review, 65,* July 1990, pp. 696–709.

Davis, Michael L., "The Purchase vs. Pooling Controversy: How the Stock Market Responds to Goodwill," *Journal of Applied Corporate Finance,* 9, Spring 1996, pp. 50–59.

Jenkins, Edmund L., "New Standards for Business Combinations, Presentation to the Committee on Banking, Housing, and Urban Affairs, March 2, 2000. Available: www.fasb.org

Lys, Thomas, and Linda Vincent, An Analysis of Value Destruction in AT&T's Acquisition of NCR," *Journal of Financial Economics,* vol. 39, 2–3, 1995, pp. 353–378.

Pahler, Arnold J., and Josept E. Mori, *Advanced Accounting,* Fort Worth, TX: The Dryden Press, 1997.

Robinson, John R., and Phillip B. Shane, "Acquisition Accounting Method and Bid Premia for Target Accounting," *The Accounting Review,* January 1990, pp. 25–48.

Scholes, Myron, and Mark A. Wolfson, *Taxes and Business Strategy,* Englewood Cliffs, NJ: Prentice-Hall 1992.

Sherman, Andrew J., *Mergers and Acquisitions: From A to Z,* New York: AMACOM Publishing, 1998, pp. 95–122.

Tillinghast, David R. "Tax Aspects of Inbound Merger and Acquisition and Joint Venture Transactions," In David J. BenDaniel and Arthur H. Rosenbloom, (Eds.), *International M&A, Joint Ventures, and Beyond: Doing the Deal,* New York: John Wiley & Sons, Inc., 1998, pp. 151–164.

ALTERNATIVE
STRATEGIES AND
STRUCTURES

11

LEVERAGED BUYOUT STRUCTURES AND VALUATION

—A billion dollars isn't what it used to be.
—Nelson Bunker Hunt

Chuck Brennan, CEO of Byzantine International, had completed the transaction after several months of hard negotiating with the firm's board of directors. Along with other senior members of management, he had proposed to take the company private by offering shareholders a substantial premium to the current market price. Although the initial offer was met with significant skepticism from the board, he was able to gain considerable credibility by obtaining financing from Jacob Carter of Carter and Associates, a well-known investor in highly leveraged "middle-market" transactions.

Jacob Carter had been able to finance about ten similar transactions in related industries during the 1980s and 1990s using relatively little capital. The methodology had been simple. Find target firms with consistent historical earnings growth, solid management, little debt, substantial tangible assets, and mature technologies and production processes in industries with largely stable growth rates. Such firms often displayed predictable cash flows well in excess of their reinvestment requirements. Carter reasoned that the unencumbered assets could be used as collateral for new borrowing, and the excess cash flow could be used to cover the subsequent increase in debt service requirements.

The remaining ingredient for the success of Carter and Associates was to motivate the management of the target firm through generous performance bonuses and stock options. Jacob Carter knew that the prospect of substantial wealth would be likely to cause management to stay focused on improving the operating performance of the highly leveraged firm to meet the quarterly interest and principal repayments. Moreover, earnings resulting from improving performance would be largely tax-free, sheltered by the deductibility of interest payments. As the outstanding debt was paid off, the target firm would then be taken public through a re-issuance of stock or sold to a strategic buyer. The lenders would be repaid from the proceeds of the sale and the equity investors would be handsomely compensated for their efforts.

Chuck Brennan was a convert to this line of reasoning and in concert with Jacob Carter was able to convince Byzantine's board that their offer was not only fair for the firm's shareholders but also that it could be readily financed. The celebration following closing was short-lived, as the enormity of the task that lay before management began to sink in. The methodology employed in the takeover was indeed conceptually simple. The challenge would be to make it all happen according to plan.

OVERVIEW

In a *leveraged buyout* (LBO), borrowed funds are used to pay for all or most of the purchase price. Historically, as much as 90% or more of the purchase price is financed with debt. Typically, the tangible assets of the firm to be acquired are used as collateral for the loans. Bank loans are often secured by the most liquid assets, such as receivables and inventory. A portion of long-term senior financing may be secured by the firm's fixed assets. Subordinated debt, either unrated on low-rated debt, is used to raise the balance of the purchase price. This debt is often referred to as *junk bond* financing.

When a public company is subject to an LBO, it is said to be *going private,* because the equity of the firm has been purchased by a small group of investors and is no longer publicly traded. Ultimately, the investor group will attempt to realize a return on their investment by once again taking the company public through an initial public offering (IPO) or by selling to a strategic buyer. Buyers of the firm targeted to become an LBO often consist of managers from the firm that is being acquired. An LBO that is initiated by the target firm's incumbent management is called a *management buyout* (MBO).

This chapter begins with a discussion of the evolution of LBOs (i.e., highly leveraged transactions) in the context of the risks associated with alternative financing options from asset-based or secured lending to pure cash flow-based lending. Subsequent sections discuss typical LBO structures, the risks associated with improperly constructed deals, and how to take a company private. Key shareholder and public policy issues are illustrated in this chapter by a case study of the largest LBO in history, RJR Nabisco. Empirical studies of pre- and postbuyout returns to shareholders are also reviewed. The chapter concludes with a discussion of how to analyze and value LBO transactions.

THE ORIGINS OF
LEVERAGED TRANSACTIONS

THE EARLY YEARS: 1950s AND 1960s

Entrepreneurs in the immediate post-World War II era, who were considering retirement, were often concerned that the continuity of the family business was not assured. They were also worried about the impact of estate taxes upon their death. Consequently, in the 1950s and early 1960s, they were often willing to sell their businesses at or below book value to younger individuals who were willing to expand the entrepreneur's business (Reisman: 1981). Generally, the buyer provided equity amounting to only 20–25% of the purchase price and borrowed the remainder from commercial finance companies using the assets of the target firm to secure the borrowing. The portion of the purchase price that was paid in cash would help to pay any taxes owed by the seller following the sale or any estate taxes following their death. Most of these leveraged transactions were of privately held, small-to-medium-sized businesses.

Commercial finance companies were specialists in short- and medium-term lending against accounts receivable, inventory, equipment, and real estate. They had the expertise to determine the market value of these assets, verify and monitor their status, obtain a legally enforceable security interest in them and, in the event of default, obtain their maximum liquidation value. Banks and insurance companies had tended to shy away from highly leveraged transactions with little equity investment because of their perceived high risk.

A bull market in stocks during the 1960s encouraged many businesses to go public during this period rather than to get involved in highly leveraged transactions. Thus, LBO activity tampered off during the late 1960s; however, by the early 1970s, the public euphoria for new equity issues had abated in the wake of escalating bankruptcies and sky-high price-to-earnings (P/E) ratios. Renewed interest in LBOs emerged by the late 1980s. Conglomerates that had amassed large portfolios of businesses during the 1960s and early 1970s began to divest many of their holdings. The size of these divested units usually ranged in annual sales from $5 million to more than $250 million. Leveraged buyouts were an increasingly common way to finance these transactions. Investors saw an opportunity to generate unusually large financial returns by using creatively structured highly leveraged transactions.

FINANCIAL BUYERS

Investors in LBOs are frequently referred to as financial buyers, because they are primarily focused on relatively short- to intermediate-term financial returns. Such buyers tend to hold their investments for 5–7 years. Financial buyers tend to concentrate on actions that enhance the target firm's ability to generate cash flow in order to satisfy their substantial debt service requirements. The existence of substantial leverage made the potential returns to equity much more attractive than less leveraged transactions (Table 11-1). Financial buyers with a demonstrated ability to identify attractive LBO candidates were frequently able to attract sufficient funding such that they could offer target company shareholders a substantial premium over the target's current public market value.

CHARACTERISTICS OF LBOs IN THE LATE 1970s AND EARLY 1980s

Debt was normally four to five times equity (Lehn and Poulsen: 1988). Debt was likely to be amortized over a 5–7-year period and certainly no more than 10 years. The LBO firm was generally taken public or divested to a corporate buyer whenever the tax benefits provided by the leverage started to diminish. Existing corporate management was encouraged to participate as equity owners. The skill of the financial buyer during this period was largely in constructing a capital structure that would allow for the highest possible leverage while still enabling the firm to meet debt service requirements through improvements in operating performance. The transactions were normally characterized by complex capital structures consisting of senior bank debt secured by the target's assets, subordinated unsecured debt, preferred stock, and common equity. Secured debt often comprised about 60% of the total purchase price with unsecured debt accounting for about 20–25%. The remainder of the purchase price consisted of preferred and common equity.

LBOS IN THE MID-TO-LATE 1980s

LBOs during this period had many of the same characteristics of earlier LBOs, with two notable differences. First, debt was serviced from both operating cash flow and asset sales. Changes in the tax laws reduced the popularity of divesting assets to reduce leverage, as asset sales immediately upon the closing of the transaction are no longer deemed tax-free. Previously, it was possible to buy stock in a

TABLE 11-1.   Impact of Leverage on Return to Shareholders

	All cash purchase ($)	Cash (50%)/ debt (50%)	Cash (20%)/ debt (80%)
Purchase price	$100	$100	$100
Equity (cash investment)	100	50	20
Borrowings	0	50	80
Earnings before interest and taxes	20	20	20
Interest @ 10%	0	5	8
Income before taxes	20	15	12
Less income taxes @ 40%	8	6	4.8
Net Income	12	9	7.2
After-tax return on equity	12%	18%	36%

company, sell the assets, and any gain on asset sales was offset by a mirrored reduction in the value of the stock. This was made illegal as a result of the Tax Act of 1986 (see Chapter 10, this volume).

The second half of the 1980s saw the emergence of the nontraditional sources of LBO financing from LBO funds. They provided both secured and unsecured financing. Their sources of funding came from large institutional investors such as life insurance companies and pension funds. These institutional investors would also lend directly to the LBO.

LBOs IN THE 1990s

Reflecting the powerful equity markets of the period, the primary exit strategy during this decade was through stock offerings to the public. Debt-to-equity ratios were typically more conservative than during the 1980s. Equity as a percent of debt increased to about 30% as compared to 5–10% in the late 1980s. Deals were often structured so that debt repayment was not required until 10 years after the transaction was structured. This tended to reduce pressure on near-term earnings performance. The LBO firm's strategy was to enable the target firm to establish a period of escalating reported earnings to make it more attractive whenever it was ultimately taken public. Moreover, LBO firms often purchased a firm to use as a platform to undertake other leveraged buyouts in the same industry. The acquired firms would then be merged and taken public at a later date.

A common technique employed during the 1990s was to wait for favorable periods in the stock market to sell a portion of the LBO's equity to the public. The proceeds of the issue would be used to repay debt, thereby reducing the LBO's financial risk. Once the LBO's shares had traded for a few months, secondary stock offerings were often made as the initial investors liquidated some portion of their equity positions. Whenever the firm had paid off a sufficient portion of its debt, a search was initiated for a strategic buyer willing to pay a premium to the LBO's investors to gain a controlling interest.

ALTERNATIVE FINANCING OPTIONS

Once a prospective target has been identified, the buyer has a number of alternative financing options. The ideal mechanism might be to finance the transaction out of cash held by the target in excess of normal working capital requirements. Such situations are usually very difficult to find. Venture capital investors may also be available to fund the transaction. However, this may represent very expensive financing, since the buyer may have to give up as much as 70% of the ownership of the acquired company. Use of the buyer's stock may be an appropriate way to minimize the initial cash outlay, but such an option is rarely available in an MBO or a buyout by privately held companies.

The seller may be willing to accept debt issued by the buyer if an up-front cash payment is not important. This may be highly disadvantageous to the buyer if the seller places substantial restrictions on how the business may be managed. The use of a public issue of long-term debt to finance the transaction may minimize the initial cash outlay, but it is also subject to restrictions placed on how the business may be operated by the investors buying the issue. Moreover, public issues are expensive in terms of administrative, marketing, and regulatory reporting costs. For these reasons, asset-based lending has emerged as an attractive alternative to the use of cash, stock, or public debt issues, if the target had sufficient tangible assets to serve as collateral.

ASSET-BASED OR SECURED LENDING

Under asset-based lending, the borrower pledges certain assets as collateral. Asset-based lenders look at the borrower's assets as their primary protection against the borrower's failure to repay. Such loans are often short-term (i.e., less than 1 year in maturity) and secured by assets that can be easily liquidated such as accounts receivable and inventory. Loans maturing in more than 1 year are often referred to as term loans. Acquiring firms generally prefer to borrow funds on an unsecured basis, because the added administrative costs involved in pledging assets as security raise the total cost of borrowing significantly. Secured borrowing can also be onerous because the security agreements can severely limit a company's future borrowing. However, in many instances, borrowers may have little choice but to obtain secured lending for a least a portion of the purchase price.

By the early 1970s, many banks had begun to engage in commercial financing as an adjunct to other types of more traditional lending. The adoption of the Uniform Commercial Code in the 1960s greatly simplified and made uniform techniques for obtaining and administering legally enforceable security interests in accounts receivables, inventory, and other types of collateral (Reisman: 1978).

Loan Documentation

The lending process entails the negotiation of a loan agreement, security agreement, and a promissory note. The *loan agreement* stipulates the terms and conditions under which the lender will loan the firm funds. The *security agreement* specifies which of the borrower's assets will be pledged to secure the loan. The *promissory note* commits the borrower to repay the loan, even if the assets when liquidated do not fully cover the unpaid balance. These agreements contain certain security provisions and protective covenants limiting what the borrower may do as long as the loan is outstanding. These provisions and covenants will be described in more detail in the next section.

The security agreement is subsequently filed at a state regulatory office in the state where the collateral is located. Future lenders can check with this office to see which assets a firm has pledged and which are free to be used as future collateral. The filing of this security agreement legally establishes the lender's security interest in the collateral. If the borrower defaults on the loan or otherwise fails to honor the terms of the agreement, the lender can seize and sell the collateral to recover the value of the loan.

The process of determining which of a firm's assets are free from liens is made easier today by commercial credit reporting repositories such as Dun & Bradstreet and Experian. These firms collect such information from commercial creditors, consolidate an individual firm's credit relationships with all its credit grantors, and provide a complete picture of how a business is paying its bills with respect to all its creditors. These reports also indicate which of the firm's assets are currently pledged as collateral.

Pledging Accounts Receivable

Accounts receivable are commonly used as collateral to obtain secured short-term financing. Accounts receivable represent a highly desirable form of collateral from the lender's viewpoint, because they are generally very liquid. However, the lender may encounter problems if the borrower pledges nonexistent accounts, the customer returns the merchandise, or the customer files a claim that the merchandise is defective. Depending upon the extent to which they are collectable, lenders may lend up to 75–80% of the book value of the receivables (Kretlow, McGuigan, and Moyer: 1998a).

Pledging Inventory

Inventories are also commonly used to provide collateral for LBO transactions. As is true of receivables, inventories are often highly liquid. Inventory consists of raw material, work-in-process, and finished goods. Only raw material and finished goods inventories are normally considered by lenders as suitable for collateral. The amount that a lender will advance against the book value of inventory depends upon its characteristics: ease of identification, liquidity, and marketability. In general, lenders will loan between 50 and 80% of the value of inventory.

Pledging Equipment and Real Estate to Support Term Loans

A term loan or intermediate term credit is a loan with a maturity of from 1 to 10 years. Borrowers often prefer term loans, because they do not have to be concerned that the loan will have to be renewed. A term loan can be structured in such a way that the term of the loan corresponds with the economic life of the item being financed. Durable equipment and real estate are often used to secure real estate. Lenders are frequently willing to lend up to 80% of the appraised value of equipment and 50% of the value of land. The cash flows generated by the assets will be used to pay off the loan. Term loans are sometimes employed in LBO transactions to reduce the overall cost of borrowing. Because term loans are privately negotiated between the borrower and the lender, they are much less expensive than the costs associated with floating a public debt or stock issue.

SECURITY PROVISIONS AND PROTECTIVE COVENANTS

Security provisions and protective covenants are included in loan documents to increase the likelihood that the interest and principal of outstanding loans will be repaid in a timely fashion. The number and complexity of security provisions depends on the size of the firm. Loans to small firms tend to be secured more often than term loans to large firms.

Security Provisions

Typical security features include the assignment of payments due under a specific contract to the lender, an assignment of a portion of the receivables or inventories, and a pledge of marketable securities held by the borrower. Other features include a mortgage on property, plant, and equipment held by the borrower and the assignment of the cash surrender value of a life insurance policy held by the borrower on key executives.

Affirmative Covenants

An affirmative covenant is a portion of a loan agreement that specifies the actions the borrowing firm agrees to take during the term of the loan. These typically include furnishing periodic financial statements to the lender, carrying sufficient insurance to cover insurable business risks, maintaining a minimum amount of net working capital, and retention of key management personnel acceptable to the lending institution.

Negative Covenants

Such covenants restrict the actions of the borrower. They include limiting the amount of dividends that can be paid, the level of salaries and bonuses that may be given to the borrower's employees, the total amount of indebtedness that can be assumed by the borrower, and investments in plant and equipment and acquisitions. The borrower may also be required to obtain the lender's approval before certain assets can be sold.

Default Provisions

All loan agreements have default provisions permitting the lender to collect the loan immediately under certain conditions. These conditions might include the borrower failing to pay interest, principal, or both in accordance with the terms of the loan agreement, the borrower materially misrepresenting information on the firm's financial statements, and the borrower failing to observe any of the affirmative or negative covenants. Loan agreements also commonly have cross-default provisions allowing a lender to collect its loan immediately if the borrower is in default on a loan to another lender.

CASH FLOW OR UNSECURED LENDERS

Cash flow lenders view the borrower's future cash flow generation capability as the primary means of recovering a loan and the borrower's assets as a secondary source of funds in the event of default by the borrower. Generally large firms with relatively little leverage and with favorable cash flows are able to borrow from cash flow lenders, such as commercial banks, at relatively low interest rates. Smaller, more highly leveraged businesses with less certain cash flows often have to borrow on a secured basis from traditional asset-based lenders, such as commercial finance companies, at relatively high rates.

Cash flow-based lending for LBOs became more commonplace during the mid-to-late 1980s. Aggressive bidding began to force purchase prices to levels well in excess of the value of the target's tangible assets. Borrowers were increasingly seeking funding for amounts well in excess of what traditional asset-based lenders would provide. Consequently, many LBOs' capital structures assumed increasing amounts of unsecured debt. To compensate for additional risk, the unsecured lenders would receive both a higher interest rate and warrants that were convertible into equity at some future date.

Unsecured debt is often referred to as *mezzanine financing,* because it has both equity and debt characteristics. In liquidation, it lies between the secured or asset-based debt and preferred and common equity. Unsecured financing often consists of several layers of debt each subordinate in liquidation to the next most senior issue. Those with the lowest level of security normally offer the highest yields to compensate for their higher level of risk in the event of default.

Types of Long-Term Financing

Long-term debt is generally classified according to whether it is secured or not. Secured debt issues are usually called mortgage bonds or equipment trust certificates. Issues not secured by specific assets are called debentures. Because debentures are unsecured, their quality depends on the general credit worthiness of the issuing company. The attractiveness of long-term debt is its relatively low after-tax cost due to the tax deductibility of interest. In addition, leverage can help improve earnings per share and returns on equity. However, too much debt can increase the risk of default on loan repayments and eventual bankruptcy.

Senior and Junior Debt

Long-term debt issues are also classified by whether they are senior or junior in liquidation. Senior debt has a higher priority claim to a firm's earnings and assets than junior debt. Unsecured debt may also be classified according to whether it is subordinated to other types of debt. In general, subordinated debentures are junior to other types of debt, including bank loans, and may even be junior to all of a firm's other debt. The extent to which a debt issue is junior to other debt depends upon the restrictions placed on the company by the purchasers of the issue in an agreement called an indenture.

Indentures

An *indenture* is a contract between the firm that issues the long-term debt securities and the lenders. The indenture details the nature of the issue, specifies the way in which the principal must be repaid, and specifies affirmative and negative covenants applicable to the long-term debt issue. Typical negative covenants include maintaining a minimum interest coverage ratio, a minimum level of working capital, a maximum amount of dividends that the firm can pay, and restrictions on equipment leasing and issuing additional debt (Emery and Finnerty: 1992).

Bond Ratings

Debt issues are rated by various rating agencies according to their relative degree of risk. These agencies include Moody's Investors Services and Standard and Poor's (S&P) Corporation. Factors considered by these agencies when assessing risk include a firm's earnings stability, interest coverage ratios, the relative amount of debt in the firm's capital structure, the degree of subordination of the issue being rated, and the firm's past performance in meeting its debt service requirements. Each rating agency has a scale for identifying the risk of an issue. For Moody's, the ratings are Aaa, Aa, A, Baa, Ba, B, Caa, Ca, and C, with Aaa the lowest and C the highest risk category. AAA denotes the lowest risk category for S&P. This rating is followed by AA, A, BBB, BB, B, CCC, CC, C, and D.

JUNK BONDS

Junk bonds are high-yield bonds either rated by the credit-rating agencies as below investment grade or not rated at all. Noninvestment grade bonds are usually rated Ba or lower by Moody's or BB or lower by S&P. When originally issued, junk bonds typically yield more than four percentage points above the yields on U.S. Treasury debt of comparable maturity. At the end of the 1990s, there was about $600 billion in high-yield debt outstanding in the United States.

Junk bond financing exploded in the 1980s. Between 1970 and 1977, junk bond issues accounted for about 3–4% of total publicly issued corporate bonds; by 1985, their share of corporate debt issues rose to more than 14%. The sharp growth of junk bonds reflected their growing acceptance by the public debt market to finance the internal growth requirements of high-growth corporations and to finance corporate takeovers, particularly LBOs. Although junk bonds were a popular source of financing for takeovers, about three-fourths of the total proceeds of junk bonds issued between 1980 and 1986 were used to finance the capital requirements of high-growth corporations such as MCI (Yago: 1991). The remainder was used to finance corporate takeovers.

This source of LBO financing dried up due to a series of defaults of over-leveraged firms in the late 1980s, coupled with alleged insider trading and fraud at such companies as Drexel Burnham, the primary market maker for junk bonds. The collapse of several large savings and loans, which had been major investors in junk bonds, and the onslaught of the 1990–1991 recession compounded these problems.

Concerns about Quality

The rapid growth of the junk bond market coincided with a growing deterioration in the quality of such issues. Wigmore (1994) found that the quality of the junk bonds issued during the 1980s deteriorated in terms of such measures as interest coverage ratios (i.e., EBIT/interest expense, debt/net tangible book value, and cash flow as a percentage of debt). Hence, it is not surprising that junk bond default rates reached record levels of more than 10% during the 1990–1991 recession.

Cumulative default rates for junk bonds issued in the late seventies reached as high as 34% by 1986 (Asquith, Mullins, and Wolff: 1989). Despite these high default rates, some portion of the face value of the junk bond issues was often recovered, as firms formerly in default emerged from bankruptcy. Altman and Kishore (1996) found that recovery rates for senior secured debt averaged about 58% of the original principal. Taking recovery rates into consideration, they found the actual realized spread between junk bonds and 10-year U.S. Treasury securities was actually about two percentage points between 1978 and 1994 rather than more than four percentage points when they were originally issued.

Empirical Studies of the Junk Bond Market

Early studies of the junk or high-yield bond market suggested that bonds that were considered below investment grade showed higher returns than those considered investment grade even after the losses due to default were deducted from the junk bond yields (Hickman: 1958). Consequently, it made sense for investors to purchase the lower rated bonds, as long as their higher yields more than offset default losses. Although a study by Fraine and Mills (1961) showed that Hickman's conclusions could have been biased, a later study by Altman and Namacher (1985) suggested that default rates on junk bonds were indeed only 2.1% as compared to about zero on investment-grade bonds during the 1970–1984 period. These low default rates were consistent with other studies by Fitzpatrick and Severiens (1984) and Fridson (1984).

These early studies often did not account for the possibility that the default risk associated with a noninvestment grade bond may increase the longer the elapsed time since its original issue date. Consequently, during periods like the late 1980s when the issuance of junk bonds reached record levels, the average default rate on junk bonds appeared to be low primarily because newly issued bonds were more likely to have relatively low default rates.

Reflecting the impact of the higher default rates on bonds issued in the early 1980s, junk bond default rates reached a record 10% in the early 1990s. Since then, default rates stabilized at their long-term rate of about 2% during the mid-to-late 1990s. However, the difference on yields between junk bonds and 10-year Treasury securities rose to more than 5 percentage points by the end of the decade due to the increasing default rate on high-yield bonds to more than 6% in 1999 (*Business Week:* 1999a). Concerns about the rising default rate were exacerbated as a result of worries about the impact of increasing interest rates on slowing the economy. These spreads had not been seen since the Russian government defaulted on its international debt and several well-known hedge funds nearly went bankrupt in 1998. Such spreads underscore the sensitivity of these types of bonds to changes in the economic cycle.

OTHER SOURCES OF FUNDS

Unlike debt and preferred stock, which are fixed income securities, common stock is a variable income security. Common stockholders participate in the firm's future earnings because they may receive a larger dividend if earnings increase. Preferred stock has both debt and common equity characteristics. Like common stock, preferred stock is part of shareholders' equity.

Although preferred stockholders receive dividends instead of interest payments, it is considered a fixed income security. Dividends on preferred stock are generally constant over time, like interest payments on debt, but the firm is generally not obligated to pay them at a specific point in time. Unpaid dividends may cumulate for eventual payment by the issuer if the preferred stock is a special cumulative issue. In liquidation, bondholders are paid first, then preferred stockholders, and common stockholders last. Preferred stock is often issued in LBO transactions, because it provides investors a fixed income security, which has a claim that is senior to common stock in the event of liquidation. Table 11-2 summarizes the key characteristics of an LBO's capital structure.

COMMON FORMS OF LEVERAGED BUYOUT STRUCTURES

As noted previously, LBOs are either asset or cash flow based. As a result of the epidemic of bankruptcies of overleveraged cash flow-based LBOs in the late 1980s, the most common form of LBO today is the asset-based LBO. This type of LBO can be accomplished in two ways: (1) the sale of assets by the target to the acquiring company or (2) a merger of the target into the acquiring company (direct merger) or a wholly owned subsidiary of the acquiring company (subsidiary merger). The direct and subsidiary merger structures are illustrated in Figure 11-1.

LENDER COMMITMENT LETTERS

The typical transaction begins with a letter of intent between the seller and buyer setting forth such basic items as price, terms of sale, assumption of liabilities, and closing deadlines. The acquirer is often asked for a *commitment letter* from a recognized lender for the loans required to fund the acquisition. Closing is generally conditioned upon the acquirer's ability to obtain financing. The commitment letter allows the lender to have access to the target company's records for credit evaluation and to conduct asset appraisals. It outlines the maximum loan amounts, interest charges, repayment schedule, and ratio of advances to assets pledged. The commitment letter is conditioned upon the lender having performed adequate due diligence and the execution of an agreement of purchase and sale between the buyer and seller.

TABLE 11-2. Leveraged Buyout Capital Structure

Type of security	Backed by	Lenders loan up to	Lending source[a]
Debt			
Secured debt (asset-based lending)			
Short-term (<1 yr.) debt	Liens generally on receivables and inventories	50–80% depending upon quality	Commercial banks and finance companies
Intermediate term (1–10 yrs.) debt	Liens on land and equipment	Up to 80% of appraised value of equipment and 50% of real estate	Life insurance companies and LBO funds
Unsecured or mezzanine debt (subordinated and junior subordinated debt) First layer Second layer Etc.	Cash-generating capabilities of the borrower	Face value of securities	Life insurance companies and LBO funds
Equity			
Preferred stock	Cash-generating capabilities of the borrower		Life insurance companies and LBO funds
Common stock	Cash-generating capabilities of the borrower		Life insurance and venture capital funds

[a] LBO, leveraged buyout.

DIRECT MERGER

If the LBO is structured as a direct merger in which the seller receives cash for stock, the lender will then make the loan to the buyer once the appropriate security agreements are in place and the target's stock has been pledged against the loan. The target is then merged into the acquiring company, which is the surviving corporation. Payment of the loan proceeds is made directly to the seller in accordance with a letter of direction drafted by the buyer. For closely held corporations, the lender may make the loan directly to the selling corporation, which then transfers the proceeds as a dividend to its stockholders, or to the buyer who has responsibility for paying the selling corporation's stockholders. All of these activities, including the closing of the acquisition, the asset-based loan closing, the distribution to the shareholders, and the merger of the target into the acquiring firm, take place simultaneously at the closing.

Direct Merger: Acquirer Purchases Stock and Merges with Target

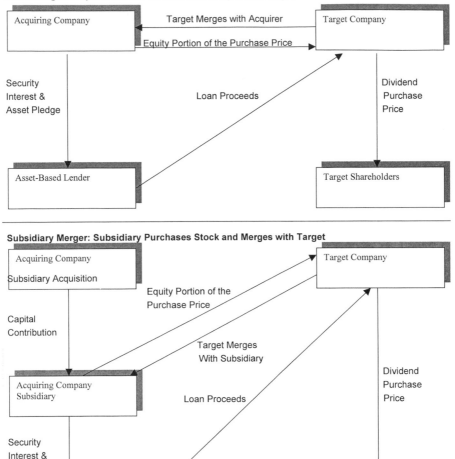

FIGURE 11-1.   Structuring an asset-based leveraged buyout.

SUBSIDIARY MERGER

LBOs may be consummated by establishing a new subsidiary that merges with the target. This may be done to avoid any negative impact that the new company might have on existing customer or creditor relationships. If some portion of the parent's assets are to be used as collateral to support the ability of its operating subsidiary to fund the transaction, both the parent and the subsidiary may be viewed as having a security interest in the debt. As such, they may be held jointly and severally liable for the debt. To avoid this situation, the parent may make a capital contribution to the subsidiary rather than provide collateral or a loan guarantee.

LEGAL PITFALLS OF IMPROPERLY STRUCTURED LBOS

Fraudulent conveyance laws take effect whenever a company goes into bankruptcy following a highly leveraged transaction. Under the law, the new company created by the LBO must be strong enough to meet its obligations to current and future creditors. If the new company is found by the court to have been inadequately capitalized to remain viable, the lender could be stripped of its secured position in the assets of the company or its claims on the assets could be made subordinate to those of the general creditors. General creditors could be compensated by other lenders, sellers, directors, and even their agents, such as auditors and investment bankers. Fraudulent conveyance laws are intended to preclude shareholders, secured creditors, and others from benefiting at the expense of unsecured creditors. The legal basis for these concerns are embodied in the U.S. Bankruptcy Code, the Uniform Fraudulent Conveyance Act, the Uniform Fraudulent Transfer Act, as well as other state statutes pertaining to fraudulent conveyance.

Avoiding Fraudulent Conveyance

A properly structured LBO should have a balance sheet that clearly indicates solvency at the time of closing. Reasonable cash flow projections should show the generation of sufficient cash to repay the firm's obligations in the ordinary course of business for at least 1 year after the acquisition. In the case of corporate divestitures, the projected cash flows should include the effect of additional interest and principal repayment and the cost of services previously provided by its parent corporation. Finally, the cash impact of off-balance sheet liabilities, such as pending litigation, should also be quantified and included in the projections.

Lender Due Diligence

The lender can be expected to make a careful evaluation of the quality of the assets to be used as collateral. Receivables will be analyzed to determine the proportion beyond normal collection terms. An assessment of the likelihood that the receivables can be realistically converted to cash will also be made. The receivables will also be evaluated for consignments, bill and hold sales, allowances and discounts, potential bad debts, and unapplied credits or charge-backs. A physical inspection of the inventory and inventory records will be made to establish both the quantitative and qualitative values of the inventory. Obsolete and unmarketable goods will be written down in value. Fixed assets will be appraised at their realistic "quick-sale" values by professional appraisers. Values should also be placed on off-balance sheet assets such as patents, trademarks, licenses, franchises, copyrights, and blueprints. Under a fair market value test, which is the standard applied to determine fraudulent conveyance, the new firm's solvency including both assets on and off the balance sheet may substantially exceed that reflected in its book value.

CRITICAL SUCCESS FACTORS

Factors critical to the success of an LBO include knowing what to buy, not overpaying, and the ability to improve operating performance.

KNOWING WHAT TO BUY

Firms that represent good candidates for an LBO are those that have substantial tangible assets, unused borrowing capacity, predictable positive operating cash flow, and assets that are not critical to the continuing operation of the business. Competent and highly motivated management is always crucial to the eventual success of the LBO.

Unused Borrowing Capacity, Tax Shelter, and Redundant Assets

Factors that enhance borrowing capacity include cash balances on the books of the target company in excess of working capital requirements, a low debt-to-total capital ratio when compared to the industry average, and a demonstrated long-term track record of consistent earnings and cash flow growth. Firms with under-valued assets may use such assets as collateral for loans from asset-based lenders. Such assets also provide a significant tax shelter as they may be revalued and depreciated or amortized over their allowable tax lives. In addition, operating assets, such as subsidiaries that are not germane to the target's core business and which can be quickly sold for cash, can be divested to accelerate the payoff of either the highest cost debt or the debt with the most restrictive covenants.

Management Competence and Motivation

Although the quality of management is always an important factor in the eventual success of a merger or acquisition, it tends to be critical to LBOs. Although management competence is a necessary condition for success, it does not ensure that the firm's performance will meet investor expectations. Management must be highly motivated by the prospect of abnormally large returns in a relatively short period of time. Consequently, management of the firm to be taken private is normally given an opportunity to own a significant portion of the equity of the firm.

Attractive Industries

Typical targets are in mature industries such as manufacturing, retailing, textiles, food processing, apparel, and soft drinks. Such industries are usually characterized by large tangible book values, modest growth prospects, relatively stable cash flow, and limited research and development (R&D), new product, or technology requirements. Such industries are generally not dependent on technologies and production processes that are subject to rapid change.

Large Company Operating Divisions

The best candidates for management buyouts are often underperforming divisions of larger companies in which the division is no longer considered critical to the parent firm's overarching strategy. Frequently, such divisions are saddled with excessive administrative overhead, often required by the parent, and expenses allocated to the division by the parent for services such as legal, auditing, and treasury functions that could be purchased less expensively from sources outside the parent firm. These often represent excellent cost-reduction opportunities once the division becomes independent of the parent. Moreover, lack of attention by the parent often results in missed opportunities for the division, because the parent is unlikely to fully fund investment opportunities that it does not consider critical to its overall business strategy.

NOT OVERPAYING

The key to a successful LBO is not to overpay for the acquisition. Although overpaying for any acquisition, highly leveraged or otherwise, almost always impairs the ability of the acquiring firm to achieve expected financial returns, it can be disastrous for LBOs. Forecasted cash flows are often subject to significant error. If the firm's projected operating earnings are even slightly lower than projected, its ability to meet interest and principal payments is jeopardized.

Failure to meet debt service obligations in a timely fashion often requires that the LBO firm re-negotiate the terms of the loan agreements with the lenders. In exchange for deferring debt repayments or for reducing interest payments, lenders will demand concessions in the form of increased equity ownership in the LBO firm. The issuance of additional shares to accommodate the lenders' demands for increased ownership dilutes the ownership position of the initial investors. If the parties to the transaction cannot reach a compromise, the firm may be forced to file for bankruptcy. In this circumstance, the value of the initial investors' investment may be wiped out as the firm is forced to reorganize under the protection of the bankruptcy court (see Chapter 13, this volume).

Highly leveraged firms are often subject to aggressive tactics from major competitors. Such competitors understand that taking on large amounts of debt will raise the break-even point for the firm. If the amount borrowed is made even more excessive due to having paid more than the economic value of the target firm, the competitors may opt to gain market share by cutting product prices. The ability of the LBO firm to match such price cuts is limited because of the need to maintain enough cash flow to meet required interest and principal repayments.

IMPROVING OPERATING PERFORMANCE

Financial buyers succeed through improving operational performance. The discipline imposed by the need to satisfy debt service requirements focuses management's attention on maximizing operating cash flows. Standard tactics include attempting to negotiate employee wage and benefit concessions in exchange for a profit sharing or stock ownership plan. Outsourcing services once provided by the parent often result in significant savings. Other cost-cutting tactics include moving the corporate headquarters to a less expensive location or to a more functional facility and aggressively pruning marginally profitable customer accounts. It is also commonplace for management to eliminate "loss leader products," those that supposedly facilitate the sale of more profitable products, and to cancel "frivolous" perks such as corporate aircraft.

Often operating performance can be improved simply by paying more attention to short-term considerations rather than focusing on more involved long-term strategies. This switch in emphasis may result in less money being spent on R&D, new product development, and on new technologies. This behavior does not necessarily imply that the LBO firm is mortgaging its future. It may mean that the discipline imposed by debt may compel managers to more clearly prioritize investment opportunities and to concentrate their available resources on those with the shortest payback period. Holthausen and Larker (1996) found that LBOs after being taken public tended to increase capital expenditures and working capital, while they were outperforming their industry competitors.

KEY SHAREHOLDER AND PUBLIC POLICY ISSUES

RJR NABISCO GOES PRIVATE

Although many LBOs involve relatively small companies, a number have involved very large companies. The largest on record occurred in 1988 when the investment firm of Kohlberg Kravis & Roberts (KKR) used an LBO to purchase RJR Nabisco for $24.6 billion. The transaction caught the attention of the public because of what at the time was its staggering size and because of the antics of many of the key players involved in the transaction. The transaction was made famous in both a best-selling novel and a movie entitled "Barbarians at the Gates."

Case Study 11-1 illustrates several important issues associated with MBOs in particular and LBOs in general. These issues deal with the potential conflict of interest facing the management team of a firm that is proposing to take the firm private and the potential wealth transfer that takes place among stakeholders of the firm undergoing an LBO.

CASE STUDY 11-1. RJR NABISCO GOES PRIVATE

BACKGROUND

The largest LBO in history is as well known for its theatrics as it is for its substantial improvement in shareholder value. In October 1988, H. Ross Johnson, then CEO of RJR Nabisco, proposed an MBO of the firm at $75 per share. His failure to inform the RJR board before publicly announcing his plans alienated many of the directors.

THE BOARD'S DILEMMA

Analysts outside the company placed the breakup value of RJR Nabisco at more than $100 per share, almost twice its then current share price. Johnson's bid was immediately countered by a bid by the well-known LBO firm, Kohlberg, Kravis, and Roberts (KKR), to buy the firm for $90 per share. The firm's board was immediately faced with the dilemma of whether to accept the KKR offer or to consider some other form of restructuring of the company. The board appointed a committee of outside directors to assess the bid in order to minimize the appearance of a potential conflict of interest in having current board members, who were also part of the buyout proposal from management, vote on which bid to select.

AN AUCTION ENVIRONMENT

The bidding war soon escalated with additional bids coming from Forstmann Little and First Boston, although the latter's bid was never really taken very seriously. Forstmann Little later dropped out of the bidding as the purchase price rose. Although the firm's investment bankers valued both the bids by Johnson and KKR at about the same level, the board ultimately accepted the KKR bid largely because of Johnson's antics.

The winning bid was set at almost $25 billion, the largest transaction on record at that time. Banks provided about three-fourths of the $20 billion that was borrowed to complete the transaction. The remaining debt was supplied by junk bond financing. The RJR shareholders were the real winners, as the final purchase price constituted a more than 100% return from the $56 per share price that existed just prior to the initial bid by RJR management.

Aggressive pricing actions by such competitors as Phillip Morris threatened to erode RJR Nabisco's ability to service its debt. Complex securities such as "increasing rate notes," whose coupon rates had to be periodically reset to ensure that these notes would trade at face value, ultimately forced the credit rating agencies to downgrade the RJR Nabisco debt. As market interest rates climbed, RJR Nabisco did not appear to have sufficient cash to accommodate the additional interest expense on the increasing return notes. To avoid default, KKR recapitalized the company by investing additional equity capital. KKR eventually liquidated its position in RJR Nabisco for a far smaller profit than expected.

The publicity surrounding the transaction did not cease with the closing of the transaction. Dissident bondholders filed suits alleging that the payment of such a large premium for the company represented a "confiscation" of bondholder wealth by shareholders.

Source: Burrough and Helyar, 1990; Wasserstein, 1998.

POTENTIAL CONFLICTS OF INTERESTS (AGENCY COSTS)

In any MBO, management is confronted by a potential conflict of interest. Their fiduciary responsibility to the shareholders is to take actions to maximize shareholder value; yet in the RJR Nabisco case, the management bid appeared to be well below what was in the best interests of shareholders. Several proposals have been made to minimize the potential for conflict of interest in the case of an MBO. Borden (1987) proposed that directors, who are part of an MBO effort, not be allowed to participate in voting on bids and that fairness opinions be solicited from independent financial advisors. Lowenstein (1987) proposed that a firm receiving an MBO proposal be required to hold an auction for the firm.

WEALTH TRANSFER EFFECTS

Wealth transfer effects refer to the alleged shift of wealth from various stakeholders to the firm's shareholders. The most contentious discussion immediately following the closing of the RJR Nabisco buyout centered on the alleged transfer of wealth from bond and preferred stockholders to common stockholders when a premium was paid for the shares held by RJR Nabisco common stockholders. It is often argued that at least some part of the premium is offset by a reduction in the value of the firm's outstanding bonds and preferred stock because of the substantial increase in leverage that takes place in an LBO. However, empirical studies of the change in the value of a firm's outstanding debt at the time of an LBO announcement provide mixed results. In their studies of numerous LBOs during the 1980s, Lehn and Poulsen (1988) found no evidence that bondholders lose value; however, Travlos and Cornett (1993) found statistically significant losses associated with the announcement of going private. In a lawsuit against RJR Nabisco, it was alleged but never proven that its $5 billion in bonds outstanding at the time of the announcement lost more than 20% of their value (Greenwald: 1988, p. 69).

Other critics of LBOs argue that a wealth transfer also takes place in LBO transactions when LBO management is able to negotiate wage and benefit concessions from current employee unions. LBOs are under greater pressure to seek such concessions than other types of buyouts, because they are under greater pressure to meet debt service requirements than less leveraged transactions. Empirical studies suggest that employment in an LBO firm does grow more slowly than for other firms in the same industry (Kaplan: 1989a; Muscarella and Vetsuypens: 1990); however, this appears to result from the more efficient use of labor and the sale of nonstrategic assets following the LBO.

Lowenstein (1985) has argued that the tax benefits associated with LBOs represent a subsidy of the premium paid to the shareholders of the firm subject to the buyout. However, this subsidy is offset by the taxes paid by the shareholders when they sell their stock (Morrow: 1988). If the LBO firm is actually made stronger as a result of the transaction, taxes paid may actually be higher than they would have been if the transaction had not occurred. Furthermore, the eventual sale of the LBO either to a strategic buyer or in a secondary public offering will also generate additional taxes.

IMPACT ON SHAREHOLDER RETURNS OF LEVERAGED BUYOUTS

RETURNS TO TARGET SHAREHOLDERS (PREBUYOUT RETURNS)

The studies cited in Table 11-3 show that the premium paid by LBOs and MBOs to target company shareholders consistently exceed 40%. The distinction made in these studies of highly leveraged transactions between MBOs and LBOs is that in the MBO there is not third-party equity participation in the firm that is being taken private. The management group organizing the MBO provides equity. These empirical studies also include so-called *reverse LBOs*. These are public companies that are taken private and later are again taken public. The second effort to take the firm public is called a *secondary initial public offering* (IPO).

As noted previously, *divisional buyouts* represent opportunities for improved operating efficiency as the division is removed from the bureaucracy of the parent corporation. Although this may be a source of gain for the acquirer, it does not seem to be true for the shareholders of the parent firm divesting the division. The parent firm's shareholders seem to receive only miniscule returns. The small size of these returns may reflect the division's relatively small share of the parent corporation's total market value. Alternatively, the parent's management may forego the auction process in favor of the division's management. In either case, the parent corporation's share price is unlikely to materially benefit from the divestiture. The fact that parent shareholders experience any gain at all may suggest that the parent's resources are re-deployed to higher return investments.

TABLE 11-3.   Returns to Target Shareholders (Prebuyout Returns)

Empirical study[a]

Nondivisional buyouts	Premium paid to target shareholders (%)[b]
DeAngelo, DeAngelo, and Rice (1984) (Sample size = 72 MBOs)	56% (1973–1983) 76% (when there are three or more bids)
Lowenstein (1985) (Sample size = 28 MBOs)	48% (1979–1984)
Lehn and Poulsen (1988) (Sample size = 92 LBOs)	41% (1980–1984)
Divisional buyouts	Return to parent corporation shareholders
Hite and Vetsuypens (1989) (Sample = 151 MBOs)	.55% (1983–1987)
Muscarella and Vetsuypens (1990) (Sample size = 45 MBOs)	1.98% (1983–1988)

[a] MBO, management buyout; LBO, leveraged buyout.
[b] The years in parentheses represent the time period in which the study took place.

FACTORS DETERMINING PREBUYOUT RETURNS

Table 11-4 summarizes the empirical research, which attempts to identify the factors that explain sizable gains in share price that accrue to prebuyout shareholders.

Anticipated Improvement in Efficiency and Tax Benefits

The most often cited sources of these returns are from expected post-LBO improvements in efficiency due to management incentives and the discipline imposed by the need to repay debt, which motivate aggressive cost cutting, as well as from tax benefits. Michael Jensen (1986) argues that managers cannot be trusted to invest free cash flows in a manner that is necessarily in the best interests of the stockholders; debt imposes a discipline that forces them to stay focused on maximizing operating cash flows. Tax benefits are largely predictable and are built into the premium offered for the public shares of the target firm as a result of the negotiation process (Kaplan: 1989b).

Wealth Transfer Effects

The evidence supporting wealth transfer effects is mixed for most LBO transactions. The exception may be for very large LBOs such as RJR Nabisco, where largely anecdotal evidence seems to suggest that a significant transfer of wealth may have taken place between the firm's pre-LBO debt holders and shareholders.

Superior Knowledge

It is sometimes argued that LBO investors have knowledge of a business that is superior to that held by the firm's public shareholders. Therefore, the LBO investors are motivated to pay such high premiums because they understand more effective ways to use the firm's resources. This argument has some intuitive appeal when the firm's management is involved in the proposed buyout. However, there is little empirical evidence to support this proposition.

More Efficient Decision Making

There is also little empirical evidence to support the notion that decision making is more efficient. Nonetheless, the intuitive appeal of the simplified decision-making process of a private company is compelling when contrasted to a public company with multiple constituents directly or indirectly impacting decision making. Such constituents include a board of directors with outside directors, public shareholders, and Wall Street analysts.

FACTORS DETERMINING POSTBUYOUT RETURNS

Table 11-5 summarizes the studies on returns to shareholders following an LBO. A number of empirical studies suggest that investors in LBOs have earned abnormal profits on their initial investments. The presumption in these studies seems to be that the full effect of increased operating efficiency following an LBO is not fully reflected in the pre-LBO premium. These studies may be subject to selection bias in that only LBOs that are successful in significantly improving their operating performance are able to undertake a secondary public offering. Mian and Rosenfeld (1993) noted that in many instances the abnormal returns earned by postbuyout shareholders were due to the LBO being acquired by another firm in the 3 years immediately following the LBO announcement.

ANALYZING LEVERAGED BUYOUTS

An LBO can be evaluated from the perspective of common equity investors only or from the perspective of all investors, including preferred stockholders and debt holders. Because common equity investors often represent less than 10% of the total financing required to complete the transaction, it normally makes sense to evaluate the transaction from the standpoint of all investors in the LBO.

CAPITAL BUDGETING METHODOLOGY

Conventional capital budgeting procedures may be used to evaluate the LBO. The transaction makes sense from the viewpoint of all investors in the transaction if the present value of the cash flows to the firm (PV_{FCFF}), discounted at the

TABLE 11-4. Factors Contributing to Preleveraged Buyout Returns to Shareholders

Factor	Theory	Evidence[a]
Management incentives		
Equity ownership Kaplan (1989, 1991) (Sample size = 76 MBOs)	Management will improve performance when their ownership stake increases.	Management ownership increased for MBOs between 1980 and 1986 from 8.3% before the buyout to 29% after the buyout.
Incentive (profit sharing) plans Muscarella and Vetsuypens (1990) (Sample size = 72 reverse LBOs)	Stock option and share appreciation plans motivate management to take cost-cutting actions that might otherwise have been unacceptable.	96% of LBOs had at least one and 75% had two incentive plans in place during the 1983–1988 period. Moreover, the change in shareholder gain is positively correlated with the fraction of shares owned by LBO's officers.
Improved operating performance Holthausen and Larker (1996) (Sample size = 90 reverse LBOs)	Equity ownership and incentive plans motivate management to initiate aggressive cost reduction plans and to change marketing strategies.	For the 1983–1988 period, sales were up by 9.4% in real terms and operating profits by 45.4% between the LBO announcement date and the secondary initial public offering. Firm performance was also highly correlated with the amount of ownership by officers and directors.

Kaplan (July 1989) — Operating income in LBO firms increased more than in other firms in the same industry during 2 years following the LBO.

Tax shelter benefits

Kaplan (1989a) — An LBO can be tax free for as long as 5–7 years. — Median value of tax shelter contributed 30% of the premium.

Lehn and Poulsen (1988) — Premium paid to pre-LBO shareholders positively correlated with pre-LBO tax liability and equity.

Wealth transfer effects

Lehn and Poulsen (1988) — Premiums represent a transfer of wealth from bondholders to common stockholders. — Found no evidence that bond holders and preferred stockholders lose value when an LBO is announced.

Travlos and Cornett (1993) — Found small losses associated with the LBO announcement.

Investor group has better information (asymmetric information) on MBO target

Kaplan (1988) and Smith (1990) — Investor group believes target worth more than shareholders. — Found no evidence to support this theory.

Improved efficiency in decision making

Travlos and Cornett (1993) — Private firms are less bureaucratic and do not incur reporting and servicing costs associated with public shareholders. — Shareholder-related expenses are not an important factor; difficult to substantiate more efficient decision making.

---

[a] MBO, managed buyout; LBO, leveraged buyout.

TABLE 11-5.   Postbuyout Returns to Leveraged Buyout Shareholders[a]

Empirical study	Impact on postbuyout performance
Muscarella and Vetsuypens (1990) (Sample size = 45 MBOs from 1983–1987)	Of 41 firms going public, median annual return was 36.6% in 3 years following buyout.
Kaplan (October 1991) (Sample size = 21 MBOs from 1979–86)	Median annualized return was 26% higher than the gain on the Standard & Poor's 500 during the 3-year postbuyout period.
Mian and Rosenfeld (1993) (Sample size = 85 reverse LBOs from 1983–1989)	Of the 33 LBOs that were acquired by another firm during the three years following the LBO, cumulative abnormal returns exceeded 21%. Of those not acquired, cumulative returns were zero.
Holthausen and Larcker (1996) (Sample size = 90 reverse LBOs from 1983–1988)	Firms outperformed their industries over the 4 years following the secondary initial public offering.

[a] MBO, managed buyout; LBO, leveraged buyout.

weighted average cost of capital, equals or exceeds the total investment consisting of debt, common equity, and preferred equity ($I_{D+E+PFD}$) required to buy the outstanding shares of the target company.

$$PV_{FCFF} - I_{D+E+PFD} \geq 0$$

If this is true, the target firm can earn its cost of capital and return sufficient cash flow to all parties to the transaction, enabling them to achieve their required returns.

If the PV_{FCFE}, discounted at the cost of equity, equals or exceeds the common equity investment (I_E) in the transaction, common equity investors are able to earn or exceed their required returns.

$$PV_{FCFE} - I_E \geq 0$$

However, it is possible for an LBO to make sense to common equity investors but not to other investors such as pre-LBO debt holders and preferred stockholders.

The market value of the debt and preferred stock on the books of the target firm prior to the announcement of the LBO reflects the perceived ability of the firm to repay the principal and interest on the debt in a timely fashion and to continue to make required dividend payments on preferred equity. The ability to meet these obligations is often measured by comparing such ratios for the target firm as debt-to-equity and interest coverage with those of comparable firms. Once the LBO has been consummated, the firm's perceived ability to meet these obligations will often deteriorate, as the firm takes on a substantial amount of new debt. The firm's pre-LBO debt and preferred stock may be revalued in the open market by investors to reflect this higher perceived risk, resulting in a significant reduction in the market value of both debt and preferred equity owned by pre-LBO investors. Although there is little empirical evidence to show that this is typical of LBOs, this revaluation may characterize large LBOs such as RJR Nabisco (see Table 11-4 and Case Study 11-1).

A VARIABLE RISK APPROACH TO ANALYZING LBOs

What follows is a seven-step procedure to determine if an LBO opportunity makes sense from the viewpoint of all investors to the transaction. Although the discount rate employed in calculating the terminal value may change, conventional discounted cash flow valuation normally assumes that the discount rate remains constant during the cash flow forecast period. Although this may be sensible for many valuation situations, it is inappropriate for valuing highly leveraged transactions. LBO strategy calls for a rapid reduction of debt and a concomitant buildup of equity. This implies that declining leverage will reduce the cost of equity by lowering the magnitude of the firm's levered beta each period during which the outstanding debt is paid off. If the firm's target debt-to-total capital ratio is used to calculate the weights, the firm's total cost of capital will also decline.

Estimating the Total Cost of the Transaction (Step 1)

The total cost of the transaction is normally viewed as the purchase price of the target firm's outstanding shareholders' equity plus any debt on the target's books that is assumed by the acquirer. For simplicity, we will assume that the LBO target has no outstanding debt. Thus, the first step involves the estimation of the total cost of buying the stock of the current shareholders of the target firm (see Table 11-6).

Determining the Preliminary Mix of Debt and Equity (Step 2)

This step requires the analyst to estimate the borrowing capacity of the firm and to make an assumption about the amount of equity to be invested in the LBO as a percentage of the total purchase price.

TABLE 11-6.   Estimating the Total Cost of a Leveraged Buyout

Total cost (assuming the target firm has no debt)	$ Millions
Buy back 10 million shares @$50 / share	500.00
Transaction expenses (2% of transaction value)	10.00
Total purchase price of equity	510.00

Estimating Borrowing Capacity

The amount of total debt the target firm may be able to borrow can be approximated using the average interest coverage ratio (earnings before interest and taxes [EBIT]/interest expense) for other firms in the same industry or by using the interest coverage ratio for recent comparable transactions. If the target firm has a sustainable annual EBIT of $65 million and the industry average interest coverage ratio (EBIT/interest expense) is 1.3, the firm can support up to $50 million in annual interest expense ($65/1.3). If the current prevailing average market rate of interest on transactions of this type is 11%, the firm has a potential capacity to borrow up to $455 million ($50/.11).

In theory, the firm could borrow as much as 89% ($455/$510) of the total purchase price. In practice, it is likely to borrow less. Any shortfall between projected and actual cash flows could result in the firm having to borrow additional funds to satisfy working capital requirements. The firm may be able to exceed its potential borrowing capacity only by paying a significantly higher interest rate to compensate lenders for the increase in perceived risk. The increase in interest expense could trigger a downward spiral toward default if the firm is unable to improve operating cash flows.

Estimating the Equity Contribution

For purposes of illustration, the preliminary financing mix is displayed in Table 11-7 using a percentage distribution of debt and equity similar to that used by LBOs during the 1980s. According to a study of 107 LBOs formed between 1981 and 1990 by Roden and Lewellen (1995), debt comprised about 85% and equity 15% of the total cost of the average transaction. These transactions accounted for about two-thirds of the total dollar volume of LBOs during that period. Note that in our illustration borrowing 85% of the purchase price of $510 million gives the LBO investors a small 5% margin of error ($433.5/$455).

Projecting Annual Cash Flows (Step 3)

This step involves projecting free cash flow to the firm (FCFF) and to equity (FCFE). FCFF measures the cash flow available to pay interest and principal repayments, preferred dividends, and common dividends after all other obligations of the firm have been met. FCFE measures the cash flow available for common

TABLE 11-7.   Approximating the Mix of Debt and Equity

Preliminary financing mix	$ Millions
Debt @ 85% of the total cost of the transaction	433.50
Equity @ 15% of total cost	76.50
Total proceeds	510.00

TABLE 11-8.   Alternative Cash Flow Definitions[a]

FCFF calculation	FCFE calculation
EBIT	FCFF
− EBIT (t)	− Interest $(1 - t)$
= EBIT $(1 - t)$	− Principal repayment
+ Depreciation	+ New debt issues
− Gross capital expenditures	− Preferred stock dividends
− Δ Working capital	
= FCFF	= FCFE

[a] FCFF, free cash flows to the firm; FCFE, free cash flows to equity holders; EBIT, earnings before interest and taxes.

equity investors after all other financing obligations have been satisfied (Table 11-8). See Chapter 7 (this volume) for additional detail on these definitions of free cash flow.

These cash flows should be projected annually until the LBO has achieved its target debt-to-equity ratio. Because the LBO wishes to recover its investment and required return by either selling to a strategic buyer or engaging in a secondary public offering, the LBO must make two calculations to determine its target debt-to-equity ratio. The first is to determine at what level of debt relative to equity the firm will have to resume paying taxes. The point at which this occurs depends on the firm's debt repayment schedule and projected pretax income. The second calculation is highly subjective and involves estimating the amount of leverage that may be acceptable to strategic buyers or investors in a secondary public offering at some point in the future. Thus, the target debt-to-equity ratio is that level of outstanding debt relative to equity at which the firm resumes paying taxes and which appears to be acceptable to strategic buyers or investors in a secondary public offering.

Projecting Debt-to-Equity Ratios (Step 4)

The decline in debt-to-equity ratios depends on known debt repayment schedules and the projected growth in shareholders' equity. The change in shareholders' equity is equal to net income (NI) less dividends paid to shareholders. Therefore, year-end shareholders' equity (SE) can be projected in future years assuming no dividends will be paid to equity investors of the LBO as $SE_t = NI_t + SE_{t-1}$.

Calculating Terminal Values (Step 5)

Calculate the terminal value of equity and of the firm in year t.

$$\text{Terminal value of equity (TVE)} = FCFE_{t+1}/(k_e - g)$$

$$\text{Terminal value of the firm (TVF)} = TVE + D_t + PS_t$$

The cost of equity, k_e, and g represent the cost of equity and cash flow growth rate during the stable growth period. D_t and PS_t are the amount of debt and preferred stock outstanding at the end of year t. TVF represents present value of the the proceeds available to the firm at time t generated by selling equity to the public or to a "strategic buyer" and by "rolling-over" the book value of outstanding debt and preferred stock at time t. Alternatively, the terminal value of debt could be calculated by computing the present value of the estimated weighted average coupon rate on total debt outstanding at time t, where the weights represent the percentage each type of debt is of total debt. The terminal value of preferred stock could also be calculated as the present value of preferred stock dividends discounted in perpetuity at the preferred stock's dividend yield.

Adjusting the Discount Rate to Reflect Changing Risk (Step 6)

The high leverage associated with an LBO increases the risk of the cash flows available for equity investors by increasing debt service requirements. As the LBO's extremely high initial debt level is reduced, the firm's cost of equity needs to be adjusted to reflect the decline in risk, as measured by the firm's levered beta (β_{FL}). This adjustment may be estimated starting with the firm's levered beta in period 1 (β_{FL1}) as follows:

$\beta_{FL1} = \beta_{IUL1} (1 + (D/E)_{F1}(1 - t_F))$,
    where β_{IUL1} is industry unlevered β in period 1;
    $(D/E)_{F1}$ and t_F are the firm's debt/equity ratio and tax rate, prespectively,
    and $\beta_{IUL1} = \beta_{IL1}/(1 + (D/E)_{I1}(1 - t_I))$;

$\beta_{FL2} = [(D/E)_{F2} - (D/E)_{F1}] (1 - t_F) + \beta_{FL1}$

$\vdots$

$\beta_{FLN} = [(D/E)_{FN} - (D/E)_{FN-1}] (1 - t_F) + \beta_{FLN-1}$

Generalizing $\Delta\beta_{FL} = (D/E)_F \times (1 - t_F)$

The firm's cost of equity (k_{eF}) may be adjusted as follows:

$\Delta k_{eF} = \Delta\beta_{FL} (R_M - R_{FR})$,
where $R_M - R_{FR}$ is an historical average spread between the return on stocks and the risk free rate of return

This implies a changing cost of equity and weighted average cost of capital over time. The cost of equity declines in line with the reduction in the levered beta. Using the firm's target debt-to-equity ratio to calculate the weights, the weighted average cost of capital also declines as the cost of equity falls. The use of the target debt-to-equity ratio, rather than the projected actual ratio, is appropriate to eliminate gyrations in the cost of capital due to simple fluctuations in the market value of debt and equity. The beta should continue to be adjusted until the LBO's actual debt-to-equity ratio equals the industry average ratio. At this point, the LBO firm's levered beta should approximate the industry average levered beta.

Because the firm's weighted average cost of capital (WACC) changes over time, the firm's cumulative cost of capital is used to discount projected cash flows. The cumulative cost of capital is represented as follows:

$$PV_1 = FCFF_1/(1 + WACC_1)$$
$$PV_2 = FCFF_2/[(1 + WACC_1)(1 + WACC_2)]$$
$$\vdots$$
$$PV_N = FCFF_N/[(1 + WACC_1)(1 + WACC_2)\ldots(1 + WACC_N)]$$

Making Sense of the Deal (Step 7)

Making sense of the deal requires calculating the PV of FCFF and FCFE including the terminal values estimated in Step 5 and comparing it to the total cost of the transaction. The deal makes sense to common equity investors if the PV of FCFE exceeds the value of the equity investment in the deal and the PV of FCFF exceeds the total cost of the deal, equity plus debt and preferred stock. These conditions suggest that the firm has achieved returns, which exceed the minimum returns required by equity investors as well as debt and preferred stock holders.

For more information on valuing LBOs, see Damadoran (1997); Kretlow, McGuigan, and Moyer (1998b); and Westin, Chung, and Siu (1998).

AN LBO EXAMPLE

Pacific Investors (PI) is a small investment management group with $100 million under management. The objective of their fund is to return investors at least a 30% annual average return on their investment by judiciously investing these funds in highly leveraged transactions. Investors are required to remain in the fund for at least 5 years.

PI has been able to realize such returns over the last decade because of their focus on investing in industries which have slow but predictable growth in cash flow, modest capital investment requirements, and relatively low levels of research and development spending. In the past, PI has made several lucrative investments in the contract packaging industry, which provides packaging for beverage companies that produce various types of noncarbonated and carbonated beverages. Because of its commitments to its investors, PI likes to liquidate its investments within 5 years through a secondary public offering or sale to a strategic investor and to use the proceeds of the sale to repay any outstanding debt and return the remainder to its investors.

Following its past success in the industry, PI is currently negotiating with California Kool (CK), a privately owned contract beverage packaging company with the technology required to package many different types of noncarbonated drinks. CK's 1999 revenue, EBIT, and net income are $47.8 million, $7.8 million, and $2.1 million, respectively. CK does not have any debt on its balance sheet. With a reputation for effective management, CK is a medium-sized contract packaging company that owns its own plant and equipment and has a history of continually increasing cash flow. The company also has significant unused excess capacity, suggesting that production levels can be increased without a major new capital spending program. Its major customers are the large beverage companies that out-source some or all of their bottling operations to contract packaging companies as well as small start-up specialty beverage companies, which devote most of their resources to marketing rather than manufacturing their products. Contract pack-aging companies give a beverage company a presence in a market where it would be impossible to serve without incurring a substantial capital investment to build a packaging operation on location.

The owners of CK are demanding a purchase price of at least $53.5 million. The purchase price represents a multiple of about 7 times EBIT and 26 times net income. These are significantly above multiples for comparable publicly traded companies, which are selling for about 6 times 1999 EBIT and 23 times 1999 net income. PI believes that it can finance the transaction through an equity invest-ment of $13.5 million and a $40 million, 15-year level payment loan from an insurance company. The loan would be secured by the fixed assets, consisting of both manufacturing facilities and land, of the target company. The annual rate of interest on the loan is 11%. If it proceeds with the transaction, PI would borrow the money at the end of 1999. (See Table 11-9.)

TABLE 1 1 -9.   Debt Amortization Table[a]

Year	Annual payment[b]	Interest[c]	Principal[d]	Ending balance[e]
1	5.56	4.40	1.16	38.84
2	5.56	4.27	1.29	37.55
3	5.56	4.13	1.43	36.12
4	5.56	3.97	1.59	34.54
5	5.56	3.80	1.76	32.78
6	5.56	3.61	1.95	30.82
7	5.56	3.39	2.17	28.65
8	5.56	3.15	2.41	26.24
9	5.56	2.89	2.67	23.57
10	5.56	2.59	2.97	20.60
11	5.56	2.27	3.29	17.31
12	5.56	1.90	3.66	13.65
13	5.56	1.50	4.06	9.59
14	5.56	1.05	4.51	5.01
15	5.56	0.55	5.01	0.00

[a] Fifteen-year $40 million loan at an 11% annual rate of interest.

[b] Equal annual payments including principal and interest are calculated by solving the following equation for the annual payment (PMT):

$$\text{PVA (present value of an annuity)} = \text{PMT} \times \text{FVIAF}_{11,15}$$
(future value interest factor for an annuity for 15 years at 11% interest)

[c] Loan balance times annual rate of interest.

[d] Annual payment less interest payment.

[e] Beginning loan balance less principal repayment.

Revenue for CK is projected to grow at 5% annually through 2004 and then 4% per year thereafter. The deceleration in the growth rate is in line with the overall aging of the population and a slower overall population growth rate. Operating expenses, capital spending, and working capital are expected to grow at the same rate as revenue. The target debt-to-equity ratio for the firm is .5. The cost of equity and capital declines in line with the reduction in the firm's beta as the debt is repaid. The cost of equity during the terminal period is assumed to be 10%. The industry average beta is 1.3 and debt-to-equity ratio is .5. In Tables 11-10, 11-11, and 11-12, PI treats 1999 as the base year or year zero in its calculations.

Since the PV of FCFF exceeds the cost of capital, the deal makes sense from the standpoint of both lenders and equity investors. If PI were to sell the business at the end of 2004, equity investors would receive a compound annual average return of 48.3% [($65.33/$13.5)$^{.25}$] over 5 years on their initial investment of $13.5 million. This is well above the 30% return promised by PI to its fund investors. Therefore, PI should do the deal.

THINGS TO REMEMBER

The underlying motivation in structuring an LBO is to finance the transaction with as much debt as possible. Much of the debt will be secured with the assets of the target firm. Often, the proceeds from the sale of "redundant" assets are used to pay off debt as quickly as possible. Success in structuring an LBO is a result of knowing what to buy, not overpaying, and being able to substantially improve operating performance. Firms that represent good LBO candidates are those that have substantial tangible assets, unused borrowing capacity, predictable positive operating cash flow, and assets that are not critical to the continuing operation of the business. While overpaying for any acquisition, highly leveraged or otherwise, almost always impairs the ability of the acquiring firm to achieve expected financial returns, it can be disastrous for highly leveraged transactions. If the firm's projected operating earnings are even slightly lower than projected, its ability to meet interest and principal payments is jeopardized.

Successful LBOs rely heavily on management incentives to improve operating performance and the discipline imposed by the demands of satisfying interest and principal repayments. The premium paid to target company shareholders by LBO and MBO investors consistently exceeds 40%, substantially above the average 33% paid to the target shareholders in less leveraged transactions. The most often cited sources of these returns are from improvements in efficiency and tax benefits. Tax benefits are largely predictable and are built into the premium offered for the public shares of the target firm as a result of the negotiation process. Post-LBO abnormal returns average between 30 to 40% during the 3 years following the announcement of the LBO. The primary reason for these gains seems to be improvements in operating efficiency whose value was not captured in the premium paid to pre-LBO stockholders.

An LBO can be evaluated from the perspective of common equity investors

TABLE 11-10.   Summary Pro Forma Financial Tables[a]

	1999	2000	2001	2002	2003	2004
Revenue	47.80	50.19	52.70	55.33	58.10	61.01
Less: operating expenses	35.00	36.75	38.59	40.52	42.54	44.67
Less: depreciation	4.90	5.15	5.40	5.67	5.96	6.25
Equals: EBIT	7.90	8.30	8.71	9.15	9.60	10.08
Less: interest	0.00	4.40	4.27	4.13	3.97	3.80
Equals: EBT	7.90	3.90	4.44	5.02	5.63	6.28
Less: taxes @ 40%	3.16	1.56	1.78	2.01	2.25	2.51
Equals: net income	4.74	2.34	2.66	3.01	3.38	3.77
Plus: depreciation	4.90	5.15	5.40	5.67	5.96	6.25
Less: capital expenditures	1.40	1.47	1.54	1.62	1.70	1.79
Less: Δ working capital	0.20	0.21	0.22	0.23	0.24	0.26
Less principal repayment[b]	0.00	1.16	1.29	1.43	1.59	1.76
Equals: FCFE	8.04	4.65	5.01	5.40	5.81	6.21
Plus: interest $(1 - t)$	0.00	2.64	2.56	2.47	2.38	2.28
Plus principal repayment	0.00	1.16	1.29	1.43	1.59	1.76
Equals: FCFF	8.04	8.45	8.86	9.30	9.78	10.25
Equity	13.50	15.84	18.58	21.76	25.41	29.56
Debt	40.00	38.84	37.55	36.12	34.53	32.77
D/E	2.96	2.45	2.02	1.66	1.36	1.11
Beta[c]	2.78	2.47	2.21	1.99	1.81	1.66
Cost of equity[d]	21.30	19.59	18.16	16.95	15.96	15.14
After-tax int. @ 11%[e]	7.00	7.00	7.00	7.00	7.00	7.00
WACC @ D/E = .5[f]	16.58	15.44	14.48	13.67	13.00	12.46

[a] EBIT, earnings before interest and taxes; FCFE, free cash flow to the firm; FCFF, free cash flow to the firm; WACC, weighted average cost of capital; D/E, debt/equity.

[b] From debt amortization table interest and principal payment columns.

[c] Industry unlevered $\beta_u = \beta_L / (1 + (D/E)(1 - t)) = 1.3 / (1 + .5 (.6)) = 1.0$
LBO levered $\beta_L = \beta_u (1.0 + (D/E)(1 - t)) = 1.0 (1.0 + 2.96 (.6)) = 2.78$
$\Delta\beta = \Delta(D/E) \times (1 - t)$

[d] $k_e = 6.0 + 2.78 (5.5) = 21.3$
$\Delta k_e = \Delta\beta (5.5)$

[e] Rounded.

[f] LBO's target debt-to-total capital (DTC) ratio used to calculate weights for the weighted average cost of capital. The weights are calculated as follows:

$$DTC = D / (D + E)$$
$$= D / (D + D/.5), \text{ since } D/E = .5 \text{ and } E = D /.5$$
$$= .5D / (.5D + D)$$
$$= .5D / 1.5D$$
$$= .33$$
$$\text{Equity-to-Total Capital (ETC)} = 1 - DTC = .67$$

TABLE 11-11. Leveraged Buyout with Free Cash Flow to the Firm Valuation[a]

Year	FCFF	$\times$	PV factor	$=$	PV
2000	$8.45		$\dfrac{\$8.45}{(1.1544)}$		$7.32
2001	$8.86		$\dfrac{\$8.86}{(1.1544)(1.1448)}$		$6.71
2002	$9.30		$\dfrac{\$9.30}{(1.1544)(1.1448)(1.1367)}$		$6.19
2003	$9.78		$\dfrac{\$9.78}{(1.1544)(1.1448)(1.1367)(1.1300)}$		$5.76
2004	$10.25		$\dfrac{\$10.25}{(1.1544)(1.1448)(1.1367)(1.1300)(1.1246)}$		$5.37
			Sum of PV of $FFCF_{1-5}$ =		$31.35

$$TVF = TVE + D$$

$$= \frac{\$6.21\ (1.04)}{.10 - .04} + \$32.77 = \$140.41$$

$$PV_{TVF} = \$140.41/(1.1544)(1.1448)(1.1367)(1.1300)(1.1246) = \$73.55$$

Total PV = $31.35 + $73.55 = $104.90

[a] FCFF, free cash flow to the firm; PV, present value; TVF, terminal value of the firm; TVE, terminal value of equity; D, debt.

TABLE 11-12. Leveraged Buyout with Free Cash Flow to the Equity Valuation[a]

Year	FCFE	$\times$	PV factor	$=$	PV
2000	$4.65		$\dfrac{\$4.65}{(1.1959)}$		$3.89
2001	$5.01		$\dfrac{\$5.01}{(1.1959)(1.1816)}$		$3.55
2002	$5.40		$\dfrac{\$5.40}{(1.1959)(1.1816)(1.1695)}$		$3.27
2003	$5.81		$\dfrac{\$5.81}{(1.1959)(1.1816)(1.1695)(1.1596)}$		$3.03
2004	$6.21		$\dfrac{\$6.21}{(1.1959)(1.1816)(1.1695)(1.1596)(1.1514)}$		$2.81
			Sum of PV of $FFCF_{1-5}$ =		$16.55

$$TVF = TVE = \frac{\$6.21\ (1.04)}{.10 - .04} = \$107.64$$

$$PV_{TVF} = \$107.64/(1.1872)(1.1696)(1.1510)(1.1389)(1.1296) = \$48.78$$

Total PV = $16.55 + $48.78 = $65.33

[a] FCFE, free cash flow to equity; PV, present value; TVF, terminal value of the firm; TVE, terminal value of equity.

only or from the perspective of all investors, including preferred stockholders and debt holders. Because common equity investors often represent less than 10% of the total financing required to complete the transaction, it normally makes sense to evaluate the transaction from the standpoint of all investors in the LBO. The high leverage associated with an LBO increases the risk of the cash flows available for equity investors by increasing debt service requirements. As the LBO's extremely high initial debt level is reduced, the firm's cost of equity needs to be adjusted to reflect the decline in risk. This implies a changing cost of equity and weighted average cost of capital over time. Excessive leverage and the resultant higher level of fixed expenses makes LBOs vulnerable to business cycle fluctuations and aggressive competitor actions, which LBOs cannot counteract.

CHAPTER DISCUSSION QUESTIONS

11.1   What potential conflicts arise between management and shareholders in an MBO? How can these conflicts be minimized?

11-2.   Describe how and why LBO strategies have changed since the early 1970s.

11-3.   What are the primary ways in which an LBO is financed?

11-4.   How do loan and security covenants affect the way in which an LBO is managed? Note the differences between positive and negative covenants.

11-5.   What are the primary factors that explain the magnitude of the premium paid to pre-LBO shareholders?

11-6.   What are the primary uses of junk bond financing?

11-7.   Describe a typical LBO's preferred capital structure in the 1970s and early 1980s and compare it to what you think the structure would look like today. Explain any changes between the two periods.

11-8.   Describe some of the legal problems that can arise as a result of an improperly structured LBO.

11-9.   Is it possible for an LBO to make sense to equity investors but not to other investors in the deal? If so, why? If not, why not?

11-10.   How does the risk of an LBO change over time? How can the impact of changing risk be incorporated into the valuation of the LBO?

CHAPTER BUSINESS CASE

CASE STUDY 11-2. EVALUATING A LEVERAGED BUYOUT OPPORTUNITY

An LBO firm is considering acquiring Nexus Enterprises. Revenue in the current year is $3,000,000. Current operating expenses before depreciation are $2,100,000. Revenue and operating expenses are projected to grow at 15% per year for the next 5 years and 5% annually thereafter. Capital expenditures and depreciation in the current year are $250,000 and $200,000, respectively, and they are expected to grow at the same rate as revenue through the forecast period. The annual change in working capital is expected to be 5% of revenue based on the firm's historical performance. Nexus does not pay any dividends during the forecast period.

Discussions with local lenders suggest that the LBO can be financed with $1,000,000 in equity capital and $5,500,000 in debt. Thus, if the transaction were completed at the end of year 0, Nexus's capital structure would consist of $1,000,000 in equity and $5,500,000 in debt. The interest rate on the debt is 10% annually. Principal repayments on the debt will be $500,000 annually through the forecast period. At the end of the fifth year, the remaining debt is expected to be refinanced at the same rate of interest in perpetuity.

Based on an examination of similar firms, the beta of the firm in the first year of operation is estimated to be 3.00 and the cost of equity to be 23.5%. The spread between the return on stocks and the risk-free rate is 5.5%. The firm's combined federal, state, and local marginal tax rate is 40%. The risk-free interest rate is expected to remain at its current level of 7.0% throughout the forecast period.

Despite its high leverage, Nexus pays some taxes from the outset. Its tax liability grows rapidly due to the firm's rapid payoff of debt. In estimating its WACC, the LBO firm uses its long-term target debt-to-equity ratio of $1 of equity for each dollar of debt to calculate the weights associated with debt and equity. This is the ratio that Nexus believes it must achieve to attract a strategic buyer or investors in a secondary public offering.

Nexus provides the following financial information. Based on this information, will the buyout generate sufficient cash to cover interest and principal payments and to provide an appropriate return to LBO firm's equity investors?

1. Calculate free cash flow to equity holders (FCFE) and the firm (FCFF).
2. Calculate the weighted average cost of capital (WACC) using a target debt to equity ratio of 1 : 1.
3. Calculate the terminal values.
4. Calculate present values.

Year	1	2	3	4	5	Terminal value
Revenues	$3,000,000	$3,450,000	$3,967,500	$4,562,625	$5,247,019	$5,509,370
Less: operating expenses	$2,100,000	$2,415,000	$2,777,250	$3,193,834	$3,672,913	$3,856,559
Less: depreciation	$ 200,000	$ 230,000	$ 264,500	$ 304,175	$ 349,801	$ 367,291
= EBIT	$ 700,000	$ 805,000	$ 925,750	$1,064,616	$1,224,305	$1,285,520
Less: interest	$ 550,000	$ 500,000	$ 450,000	$ 400,000	$ 350,000	$ 300,000
= Pretax income	$ 150,000	$ 305,000	$ 475,750	$ 664,616	$ 874,305	$ 985,520
Less tax	$ 60,000	$ 122,000	$ 190,300	$ 265,846	$ 349,722	$ 394,208
= Net income	$ 90,000	$ 183,000	$ 285,450	$ 398,770	$ 524,583	$ 591,312

A solution to this case is provided in the back of this book.

REFERENCES

Altman, Edward I., and Scott A. Namacher, *The Default Rate Experience on High Yield Corporate Debt,* New York: Morgan Stanley & Co., 1985.

Altman, Edward I., and Vellore M. Kishore, "Almost Everything You Wanted to Know about Recoveries on Defaulted Bonds," *Financial Analysts Journal,* November/December 1996, pp. 57–64.

Asquith, Paul, David Mullins, and Eric Wolff, "Original Issue High Yield Bonds: Aging Analysis of Defaults, Exchanges and Calls," *Journal of Finance, 44,* (4), September 1989, pp. 923–952.

Borden, Arthur M., *Going Private,* New York: Law Journal Seminar Press, 1987, pp. 1–6.

Burrough, Bryan, and John Helyar, *Barbarians at the Gate: The Fall of RJR Nabisco,* New York: Harper & Row, 1990.

Business Week, November 1, 1999a, p. 220.

Damadoran, Aswath, *Corporate Finance: Theory and Practice,* New York: John Wiley & Sons, 1997, pp. 502–537.

DeAngelo, Harry, Linda DeAngelo, and Edward Rice, "Going Private: Minority Freezeouts and Stockholder Wealth," *Journal of Law and Economics, 27,* October 1984, pp. 367–401.

Emery, Douglas R., and John D. Finnerty, "A Review of Recent Research Concerning Corporate Debt provisions," *Financial Markets, Institutions, and Instruments, 1,* (5), December 1992, pp. 23–39.

Fitzpatrick, J. D., and J. T. Severiens, *Hickman Revisited: The Case for Junk Bonds,* New York: Salomon Brothers, March 1984.

Fraine, Harold G., and Robert H. Mills, "The Effects of Defaults and Credit Deterioration on Yields of Corporate Bonds," *Journal of Finance,* September 1961, pp. 423–434.

Fridson, Martin, *Default Experience of Corporate Bonds,* New York: Salomon Brothers, March 1984.

Greenwald, J., "Where's the Limit?" *Time,* December 5, 1988, pp. 66–70.

Hickman, W. B., *Corporate Bond Quality and Investor Experience,* Princeton, NJ: Princeton University Press, 1958.

Hite, G. L., and M. R. Vetsuypens, "Management Buyouts of Divisions and Shareholder Wealth," *Journal of Finance, 44,* 1989, pp. 953–970.

Holthausen, Robert W., and David F. Larker, "The Financial Performance of Reverse Leveraged Buyouts," *Journal of Financial Economics, 42,* 1996, pp. 293–332.

Jensen, Michael C., "Agency Costs of Free Cash Flow, Corporate Finance, and Takeovers," *American Economic Association Papers and Proceedings,* May 1986, pp. 323–329.

Kaplan, Steven, "The Staying Power of Leveraged Buyouts," *Journal of Financial Economics, 29,* October 1991, pp. 287–314.

Kaplan, Steven, "The Effects of Management Buyouts on Operating Performance and Value," *Journal of Financial Economics, 24,* 1989a, pp. 217–254.

Kaplan, Steven, "Management Buyouts: Efficiency Gains or Value Transfers," *Journal of Finance, 3,* July 1989b, pp. 611–632.

Kaplan, Steven, "Management Buyouts: Efficiency Gains or Value Transfers," *University of Chicago Working Paper,* No. 244, October 1988.

Kretlow, James R., James R. McGuigan, and R. Charles Moyer, *Contemporary Financial Management* (7th ed.), Georgetown, TX: Southwestern College Publishing, 1998a, pp. 681–711.

Kretlow, James R., James R. McGuigan, and R. Charles Moyer, *Contemporary Financial Management* (7th ed.), Georgetown, TX: Southwestern College Publishing, 1998b, pp. 796–831.

Lehn, Ken, and Annette Poulsen, "Leveraged Buyouts: Wealth Created or Wealth Redistributed?" In M. Weidenbaum and K. Chilton (eds.), *Public Policy Towards Corporate Takeovers,* New Brunswick, NJ: Transaction Publishers, 1988.

Lowenstein, Louis, *What's Wrong with Wall Street?* Reading, MA: Addison-Wesley, 1987, p. 184.

Lowenstein, Louis, "Management Buyouts," *Columbia Law Review, 85,* 1985, pp. 730–784.

Mian, Shedhzad, and James Rosenfeld, "Takeover Activity and the Long-Run Performance of Reverse Leveraged Buyouts," *Financial Management, 22,* Winter 1993, pp. 46–57.

Morrow, D. J., "Why the IRS Might Love Those LBOs," *Fortune,* December 5, 1988, pp. 145–146.

Muscarella, C. J., and M. R. Vetsuypens, "Efficiency and Organizational Structure: A Study of Reverse LBOs," *Journal of Finance, 45,* December 1990, pp. 1389–1413.

Reisman, Albert F., "Leveraged Business Transactions." In Steven James Lee and Robert Douglas Colman (eds.), *Handbook of Mergers, Acquisitions, and Buyouts,* Englewood Cliffs, NJ: Prentice-Hall, 1981, pp. 313–327.

Reisman, Albert F., "The Challenge of the Proposed Bankruptcy Act to Accounts Receivable and Inventory Financing of Small-to-Medium-Sized Business, 83," *Commercial Law Journal, 169,* 1978, pp. 177–180.

Roden, Dianne M., and Wilbur G. Lewellen, "Corporate Capital Structure Decisions: Evidence from Leveraged Buyouts," *Financial Management, 24,* Summer 1995, pp. 76–87.

Smith, Abbie, "Corporate Ownership Structure and Performance: The Case of Management Buyouts," *Journal of Financial Economics, 27,* September 1990, pp. 143–164.

Travlos, N. G., and M. N. Cornett, "Going Private Buyouts and Determinants of Shareholders' Returns," *Journal of Accounting, Auditing and Finance, 8,* 1993, pp. 1–25.

Wasserstein, Bruce, *Big Deal: The Battle for Control of America's Leading Corporations,* New York: Warner Books, 1998, pp. 113–116.

Westin, J. Fred, Kwang S. Chung, and Juan A. Siu, *Takeovers, Restructuring, and Corporate Governance,* 2nd ed., New York: Prentice-Hall, 1998, pp. 316–343.

Wigmore, Barry, "The Decline in Credit Quality of Junk Bond Issues: 1980–1988." In Patrick A. Gaughan (Ed.), *Readings in Mergers and Acquisitions,* Cambridge: Basil Blackwell, 1994, pp. 171–184.

Yago, Glenn, *Junk Bonds: How High Yield Securities Restructured Corporate America,* New York: Oxford University Press, 1991.

12

SHARED GROWTH AND SHARED CONTROL STRATEGIES:

JOINT VENTURES, PARTNERSHIPS, AND ALLIANCES

Humility is not thinking less of yourself.
It is thinking less about yourself.

—*Rick Warren*

When it was formed in early 1998, executives at Spanish phone operator Telefonica de Espana and U.S. long-distance giant MCI WorldCom were all smiles as they unveiled a partnership to provide telecommunications services to customers worldwide. They declared in no uncertain terms that the partners would substantially improve the value of their companies. Or would they?

Since then the grand global alliance appears to have stalled. Of the dozen or so initiatives that have been announced by the two partners, none has been implemented. In many markets MCI WorldCom and Telefonica look more like archrivals than allies. For example, MCI WorldCom bought a controlling interest in Brazilian long-distance carrier, Embratel, putting it into direct competition with Telesp, a network operator in Sao Paolo that is owned by Telefonica.

On the surface, the partnership would seem to offer both parties tremendous opportunities. Telefonica is the strongest player in the $50 billion Latin American telecommunications market and could help MCI grow beyond its current position in Brazil and Mexico. In turn, MCI WorldCom is among the strongest players in telecommunications in the United States, the United Kingdom, France, and Germany. The partnership should give Telefonica a much-needed boost in these geographic areas.

Caution by both parties seems to have prevented them from integrating operations or from sharing competitive information. Neither company seems to have been willing to relinquish control over resources. Moreover, MCI WorldCom's largely "go-it-alone" culture does not seem to be compatible for a partnership whose long-term success requires substantial cooperation. What started out in marital bliss may be ultimately doomed by a failure to communicate. How ironic for firms whose primary business is to help others to communicate.

OVERVIEW

Business alliances are ubiquitous. They come in many forms and perform many different functions. The gas we put in our car before going to the airport could come from an alliance between Shell and Texaco. The credit card used to pay for the gas could be a co-branded credit card between Citibank and America Airlines. Upon arriving at the airport, the Starbuck's coffee we might drink is sold through an alliance with Host Marriott. Our trip from Los Angeles on United Airlines to New York and then on to London on British Airways could be part of a global coalition consisting of seven other airlines called the Star Alliance.

For many years, joint ventures (JVs) and alliances have been commonplace in high-technology industries; many segments of manufacturing; the oil exploration, mining, and chemical industries; media and entertainment; financial services; among pharmaceutical and biotechnology firms, and in real estate. They have taken the form of licensing, distribution, co-marketing, research and development agreements, as well as equity investments.

According to *Business Week* (1999), high-technology companies engage in literally thousands of alliances with their customers as part of their normal marketing strategies. Oracle claims to have as many as 15,000 to 16,000 alliances with their business customers. IBM announced $30 billion worth of alliances during 1999 with companies like Dell Computer and Cisco. AT&T announced deals with behemoths like British Telecom and Microsoft.

In manufacturing, General Motors and Toyota entered into an unprecedented JV agreement in 1982. For the first time in 60 years, GM accepted something other than controlling interest in a relationship with another major automotive company. GM believed it could enhance its manufacturing processes and product quality by learning and adopting Toyota's quality manufacturing processes. In turn, Toyota saw an opportunity to gain access to new markets for its products in the United States and in other countries in which GM was well established. Corning has created numerous JVs in genetic enzymes, fiber optics, hollow glass building blocks, and through Owens-Corning in fiberglass insulation.

Largely driven by the risks of oil exploration and by the large capital expenses inherent in this activity, the oil and gas industry has been characterized by numerous JVs. Chemical companies, such as Dow, Hercules, Olin, and ARCO, have used JVs to build new plants throughout the world. When shortages of raw materials threaten future production, these firms commonly form JVs to secure future sources of supply. Shell and Amoco have pooled most of their West Texas oilfields to become the first major oil companies to combine operations across an entire region. Shell and Mobil are doing the same on the West Coast.

The use of alliances in the oil and gas industry is expected to expand in the future. Eighty-four percent of senior managers from leading U.S. and Canadian oil companies expect alliances rather than internal operations to be the main source of performance improvements. Alliances are often preferred to acquisitions and divestitures because they bypass or reduce the valuation, tax, and regulatory issues associated with outright changes in control. They also rationalize overlapping oilfield assets and operations, while allowing both parents to retain oil reserves as a hedge against oil price increases (Ernst and Stenhubl: 1997).

Concerned about the loss of viewers to cable TV and the Internet, NBC, a unit of General Electric, and Microsoft each invested $500 million in 1995 to create a new news channel available both on cable and the Internet. The JV was intended to provide programming for the expected convergence of TV and the Internet. By early 1999, NBC owned minority positions in Bravo and the America Movie Classics channels; autobytel.com; and Intervu, a video streaming company. In mid-1999, NBC merged several of its key Internet properties with XOOM.com and Snap.com to form the then seventh largest Internet site and the first publicly traded Internet company partially owned by a major broadcaster.

Although many alliances are created to share risks, others involve partners with complementary skills or operations. Global competition, more sympathetic regulators, and the desire to gain access to technology are also factors contributing to the dizzying pace at which new alliances are being formed. Business alliances may also span several different industries. Despite competing directly with Canon printers, Hewlett Packard has sold more than 20 million laser printers that use a motor made by Canon.

The term *business alliance* will be used throughout this chapter to include JV corporations, partnerships, strategic alliances, equity partnerships, licensing agreements, and franchise alliances. The primary theme of this chapter is that well-constructed business alliances often represent viable alternatives to mergers and acquisitions and that they should always be considered as one of the many options available to achieving strategic business objectives. This chapter discusses the wide variety of motives for business alliances and the factors that are common to most successful alliances. Also addressed are alternative legal structures, important deal-structuring issues, and empirical studies, which attempt to measure the contribution of business alliances to creating shareholder wealth.

ALTERNATIVES TO MERGERS AND ACQUISITIONS

One of the most confusing aspects of business alliances is the many forms and functions they may take. Although the distinctions may appear to be largely superficial or based more on semantics than substance, the various forms of business alliances can have very different implications from the standpoint of taxes, control, resource commitment, risk/reward sharing, and ease of termination. The purpose of this section is to clarify the characteristics of the more commonly used strategic forms of business alliances. The legal and tax implications of the various forms of alliances are discussed in more detail later in this chapter.

JOINT VENTURES

A JV is a cooperative business relationship formed by two or more separate organizations to achieve common strategic objectives. The JV is usually an independent legal entity in the form of a corporation or partnership. As part of the JV agreement, ownership, operational responsibilities, and financial risks and rewards are allocated to each member. Each member preserves its own corporate identity and autonomy.

STRATEGIC ALLIANCES

Strategic alliances and JVs are often strategically similar, but they differ in one important aspect. Strategic alliances do not create separate legal entities. Examples include a corporation signing an agreement with another to transfer technology, research and development (R&D) services, and marketing rights or to assume a minority equity position without a separate business being formed. The strategic alliance may be a precursor to a JV corporation or partnership or an acquisition. JVs and strategic alliances are not passive investments or conventional vendor–customer relationships. Alliances often involve cross-training, coordinated product development, and long-term contracts based on such performance metrics as product quality rather than just price.

EQUITY PARTNERSHIPS

Equity partnerships are somewhat more complicated than strategic alliances. They have all the characteristics of an alliance. However, they also involve one party taking a minority equity stake in the other party, often 5–10%. The minority investor may also have an option to purchase a larger stake. In many international partnerships, it is commonplace for the partners to take equity positions in each other's operations.

LICENSING

There are two primary types of licensing. The first involves licensing a specific technology, product, or process to exploit a perceived opportunity. The second involves merchandise and character licensing in which a firm licenses a recognizable trademark or copyright to a manufacturer of consumer goods in markets not currently served by the licensee.

Royalties and Fees

The company owning the patent, trademark, or copyright may license these rights to other firms for a fee or royalty. Although licensing requires cooperation, unlike a JV or alliance, there is no sharing of risk or reward. A licensing agreement normally stipulates what is being sold, how and where it can be used, and for how long the licensee is authorized to use it. Payments to the licensor typically include an upfront fee coupled with royalty payments based on a percentage of future licensee sales. In addition to royalty payments, a licensing alliance with a larger company may involve fees for consulting, training, further product development or enhancement, and manufacturing rights.

Risk Characteristics

Licensing can provide a comparatively safe, low-risk method of cooperation, with little upfront investment. Small firms may find licensing of their proprietary know-how to larger companies as a way to rapidly recover their initial investment made to develop the know-how. As part of the licensing agreement, the licensee may also be required to make a minority investment in the licensor.

FRANCHISING ALLIANCES

Franchising alliances are systems or networks of alliances in which the partners are linked together through various licensing agreements. For example, a parent firm could have multiple smaller geographic franchisees or several equal cross-licensors. Such agreements often grant rights to offer, sell, or distribute goods and services. They often come with the obligation to purchase in return goods and services from other firms in the alliance. The arrangement could also include "master licenses" providing access to all new products and future technologies.

NETWORK ALLIANCES

A network alliance is an array of interconnecting alliances among companies. It often crosses international and industrial boundaries. Such arrangements may result in two companies collaborating in one market while competing in another. Network alliances are most commonly used to access skills from different but converging industries. The multimedia and computer industries are full of examples, such as the Network Computer consortia launched by Oracle and others to challenge the dominance of the personal computer. Network alliances may also be used to achieve global coverage. In the airline and telecommunications industries, national companies have formed alliances with groups of similar firms in other geographic markets to expedite global air travel and wireless communication.

MOTIVATIONS FOR BUSINESS ALLIANCES

Business alliances are generally not created as a result of one company making a passive investment in another. Money alone rarely provides the basis for a successful long-term business alliance. A partner can often obtain funding from a variety of sources but may be able to obtain access to a set of skills or nonfinancial resources only from a specific source. Obviously, alliances are likely to be lasting only if both parties find the relationship to be a mutually beneficial union. The basis of this union can include risk sharing, gaining access to new markets, accelerating the introduction of new products, technology sharing, globalization, cost reduction, a desire to acquire (or exit) a business, or the favorable regulatory treatment they often receive as compared to mergers and acquisitions.

RISK SHARING

Risk is the potential for losing, or at least not gaining, value. Risk is often perceived to be greater the more money, management time, or other resources a company has committed to an endeavor and the less certain the outcome. In order to mitigate perceived risk, companies often enter into alliances to gain access to know-how and scarce resources or to reduce the amount of resources they would have to commit if they were to do it on their own.

Sharing Proprietary Knowledge

The driving force behind one-half of all JVs is to acquire proprietary know-how (Berg, Duncan, and Friedman: 1982). Developing new technologies can be extremely expensive. Given the pace at which technology changes, the risk is high that a competitor will be able to develop a superior technology before a firm can bring its own new technology to market. Consequently, high-technology companies with expertise in a specific technology segment often combine their efforts with another company or companies with complementary know-how to reduce the risk of failing to develop the "right" technology.

Moreover, by having multiple contacts throughout an industry, it is unlikely that a firm will overlook new innovations or best practices. For example, TiVo, a small manufacturer of set-top boxes that provide interactive TV service, raised $32 million in 1999 through a series of private placements with CBS, NBC, Disney/ABC, Hughes's Direct TV satellite service, and Comcast, a leading cable TV service. By lending to TiVo, these companies would be able to obtain access to the latest technologies that may someday be necessary to remain competitive in their respective markets.

In 1983, Rockwell, Sperry, Boeing, Control Data, Honeywell, Digital Equipment, Kodak, Harris, Lockheed, Martin Marietta, 3M, Motorola, NCR, National Semiconductor, and RCA formed Micro-Electronics Computer Corporation (MCC). MCC was formed to share the cost of developing semiconductor, computer, and software technology that could not otherwise be developed cost effectively by these companies. In 1988, Sematech was founded as a research alliance consisting of IBM, National Semiconductor, Advanced Micro Devices, and other major companies.

The Microsoft and Intel relationship is one of the more well-known technology partnerships; it is also one of the more confusing. The two cooperate to enhance the "Wintel" world, which combines Windows operating systems with Intel microchips. Although the partnership is viewed as highly successful, there have been disagreements. For example, Intel wants more competition and lower prices on software bundled with personal computers to reduce the pricing pressure on PC components such as microchips as PC prices decline. Microsoft has been very slow to reduce the price of its Windows operating system software presumably to maintain profit margins.

Sharing Management Skills and Resources

Firms often lack the management skills and resources to solve complex tasks and projects. These deficiencies can be remedied by aligning with other firms, which possess the requisite skills and proprietary knowledge. Building contractors and real estate developers have collaborated for years by pooling their resources to construct, market, and manage large, complex commercial projects. Similarly, the contribution of Dow Chemical personnel to a JV with Cordis, a small pacemaker manufacturer, enabled the JV to keep pace with accelerating production.

GAINING ACCESS TO NEW MARKETS

Gaining access to new customers is often a highly expensive proposition involving substantial up-front marketing costs such as advertising, promotion, warehousing, and distribution expenses. The cost may be prohibitive unless alternative distribution channels providing access to the targeted markets can be found.

Using Another Firm's Distribution Channel

To solve this problem, a company may enter into an alliance to sell its products through another firm's direct sales force, telemarketing operation, retail outlets, or Internet site. The alliance may involve the payment of a percentage of revenue generated in this manner to the firm whose distribution channel is being used. Alternatively, firms may enter into a "cross-marketing" relationship in which they agree to sell the other firm's products through their own distribution channels. The profitability of these additional sales can be significant since neither firm has to add substantially to its overhead expense or to its investment in building or expanding its distribution channels.

The Convergence of "Bricks and Clicks"

Although marketing alliances have been commonplace for years, we are now seeing a convergence of conventional brick-and-mortar retail operations and cyberspace distribution channels. Companies are using their recognizable consumer brands and complementary sales and distribution channels to co-market their products and services. About one-half of U.S. consumers were online by the end of 1999. Most of these tended to be wealthier consumers. Retailers and Internet companies are now trying to gain access to consumers who are not currently online. During late 1999 and early 2000, a slew of partnerships were announced between major retail outlets and Internet players (see Case Study 12-1).

CASE STUDY 12-1. WAL-MART–AMERICA ONLINE AND OTHER INTERNET MARKETING ALLIANCES

During the second half of 1999, the number of marketing alliances between major retailers and Internet companies exploded. Wal-Mart Stores, the world's biggest retailer, and Circuit City, a large consumer electronics retailer, announced partnerships with America Online (AOL). Best Buy, the largest U.S. consumer electronics chain, partnered with Microsoft, which had previously joined with Tandy Corporation's RadioShack stores. Kmart Corp allied with Yahoo! and Softbank Corporation in starting a service to offer free access to the Internet. Signaling its own strategy of bringing its service to anyone, anywhere, AOL announced in March 2000 partnerships with Sprint PCS and Nokia to help move AOL's service from the desktop to phones, pagers, organizers, and even TVs.

WAL-MART AND AOL

Wal-Mart and AOL have agreed to create a low-cost web service for consumers who lack access and also promote each other's services. Wal-Mart customers will get software that allows them to set up the service through AOL's CompuServe service. The retailer will also distribute AOL's software with a link to Wal-Mart's web site, Wal-Mart.com. The Internet access service will be geared to Wal-Mart customers in smaller towns that currently do not have local numbers to dial for online connections. Wal-Mart wants to funnel as many customers as possible to its revamped web site, which contains a pharmacy, a photo center, and travel services in addition to general merchandise. The alliance gives AOL access to the 90 to 100 million people who shop at Wal-Mart weekly.

MICROSOFT, BEST BUY, AND RADIOSHACK

Through its alliance with Best Buy, Microsoft is selling its products, including Microsoft Network (MSN) Internet-access services and hand-held devices such as digital telephones, hand-held organizers, and WebTV that connect to the Web, through kiosks in Best Buy's 354 stores nationwide. In exchange, Microsoft has invested $200 million in Best Buy. Microsoft has a similar arrangement with Tandy Company's RadioShack stores in which it agreed to invest $100 million in Tandy's online sales site in exchange for in-store displays promoting Microsoft products and services. Both Best

Buy and RadioShack are major advertisers on the MSN and share in the monthly revenue from some of the Microsoft Internet access services they sell through their stores. Best Buy has issued 4 million new shares of common stock to Microsoft in exchange for its investment, giving Microsoft approximately a 2% ownership position in Best Buy. Best Buy is using the proceeds from the Microsoft investment to revamp its electronic commerce operation and to fund new store openings. The multiyear pact is nonexclusive.

KMART AND YAHOO

Kmart has formed its own Internet JV with Yahoo to provide consumers with free web access, personalized content, and shopping services. The electronic commerce offering, BlueLight.com, is being promoted by Yahoo throughout its network of Internet properties. All users of the service are greeted by a co-branded BlueLight.com/My Yahoo start page, which includes personalized relevant news, sports, and weather, as well as Blue-Light.com featured products. BlueLight users can also sign up for a Yahoo mail account as well as Yahoo's instant messaging service. Bluelight.com endeavors to combine the strength of the Kmart brand, its merchandising expertise, and Yahoo's leading Internet portal brand to create a highly differentiated web experience. "Blue Light" promotions are expected to remind consumers of Kmart's discounted special offers.

CIRCUIT CITY AND AMERICA ONLINE

AOL and Circuit City entered a strategic alliance to provide in-store promotion of AOL products and services to Circuit City shoppers nationwide, to make AOL Circuit City's preferred Internet online service, and to feature Circuit City as an anchor tenant in AOL's shopping mall. Under the agreement, AOL products and services are prominently displayed in dedicated retail space in Circuit City's 615 stores across the nation. Circuit City will be able to offer consumers everything they need to connect their homes to the Internet. Access to the Internet is available via AOL through dial-up service and developing broadband technologies, including digital subscriber line and satellite, as well as wireless interactive devices. Circuit City is promoting AOL and its in-store offerings in its print and television advertising programs and in other promotional and marketing campaigns. As an anchor tenant on AOL's shopping mall, Circuit City will have access to AOL's more than 22 million subscribers.

GLOBALIZATION

The dizzying pace of international competition has increased the demands for alliances and JVs to enable companies to enter markets in which they lack production or distribution channels or in which laws prohibit 100% foreign ownership of a business. Moreover, a major foreign competitor might turn out to be an excellent partner in fighting domestic competition. Alternatively, a domestic competitor could become a partner in combating a foreign competitor.

The automotive industry uses alliances to provide additional production capacity, distribution outlets, technology development, and parts supply. Many companies, such as General Motors and Ford, take minority equity positions in other companies within the industry to gain access to foreign markets (see Case Study 12-2). Other companies choose to assume a controlling interest (i.e., 51% or more). Exhibit 12-1 illustrates ownership ties between major automotive makers in which one company owns less than 100% of another as of mid-2000.

CASE STUDY 12-2. GENERAL MOTORS BUYS 20% OF SUBARU

In late 1999, General Motors (GM), the world's largest auto manufacturer, agreed to purchase 20% of Japan's Fuji Heavy Industries, Ltd., the manufacturer of Subaru vehicles, for $1.4 billion. GM's objective is to accelerate GM's push into Asia. The investment gives GM an interest in an auto manufacturer known for four-wheel drive vehicles. In combination with its current holdings, GM now has a position in every segment of Japan's auto market, including minivans, small and midsize cars, and trucks. GM already owns 10% of Suzuki Motor Corporation and 49% of Isuzu Motors Ltd. GM can now expand in Asia more quickly and at a lower cost than if it developed products independently.

GM has been collaborating with Fuji on various products since 1995. The move underscores GM's commitment to expanding its current modest position in the Asian market, which is expected to be the fastest growing market during the next decade. GM has sold less than 500,000 in the Asia-Pacific region in 1999, including about 60,000 in Japan.

Source: Bloomberg.com, 1999a.

COST REDUCTION

Cost reduction through business alliances may come about in a number of ways, such as purchaser–supplier relationships and sharing or combining facilities in joint manufacturing operations.

Purchaser–Supplier Relationships

During the 1990s, firms became increasingly involved in purchaser–supplier relationships. These are also called logistics alliances. Companies across the spectrum from retailers to computer manufacturing are increasingly forming alliances

---

EXHIBIT 12-1. OTHER AUTOMOTIVE INDUSTRY INVESTMENTS

General Motors: Owns

49% of Isuzu Motors
20% of Fiat Auto SPA
20% of Fuji Heavy Industries Ltd. (see Case Study 12-2)
9.9% of Suzuki Motors Company

Ford Motor Company: Owns 33.4% of Mazda
Daimler-Chrysler AG: Owns 34% of Mitsubishi Motors Company
Renault SA: Owns 36.8% of Nissan Motor Company
Fiat SPA: Owns

5% of GM
80% of Fiat Auto, Alfa Romeo, and Lancia

Mitsubishi Motor Company: Owns 13% of Hyundai Motors
Hyundai Motors: Owns 51% of Kia Motor Company
Toyota Motor Company: Owns 51% of Daihatsu Motor Company

---

with providers of "logistics" services. These alliances generally cover both transportation and warehousing services and utilize a single provider for these services.

In a survey of 50 companies and 20 logistics service providers, Van Laarhoven and Sharman (1994) found that most believed that as a result of logistics alliances, delivery service exceeded their expectations, although cost reductions, while significant, did not meet expectations. Service improvements resulted from better on-time delivery, and cost reductions came mostly from sharing of resources with other client companies. Forty-three percent of respondents to the survey indicated that the alliance was clearly successful; 33 percemt said it was moderately so.

The increased use of the Internet for commercial purposes is widely expected to enable businesses to realize the substantial cost savings that to date have been less than expected by more effectively managing their supplier relationships. The global telecommunications network that comprises the Internet is making electronic business to business communication increasingly possible for businesses of all sizes. The inherent efficiencies of converting data to electronic form expedites data transmission, storage, retrieval, updating, and analysis. These capabilities now make possible instantaneous communication with a massive number of suppliers. The desire to more efficiently manage the corporate supply chain drove the major auto manufacturers to create what could become the largest online business in terms of revenue (see Case Study 12-3). By increasing the efficiency of the purchasing process, both purchasers and suppliers are likely to benefit. Note how the JV concept is used to achieve the desired neutrality and confidentiality demanded by all participants.

CASE STUDY 12-3. AUTOMOTIVE MANUFACTURERS JOIN FORCES IN ONLINE PURCHASING CONSORTIUM

In late February 2000, GM, Ford, and Daimler-Chrysler announced the formation of a JV corporation intended to streamline the process of purchasing materials and services from external vendors. The new company is expected to manage the purchasing of the bulk of the $240 billion in raw materials, parts, and office supplies used annually by the three auto manufacturers. All ordering will be done via the Internet.

By using the Internet, the auto makers believe that they, as well as suppliers, can experience substantial cost savings by reducing the time, paperwork, and error rate associated with literally millions of purchases made with more than 30,000 suppliers. By automating much of the purchasing process, the auto makers will be able to automatically reorder parts when inventories drop below desired levels, facilitating efforts to minimize inventory investment. Moreover, tracking systems can be put in place to determine the status of orders and to confirm delivery dates. Estimates of the savings that could be realized in the cost of processing a purchase order range as high as 90%. The resulting cost savings to purchasers and suppliers can contribute to profit margin improvements for both parties. Suppliers could also be allowed to do purchasing online through this JV purchasing corporation.

GM, Ford, and Daimler-Chrysler have equal equity stakes in the JV company. However, the JV will be managed as an independent entity. Other investors with smaller stakes include Oracle and Commerce One, which will provide software required to automate the purchasing process. The JV company will be opened to other auto manufacturers, which may choose to make investments in the company. Eventually, the focus of the company could be expanded to include other industries. Ultimately, equity in the company could be offered to the public.

By centralizing purchasing in an independently operated company, the automotive manufacturers were able to overcome previous concerns expressed by various parties. Both suppliers and auto companies had concerns about previous attempts to move purchasing into an online environment, because these efforts had involved working with parts exchanges launched by GM and Ford in 1999 using different and potentially incompatible software and systems. Moreover, auto companies were concerned about the confidentiality of the data they would be asked to place on the computer systems of companies managed by their competitors.

Source: Hyde, 2000, and various corporate GM, Ford, and Daimler-Chrysler press releases.

Joint Manufacturing

Companies may also choose to combine their manufacturing operations in a single facility with the capacity to meet the production requirements of all parties involved. By building a large facility, the firms can jointly benefit from lower production costs resulting from spreading fixed costs over larger volumes of production. This type of arrangement is commonplace within the newspaper industry in major cities in which there are several newspapers engaged in "head-to-head" competition. Similar cost benefits may be realized if one party closes its production facility and satisfies its production requirements by buying at preferred prices from another party with substantial unused capacity.

A PRELUDE TO ACQUISITION OR EXIT

Rather than acquire a company, a firm may choose to make a minority investment in another company. In exchange for the investment, the investing firm may receive board representation, preferred access to specified proprietary technology, and an option to purchase a controlling interest in the company. The investing firm is able to assess the quality of management, cultural compatibility, and the viability of the other firm's technology without having to acquire a controlling interest in the firm.

Alternatively, JVs or strategic alliances may be used as a means of exiting a business. TRW entered into a JV with Elsevier, a large Dutch publishing company in 1990, in which both companies contributed their residential property information companies to form TRW REDI. The property information included data on the physical characteristics of homes and home-selling prices in selected regions throughout the United States. Neither business had been achieving what their parents considered adequate financial returns. Although divestiture was an option open to both TRW and Elsevier, the individual operations had limited value to potential acquirers due to inadequate geographic coverage. However, in combination, the two operations could experience significant cost savings by eliminating overlapping overhead and achieving economies of scale in selling the same data to more customers over a broader geographic area. Moreover, the combined operations could achieve increased purchasing leverage in negotiating with suppliers of unique types of data. TRW REDI's financial performance improved to the point where it could be sold at what the parents considered an acceptable price. First American Title Company eventually acquired the partnership in 1996.

Case Study 12-4 illustrates how a JV may be used to acquire selected assets of another company. In an "acquisition JV," one company purchases a controlling interest in an existing subsidiary of another company. The former wholly owned subsidiary is subsequently managed as a JV corporation.

CASE STUDY 12-4. BRIDGESTONE ACQUIRES FIRESTONE'S TIRE ASSETS

Bridgestone Tire, a Japanese company, lacking a source of retail distribution in the United States, approached its competitor, Firestone to create a JV whose formation involved two stages. In the first stage, Firestone, which consisted of a tire manufacturing and distribution division and a diversified rubber products division, agreed to transfer its tire manufacturing operations into a subsidiary. This subsidiary owned and operated Firestone's worldwide tire business. In the second stage, Firestone sold three-quarters of its equity in the tire subsidiary to Bridgestone, making the subsidiary a JV corporation. Firestone received $1.25 billion in cash, $750 million from Bridgestone and $500 million from the JV. Firestone also retained 100% ownership in the diversified products division and 25% of the tire JV corporation. For its investment, Bridgestone acquired a 75% ownership interest in a worldwide tire manufacturing and distribution system.

FAVORABLE REGULATORY TREATMENT

As noted in Chapter 2, the Department of Justice (DoJ) has looked upon JVs far more favorably than mergers or acquisitions. Mergers result in the reduction in the number of firms. In contrast, JVs increase the number of firms, as the parents continue to operate while another firm is created. Project-oriented JVs are looked at most favorably. Collaborative research is encouraged by the regulatory authorities, particularly when the research is shared among all the parties to the JV.

CRITICAL SUCCESS FACTORS FOR BUSINESS ALLIANCES

Robert Lynch (1990) argues that the probable success of a JV or alliance is dependent on a specific set of identifiable factors. A successful business alliance is most often characterized by the following factors: synergy; risk reduction; accountability; clarity of purpose, roles and responsibilities; a "win–win" situation; compatible time frames for the partners; support from top management; and similar financial expectations.

SYNERGY

To be successful, the partners should have attributes that either complement existing strengths or offset significant weaknesses. Examples include economies of scale and scope, access to new products, distribution channels, and proprietary know-how. As with any merger or acquisition, the perceived synergy should be measurable to the extent possible.

RISK REDUCTION

Product introduction costs can be exorbitant in terms of development and manufacturing costs. By sharing these costs with others, the amount of capital any single partner has at risk is reduced. Risk may be further mitigated by reducing the likelihood of making poor business decisions by allying with those who have access to better information or proprietary knowledge. Risk can also be viewed as the cost of missing an attractive opportunity. This risk may be lessened by having access to a sufficient number of the right resources needed to exploit a perceived opportunity in a timely fashion.

COOPERATION

All parties involved must have the ability to cooperate with one another. A lack of consistent cooperation will result in poor internal communications and reduce the likelihood that the objectives of the JV or alliance will be met. Companies with similar philosophies, goals, rewards, operating practices, and ethics are more likely to be able to cooperate over the long-run.

CLARITY OF PURPOSE, ROLES, AND RESPONSIBILITIES

The purpose of any business alliance must be crystal clear. A well-understood purpose drives timetables, division of responsibility, commitments to milestones, and measurable results. Poorly defined roles and responsibilities of the participants inevitably lead to internal conflict and lethargic decision making.

WIN–WIN SITUATION

All parties involved must see the apportionment of risk and awards as equitable. No matter how clear the purpose of the JV or alliance, the ability to achieve objectives will be retarded if middle-level management on down believes that they are being treated unfairly. Internal dissent can result in lower productivity or even outright sabotage.

Johnson & Johnson's (J&J) alliance with Merck & Company in the marketing of Pepcid AC is a classic win–win situation. Merck contributed its prescription drug Pepcid to the alliance so that J&J could market it as an over-the-counter drug. With Merck as the developer of the upset stomach remedy and J&J as marketer, the product became the market share leader in this drug category.

COMPATIBLE TIME FRAMES FOR THE PARTNERS

The length of time an alliance agreement remains in force depends on the partners' objectives, the availability of resources needed to achieve these objectives, and the accuracy of the assumptions on which the alliance's business plans are based. Incompatible time frames are a recipe for disaster. The management of a small Internet business may want to "cash out" within the next 12 to 18 months, whereas a larger firm may wish to gain market share over a number of years. Unfortunately, even though time frames may initially be compatible, short-run profit pressures may force the alliance to dissolve, because one or more of the partners is no longer able to meet its commitments for the duration of the time period stipulated in the alliance agreement.

SUPPORT FROM THE TOP

It is imperative that top management of the parents of a business alliance be involved aggressively and publicly. Tepid support or worse, indifference, will filter down to lower level managers and prove to be highly de-motivating. Middle-level managers will tend to focus their time and effort on those activities that tend to maximize their compensation and likelihood of promotions. These activities may divert time and attention from the business alliance.

SIMILAR FINANCIAL EXPECTATIONS

Partners must be in agreement with the goals of the JV or alliance. A goal of gaining market share will have very different financial implications than one focused on quarterly earnings targets. The parties to the venture must agree on what constitutes success. If objectives are quantifiable and milestones identifiable, success may be defined in terms of how well the venture is doing in meeting these objectives and milestones.

ALTERNATIVE LEGAL FORMS OF BUSINESS ALLIANCES

As is true of mergers and acquisitions, determining the form of a business alliance should follow the creation of a coherent business strategy. The choice of legal structure should be made only when the parties to the business alliance are comfortable with the venture's objectives, potential synergy, and preliminary financial analysis of projected returns and risk.

Business alliances may assume a variety of different legal structures. These include the following: corporate, partnership, franchise, equity partnership, or written contract. Technically, a handshake agreement is also an option. However, given the inordinate risk associated with the lack of a written agreement, those seeking to create a business alliance are encouraged to avoid this type of arrangement.

The five basic legal structures, excluding the handshake agreement, are discussed in detail in the following section. Each has its own implications with respect to taxation, control by the owners, ability to trade ownership positions, limitations on liability, duration, and raising capital. The relative merits of each legal form are summarized in Table 12-1.

CORPORATE STRUCTURES

A corporation is a legal entity created under state law in the United States with an unending life and limited financial liability for its owners. Corporate legal structures include a generalized corporate form, the subchapter S (S-type) corporation, and the limited liability corporation (LLC). The S-type corporation contains certain tax advantages intended to facilitate the formation of small businesses, which are perceived to be major contributors to job growth. The LLC is a hybrid structure that contains some of the benefits of both a corporate and a partnership structure.

Corporations

A JV corporation normally involves a stand-alone business. The corporation's income will be taxed at the prevailing corporate tax rates. Corporations, other than S-type Corporations, are subject to "double" taxation. Taxes are paid by the corporation when profits are earned and a second time by the shareholders when the corporation distributes dividends. Moreover, setting up a corporate legal structure may be more time-consuming and costly than other legal forms due to legal expenses incurred in drafting a corporate charter and bylaws.

Although the corporate legal structure does have adverse tax consequences and may be more costly to establish, it does offer a number of important advantages over other legal forms, as discussed next.

Managerial Autonomy

This is most often employed when the JV is large or complex enough to require a separate or centralized professional management organization. The corporate structure works best when the JV requires a certain amount of operational autonomy to be effective. The parent companies would continue to set strategy, but the JV's management would manage the day-to-day operations.

Continuity of Ownership

Continuity refers to the continuation of the corporation's existence over a long period of time. Unlike other legal forms, the corporate structure does not have to be dissolved as a result of the death of the owners or if one of the owners wishes to liquidate their ownership position. A corporate legal structure may be warranted if the JV's goals are long-term and if the parties choose to contribute cash directly to the JV. In return for the cash contribution, the JV partners receive stock in the new company. If the initial strategic reason for the JV change and the JV no longer

TABLE 12-1.   Alternative Legal Forms Applicable to Business Alliances

Legal form	Advantages	Disadvantages
Corporate structures		
Generalized	Continuity of ownership Limited liability Provides operational autonomy Facilitates funding	Double taxation High set-up costs including charter and bylaws
Sub-Chapter S	Avoids double taxation Limited liability	Maximum of 10 shareholders Excludes corporate shareholders Must distribute all earnings Allows only one class of stock

Limited liability	Limited liability
	Owners can be managers without
	   losing limited liability
	Avoids double taxation
	Allows an unlimited number of
	   stockholders
	Allows corporate shareholders
	Can own more than 80% of an-
	   other company
	Allows flexibility in allocating
	   profits and losses
		Lacks continuity of generalized
		   corporate structure
		Owners must also be active par-
		   ticipants in the firm

Partnership structures		

General partnerships	Avoids double taxation
	Allows flexibility in allocating
	   profits and losses
		Partners have unlimited liability
		Lacks continuity of generalized
		   corporate structure
		Partnership interests illiquid

Limited partnerships	Limits partner liability (except
	   for general partner)
	Avoids double taxation
		Lacks continuity of generalized
		   corporate structure
		Partnership interests illiquid

Franchise alliances	Allows repeated application of
	   successful business model
	Minimizes start-up expenses
	Facilitates communication of
	   common brand and marketing
	   strategy
		Success depends on quality of
		   franchise sponsor support
		Royalty payments (3–7% of
		   revenue)

Equity partnerships	Facilitates close working relationship Potential prelude to merger May preempt competition	Limited control Lacks close coordination
Written contracts	Easy start-up Potential prelude to merger	Limited control Lacks close coordination Potential for limited commitment

benefits one of the partners, the stock in the JV can be sold. Alternatively, the partner can withdraw from active participation in the JV, but it can remain a passive shareholder in anticipation of potential future appreciation of the stock. In practice, the transferability of ownership interests is strictly limited by the stipulations of a shareholder agreement created when the corporation is formed.

Ease of Raising Money

A corporate structure may also be justified if the JV is expected to have substantial future financing requirements. A corporate structure provides a broader array of financing options than other legal forms. These include the ability to sell interests in the form of shares, and the issuance of corporate debentures and mortgage bonds. The ability to sell new shares enables the corporation to raise funds to expand while still retaining control if less than 51% of the corporation's shares are sold.

Limited Liability

Under the corporate structure, the parent's liability is limited to the extent of its investment in the corporation. Consequently, an individual stockholder cannot be held responsible for the debts of the corporation or of other shareholders. Creditors cannot take the personal assets of the owners.

Chapter S Corporations

A firm having 10 or fewer shareholders may qualify as an S-type corporation and may elect to be taxed as if it were a partnership and thus avoid double taxation. The major disadvantages to an S-type corporation is the exclusion of any corporate shareholders, the requirement to issue only one class of stock, and the necessity of distributing all earnings to the shareholders each year.

Limited Liability Corporations

LLCs were first recognized for tax purposes in 1988. As of the end of 1999, they were permissible in 36 states. The LLC combines features of the corporation and the limited partnership and offers both tax and nontax benefits. Like a corporation, the LLC protects all its owners from liability, whether or not they participate in the management of the company. This feature enables owners to also be managers without running the risk of losing their limited liability protection. Like a limited partnership, the LLC passes through all the profits and losses of the entity to its owners without itself being taxed. Unlike S-type corporations, LLCs can own more than 80% of another corporation, have an unlimited number of shareholders, and corporations as well as non-U.S. residents can own LLC shares. The LLC can also sell shares without completing the costly and time-consuming process of registering them with the Securities Exchange Commission (SEC), which is required for corporations that sell their securities to the public. This arrangement works well for corporate JVs or projects developed through a subsidiary or affiliate. The parent corporation can separate a JV's risk from its other businesses while getting favorable tax treatment and greater flexibility in allocation of revenues and losses. Finally, LLCs can incorporate before an initial public offering (IPO) tax-free.

The LLC's drawbacks are evident if one owner decides to leave. All other owners must formally agree to continue the firm. Also, all of the LLC's owners must take active roles in managing the firm.

PARTNERSHIP STRUCTURES

Partnership structures are frequently used as an alternative to a corporation. Partnership structures include general partnerships and limited partnerships.

General Partnerships

Under the general partnership legal structure, investment, profits, losses, and operational responsibilities are allocated to the partners. The arrangement has no effect on the autonomy of the partners. Because profits and losses are allocated to the partners, the partnership is not subject to tax. The partnership structure also offers substantial flexibility in how the profits and losses are allocated to the partners.

Typically, a corporate partner will form a special-purpose subsidiary to hold its interest. This not only limits liability but also may facilitate disposition of the JV interest in the future. The partnership structure is preferable to the other options when the business alliance is expected have a short 3–5-year duration and if high levels of commitment and management interaction are necessary for short time periods.

The primary disadvantages of the general partnership are that all the partners have unlimited liability and may have to cover the debts of the other, less financially sound partners. Each partner is said to be jointly and severally liable for the partnership's debts. For example, if one of the partners negotiates a contract that results in a substantial loss, each partner must pay for a portion of the loss, based on a previously determined agreement on the distribution of profits and losses. Because each partner has unlimited liability for all the debts of the firm, creditors of the partnership may claim assets from one or more of the partners if the remaining partners are unable to cover their share of the loss. The other partners may sue the offending partner if there is any violation of the articles of partnership.

Moreover, the entity lacks continuity in that it must be dissolved if a partner dies or withdraws, unless a new partnership agreement can be drafted. Therefore, the partnership structure lacks the continuity of the corporate form. Partnership interests may also be difficult to sell, thus making the partnership difficult to liquidate or transfer partnership. Partnership interests are often sold at a discount that reflects their lack of liquidity, their lack of majority control over the firm, and the need for the new partner to be compatible with the existing partners.

Limited Partnerships

A limited liability partnership is one in which one or more of the partners can be designated as having limited liability as long as at least one partner has unlimited liability. Limited partners usually cannot lose more than their capital contribution. Those who are responsible for the day-to-day operations of the partnership's activities, whose individual acts are binding on the other partners, and who are personally liable for the partnership's total liabilities are called general partners. Those who contribute only money and who are not involved in management decisions are called limited partners. Limited partners, who participate in managing the partnership, run the risk of being subject to general liability as if they were general partners.

Usually limited partners receive income, capital gains, and tax benefits, while the general partner collects fees and a percentage of the capital gain and income. Typical limited partnerships are in real estate, oil and gas, and equipment leasing, but they are also used to finance movies, research and development, and other projects. Public limited partnerships are sold through brokerage firms, financial planners, and other registered securities representatives. Public partnerships may have an unlimited number of investors and their partnership plans must be filed with the SEC. Private limited partnerships are constructed with fewer than 35 limited partners who each invest more than $20,000. Their plans do not have to be filed with the SEC.

FRANCHISE ALLIANCE

Franchises typically involve a franchisee making an initial investment to purchase a license, plus additional capital investment for real estate, machinery, and working capital. For this up-front investment, the franchisor provides training, site-selection assistance, and economies of scale in purchasing. Royalty payments for the license typically run 3–7% of annual franchisee revenue. Franchise success rates exceed 80% over a 5-year period as compared to start-ups, which have success rates of less than 10% after 5 years (Lynch: 1990, p. 253).

The franchise alliance is preferred when a given business format can be replicated many times, when there needs to be a common, recognizable identity presented to customers of each of the alliance partners, and when close operational coordination is required. In addition, a franchise alliance may be appropriate when a common marketing program needs to be coordinated and implemented by a single partner.

EQUITY PARTNERSHIP

An equity partnership involves a company's purchase of stock in another company or a two-way exchange of stock by the two companies. It is often referred to as a partnership because of the equity ownership exchanged. However, it is not a partnership in a legal sense. Equity partnerships are commonly used in purchaser–supplier relationships, technology development, marketing alliances, and in situations where a larger firm makes an investment in a smaller firm to ensure its continued financial viability. In exchange for an equity investment, a firm normally receives a seat on the board of directors and possibly an option to buy a controlling interest in the company.

The equity partnership may be preferred when there is a need to have a long-term or close strategic relationship, to preempt a competitor from making an alliance or acquisition, or as a prelude to a possible acquisition or merger.

WRITTEN CONTRACT

The written contract is the simplest form of legal structure. This form is used most often with strategic alliances, because it maintains an "arms-length" relationship between the parties to the contract. The contract normally stipulates such things as how the revenue is divided as well as the responsibilities of each party, the duration of the alliance, and confidentiality requirements. No separate business entity is established for legal or tax purposes. The written contract is most often used when the business alliance is expected to last less than 3 years, when frequent close coordination is not required, when capital investments are made independently by each party to the agreement, and when the parties have had little previous contact. This type of legal structure may evolve into a partnership or corporate structure at a later date once the parties to the agreement feel more comfortable with each other or the original reasons for the written contract change.

STRATEGIC AND OPERATIONAL PLANS

Planning should precede deal-structuring activities. Too often, the parties to a proposed alliance get bogged down early in the process in such details as legal structure, control, ownership, and other deal-structuring issues. They do not spend sufficient energy in determining if the proposal makes good strategic and operational sense in terms of the participants' financial and nonfinancial objectives. Before any deal-structuring issues are addressed, the prospective parties must agree on the basic strategic direction and purpose of the alliance as defined in the alliances' strategic plan, as well as the financial and nonfinancial goals and milestones established in the operations plan.

STRATEGIC PLAN

The strategic plan identifies the primary purpose or mission of the business alliance; communicates specific quantifiable targets such as financial returns or market share and milestones; and analyzes the business alliance's strengths and weaknesses relative to the competition as well as opportunities and threats. The purpose of a business alliance could take various forms as diverse as research and development, cross-selling the partners' products, or jointly developing an oil field. Chapter 4 (this volume) describes tools and methods for developing strategic business plans.

OPERATIONS PLAN

The roles and responsibilities of each partner in conducting the day-to day operations of the business alliance are stipulated in an operations plan. Teams representing all parties to the alliance should be involved from the outset of the discussions in developing both a strategic and operations plan for the venture. The operations plan should reflect the specific needs of the proposed business alliance. It is crucial that the operations plan be written by those implementing the plan. Strict attention to details before the business alliance is put in place is crucial to its eventual success.

The operations plan is typically a 1-year plan that outlines for managers what is to be accomplished, when it is to be accomplished, and what resources are required. The operations plan is also referred to as the annual operating budget. The short-term objectives of the operations plan must be consistent with the more long-term objectives of the strategic plan. The standard operations plan contains the following elements:

1. An analysis of the current external competitive environment
2. A statement of critical success factors, such as product performance specifications and service and support levels
3. Key objectives and milestones
4. Marketing plan with projected product prices, unit volumes, and net revenue
5. Manufacturing/production/engineering plans
6. A purchasing plan, including the source of needed inputs and their purchase price
7. Implementation schedule with completion dates and the names of individuals responsible for each major activity
8. Contingency plan
9. Financial forecasts for the enterprise, including a monthly budget statement
10. A performance-tracking system to compare actual performance with the budget statement

Note that some deal-structuring decisions, such as the legal form, may impact the financial analysis because of the their tax implications for the cash flow of the business alliance. Nonetheless, the decision to proceed with forming the alliance should never be justified based on tax benefits alone but rather on the overall strategic value of the alliance to the participants.

BUSINESS ALLIANCE DEAL STRUCTURING

Generally speaking, the purpose of deal structuring in a business alliance is to allocate fairly risks, rewards, resource requirements, and responsibilities among participants. The formation of a successful alliance requires that a series of issues be resolved prior to signing an alliance agreement. Table 12-2 summarizes the key issues and related questions that need to be addressed as part of the business alliance deal-structuring process. This section discusses how these issues are commonly resolved. For an excellent discussion of deal structuring in this context, see Ebin (1998), Freeman and Stephens (1994), Fusaro (1995), and Lorange and Roos (1992).

SCOPE

A basic question in setting up a business alliance involves which products are specifically included and excluded from the business alliance. This question deals with defining the scope of the business alliance. Scope outlines how broadly the alliance will be applied in pursuing its purpose. For example, an alliance whose purpose is to commercialize products developed by the partners could be broadly or narrowly defined in specifying what products or services are to be offered, to whom, in what geographic areas, and for what period of time. Failure to define scope adequately can lead to situations in which the alliance may be competing with the products or services offered by the parent firms. Furthermore, alliances are not static. Products developed for one purpose may prove to have other applications in the future. With respect to both current and future products, the alliance agreement should identify who receives rights to market or distribute products, manufacture products, acquire or license technology, or purchase products from the venture.

In certain types of alliances, intellectual property may play a very important role. It is common for a share in the intangible benefits of the alliance, such as rights to new developments of intellectual property, to be more important to an alliance participant than its share of the alliance's profits.

What started out as a symbiotic marketing relationship between two pharmaceutical powerhouses, Johnson & Johnson (J&J) and Amgen, deteriorated into a highly contentious feud (see Case Study 12-5). During the formation of the business alliance, the failure to properly define which parties would have the rights to sell certain drugs for certain applications and to sell future drugs that may have been developed as a result of the alliance laid the groundwork for a lengthy legal battle between these two corporations.

TABLE 12-2. Business Alliance Deal-Structuring Issues

Issue	Key questions
Scope	What products are included and what are excluded? Who receives rights to distribute, manufacture, acquire orlicense technology, or purchase future products ortechnology?
Duration	How long is the alliance expected to exist?
Legal form	What is the appropriate legal structure? Stand-alone entity or contractual?
Governance	How are the interests of the parents to be protected? Who is responsible for specific accomplishments?
Control	How are strategic decisions to be addressed? How are day-to-day operational decisions to be handled?
Resource contributions and ownership determination	Who contributes what and in what form? Cash? Assets? Guarantees/loans? Technology including patents, trademarks, copyrights, and proprietary knowledge? How are contributions to be valued? How is ownership determined?
Financing ongoing capital requirements	What happens if additional cash is needed?
Distribution	How are profits and losses allocated? How are dividends determined?
Performance criteria	How is performance to plan measured and monitored?
Dispute Resolution	How are disagreements resolved?
Revision	How will the agreement be modified?
Termination	What are the guidelines for termination? Who owns the assets upon termination? What are the rights of the parties to continue the alliance activities after termination?
Transfer of interests	How are ownership interests to be transferred? What are the restrictions on the transfer of interests? How will new alliance participants be handled? Will there be rights of first refusal, drag-along, tag-along, or put provisions?
Tax	Who receives tax benefits?
Management/ organization	How is the alliance to be managed?
Confidential information	How is confidential information handled? How are employees and customers of the parent firms protected?
Regulatory restrictions and notifications	What licenses are required? What regulations need to be satisfied? What agencies need to be notified?

CASE STUDY 12-5. JOHNSON & JOHNSON SUES AMGEN

In 1999, J&J sued Amgen over their 14-year alliance to sell a blood-enhancing treatment called erythropoietin. The disagreement began when unforeseen competitive changes in the marketplace and mistrust between the partners began to strain the relationship. The relationship had begun in the mid-1980s with J&J helping to commercialize Amgen's blood-enhancing treatment, but the partners ended up squabbling over sales rights and a spin-off drug.

J&J booked most of the sales of its version of the $3.7 billion medicine by selling it for chemotherapy and other broader uses, while Amgen has been left with the relatively smaller dialysis market. Moreover, the companies could not agree on future products for the JV. Amgen won the right in arbitration to sell a chemically similar medicine that can be taken weekly rather than daily. Arbitrators ruled that the new formulation was different enough to fall outside the licensing pact between Amgen and J&J.

Source: Bloomberg.com, 1999b.

DURATION

The participants need to agree on how long the business alliance is to remain in force. Participant expectations must be compatible. The management of a large corporation may view the alliance as a pivotal part of its long-term strategy; in contrast, the management of a small, start-up operation may be interested in "cashing out" as soon as possible. The alliance's expected longevity is also an important determinant in the choice of a legal form. For example, the corporate structure more readily provides for a continuous life than a partnership structure because of its greater ease of transferring ownership interests. There is conflicting evidence on how long most business alliances actually last. Mercer Management Consulting in ongoing research concludes that most JVs last only about three years (Lajoux: 1998, p. 41), while Booz-Allen and Hamilton (1993) reported an average life span of 7 years.

LEGAL FORM

The corporation and partnership structures are the most common legal forms employed in business alliances. As noted previously, partnerships offer tax advantages and greater flexibility in allocating profits and losses than corporate structures. However, a corporate structure may be a more logical choice if the alliance is expected to be large and complex, with its own management structure requiring clearly drawn lines of authority, to have an indefinite life span, and to have substantial future capital requirements. If the corporate structure is selected, the participants also need to determine the state of incorporation.

GOVERNANCE

In the context of a business alliance, governance may be broadly defined as an oversight function providing for efficient, informed communication between two or more parent companies. Governance makes those who control the alliance accountable. The primary responsibilities of this oversight function are to protect the interests of the corporate parents, approve changes to strategy and annual operating plans, allocate resources needed to make the alliance succeed, and to arbitrate conflicts among lower levels of management.

Traditional Approaches to Governance

Historically, governance of business alliances has followed either a quasi-corporate or quasi-project approach. For example, the oil industry has traditionally managed alliances by establishing a board of directors to provide oversight of managers and to protect the interests of nonoperating owners. In contrast, in the pharmaceutical and automotive industries where nonequity alliances are common, firms treat governance like project management by creating a steering committee that allows all participants to provide input into issues confronting the alliance.

The Need to Modify Traditional Approaches

As companies pursue alliances with different goals, duration, resource contributions, and potentially greater contributions to shareholder value, the traditional governance models will have to be modified. In the past, alliances have often been treated as a sideline by senior management. However, today alliances are often formed to augment a firm's core competencies by drawing upon the primary skills of other alliance partners. Consequently, alliances are becoming a key underpinning of a firm's overall business strategy. For highly complex alliances, governance may have to be practiced through multiple boards of directors, steering committees, operating committees, alliance managers, and project committees. For example, the General Electric and Honeywell industrial controls JV recognized that the interaction required to manage the JV was too extensive to be managed by a single board. Consequently, an operating committee and several project committees were established to address issues involving specialized expertise (Kalmbach and Roussel: 1999).

RESOURCE CONTRIBUTIONS AND
OWNERSHIP DETERMINATION

As part of the negotiation process, the participants must agree on a fair value for all tangible and intangible assets contributed to the business alliance. The valuation of partner contributions is important in that it often provides the basis for determining ownership shares in the business alliance. The shares of the corporation or the interests in the partnership will be distributed among the owners in accordance with the value contributed by each participant. The partner with the largest risk or the largest contributor of cash is generally given the greatest equity share of a JV.

Valuing Tangible Contributions

It is easy to value tangible or "hard" contributions such as cash, promissory cash commitments, contingent commitments, stock of existing corporations, and assets and liabilities associated with an ongoing business in terms of actual dollars or their present values. A party contributing "hard" assets such as a production facility may want the contribution valued in terms of the value of increased production rather than its replacement cost or lease value. The contribution of a fully operational, nonobsolete facility to a venture interested in being first to market with a particular product may provide far greater value than if the venture attempted to build a new facility due to the normal "break-in" period associated with new operations.

Valuing Intangible Contributions

In contrast, intangible or "soft" or "in-kind" contributions such as skills, knowledge, services, patents, licenses, brand names, and technology are often much more difficult to value. Partners providing such services are often compensated by having the business alliance pay a market-based royalty or fee for such services. If the royalties or fees paid by the alliance are below standard market prices for comparable services, the difference between the market price and what the alliance is actually paying may become taxable income to the alliance. Alternatively, contributors of intellectual property may be compensated by receiving rights to future patents or technologies developed by the alliance. Participants in the business alliance contributing brand identities, which facilitate the alliance's entry into a particular market, may require assurances that they can purchase a certain amount of the product or service, at a guaranteed price, for a specific time period.

FINANCING ONGOING CAPITAL REQUIREMENTS

The business alliance may finance future capital requirements that cannot be financed out of operating cash flow by calling upon the participants to make a capital contribution, issuing additional equity or partnership interests, or by borrowing. If it is decided that the alliance should be able to borrow, the participants must agree on an appropriate financial structure for the enterprise. Financial structure refers to the amount of equity that will be contributed to the business alliance and how much debt it will carry. The financial structure will differ with the type of legal structure selected for the business alliance. Alliances established through a written contract obviate the need for such a financing decision because each party to the contract will finance their own financial commitments to the alliance.

Because of their more predictable cash flows, project-based JVs, particularly those that create a separate corporation, sometimes sell equity directly to the public or though a private placement. Banks and insurance companies may also be a source of funding.

OWNER OR PARTNER FINANCING

The equity owners or partners may agree to make contributions of capital in addition to their initial investments in the enterprise. The contributions are usually made in direct proportion to their equity or partnership interests. If one party chooses not to make a capital contribution, the ownership interests of all the parties are adjusted to reflect the changes in their cumulative capital contributions. This adjustment results in an increase in the ownership interests of those making the contribution and a corresponding reduction in the interests of those not making contributions.

EQUITY FINANCING

JVs formed as a corporation may issue different classes of either common or preferred stock. JVs established as partnerships raise capital through the issuance of limited partnership units to investors, with the sponsoring firms becoming general partners. When a larger company aligns with a smaller company, it may make a small equity investment in the smaller firm to ensure it remains solvent or to benefit from potential equity appreciation. Such investments often include an option to purchase the remainder of the shares, or at least a controlling interest, at a predetermined price if the smaller firm or the JV satisfies certain financial targets. In some instances, the general partner may be required, as part of the original agreement, to invest specific amounts of capital in the venture at regular intervals or when certain milestones are reached. These requirements are normally stipulated in the original articles of partnership.

DEBT FINANCING

Nonproject-related alliances or alliances without financial track records will generally find it very difficult to borrow. Banks and insurance companies will generally require loan guarantees from the participating partners. Such guarantees give lenders recourse to the participating partners in the event the alliance fails to repay its debt. The amount that the alliance can ultimately borrow is likely to be based more on the financial viability of the partners than on the venture's cash flows. Nonrecourse financing (i.e., loans granted to the venture without partner guarantees) is usually reserved for ventures that have already demonstrated that they are viable businesses.

CONTROL

Control is distinguishable from ownership by the use of shareholder agreements or voting trusts or by issuing different classes of shares. Control issues should be negotiated with an eye to differentiating between day-to-day management and major strategic decisions. The most successful JVs are those in which one party is responsible for most routine management decisions, with the other parties participating in decision making only when the issue is fundamental to the success of the business alliance.

The business alliance agreement must define what issues are to be considered fundamental to the business alliance and address how they are to be resolved, either by majority votes or by veto rights given to one or more of the parties. Whichever partner is responsible for the results of the alliance will want operational control. Operational control should be placed with the partner most able to manage the JV. In some cases, the partner with operational control could be a minority owner.

If the partner having the largest equity share does not also have operational control, the partner will generally insist on being involved in the operations of the business alliance by having a seat on the board of directors or steering committee. The partner may also insist on having veto rights over issues it views as fundamental to the success of the alliance. These issues often include changes in the alliance's purpose and scope, overall strategy, capital expenditures over a certain amount of money, key management promotions, salary increases applying to the general employee population, the amount and timing of dividend payments, buyout conditions, and acquisitions or divestitures.

DISTRIBUTION ISSUES

Distribution issues relate to enterprise dividend policies and how profits and losses are allocated among the owners.

Dividend Policies

The dividend policy determines the cash return each partner should receive. How the cash flows of the venture will be divided generally depends on the initial equity contribution of each partner, ongoing equity contributions, and noncash contributions in the form of technical and managerial resources.

Allocation of Profit and Losses

Allocation of profits and losses will normally follow directly from the allocation of shares or partnership interests. When the profits flow from intellectual property rights contributed by one of the parties, royalties or payments for know-how may be used to compensate the party contributing the property rights. When the profits are due to distribution or marketing efforts of a partner, fees and commission can be used to compensate the partners. Similarly, rental payments can be used to allocate profits attributable to specific equipment or facilities contributed by a partner.

PERFORMANCE CRITERIA

The lack of adequate performance measurement criteria can result in significant disputes among the partners and eventually contribute to the termination of the venture. Performance criteria should be both measurable and simple enough to be understood and used by managers at all levels. Performance criteria should be clearly spelled out in the business alliance agreement. Nonfinancial performance measures should be linked to financial return drivers. For example, factors such as market share, consistent product quality, and customer service may be critical to success in the marketplace. Improvements in the venture's performance against these critical success factors should ultimately result in increasing financial returns to the partners.

Balanced Scorecard

The balanced scorecard technique is a widely used performance measurement tool in cross-functional corporate work teams. The concept can also be applied to measuring alliance performance by having the partners agree on a small number (i.e., 5–10) of relevant indicators. The number of indicators must be limited so that they can be easily tracked by alliance managers. They should include financial and nonfinancial, short- and long-term, and internal and customer-focused indicators. Examples of performance measures include return on investment, operating cash flow, profit margins, asset turnover, market share, on-time delivery, and customer satisfaction survey results.

Linking Performance to Individual Incentives

Managers will ignore performance measures if their compensation is not linked to their actual performance against these measures. The top alliance managers should be evaluated against the full list of balanced scorecard performance measures. The performance of lower level managers should be evaluated only against those measures over which they have some degree of control.

DISPUTE RESOLUTION

No matter how well the participants draft the venture agreement, disputes between parties to the agreement will arise. There are several ways to resolve such disputes. One is a "choice of law provision" in the alliance agreement indicating which state's or country's laws will have jurisdiction in settling disputes. This provision should be drafted with an understanding of the likely outcome of litigation in any of the participants' home countries or states and the attitude of these countries' or state's courts in enforcing "choice of law provisions" in the JV agreements.

Another important clause is the definition of what constitutes a deadlock when a disagreement arises. This clause should include a clear statement of what events trigger various types of dispute-resolution procedures. Care should be taken not to define the events triggering dispute-resolution procedures so narrowly that even a minor disagreement is subject to the dispute mechanism. Finally, an arbitration clause is usually employed to address major disagreements. Such a clause should define the type of dispute subject to arbitration and how the arbitrator will be selected.

REVISION

No matter how well conceived the business alliance was at the time of formation, changing circumstances and partner objectives may prompt a need to revise the objectives of the business alliance. If one of the parties to the agreement wishes to withdraw, the participants should have agreed in advance how the withdrawing party's ownership interest would be divided among the remaining parties. Moreover, a product or technology may be developed that was not foreseen when the alliance was first conceived. The alliance agreement should indicate that the rights to manufacture and distribute the product or technology might be purchased by a specific alliance participant. If revisions cannot be made to meet the needs of the partners, it may be necessary to terminate the enterprise. The events triggering dissolution are usually spelled out in the "deadlock" clause.

TERMINATION

In general, business alliances are not intended to become permanent arrangements. A business alliance may be terminated as a result of the completion of a project, successful operations resulting in merger of the partners, diverging strategic objectives of the partners, and failure of the alliance to achieve stated objectives. Termination provisions in the alliance agreement should include buyout clauses enabling one party to purchase another's ownership interests, prices of the buyout, as well as how assets and liabilities are to be divided if the venture fails or the partners elect to dissolve the operation. What will happen to key personnel and who owns tangible and intangible property such as trade secrets and patents should also be considered in the termination provisions. In some instances, a JV may convert to a simple licensing arrangement. Consequently, the partner may disengage from the JV without losing all benefits by purchasing rights to the product or technology.

The events leading to termination are usually the same as those stipulated in the "deadlock" clause. Moreover, the parties will normally be entitled to terminate the venture by mutual consent. But whether it is by mutual consent or through a failure of the dispute resolution mechanism, the business alliance agreement should include detailed provisions for terminating the agreement.

TRANSFER OF INTERESTS

JV and alliance agreements often limit how and to whom parties to the agreements can transfer their interests. This is justified by noting that each party entered the agreement with the understanding of who their partners would be. In agreements that permit transfers under certain conditions, the partners or the JV itself may have rights of first refusal (i.e., the party wishing to leave the JV must first offer their interests to other participants in the JV). Usually, the agreement will permit the parties to transfer their interests to corporate affiliates without restrictions. Parties to the agreement may have the right to "put" or sell their interests to the venture, and the venture may have a call option or right to purchase such interests. There may also be "tag-along" and "drag-along" provisions, which have the effect of a third-party purchaser acquiring not only the interest of the JV party whose interest it seeks to acquire but also the interests of other parties as well. A drag-along provision specifically requires a party not otherwise interested in selling its ownership interest to the third party to do so. A tag-along provision allows a participant, who was not originally targeted by the third party, to join the targeted party in conveying its interest to the third party.

TAXES

Each of the different types of business alliance legal structures has different tax implications. Although tax considerations should never drive the transaction, failure to explore their different implications can have painful financial consequences for all parties involved. As is true for a merger, the primary tax concerns of the JV partners will be to avoid the recognition of taxable gains on the formation of the venture and to minimize taxes imposed on the distribution of its earnings.

Corporation

In addition to the double taxation of dividends discussed earlier, the corporate structure may have other adverse tax consequences. Assuming that the partner's interest in the business alliance is less than 80%, its share of the alliance's results cannot be included in its consolidated income tax return. This has two effects. First, when earnings are distributed, they will be subject to an intercorporate dividend tax, 7% if the partner's interest in the venture is 20% or more. Second, losses of the business alliance cannot be used to offset other income earned by the participant (Tillinghast: 1998, pp. 163–164). For tax purposes, the preferred alternative to a corporate legal structure is to use a "pass-through" legal structure such as a partnership.

Partnership

Since the profits and losses are allocated directly to the partners, the partnership does not have to pay taxes. Each partner in the JV will report its share of the enterprise's income or loss in its own consolidated return, and no intercorporate dividend tax will be imposed. In addition, the partnership can be structured in such a way that some partners can receive a larger share of the profits while others receive a larger share of the losses. This flexibility in tax planning is an important factor stimulating the use of partnerships and LLCs. These entities can allocate to each JV partner a portion of a particular class of revenue, income, gain, loss, or expense. These "special allocations" can be made in the documents governing the creation of the partnership. Thus, partners need not share the results of the venture on a pro rata basis.

However, to be considered legitimate by the IRS, the special allocations must have an economic impact on the parties receiving the allocation. Therefore, it is not possible to allocate tax losses to a partner that can use them in its consolidated return without requiring that the participant actually bear the loss by experiencing a reduction in the amount it will receive on dissolution of the venture.

Written Contract

The business alliance does not incur any tax because no separate legal entity has been created. Any profits earned or losses incurred by parties to the alliance are taxed at their own effective tax rates.

Noncash Contributions

When one of the partners contributes technology, patent rights, or other property to the JV, the contribution may be structured so that the partner receives equity in exchange for the contribution. Otherwise, it will be viewed by the IRS as an attempt to avoid making a cash contribution and will be treated as taxable income to the enterprise.

Startup Expenses

If a new corporation has been created, expenses related to the start-up (e.g., advertising, training, and equipment/facility lease payments) are capitalized as deferred expenses and amortized over a 5-year period rather than expensed in the first year. However, once the venture is actively engaged in business, these types of expenses can generally be treated as operating expenses and deducted for tax purposes.

Parent Services Provided to Joint Ventures

Services provided to the JV, such as accounting, auditing, legal, human resource, and treasury services are not viewed by the IRS as being "at risk" if the JV fails. The JV should pay prevailing market fees for such services. Services provided to the JV in return for equity may be seen as taxable to the JV by the IRS if such services are not truly "at risk."

MANAGEMENT AND ORGANIZATIONAL ISSUES

Before a business alliance agreement is signed, the partners must decide what type of organizational structure will provide the most effective management and leadership.

Steering or Joint Management Committee

Control of business alliances is most often accomplished through a steering committee. The steering committee is the ultimate authority for ensuring that the venture stays focused on the strategic objectives agreed to by the partners. To maintain good communication, coordination, and teamwork, the committee should meet at least monthly. The committee should provide operations managers with sufficient autonomy so they can take responsibility for their actions and be rewarded for their initiative.

Methods of Dividing Ownership and Control

Majority–Minority Framework

The first method of control is the majority–minority framework, which relies on identifying a clearly dominant partner. A dominant partner is defined as having at least a 51% ownership stake in the enterprise. In this scenario, the equity, control, and distribution of rewards reflect the majority–minority relationship. This type of structure fosters clear decision making, the ability to make rapid midcourse corrections, and an undeniable understanding of who is in charge. This framework is most appropriate for high-risk ventures where quick decisions are often required. The major disadvantage of this approach is that the minority partner may feel powerless and become passive or alienated.

Equal Division of Power Framework

The second method is the equal division of power framework, which usually means that equity is split 50/50. This assumes that the initial contribution, distribution, decision making, and control are split equally. This approach helps keep the partners actively engaged in the management of the venture. This is best suited for partners sharing a strong common vision for the venture and possessing similar corporate cultures. However, this approach can lead to deadlocks and to the eventual dissolution of the alliance, in the absence of mutual respect, good problem-solving skills, and patience by the partners.

"Majority Rules" Framework

Under this arrangement, the equity distribution may involve three partners. Two of the partners have large equal shares, while the third partner may have less than 10%. The minority partner is used to break deadlocks. This approach enables the primary partners to remain actively engaged in the enterprise without stalemating the decision-making process. However, it may be difficult to keep the minority partner motivated to remain abreast of all the issues because their share of equity is too small.

Multiple Party Framework

In this framework, no partner has control. Instead, control resides with the management of the venture. Consequently, decision making can be nimble and made by those that best understand the issues. This framework is well suited for international ventures where a country's laws may prohibit a foreign firm from having a controlling interest. In this instance, it is commonplace for a domestic company to own the majority of the equity but the operational control of the venture resides with the foreign partner. In addition to a proportional split of the dividends paid, the foreign company may receive additional payments in the form of management fees and bonuses.

The creation of the NBC Internet (NBCi) JV corporation in 1999 illustrates a multiple-party framework in which the management of the JV appears to have control over the decision-making process in that there is no dominant party. However, if NBC exercises its option to convert its debt to equity, giving it a controlling interest, the organizational structure could convert to a more traditional majority–minority framework (see Case Study 12-6). The NBCi management challenges could be daunting in view of the disparate size of the parties involved and the potentially major cultural differences. For an interesting perspective on these types of arrangements, see Armstrong and Hagel (1997).

CASE STUDY 12-6. NBC CREATES NBC INTERNET (NBCI)

On May 10, 1999, NBC announced that it would contribute key Internet properties into a JV with CNET and XOOM.com, Inc. The new company will be NBC's exclusive portal/virtual community and electronic commerce investment. NBCi will use Snap as its consumer brand and integrate broadcast, portal, and electronic commerce for more than 18 million unique users per month.

COMPOSITION

NBCi will consist of NBC and CNET's Snap.com, an Internet portal and the first to launch a broadband service, XOOM.com, a community-based web site, and several NBC Internet properties. The NBC properties include NBC.com, NBC's Interactive Neighborhood, Videoseeker.com, and a 10% ownership stake in the new CNBC.com launched in mid-1999. NBCi has agreed to purchase $380 million in NBC TV network advertising over the next 4 years. The agreement calls for NBCi to purchase an additional $500 million in advertising in the subsequent 6-year period.

In 1998, NBC purchased 19% of the equity of CNET's Snap.com Internet portal. Snap.com was ranked the 11th most heavily visited Internet site, with 9.75 million unique visitors per month at the end of 1999. XOOM.com has 9.69 million unique visitors per month making it the 12th-ranked Internet site.

XOOM offers consumers free services over the web, including homepage building, chat rooms, message boards, email, online greeting cards, clip art, and downloadable software. XOOM also targets its visitors with product and service offerings tailored to their tastes. Owned by NBC and CNET, Snap.com provides portal services, content from 100 leading web publishers, and offers high-speed, broadband user access.

PRODUCT/SERVICE OFFERING

NBCi will offer high-quality free web services, such as search and navigation services, a directory of web sites, home page building, chat rooms, downloadable software, message boards, and greeting cards. The company will also offer NBC content, including certain full-motion video programming, original extensions of NBC shows, including sites for *Saturday Night Live* and *The Tonight Show with Jay Leno,* and guides tailored for local communities. Revenue will be generated from visitor transactions and advertising.

PRESUMED COMPETITIVE EDGE

The partners believe that the integration of NBC's content and promotional strengths with XOOM's expertise in direct e-commerce and Snap's navigational strengths will cause NBCi to stand out among its competitors. Site users will only have to go to one location to search, chat with other users, send e-mail, receive faxes, watch videos, create their own web page, personalize their own page, and purchase products.

DEAL STRUCTURE

NBC will own a 49.9% stake in NBCi and will have 6 of the 13 board of directors seats. NBC will also purchase convertible debt, which when fully converted will increase NBC's ownership to 53% and give it majority representation on the board. Assuming NBC converts the debt, CNET and SNAP.com option holders would own 13% and XOOM shareholders and its option holders would own 34% of NBCi's equity.

MSNBC.com is not part of the transaction and will remain a 50–50 JV between NBC and Microsoft. Snap.com will give MSNBC.com preferred positioning on the NBCi site.

Source: NBC, 1999.

CONFIDENTIAL INFORMATION

Parties to a business alliance will have access to a substantial amount of confidential information, including proprietary know-how, customers, and employees. The alliance agreement should specify how such information should be treated. Confidential information should never be released without the consent of all parties involved. Moreover, the alliance agreement should also contain clauses preventing the various partners from soliciting the other's employees for purposes of employment or from soliciting the other partner's customers.

REGULATORY RESTRICTIONS AND NOTIFICATIONS

This section provides a brief overview of the regulatory issues confronting business alliances. See Chapter 2 (this volume) for a more detailed discussion of regulations covering business combinations.

Antitrust Policy

The DoJ has historically looked upon business alliances far more favorably than mergers or acquisitions. Nonetheless, JVs may be subject to Hart-Scott-Rodino filing requirements, since the parties to the JV are viewed as acquirers and the JV itself as a target.

For JVs between competitors to be acceptable to regulators, competitors should be able to do something together that they could not do alone. In general, competitors can be relatively confident that a partnership will be acceptable to regulators, if in combination they do not control more than 20% of the market. Project-oriented ventures are looked at most favorably. Collaborative research is encouraged, particularly when the research is shared among all the parties to the alliance. However, regulators will move aggressively to investigate any perceived restraint of competition between partners, such as price fixing and market allocation, or any effort to deprive competitors from accessing a much needed resource.

The regulatory guidelines for joint marketing arrangements are still ambiguous. Such agreements, particularly between competitors, are likely to spark a review by the regulators, since they have the potential to result in price fixing and dividing up the market.

Securities and Exchange Commission

If the corporate partners make a public stock offering or a private placement of partnership shares in addition to the infusion of capital, the JV must comply with prevailing federal and state securities laws.

EMPIRICAL FINDINGS

EXCESS RETURNS

There is empirical evidence that JVs create value for their participants. In a study of 136 JVs between 1972 and 1979, McConnell and Nantell (1985) found that excess returns (i.e., the amount of return above what the capital asset pricing model would have predicted) to venture participants averaged 2.15% during the 62 days prior to the announcement of the JV. In a more recent study, Chan,

Kensinger, Keown, and Martin (1997) support these findings. The authors track share price response to the formation of 345 strategic alliances spanning 1983 to 1992 and conclude that the stock price response was positive for both horizontal alliances involving partner firms in the same industries as well as nonhorizontal alliances. Notably, the increase in share price is greater for horizontal alliances involving the transfer of technical knowledge than with nontechnical alliances. Finally, partnering firms tend to display better operating performance than their industry peers do over the 5-year period surrounding the year in which an alliance is formed.

IMPACT ON MARKET VALUE

There is also evidence that business alliances may account for a significant amount of the market value of participants. Kalmbach and Roussel (1999) of Andersen Consulting found that alliances account for about 6–15% of the market value of the typical large company in a sample of 870 JVs and 1,106 licensing arrangements studied over a 4-year period.

THE GROWING ROLE OF BUSINESS ALLIANCES

The average large company, which may have had no alliances in 1990, now has more than 30 (Kalmbach and Roussel: 1999). Over the last decade, the number of reported alliances has been increasing at about 30% per year. Despite rapid growth, there is evidence that most companies have yet to develop the skill to successfully implement alliances. The Kalmbach and Roussel study indicates that 61% of the alliances are viewed as either disappointments or outright failures. This figure substantiates earlier findings by Robert Spekman of the Darden Graduate School of Business Administration that 60% of all ventures fail (Ellis: 1996).

These studies do not make allowances for different levels of experience in forming and managing alliances among the firms in their samples. As is true for mergers and acquisitions, cumulative experience is an important factor in increasing the likelihood that an alliance will meet expectations. According to a Booz-Allen survey of 700 alliances (Booz-Allen and Hamilton: 1993), financial returns on investment are directly related to a company's experience in forming and managing business alliances. Companies with one or two alliances in place tended to earn a 10% average return on investment as compared to 15% for those with three to five, 17% for those with six to eight, and 20% for those with nine or more.

THINGS TO REMEMBER

Business alliances may represent attractive alternatives to mergers and acquisitions. The motivations for business alliances can include risk sharing, gaining access to new markets, accelerating the introduction of new products, technology sharing, cost reduction, globalization, a desire to acquire (or exit) a business, or their perceived acceptability to regulators.

Business alliances may assume a variety of different legal structures. These include the following: corporate, partnership, franchise, equity partnership, written contract, or handshake agreements. Handshake agreements should be avoided in view of their inherent ambiguity. Corporate legal structures include a generalized form, S-type, and LLCs, which contain some of the benefits of both the corporate and partnership structures. Although the corporate structure is subject to double taxation, it does provide for centralized management, continuity of ownership, ease of raising capital, and limited liability. Partnerships are frequently used as an alternative to the corporate structure because of their greater flexibility in allocating gains and losses and their more favorable tax treatment. The written contract is the simplest legal structure and is most often used in strategic alliances.

As is true of mergers and acquisitions, planning should always precede concerns about how the transaction should be structured. All parties must agree on the basic strategic direction and purpose of a proposed alliance as well as the financial and nonfinancial goals and milestones used in establishing the first year's operating plan or budget.

Deal structuring in the context of a business alliance concerns the fair allocation of risks, rewards, resource requirements, and responsibilities among participants. Key issues that must be resolved include the alliance's scope, duration, legal form, governance, and control mechanism. The valuation of resource contributions ultimately determines ownership interests. How profits and losses will be distributed and performance measured must also be determined. Alliance agreements must also be flexible enough to be revised when necessary and contain mechanisms for breaking deadlocks, transferring ownership interests, and dealing with the potential for termination.

Empirical studies suggest that business alliances contribute to shareholder value and that they are likely to become increasingly popular in the future. Nonetheless, their success rate in terms of meeting participants' expectations does not seem to be materially different from that of mergers and acquisitions.

CHAPTER DISCUSSION QUESTIONS

12-1.   Under what circumstances does a business alliance represent an attractive alternative to a merger or acquisition?

12-2.   Compare and contrast a corporate and partnership legal structure.

12-3.   What are the primary motives for creating a business alliance? How do they differ from the motives for a merger or acquisition?

12-4.   What factors are critical to the success of a business alliance?

12-5.   Why is a handshake agreement a potentially dangerous form of business alliance?

12-6.   What is a limited liability corporation? What are its advantages and disadvantages?

12-7. Why is defining the scope of a business alliance important?

12-8. Discuss ways of valuing tangible and intangible contributions to a JV.

12-9. What are the advantages and disadvantages of the various organizational structures that could be employed to manage a business alliance?

12-10. What are the common reasons for the termination of a business alliance?

CHAPTER BUSINESS CASE

CASE STUDY 12-7. BELL ATLANTIC AND VODAFONE FORM WIRELESS JV

Bell Atlantic and Vodafone agreed to a JV that creates the largest wireless phone company in the United States. This announcement came shortly after AT&T and British Telecommunications formed a global alliance to link their wireless telephone operations with roaming agreements and other unified services in September 1999. AT&T and British Telecom will provide wireless service to a customer base of 41 million in seventeen countries.

Bell Atlantic, the largest local telephone company in the U.S., will connect its East Coast network with the West Coast network of VodafoneAirTouch, the world's largest wireless telephone company. Together, their combined 20 million customers will be able to buy cheaper wireless phones and make calls from almost anywhere in the country without having to pay "roaming" charges for out-of-area calls.

The driving force behind the creation of the JV was to create a national wireless phone network that will give both companies access to a larger pool of customers. Bell Atlantic gets to reach a national market and Vodafone is able to fill a serious gap in its global coverage.

Vodafone's West Coast network is valued at $15 billion. In exchange for this network, Bell Atlantic gave Vodafone a 45% stake in the new company. Bell Atlantic will manage the New York-based JV and control a majority of the seats on the board of directors. The total assets of the JV will exceed $28 billion. The parent companies are expecting to sell a stake in the new company to the public within two or three years.

CASE STUDY DISCUSSION QUESTIONS

1. What did Bell Atlantic and Vodafone expect to get out of the JV?

2. Do you think this JV will promote or reduce competition in the wireless phone market?

3. Why would Bell Atlantic and Vodafone want to sell a portion of the new JV to the public?

4. In your judgment, how do you think ownership in the JV was determined?

5. What type of JV legal structure was selected by the parent companies? Why was this particular type of legal structure chosen?

A solution to this case study is given in the back of the book.

REFERENCES

Armstrong, Arthur, and John Hagel, *Net Gain: Expanding Markets through Virtual Communities,* Harvard Business School Press, 1997.

Berg, Sanford V., Jerome Duncan, and Philip Friedman, *Joint Venture Strategies and Corporate Innovation,* Cambridge, MA: Oelgeschlager, Gunn & Hain, 1982.

Bloomberg.com, "GM Invests in Fuji," December 17, 1999a.

Bloomberg.com, "J&J Sues Amgen," December 11, 1999b.

Booz-Allen & Hamilton, *A Practical Guide to Alliances: Leapfrogging the Learning Curve,* Los Angeles, 1993.

Chan, Su Han, John W. Kensinger, Arthur J. Keown, and John D. Martin, "Do Strategic Alliances Create Value?" *Journal of Financial Economics, 46,* (2), November 1997, pp. 199–221.

Ebin, Robert F., "Legal Aspects of International Joint Ventures and Strategic Alliances," in *International M&A, Joint Ventures and Beyond: Doing the Deal,* edited by David J. BenDaniel and Arthur H. Rosenbloom, (eds.), New York: John Wiley & Sons, 1998, pp. 315–360.

Ellis, Caroline, "Briefings from the Editors," *Harvard Business Review, 74,* (1), July/August 1996, p. 8.

Ernst, David, and Andrew M. S. Steinhubl, Alliances in Upstream Oil and Gas, *The McKinsey Quarterly,* 1997, Number 2, pp. 144–155.

Freeman, Louis S., and Thomas M. Stephens, "Advantages, Key Issues, and Tax Strategies in the Use of Partnerships by Corporate Joint Ventures," in *Tax Strategies for Corporate Acquisitions, Dispositions, Spin-Offs, Joint Ventures and Other Strategic Alliances, Financings, Reorganizations, and Restructurings,* New York: Practising Law Institute, 1994.

Fusaro, Robert F. X., "Issues to Consider in Drafting Joint Venture Agreements," in *Drafting Corporate Agreements,* New York: Practising Law Institute, 1995.

Hyde, Justin, "GM, Ford, DaimlerChrysler Join Online Ordering Forces," CNNfn, February 22, 2000.

Kalmbach Jr., and Charles Roussel, *Dispelling the Myths of Alliances,* Andersen Consulting, 1999. Available: www.ac.com/showcase/alliances/exec_summ.html

Lajoux, Alexandra Reed, *The Art of M&A Integration,* New York: McGraw-Hill, 1998, p. 41, note 7.

Lorange, Peter, and Hohan Roos, *Strategic Alliances: Formation, Implementation, and Evolution,* Oxford: Blackwell, 1992.

Lynch, Robert Porter, *The Practical Guide to Joint Ventures and Corporate Alliances,* New York: John Wiley & Sons, 1990.

McConnell, John J. and Timothy J. Nantell, "Corporate Combinations and Common Stock Returns: the Case of Joint Ventures," *Journal of Finance, 40,* June 1985, pp. 519–536.

NBC, Press release May 10, 1999.

Rigby, Darrell K. and Robin W. T. Buchanan, "Putting More Strategy in Strategic Alliances," *Directors and Boards,* Winter 1994, pp. 14–19.

Tillinghast, David R., "Tax Aspects of Inbound Merger and Acquisitions and Joint Venture Transactions," In David J. BenDaniel and Arthur H. Rosenbloom (eds.), *International M&A, Joint Ventures and Beyond: Doing the Deal,* New York: John Wiley & Sons, 1998, pp. 151–180.

Van Laarhoven, Peter, and Graham Sharman, Logistics Alliances: The European Experience, *The McKinsey Quarterly, 1,* 1994, pp. 39–49.

13

ALTERNATIVE EXIT AND RESTRUCTURING STRATEGIES:

DIVESTITURES, SPIN-OFFS, CARVE-OUTS, SPLIT-UPS, BANKRUPTCY, AND LIQUIDATION

Experience is the name everyone gives to their mistakes.
—Oscar Wilde

Stunned by the continued decline in the firm's share price, Joe leaned forward in his chair as he passionately directed his division general managers to improve their units' operating performance. Wall Street had concluded that the conglomerate had become too highly diversified with significant investments in seven different industries. Management had hoped that by diversifying their operations in industries whose fortunes were tied to different stages of the business cycle, the firm would be able to make earnings growth more predictable. In fact, senior management found it increasingly difficult to understand the nuances of the competitive dynamics of so many different industries. This lack of understanding resulted in missed opportunities and poorly performing investments. Consequently, Joe was under considerable pressure to improve consolidated performance, to increase the firm's overall focus, or perhaps even to completely liquidate the business and distribute the cash proceeds to the shareholders.

Last year at this time, Joe's division managers had assured him that plans were in place to materially improve operating performance. Despite a robust economy, the promised improvement did not take place. Joe had lost all patience. His directive to his managers was simple. Improve performance during the coming fiscal year or be divested. Joe was not confrontational by nature, but he felt he had to do something to get his managers' attention. Joe's finance and planning staffs were already using projections submitted by his division managers to value each of the firm's operations as if it were operating independently from the parent. Concurrently, an investment banker had been hired to estimate the after-tax value of each operation as if it had been sold. By comparing the present value of each operation to its sale value, Joe would have some indication of which of his firm's operations should be sold and which retained.

The investment banker concluded that one unit would require substantial additional funding if it were to realize the full potential of its technology. Although a cutting-edge unit, few firms seemed to show any real interest in acquiring the largely untested technology. Consequently, the outright sale of the unit did not appear to be an attractive option. However, the stock market was setting new records and many investors seemed to be hungry for "emerging" technology investment opportunities. Consequently, the investment banker recommended that the unit be converted to a wholly owned subsidiary and that a portion of its stock be sold to the public. The resulting proceeds could be used to fund further development of the technology and to establish a market value for the unit. Once established, the balance of the unit's stock could be sold to the public and the proceeds used to fund opportunities in the parent firm's remaining operations.

Joe carefully considered his options. Under fire from Wall Street and increasing pressure from his board of directors, he knew he would have to make some very difficult decisions. He knew he was going to face a number of sleepless nights in the coming months.

OVERVIEW

Many corporations, particularly large, highly diversified organizations, are constantly reviewing ways in which they can enhance shareholder value by changing the composition of their assets, liabilities, equity, and operations. These activities are generally referred to as restructuring strategies. Restructuring may embody both growth and exit strategies. Growth strategies have been discussed elsewhere in this book. The focus in this chapter is on those strategic options that allow the firm to maximize shareholder value by re-deploying assets through contraction and downsizing of the parent corporation.

Although asset sales may occur to fund growth investments, the motivations for most of the strategies discussed in this chapter involve a desire to withdraw from underperforming, undervalued, or nonstrategic businesses. Empirical studies show that exit strategies, which return cash to shareholders, tend to have a highly favorable impact on shareholder wealth creation. The share prices of firms that return cash or noncash assets to their shareholders tend to respond much more positively than for those firms that retain cash generated from the sale of assets for reinvestment in the parent firm (Lang, Poulsen, and Stulz: 1995; Allen and

McConnell: 1998). These results suggest that investors apparently have little confidence in management's ability to invest the funds wisely.

Divestitures, spin-offs, equity carve-outs, split-ups, split-offs, and bust-ups are commonly used strategies to exit businesses and to redeploy corporate assets by returning cash or noncash assets through a special dividend to shareholders. The intent of this chapter is to discuss why parent corporations may choose to exit certain businesses, how this may be achieved, and the impact on shareholder value of such actions. This chapter also addresses how firms deal with business failure through voluntary or involuntary reorganization and in some instances liquidation. Figure 13-1 summarizes commonly used exit restructuring strategies.

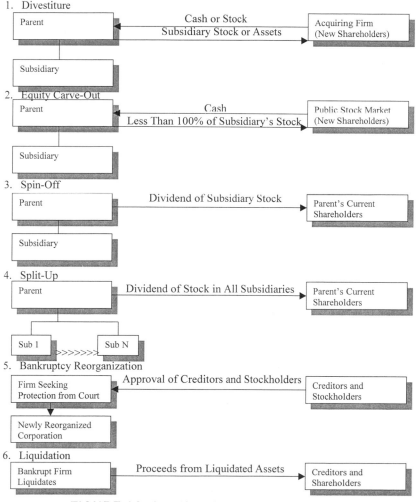

FIGURE 13–1. Alternative exit restructuring strategies.

MOTIVES FOR EXITING BUSINESSES

The motives for exiting businesses are both numerous and diverse. These include changing corporate strategy or focus, a desire to exit underperforming businesses, a lack of fit, regulatory concerns, and tax considerations. Other motives include a need to raise funds, reduce risk, move away from the core business, discarding unwanted businesses from prior acquisitions, and avoiding conflicts with customers. Although there is empirical evidence to demonstrate that changing corporate strategies or focus are common reasons for firms to exit businesses, support for the other motives is largely anecdotal.

CHANGING CORPORATE STRATEGY OR FOCUS

Firms may change strategies or focus as a result of a changing competitive or regulatory environment or simply as a result of having learned from past mistakes. Managing highly diverse and complex portfolios of businesses is both time-consuming and distracting. This is particularly true when the businesses are in largely unrelated industries. There is a limited understanding by senior management of the nuances of each business and of what constitutes worthwhile opportunities for the parent to adequately fund. A unit may be a small portion of a parent company's sales and may not be receiving adequate time or attention from management at the corporate level. Often, senior management may not completely understand the opportunities facing such a business, resulting in limited funding of potentially attractive opportunities. A business that is rich in high-growth opportunities may be an excellent candidate for divestiture to a strategic buyer with significant cash resources and limited growth opportunities.

Empirical Evidence

The difficulty in managing diverse portfolios of businesses in many different industries and the difficulty in accurately valuing these portfolios contributed to the "de-conglomeration" movement of the 1970s and 1980s. Sixty percent of acquisitions made between 1970 and 1982 by companies in industries unrelated to the acquirer's primary industry focus were divested by 1989 (Petty, Keown, Scott, and Martin: 1993). John and Ofek (1995) found that abnormal returns earned by the shareholders of a firm divesting a business result largely from improved management of the assets that remain after the divestiture is completed. They attributed these returns to increased focus and the ability of management to understand fewer lines of business. As evidence of the challenges of understanding businesses in diverse industries, they also found that 75% of divested units were unrelated to the selling company.

More recently, these conclusions were supported by Krishnaswami and Subramaniam (1999), who noted that reducing complexity significantly increases returns to shareholders. They also found that gains experienced by spin-offs were greater the more complex the parent was before the spin-off.

Examples of Achieving Greater Focus

In the late 1980s, TRW divested many of its lower technology businesses to shift into high-technology segments of the information systems and services, space and defense, and automotive parts industries. In 1987, Allegis Corporation reversed its previous strategy of providing a broader range of travel services by selling its hotel and car rental businesses to become UAL Corporation and to concentrate on operating United Airlines. In the late 1990s, General Motors spun off its Hughes Electronics and Delphi Automotive Parts operations to focus on its passenger car and light truck businesses. In 1999, Allegheny Teledyne spun off its software and engineering systems, communication and electronics, and aircraft engine businesses to focus on its specialty metals businesses.

UNDERPERFORMING BUSINESSES

Parent firms often exit businesses that consistently fail to meet or exceed the parent's hurdle rate requirements. These hurdle rates frequently consist of the parent's cost of capital adjusted for any special risks associated with the business or the industry in which it competes. Baxter International Inc. announced in late 1999 its intention to spin off its underperforming cardiovascular business, creating a new company that will specialize in treatments for heart disease.

Frequently, a parent firm may hang on to operations that have been underperforming for years. The reluctance to sell a poor performer can reflect the parent's emotional attachment due to its long history in the business or its unwillingness to admit to mistakes in managing the business. In the instance of an acquisition, management may not want to admit to having paid too much for the business or to having been unable to manage the business effectively (Boot: 1992).

REGULATORY CONCERNS

A firm with substantial market share purchasing a direct competitor may create concerns about violations of antitrust laws. Regulatory agencies may still approve the merger if the acquiring firm is willing to divest certain operations, which in combination with similar units in the acquiring company, are deemed to be anti-competitive. As a result of an antitrust suit filed by the Department of Justice (DoJ), the government and AT&T reached an agreement effective January 1, 1984, to breakup AT&T's 22 operating companies into seven regional Bell operating companies (RBOCs). The RBOCs became responsible for local telephone service, and AT&T kept responsibility for long-distance service.

LACK OF FIT

Individual businesses may be undervalued because investors believe that there are insufficient benefits from synergy to offset the overhead expenses associated with being part of a holding company. This may have been a factor in AT&T's

choice to implement a split-up of its business in the mid-1990s into three separate entities, each with its own stock traded on the public exchanges.

Companies may divest units after they have had time to learn more about the business. In 1995, Raytheon sold its D.C. Heath textbook publishing company to Houghton Mifflin Company for $455 million. Although a sizable publishing business on a stand-alone basis, D.C. Heath never quite fit with the three larger core businesses of Raytheon which included defense electronics, engineering, and avionics. Similarly, TRW's decision to sell its commercial information services businesses in 1997 came after years of trying to find a significant fit with its space and defense businesses.

TAX CONSIDERATIONS

Restructuring actions may provide tax benefits that cannot be realized without undertaking a restructuring of the business. Marriot Corporation contributed its hotel real estate operations to a Real Estate Investment Trust (REIT) in 1989 through a spin-off. Because REITs do not have to pay taxes on income that is distributed to shareholders, Marriot was able to enhance shareholder value by eliminating the double taxation of income, once as rental income to the parent and again when distributed to shareholders.

RAISING FUNDS

Parent firms may choose to fund new initiatives or acquisitions or reduce leverage through the sale or partial sale of units that are no longer considered strategic or are underperforming corporate expectations. Such sales may also result from the need to improve near-term cash flow. Examples include Chryler's sale of its highly profitable tank division to avoid bankruptcy in the early 1980s. Similarly, Navistar, formerly International Harvester, sold its profitable Solar Turbines operation to Caterpillar Tractor to reduce its indebtedness.

RISK REDUCTION

A firm may reduce its perceived risk associated with a particular unit by selling a portion of the business to the public. Shearson Lehman was viewed by American Express as riskier than its core credit card business. Although the firm believed that there were opportunities to sell its credit cards to Shearson Lehman customers, it decided to reduce its exposure to the cyclical variation of the securities business by selling a portion of the unit in 1987. Major tobacco companies have been under pressure for years to divest or spin off their food businesses because of the litigation risk associated with their tobacco subsidiaries. RJR Nabisco bowed to such pressure in 1998 with the spin-off of Nabisco Foods.

MOVING AWAY FROM THE CORE BUSINESS

Management may not believe that investment opportunities in their current core business are attractive. They may believe that their firm's core skills or competencies in manufacturing or distribution can be used to pursue growth opportunities in other industries. Consequently, assets in the current core business may be sold to fund these diversification opportunities. An example would be Dial Corporation's sale of its Greyhound bus operations in 1987.

DISCARDING UNWANTED BUSINESSES FROM PRIOR ACQUISITIONS

Acquiring companies often find themselves with certain assets and operations of the acquired company that do not fit their primary strategy. These redundant assets may be divested to raise funds to help pay for the acquisition and to enable management to focus on integrating the remaining businesses into the parent without the distraction of having to manage nonstrategic assets. Upon acquiring Allied Stores in the mid-1980s, Campeau Corporation announced that it would sell sixteen Allied operations that were not critical to the firm's overall strategy to help reduce its indebtedness. Campeau undertook a similar strategy after its acquisition of Federated Department Stores in 1989.

AVOIDING CONFLICTS WITH CUSTOMERS

For years, many of the RBOCs spun off by AT&T in 1984 have been interested in competing in the long-distance market, which would put them in direct competition with their former parent. Similarly, AT&T sought to penetrate the regional telephone markets by acquiring access to millions of households by acquiring cable TV companies. In preparation for the implementation of these plans, AT&T announced in 1995 that it would split up the company into three publicly traded global companies. The three companies included Communications Services (long-distance services), Communications Systems (later renamed Lucent Technologies, a provider of network switches and transmission equipment), and Global Information Solutions (later renamed NCR, a provider of systems integration services). The primary reason for the split up was to avoid possible conflicts between AT&T's former equipment manufacturer and its main customers, the RBOCs.

DIVESTITURES

A divestiture is the sale of a portion of the firm to an outside party generally resulting in a cash infusion to the parent. Divestitures are generally the least complex of the exit-restructuring activities to understand. A firm may choose to sell an undervalued operation that it determined to be nonstrategic or unrelated to the core business and to use the proceeds of the sale to fund investments in potentially higher return opportunities. Alternatively, the firm may chose to divest the undervalued business and return the cash to shareholders either through a liquidating dividend or share repurchase.

HISTORICAL TRENDS

Between 1970 and 1999, divestitures averaged about 40% of total transactions (Thomson Financial Securities Data). Divestitures reached a peak of 54% in 1975, the trough of the worst recession since World War II. The surge in divestitures in the early-to-mid 1970s and again in the early 1990s followed the merger boom periods of the late 1960s and the 1980s (Gaughan: 1999).

EMPIRICAL STUDIES

Studies suggest that the more unrelated an operating unit is to the parent's core business the more likely it is to be divested. For a sample of 271 acquisitions between 1971 and 1982, Kaplan and Weisbach (1992) found that 119 were divested by 1989. Of the firms in the sample, 60% of the acquisitions in which the acquirer and the target are not highly related were divested; less than 20% of highly related acquisitions were divested. The conclusion that largely unrelated businesses were more likely to be divested was also supported in a more recent study in which the authors concluded that three-fourths of divested businesses are unrelated to the core business of the seller (John and Ofek: 1995).

DECIDING WHEN TO SELL

Many corporations review their business portfolio periodically to determine which operations continue to fit their core strategies. As noted earlier in this chapter, changes in the parent's strategy or a desire to achieve a more focused business portfolio can result in certain operations becoming strategically redundant. Such operations become prime candidates for divestiture. Even if a business "fits" within the parent corporation's current strategy, the business may not be earning the financial rates of return required by the parent. Consequently, the parent will conduct a financial analysis to determine if the business is worth more to shareholders if it is sold and the proceeds either returned to the shareholders or reinvested in opportunities offering potentially higher rates of return.

Financial Issues

An analysis undertaken to determine if a business should be sold requires the estimation of four key elements. These elements include the of after-tax cash flows generated by the unit, an appropriate discount rate reflecting the risk of the business, the after-tax market value of the business, and the after-tax value of the business to the parent. The decision to sell or to retain the business depends on a comparison of the after-tax value of the business to the parent with the after-tax proceeds from the sale of the business.

Calculating After-Tax Cash Flows

To decide if a business is worth more to the shareholder if sold, the parent must first estimate after-tax cash flows of the business viewed on a stand-alone basis (i.e., as if it were operated as an independent operating unit). This requires that the cash flows be adjusted for intercompany sales and the cost of services (e.g., legal, treasury, and audit provided by the parent).

Intercompany sales refer to operating unit revenue generated by selling products or services to another unit owned by the same parent. For example, in a vertically integrated business, such as a steel manufacturer that obtains both iron ore and coal from its operating subsidiaries, the majority of the revenue generated by the iron ore and coal operations often comes from sales to the parent company's steel-making operations. The parent may value this revenue for financial reporting purposes using product transfer prices, which may reflect current market prices or some formula such as a predetermined markup over the cost of production. If the transfer prices do not reflect actual market prices, intercompany revenue may be artificially high or low, depending on whether the transfer prices are higher or lower than actual market prices. Intercompany revenues associated with the operating unit should be restated to reflect actual market prices.

Services provided by the parent to the business may be subsidized (i.e., provided at below actual cost) or at a markup over actual cost. To reflect these factors, the cash flows of the business should be adjusted for services provided by the parent at more or less than what the business would have to pay for them if it were operating as an independent organization. Operating profits should be reduced by the amount of any subsidies and increased by any markup over what the business would have to pay if it purchased comparable services from sources outside of the parent firm.

Estimating the Discount Rate

Once the after-tax stand-alone cash flows have been determined, a discount rate should be determined that reflects the risk characteristics of the industry in which the business competes. The cost of capital of other firms in the same industry is often a good proxy for the business' discount rate.

Estimating the After-Tax Market Value of the Business

The discount rate is then used to estimate the present or market value (MV) of the projected after-tax cash flows of the business as if it were a stand-alone business. The valuation is based on cash flows that have been adjusted for intercompany revenues not on the books at market prices and services provided to the operating unit by the parent firm at something other than actual cost.

Estimating the Value of the Business to the Parent

The after-tax equity value (EV) of the business as part of the parent is estimated by subtracting the market value of the business' liabilities (L) from its MV as a stand-alone operation. (To determine how to calculate the market value of the business' liabilities, see the discussion on valuing liabilities in the section on purchase accounting in Chapter 10, this volume.) This relationship can be expressed as follows:

$$EV = MV - L$$

EV is a measure of the after-tax market value of shareholder equity of the business, where the shareholder is the parent firm.

Deciding to Sell

The decision to sell or retain the business is made by comparing EV with the after-tax sale value (SV) of the business. Assuming other considerations do not outweigh any after-tax gain on the sale of the business, the decision to sell or retain can be summarized as follows:

If SV > EV, divest.

If SV < EV, retain.

Timing

Timing often has a major influence on the decision to sell a business. Obviously, the best time to sell a business is when the owner does not need to sell to raise new capital or to repay creditors. The sell decision should also reflect the broader financial environment. Selling when business confidence is high and stock prices are rising and interest rates are low is likely to fetch a higher price for the unit.

If the business to be sold is highly cyclical, the sale should be timed to coincide with the firm's peak year earnings. Businesses can also be timed to sell when they are considered most popular. In 1980, the oil exploration business was booming; by 1983 it was in the doldrums. It recovered again by the mid-1990s. What's hot today can be a fizzle tomorrow. A similar story could be told about many of today's high-flying Internet-related companies.

CASE STUDY 13-1. GILLETTE ANNOUNCES DIVESTITURE PLANS

With 1998 sales of $10.1 billion, Gillette is the world leader in the production of razor blades, razors, and shaving cream. Gillette also has a leading position in the production of pens and other writing instruments. Gillette's consolidated operating performance during the first 9 months of 1999 continued to be carried by the core razor blade and razor, Duracell battery, and oral care businesses. Excluding certain one-time adjustments, total corporate sales for the first 9 months of 1999 increased by 5% when compared to the same period in 1998; however, operating profits dropped by 5%.

In contrast to Gillette's core product areas, sales of Braun products, including electric shavers and oral care products, dropped by 11% and operating profits by 43% during the first 9 months of 1999 over the same period in 1998. Similarly, sales of toiletries and operating profits declined by 5%

and 6%, respectively, during the same period. Sales and operating profits of stationery products, which include pens, fell by 11% and 78%, respectively, through the first three-quarters of 1999.

Reflecting disappointment in the performance of certain operating units, Gillete's CEO, Michael Hawley, announced in October 1999 his intention to divest poorly performing businesses, unless he could be convinced by early 2000 that they could be turned around. The businesses under consideration comprise about 15% of the company's $10 billion in annual sales. Hawley sees the new focus of the company to be in razor blades, batteries, and oral care.

To achieve this new focus, Hawley intends to prune the firm's product portfolio. The most likely targets for divestiture include pens (i.e., Paper-Mate, Parker, and Waterman). With operating earnings for these businesses down 78% during the first 9 months of 1999, the prospects are for continuing deterioration.

Other units under consideration include Braun and toiletries. With respect to these businesses, Hawley apparently intends to be selective. At Braun, where overall operating profits plunged 43% in the first three quarters of 1999, Hawley has announced that Gillette will keep electric shavers and electric toothbrushes. However, the household and personal care appliance units are likely divestiture candidates.

The timing of these sales may be poor. A decision to sell Braun at this time would compete against Black & Decker's recently announced decision to sell its appliance business.

Although Gillette would be smaller, the firm believes that its margins will improve and that its earnings growth will be more rapid. Moreover, divesting such problem businesses as pens and appliances would let management focus on the units whose prospects are the brightest. These are businesses that Gillette's previous management was simply not willing to sell because of their perceived high potential.

Source: *Business Week,* 1999a, p. 86; Gillette, 1999.

SPIN-OFFS AND SPLIT-UPS

SPIN-OFFS

A spin-off is a transaction in which a parent creates a new legal subsidiary and distributes shares it owns in the subsidiary to its current shareholders as a stock dividend. The shares are distributed in direct proportion to the shareholders current holdings of the parent's stock. Consequently, the proportional ownership of shares in the new legal subsidiary is the same as the stockholders' proportional ownership of shares in the parent firm. The new entity has its own management and is run independently from the parent company. Unlike the divestiture or equity carve-out, the spin-off does not result in an infusion of cash to the parent company. The average size of spin-offs is 20% of the parent's original market value (Schipper & Smith: 1983). Some of the more notable spin-offs include the spin-off of Allstate by Sears, Payless by May Department Stores, Dean Witter/Discover by Sears, CBS by Westinghouse, and Pizza Hut, KFC, and Taco Bell by Pepsico.

SPLIT-UPS

A split-up involves the creation of a new class of stock for each of the parent's operating subsidiaries, paying current shareholders a dividend of each new class of stock, and then dissolving the remaining corporate shell. Stockholders in the new companies may be different as shareholders in the parent company may exchange their stock for stock in one or more of the spin-offs. Some of the most famous split-ups in recent years include ITT, Grace, AT&T, 3M, Baxter, Tenneco, Anheuser Busch, Ralston Purina, General Motors, Corning, Dial, Dun & Bradstreet, and Aetna.

TAX CONSIDERATIONS

If properly structured, spin-offs or split-ups, which consist of multiple spin-offs, are generally not taxable to shareholders. To avoid being subject to ordinary income tax rates, the parent and the subsidiary must have been engaged in business for the 5 years prior to the spin-off. The subsidiary must also be at least 80% owned by the parent, and the parent has to distribute the shares in the subsidiary without a prearranged plan for these securities to be resold. These conditions have been included in the U.S. Tax Code to ensure that there is a sound business purpose for the spin-off other than to avoid the payment of taxes.

CHOOSING BETWEEN SPIN-OFFS AND DIVESTITURES

On the surface, it may seem that a divestiture would generally be preferable to a spin-off, if the after-tax proceeds from the sale of an operating unit or selected assets exceed their after-tax equity value to the firm. Unlike a spin-off, a divestiture generates a cash infusion to the firm, which can either be reinvested or paid to shareholders as a dividend or share buyback.

In fact, a spin-off may create greater shareholder wealth for several reasons. First, a spin-off is tax-free to the shareholders if it is properly structured. In contrast, the cash proceeds from an outright sale may be taxable to the extent a gain is realized. Moreover, management must be able to reinvest the after-tax proceeds in a project that has a reasonable likelihood of returning the firm's cost of capital. If management chooses to return the cash proceeds to shareholders as a dividend Second, a spin-off enables the shareholder to determine when to sell their shares.

CASE STUDY 13-2. BAXTER TO SPIN-OFF
HEART CARE UNIT

Baxter International Inc. announced in late 1999 its intention to spin off its underperforming cardiovascular business, creating a new company that will specialize in treatments for heart disease. The new company will have 6,000 employees worldwide and annual revenue in excess of $1 billion. The unit sells biological heart valves harvested from pigs and cows, catheters and other products used to monitor hearts during surgery, and heart-assist devices for patients awaiting surgery.

Baxter conceded that they have been "optimizing" (harvesting) the cardiovascular business by not making the necessary investments to grow or through a stock repurchase, taxes must again be paid by the shareholders. the unit. The unit's primary competitors, Guidant, Medtronic, and Boston Scientific, are spending more on research and investing more on start-up companies that are developing new technology than is Baxter.

With the spin-off, the new company will have the currency (i.e., stock and financial resources) that had formerly been siphoned off by the parent to create an environment that will more directly encourage the speed and innovation necessary to compete effectively in this industry. The unit's stock will be used to provide additional incentive for key employees and to serve as a means of making future acquisitions of companies necessary to extend the unit's product offering.

Source: *Wall Street Journal,* 1999a; *Orange County Register,* 1999.

Studies show that spin-offs may produce abnormal returns for shareholders of as much as 3–4 percentage points (see Table 13-2). Consequently, shareholders may benefit more from a spin-off than an attempt by management to reinvest the after-tax proceeds from a divestiture in the parent firm. Third, a spin-off may be less traumatic for an operating unit than a divestiture. The divestiture process can degrade value if it is lengthy. Employees leave, worker productivity generally suffers, and customers may not renew contracts until the new owner is known.

EQUITY CARVE-OUTS AND SPLIT-OFF
INITIAL PUBLIC OFFERINGS

Equity carve-outs are often difficult to define. They are most appropriately viewed as hybrid or intermediate transactions. They are hybrid transactions in that they are similar to spin-offs as both result in the subsidiary's stock being traded separately from the parent's stock; to divestitures as they both result in a cash infusion; and to initial public offerings (IPOs) as cash is raised through the sale of equity to the public. However, unlike the spin-off or divestiture, the parent generally retains control of the subsidiary in a carve-out transaction. They are intermediate transactions in that they are often simply a prelude to another transaction (i.e., the issuance of another portion of or all of the remaining equity in the subsidiary).

There are two basic forms of an equity carve-out: the subsidiary equity carve-out and the split-off IPO. These are discussed below.

SUBSIDIARY EQUITY CARVE-OUT

The subsidiary carve-out is a transaction in which the parent creates a wholly owned independent legal subsidiary, with a management team that is different from the parent's, and issues a portion of the subsidiary's equity to the public. Usually only a minority share of the parent's equity in the subsidiary is issued to the public (Schipper and Smith: 1986). Although the parent retains control, the shareholder base of the subsidiary may be different than that of the parent as a result of the public sale of equity. The cash raised may be retained in the subsidiary or transferred to the parent as a dividend, as a stock repurchase, or as an intercompany loan. The return of any portion of the proceeds to the shareholder is taxable to the shareholder.

SPLIT-OFF INITIAL PUBLIC OFFERING

A split-off IPO is a transaction in which a privately held firm "splits off" a portion of the stock of the consolidated entity and offers it to the general public. Such transactions are often referred to as IPOs, because they resemble an IPO in which the parent's stock is traded for the first time on a public exchange. The sale of the stock provides an infusion of cash to the parent. As with the subsidiary equity carve-out, this cash may be retained by the parent or returned to shareholders. United Parcel Services' IPO of a small share of its stock in 1999 is an example of a split-off IPO (see Case Study 13-3).

STAGED TRANSACTIONS

Equity may be sold to the public in several stages. A partial sale of equity either in a wholly owned subsidiary (a subsidiary equity carve-out) or in the price of $50 per share in the biggest IPO by any U.S. company in history. consolidated business (a split-off IPO) may be designed to both raise capital and to establish a market price for the stock. Later, once a market has been established for the stock, the remainder of the subsidiary's stock may be issued to the public.

CASE STUDY 13-3. UNITED PARCEL
SERVICES GOES PUBLIC IN AN EQUITY
SPLIT-OFF IPO

On November 10, 1999, United Parcel Services (UPS) raised $5.47 billion by selling 109.4 million shares of Class B common stock at an offering The IPO represented 9% of the firm's stock and established the firm's total market value at $81 billion.

The share price exploded to $67.38 at the end of the first day of trading. This represented an increase of $17.38 from its initial offering price. With 1998 revenue of $24.8 billion, UPS transports more than 3 billion parcels and documents annually. The company provides services in more than 200 countries.

By splitting off only a portion of the stock for sale to the public, UPS ensured that control would remain in the hands of current management. The proceeds of the stock issue will be used to buy back about 9% of the Class A voting stock held by employees and by heirs to the founding Casey family. The Class B shares have one vote each, whereas the Class A shares have ten votes. The stock buyback will keep the number of shares outstanding constant at about 1.2 billion shares. The proceeds will also be used to acquire businesses, as firms that UPS has approached to date have wanted shares in the company instead of cash.

The beneficiaries of the sale include UPS employees from top management to workers on the loading docks. In a growing trend in U.S. companies to generate greater employee loyalty and productivity, UPS offered all 330,000 employees worldwide an opportunity to buy shares in this highly profitable company at prices as low as $20 per share.

Before UPS, the largest IPOs included Conoco in October 1998 at $4.40 billion, Goldman Sachs in May 1999 at $3.66 billion, Charter Communications in November 1999 at $3.23 billion, and Lucent Technologies in April 1996 at $3 billion.

Source: *Wall Street Journal,* 1999b.

Alternatively, the parent may choose to spin off its remaining shares in thesubsidiary to the parent's shareholders as a dividend.

Hewlett Packard's (HP) 1999–2000 staged spin-off of its Agilent Technologies subsidiary is an example of a staged transaction. It began with an equity carve-out of a minority position in its wholly owned Agilent subsidiary in late 1999. The spin-off was completed in 2000 when HP issued the remainder of its shares in Agilent to HP shareholders in the form of a tax-free dividend (see Case Study 13-4).

CASE STUDY 13-4. HEWLETT PACKARD
SPINS OUT ITS AGILENT
IN A STAGED TRANSACTION

Hewlett Packard announced the spin-off of its Agilent Technologies unit to focus on its main business of computers and printers, where sales have been lagging behind such competitors as Sun Microsystems. Agilent makes test, measurement, and monitoring instruments, semiconductors, and optical components. It also supplies patient-monitoring and ultrasound-imaging equipment to the health-care industry. Agilent earned $257 million in net income on sales of about $8 billion for the fiscal year ended October 31, 1998. For the 9 months ending July 31, 1999, net income rose 19% to $366 million from $308 million during the same period in 1998. However, revenue fell by 1.4% to $5.88 billion from $5.97 billion, reflecting weakness in the Asian markets during the first half of 1999.

Hewlett Packard will retain an 85% stake in the company. The cash raised through the 15% equity carve-out will be paid to HP as a dividend from the subsidiary to the parent. Hewlett Packard will provide Agilent with $983 million in start-up funding. HP will retain a controlling interest until mid-2000 when it intends to spin off the rest of its shares in Agilent to HP shareholders as a tax-free transaction.

Source: Bloomberg News and Dow Jones (www.dowjones.com) Newswire, November 18, 1998.

TRACKING OR TARGETED STOCKS

Tracking or targeted stock transactions are those in which a parent divides its operations into two or more operating units and assigns a common stock to each operation. The concept was introduced in the mid-1980s by General Motors (GM) to track the performance of two of its subsidiaries, Electronic Data Systems and Hughes Electronics Corporation. Although tracking stocks may not be created initially for the purpose of exiting a business, they make such a move easier for the parent at a later date. Following a restructure of its Hughes Electronics subsidiary, GM spun off and subsequently merged its defense electronics unit with Raytheon Corporation in 1997.

TAX AND OWNERSHIP CONSIDERATIONS

Tracking stocks may be issued as dividends to the parent's current shareholders. Unlike the case with spin-offs, the IRS does not currently require the business for which the tracking stock is created to be at least 5 years old and that the parent retains a controlling interest in the business for the stock to be exempt from capital gains taxes. Unlike a spin-off or carve-out, the parent retains complete ownership of the business. Each tracking stock is considered as common stock for the consolidated parent company and not of the subsidiary. Examples of firms with tracking stocks include USX's three different stocks and General Motor's Class H (Hughes) stock. USX's tracking stocks include USX-Marathon, USX-U.S. Steel, and USX-Delhi. Dividends paid on the tracking stocks for both USX and GM are based on the performance of each individual operation.

THE MOTIVATION FOR TRACKING STOCKS

The purpose in creating tracking stock is to enable the financial markets to value the different operations within a corporation based on their own performance. Tracking or targeted stocks provide the parent company with an alternative means of raising capital for a specific operation by selling a portion of the stock to the public and an alternative "currency" for making acquisitions. In addition, stock-based incentive programs to attract and retain key managers can be implemented for each operation with its own tracking stock.

PROBLEMS WITH TRACKING STOCKS

Tracking stocks may create internal operating conflicts among the parent's business units. Such conflicts arise in determining how the parent's overhead expenses will be allocated to the business units and what price one business unit is paid for selling products to other business units. As of June 1999, there were 36 tracking stocks on public exchanges including AT&T, Perkin-Elmer, Ziff-Davis, and Donaldson, Lufkin & Jenrette (*Business Week,* 1999b).

In addition to creating internal problems, tracking stocks can stimulate shareholder lawsuits. Although the unit for which a tracking stock has been created may be largely autonomous, the potential for conflict of interest is substantial because the parent's board and the target stock's board are the same. The parent's board approves overall operating unit and capital budgets. Decisions made in support of one operating unit may appear to be unfair to those holding a tracking stock in another unit. Thus, tracking stocks can pit classes of shareholders against one another and lead to lawsuits. When GM sold part of its Hughes unit and all of EDS, holders of H shares sued the GM board of directors, complaining that they were underpaid. Although the suits were dismissed in a lower court in Delaware, they have been appealed to the Delaware Supreme Court. The decision has not yet been resolved. Although shareholders may be less concerned with potential conflicts of interest when they first receive tracking stocks, the potential for antagonism among different classes of stockholders often grows with time.

Tracking stocks may offer investors the opportunity to invest in a "pure play," but they also may have several unattractive features. Tracking stocks may be penalized if the parent's management continues to operate them conservatively. With a spin-off, the firm has a separate board of directors that can introduce a more aggressive management style than the parent may have been willing to tolerate. Also, tracking stocks may not have voting rights. Finally, because a company with a tracking stock is controlled by the parent, the chances of a hostile takeover are virtually zero. Hence, there is no takeover premium built into the stock price.

VOLUNTARY LIQUIDATIONS (BUST-UPS)

Involuntary liquidations, normally associated with bankruptcy, are discussed later in this chapter and occur when creditors and the bankruptcy court concur that they will realize more value through liquidation than by reorganizing the firm. Voluntary liquidations reflect the judgment that the sale of individual parts of the firm could realize greater value than the value created by a continuation of the combined corporation. This may occur when management views the firm's growth prospects as limited. This option is generally pursued only after other restructure actions have failed to provide a significant improvement in the firm's overall market value.

Managers may be encouraged to liquidate because of the threat that an acquirer will mount a proxy contest for control or launch a tender offer to buy the firm and then liquidate it. Many of the tax advantages to bust-ups compared to nontaxable mergers were removed by the 1986 Tax Reform Act. Prior to the change in the law, capital gains to the selling firm were not taxable if it adopted a plan of liquidation and all proceeds were paid out to the shareholders within 12 months after the plan was adopted.

In general, a merger has the advantage over the voluntary bust-up of deferring the recognition of a gain by the stockholders of the selling company until they eventually sell the stock. In liquidation, the selling shareholders must recognize the gain immediately. Unused tax credits and losses belonging to either of the merged firms are carried over in a nontaxable merger but are lost in liquidation (see Table 13-1).

RETURNS TO SHAREHOLDERS

PREANNOUNCEMENT ABNORMAL RETURNS

Empirical studies indicate that the alternative exit restructure strategies discussed in this chapter generally provide positive abnormal returns to the shareholders of the company implementing the strategy. However, the size of the ab-

TABLE 13-1.   Key Characteristics of Alternative Exit Restructuring Strategies

| Characteristics | Alternative strategy | | | | |
	Divestitures	Equity carve-outs/split-off IPOs	Spin-offs	Split-ups	Voluntary liquidations (bust-ups)
Cash infusion to parent	Yes	Yes	No	No	No
Change in equity ownership	Yes	Yes	No	No	Yes
Parent ceases to exist	No	No	No	Yes	Yes
New legal entity created	Sometimes	Yes[a]	Yes	Yes	No
New shares issued	Sometimes	Yes	Yes	Yes	No
Parent remains in control	No	Generally	No	No	No
Taxable to shareholders	Yes[b]	Yes[b]	No[c]	No[c]	Yes

[a] Applies to subsidiary carve-outs only.

[b] The proceeds are taxable if returned to shareholders as a dividend or used to repurchase the parent's stock.

[c] The transaction is generally not taxable if properly structured.

normal returns varies widely among the alternative exit strategies (see Table 13-2).

Divestitures

Abnormal returns for shareholders of firms divesting businesses tend to be about 1–2%, although the return can be as high as 8% whenever the divesting firm is selling an operation comprising more than one-half of its equity value (Klein: 1986). Firms that intend to pay out the proceeds from the sale to shareholders tend to experience abnormal returns of at least 2%, although those that reinvest the funds display negative .5% returns (Lang, Poulsen, and Stulz: 1995).

Spin-offs

Abnormal returns average about 3–3.5%, but they can get as high as 6% whenever the business the parent is spinning off comprises more than 10% of the parent's equity (J.P. Morgan: 1995).

Tracking Stocks

Although the empirical evidence is very limited, abnormal returns average about 3%.

TABLE 13-2.　Returns to Shareholders of Firms Undertaking Restructuring Actions

Study	Preannouncement abnormal returns[a]
Divestitures	
Alexander, Benson, and Kampmeyer (1984): 53 from 1964–1973	.17
Linn and Rozeff (1984): 77 from 1977–1982	1.45
Jain (1985): 1,107 from 1976–1978	.70
Klein (1986): 202 from 1970–1979	1.12
	When percent of equity sold is
	< 10%: None
	> 10 < 50%: 2.53%
	> 50%: 8.09%
Lang, Poulsen, and Stulz (1995): 93 from 1984–1989	2% for firms distributing proceeds to shareholders; (.5)% for those reinvesting proceeds
Spin-Offs	
Hite and Owers (1983): 56 from 1963–1979	3.8%
Miles and Rosenfeld (1983): 62 from 1963–1981	2.33
Michaely and Shaw (1995): 91 master limited partnerships from 1981–1989	4.5%
Loh, Bezjak, and Toms (1995): 59 from 1982–1987	1.5
J. P. Morgan (1995): 77 since beginning of 1995	5%
	6% if spin-off > 10% of parent's equity
	4% if spin-off < 10% of parent's equity
Tracking Stocks	
Logue, Seward, and Walsh (1996): 9 from 1991–1995	2.9%
Equity carve-outs (split-off IPOs)	
Schipper and Smith (1986): 81 for 1965–1983	1.7%
Michaely and Shaw (1995): 91 limited partnerships from 1981–1989	.4%
Allen and McConnell (1998): 188 from 1978–1993)	6.63% when proceeds used to pay off debt; zero otherwise
Voluntary liquidations	
Skantz and Marchesini (1987): 37 from 1970–1982	21.4%[b]
Hite, Owers, and Rogers (1987): 49 from 1966–1975	13.62%[b]
Kim and Schatzberg (1987): 73 from 1963–1981	14%
Erwin and McConnell (1997): 61 from 1970–1991	20%

[a] Abnormal returns measured from 1–3 days prior to and including announcement date of restructure action.

[b] Abnormal returns measured during the month of the announced restructure action.

Equity Carve-Outs

Abnormal returns average about 3%, although there is evidence that the returns may be as high as 6% if the parent uses the proceeds to reduce debt (Allen and McConnell: 1998). Equity carve-outs are undertaken to raise capital. The increase in the abnormal return may reflect the lack of confidence investors have in the parent's management ability to invest the proceeds appropriately.

Voluntary Bust-Ups

Abnormal returns average about 17%. The market's very positive reaction to the announcement of "bust-ups" may reflect investors' concurrence with management that continued operation of the firm is likely to erode shareholder value. Liquidation of the firm results in the firm's assets being redeployed to potentially higher alternative financial returns. The magnitude of the returns may also have been influenced by their announcement following closely after merger proposals and tender offers.

POST-SPIN-OFF RETURNS TO SHAREHOLDERS

Empirical studies show that shares in carve-outs and spin-offs tend to significantly outperform the Standard & Poor's (S&P) 500 during the 2 years following the announcement (see Table 13-3). Carve-outs tend to outperform spin-offs by about 1–3%, because the market is able to value the stocks before additional

TABLE 13-3.   Returns to Postrestructuring Shareholders

Study	Average annual returns[a]
Spin-offs, carve-outs, and tracking stocks	
Oppenheimer (1981): 19 spin-offs from 1970–1979	44% during 1970s
Cusatis, Miles, and Wollridge (1993): 300 spin-offs from 1965–1988	76% for 3 years following spin-off (one-third of spin-offs and their former parents involved in takeovers 2–3 years after spin-off). These returns are < IPOs, which have higher initial returns but lower longer-term returns.
J. P. Morgan (1999): 231 spin-offs and carve-outs from 1985–1998	During 18 months following spin-off, Spin-offs exceeded S&P by 11.3% Carve-outs exceeded S&P by 10.1%
McKinsey & Co. (1999): 168 spin-offs, carve-outs, and tracking stocks from 1988–1998	During first two years announcement, Spin-offs averaged 27% Carve-outs averaged 24% Tracking stocks averaged 19% S&P 500 averaged 21%

[a] IPO, initial public offering; S&P, Standard & Poor's.

shares are issued and initially tend to get more analyst attention than spin-offs (McKinsey & Company: 1999c). In contrast to spin-offs and carve-outs, tracking stocks tend to underperform the gains in the S&P 500.

Carve-outs and spin-offs may also tend to outperform the broader stock market indices, because their share prices reflect speculation that they will be acquired. One-third of spin-offs are acquired within 3 years after the unit is spun off by the parent. Once those spin-offs that have been acquired have been removed from the sample, the remaining spin-offs do not perform better than their peers (Cusatis, Miles, and Wollridge: 1993). Spin-offs may simply create value by providing an efficient method of transferring corporate assets to acquiring companies.

Smaller spin-offs (i.e., those with a market cap of less than $200 million) tend to outperform larger ones (i.e., those with a market cap greater than $200 million) (J. P. Morgan: 1999). This may be a result of a tendency of investors relatively unfamiliar with the business that is spun off by the parent to undervalue the spin-off.

BUSINESS FAILURE

The leading causes of business failure in order of priority include economic factors such as recession, financial factors such as excess operating expenses and excessive leverage, and lack of business or managerial experience (Dun & Bradstreet: 1997). It is easy to understand the role of economic factors as the leading cause of business failure. The onset of recessions tends to compound problems relating to mismanagement and excessive leverage. Firms with high fixed costs frequently fail when confronted with falling revenue during a recession. The cash flow problems resulting from the recession are exacerbated by the normal increase in interest rates just prior to the downturn. This makes it more expensive for the firm to obtain additional financing at the very time when it needs it most.

A study by the U.S. Small Business Administration (1999) traced the experience of 3,377 small businesses, which had declared bankruptcy between 1994 and 1997. The results are consistent with the study by Dun & Bradstreet (1997). In order of importance, the reasons for filing for bankruptcy include outside business conditions, financing problems, and problems that reflect inexperience, such as selecting a poor location, an inability to manage people, the loss of major clients, and an inability to collect accounts receivable.

INSOLVENCY VERSUS BANKRUPTCY

When a firm is unable to pay its liabilities as they come due, it is said to *be technically insolvent*. *Legal insolvency* occurs when a firm's liabilities exceed the fair market value of its assets. Creditors' claims cannot be satisfied unless the firm's assets can be liquidated for more than their book value. The U.S. court system treats both technical insolvency and legal insolvency as a financial failure of the firm. *Bankruptcy* is a federal legal proceeding designed to protect the technically or legally insolvent firm from lawsuits by its creditors until a decision can be made to shut down or to continue to operate the firm. A firm is not considered to be bankrupt or in bankruptcy until it or its creditors file a petition for reorganization or liquidation with the federal bankruptcy courts.

VOLUNTARY SETTLEMENTS WITH CREDITORS OUTSIDE OF BANKRUPTCY

An insolvent firm may reach an agreement with its creditors to restructure its obligations out of court to avoid the costs of bankruptcy proceedings. The voluntary settlement process is usually initiated by the debtor firm, because it generally offers the best chance for the current owners to recover a portion of their investments either by continuing to operate the firm or through a planned liquidation of the firm. This process normally involves the debtor firm requesting a meeting with its creditors. At this meeting, a committee of creditors is selected to analyze the debtor firm's financial position and to recommend an appropriate course of action. The recommendation can either involve a continuation of the firm or its liquidation.

Voluntary Settlement Resulting in Continued Operation

Creditors may decide to allow the insolvent firm to continue to operate, because they believe that they are most likely to recover more of what they are owed than if they force the firm to liquidate its assets. Because of the firm's weak financial position, the creditors must be willing to restructure the insolvent firm's debts to enable it to sustain its operations. *Debt restructuring* involves concessions by creditors that will lower an insolvent firm's payments so that it may remain in business. Restructuring is normally accomplished in three ways: an extension, a composition, or a debt-for-equity swap.

An *extension* occurs when creditors agree to lengthen the period of time during which the debtor firm can repay its debt. Creditors often agree to temporarily suspend both interest and principal repayments. A *composition* is an agreement in which creditors agree to settle for less than the full amount they are owed. A *debt-for-equity swap* occurs when creditors surrender a portion of their claims on the firm in exchange for an ownership position in the firm. If the reduced debt service payments enable the firm to prosper, the value of the stock may in the long run far exceed the amount of debt the creditors were willing to forgive.

Exhibit 13-1 illustrates a debt restructure or composition of a bankrupt company that will enable the firm to continue operation by converting debt to equity. Although the firm, Survivor Incorporated, has positive earnings before interest and taxes, it is not enough to meet its interest payments. When principal payments are considered, cash flow becomes significantly negative. Therefore, it is technically insolvent. As a result of the restructuring of the firm's debt, Survivor Incorporated is able to continue to operate. However, the firm's lenders now have a controlling interest in the firm. Note the same type of restructuring could take place either voluntarily outside the courts or as a result of reorganizing under the protection of the bankruptcy court. The latter scenario will be discussed later in this chapter.

EXHIBIT 13-1. SURVIVOR INC. RESTRUCTURES ITS DEBT

Survivor Inc. currently has 400,000 shares of common equity outstanding at a par value of $10 per share. The current rate of interest on its debt is 8% and the debt is amortized over 20 years. The combined federal, state, and local tax rate is 40%. The firm's cash flow and capital position are shown below.

Income and cash flow		Total capital	
Earnings before interest & taxes	$ 500,000	Debt	$10,000,000
Interest	800,000	Equity	4,000,000
Earnings before taxes	(300,000)	Total	$14,000,000
Taxes			
Earnings after taxes	(300,000)	Debt/total capital	71.4%
Depreciation	400,000		
Principal repayment	(500,000)		
Cash flow	(400,000)		

Assume that bondholders are willing to convert $5,000,000 in debt to equity at the current par value of $10 per share. This necessitates that Survivor Inc. issues 500,000 new shares. These actions result in positive cash flow, a substantial reduction in the firm's debt-to-total capital ratio, and a transfer of control to the bondholders. The former stockholders now own only 44.4% (4,000,000/9,000,000) of the total company.

Income and cash flow		Total capital	
Earnings before interest & taxes	$ 500,000	Debt	$ 5,000,000
Interest	400,000	Equity	9,000,000
Earnings before taxes	100,000	Total	$14,000,000
Taxes	40,000		
Earnings after taxes	60,000	Debt/total capital	35.7%
Depreciation	400,000		
Principal repayment	(250,000)		
Cash flow	$ 210,000		

Voluntary Settlement Resulting in Liquidation

If the creditors conclude that the insolvent firm's situation cannot be resolved, liquidation may be the only acceptable course of action. Liquidation can be conducted outside the court in a private liquidation or through the U.S. bankruptcy court. If the insolvent firm is willing to accept liquidation and all creditors agree, legal proceedings are not necessary. Creditors normally prefer private liquidations to avoid lengthy and costly litigation.

Through a process called an *assignment,* a committee representing creditors grants the power to liquidate the firm's assets to a third party called an *assignee or trustee.* The responsibility of the assignee is to sell the assets as quickly as possible while obtaining the best possible price. Once the assets have been sold, the assignee distributes the proceeds to the creditors and to the firm's owners if any monies remain. The private liquidation concludes when all creditors sign a release indicating their satisfaction with the settlement.

REORGANIZATION AND LIQUIDATION IN BANKRUPTCY

In the absence of a voluntary settlement out of court, the debtor firm may seek protection from its creditors by initiating bankruptcy or be forced into bankruptcy by its creditors (Case Study 13–5). When the debtor firm files the petition with the bankruptcy court, the bankruptcy is said to be *voluntary.* When creditors do the filing, the action is said to be *involuntary.* It takes only a group of three creditors who are owed a total of $5,000 to place a firm in involuntary bankruptcy. Once either a voluntary or involuntary petition is filed, the debtor firm is protected from any further legal action related to its debts until the bankruptcy proceedings are completed. The filing of a petition allows the debtor firm to stop all principal and interest payments owed to creditors, while preventing secured creditors from taking possession of their collateral.

CASE STUDY 13-5. IRIDIUM FILES FOR CHAPTER 11

After its bondholders and its biggest investor, Motorola, could not agree on a plan to reorganize Iridium, the satellite/communications company filed for Chapter 11 protection from creditors in Delaware's bankruptcy court in August 1999. This action came hours after a group of the firm's bondholders filed for an involuntary bankruptcy in the U.S. Bankruptcy Court in the Southern District of New York. This group owns about 25% of the firm's $1.45 billion in senior subordinated debt. Iridium had already defaulted on $1.55 billion in bank loans after failing to attract enough subscribers for

---

their satellite-based wireless phone service. Lenders had wanted Motorola to guarantee any additional loans to Iridium.

After spending more than $1 billion, Iridium had attracted by August only about 20,000 of the 500,000 subscribers it expected to have by the end of 1999. Iridium was also confronted with the prospect of increasing competition from other start-ups including Teledesic and Globalstar.

Despite 35,000 new subscribers by early 2000, the subscriber base was still not nearly enough to service the firm's outstanding debt. By March 18, 2000, Iridium gave up its search for new backers, and a U.S. Bankruptcy Court judge gave the firm permission to cut off service to 55,000 customers and to destroy its $5 billion constellation of 66 satellites. In all, more than 80 parties had been contacted in a futile search for new investors.

Source: *Business Week,* 1999c, p. 48; *Bloomberg News,* 1999; *Orange County Register,* 2000.

BANKRUPTCY LAWS AND PROCEDURES

The Bankruptcy Reform Act of 1978 was enacted to make bankruptcy proceedings more flexible than previous laws, which dictated that creditor claims took absolute priority over ownership claims. Moreover, under the 1978 Act, the conditions under which companies could file were broadened such that a firm could declare bankruptcy without having to wait until it was virtually insolvent. The intent of making the bankruptcy code less rigid was to increase the likelihood that creditors and owners would reach agreement on plans to reorganize rather than liquidate insolvent firms. Although most companies that file for bankruptcy do so as a result of their deteriorating financial position, there is evidence that some firms are using the bankruptcy code for purposes for which it was not intended.

Companies are increasingly seeking bankruptcy protection to avoid litigation and hostile takeovers. In the mid-1980s, Johns Manville Corporation used bankruptcy to negotiate a reduction in huge liability awards granted in the wake of asbestos-related lawsuits. Similarly, Texaco used the threat of bankruptcy in the early 1990s as a negotiating ploy to reduce the amount of court-ordered payments to Occidental Petroleum resulting from the court's determination that Texaco had improperly intervened in a pending merger transaction. To protect themselves from litigation, Washington Construction Group required Morrison Knudsen Corporation to file for bankruptcy as a closing condition before acquiring the firm to protect the acquirer from certain liabilities (*Business Week:* 2000).

The two key chapters in the Bankruptcy Reform Act are Chapters 7 and 11. Chapter 7 deals with liquidation and provides for a court-appointed interim trustee with broad powers and discretion to operate the debtor firm in such a way to prevent further deterioration in the overall financial position of the firm and the removal of assets by owners prior to liquidation. The debtor is able to regain control from the trustee only by posting an appropriate bond. Chapter 11 deals with reorganization, which provides for the debtor to remain in possession, unless the court rules otherwise, of the business and in control of its operations. The debtor and creditors are permitted considerable flexibility in working together, enabling them to negotiate debt repayment schedules, the restructuring of debt, and even the granting of loans by the creditors to the debtor. If a workable plan cannot be formulated, the firm will be liquidated in accordance with the procedures outlined in Chapter 7.

Figure 13-2 summarizes the process for filing for reorganization under Chapter 11. The process begins by filing in a federal bankruptcy court. In the case of an involuntary petition, a hearing must be held to determine whether the firm is insolvent. If the firm is found to be insolvent, the court enters an *order for relief* that initiates the bankruptcy proceedings. Upon the filing of a reorganization petition, the filing firm becomes the *debtor in possession* (DIP) of all the assets. The debtor firm's managers are able to continue to make operating decisions, and they have the exclusive right to propose a reorganization plan during the 120 days following filing for Chapter 11 bankruptcy. The court often grants several extensions if requested by management. Management has 180 days from the filing date to obtain creditor and shareholder approval of a proposed reorganization plan. If management does not propose a plan or their plan is rejected, creditors can propose their own plan. The creditors may request that the court appoint a trustee instead of the debtor to manage the firm (see Case Study 13-6).

Following a thorough analysis of the debtor firm's position, the DIP or court-appointed trustee must submit a plan to the bankruptcy court to reorganize the firm. Federal bankruptcy courts evaluate reorganization plans in terms of their fairness and feasibility. Fairness means that the creditor claims are to be satisfied in accordance with the order of priorities listed in the bankruptcy laws. Feasibility refers to whether the assumptions underlying the plan are viewed by the court as being realistic.

When the plan is approved by the court, creditors and owners are placed in groups with similar claims. In the case of creditors, the plan must be approved by holders of at least two-thirds of the dollar value of the claims as well as a simple majority of the creditors in each group. In the case of owners, two-thirds of those in each group (e.g., common and preferred shareholders) must approve the plan. Once approved by all claimant groups, the plan is put into effect. Finally, the

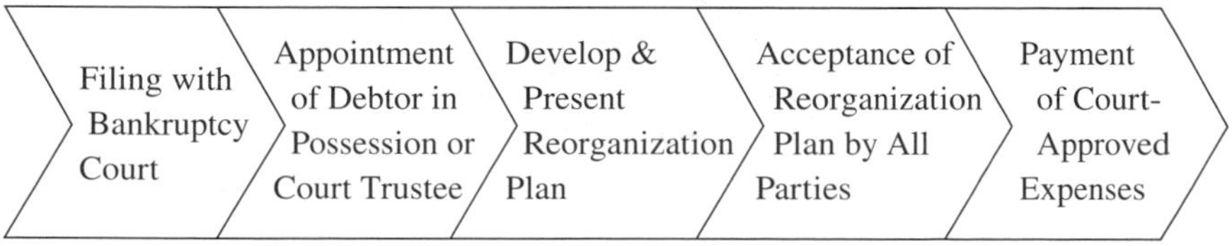

FIGURE 13-2.   Procedures for reorganizing in bankruptcy.

debtor is responsible for paying the expenses approved by the court of all parties whose services contributed to the approval or disapproval of the plan.

CASE STUDY 13-6. DEBTORS IN POSSESSION—PUTTING THE FOX IN CHARGE OF THE CHICKEN COOP

In rewriting the bankruptcy code in 1978, Congress introduced the concept of debtor in possession (DIP) with the belief that the debtor firm's current managers are best able to deal with the firm's current problems. The assumption is that they would be more knowledgeable than any court-appointed trustee. It was also believed that the debtor's interests would be protected, because the lawyers appointed by the court would closely monitor the DIP's actions.

Critics of the DIP concept point out that the managers, who are put in charge of managing the failed firm during the legal proceedings, are frequently the same ones who made the company insolvent in the first place. In some instances, managers and owners have conspired to "hide" the debtor firm's assets during the period of Chapter 11 bankruptcy protection. In many bankruptcies, critics point out that creditors would have a better chance of recovering what is owed them if the court appointed a trustee to oversee the business while it is under the protection of Chapter 11. The trade-off, of course, is the difficulty of finding and the expense associated with appointing an appropriate trustee for each bankruptcy.

Liquidation in Bankruptcy

If the bankruptcy court determines that reorganization is not feasible, the failing firm may be forced to liquidate. A trustee is appointed by the court to handle the administrative aspects of the liquidation. The trustee convenes a meeting of all creditors to apprise them of the prospects for liquidation. The trustee is then given the responsibility to liquidate the firm's assets, keep records, examine creditors' claims, to disburse the proceeds, and to submit a final report on the liquidation.

The priority in which the claims are paid is stipulated in Chapter 7 of the Bankruptcy Reform Act, which must be followed by the trustee when the firm is liquidated. All secured creditors are paid when the firm's assets that were pledged as collateral are liquidated. If the proceeds of the sale of these assets are inadequate to satisfy all of the secured creditors' claims, they become unsecured or general creditors for the amount that was not recovered. If the proceeds of the sale of pledged assets exceed secured creditors' claims, the excess proceeds are used to pay general creditors.

The order of priority of payment of claims after the pledged assets have been sold is as follows:

1. Secured creditors up to the proceeds of the sale of pledged assets; unpaid portions of secured claims become unsecured claims
2. Bankruptcy proceedings expenses
3. Any unpaid expenses incurred between the filing of the bankruptcy petition and the court's granting of an order of relief
4. Wages not to exceed $2000 per worker that are owed to those employed by the firm during the 90 days preceding the initiation of bankruptcy proceedings
5. Unpaid employee benefit plan contributions, up to $2000 per worker, that were to have been paid during the 6 months prior to the initiation of bankruptcy proceedings
6. Unsecured customer deposits, of $900 or less, resulting from purchasing or leasing a product or service from the firm
7. Taxes owed to federal, state, or local governments
8. Underfunded pension liabilities up to 30% of the book value of preferred and common equity; unpaid portions become unsecured claims
9. Unsecured creditors, including claims of secured creditors that were not fully satisfied by the sale of pledged assets. All such claimants are paid from available proceeds on a pro rata basis
10. Preferred stockholders, who are paid up to the par value of their stock
11. Commons shareholders, who are paid out of the remaining funds on an equal per share basis

Exhibit 13-2 illustrates how a legally bankrupt company could be liquidated with the proceeds distributed in order of priority. The bankruptcy court, owners, and creditors could not agree on an appropriate reorganization plan for DOA Inc. Consequently, the court has ordered that the firm be liquidated in accordance with Chapter 7. Note that this illustration would differ from a private liquidation in two important respects. First, the expenses associated with conducting the liquidation would be lower, because the liquidation would not involve extended legal proceedings. Second, the distribution of proceeds could reflect a prioritization of claims negotiated between the creditors and the owners that differs from that set forth in Chapter 7 of the Bankruptcy Reform Act.

EXHIBIT 13-2. LIQUIDATION OF DOA, INC. UNDER CHAPTER 7

DOA has the following balance sheet. The only liability that is not shown on the balance sheet is the cost of the bankruptcy proceedings, which are treated as expenses and are not capitalized.

Balance sheet

Assets		Liabilities	
Cash	$ 35,000	Accounts payable	$ 750,000
Accounts receivable	2,300,000	Bank notes payable	3,000,000
Inventories	2,100,000	Accrued salaries	720,000
Total current assets	$4,435,000	Unpaid benefits	140,000
Land	1,500,000	Unsecured customer deposits	300,000
Net plant & equipment	2,000,000	Taxes payable	400,000
Total fixed assets	$3,500,000	Total current liabilities	$5,310,000
Total assets	$7,935,000	First mortgage	2,500,000
		Unsecured debt	200,000
		Total long-term debt	2,700,000
		Preferred stock	50,000
		Common stock	100,000
		Paid in surplus	500,000
		Retained earnings	(725,000)
		Total stockholders' equity	$ (75,000)
		Total shareholders' equity & total liabilities	$7,935,000

The sale of DOA's assets generates $5.4 million in cash. The distribution of the proceeds results in the following situation. Note that the proceeds are distributed in accordance with the priorities stipulated in the current commercial bankruptcy law and that the cost of administering the bankruptcy totals 18% of the proceeds from liquidation.

Distribution of liquidation proceeds

Proceeds from liquidation	$5,400,000
Expenses of administering bankruptcy	972,000
Salaries owed employees	720,000
Unpaid employee benefits	140,000
Unsecured customer deposits	300,000
Taxes	400,000
Funds available for creditors	$2,868,000
First mortgage (from sale of fixed assets)	1,500,000
Funds available for unsecured creditors	$1,368,000

Once all prior claims have been satisfied, the remaining proceeds are distributed to the unsecured creditors. The pro-rata settlement percentage of 27.64% is calculated by dividing funds available for unsecured creditors by the amount of unsecured creditor claims. The shareholders receive nothing, since not all unsecured creditor claims have been satisfied.

Pro rata distribution of funds among unsecured creditors

Unsecured creditor claims	Amount	Settlement at 27.64%
Unpaid balance from first mortgage	$1,000,000	$ 276,400
Accounts payable	750,000	207,300
Notes payable	3,000,000	829,200
Unsecured debt	200,000	55,280
Total	$4,950,000	$ 1,368,000

STRATEGIC OPTIONS FOR FAILING FIRMS

A failing firm's strategic options are to merge with another firm, reach an out-of-court voluntary settlement with creditors, or file for Chapter 11 bankruptcy. The firm may voluntarily liquidate as part of an out-of-court settlement or be forced to liquidate under Chapter 7 of the bankruptcy code. The implications of each of these options are summarized in Table 13-4. The choice of which option to pursue is critically dependent on which provides the greatest present value for creditors and shareholders. To evaluate these options, the firm's management needs to estimate the going concern, selling price, and liquidation values of the firm.

TABLE 13-4.   Alternative Strategies for Failing Firms

Assumptions	Options: Failing firm	Outcome: Failing firm
Selling price > Going concern or liquidation value	1. Is acquired by or 2. Merges with another firm	1. Continues as subsidiary of acquirer 2. Merged into acquirer and ceases to exist
Going concern value > sale or liquidation value	1. Reaches out-of-court settlement with creditors 2. Seeks bankruptcy protection under Chapter 11	1. Continues with debt for equity swap, extension, and composition 2. Continues in reorganization
Liquidation value > sale or going concern value	1. Reaches out of court settlement with creditors 2. Liquidates under Chapter 7	1. Ceases to exist. Assignee liquidates assets and distributes proceeds to creditors on a pro-rata basis 2. Ceases to exist. Trustee supervises liquidation and distributes proceeds according to statutory priorities

Merging with Another Firm

If the failing firm's management estimates that the sale price of the firm is greater than the going concern or liquidation values, management should seek to be acquired by or merge with another firm. If a strategic buyer can be found, management must convince the firm's creditors that they will be more likely to receive what they are owed if the firm is acquired rather than liquidated or allowed to remain independent. Stockholders may be able to recover a significant portion of their cost basis in the stock of the failing company. Clark and Ofek (1994) in a study of 38 takeovers of distressed firms from 1981 to 1988 found that bidders tend to overpay for these types of firms.

The failing firm may continue to exist as a subsidiary of the acquiring company or cease to exist as a result of a merger with the acquirer. Although this strategy may benefit the failing firm's shareholders, such takeovers do not seem to benefit the acquirer's shareholders. Clark and Ofek also found that, in the majority of cases, the acquiring firms fail to successfully restructure the acquired firms.

Reaching an Out-of-Court Voluntary Settlement with Creditors

Alternatively, the going concern value of the firm may exceed the sale or liquidation values. Management must be able to demonstrate to creditors that a restructured or downsized firm will be able to repay its debts if creditors are willing to accept less, extend the maturity of the debt, or exchange debt for equity. The resulting improvement in cash flow may demonstrate to the satisfaction of the creditors that the going concern value of the firm is indeed much higher than liquidation or merger strategies. If management cannot reach agreement with the firm's creditors, it may seek protection under Chapter 11.

Holdout Problem

A voluntary settlement may be difficult to achieve because the debtor often needs the approval of all of its creditors. Smaller creditors sometimes have an incentive to attempt to hold up the agreement unless they receive special treatment. The situation may become untenable if there are a large number of creditors with similar motivations. Consensus may be accomplished by paying all small creditors 100% of what they are owed and the larger creditors an agreed upon percentage. A preference on the part of certain institutions for debt rather than equity and inadequate access by creditors to the necessary information to enable them to properly value the equity they are being offered in a debt-for-equity swap also limit the use of voluntary agreements. Because of these factors, there is some evidence that firms that attempt to restructure outside of Chapter 11 bankruptcy have more difficulty in reducing their leverage than those that tend to negotiate with creditors while under the protection of Chapter 11 (Gilson: 1997).

Prepackaged Bankruptcies

Prepackaged bankruptcies start with the failing firm negotiating with its creditors well in advance of filing for a Chapter 11 bankruptcy. Preferably, the failing company will have unanimous approval of the proposed reorganization plan before any formal filing is made. Because there is general approval of the plan before the filing, the formal Chapter 11 reorganization that follows generally averages only a few months and results in substantially lower legal and administrative expenses (Altman: 1993; Betker: 1995).

Voluntary and Involuntary Liquidations

The failing firm's management, shareholders, and creditors may agree that the firm is worth more in liquidation than in sale or as a continuing operation. All parties involved may believe that continued operation of the firm may cause the value of the firm's assets to deteriorate further. As noted earlier in this chapter, studies show that voluntary liquidations often result in significant returns to the shareholders of the failing firm.

If management cannot reach agreement with its creditors on a private liquidation, the firm may seek to liquidate under Chapter 7 of the 1978 Bankruptcy Law. However, the expenses associated with the legal proceedings can result in the creditors receiving much less than with a voluntary liquidation and in the shareholders receiving nothing.

RETURNS TO FIRMS EMERGING FROM BANKRUPTCY

When firms emerge from bankruptcy, they often cancel the old stock and issue new common stock. Empirical studies show that firms emerging from bankruptcy often show very attractive returns to holders of the new stock in the period immediately following the announcement.

Focusing on total cash flows generated by the firm, Alderson and Betker (1996) found that between 1983 and 1993, for 89 firms returns on average exceeded the returns on the S&P 500 index. These findings were supported in a study by Eberhart, Altman, and Aggarwal (1999) of 546 firms emerging from bankruptcy at various times between 1980 and 1993. They found that excess returns ranged from 24.6% to 138.8% depending on how they were measured during the 200 days following the firm's emergence from bankruptcy. They also found some evidence that the willingness of informed institutional investors such as banks to accept only equity in the new firm in exchange for debt contributes to the excess returns. The latter conclusion may reflect the willingness of the bankers with access to the necessary information about the firm's financial condition to significantly restructure debt and improve the firm's cash flow.

Despite the short-term favorable results, the more long-term performance of these firms often deteriorates in terms of standard accounting measures such as operating profit. For a sample of firms emerging from bankruptcy between 1979 and 1988, Hotchkiss (1995) found that 40% of the firms studied continued to experience operating losses in the 3 years after emergence from Chapter 11. Almost one-third subsequently file for bankruptcy again or have to again restructure their debt.

THINGS TO REMEMBER

Divestitures, spin-offs, equity carve-outs, split-ups, and voluntary bust-ups are commonly used exit strategies to redeploy assets by returning cash or noncash assets through a special dividend to shareholders. Empirical studies show that these restructuring actions can have a highly favorable impact on shareholder returns. Abnormal returns for divestitures average about 1–2%; about 3–3.5% for equity carve-outs, spin-offs, and split-ups; and about 17% for bust-ups.

The motives for firms undertaking these strategies include a changing corporate strategy or a desire to exit underperforming businesses. Tax and regulatory considerations, a desire to reduce risk, abandoning the core business, discarding unwanted businesses from prior acquisitions; and avoiding conflicts with customers are also factors causing firms to restructure.

A divestiture is the sale of a portion of the firm to an outside party generally resulting in a cash infusion to the parent. Studies suggest that the more unrelated a business is to the parent's core business the more likely it is to be divested. Once a business has been determined to be nonstrategic, the decision to sell an operating unit can be reduced to simply comparing the division's "stand-alone" value less its operating liabilities with the after-tax proceeds of the sale value of the operation. If the after-tax sale value exceeds the equity value to the parent, the business should be sold.

Equity carve-outs tend to fall into two categories. The first category involves a parent selling a portion of the stock in a newly created, wholly owned subsidiary to the public. The second type involves a transaction in which a privately held firm "splits-off" a portion of the stock of the consolidated entity and offers it to the general public. As is true with equity carve-outs, spin-offs entail the creation of a new legal entity. However, there is no cash infusion to the parent as these new shares are distributed, as a stock dividend, to the parent's current shareholders in direct proportion to their current holdings of the parent's stock. In a split-up, the entire company is broken up into a series of spin-offs or newly formed companies and returned to the shareholders as dividends. The parent ceases to exist.

Tracking or target stock transactions are those in which a parent divides its operations into two or more operating units and assigns a common stock to each operation. The tracking stock is owned by the parent and not by the subsidiary. Voluntary liquidations or bust-ups reflect the judgment that the sale of individual parts of the firm could realize greater value than the value created by a continuation of the combined corporation.

A failing firm's strategic options are to merge with another firm, reach an out-of-court voluntary settlement with creditors, or file for Chapter 11 bankruptcy. The firm may voluntarily liquidate as part of an out-of-court settlement or be forced by its creditors to liquidate. The choice of which option to pursue depends upon which provides the greatest present value for creditors and shareholders.

A technically insolvent firm is unable to pay its liabilities as they come due; a legally insolvent is one in which the firm's liabilities exceed the fair market value of its assets. The firm is not bankrupt or in bankruptcy until a petition for bankruptcy is filed in the federal bankruptcy court. A failing firm or its creditors may file a bankruptcy petition. Once filed, the bankruptcy procedures normally involve a reorganization, debt restructuring, or liquidation. A reorganization is a business plan, which, if acceptable to the court, creditors, and shareholders, allows the failing firm to continue to operate. Before the firm is able to emerge from bankruptcy, the firm's debt is usually restructured with creditors granting concessions that will lower an insolvent firm's payments so that it may remain in business. Finally, liquidation involves closing the firm, selling its assets, and distributing the proceeds to its creditors and owners. There is usually nothing left for common shareholders.

CHAPTER DISCUSSION QUESTIONS

13-1. How do tax and regulatory considerations influence the decision to exit a business?

13-2. How would you decide when to sell a business?

13-3. What are the major differences between a spin-off and an equity carve-out?

13-4. Under what conditions is a spin-off tax-free to shareholders?

13-5. Why would a firm decide to voluntarily split up?

13-6. What are the advantages and disadvantages of tracking or target stocks to investors and to the firm?

13-7. What factors contribute to the high positive abnormal returns to shareholders prior to the announcement of a voluntary bust-up?

13-8. What are the primary factors contributing to business failure?

13-9. Why would creditors make concessions to a failing firm?

13-10. What are the primary options available to a failing firm? What criteria might the firm use to select a particular option?

CHAPTER BUSINESS CASE

CASE STUDY 13-7. ALLEGHENY TELEDYNE RESTRUCTURES

Allegheny Teledyne is the creation of the 1996 merger of Allegheny Ludlum Corporation and Teledyne Inc. In 1999, Allegheny Teledyne Inc. reconfigured its operations by creating a new independent company to be spun-off to its shareholders. The new company would comprise four former Teledyne units in aerospace and electronics. Combined 1998 revenues of these businesses were approximately $800 million. The intent is to focus the new company on its high-technology competencies and markets in software and engineering systems, communication and electronics, and aircraft engines and components.

Allegheny Teledyne is simultaneously considering a spin-off and public offering of its consumer segment into a free-standing public company. Its 1998 revenues were $250 million.

Allegheny Teledyne has received approval for the proposed tax-free spin-offs of its aerospace/electronics and consumer products business from the IRS. After the spin-offs, Allegheny Teledyne will have six units. These units include a specialty metals, stainless steel, and flat-rolled producer; a producer of nickel-based super-alloy and titanium alloy products; a producer of zirconium, titanium, niobium, and tantalum; a tungsten mill products and tungsten carbide cutting tools manufacturer; a foundry for large gray and ductile iron castings; and a custom impression die forging company. Allegheny Teledyne will have annual sales of $2.5 billion in these businesses, which are currently the firm's highest margin businesses. Allegheny Teledyne is also exploring selling Ryan Aeronautical, Fluid Systems, and Specialty Equipment, which had combined 1998 revenues of $400 million.

Once all this restructuring has been completed, stockholders would own common stock in each of three distinct companies, each with a clear business focus and the financial ability to pursue individual strategic growth objectives. Although Richard P. Simmons will remain as chairman, the Allegheny Teledyne board announced that they will begin looking for his successor as chief executive officer.

Case Study Discussion Questions

1. What are some of the reasons that Allegheny Teledyne considered such an extensive restructuring of its operations?
2. What synergies might there be in the businesses that Allegheny Teledyne is retaining?
3. Why do you think that stockholders might be better off owning stock in each of the three new companies (consumer products, aerospace/electronics, and metals manufacturing) than just Allegheny Teledyne Inc.?
4. Why might Allegheny Teledyne be considering spinning off some units and divesting others?
5. Why might it be common for a major restructuring to come at a time when the head of a company is leaving, retiring, or assuming fewer responsibilities?

Solutions to these questions are found in the Appendix at the end of this book.

REFERENCES

Alderson, Michael J., and Brian L. Betker, "Assessing Post-Bankruptcy Performance: An Analysis of Reorganized Firms' Cash Flows," Working Paper, Saint Louis University, 1996.

Altman, E. I., *Corporate Financial Distress and Bankruptcy* (2nd ed.), New York: John Wiley & Sons, 1993.

Alexander, Gordon J., George Benson, and Joan M. Kampmeyer, "Investigating the Valuation Effects of Announcements on Valuing Corporate Sell-Offs," *Journal of Finance, 39,* June 1984, pp. 503–517.

Allen, Jeffrey, and John J. McConnell, "Equity Carve Outs and Managerial Discretion," *Journal of Finance, 53*(1), February 1998, pp. 163–186.

Betker, B., "An Empirical Examination of Prepackaged Bankruptcy," *Financial Management,* Spring 1995, pp. 3–18.

Bloomberg News, "Iridium Movies Toward Bankruptcy," September 29, 1999, www.bloomberg.com.

Boot, Arnoud W. A., "Why hang on to Losers? Divestitures and Takeovers," *Journal of Finance, 47,* no. 4, December 1992, pp. 1401–1423.

Business Week, "Gillette Slims Down," November 8, 1999a, p. 86.

Business Week, "Tread Carefully When You Buy Tracking Stocks," June 28, 1999b, pp. 98–99.

Business Week, "Iridium Files for Bankruptcy," August 30, 1999c, p. 480.

Business Week, "Chapter 11 Never Looked So Good," March 20, 2000, p. 44.

Clark, Kent, and Eli Ofek, "Mergers as a Means of Restructuring Distressed Firms: An Empirical Investigation," *Journal of Financial and Quantitative Analysis, 29,* December 1994, pp. 541–565.

Cusatis, Patrick J., James A. Miles, and J. Randall Woolridge, "Restructuring Through Spin-Offs," *Journal of Financial Economics, 33,* 1993, pp. 293–311.

Dun & Bradstreet Corporation, New York, *Business Failure Record,* 1997.

Eberhart, Allan C., Edward I. Altman, and Reena Aggarwal, "The Equity Performance of Firms Emerging from Bankruptcy," *Journal of Finance, 54*(5), October 1999.

Eberhart, Allan C., and Richard J. Sweeney, "Does the Bond Market Predict Bankruptcy Settlements?", *Journal of Finance, 47,* 1992, pp. 943–980.

Erwin, Gayle R., and John J. McConnell, "To Live or Die? An Empirical Analysis of Piecemeal Voluntary Liquidations," *Journal of Corporate Finance, 3*(4) (December 1997), pp. 325–354.

Gaughan, Patrick A., *Mergers, Acquisitions, and Corporate Restructurings,* (2nd ed.), New York: John Wiley & Sons, 1999, pp. 398–402.

Gillette Corporation, "Restructuring to Improve Performance," October 21, 1999.

Gilson, Stuart, "Transactions Costs and Capital Structure Choice: Evidence from Financially Distressed Firms," *Journal of Finance, 52*(1), March 1997, pp. 161–196.

Hite, Gailen, and James E. Owers, "Security Price Reactions around Corporate Spin-Off Announcements," *Journal of Financial Economics, 12,* 1983, pp. 409–436.

Hite, Gailen, James Owers, and Ronald Rogers, "The Market for Inter-firm Asset Sales: Partial Sell-offs and Total Liquidations," *Journal of Financial Economics, 18,* June 1987, pp. 229–252.

Hotchkiss, Edith S., "The Post-Emergence Performance of Firms Emerging from Chapter 11," *Journal of Finance, 50,* 1995, pp. 3–21.

Jain, Prem C., "The Effects of Voluntary Sell-Off Announcements on Shareholder Wealth," *Journal of Finance, 40,* March 1985, pp. 209–224.

J. P. Morgan, "Monitoring Spin-Off Performance," *Morgan Markets,* New York, June 6, 1995.

J. P. Morgan, "Monitoring Spin-Off Performances," *Morgan Markets,* New York, August 20, 1999.

Kaplan, Steven N., and Michael S. Weisbach, "The Success of Acquisitions: Evidence from Divestitures," *Journal of Finance, 47*(1), March 1992, pp. 107–138.

Kim, E. Han, and Hohn Schatzberg, "Voluntary Corporate Liquidations," *Journal of Financial Economics, 19*(2), December 1987, pp. 311–328.

Klein, A., "The Timing and Substance of Divestiture Announcements: Individual, Simultaneous and Cumulative Effects," *Journal of Finance, 41,* 1986, pp. 685–697.

Kose, John, and Eli Ofek, "Asset Sales and Increase in Focus," *Journal of Financial Economics, 37*(1), January 1995, pp. 105–126.

Krishnaswami, Sudha, and Venkat Subramaniam, "Information Asymmetry, Valuation and the Corporate Spin-off Decision," *Journal of Financial Economics, 53,* issue 1, July 1999, pp. 73–112.

Lang, Larry, Annette Poulsen, and Rene Stulz, "Asset Sales, Firm Performance, and the Agency Costs of Managerial Discretion," *Journal of Financial Economics, 37*(1), January 1995, pp. 3–37.

Linn, Scott C., and Michael S. Rozeff, "The Corporate Sell-Off," *Midland Corporate Finance Journal, 2,* Summer 1984, pp. 17–26.

Logue, Dennis E., James K. Seward, and James W. Walsh, "Rearranging Residual Claims: A Case for Targeted Stock," *Financial Management, 25*(1), Spring 1996, pp. 43–61.

Loh, Charmen, Jennifer Russell Bezjak, and Harrison Toms, "Voluntary Corporate Divestitures as an Anti-takeover Mechanism," *The Financial Review, 30*(1), February 1995, pp. 21–24.

McKinsey & Co., "Spin-offs May Overshadow Other Investments," *Business Week,* December 13, 1999, pp. 196–197.

Michaely, Roni, and Wayne H. Shaw, "The Choice of Going Public: Spin-offs vs. Carve-outs," *Financial Management, 24*(3), Autumn 1995, pp. 15–21.

Miles, James, and James Rosenfeld, "An Empirical Analysis of the Effects of Spin-off Announcements on Shareholder Wealth," *Journal of Finance, 38*(5), December 1983, pp. 15–28.

Oppenheimer & Company, "The Sum of the Parts," New York: January 14, 1981.

Orange County Register, "Baxter to Exit Heart Care Unit" July 13, 1999, Business Section, p. 2.

Orange County Register, "Iridium Gives up on Bid to Find a Savior," Business Section, p. 2, March 18, 2000.

Parrino, Robert, "Spin-offs and Wealth Transfers: The Marriott Case," *Journal of Financial Economics, 43*(2), February 1997, pp. 241–274.

Petty, J. William, Arthur J. Keown, David F. Scott, Jr., and John D. Martin, *Basic Financial Management* (6th ed.), Englewood Cliffs, NJ: Prentice-Hall, 1993, p. 798.

Schipper, Katherine, and Abbie Smith, "Effects of Recontracting on Shareholder Wealth," *Journal of Financial Economics, 12,* 1983, pp. 437–467.

Schipper, Katherine, and Abbie Smith, "A Comparison of Equity Carve-Outs and Equity Offerings: Share Price Effects and Corporate Restructuring," *Journal of Financial Economics, 15,* 1986, pp. 153–186.

Skantz, Terrance, and Roberto Marchesini, "The Effect of Voluntary Corporate Liquidation on Shareholder Wealth," *Journal of Financial Research, 10,* Spring 1987, pp. 65–75.

United States Small Business Administration, "Financial Difficulties of Small Businesses and Reasons for Their Failure," Office of Advocacy, RS 188, March 1999.

Wall Street Journal, "Baxter Spins Off Heart Care Business," July 13, 1999a.

Wall Street Journal, "UPS Goes Public," November 10, 1999b.

PUTTING IT ALL TOGETHER

14

THE ACQUISITION
PROCESS:

THE GEE WHIZ MEDIA CASE

PART I: PLANNING

THE DREAM

Like most start-up companies, Gee Whiz Media (GWM) was the product of the visionary zeal of its founder Dan Durand. Dan had a long-standing reputation in the local technology community of being a gifted visionary who put a premium on honesty. In the industry, he was known for his integrity in his relationships with employees, customers, and suppliers. This reputation had come from several successful start-ups he had taken public in the 1980s. He found that this was a particularly good way to do business, as those with whom he dealt were generally willing to accept his word at face value. This reputation was to serve him well in his next venture.

In the late 1980s, an emerging technology called multimedia caught Dan's imagination. CD-ROMs were one of the few media with the capacity to store such diverse types of information as sound, video, and text. As PCs became commonplace, Dan believed that CD-ROMs would revolutionize the home-entertainment business by allowing users to interact easily with the new media.

Dan convinced the owner of a local retail computer store to provide space for him to demonstrate the wonders of multimedia. He reasoned that if consumers saw that computers didn't need to be boring, they might buy a complete system including a CD-ROM drive, speakers, and graphics programs. Dan would get a percentage of the sale. Thus, GWM was born.

For several years, Dan evangelized about the virtues of multimedia. However, the pace of acceptance was painfully slow. To energize the growth of multimedia usage, Dan convinced Apple, IBM, Sony, and others to fund his efforts to promote their multimedia technologies. To accommodate additional employees and to gain access to a larger demo area, Gee Whiz Media moved out of the computer retail store and into a small, nearby office park early in 1991. IBM and the others paid Dan $5,000 to $15,000 per month to provide day-long seminars in a small auditorium inside GWM's offices.

With a small staff and increasing revenues, Dan had the perfect niche, promoting multimedia technology applications. They were professional evangelists. They were succeeding. But Dan knew that this success was likely to be fleeting. As CD-ROMs loaded with multimedia applications were becoming common, the need for GWM as a promotion company would end. Dan knew that just to stay in business he had to change with the industry. His dream that multimedia CD-ROMs would become the mainstay of the interactive home entertainment media and the reference manuals of the future appeared to be coming true. But to survive he had to find a new niche.

BUILDING THE BUSINESS PLAN

Dan and his staff of nine met in his home to redefine their place in the multimedia industry. Together, they attempted to summarize the dynamics underlying the multimedia industry. Early pioneers in the industry viewed it as electronic publishing, the conversion of text, video, and music to an electronic medium. Major segments included entertainment (e.g., music videos), games, sports, education, hobbies, "how-to" or training manuals, and career development applications.

More and more small companies were entering the industry. Few resources were required other than the knowledge to develop the requisite software and the creativity to develop exciting content or the rights to use existing content. No one company as of yet dominated the industry, but Dan knew that it was just a matter of time.

Game applications proved to be a hit and demonstrated that there was demand for the right content. A game named "Myst" had just been introduced. Players moved through a fantasy land by clicking a mouse and solving a series of intricate puzzles along the way. "Myst" was doing phenomenally well, and it would go on to sell nearly one million copies. Reference CD-ROMs, Dan reasoned, might do even better, since they were reusable and beautiful.

Although CD-ROMs held great promise, the risk was still great. CD-ROM drives were in less than 30% of personal computers. CD-ROM technology was still in its infancy. Video appeared very erratic rather than seamless like the big screen movie. But the format held unlimited promise. CD-ROMs could store 600 times more information than a 3-inch square diskette and could be read optically with lasers like a compact disk. Durand saw CD-ROMs as modern encyclopedias, where information could be retrieved by a click of the mouse, rather than by flipping pages. Moreover, instead of just text and pictures, a multimedia reference guide could have movies and music.

Several days of brainstorming caused Dan and his staff to agree that they could emulate Myst's success with the right kind of content. They chose to focus on the music entertainment segment, because they saw it as large and growing and subject to less intense competition than the game segment.

GWM proposed to apply multimedia technology to famous artists in the music industry. Viewers would move through buildings, clicking on objects such as guitars and sheet music that would serve as gateways to a biography of the artist, the lyrics to his songs, and his filmed interviews. None, however, would be labeled. Rather than having a menu or an index, the disk would abandon the traditional, narrative look. Symbols that represent the artist would be used as interactive icons and transitions. Buyers of the CD-ROM would simply explore the contents of the disk on their computer screens.

Dan's dream for GWM was to put a well-known artist on a CD-ROM and make it into a nationally recognized brand name. This, he thought, would move GWM from a narrow niche player into a national brand name in the CD-ROM business. It could be an Activision, a Broderbund, or maybe even a Microsoft. After some honest soul searching, Dan and his staff quickly realized that although they did have an exciting vision and some highly talented technical people and artists on staff, they lacked access to proprietary content, advertising, and a distribution channel to get the CD-ROM to market once it had been produced. Converting the dream to reality was going to take a lot of hard work and money.

ANALYZING OPTIONS

Dan decided to address the content issue first. His options were limited by the lack of funds. He could develop the content internally and then pay a license fee to utilize the artist's name. He realized that this would require substantial time and effort to hire the right talent and negotiate a license arrangement. He thought he could solve this problem and also his concerns about the lack of a cost-effective distribution channel by directly contacting major music publishing companies. Such companies frequently owned the rights to certain music libraries, were in a position to convince the artist to promote the CD-ROM, and had the financial wherewithal to aggressively advertise the product.

In January 1993, Dan approached a former college classmate at a major music company to sell him on his vision. Dan told his friend that the CD-ROM was a new type of biography and a new kind of reference guide. It could replace a *Rolling Stone* article or maybe the *World Book Encyclopedia*. In Dan's opinion, print was dead. His friend was aware that his company had an artist under contract who was curious about CD-ROMs. The company and the artist proved to be receptive to the new technology. Dan signed the contract and GWM was moving from being a single idea-promotion company into the world of publishing rock 'n' roll music.

GWM was continuing to receive significant fee income from the multiyear contracts it had signed with Apple, IBM, Sony and others to promote their multimedia products, but this was insufficient to fund GWM's move into the electronic publishing business. Dan, the consummate salesman, was able to get sufficient additional funding through an initial public offering (IPO) of the company's stock in mid-1993. The timing was right for new technology companies coming to market. Moreover, GWM was one of the few that were profitable as a result of its multi-year fee-based contracts.

By late 1993, GWM had introduced several CD-ROMs. The acceptance of the new music CD-ROMs showed great promise. Sales exploded, as they more than doubled between 1993 and 1995. Revenue and net income reached $6.8 million and $450,000, respectively, in 1995. Cash flow was growing and the company had very little debt. (See Table 14-1).

Dan and his staff worked feverishly to flesh out GWM's business expansion strategy. The essence of GWM's business plan was to grow through the rapid introduction of high-quality multimedia disks targeted at relatively narrow market segments. Dan was ready to shift into high gear by accelerating efforts to introduce new products. Revenue and profit growth would come from increasing GWM's penetration into the music entertainment CD-ROM publishing segment and then expanding into related electronic publishing segments.

The central strategic question on Dan's mind was how best to achieve this growth: through internal development, through alliance, or through acquisition.

THE INEVITABLE NEED TO FUND FUTURE GROWTH

To fuel high growth, GWM had to continue to sign more artists, expand staff, increase the size of their facility, and increase their promotion and marketing budget. To date, GWM had been able to fund its growth largely through internal cash flow. Any shortfalls were made up through bank loans. But troubling signs began to appear on the horizon.

Although the future continued to hold great promise, the dynamics of the market were changing. By late 1996, industry-wide sales began to slow. GWM's market niche was not immune. Other companies were churning out similar products. The market was getting crowded. Predictions of a multibillion dollar market by the end of the decade were simply not panning out. The entry of other companies into the marketplace coupled with slower than expected industry sales growth caused profit margins to deteriorate.

In 1996, 36,000 CD-ROM titles were published. Forty-one percent of all multimedia CD-ROM titles were for businesses to promote products or train employees. Games and tutorials for software applications comprised much of what remained. Only 8% were "miscellaneous," a group that includes everything from cookbooks to golf tutorials. GWM's titles fell into this category, a niche virtually ignored by consumers.

Dan was beginning to question whether the market was really there. The numbers were simply not supporting the dream. Between 1996 and 1998, GWM's net income (normalized to eliminate nonrecurring expenses) declined 2.7% per year. GWM responded in 1997 by conducting the first layoffs in the company's 6-year history. This was followed by additional cutbacks in 1998. Although cash flow remained positive largely on the strength of income generated from previous

TABLE 14-1. Gee Whiz Media[a] Standalone Income, Balance Sheet, and Cash Flow Statements

	1993	1994	1995	1996	1997	1998	1999	2000	2001	2002
Income statement ($ millions)										
Net sales	2.90	4.40	6.80	8.30	8.10	8.00	8.50	10.80	12.60	15.00
Cost of goods sold[b]	2.32	3.52	5.44	6.64	6.48	6.40	6.80	8.64	10.08	12.00
SG&A expense	0.15	0.22	0.34	0.42	0.41	0.40	0.43	0.54	0.63	0.75
Depreciation	0.09	0.13	0.20	0.25	0.24	0.24	0.26	0.32	0.38	0.45
Special charges[c]					0.25	0.35				
EBIT	0.35	0.53	0.82	1.00	0.72	0.61	1.02	1.30	1.51	1.80
Interest on debt	0.02	0.03	0.06	0.06	0.08	0.09	0.09	0.10	0.12	0.15
Earnings before taxes	0.33	0.50	0.76	0.94	0.64	0.53	0.93	1.20	1.39	1.65
Income taxes	0.13	0.20	0.30	0.37	0.26	0.21	0.37	0.48	0.56	0.66
Net income	0.20	0.30	0.45	0.56	0.39	0.32	0.56	0.72	0.84	0.99
EPS	1.97	2.99	2.27	1.87	1.28	0.79	1.40	1.44	1.67	1.65
Balance sheet (year ending 12/31)										
Current assets	0.17	0.26	0.41	0.50	0.49	0.48	0.51	0.65	0.76	0.90
Current liabilities	0.14	0.21	0.33	0.40	0.39	0.38	0.41	0.52	0.60	0.72
Working capital	0.03	0.05	0.08	0.10	0.10	0.10	0.10	0.13	0.15	0.18
Total assets	1.31	1.98	3.06	3.74	3.65	3.60	3.83	4.86	5.67	6.75
Long-term debt	0.20	0.30	0.60	0.60	0.80	0.85	0.90	1.00	1.20	1.50
Equity	0.97	1.47	2.13	2.74	2.46	2.37	2.52	3.34	3.87	4.53
Shares	0.10	0.10	0.20	0.30	0.30	0.40	0.40	0.50	0.50	0.60
Free cash flow										
EBIT (1 − T)	0.21	0.32	0.49	0.60	0.43	0.37	0.61	0.78	0.91	1.08
Depreciation	0.09	0.13	0.20	0.25	0.24	0.24	0.26	0.32	0.38	0.45
Capital expenditures	0.17	0.26	0.41	0.50	0.49	0.48	0.51	0.65	0.76	0.90
Change in working capital	0.02	0.02	0.03	0.02	0.00	0.00	0.01	0.03	0.02	0.03
Free cash flows	0.10	0.17	0.26	0.33	0.19	0.13	0.35	0.43	0.51	0.60

[a] Numbers subject to rounding. SG&A, sales, general and administrative; EBIT, earnings before interest and taxes; EPS, earnings per share; EBIT (1 − T), earnings before interest but after taxes.

[b] Forecasts of the cost of goods sold and other major expense categories are calculated as a percent of annual projected sales. Percentages reflect the historical ratios of the expense categories to sales.

[c] One-time severance expenses.

multiyear contracts, the trend was down. With a few exceptions, other companies in the industry were experiencing similar developments.

Because of its reputation and early leadership in the industry, GWM's long-term contracts with record companies included features that were relatively unusual in the industry. As part of the GWM contracts, the record companies were obligated to fund some of the development costs up front and to continue to make partial payments until the new title was completed. Many of GWM's later competitors did not have the market credibility that GWM had from its early successes; and, as contractors to the record companies, they were not paid until the titles were delivered. Even then, a portion of the payment would be held back until some minimum sales level had been achieved. They had to shoulder the bulk of their production costs. Moreover, in an effort to catch up with GWM, these companies had tended to overpay for artists' material and were having difficulty making a profit as the market for entertainment CD-ROMs slowed.

A review of what successful players in the industry were doing convinced Dan that he had to change GWM's formula for success. Go Go Technology (GGT), the fastest growing industry participant, and Multimedia, Inc., the largest player, were continuing to grow. Unlike others, they were focusing primarily on programming while allowing others to manufacturer the disks. Marketing was done largely through alliances with major software companies such as Broderbund, which was well known in the industry. GGT had done an excellent job in entering exclusive marketing relationships with some of the best-known software companies.

Dan was convinced that the market was moving too fast for him to outsource his development activities and to broaden his product line through purchasing or developing additional content. He felt that he did not even have the time required to enter into strategic marketing arrangements with the major software companies and publishing companies. Such arrangements could take months to negotiate, and the results were highly unpredictable.

Dan believed that the multimedia industry was ripe for consolidation. Slower growth at least in certain segments of the market would require consolidation to survive. The cost of developing, buying, or licensing content was becoming too great for the smaller players to survive. Dan carefully considered other options such as the sale of all or a portion of his company to a larger company. But GWM was still his baby. It was his dream, and he wanted to retain control until his dream was realized.

In January 1998, his worst fears were realized when Multimedia, Inc. acquired Fly-By-Nite, Inc. for $15 million. The consolidation phase in the industry that Dan had feared was underway.

GEE WHIZ MEDIA LOOKS TO GROW
THROUGH ACQUISITION

It had become clear to Durand that an acquisition would be the best route to restoring GWM's earlier meteoric growth. Dan enlisted the aid of a respected regional investment banking firm and proceeded to develop a plan involving an acquisition as the primary means of realizing GWM's business plan. As envisioned by Dan, the acquisition plan would really provide the detail required to successfully implement GWM's business plan through an acquisition strategy. The acquisition plan provided both financial (minimum return, cash flow, etc.) and nonfinancial objectives (gaining access to distribution channels, content libraries, development capacity, etc.); GWM's resource limitations; further definition of the target industry, and the primary tactics required to complete the acquisition.

As outlined in GWM's business plan, management's primary strategy was to gain market share by extending its existing product line capabilities for converting content focused on niche markets into highly entertaining and interactive multimedia experiences. The means of accomplishing this was through the medium of the CD-ROM. An acquisition was viewed as the best way to implement rapidly the business strategy.

SETTING ACQUISITION PLAN OBJECTIVES

To implement this strategy, GWM sought to identify other related companies with proprietary or access to proprietary content, effective distribution channels, and excellent design and production capabilities. GWM would look for other CD-ROM companies with widely recognized titles whose growth had matured. Dan believed that it would be easier to rejuvenate old, but well-known titles than to build widespread recognition around new ones. By adding new characters or story lines to existing development engines (i.e., the basic software code on which each title is based), it would be much faster and cheaper than starting from scratch each time the company developed a new title. Consequently, GWM could speed development time and drastically reduce its costs.

As a normal part of its internal business planning process, GWM would conduct a "peer analysis" to compare its own performance with that of other industry performers. This peer-review process would serve as an important component of the process for searching for acquisition targets. Although it was very difficult to get such data as market share, Dan had ready access to financial information on his primary competitors, which were all publicly traded companies.

Dan was aware that financial performance could fluctuate widely due to seasonal factors or accounting reserves. Therefore, he insisted on viewing the trend in key financial indicators by averaging the data over a 3-year period. This had the effect of smoothing out fluctuations in the data (see Table 14-2).

Early in the process, Dan and his board of directors decided to stay within the industry they understood. They continued to believe in the long-term promise of multimedia applications. Furthermore, they believed that by staying with what they understood they were more likely to achieve the goals laid out in GWM's acquisition plan. Kathryn Kim, GWM's investment banker, explained that numerous academic studies confirmed this belief.

As evidenced by the company's low leverage, GWM was a very conservative

TABLE 14-2. Comparative Financial Performance Ratios 1996–1998, 3-Year Average[a]

	Gee Whiz Media	Go Go Technology	Fly-By-Nite, Inc.	Hype-O-Tech	Hi Flyer Corp.	Multimedia, Inc.
Profitability ratios						
EBIT/sales	11	21.7	2.8	6.7	1.9	9.8
Net income/sales	6.7	13	0.9	4.8	0.8	7.6
EBIT/total assets	24.7	54.6	4.1	12.1	3.1	22.7
Net income/equity	21.5	38.9	6.8	16.9	5.2	24.8
Growth in net income	−2.7	31.1	−4.2	−3.6	−3.5	6.4
Activity ratios						
Sales growth	−1.8	30.4	−3.1	−2.1	−3.6	4.1
Sales/assets	2.2	2.5	1.46	1.81	1.63	2.32
Liquidity ratios						
Current assets/current liabilities	1.26	1.5	1.1	1.1	1.2	1.67
Working capital/sales	1.2	1.7	3.9	3.1	2.5	2.6
Financial leverage ratios						
Debt/total assets	0.21	0.06	0.81	0.77	0.83	0.39
Debt/total capitalization	0.3	0.07	0.9	0.83	0.89	0.45
EBIT/interest expense	12.74	89	1.8	2.7	1.9	8.9
Market-based ratios						
Price/share	$36.30	$95.10	$3.77	$9.24	$1.60	$66.22
Price/earnings	22	30	13	14	10	22
EPS	1.65	3.17	0.29	0.66	0.16	3.01
Price/revenue	1.7	5.48	0.9	1.3	0.8	0.8
Price/book	5.49	8.91	3.9	4.3	3	5.9
Price/cash flow	13.1	25	45	35	48	16
Market capitalization						
Market value[b]	$14,520,000.00	$19,020,000	$12,565,000	$8,462,000	$7,239,000	$68,990,000

[a] Based on normalized financial performance. EBIT, earnings before interest and taxes; EPS, earnings per share.
[b] Three-year average price/earnings times shares outstanding at year-end 1998.

company. The company's management was very concerned about the ability to manage the acquired company (i.e., operating risk), earnings-per-share (EPS) dilution (i.e., overpayment risk), and losing the ability to pursue unanticipated opportunities by assuming too much leverage (i.e., financial risk). These concerns drove many of their conclusions and subsequent actions in seeking an acquisition target. Having established acquisition plan objectives, resource capability limitations, and the target industry, GWM set about to define key tactics it would employ in making an acquisition.

DEFINING ACQUISITION TACTICS

Based upon the following analysis, GWM's management determined that they could not afford to pay more than $25 to $30 million for an acquisition. In determining the maximum price GWM would be willing to pay for a company, GWM's management laid out the following criteria:

- The minimum acceptable rate of return would be GWM's cost of capital, which Kathryn Kim had estimated to be 15%.
- EPS dilution of the combined organizations would be limited to no more than 2 years following the closing date.
- The maximum price-to-earings ratio (P/E) of the acquired company could not exceed 35 times the current year's earnings or 30 times next year's projected earnings.
- The interest coverage of the combined companies could not fall below the industry average of 6.2. GWM's management believed the company's highly favorable interest coverage ratio (more than 12 to 1) would not result in any reduction in their credit rating by the investor community.
- Only one-half of projected cash flow resulting from synergy would be counted in the purchase price. GWM's management believed that although they would be conservative in their estimate of synergy, history has consistently demonstrated that acquiring companies tend to realize only a portion of anticipated synergy in the desired time frame. Moreover, some portion of the projected synergy should accrue to GWM's shareholders rather than all of it going to the shareholders of the acquired company.

PART II: IMPLEMENTATION

INITIATING THE SEARCH
FOR ACQUISITION CANDIDATES

Declining cash flow from operations and a floundering stock price made it clear that GWM would have to strictly adhere to realistic expectations of what it could pay for an acquisition. With Kathryn Kim's assistance, GWM's management team set about determining appropriate criteria for selecting potential acquisition candidates. The primary selection criteria included target industry, size, price range, profitability, and growth rate. Kim cautioned against adding more criteria at this point in the search. "Too many selection criteria," she warned, "would eliminate all potential prospects."

In establishing secondary selection criteria (i.e., those used to reduce the long list developed by applying the primary criteria), Kim advised GWM to focus on targets whose cash flow, asset base, or lack of leverage could be used to finance the acquisition. This was particularly important in view of the downward trend in GWM's own cash flow.

A "short list" of potential acquisition targets was developed following a search of Kim's in-house database of companies, a review of industry literature, and confidential inquiries to GWM's board members as well as law and accounting firms. Current competitors and potential entrants into the market were given particular consideration.

GWM's management decided that control was important; therefore, they would not be interested in acquiring a minority interest in another company. In addition, they had seen how unfriendly takeovers during the 1980s had dramatically inflated acquisition purchase prices as companies were "put into play." Control premiums for multimedia companies were believed to be 25–35% of current market value, as suggested by recent transactions.

Because GWM was a publicly traded company, management believed that they had to pay close attention to EPS. Although Durand knew that GWM's true economic value was determined by discounting the firm's future cash flows, he also knew that investors and Wall Street analysts closely monitored fluctuations in EPS as a proxy for economic value. Consequently, their first preference was to acquire a company using GWM stock. An exchange of shares with another company would enable GWM, if they could qualify for "pooling of interests" accounting, to add the balance sheets of both companies at book value. This would eliminate the penalty that the write-off of goodwill imposes on future earnings.

With this information in hand, Dan Durand was prepared to initiate "first contact" with firms on the "short list." Whenever possible, contact would be made through a trusted intermediary such as a GWM board member, the company's law or accounting firm, or Kathryn Kim. He made it clear to all involved that at this stage in the process, secrecy was of paramount importance. He did not want to create concern among GWM's employees, suppliers, or customers. In addition, he did not want the "marketplace" to get wind of his intentions, which could drive up market values of potential acquisition targets. Professional arbitrageurs frequently made fortunes by buying on rumors and selling shortly before or after a transaction was complete.

FIRST CONTACT

After a somewhat frustrating 2-month search, GWM reduced what had been a lengthy list of 12 candidates to 2. The list was narrowed either because the companies did not fit the selection criteria as well as GWM had wanted, or because they had rejected GWM's initial overtures through its intermediaries. Dan Durand was not interested in an unfriendly takeover.

At Dan's request, Dana Davies, one of GWM's board members, contacted her former business associate, Barry Chang, the CEO of GGT. Chang said that GGT might be willing to be acquired under "the right conditions." Kathryn Kim recommended further research into GGT's competitive market position and the goals of major shareholders and management before approaching GGT with a formal proposal.

It became apparent that the secret to GGT's success appeared to be its ability to outsource programming activities to service bureaus employing armies of highly skilled software programmers in India and the Philippines. Their hourly rates were a fraction of what domestic software engineers demanded. Moreover, because of significant savings in developing software, GGT was able to diversify into other types of content in order to expand its product offering. GGT demonstrated its clear understanding of market segmentation as it developed titles for such niche hobbyist and educational markets as Civil War Battlefields Interactive and a series entitled the Great Works of Literature Come Alive. Finally, as previously mentioned, GGT had done an excellent job of developing marketing relationships with some of the major software companies.

GGT was following a different business model from other companies in the industry, and Wall Street analysts were taking notice. GGT's approach to this business was to program the disks and have a larger publisher (like Broderbund) distribute them. Other companies such as Fly-By-Nite, Inc., Hype-O-Tech, and Hi Flyer Corp. chose to bear nearly all of the costs for programming and distributing the discs. Rather than contracting out projects (avoiding the price of new equipment, for instance) or developing for others (avoiding the actual manufacture of the disks), these companies wanted to be major players. They also wanted control. Moreover, without a publisher, they didn't need to deal with contracts and the close scrutiny of others.

Although GGT was the industry's current "Wall Street darling" with a 52-week trailing P/E of 30, a recent speech by Barry Chang at an industry trade association meeting implied that GGT's management was anything but smug about its current market position. By "reading between the lines," Dan believed that Barry was becoming increasingly concerned that Mulitmedia, Inc., the industry's behemoth, was likely to erode GGT's position by adopting many of the tactics employed by GGT.

Multimedia, Inc. had publicly pronounced in an interview with its CEO, Carl Widman, that its strategy was to adopt the best practices in the industry and to improve upon them. Moreover, it had the financial wherewithal to do this. Finally, it was learned that Widman, who had a reputation for reneging on commitments, and Chang had a falling out following a failed co-marketing alliance. In particular, Chang believed that he had been given misleading financial forecasts, with Widman's knowledge, by Multimedia's CFO, Hank Perot.

After further conversations between Davies and Chang, Dan believed that it was time for a face-to-face meeting with Chang. At that meeting, Dan presented

the argument that together their two companies could present an effective counterweight to Mulitmedia Inc. Dan wanted to play to Chang's concerns. "Individu-
ally," he argued, "their competitive positions were questionable in the long run
given the apparent slowdown in industry demand. But together they could benefit
from Gee Whiz Media's excellent content library and GGT's lower cost of designing, developing, and marketing CD-ROM products." Chang seemed to be impressed by Durand's compelling logic.

At the end of the meeting, Dan and Barry agreed to sign a confidentiality agreement that would cover both parties and to exchange summarized business plans
and financial statements for their respective companies. (See Tables 14-1 and
14-3). Dan was very interested in seeing in more detail what GGT had done over
the last few years and thought it could do over the next few years; Barry was
interested in evaluating GWM's ability to finance a transaction. Barry had no desire to waste time with a suitor who could not complete a transaction.

Dan and Barry also laid out a timeline that would enable GWM to perform a
modest preliminary due-diligence review. At the end of 30 days, GWM would
have to provide a formal letter of intent containing a specific purchase price. Although the letter of intent would be binding, it would contain the standard protections for both parties. GGT would agree not to "shop" for another suitor during
the 60-day period the letter of intent was in force, and GWM's offer price would
be contingent upon performing a more thorough due diligence, gaining a commitment from lenders, and obtaining the requisite board and shareholder approvals.

PRELIMINARY VALUATION

Dan and his chief financial officer, Andy Perez, poured over the 5 year's of
audited statements that they had received from GGT. Dan expressed some disappointment that the cash flow numbers tended to jump around from year to year.
He was hoping that GGT could demonstrate a stable, predictable cash flow stream.
Predictable cash flows, he reasoned, would enable GWM to convince bankers that
GWM could assume significant leverage to purchase GGT for cash and still be
able to easily meet debt service requirements.

Perez was quick to point out that much of the variation in historical cash flows
was due to nonrecurring or one-time events. For example, he explained that
GGT's free cash flow tripled between 1993 and 1994 due to the sale of fully depreciated computer equipment. The next year it dropped sharply reflecting a one-
time expense associated with the out-of-court settlement of a software copyright
infringement lawsuit filed by Fly-By-Nite, Inc. Cash flow bounced around again
during the next 2 years as a result of an expense write-off associated with an
aborted new product introduction and the receipt of a one-time fee from the sale
of a proprietary software license to another firm. Perez assured Durand that if the
historical numbers were restated to eliminate the one-time occurrences, GGT's
cash flow would show a smooth upward trend. (See Tables 14-4 and 14-5 for the
restated statements).

Dan designated Perez as the acquisition project leader with clear authority to

TABLE 14-3. Go Go Technology[a] Standalone Income, Balance Sheet, and Cash Flow Statements

	1993	1994	1995	1996	1997	1998	1999	2000	2001	2002
Income statement ($ millions)										
Net sales	0.90	1.45	2.50	3.00	4.10	5.10	6.20	7.70	9.30	12.00
Cost of goods sold	0.63	1.02	1.75	2.10	2.87	3.57	4.03	5.01	6.05	7.80
SG&A expense	0.05	0.07	0.13	0.15	0.21	0.26	0.31	0.39	0.47	0.60
Depreciation	0.03	0.04	0.08	0.09	0.12	0.15	0.19	0.23	0.28	0.36
Special charges[b,c]			0.50		0.60					
Other income[d,e]		0.20		0.30						
EBIT	0.20	0.52	0.05	0.96	0.30	1.12	1.67	2.08	2.51	3.24
Interest on debt	0.00	0.00	0.00	0.00	0.01	0.01	0.01	0.02	0.02	0.03
Earnings before taxes	0.19	0.71	0.05	0.96	0.29	1.11	1.66	2.06	2.49	3.21
Income taxes	0.08	0.29	0.02	0.38	0.12	0.44	0.66	0.82	1.00	1.28
Net income	0.12	0.43	0.03	0.57	0.18	0.67	1.00	1.24	1.49	1.93
EPS	2.32	4.29	0.18	3.82	1.17	3.33	4.98	4.95	4.27	4.81
Balance sheet (year ending 12/31)										
Current assets	0.05	0.09	0.15	0.18	0.25	0.31	0.37	0.46	0.56	0.72
Current liabilities	0.04	0.06	0.11	0.13	0.17	0.21	0.24	0.30	0.36	0.47
Working capital	0.02	0.03	0.05	0.05	0.07	0.09	0.13	0.16	0.20	0.25
Total assets	0.36	0.58	1.00	1.20	1.64	2.04	2.48	3.08	3.72	4.80
Long-term debt	0.05	0.05	0.05	0.05	0.10	0.15	0.15	0.20	0.25	0.35
Equity	0.27	0.47	0.85	1.02	1.37	1.68	2.09	2.58	3.11	3.98
Shares outstanding	0.05	0.10	0.15	0.15	0.15	0.20	0.20	0.25	0.35	0.40
Free cash flow										
EBIT (1 − T)	0.12	0.31	0.03	0.58	0.18	0.67	1.00	1.25	1.51	1.94
Depreciation	0.03	0.04	0.08	0.09	0.12	0.15	0.19	0.23	0.28	0.36
Capital expenditures	0.05	0.09	0.15	0.18	0.25	0.31	0.37	0.46	0.56	0.72
Change in working capital	0.02	0.01	0.02	0.01	0.02	0.02	0.04	0.03	0.03	0.06
Free cash flow	0.07	0.26	−0.06	0.48	0.04	0.50	0.78	0.98	1.19	1.53

[a] Numbers subject to rounding. SG&A, sales, general and administrative; EBIT, earnings before interest and taxes; EPS, earnings per share; EBIT (1 − T), earnings before interest but after taxes

[b] One-time expense associated with the settlement of a software copyright infringement lawsuit filed by Fly-By-Nite, Inc.

[c] One-time expense associated with an aborted new product introduction.

[d] One-time gain on the sale of fully depreciated computer equipment.

[d] One-time fee on the sale of a proprietary software license.

[e] Cost of sales as percent of sales reduced from .7 to .65 beginning in 1999 and continued thereafter.

TABLE 14-4. Go Go Technology Normalized Income, Balance Sheet, and Cash Flow Statements [a]

	1993	1994	1995	1996	1997	1998	1999	2000	2001	2002
Income statement ($ millions)										
Net sales	0.90	1.45	2.50	3.00	4.10	5.10	6.20	7.70	9.30	12.00
Cost of goods sold	0.63	1.02	1.75	2.10	2.87	3.57	4.34	5.39	6.51	8.40
SG&A Expense	0.05	0.07	0.13	0.15	0.21	0.26	0.31	0.39	0.47	0.60
Depreciation	0.03	0.04	0.08	0.09	0.12	0.15	0.19	0.23	0.28	0.36
Special charges [b,c]										
Other income [d,e]		0.00	0.00	0.00	0.00					
EBIT	0.20	0.32	0.55	0.66	0.90	1.12	1.36	1.69	2.05	2.64
Interest on debt	0.00	0.00	0.00	0.00	0.01	0.01	0.01	0.02	0.02	0.03
Earnings before taxes	0.19	0.31	0.55	0.66	0.89	1.11	1.35	1.68	2.02	2.61
Income taxes	0.08	0.13	0.22	0.26	0.36	0.44	0.54	0.67	0.81	1.04
Net income	0.12	0.19	0.33	0.39	0.54	0.67	0.81	1.01	1.21	1.57
EPS	2.32	1.89	2.18	2.62	3.57	3.33	4.05	4.02	3.47	3.91
Balance sheet (year ending 12/31)										
Current assets	0.05	0.09	0.15	0.18	0.25	0.31	0.37	0.46	0.56	0.72
Current liabilities	0.04	0.06	0.11	0.13	0.17	0.21	0.26	0.32	0.39	0.50
Working Capital	0.02	0.03	0.05	0.05	0.07	0.09	0.11	0.14	0.17	0.22
Total assets	0.36	0.58	1.00	1.20	1.64	2.04	2.48	3.08	3.72	4.80
Long-term debt	0.05	0.05	0.05	0.05	0.10	0.15	0.15	0.20	0.25	0.35
Equity	0.27	0.47	0.85	1.02	1.37	1.68	2.07	2.56	3.08	3.95
Shares	0.05	0.10	0.15	0.15	0.15	0.20	0.20	0.25	0.35	0.40
Free cash flow										
EBIT (1 − T)	0.12	0.19	0.33	0.40	0.54	0.67	0.82	1.02	1.23	1.58
Depreciation	0.03	0.04	0.08	0.09	0.12	0.15	0.19	0.23	0.28	0.36
Capital expenditures	0.05	0.09	0.15	0.18	0.25	0.31	0.37	0.46	0.56	0.72
Change in working capital	0.02	0.01	0.02	0.01	0.02	0.02	0.02	0.03	0.03	0.05
Free cash flow	0.07	0.14	0.24	0.30	0.40	0.50	0.61	0.76	0.92	1.18

[a] Numbers subject to rounding. SG&A, sales, general and administrative; EBIT, earnings before interest and taxes; EPS, earnings per share; EBIT (1 − T), earnings before interest but after taxes.

[b] One-time expense associated with the settlement of a software copyright infringement lawsuit filed by Fly-By-Nite, Inc.

[c] One-time expense associated with an aborted new product introduction.

[d] One-time gain on the sale of fully depreciated computer equipment.

[e] One-time fee on the sale of a proprietary software license.

TABLE 14-5. Go Go Technology Normalized Financial Performance Summary in Millions[a]

	1993	1994	1995	1996	1997	1998	1999	2000	2001	2002
Original EBIT	0.20	0.52	0.05	0.96	0.30	1.12	1.67	2.08	2.51	3.24
Add back: Special charges			0.5		0.6					
Deduct: One-time gains		0.2		0.3						
Normalized EBIT	0.20	0.32	0.55	0.66	0.90	1.12	1.67	2.08	2.51	3.24
Interest on debt	0	0	0	0	0.01	0.01	0.01	0.02	0.02	0.03
Normalized earnings BT	0.20	0.32	0.55	0.66	0.89	1.11	1.66	2.06	2.49	3.21
Income taxes	0.08	0.13	0.22	0.26	0.36	0.44	0.54	0.67	0.81	1.04
Normalized net income	0.12	0.19	0.33	0.40	0.53	0.67	1.12	1.39	1.68	2.17
Shares outstanding	0.05	0.10	0.15	0.15	0.15	0.20	0.20	0.25	0.35	0.40
Normalized EPS	2.41	1.93	2.21	2.65	3.57	3.34	5.62	5.55	4.80	5.42
Original valuation CF	0.07	0.26	−0.06	0.48	0.04	0.50	0.78	0.98	1.19	1.53
Normalized valuation CF	0.07	0.14	0.24	0.30	0.40	0.50	0.61	0.76	0.92	1.18

[a]EBIT, earnings before interest and taxes; EPS, earnings per share; BT, before taxes; CF, cash flow.

draw upon others with specialized skills throughout the organization. Perez was quick to establish action teams dedicated to specific aspects of the negotiation process. These teams included financial analysts to refine the initial valuation of GGT and a combined legal and financial team to work on structuring the proposal to GGT's management. Other teams included a multidisciplined group to conduct due diligence consisting of operations, marketing, and accounting experts and a team consisting of Perez and GWM's treasurer to develop a plan for financing the acquisition.

Dan was pleased with the appearance of highly predictable cash flows for GGT between 1993 and 1998. He was, however, quite skeptical of the 30.3% and 32.3% compound growth rate GGT projected for net income and cash flow, respectively, between 1998 and 2002. Once again, Perez—being the consummate numbers person—cautioned that Dan should reserve judgement until the assumptions underlying the forecast were well understood.

Following several days of hectic number crunching by Perez's minions, Perez reported to Durand that the assumptions looked reasonable except for a five percentage point drop in the ratio of cost of goods sold to sales built into the forecast period beginning in 1999. This was evident upon examination of the "common-size income statement displayed in Table 14-6.

Chang was questioned about the realism of this assumption. "This reduction," he explained, "reflected the implementation of a modular software development system that GGT had been working on for several years. This system would enable GGT's developers to more readily reuse existing software code in new product introductions. The resulting reduction in coding time would substantially lower product introduction costs."

Dan was familiar with software development projects, and he was well aware that they frequently were implemented well behind schedule and considerably above budget. Furthermore, his experience led him to believe that these types of projects rarely provide the productivity improvements that are expected. Consequently, Dan told Perez to rerun the GGT projections but with more modest growth assumptions and with the cost of goods sold as a percent of sales in line with the company's historical performance of 70% rather than the 65% used in the forecast originally provided by GGT. This, he believed, would provide a more realistic picture that did not depend on what Dan thought were largely heroic assumptions. (See Table 14-7).

IDENTIFYING SOURCES (AND DESTROYERS) OF VALUE

With the revised forecast, Durand and Perez turned to identifying "hidden" sources of value that GWM could unlock to provide additional cash generated by the combination of GGT and GWM. To identify these sources of value (measured in terms of incremental cash flow), Perez and his associates poured over GGT's books and operations looking for assets not recorded on the books at fair value, underutilized borrowing capacity, and the potential for cost savings (e.g., shared overhead, duplicate facilities, etc.). Other potential sources of value included new

TABLE 14-6. Go Go Technology Normalized, Common-Size Income, Balance Sheet and Cash Flow Statements
Income Statement (Percent of Net Sales)[a]

	1993	1994	1995	1996	1997	1998	1999	2000	2001	2002
Net sales	1.00	1.00	1.00	1.00	1.00	1.00	1.00	1.00	1.00	1.00
Cost of goods sold	0.70	0.70	0.70	0.70	0.70	0.70	0.65	0.65	0.65	0.65
SG&A expense	0.05	0.05	0.05	0.05	0.05	0.05	0.05	0.05	0.05	0.05
Depreciation	0.03	0.03	0.03	0.03	0.03	0.03	0.03	0.03	0.03	0.03
Special charges			0.00		0.00					
Other income		0.00		0.00						
EBIT	0.22	0.22	0.22	0.22	0.22	0.22	0.27	0.27	0.27	0.27
Interest on debt	0.00	0.00	0.00	0.00	0.00	0.00	0.00	0.00	0.00	0.00
Earnings before taxes	0.22	0.22	0.22	0.22	0.22	0.22	0.27	0.27	0.27	0.27
Income taxes	0.09	0.09	0.09	0.09	0.09	0.09	0.09	0.09	0.09	0.09
Net income	0.12	0.13	0.13	0.13	0.13	0.13	0.18	0.18	0.18	0.18

[a] SG&A, sales, general and administrative; EBIT, earnings before interest and taxes.

TABLE 14-7. Go Go Technology Normalized Income, Balance Sheet, and Cash Flow Statements[a]

	1993	1994	1995	1996	1997	1998	1999	2000	2001	2002
Income statement ($ millions)										
Net sales	0.90	1.45	2.50	3.00	4.10	5.10	6.20	7.70	9.30	12.00
Cost of goods sold	0.63	1.02	1.75	2.10	2.87	3.57	4.34	5.39	6.51	8.40
SG&A expense	0.05	0.07	0.13	0.15	0.21	0.26	0.31	0.39	0.47	0.60
Depreciation	0.03	0.04	0.08	0.09	0.12	0.15	0.19	0.23	0.28	0.36
Special charges										
Other inccme		0.00	0.00	0.00	0.00					
EBIT	0.20	0.32	0.55	0.66	0.90	1.12	1.36	1.69	2.05	2.64
Interest on debt	0.00	0.00	0.00	0.00	0.01	0.01	0.01	0.02	0.02	0.03
Earnings before taxes	0.19	0.31	0.55	0.66	0.89	1.11	1.35	1.68	2.02	2.61
Income taxes	0.08	0.13	0.22	0.26	0.36	0.44	0.54	0.67	0.81	1.04
Net income	0.12	0.19	0.33	0.39	0.54	0.67	0.81	1.01	1.21	1.57
EPS	2.32	1.89	2.18	2.62	3.57	3.33	4.05	4.02	3.47	3.91
Balance sheet (year ending 12/31)										
Current assets	0.05	0.09	0.15	0.18	0.25	0.31	0.37	0.46	0.56	0.72
Current liabilities	0.04	0.06	0.11	0.13	0.17	0.21	0.26	0.32	0.39	0.50
Working capital	0.02	0.03	0.05	0.05	0.07	0.09	0.11	0.14	0.17	0.22
Total assets	0.36	0.58	1.00	1.20	1.64	2.04	2.48	3.08	3.72	4.80
Long-term debt	0.05	0.05	0.05	0.05	0.10	0.15	0.15	0.20	0.25	0.35
Equity	0.27	0.47	0.85	1.02	1.37	1.68	2.07	2.56	3.08	3.95
Shares	0.05	0.10	0.15	0.15	0.15	0.20	0.20	0.25	0.35	0.40
Free cash flow										
EBIT (1 − T)	0.12	0.19	0.33	0.40	0.54	0.67	0.82	1.02	1.23	1.58
Depreciation	0.03	0.04	0.08	0.09	0.12	0.15	0.19	0.23	0.28	0.36
Capital expenditures	0.05	0.09	0.15	0.18	0.25	0.31	0.37	0.46	0.56	0.72
Change in working capital	0.02	0.01	0.02	0.01	0.02	0.02	0.02	0.03	0.03	0.05
Free cash flow[b]	0.07	0.14	0.24	0.30	0.40	0.50	0.61	0.76	0.92	1.18

PV (1998–2002) @ 15%	3.00
PV of 6th-yr. terminal value	19.45
Sum	22.85

[a] Numbers subject to rounding. SG&A, sales, general and administrative; EBIT, earnings before interest and taxes; EPS, earnings per share; EBIT (1 − T), earnings before interest but after taxes.

[b] 15% discount rate, 5th-yr. free cash flow grown 11.7% to 6th yr.; cost of sales increased from .65 to .70 between 1999 and 2002. PV, present value.

customer relationships, opportunities for GWM to utilize new technologies and processes, as well as intellectual property such as patents, trademarks, and royalty rights. They also looked for factors that would reduce future cash flow such as product quality problems, employee turnover, duplicate customer relationships, and so on. Perez knew from past experience that finding and quantifying potential sources of value would frequently be the difference between a successful acquisition and one that failed to meet expectations. Upon completing his investigation, Perez constructed Table 14-8:

The present value of total synergy was estimated at $6.0 million. None of the synergy was expected to be realized in 1998; one-half was expected to be realized in 1999. The full $500,000 in annual synergy was expected to be realized by 2000 and each year thereafter.

From past experience, Perez was aware that he also needed to look for factors that could detract from the future cash flow of the combined entities. A third-party marketing firm was hired to interview a representative sample of GGT customers without divulging that they were hired by GWM. Rather, customers were told, with GGT's blessing, that the marketing firm was conducting a survey for GGT so that the company could better understand its customers' needs. Assumptions made about factors contributing to future cash flows of the combined firms and those detracting from future cash flows were clearly delineated in Perez's presentations to Durand. Moreover, these assumptions would be carefully validated during the more exhaustive on-site due diligence that was to take place before closing.

TABLE 14-8.   Sources of Value ($ Millions)

Item	1998	After-tax cash flow in 1999	Incremental annual operating cash flow[a] beyond 1999	Assumptions
Sale of building and land[b]	$6.8	0	0	• GGT personnel housed in surplus GWM space
Cost savings	0	$.25	$.25	• Duplicate positions eliminated without disruption during 1999 • Severance expenses less than $50,000
Incremental product-related EBIT[c]	0	$.25	$.25	• Cross selling of GWM and GGT products • No significant customer attrition

[a] Net of severance, training, and other expenses that must be incurred to realize projected synergy.

[b] GGT's headquarters building and land purchased in 1990 were on the books at historical cost; since then, they had appreciated dramatically.

[c] EBIT, earnings before interest and taxes.

DETERMINING THE INITIAL OFFER PRICE

Perez's approach to valuation involved two stages. First, he discounted projected cash flows for GGT as a stand-alone business. Second, he calculated the discounted value of the projected synergy resulting from combining GGT and GWM as described above. The difference between the stand-alone value excluding synergy and the stand-alone value including synergy constituted the price range that Durand and Perez would consider reasonable. The initial purchase price would then lie in this range.

This price range would be further validated by comparing the discounted cash flow valuations with purchase prices based on by P/E, price/revenue, and price/

TABLE 14-9.   GGT Preliminary Valuation

Valuation based on	Multiple	$ Millions
Discounted cash flow		
GGT stand-alone		22.9
GGT stand-alone + ½ of synergy [a]		25.6
GGT stand-alone + synergy		28.3
Price/earnings		
Recent transactions [b]	28.5	19.1
Industry (w/o premium)		
3-year average	18.5	12.4
1998	22.7	15.2
GGT (w/o premium)		
3-year average	30	20.1
1998	33	22.1
Price/Revenue		
Recent Transactions [b]	3.8	19.4
Industry (w/o premium)		
3-year average	1.8	9.2
1998	3.1	15.8
GGT (w/o premium)		
3-year average	5.5	28.1
1998	5.9	30.1
Price/Book		
Recent Transactions [b]	11.3	19.0
Industry (w/o premium)		
3-year average	5.2	8.7
1998	7.7	12.9
GGT (w/o premium)		
3-year average	8.9	15.0
1998	9.9	16.6
Net Liquidation Value [c]		8.9

[a] Reflects tactics outlined in GWM's acquisition plan.
[b] Fly-By-Nite, Inc. acquired by Multimedia, Inc. in early 1998.
[c] After all liquidation-related expenses (see Table 14-10).

book ratios for recent transactions involving comparable companies, the 3-year industry average, and for 1998. These ratios were then applied to GGT's current and 3-year average performance. These ratios seem to confirm for Durand and Perez that $26 million was a fair price for GGT, representing an approximate one-third premium over the current share price. Durand knew that the negotiation would not be easy. Chang would be quick to point out that the price should be between $28 and $30 million, the range implied by GGT's price-to-revenue ratios. Table 14-9 summarizes the range of valuations calculated for GGT. Both Durand and Perez were well aware that what was actually paid would reflect the outcome of hard negotiating and the findings of full diligence.

TABLE 14-10.   Go Go Technology: Calculating Liquidation Value

Assets and liabilities	Book value of assets as of 12/31/98 ($)	"Orderly sale" liquidation value ($)[a]
Current assets	310,000	280,450
Cash	28,000	28,000
Marketable securities	90,000	90,000
Receivables[b]	177,000	150,450 (2)
Inventories[c]	15,000	12,000 (3)
Fixed assets	1,712,000	9,000,000
Equipment[d]	640,000	250,000 (4)
Buildings and land[e]	1,072,000	8,750,000 (5)
Prepaids	18,000	4,500
Total assets	2,040,000	9,284,950
Less		
Current liabilities	210,000	210,000
Long-term debt	150,000	150,000
Total deduction	360,000	360,000
Liquidation value		8,924,950
Less liquidation-related expenses[f]		2,150,000
Net liquidation value		6,774,950
Total shares outstanding	200,000	200,000
Liquidation value per share		33.87

[a] Orderly sale is defined as taking place over 12–18 months. Liquidation values are likely to be much lower if the pace of liquidation had to be accelerated.

[b] Valid and collectable receivables are assumed to be 85% of book value.

[c] Inventories are assumed to be liquidated at 80% of book value.

[d] Mostly computer hardware, furniture, and fixtures. In liquidation, assets such as capitalized software generally have no value. For going concerns, the value of capitalized software is written off over what is viewed as its commercial life.

[e] The land and building were acquired prior to the commercial development of the area.

[f] Legal fees, taxes, management fees, and contractually required employee severance expenses.

DEAL STRUCTURING

Dan knew that GGT's higher P/E would make a stock-for-stock purchase problematic because of the likely dilution in GWM's EPS. GWM's declining EPS in recent years was making many Wall Street analysts nervous; nonetheless, GWM continued to show a substantial multiple largely on the past successes of its CEO, Dan Durand. However, an acquisition resulting in dilution was not likely to be acceptable to Wall Street. Early valuations of GGT suggested that to complete the acquisition GWM would have to pay something in the neighborhood of $26 million, if it were to purchase 100% of the stock. "Twenty-six million was a very big neighborhood for a company our size," gulped Durand when told by Perez what he thought it would take to complete the transaction.

Durand and Perez had to be creative to reduce the initial cash flow impact of the acquisition on GWM. They would need to know what GGT's management and shareholders would be willing to accept. This required some old-fashioned detective work, such as reading old speeches made by Widman at trade shows and shareholder meetings, reading Wall Street analysts' reports, and looking at the amount of GGT stock accumulated by the company's top management. In addition, because many of the GGT's top managers were quite young, it was possible that they would like to stay with the combined companies or even that they would be willing to hold significant amounts of stock in the new company.

Although Durand wanted to retain several key GGT managers, he believed that in the long-term, personality conflicts would arise as a result of his way of doing business and Chang's hard-charging, sometimes "bend-the-rules" approach to things. Moreover, Chang's salary was the highest in the industry; Durand thought it was out of line for what Chang could contribute as a senior manager to the combined firm's ongoing operations. Dan Durand was willing to consider management employment contracts to retain key managers, but he did not want to keep Chang.

Durand, Perez, and their investment banker began to brainstorm different scenarios involving different purchase price compositions. They knew that if an exciting "story line" could be created for the combined companies it would be possible to convince GGT's shareholders to accept something other than an all-cash offer. Furthermore, they understood that the more exciting the outlook for the combined companies the more likely they would be able to borrow money, perhaps even at a rate less than the prevailing market rate of interest. This might happen if they offered the bankers warrants or rights to buy the combined companies' stock at some point in the future at a predetermined price.

Fifteen alternative scenarios were created in order to determine the optimal composition of the purchase price from the standpoint of GWM. GWM's own analysis suggested that its EPS would exceed $1.44 by 2000 and that its net present value was $19.5 million, even without the acquisition of GGT (see Table 14-11). The most acceptable scenario would be the one that resulted in the highest net present value (NPV), the least EPS dilution initially, substantially exceeded what GWM could have done without GGT, and would most likely be acceptable

TABLE 14-11. Gee Whiz Media Valuation Based on Normalized Data[a]

	1993	1994	1995	1996	1997	1998	1999	2000	2001	2002
Normalized income statement ($ millions)[b]										
Net sales	2.90	4.40	6.80	8.30	8.10	8.00	8.50	10.80	13.60	17.00
Cost of goods sold	2.32	3.52	5.44	6.64	6.48	6.40	6.80	8.64	10.88	13.60
SG&A expense	0.15	0.22	0.34	0.42	0.41	0.40	0.43	0.54	0.68	0.85
Depreciation	0.09	0.13	0.20	0.25	0.24	0.24	0.26	0.32	0.41	0.51
Special charges				0.00	0.00	0.00				
EBIT	0.35	0.53	0.82	1.00	0.97	0.96	1.02	1.30	1.63	2.04
Interest on debt	0.02	0.03	0.06	0.06	0.08	0.09	0.09	0.10	0.12	0.15
Earnings before taxes	0.33	0.50	0.76	0.94	0.89	0.88	0.93	1.20	1.51	1.89
Income taxes	0.13	0.20	0.30	0.37	0.36	0.35	0.37	0.48	0.60	0.76
Net income	0.20	0.30	0.45	0.56	0.54	0.53	0.56	0.72	0.91	1.13
EPS	1.97	2.99	2.27	1.87	1.78	1.31	1.40	1.44	1.81	1.89
Balance sheet (year ending 12/31)										
Current assets	0.17	0.26	0.41	0.50	0.49	0.48	0.51	0.65	0.82	1.02
Current liabilities	0.14	0.21	0.33	0.40	0.39	0.38	0.41	0.52	0.65	0.82
Working capital	0.03	0.05	0.08	0.10	0.10	0.10	0.10	0.13	0.16	0.20
Total assets	1.31	1.98	3.06	3.74	3.65	3.60	3.83	4.86	6.12	7.65
Long-term debt	0.20	0.30	0.60	0.60	0.80	0.85	0.90	1.00	1.20	1.50
Equity	0.97	1.47	2.13	2.74	2.46	2.37	2.52	3.34	4.27	5.33
Shares	0.10	0.10	0.20	0.30	0.30	0.40	0.40	0.50	0.50	0.60
Free cash flow										
EBIT (1 − T)	0.21	0.32	0.49	0.60	0.58	0.58	0.61	0.78	0.98	1.22
Depreciation	0.09	0.13	0.20	0.25	0.24	0.24	0.26	0.32	0.41	0.51
Capital expenditures	0.17	0.26	0.41	0.50	0.49	0.48	0.51	0.65	0.82	1.02
Change in working capital	0.02	0.02	0.03	0.02	0.00	0.00	0.01	0.03	0.03	0.04
Free cash flow	0.10	0.17	0.26	0.33	0.34	0.34	0.35	0.43	0.54	0.67

[a]Present value (PV) (1998–2002)	1.82
PV of terminal value	18.73
Total value	$19.55

Assumptions: 15% cost of capital, 5th-year free cash flow (FCF) (2002) is grown 13% to get 6th-year FCF.

[b]SG&A, sales, general and administrative; EBIT, earnings before interest and taxes; EPS, earnings per share; EBIT (1 − T), earnings before interest but after taxes.

TABLE 14-12. GWM and GGT Combined Normalized Income, Balance Sheet, and Cash Flow Statements[a]

	1993	1994	1995	1996	1997	1998	1999	2000	2001	2002
Normalized income ($ millions)										
Net sales	3.80	5.85	9.30	11.30	12.20	13.10	14.70	18.50	22.90	29.00
Cost of goods sold	2.95	4.54	7.19	8.74	9.35	9.97	11.14	14.03	17.39	22.00
SG&A expense	0.19	0.29	0.47	0.57	0.61	0.66	0.74	0.93	1.15	1.45
Depreciation	0.11	0.18	0.28	0.34	0.37	0.39	0.44	0.56	0.69	0.87
Synergy							0.25	0.50	0.50	0.50
EBIT	0.55	0.85	1.37	1.66	1.87	2.08	2.63	3.49	4.18	5.18
Interest on debt	0.02	0.03	0.06	0.06	0.09	0.10	0.10	0.12	0.14	0.18
Earnings before taxes	0.52	0.81	1.30	1.59	1.79	1.98	2.53	3.37	4.04	5.00
Income taxes	0.21	0.33	0.52	0.64	0.71	0.79	1.01	1.35	1.61	2.00
Net income	0.31	0.49	0.78	0.95	1.07	1.19	1.52	2.02	2.42	3.00
Balance sheet (year ending 12/31)										
Current assets	0.23	0.35	0.56	0.68	0.73	0.79	0.88	1.11	1.37	1.74
Current liabilities	0.18	0.27	0.43	0.52	0.56	0.60	0.67	0.84	1.04	1.32
Working capital	0.05	0.08	0.13	0.15	0.17	0.19	0.21	0.27	0.33	0.42
Total assets	1.67	2.56	4.06	4.94	5.29	5.64	6.31	7.94	9.84	12.45
Long-term debt	0.25	0.35	0.65	0.65	0.90	1.00	1.05	1.20	1.45	1.85
Equity	1.24	1.94	2.98	3.76	3.82	4.04	4.59	5.90	7.35	9.28
Shares	0.15	0.20	0.35	0.45	0.45	0.60	0.60	0.75	0.85	1.00
Free cash flow										
EBIT (1 − T)	0.33	0.51	0.82	0.99	1.12	1.25	1.58	2.09	2.51	3.11
Depreciation	0.11	0.18	0.28	0.34	0.37	0.39	0.44	0.56	0.69	0.87
Capital expenditures	0.23	0.35	0.56	0.68	0.73	0.79	0.88	1.11	1.37	1.74
Change in working capital	0.04	0.03	0.05	0.03	0.02	0.02	0.03	0.05	0.06	0.09
Free cash flow	0.17	0.30	0.49	0.63	0.74	0.84	1.11	1.48	1.76	2.15
PV (1998–2002) @ 15%[b]	5.72									
PV of 6th-yr. terminal value	42.71									
Sum	48.43									

[a] SG&A, sales, general and administrative; EBIT, earnings before interest and taxes; EPS, earnings per share; EBIT (1 − T), earnings before interest but after taxes.

[b] Fifteen percent discount rate, 5th-yr. free cash flow grown 12.2%; cost of sales from .65 to .70. The 12.5% earnings growth rate is .5% less than the 13% used for the GGT valuation because of the lower anticipated growth of GWM's product lines.

to the GGT shareholders. Moreover, the scenario could not jeopardize the combined companies' ability to satisfy loan covenants or maintain interest coverage and debt-to-equity ratios consistent with the average for other companies in the industry. But the GGT acquisition looked attractive, promising to boost the market value of the combined companies to more than $48.4 million (see Table 14-12). This figure was about 14% more than the value of GGT plus GWM if they were operated as stand-alone businesses.

All cash and all stock offers were included (even though it was felt that neither was a realistic option) as benchmarks or baselines for comparing the other options. Three of the scenarios (i.e., all cash, all stock, and 50% cash–50% stock) are summarized in Table 14-13 in order to illustrate the process for determining the optimal financing plan. Note that all three scenarios exceed Durand's minimum acceptable NPV (see Tables 14-14 to 14-16).

THE NEGOTIATIONS HEAT UP: REFINING THE OFFER PRICE

Based on this analysis and on what Durand thought the GGT shareholders would accept, GWM decided that the proposal to GGT's board would consist of $12.5 million in cash, $6.25 million in subordinated debentures, and $6.25 million in GWM's stock for 100% of GGT's stock. This combination would not result in any appreciable dilution in the combined companies EPS and exceeded substantially GWM's stand-alone EPS performance by 2001. Furthermore, the present

TABLE 14-13.   Representative Alternative Financing Plans

Scenario	Sources of funds	Millions ($)	Implications
All cash	Net liquidation value of building Borrowing	6.8 19.2	• Severe dilution from GWM stand-alone projection in 1999 • High potential for violating loan covenants and downgrade by credit rating agencies
All stock	GWM issues 700,000 new shares of stock	26.0	• Minor dilution from GWM's stand-alone projection in 1999
50% cash–50% stock	Net liquidation value of building = $6.8 New borrowing = $6.2 GWM issues 350,000 new shares	13.0 in cash 13.0 in stock	• No dilution; EPS exceeds all alternative financing plans by 2002[b]

[a] Purchase price = $26 million.
[b] EPS, earnings per share.

TABLE 14-14. All Cash Purchase ($26 Million): GWM/GGT Combined Normalized Income, Balance Sheet, and Cash Flow Statements[a]

	1993	1994	1995	1996	1997	1998	1999	2000	2001	2002
Income statement ($ millions)										
Net sales	3.80	5.85	9.30	11.30	12.20	13.10	14.70	18.50	22.90	29.00
Cost of Goods Sold	2.95	4.54	7.19	8.74	9.35	9.97	11.14	14.03	17.39	22.00
SG&A Expense	0.19	0.29	0.47	0.57	0.61	0.66	0.74	0.93	1.15	1.45
Depreciation	0.11	0.18	0.28	0.34	0.37	0.39	0.44	0.56	0.69	0.87
Goodwill amortization							0.50	0.50	0.50	0.50
Synergy							0.25	0.50	0.50	0.50
EBIT	0.55	0.85	1.37	1.66	1.87	2.08	2.13	2.99	3.68	4.68
Interest on debt	0.02	0.03	0.06	0.06	0.09	2.22	2.15	2.06	1.98	1.91
Earnings before taxes	0.52	0.81	1.30	1.59	1.79	−0.14	−0.01	0.93	1.70	2.77
Income taxes	0.21	0.33	0.52	0.64	0.71	−0.06	−0.01	0.37	0.68	1.11
Net income	0.31	0.49	0.78	0.95	1.07	−0.08	−0.01	0.56	1.02	1.66
EPS	NA	NA	NA	NA	NA	−0.21	−0.02	1.11	2.04	2.77
Balance sheet (year ending 12/31)										
Current assets	0.23	0.35	0.56	0.68	0.73	0.79	0.88	1.11	1.37	1.74
Current liabilities	0.18	0.27	0.43	0.52	0.56	0.60	0.67	0.84	1.04	1.32
Working capital	0.05	0.08	0.13	0.15	0.17	0.19	0.21	0.27	0.33	0.42
Total assets[c]	1.67	2.56	4.06	4.94	5.29	30.54	31.75	32.97	33.05	34.13
Long-term debt[d]	0.25	0.35	0.65	0.65	0.90	18.50	17.90	17.19	16.50	15.90
Equity	1.24	1.94	2.98	3.76	3.82	11.44	13.18	14.94	15.51	16.91
Shares	0.15	0.20	0.35	0.45	0.75	0.40	0.40	0.50	0.50	0.60
Free cash flow										
EBIT (1 − T)	0.33	0.51	0.82	0.99	1.12	1.25	1.28	1.79	2.21	2.81
Depreciation	0.11	0.18	0.28	0.34	0.37	0.39	0.44	0.56	0.69	0.87
Goodwill amortization						0.50	0.50	0.50	0.50	0.50
Capital expenditures	0.23	0.35	0.56	0.68	0.73	0.79	0.88	1.11	1.37	1.74
Change in working capital	0.04	0.03	0.05	0.03	0.02	0.02	0.03	0.05	0.06	0.09
Principal repayment						0.67	0.67	0.67	0.67	0.67
Free cash flow	0.17	0.30	0.49	0.63	0.74	0.17	0.64	1.01	1.29	1.68

[a] SG&A, sales, general and administrative; EBIT, earnings before interest and taxes; EPS, earnings per share; EBIT (1 − T), earnings before interest but after taxes.

[b] Total assets increase to $30.54 million, equal to $5.64 million in total assets at Y/E 98 of combined companies less $1.1 million book value of GGT building plus the $26 million purchase price. Equity equals total assets less current liabilities and long-term debt.

[c] Following allocation of purchase price, goodwill is assumed to be $20 million. See notes to Table 14-16 for explanation of methodology.

[d] Total debt increases from $1 million at Y/E 98 for combined companies to $20.2 million reflecting additional borrowing of $19.2 million. Total debt of $20.2 million is assumed to be amortized over 30 years.

TABLE 14-15. All Stock Purchase ($26 Million): GWM/GGT Combined Normalized Income, Balance Sheet, and Cash Flow Statements[a]

	1993	1994	1995	1996	1997	1998	1999	2000	2001	2002
Income statement ($ millions)										
Net sales	3.80	5.85	9.30	11.30	12.20	13.10	14.70	18.50	22.90	29.00
Cost of goods sold	2.95	4.54	7.19	8.74	9.35	9.97	11.14	14.03	17.39	22.00
SG&A expense	0.19	0.29	0.47	0.57	0.61	0.66	0.74	0.93	1.15	1.45
Depreciation	0.11	0.18	0.28	0.34	0.37	0.39	0.44	0.56	0.69	0.87
Synergy							0.25	0.50	0.50	0.50
EBIT	0.55	0.85	1.37	1.66	1.87	2.08	2.63	3.49	4.18	5.18
Interest on debt	0.02	0.03	0.06	0.06	0.09	0.10	0.10	0.12	0.14	0.18
Earnings before taxes	0.52	0.81	1.30	1.59	1.79	1.98	2.53	3.37	4.04	5.00
Income taxes	0.21	0.33	0.52	0.64	0.71	0.79	1.01	1.35	1.61	2.00
Net income	0.31	0.49	0.78	0.95	1.07	1.19	1.52	2.02	2.42	3.00
EPS	.28	.46	.71	.86	.97	1.08	1.38	1.84	2.20	2.73
Balance sheet (year ending 12/31)										
Current assets	0.23	0.35	0.56	0.68	0.73	0.79	0.88	1.11	1.37	1.74
Current liabilities	0.18	0.27	0.43	0.52	0.56	0.60	0.67	0.84	1.04	1.32
Working capital	0.05	0.08	0.13	0.15	0.17	0.19	0.21	0.27	0.33	0.42
Total assets	1.67	2.56	4.06	4.94	5.29	5.64	6.31	7.94	9.84	12.45
Long-term debt	0.25	0.35	0.65	0.65	0.90	1.00	1.05	1.20	1.45	1.85
Equity	1.24	1.94	2.98	3.76	3.82	4.04	4.59	5.90	7.35	9.28
Shares [b]	1.10	1.10	1.10	1.10	1.10	1.10	1.10	1.10	1.10	1.10
Free cash flow										
EBIT (1 − T)	0.33	0.51	0.82	0.99	1.12	1.25	1.58	2.09	2.51	3.11
Depreciation	0.11	0.18	0.28	0.34	0.37	0.39	0.44	0.56	0.69	0.87
Capital expenditures	0.23	0.35	0.56	0.68	0.73	0.79	0.88	1.11	1.37	1.74
Change in working capital	0.04	0.03	0.05	0.03	0.02	0.02	0.03	0.05	0.06	0.09
Free cash flow	0.17	0.30	0.49	0.63	0.74	0.84	1.11	1.48	1.76	2.15

[a] Numbers subject to rounding. SG&A, sales, general and administrative; EBIT, earnings before interest and taxes; EPS, earnings per share; EBIT (1 − T), earnings before interest but after taxes.

[b] 700,000 new share issued to purchase GGT's stock. GWM's shares outstanding increase from .4 million to 1.1 million. GGT's shares are retired. Unlike purchase accounting, historical data are restated to show continuity of interest of all shareholders in the combined companies. Therefore, historical EPS is recalculated using 1.1 million shares outstanding.

TABLE 14-16. Fifty Percent Stock–Fifty Percent Cash Purchase ($26 Million) GWM/GGT Combined Normalized Income, Balance Sheet, and Cash Flow Statements

	1993	1994	1995	1996	1997	1998	1999	2000	2001	2002
Income statement ($ millions)										
Net sales	3.80	5.85	9.30	11.30	12.20	13.10	14.70	18.50	22.90	29.00
Cost of goods sold	2.95	4.54	7.19	8.74	9.35	9.97	11.14	14.03	17.39	22.00
SG&A expense	0.19	0.29	0.47	0.57	0.61	0.66	0.74	0.93	1.15	1.45
Depreciation	0.11	0.18	0.28	0.34	0.37	0.39	0.44	0.56	0.69	0.87
Goodwill amortization							0.25	0.25	0.25	0.25
Synergy[b]							0.25	0.50	0.50	0.50
EBIT	0.55	0.85	1.37	1.66	1.87	2.08	2.38	3.24	3.93	4.93
Interest on debt	0.02	0.03	0.06	0.06	0.09	0.64	0.56	0.48	0.40	0.32
Earnings before taxes	0.52	0.81	1.30	1.59	1.79	1.44	1.82	2.76	3.53	4.61
Income taxes	0.21	0.33	0.52	0.64	0.71	0.58	0.73	1.10	1.41	1.84
Net income	0.31	0.49	0.78	0.95	1.07	0.87	1.09	1.66	2.12	2.77
EPS	NA	NA	NA	NA	NA	1.15	1.46	2.21	2.82	3.69
Balance sheet (year ending 12/31)										
Current assets	0.23	0.35	0.56	0.68	0.73	0.79	0.88	1.11	1.37	1.74
Current liabilities	0.18	0.27	0.43	0.52	0.56	0.60	0.67	0.84	1.04	1.32
Working capital	0.05	0.08	0.13	0.15	0.17	0.19	0.21	0.27	0.33	0.42
Goodwill[c]						10.00	9.75	9.50	9.25	9.00
Total assets[d]	1.67	2.56	4.06	4.94	5.29	30.54	31.75	32.97	33.05	34.13
Long-term debt[e]	0.25	0.35	0.65	0.65	0.90	6.40	5.60	4.80	4.00	3.20
Equity[f,g]	1.24	1.94	2.98	3.76	3.82	23.54	25.48	27.33	28.01	29.61
Shares	0.15	0.20	0.35	0.45	0.45	0.75	0.75	0.75	0.75	0.75
Free cash flow										
EBIT (1 − T)	0.33	0.51	0.82	0.99	1.12	1.25	1.43	1.94	2.36	2.96
Depreciation	0.11	0.18	0.28	0.34	0.37	0.39	0.44	0.56	0.69	0.87
Goodwill amortization							0.25	0.25	0.25	0.25
Capital expenditures	0.23	0.35	0.56	0.68	0.73	0.79	0.88	1.11	1.37	1.74
Change in working capital	0.04	0.03	0.05	0.03	0.02	0.02	0.03	0.05	0.06	0.09
Principal repayment						0.80	0.80	0.80	0.80	0.80
Free cash flow	0.17	0.30	0.49	0.63	0.74	0.04	0.41	0.78	1.06	1.45

a SG&A, sales, general and administrative; EBIT, earnings before interest and taxes; EPS, earnings per share; EBIT (1 − T), earnings before interest but after taxes.

b Acquisition expenses are assumed to net to zero as the gain on the sale of GGT's building/land offsets such expenses as costs of furnishing information to shareholders, consultant's fees, and other expenses associated with revaluation of assets (e.g., write-downs of inventories or receivables) and liabilities (e.g., under-funded pension plans).

c Costs associated with realizing synergy (e.g., training, severance, etc.) have already been deducted from estimated pretax profits from synergy. Receivables are reduced by reserves for doubtful accounts, inventories are valued at current selling prices, and P&E is valued at replacement cost. Intangibles are measured at appraised values. Accounts/notes payable and long-term debt are valued at PV using current interest rates. Other liabilities and accruals such as pension cost and litigation accruals, warranties, vacation pay and deferred compensation are valued at PV of amounts to be paid using current interest rates.

Calculation of goodwill:	Purchase price		$26.00
	Less: 100% interest in GGT (total stockholder equity)		1.68
	Equals: Cost (purchase price) over book value		$24.32
	Less: Portion of purchase price allocated to:		14.32
	Tangible assets (i.e., inventory and P&E)		
	Non-goodwill-related intangible assets such as customer list, distributor contracts, copyrights, capitalized software, patents, etc.		
	Equals: Goodwill		$10.00

d Total assets at Y/E 98 equal $5.68 million less $1.1 million book value of building sold plus $26 million purchase price.

e Borrow $6.2 million of the purchase price plus $1.0 in the combined debt of the two companies outstanding at the end of 1998. Principal repaid at a rate of $.8 million per year.

f GWM's shares increase by 350,000 from .4m in 1998 to .75m in 1998. GGT's .2m are retired. The 350,000 new GWM shares are valued at GWM's market price per share of $37.14 at the time of closing.

Offer price per share of GGT stock ($130/share or $130 × .2 million shares = $26 million purchase price)

50% cash		$65.00
50% in GWM stock ($65.00/$37.14 = 1.75 shares of GWM stock for each share of GGT stock)		65.00
Total		$130.00

g Equity equals total assets less current liabilities and long-term debt. Equity increases by $19.72 million. Equity increases by $19.72 million (i.e., $3.82 million to $23.54 million) between yearend 1997 and yearend 1998. Of this increase, $13 million is allocated to the par value of the new GWM shares and to paid in capital in excess of par. The remainder is allocated to retained earnings.

value of this offer to GGT was only $24 million because of the inclusion of the debt, which had a present value of $5.25 million as compared to a face value of $6.25 million.

While this offer had great appeal from GGT's perspective, the transaction would create a significant tax liability for GGT's shareholders. Dan knew that this could be a stumbling block. Although he did not mention it to Chang at this point, Dan was willing to share up to one half of the expected $5.4 million in synergy from the combination of the two companies with GGT stockholders. However, he would only play that card if he were forced to do so.

Chang made it clear that although Dan's proposal was "in the ballpark" on a pretax basis it was wholly inadequate on an after-tax basis. Much of GGT's stock was held by a relatively few shareholders that had a very low tax basis in the stock. Consequently, their tax liabilities from a taxable transaction would be substantial. Chang indicated that Dan would either have to raise the total price on a pretax basis to compensate for any tax liability or construct a purchase price that would be nontaxable to the GGT shareholders.

Dan agreed to review his options and get back to Chang. Dan knew that "in the ballpark" meant that Chang was looking for a higher price on both a pre- and after-tax basis. He and Perez would have to be creative to satisfy Chang's demands.

DEVELOPING COUNTER-OFFERS

Perez knew that at the end of 1997, GGT had 150,000 shares outstanding (with another 50,000 in unexercised "in-the-money" management stock options) and that at current share prices GWM would have to issue three and one-half shares of its stock for each share of GGT's stock (including a 33% control premium) if an all-stock transaction were to be undertaken. This meant that GWM would have to issue 700,000 shares (3.5 × 200,000), bringing GWM's total shares outstanding to 1.1 million shares. Under this scenario, EPS for the combined companies would remain below what GWM believes it could have achieved independently throughout the foreseeable future. This scenario was clearly unacceptable to GWM shareholders. Where would Dan find the money to sweeten the purchase price while still making it attractive to GWM shareholders? Dan looked to the projected cash flow from anticipated synergy.

Incremental after-tax cost savings and after-tax profits from product sales from combining the two companies were expected to be $500,000 annually. Because of implementation delays, the best Dan could hope for was about 50% of the projected synergy gains in 1999. From then on, he expected to realize 100% of the synergy. Dan could only raise the bid to GGT if he surrendered a significant portion of projected synergy. But should Dan take the risk that the projected synergy would be realized?

Dan was not a gambler by nature. This was a very difficult decision for him. He knew that Wall Street investors were very unforgiving about missed EPS forecasts. By betting that he would realize 50% of the synergy in 1999, he was giving himself little margin for error. It had been Perez's experience that this might be an optimistic assumption. Nonetheless, Dan wanted GGT. It would enable him to realize his dream. He decided to take the risk.

After recasting the offer, Durand and Chang hashed out an agreement whereby GWM would offer each GGT shareholder $130 for each share of stock they owned. The purchase price would consist of $65 in cash and $65 in GWM stock. The 3.5 exchange rate of GWM stock for each share of GGT stock was based on the prevailing price of GGT stock on October 19. This implied a 33% premium over GGT's current stock price. Moreover, the deal would be partially nontaxable for GGT's shareholders. The deal would be valued at $26 million. Chang was happy because he could present his board of directors and shareholders with a transaction that was partially nontaxable and that offered a substantial premium over the current share price. Durand was happy because he was able to move the deal along without raising the total purchase price to levels that were clearly unjustifiable.

The GWM management team celebrated. They were on the verge of closing the transaction. Dan knew the success of the transaction in the eyes of the GWM shareholder rested on his and his management team's ability to realize the projected synergy. He did not really know if this would be doable, but he was willing to savor the moment and worry about that later. There was much work remaining to be done.

Durand and Perez would have to devote more time to conducting due diligence and developing a financing plan. Now that he and Perez had resolved the major business issues, the lawyers could draft the necessary legal documents.

DUE DILIGENCE:
LOOKING FOR A NEEDLE IN A HAYSTACK

Durand was a "big picture" guy. He had little interest in details. He understood intuitively the need for thorough due diligence, but he did not have the temperament to actively participate in such a time-consuming and laborious process. "Andy, you take the lead in due diligence," he barked. "I will attend to the day-to-day operations of GWM that have been neglected during the negotiations." Perez reminded him that due diligence was extremely important in order confirm the "sources of value" assumed in the valuation, identify other potential sources of value, and to identify any "fatal flaws" that would reduce future cash flows. Perez urged him to participate at least in the interviews of senior GGT managers. Perez quipped "What we don't know can hurt us." Dan reluctantly agreed to participate.

Perez organized three teams to conduct due diligence: a financial team, a strategy team, and a legal team. He asked Dan to direct the strategy group while he would handle financial matters and the attorneys would handle the legal affairs. The strategy and operations teams' responsibilities were to review past business and operating plans to evaluate actual performance to plan (a measure of management competence), to evaluate the effectiveness of sales and marketing plans, and to assess customer relationships. In addition, the team was to evaluate the integrity of operations in terms of facility design and layout, software design and development capabilities, and project management skills. Much of this was to be accomplished through a series of personal interviews with midlevel and senior management.

The financial team would concern itself with the integrity of GGT's books (i.e., are they stated in a manner consistent with generally accepted accounting principles) and would conduct an inventory of assets to substantiate their existence and to evaluate their quality. The legal team would review corporate records, material contracts and obligations of the seller, as well as current and pending litigation and claims. Each team developed a question checklist to ensure that the due-diligence activity was comprehensive.

Following an extensive review of GGT's operations and books, several areas of concern as well as opportunities emerged. Revenue recognition appeared that it might become an issue. This has traditionally been a problem with software companies where products are frequently shipped to distributors on consignment or where service contracts and upgrades can stretch revenue out for years. GWM accountants noted that GGT might have been booking revenue too quickly. When disks were sent to retailers, allowance for the return of unsold disks from the retailers should have been taken into account. Booking revenue too early provides an opportunity to inflate current sales and earnings at the expense of future earnings.

Areas that provided an opportunity for GWM included in-process research and development (R&D) charges. These could be taken by GWM at the time of the acquisition. These charges represent the estimated value of R&D at the target company. Because it is still "in process," the research is not yet commercially viable. Since it may prove worthless, it can all be written off. But by separating the expenses from revenues that might be gained in the future from the R&D, future earnings can get a big boost. Moreover, some portion of goodwill arising from the purchase could be offset by the increasingly common practice of writing off in-process R&D charges.

As a result of its own internal due-diligence activity, GGT felt comfortable with the accuracy of the representations and warranties it was prepared to make in the agreement of purchase and sale. Because GWM was well known to Chang and his management team, the review of GWM's ability to finance the acquisition was limited.

OBTAINING FINANCING:
LEND ME THE MONEY, STUPID!

"It's a great deal, just lend me the money you dunderheads," thought Dan as he and Perez pitched the acquisition proposal to lenders. To raise money, Durand

and Perez had to go on the typical road show to make presentations to banks, insurance companies, pension funds, etc., to raise funding. They would need to borrow $6.2 million to complete the transaction. Their challenge was to convince bankers that the cash flow of the combined companies could meet debt service requirements. In the electronic publishing business, few companies had a sufficient amount of tangible assets to serve as collateral. Consequently, lenders focus on the amount and predictability of free cash flow (i.e., cash generated in excess of normal working capital, capital expenditures, and other fixed obligations).

The combined companies' total debt would reach $7.2 million at the end of 1998. This consisted of $6.2 million in debt to finance one-half of the cash portion of the purchase price and $1 million in preexisting debt on the books of the two companies.

After extended negotiations, a bank agreed to an unsecured loan to GWM of $6.2 million amortized over 8 years at 10% annum. The loan was subject to normal covenants, which restricted the amount GWM could borrow in the future, and the types of spending it could undertake without the bank's approval. Furthermore, GWM would have to ensure that certain financial ratios such as debt-to-total capital did not exceed some threshold and that earnings before interest and taxes (EBIT) as a multiple of interest expense did not fall below a contractually determined multiple. Durand felt the covenants would restrict his ability to manage GWM in the future as aggressively as he might want. This provided an incentive for him to use the majority of future free cash flow to accelerate repayment of the loan. He knew that the loss of some control and strategic flexibility was the price he would have to pay to complete the transaction.

CONSOLIDATING THE ORGANIZATIONS: COMMUNICATE! COMMUNICATE! COMMUNICATE!

On the surface, the cultures of the two companies seemed to be quite compatible. Although one could expect to lose some key employees to competitors following the acquisition, Durand felt that the situation was manageable if the proper planning was done ahead of time. He had to start by clearly communicating his own priorities to his subordinates and establishing an appropriate integration team infrastructure.

Prior to closing, he appointed Amy Pettibone, one of his best operating and project managers, to oversee the operational combination of the two firms once the transaction had been completed. Perez was disappointed that he did not get this assignment, but he understood that spearheading the activities prior to closing frequently took a different set of skills than those required during the integration of the two companies.

Amy had a demonstrated ability to set and communicate priorities, to size up people accurately, to make tough but fair decisions, to establish a timeline, and to stick to even the most ambitious schedule. These were managerial skills crucial to successfully integrating businesses where differences in corporate cultures could be significant. Meshing the software development teams of the two companies would be critical to ensuring that the productivity improvements and acceleration of new product introductions envisioned in GWM's acquisition strategy would be realized. Amy was assigned to head the strategy and operations team during due diligence in order to familiarize herself with the challenges of integration.

Based upon the information collected during due diligence, Pettibone and Perez worked closely to determine what near-term expenditures might be required to ensure that GGT's operations would continue without interruption during the next 12 to 24 months. This included the identification of key managers that were to be retained, key technologies, a review of vendors, and of customers. The pair also reviewed industry operating norms to determine other adjustments that might have to be made in the immediate future. These norms included executive compensation, billing procedures, product delivery times, quality metrics, and employee benefit and compensation packages.

GWM's management knew that the time to address these issues was prior to the closing. Issues such as severance expenditures, pension plan buyouts, employment contracts, capital expenditures that should have been made by GGT as part of the "normal course of business," and so on, should be addressed as part of the negotiation process. When appropriate, GWM would seek a reduction in the purchase price as at least a possible offset to these types of expenses that were not apparent when the preliminary indication of value for GGT was given in the letter of intent.

Key managers at GGT were offered 1-year employment contracts with GWM. Retaining key GGT managers was considered important enough that Durand instructed his attorneys to make the acceptance of employment contracts by designated employees a "condition" of closing.

Finally, a detailed communications plan was devised for use immediately following closing. The plan included press releases and announcements to employees (addressing questions about job security, compensation, and benefits), customers (providing assurances of an uninterrupted service), and vendors. Dan Durand would speak to GGT employees at their headquarters to answer questions and provide reasonable assurances of continuity of pay and benefits. The lawyers cautioned Dan about not making verbal commitments about job security, which could result in litigation at a later date. In addition, "talk tracks" were written for the sales force, who were instructed to contact all major customers directly on the day of the announcement of the acquisition of GGT.

Nothing was to be left to chance!

THE DREAM COMES TRUE

The stress level rose sharply doing the days just prior to closing. Heated negotiations were taking place around a number of issues that surfaced during due diligence. The results of the marketing consultant's report on GGT's customers indicated that several large GGT customers were unhappy with GGT's delivery performance and were likely to transfer their business to Mulitmedia. Several major customer and vendor contracts were either missing or unsigned. These customers and vendors were expected to take the change of ownership as an excuse to change payment terms. The reserve for doubtful accounts was also viewed to be inadequate. Finally, several hundred thousand dollars would have to be spent in normal maintenance and repair of the GGT operations. GGT management had postponed these expenditures when the prospect of sale came up.

The combination of lost revenue, uncollectable accounts, and deferred maintenance was estimated to have a present value of $750,000. Durand was concerned enough about what was uncovered during due diligence that he wanted Chang to agree to put 5% of the purchase in escrow for at least 1 year until all the surprises were known.

Despite several days of aggressive negotiating, Durand capitulated and agreed to absorb these additional costs without any reduction in purchase price. Durand believed that the $750,000 could be financed out of cash flow from operations during the next 5 years. Besides, he was tired. He wanted the negotiations to end so that he could get on with the business of growing the combined businesses.

In the final agreement of purchase and sale, the purchase price was stated as $26 million plus assumed debt of $150,000, which was on the books of GGT as of the closing date. From GWM's viewpoint the actual purchase price was $26,900,000 (i.e., $26 million plus assumed debt of $150,000 and retained expenses of $750,000).

Once the respective companies' boards of directors and shareholder approvals were received, customer and vendor contracts assigned, financing in place, and other closing conditions satisfied, the closing finally took place. For the first time in 6 months both parties could relax. Congratulations were in order for all participants. While Perez's stress level eased, Pettibone's escalated as she faced the challenges of meeting the demanding integration schedule.

Durand's role changed from that of the deal maker to that of the chief executive charged with meeting the expectations of his shareholders and Wall Street analysts. As the CEO of one of the major firms in his industry, Durand was trading one set of challenges for another. But he was happy; he was living his dream.

GEE WHIZ MEDIA CASE STUDY QUESTIONS

PART I: PLANNING

1. Describe the industry or market in which GWM competed in terms of the following: customers, suppliers, current competitors, potential entrants, and product substitutes. How should this information be used by GWM management to develop a long-term strategy?

2. Identify GWM's primary strengths and weaknesses as compared to the competition. How can this information be used to identify threats to and opportunities for GWM?

3. Identify the range of reasonable options available to GWM to grow its business. Discuss the key advantages and disadvantages of each option. Of the available options, which would you have selected and why?

4. GWM's acquisition plan identified key objectives, resource capability, the target industry, and appropriate tactics for completing an acquisition. Were all the objectives adequately quantified and did they have associated completion dates? What other key objectives and tactics might GWM have included? Discuss the importance of these additional objectives and tactics.

5. What were the key assumptions made in the GWM business plan used to justify the acquisition of GGT? Consider key assumptions, both explicit and implicit, with respect to the following areas: the market, financial performance, acquisition tactics, valuation, and integration.

PART II: IMPLEMENTATION

6. In valuing GGT, Perez used various valuation techniques including P/E ratios for publicly traded companies, liquidation value, price to book and price to revenue ratios, and PV calculations. What are the strengths and weaknesses of the alternative valuation approaches? What might you have done differently to value GGT? Are there any factors that might lead you to believe that Durand paid too much for GGT?

7. What factors did Durand consider in structuring the initial purchase price offer to Chang? What other factors should he have considered?

8. Suppose that another CD-ROM media company is sold during the negotiations between GWM and GGT and that the P/E was 40 (vs. 33 for GGT). How would this information affect negotiations? What would Chang's likely position be? How would Durand counter Chang's arguments? Assuming Durand still wanted to complete the transaction, how might he have restructured the purchase price to make it acceptable to both firms' shareholders?

9. What additional information would you like to have to make a more informed valuation of GGT?

10. Using Table 14-7 as an example and showing your work on a spreadsheet, calculate the standalone value of GGT using the following assumptions applied to 1997 in Table 14-7 as the base year:
   a. Sales grow at 30% per year for the 5-year period from 1998 through 2002 and 10% thereafter.
   b. Cost of sales and SG&A equal 70% and 10% of sales, respectively.
   c. Depreciation expense equals 3% of sales.
   d. GGT has no debt. (Note: Remove all interest and debt in Table 14-7 from 1997.)
   e. The marginal tax rate is 40%.
   f. Current assets and liabilities equal 8% and 5% of sales, respectively.
   g. Capital expenditures equal 5% of sales.
   h. Shares outstanding are constant at 300,000.

   i. Total assets are equal to 50% of sales.

   j. Equity equals total assets − current liabilities

   k. The risk-free rate of return is 5%, the β is 1.5 (from 1998 through 2002 and 1.25 thereafter), and the spread between the return on stocks and the risk-free rate is 5.5%.

Solutions to these questions are found in the Appendix at the back of this book.

APPENDIX

SOLUTIONS TO CHAPTER BUSINESS CASE STUDY DISCUSSION QUESTIONS

CASE STUDY 1-5.
AMERICA ONLINE ACQUIRES TIME WARNER

1. *What were the primary motives for this transaction? How would you categorize them in terms of the historical motives for mergers and acquisitions discussed in this chapter?*

American Online (AOL) is buying access to branded products, a huge potential subscriber base, and broadband technology. The new company will be able to deliver various branded content to a diverse set of audiences using high-speed transmission channels (e.g., cable).

This transaction reflects many of the traditional motives for combining businesses:

    a. *Improved operating efficiency resulting from both economies of scale and scope.* With respect to so-called back office operations, the merging of data, call centers, and other support operations will enable the new company to sustain the same or a larger volume of subscribers with lower overall fixed expenses. Time Warner will also be able to save a considerable amount of expenditures on information technology by sharing AOL's current online information infrastructure and network to support the design, development, and operation of web sites for its various businesses. Advertising and promotion spending should be more efficient, because both AOL and Time Warner can promote their services to the other's subscribers at minimal additional cost.

    b. *Diversification.* From AOL's viewpoint, it is integrating down the value chain by acquiring a company that produces original, branded content in the form of magazines, music, and films. By owning this content, AOL will be able to distribute it without having to incur licensing fees.

    c. *Changing technology.* At least two profound changes in technology are promoting these types of business combinations. First, the trend toward the use of digital rather than analog technology is causing many media and entertainment firms to look to the Internet as a highly efficient way to market and distribute their products. Time Warner had for several years been trying to develop an online strategy with limited success. AOL represented an unusual opportunity to "leap frog" the competition. Second, the market for online services is clearly shifting away from current dial-up access to high-speed transmission. AOL had been attempting to lobby the government to require that access to the Internet via cable systems be open to the subscribers of any Internet service provider (ISP). As a contingency plan if it could not get "open access" on cable systems, it was developing alliances with local phone companies to utilize their high-speed digital subscriber line (DSL) service. By gaining access to Time Warner's cable network enhanced to carry voice, video, and data, AOL will be able to improve both upload or access and download speeds for its subscribers. AOL has indicated that subscription to this broadband service will be priced at a premium to regular dial-up subscriptions.

    d. *Hubris.* AOL was willing to pay a 71% premium over Time Warner's current share price to gain control. This premium is very high by historical standards and seems to assume that the challenges inherent in making this merger work can be overcome. The overarching implicit assumption is that somehow the infusion of new management into Time Warner can result in the conversion of what is essentially a traditional media company into an Internet powerhouse. Not only did this result in the most expensive merger up to that time, but it also created the most unique and the biggest media and entertainment company in the world. Investor confusion following the announcement underscored the difficulty in valuing something that had never been done before.

    e. *A favorable regulatory environment.* Growth on the Internet has been fostered by the lack of government regulation. The Federal Communication Commission (FCC) has ruled that ISPs are not subject to local phone company access charges, e-commerce transactions are not subject to tax, and restrictions on the use of personal information have been limited.

  2. Although the AOL–Time Warner deal is referred to as an acquisition in the case, why is it technically more correct to refer to it as a consolidation? Explain your answer.

  A consolidation refers to two or more businesses combining to form a third company. The newly formed company assumes all the assets and liabilities of both companies. Shareholders in both companies exchange their shares for shares in the new company.

3. *Would you classify this business combination as a horizontal, vertical, or conglomerate transaction? Explain your answer.*

If one defines the industry broadly as media and entertainment, this transaction could be described as a vertical transaction in which AOL is backward integrating along the value chain to gain access to Time Warner's proprietary content and broadband technology. However, a case could be made that it also has many of the characteristics of a conglomerate. If industries are defined more narrowly as magazine and book publishing, cable TV, film production, and music recording, the new company could be viewed as a conglomerate.

4. *What are some of the reasons AOL Time Warner may fail to satisfy investor expectations?*

Although AOL has control of the new company in terms of ownership, the extent to which they can exert control in practice may be quite different. AOL could become a captive of the more ponderous Time Warner empire and its 82,000 employees. Time Warner's management style and largely independent culture, as evidenced by their limited success in leveraging the assets of Time and Warner Communications following their 1990 merger, could rob AOL of its customary speed, flexibility, and entrepreneurial spirit. The key to the success of the new companies will be how quickly they will be able to get new web applications involving Time Warner content up and operating.

Decision making may slow to a halt if top management cannot cooperate. Roles and responsibilities at the top were ill defined in order to make the combination acceptable to senior management at both firms. It will take time for the managers with the dominant skills and personalities to more clearly define their roles in the new company.

To their credit, AOL has a good track record in acquiring and integrating companies in a rapidly changing environment. However, it has never before attempted to absorb a company of this size and complexity. If earnings growth slows from historical rates, it is unlikely that investors will assign the excessively high price-to-earnings (P/E) ratios characteristic of Internet firms to the newly formed company.

5. *What would be an appropriate arbitrage strategy for this all-stock transaction?*

Arbitrageurs make a profit on the difference between a deal's offer price and the current price of the target's stock. Following a merger announcement, the target's stock price normally rises, but not to the offer price reflecting the risk that the transaction will not be consummated. The difference between the offer price and the target's current stock price is called a discount or spread. In a cash transaction, the arb can lock in this spread by simply buying the target's stock. In a share-for-share exchange, the arb protects or hedges against the possibility that the acquirer's stock might decline by selling the acquirer's stock short. In the short sale, the arb instructs her broker to sell the acquirer's shares at a specific price. The broker loans the arb the shares and obtains the stock from its own inventory or borrows it from a customer's margin account or from another broker. If the acquirer's stock declines in price, the short seller can buy it back at the lower price and make a profit; if the stock increases, the short seller incurs a loss.

CASE STUDY 2-8.
EXXON AND MOBIL MERGER

1. *How does the Federal Trade Commission (FTC) define market share?*

The market is generally defined by the regulators as a product or group of products offered in a specific geographic area. Market participants are those currently producing and selling these products in this geographic area as well as potential entrants. Regulators calculate market shares for all firms identified as market participants based on total sales or capacity currently devoted to the relevant markets. In addition, the market share estimates include capacity that is likely to be diverted to this market in response to a small, but significant and sustainable, increase in price.

2. *Why might it be important to distinguish between a global and a regional oil and gas market?*

The value chain for a fully integrated oil and gas company consists of the following segments: exploration, production, transmission, refining, and distribution. Oil and gas exploration and production is largely a global market subject to substantial competition from numerous competitors. In contrast, the refining and distribution segments of the business can be highly concentrated in the hands of a few oil and gas companies. Such concentration may give the oil and gas company substantial pricing power within a specific region for various types of refined products by owning substantially all of the refining capacity, distribution points, such as gas stations, or both.

3. *Why are the Exxon and Mobil executives emphasizing efficiencies as a justification for this merger?*

Current antitrust guidelines recognize that the efficiencies associated with a business combination may offset the potential anticompetitive effects of increased concentration. The guidelines call for an examination of the net effects of the proposed combination. Proving that the presumed efficiencies justify the merger is difficult, because most synergies will not be realized for a number of years. It is therefore difficult to measure their true impact.

4. *Should the size of the combined companies be an important consideration in the regulators' analysis of the proposed merger?*

Size alone should not be a criterion unless it results in anticompetitive practices. Because of the increasing cost of oil and gas exploration and development worldwide, increasing size to realize economies of scale is becoming more important if increasingly scarce world energy resources are to be recovered.

5. *How do the divestitures address perceived anticompetitive problems?*

Increased concentration can be reduced by requiring one or both of the parties to the merger to sell assets such as refineries or gas stations to competing firms.

Such actions will tend to restore competition within a heavily concentrated market.

CASE STUDY 3-2.
TYCO SAVES AMP FROM ALLIED SIGNAL

1. *What types of takeover tactics did AlliedSignal employ?*

AlliedSignal reinforced its bear hug of AMP with its public announcement of its intent to initiate a tender offer for all of AMP. The move was designed to put pressure on the AMP board and management. Following AMP's rebuff, Allied-Signal initiated a "creeping" tender offer for a portion of AMP's outstanding shares. AlliedSignal also employed a consent solicitation to gain effective control of the AMP board through "packing" the board with sympathetic representatives and to neutralize the AMP rights agreement (poison pill) without having to call a special AMP shareholders' meeting. AlliedSignal also used litigation to attempt to thwart AMP's efforts to prevent AlliedSignal from voting its shares.

2. *What steps did AlliedSignal take to satisfy federal securities laws?*

As required by federal securities laws, AlliedSignal informed the AMP board of its intentions to acquire AMP through a hostile tender offer and to file the appropriate schedules with the Securities Exchange Commission (SEC). AlliedSignal proceeded to file the necessary disclosure documents and consent solicitation materials to be used to obtain consents from AMP shareholders with respect to a series of proposals with the SEC.

3. *What antitakeover defenses were in place at AMP prior to AlliedSignal's offer?*

The AMP rights agreement, a poison pill, was its primary defense in place before the bid.

4. *How did the AMP board use the AMP rights agreement to encourage AMP shareholders to vote against AlliedSignal's proposals?*

If the AMP board lost majority control following the purchase of more than 20% of AMP's stock by a single individual or entity, the rights could not be redeemed.

5. *What options did AlliedSignal have to neutralize or circumvent AMP's use of the rights agreement?*

AlliedSignal chose to reduce the number of shares it would purchase through its partial tender offer to ensure that it stayed below the 20% ownership threshold. However, AlliedSignal could have increased its offer price to put more pressure on the AMP board to accept its unsolicited bid.

6. *After announcing it had purchased 20 million AMP shares at $44.50, why did AlliedSignal indicate that it would reduce the price paid in any further offers it might make?*

AlliedSignal was trying to frighten AMP shareholders into tendering their shares at $44.50. This may have been a prelude to a tender offer for more shares at a later date.

7. *What other takeover defenses did AMP employ in its attempt to thwart AlliedSignal?*

Initially, AMP employed the "just say no" defense to buy time to add more defenses. The board cleverly used the AMP rights plan to discourage AlliedSignal from immediately moving ahead with its proposed $10 billion tender offer for all of AMP's shares. The board initiated a stock buyback plan for 30 million shares at $55.00. This was intended to reduce the number of shares available for purchase by AlliedSignal and to communicate to the market what AMP thought its shares were worth. In addition, AMP set up an employee stock ownership plan (ESOP) enabling it to place some number of AMP shares in "friendly" hands. Finally, AMP used litigation to attempt to block AlliedSignal from voting its shares. Note that as part of the merger agreement with Tyco, these defenses were deactivated. The self-tender and ESOP were terminated and the rights plan amended so that it would not apply to the merger with Tyco.

8. *How did both AMP and AlliedSignal use litigation in this takeover battle?*

AMP used Pennsylvania antitakeover statutes to try to block Allied Signal's ability to vote its shares and to prevent AlliedSignal from taking control of the AMP board through its consent solicitation. Both sides used lawsuits to increase the cost of the acquisition and to wear down their opponents.

9. *Should state laws be used to protect companies from hostile takeovers?*

The empirical evidence suggests that target shareholders benefit greatly from a hostile takeover, whereas the acquirer's shareholders may experience modest negative returns. Some may argue that the gains to the target shareholders are more than offset by the damage to other constituent groups including employees, communities, customers, and suppliers.

10. *Was AMP's board and management acting to protect their own positions (i.e., the management entrenchment hypothesis) or in the best interests of the shareholders (i.e., the shareholder interests hypothesis)?*

As a result of their resistance, AMP's Board was able to secure for its shareholders an additional 15% premium to the original AlliedSignal offer.

CASE STUDY 4-3.
CONSOLIDATION IN THE GLOBAL PHARMACEUTICAL
INDUSTRY CONTINUES: THE GLAXO WELLCOME
AND SMITHKLINE BEECHAM EXAMPLE

1. *What drove change in the pharmaceutical industry in the late 1990s?*

Profit margin pressures continued to mount on drug companies due to the proliferation of managed care, reductions in the number of "me-too" drugs, and new medical breakthroughs in human genome research. The cost of supporting the drug trials necessary to bring new drugs to market based on this research continued to grow. The potential for government intervention further complicated efforts to increase selling prices. Finally, the loss of patent protection for many "blockbuster" drugs and the dearth of such drugs in the pipeline encouraged the remaining independent companies to rethink their strategies of staying independent.

2. *In your judgment, what are the likely strategic business plan objectives of the major pharmaceutical companies and why are they important?*

Major strategic objectives are likely to include the following: (1) gaining access to current patents for drugs that are already generating substantial cash flow or show significant promise of doing so; (2) gaining access to proprietary research pertaining to drugs currently under development; (3) increasing returns on R&D spending; (4) obtaining access to new distribution channels for current and new products; and (5) reducing the overall cost of doing business.

3. *What are the alternatives to merger's available to the major pharmaceutical companies? What are the advantages and disadvantages of each alternative?*

Drug companies could enter joint ventures (JVs) or partnerships or make minority investments in research oriented biotechnology companies. Although such options are generally less costly, the degree of control is also substantially less. It may be possible to gain access to new distribution channels through partnering, but such arrangements do not address the immediate needs of companies whose backlog of new drugs is limited. Finally, partnering rarely provides the degree of cost savings that can be realized through the consolidation of overlapping portions of merged companies.

4. *How would you classify the typical drug company's strategy in the 1970s and 1980s: cost leadership, differentiation, focus, or hybrid? Explain your answer. How have their strategies changed in recent years?*

Historically, drug companies tended to pursue differentiation strategies that were heavily dependent on the ability of their sales forces to convince physicians, hospitals, and pharmacies to buy their drugs. Although "me-too" drugs were heavily promoted, the sales force had to be able to convince the customers that there were legitimate reasons to buy them. Today, drug companies seem to be moving toward hybrid strategies involving a combination of differentiation and cost leadership in their targeted markets. Margin pressure continues to force companies to look for ways to reduce operating expenses and to improve productivity.

5. *What do you think was the major motivating factor behind the Glaxo SmithKline merger and why was it so important?*

The primary factor seems to be the desire to achieve sufficient scale to support the necessary R&D to commercialize new products based on advances made in gene sequencing. While cost savings continue to be important, it is likely to have played a secondary consideration. The estimated annual cost savings of $1.7 billion after 3 years represents less than 5% of the combined companies' total cost base.

CASE STUDY 5-5.
MATTEL ACQUIRES THE LEARNING COMPANY

1. *Why was Mattel interested in diversification?*

With more than one-third of its revenue coming from a mature product like Barbie, Mattel was hoping to take advantage of the children's software market that was growing at 20% per year, about four times the growth rate of the traditional toy market.

2. *What alternatives to acquisition could Mattel have considered? Discuss the pros and cons of each alternative?*

Mattel could have considered building the capability internally by leveraging its small, but growing software division. Alternatively, Mattel could have considered creating a joint venture corporation with a leading "edutainment" software company. Both parties would contribute certain assets. Mattel could contribute certain of its most recognized brand name products and the software company could contribute its technical expertise. Mattel could also have considered licensing certain software products from other companies for distribution under its own brand or taking minority positions in software companies that would develop products for distribution by Mattel.

Developing the capability internally may be a high-risk proposition, since given its limited technical resources Mattel may have missed the opportunity to participate in the accelerating market for interactive children's toys. A joint venture or partnering arrangement may not provide the control Mattel may want in order to market globally and to produce only products that would not compete directly with Mattel's current products. Licenses and minority investments both suffer from limited control and may be difficult to manage.

3. *How might the Internet affect the toy industry? What potential conflicts with customers might be created?*

As illustrated by eToy's success, the Internet poses an interesting new distribution channel for Mattel. However, efforts to exploit this new technology put Mattel in direct competition with its customers who are already online.

4. *What are the primary barriers to entering the toy industry?*

Barriers to entry include the well-established distribution channels of the major manufacturers, based on long-standing relationships with retailers such as Wal-Mart and Toys 'R' Us. Companies like Mattel and Hasbro have substantial brand recognition created over the years by spending tens of millions of advertising dollars. Furthermore, brand names are protected by patents and proprietary knowledge. Finally, the top manufacturers have licensing arrangements granting them the exclusive right to market toys based on products provided by the major entertainment companies.

5. *What could Mattel have done to protect itself against risks uncovered during due diligence?*

Mattel could have protected itself by shifting some of the risk to The Learning Company (TLC). This could have been achieved by making part of the purchase price contingent on TLC hitting certain future performance targets defined in terms of profits or revenue. Alternatively, Mattel could have insisted that a portion of the purchase price be put into an escrow account until the full extent of the problems uncovered during due diligence were understood.

CASE STUDY 6-7.
DAIMLER ACQUIRES CHRYSLER—ANATOMY OF
A CROSS-BORDER TRANSACTION

1. *Identify ways in which the merger combined companies with complementary skills and resources.*

Germany's world-renowned reputation in engineering could be employed to raise the overall quality of Chrysler products, while Chrysler's project management skills could be used to shorten the new product introduction cycle. In addition, Daimler's distribution network in Europe could provide access to the European market for Chrysler products. Chrysler dealerships could be used to service Daimler cars in the United States. Finally, greater access to capital markets and the combined operating cash flow of the two companies could give Daimler-Chrysler the financial strength to build assembly plants and develop distribution networks in Asia.

2. *What are the major cultural differences between Daimler and Chrysler?*

Daimler is largely a conglomerate in which management is decentralized. In contrast, Chrysler's management and decision-making process tended to be highly centralized. Daimler, like many European companies, tended to be very detail oriented. The reference to lengthy meetings and big reports suggests a very cumbersome and bureaucratic decision-making process. The replacement of key Chrysler managers by Daimler managers may have left many Chrysler managers feeling alienated. The small number of former Chrysler managers reporting directly to the top may have added to a sense of powerlessness. Differences in customs and habits may also have contributed to poor communications. All of these factors tended to reduce loyalty by Chrysler managers to the newly created corporation.

3. *What were the principal risks to the merger?*

The risks to the merger included the loss of key Chrysler operating managers, who were enriched by the merger, and a loss of corporate continuity. Moreover, the lengthy time period required to integrate manufacturing operations and purchasing makes the recovery of the premium paid for Chrysler that much more difficult.

4. *Why might it take so long to integrate manufacturing operations and certain functions such as purchasing?*

Changing manufacturing operations requires changing union work rules, which are set by contract. Such rules could only be renegotiated when current contracts covering the plants expire. Before any significant changes could be made, Daimler-Chrysler would have to inventory/catalogue equipment and procedures by plant, benchmark performance, identify best practices, and convince workers at the plant level to change their methods. Purchasing represented both a significant opportunity and major challenge for Daimler-Chrysler. Spending on purchased materials for automotive companies represents a major portion of their total cost of production. Therefore, opportunities to buy in bulk offer substantial cost savings. However, integrating purchasing, which is often dispersed across various countries or even plants, could only be done as contracts with existing vendors expire. In addition, much purchasing is done at the plant level where purchasing agents are accustomed to significant autonomy.

CASE STUDY 7-2.
@HOME AND EXCITE FORM EXCITE@HOME

1. *Did @Home overpay for Excite?*

To answer the question of whether @Home overpaid, it is necessary to estimate the value of synergy, add this estimate to the market value of Excite, and compare the resulting sum to the $6.7 billion purchase price. Note that free cash flow to the firm in the first full year of operation following the merger equals ($500 − $50) × (1 − .4) × 340,000 or $91.8 million.

Using the variable growth model, we can calculate the present value of potential synergy (P_0) as follows:

Year	FCFF ($millions)	Present value interest factor	Present value ($millions)
1	91.8	.83	76.2
2	105.6	.69	73.3
3	121.4	.58	70.4
4	139.6	.48	67.0
5	160.6	.40	64.2
6	184.6	.33	61.8
7	212.3	.28	59.4
8	244.2	.23	56.2
9	280.8	.19	53.4
10	322.9	.16	51.7
			$633.6

$$\text{Terminal value} = \frac{\$322.9 \times (1.05)/(.10 - .05)}{(1.20)^{10}} = \frac{\$6,780.90}{6.19} = \$1,095.5$$

$$P_0 = \$633.6 + \$1,095.5 = \$1,729.1$$

Maximum purchase price for Excite (including present value of synergy):

$$\$1,729.1 + \$3,500.0 = \$5,229.1 \text{ (vs. \$6,700.0)}$$

2. *What other assumptions might you consider?*

Other sources of profitable revenue could be considered, such as selling additional products and services to the Excite customer base and revenue from selling advertising space on the site.

3. *What are the limitations of the valuation methodology employed in this case?*

The valuation is heavily dependent on the choice of assumptions concerning growth rates during the high-growth and stable growth periods and the discount rates for each period. Almost two-thirds of the total valuation is dependent on the estimation of the residual value or the value of cash flows beyond the tenth year, which is likely to be less accurate than estimates of cash flows during the earlier years of the forecast period.

4. *What alternative valuation techniques could you utilize?*

The analyst could examine recent transactions of similar companies or consider market valuations of similar companies in the same industry. The latter would have to be adjusted to reflect premiums paid for these types of companies.

CASE STUDY 8-2.
MAINTAINING SHAREHOLDER VALUE
IN A STOCK-FOR-STOCK EXCHANGE

1. *What is the share exchange ratio (SER) of Company B's stock in terms of Company A's stock?*

Exchange ratio of Company B's stock in terms of Company A's stock is

$$50/100 = 1/2$$

2. *What is the dollar value of A's shares exchanged for 100 shares of B's stock?*

The dollar value of A's shares exchanged for 100 shares of B's stock is $5,000 (i.e., 50×100 shares).

3. *What is the new SER?*

The new exchange ratio would be $50/75 = 2/3$.

4. *What is the dollar value of A's shares received by a holder of 100 shares of B's stock?*

The dollar value of A's shares received by a holder of 100 shares of B's stock would still be $5,000 (i.e., 66.66 shares of A $\times$ $75).

CASE STUDY 9-2.
VALUING A PRIVATELY HELD COMPANY

Note: To estimate the cost of capital (COC) for a leveraged private firm, it is necessary to calculate the firm's leveraged β. This requires an estimate of the firm's unleveraged β, which can be obtained by estimating the unleveraged β for similar firms in the same industry. Also, the value of debt and equity in calculating the cost of capital should be expressed as market rather than book values.

Calculating cost of equity (COE) and COC:

1. Unlevered β for publicly traded firms in the same industry $= 2.00/(1 + .6 \times .4) = 1.61$, where 2.00 is the levered β, .6 is (1-tax rate), and .4 is the average debt ratio for firms in this industry.

2. Debt/Equity ratio for the private firm $= 5/(2 \times 4) = .625$ where 5, 4, and 2 are the private firm's debt, book value of equity, and the ratio of market value to book value for similar firms.

3. Levered beta for the private firm $= 1.61 \times (1 + .6 \times .625) = 2.21$.
4. Cost of equity for the private firm $= 6 + 2.21 \times 5.5 = 18.16$.
5. After-tax cost of debt $= .10 \times (1 - .4) = 6.0$.
6. COC for the private firm $= 18.16 \times \frac{2 \times 4}{2 \times 4 + 5} + 6.00 \times \frac{5}{2 \times 4 + 5}$.

$$= 18.16 \times 615 + 6.00 \times 385$$
$$= 13.48$$

Valuing the business using the FCFF model

Year	1	2	3	4	5	6
EBIT (EBIT grows at 15% for the first 5 years and 5% thereafter).	$2.30	$2.65	$3.04	$3.50	$4.02	$4.22
EBIT (1 − tax rate)	$1.38	$1.59	$1.82	$2.10	$2.41	$2.53
Less						
(Cap. expenditures-depreciation) grows at same 15% annual rate as revenue for 5 years and are offsetting thereafter)	$ .115	$ .132	$ .152	$ .175	$ .201	$0.00
Equals						
Free cash flow to the firm (FCFF)	$1.26	$1.46	$1.67	$1.93	$2.21	$2.53

Terminal value $= \$2.53/(.1348 - .05) = \$29.83$

$$\text{Present Value of FCFF} = \frac{\$2.30}{1.1348} + \frac{\$2.65}{1.1348^2} + \frac{\$3.04}{1.1348^3} + \frac{\$3.50}{1.1348^4}$$
$$+ \frac{\$4.02}{1.1348^5} + \frac{\$29.83}{1.1348^5}$$
$$= \$2.03 + \$2.06 + \$2.08 + \$2.11 + \$2.14 + \$15.85$$
$$= \$26.27$$

Value of equity $= \$26.27$ (MV of the firm) $- \$5$ (MV of debt) $= \$21.27$

CASE STUDY 10-1.
VODAFONE ACQUIRES AIRTOUCH

1. *Did the AirTouch Board make the right decision? Why or why not?*

Only time will tell which stock, Vodafone or Bell Atlantic's, will outperform the other. Morgan Stanley concluded that the Vodafone offer was likely to have the higher overall value at the time of the closing. AirTouch shareholders could lock in this higher value if they choose to sell the shares of Vodafone they receive for each share of AirTouch. In addition, the anticipated earnings dilution through 2002 would probably cause the gap between the values of Vodafone's and Bell Atlantic's offers to widen. Intangible arguments for accepting the Vodafone proposal include the probability that Vodafone had the more compatible corporate culture. Both companies shared the same vision and appear to be relatively decentralized in terms of management style. In contrast, Bell Atlantic is still emerging from the highly regulated environment of the landline carriers.

2. *How valid are the reasons for the proposed merger?*

The justification for the merger rests more on faith in the continued expansion of the wireless communication market than on factual evidence. To date, it remains unclear how much business travelers and travel-oriented consumers are willing to pay for wireless communication services. Establishing a global wireless network with global roaming capability is going to be a very expensive proposition. In late 1999, Iridium LLC, a satellite phone venture backed by Motorola, which has an 18% stake in the venture, went into default on an $800 million syndicated loan. Default on this loan automatically placed Iridium in violation of loan covenants on $700 million in other loans. At the same time, Chase Manhattan Bank demanded that Motorola guarantee at least $300 million of the $800 million syndicated loan. On August 13, 1999, Iridium filed for protection under Chapter 11 of the U.S. Bankruptcy Code because Motorola and Iridium's creditors could not agree on a plan for repaying Iridium's debt. While this will give Iridium some breathing space, it does not address its key problems, a lack of paying customers. As of August 13, Iridium had signed 20,000 of the 500,000 new customers it had projected for 1999. In March 2000, Iridium filed for Chapter 7 liquidation.

3. *What are the potential risk factors related to the merger?*

Cost savings may not be realized. Even if they are, they represent only about 6% of the total purchase price. Because of the absence of a collar, the AirTouch shareholders could be hurt if Vodafone ADSs decline in value before the closing date. Projected earnings may not be realized as a possible global recession slows the growth of international travel. Achieving global coverage may be more expensive than anticipated. Increased competition from other vendors may cause reductions in the price per minute of usage, which more than offset the projected increase in the number of minutes used.

4. *Why did the merger happen so quickly?*

Once a target announces that it has received an offer from a legitimate potential acquirer, the target has been "put into play." Other potential suitors may make bids for the target, boosting the potential purchase price in an auction-like environment. The key is for the initial bidder to move quickly enough and to make the proposed price attractive enough to preclude others from making a bid.

5. *Why was Bell Atlantic interested in a pooling-of-interest accounting treatment? Why was this a concern about Bell Atlantic's purchase price?*

The Bell proposal was already dilutive. Purchase accounting would have created substantial annual goodwill charges, which would have exacerbated this situation. AirTouch's Board was concerned about this closing condition, because its failure to qualify for pooling of interests would have removed Bell from the bidding. The remaining bidder(s) could have found some pretext to lower their offering prices.

6. *The Vodafone merger will be treated as a purchase of assets under GAAP and create $3.4 billion in annual goodwill expenses. Why might the merger have been accounted for financial reporting purposes using the purchase method of accounting?*

The purchase method improves after-tax cash flow by allowing the acquiring corporation to write off the excess of the fair market value of acquired assets over their book values.

7. *Is this merger likely to be tax-free, partially tax free, or taxable?*

The merger is partially taxable. Cash received will be taxed at the capital gains tax rate because it does not exceed the AirTouch shareholder cost basis in the stock.

8. *What are some of the challenges the two companies are likely to face while integrating the businesses?*

Although the two companies appear to have been managed somewhat similarly in the past and both seem somewhat entrepreneurial, they are likely to suffer the same challenges others experience in international mergers. This includes diminished control over widely dispersed operations, a lack of loyalty or commitment to the parent company, jealousies created by differences in salary and benefit levels, lack of a shared vision in remote operations, and increasingly large percentages of profits whipsawed by currency fluctuations. More specifically, most of the anticipated $3.5 billion in cost savings is expected from economies realized through bulk purchases. This presumes that most of the purchasing can be coordinated sufficiently to realize this objective. This is frequently extraordinarily difficult to implement in highly decentralized operations.

9. *How would the collar protect AirTouch shareholders from a decline in Bell Atlantic's stock?*

The collar guarantees the price of Bell Atlantic stock for the AirTouch shareholders since 48×1.6683 and 52×1.54 both equal $80.08.

CASE STUDY 11-2.
EVALUATING A LEVERAGED BUYOUT OPPORTUNITY

Based on the information given in the case, will the buyout generate sufficient cash to cover interest and principal payments and to provide an appropriate return to the LBO firm's equity investors?

1. Calculate free cash flow to equity holders (FCFE) and to the firm (FCFF).

Year	1	2	3	4	5	Terminal year
Revenues	$3,000,000	$3,450,000	$3,967,500	$4,562,625	$5,247,019	$5,509,370
− Expenses	$2,100,000	$2,415,000	$2,777,250	$3,193,834	$3,672,913	$3,856,559
− Depreciation	$ 200,000	$ 230,000	$ 264,000	$ 304,175	$ 349,801	$ 367,291
= EBIT	$ 700,000	$ 805,000	$ 925,750	$1,064,616	$1,224,305	$1,285,520

− Interest	$ 550,000	$ 500,000	$ 450,000	$ 400,000	$ 350,000	$ 300,000
= Taxable income	$ 150,000	$ 305,000	$ 475,750	$ 664,616	$ 874,305	$ 985,520
− Tax	$ 60,000	$ 122,000	$ 190,300	$ 265,846	$ 349,722	$ 394,208
= Net income	$ 90,000	$ 183,000	$ 285,450	$ 398,770	$ 524,583	$ 591,312
+ Depreciation	$ 200,000	$ 230,000	$ 264,500	$ 304,175	$ 349,801	$ 367,291
− Capital Expenditures	$ 250,000	$ 287,500	$ 330,625	$ 380,219	$ 437,252	$ 459,114
− Chg. WC	$ 150,000	$ 172,500	$ 198,375	$ 228,131	$ 262,350	$ 275,468
− Principal Repaid	$ 500,000	$ 500,000	$ 500,000	$ 500,000	$ 500,000	$ 0
= FCFE	$ (610,000)	$ (547,000)	$ (479,050)	$ (405,405)	$ (325,218)	$ 224,021
+ Interest × (1 − t)	$ 330,000	$ 300,000	$ 270,000	$ 240,000	$ 210,000	$ 180,000
+ Principal Repaid	$ 500,000	$ 500,000	$ 500,000	$ 500,000	$ 500,000	$ 0
= FCFF	$ 220,000	$ 253,000	$ 290,950	$ 334,595	$ 384,782	$ 404,021

2. *Calculate the weighted average cost of capital (WACC) using a target debt to equity ratio of 1:1.*

Equity (year/end)	$1,090,000	$1,273,000	$1,558,450	$1,957,220	$2,481,803	$3,073,115
Debt (Y/E)	$5,000,000	$4,500,000	$4,000,000	$3,500,000	$3,000,000	$2,500,000
D/E ratio	4.59	3.54	2.57	1.79	1.21	.81
Beta	3.00	2.37	1.79	1.32	.97	.73
Cost of equity	23.50%	20.04%	16.85%	14.27%	12.35%	10.15%
WACC	14.75%	13.02%	11.43%	10.14%	9.18%	8.08%

Note the following:

1. Equity at the end of year 1 = net income + Equity at the end of year 0.
   $$= \$90,000 + \$1,000,000$$
   $$= \$1,090,000.$$

2. β_L in year 2: $\beta_{L2} - \beta_{L1} = (1 - t) \times (D_2/E_2 - D_1/E_1)$ and
   $$\beta_{L2} = (1 - t) \times (D_2/E_2 - D_1/E_1) + \beta_{L1}$$
   $$= (.6) \times (-1.05) + 3.00 = 2.37$$

3. COE in year 2: $COE_2 - COE_1 = (B_{L2} - B_{L1}) \times 5.5$ and
   $$COE_2 = (B_{L2} - B_{L1}) \times 5.5 + COE_1$$
   $$= (2.37 - 3.00) \times 5.5 + 23.50$$
   $$= 20.04\%$$

4. After-tax interest cost on debt is $10\% \times (1 - t) = 6\%$

3. Calculate terminal values:
   a. Terminal Value of Equity = $\$224,021/(.1015 - .05) = \$4,349,922$
   b. Terminal Value of Firm = Terminal Value of Equity
      + Outstanding Debt
      $$= \$4,349,922 + \$2,500,000$$
      $$= \$6,849,922$$

4. Calculate present values:

PV to equity investors =

$$-\frac{\$610,000}{(1.2350)} - \frac{\$547,000}{(1.2350)(1.2004)}$$

$$-\frac{\$479,050}{(1.2350)(1.2004)(1.1685)}$$

$$-\frac{\$405,405}{(1.2350)(1.2004)(1.1685)(1.1427)}$$

$$+\frac{(\$4,349,922 - \$325,218)}{(1.2350)(1.2004)(1.1685)(1.1427)(1.1235)}$$

$$= -\$493,927 -\$368,973 - \$276,541 - \$204,552 + \$1,809,702$$

$$= \$465,709 < \$1,000,000 \text{ (equity investment in the LBO)}$$

PV of Deal to Firm =

$$\frac{\$220,000}{(1.1475)} + \frac{\$253,000}{(1.1475)(1.1302)}$$

$$+\frac{\$290,950}{(1.1475)(1.1302)(1.1143)}$$

$$+\frac{\$334,595}{(1.1475)(1.1302)(1.1143)(1.1014)}$$

$$+\frac{(\$384,782 + \$6,849,922)}{(1.1475)(1.1302)(1.1143)(1.1014)(1.0918)}$$

$$\$191,721 + \$195,080 + \$201,330 + \$210,215 + \$4,163,154$$

$$= \$4,961,500 < \$6,500,000 \text{ (total cost of the LBO}$$

including both debt and equity)

Conclusion: The proposed LBO does not make sense because neither equity investors nor lenders can recover their original investment or loans plus their required rates of return.

CASE STUDY 12-7.
BELL ATLANTIC AND VODAFONE
FORM WIRELESS JOINT VENTURE

1. *What did Bell Atlantic and Vodafone expect to get out of the JV?*

A substantial number of users of wireless devices are business travelers. Securing widespread geographic coverage would give both companies access to more customers. By utilizing existing networks, the two companies could gain access to these new customers far less expensively than if they were to attempt to build their own networks. (It is unclear if the two companies could not simply have cross-licensed access to their respective networks.) In particular, although Vodafone is the world's largest wireless company, it did not have complete geographic coverage in the U.S. This significantly reduced the value of the Vodafone franchise given the size of the U.S. market.

2. *Do you think this JV will promote or reduce competition in the wireless phone market?*

The JV is likely to be procompetitive, because it will put the partners on a more equal footing with other global competitors such as MCIWorldcom/Sprint as well as AT&T and British Telecom. The JV made it possible for the two partners to achieve national coverage at a price that is far less than if they had tried to build their own networks. Antitrust regulators generally look more favorably on alliances that make it possible for companies to do something that they could probably not have done on their own.

3. *Why would Bell Atlantic and Vodafone want to sell a portion of the new JV to the public?*

Selling equity to the public will enable the JV to finance future capital expenditures, provide a currency for future acquisitions, and will place a value on the JV that might help to boost the share prices of both companies. The two partners may eventually wish to sell the entire JV to the public.

4. *In your judgment, how do you think ownership in the JV was determined?*

The distribution of ownership appears to have been based on the valuation of the assets contributed by each party to the JV. Each party contributed their network assets, which could be valued either by discounting future cash flows generated by each network or by estimating the cost of building a network in the geographic areas that were not currently covered by Bell Atlantic and Vodafone.

5. *What type of JV legal structure was selected by the parent companies? Why was this particular type of legal structure chosen?*

The partners selected a corporate legal structure because of their desire to issue equity in the future. The corporate structure is often selected if the proposed alliance is large and complex such that it requires its own organizational structure and internal management. The equity structure of the corporation will also facilitate the sale of the partners' interest in the business if they should choose to exit the business at some point in the future. These benefits are negated by the double taxation of dividends that could have been avoided if a partnership had been the preferred legal structure. Moreover, both companies lose the flexibility associated with the partnership structure, which enables creative ways to distribute profits and losses from the venture in amounts that are disproportionate to their respective ownership shares.

CASE STUDY 13-7.
ALLEGHENY TELEDYNE RESTRUCTURES

1. *What are some of the reasons that Allegheny Teledyne considered such an extensive restructuring of its operations?*

Allegheny Teledyne had a desire to achieve greater focus and to improve its overall profitability and growth potential by exiting underperforming businesses.

2. *What synergies might there be in the businesses that Allegheny Teledyne is retaining?*

All remaining businesses are in some segment of the metals manufacturing or fabrication business, which should facilitate management's understanding of specific business problems and opportunities. In addition, some of the metal alloy products may be used in the production of specialty metals.

3. *Why do you think that stockholders might be better off owning stock in each of the three new companies (consumer products, aerospace/electronics, and metals manufacturing) than just in Allegheny Teledyne Inc.?*

They are pure plays and may be more accurately valued by analysts and investors. Moreover, they will have their own management, who will be focused on operating a single business, and they will not be burdened by Allegheny Teledyne's corporate overhead structure.

4. *Why might Allegheny Teledyne be considering spinning off some units and divesting others?*

The decision to spin off rather than to divest a business may reflect the lack of buyers for the business or a concern that the divestiture process will be too disruptive to the employees, customers, and suppliers of the business.

5. *Why might it be common for a major restructuring to come at a time when the head of a company is leaving, retiring, or assuming fewer responsibilities?*

The CEO may be retiring rather than face a firing following the poor performance of the corporation. The CEO may also see this as an appropriate time to retire, because a successful restructuring may be viewed as his legacy to the company.

CHAPTER 14
GEE WHIZ MEDIA (GWM) ACQUIRES
GO-GO TECHNOLOGY (GGT)

1. *Describe the industry or market in which GWM competed in terms of the following: customers, suppliers, current competitors, potential entrants, and product substitutes. How should this information be used by GWM's management to develop a long-term strategy?*

a. *Customers:* Electronic publishing companies (e.g., Activision and Broderbund) and distributors

b. *Suppliers:* Primarily content owners including Prince, famous artists, and record companies. Suppliers had market power and could exact high prices from CD programming companies.

c. *Current competitors:* GGT and Multimedia Corp were focusing on what they did best (i.e., converting content to electronic media such as CD-ROMs), allowing others to manufacture the disks, and aligning with distribution companies such as Broderbund for marketing, distribution, and advertising.

    d. *Potential entrants:* Few barriers to entry. Many small companies were entering the multimedia industry segment to convert content to CD-ROMs

    e. *Product substitutes:* Virtually all types of entertainment (e.g., books, tapes, TV, other game CDs, etc).

    f. This information could be used by GWM management in developing a long-term strategy by helping to define their customers needs, suppliers' requirements, relative strengths versus the competition, potential threats and opportunities, and ways in which they can satisfy customer needs better than the competition.

2. *Identify GWM's primary strengths and weaknesses as compared to the competition. How can this information be used to identify threats to and opportunities for GWM?*

    a. Strengths:

        i. market recognition that comes from being first (i.e., "first mover advantage)

        ii. reputation for honesty

        iii. multiyear licenses with major software companies (Sony, IBM and Apple) to promote their multimedia products

    b. Weaknesses:

        i. undercapitalized

        ii. poor project management skills, including few controls and an inability to meet deadlines

        iii. excessive spending

        iv. limited access to distribution channels

        v. no proprietary content

3. *Identify the range of reasonable options available to GWM to grow its business. Discuss the key advantages and disadvantages of each option. Of the available options, which would you have selected and why?*

Rapid industry consolidation suggested that acquisition was the most attractive route for GWM. Time was not on their side. Organic or internal growth through reinvestment of excess cash flow involved significant investment in marketing programs and in developing proprietary content. This would also require substantial time to assemble the right content. An alliance or JV with another competitor or a publisher to obtain content would initiate control issues and require significant amounts of time to negotiate, especially if it involved multiple content suppliers.

4. *GWM's acquisition plan identified key objectives, resource capability, the target industry, and appropriate tactics for completing an acquisition. Were all of the objectives adequately quantified and did they have associated completion dates? What other key objectives and tactics might GWM have included? Discuss the importance of these additional objectives and tactics.*

    a. GWM's stated objectives in its acquisition plan included the following:

        i. Acquiring companies with proprietary or access to proprietary content, effective distribution channels, and excellent design and production capabilities

      ii. Acquiring companies with widely recognized CD titles

      iii. Staying within the multimedia industry that they knew.

  b. GWM's stated tactics in its acquisition plan included the following:

      i. GWM not paying more than they could afford, which was estimated to be $25 to $30 million for an acquisition

      ii. Achieving a minimum acceptable rate of return equal to its cost of capital of 15%

      iii. A maximum P/E for the target company of not more than 35 times current year's earnings or 30 times next year's earnings

      iv. An interest coverage ratio of the combined companies that would not fall below the industry average of 6.2

      v. Counting only one-half of the projected cash flow resulting from synergy as part of the purchase price

  c. Other tactics could have included a target debt-to-equity ratio.

  5. *What were the key assumptions made in the GWM business plan used to justify the acquisition of GGT? Consider key assumptions, both explicit and implicit, with respect to the following areas: the market, financial performance, acquisition tactics, valuation, and integration.*

  a. Market

      i. CD-ROM technology would improve and proliferate.

      ii. People would use this medium to play games and for reference material.

      iii. The market would be large and growing.

  b. Financial performance

      i. They could make money without owning content.

      ii. Initially they felt they could distribute the disks on their own.

      iii. Growth through acquisition is preferable to organic, JVs, or alliances.

      iv. Easier to rejuvenate existing products than to introduce new ones and build a brand image.

      v. Even though the number of titles produced in the industry in 1996 slowed to 360,000, Durand believed the combined companies could grow faster than the industry.

      vi. The potential loss of customers and other unanticipated expenses discovered during due diligence could be made up from future cash flows.

  c. Acquisition tactics

      i. Acquiring something in their same industry would heighten their chances of success.

      ii. A friendly acquisition was superior to a hostile one.

      iii. Wall Street would accept 2 years of earnings dilution.

  d. Valuation

      i. GWM could raise $6.8 million by selling GGT's building and land.

      ii. GWM could realize $5.4 million in synergy.

     iii. GMW could realize $500,000 in annual synergy, but not until the second year.

     iv. GGT had not been booking revenue too quickly.

      v. They could finance the $750,000 in retained expenses from internal cash flow.

     vi. Only a few customers would leave.

    vii. The loan covenants would not prove to be too burdensome.

   viii. They would generate sufficient cash flow to meet debt service requirements.

     ix. Discount rate is 15%, and the conventional valuation techniques are adequate to measure value.

      x. GGT's software development program would not realize the cost savings embodied in the GGT forecast (COS reduced from 70 to 65%) by Chang.

  e. Integration

      i. The cultures of the two companies are compatible.

     ii. The software development teams could work together.

    iii. The two businesses could be quickly integrated.

    iv. Severance expenses were adequately estimated.

     v. GGT personnel could be housed in surplus GWM headquarters space once the GGT building and land were sold.

    vi. Duplicate personnel positions could be eliminated without disruption.

6. *In valuing GGT, Perez used various valuation techniques including P/E ratios for publicly traded companies, liquidation value, price-to-book and price-to-revenue ratios, and PV calculations. What are the strengths and weaknesses of the alternative valuation approaches? What might you have done differently to value GGT? Are there factors that might lead you to believe that Durand paid too much for GGT? What are the strengths and weaknesses of the alternative approaches?*

  a. P/Es for publicly traded companies are accounting based but represent values the stock market currently places on similar types of companies.

  b. *Liquidation value:* These types of companies have few hard assets. Most of GGT's hard assets were sold and would not be available in liquidation.

  c. *Price-to-book:* Accounting based and not useful for companies with few hard assets.

  d. *Price to revenue:* Same as P/Es

  e. *Value of recent transactions:* Best method if the recent transactions are very similar.

  f. *NPV:* Assumes accurate projections of the magnitude and timing of future cash flows as well as the discount rate.

What would you have done differently to value GGT?
   a. Weighted each valuation technique and computed a weighted average going concern value.
   b. Ignored liquidation value for this type of business.

Are there any factors that might lead you to believe that Durand paid too much? Yes.
   a. Willingness to retain $750,000 in expenses.
   b. Inability to get Chang to put some portion of the purchase price in escrow in view of the anomalies found during due diligence.

7. *What factors did Durand consider in structuring the initial purchase price offer to Chang? What other factors should he have considered?*
   a. Impact on GWM shareholders in terms of extent of initial dilution of EPS (his first inclination was to dismiss an all-stock purchase as being too dilutive.)
   b. Ability to enable the combined companies to outperform what GWM could have done on its own in terms of EPS.
   c. Acceptability to GGT management and stockholders
        i. Durand knew that many GGT managers were young and would be receptive to a deferred purchase price or options.
        ii. He also knew that many large shareholders had been shareholders for a long time and probably had a low tax basis in the business.

8. *Suppose that another CD-ROM media company is sold during the negotiations between GWM and GGT and the P/E was 40 (vs. 33 for GGT). How would this information affect negotiations?*

What would Chang's likely position be? How would Durand counter Chang's arguments?

Assuming Durand still wanted to complete the transaction, how might he have restructured the purchase price to make it acceptable to Chang while still making the transaction attractive to the GWM shareholders?

How would this information affect negotiations?
   a. Chang would want GWM to raise the purchase price for GGT.

How would Durand counter Chang's arguments?
   a. Point out the concessions Durand has already made (e.g., retention of $750,000 and willingness to forego escrowing some portion of the purchase price) and argue that the recent transaction is not really comparable.
   b. Together the two firms represented a counterweight to Multimedia, the industry's behemoth.

Assuming Durand still wanted to complete the transaction, how might he have restructured the purchase price to make it acceptable to both firms' shareholders?
   a. Offer to increase the purchase price based on an earn-out formula.
   b. Defer a portion of the purchase price payment to some future period, which would offer a higher future but a lower present value of the transaction.

9. *What additional information would you like to have to make a more informed valuation of GGT?*

a. More comparable, recent transactions

b. Profitability by customer and product to generate more reliable cash flow estimates

c. Listing of informal commitments made to customers and vendors

d. Listing of pot ential lawsuits

10. Using Table 14-7 as an example and showing your work on a spreadsheet, calculate the stand-alone value of GGT using the following assumptions applied to 1997 as the base year:

a. Sales grow at 30% per year for the 5-year period from 1998 through 2002 and 10% thereafter.

b. Cost of sales and SG&A equal 70% and 10% of sales, respectively.

c. Depreciation expense equals 3% of sales.

d. GGT has no debt. (Note: Delete interest expense and debt in Table 14-7 from 1997.)

e. The marginal tax rate is 40%.

f. Current assets and liabilities equal 8% and 5% of sales, respectively.

g. Capital expenditures equal 5% of sales.

h. Shares outstanding are constant at 300,000.

i. Total assets are equal to 50% of sales.

j. Equity equals total assets − current liabilities.

k. The risk-free rate of return is 5%, the β is 1.5 (from 1998 through 2002 and 1.25 thereafter), and the spread between the return on stocks and the risk-free rate is 5.5%.

TABLE 14-7. Solution to Question 10 for GWM Business Case Go Go Technology Normalized Income, Balance Sheet, and Cash Flow Statements[a]

	1993	1994	1995	1996	1997	1998	1999	2000	2001	2002
Income statement (thousands $)										
Net sales	0.90	1.45	2.50	3.00	4.10	5.10	6.63	8.62	11.20	14.57
Cost of goods sold	0.63	1.02	1.75	2.10	2.87	3.57	4.64	6.83	7.84	10.20
SG&A expense	0.05	0.07	0.13	0.15	0.21	0.26	0.66	0.86	1.12	1.46
Depreciation	0.03	0.04	0.08	0.09	0.12	0.15	0.20	0.26	0.34	0.44
EBIT	0.20	0.32	0.55	0.66	0.90	1.12	1.13	1.47	1.90	2.48
Income taxes	0.08	0.13	0.22	0.26	0.36	0.45	0.45	0.59	0.79	0.99
Net income	0.12	0.19	0.33	0.39	0.54	0.67	0.68	0.88	1.14	1.49
Earnings per share	2.38	1.91	2.20	2.64	3.61	2.24	2.25	2.93	3.81	4.95
Balance sheet (year ending 12/31)										
Current assets	0.05	0.09	0.15	0.18	0.25	0.41	0.53	0.69	0.90	1.17
Current liabilities	0.05	0.09	0.15	0.18	0.25	0.26	0.33	0.43	0.56	0.73
Working capital	0.00	0.00	0.00	0.00	0.00	0.15	0.20	0.26	0.34	0.44
Total assets	0.36	0.58	1.00	1.20	1.64	2.55	3.32	4.31	5.60	7.28
Equity	0.31	0.49	0.85	1.02	1.39	2.30	2.98	3.88	5.04	6.55
Shares	0.05	0.10	0.15	0.15	0.15	0.30	0.30	0.30	0.30	0.30
Free cash flow										
EBIT (1 − T)	0.12	0.19	0.33	0.40	0.54	0.67	0.68	0.88	1.14	1.49
Depreciation	0.03	0.04	0.08	0.09	0.12	0.15	0.20	0.26	0.34	0.44
Capital expenditures	0.05	0.09	0.15	0.18	0.25	0.26	0.33	0.43	0.56	0.73
Change in working capital	0.00	0.00	0.00	0.00	0.00	0.15	0.05	0.06	0.08	0.10
Free cash flow	0.07	0.15	0.26	0.31	0.42	0.42	0.50	0.65	0.84	1.09
PV (1998–2002) @. 1325%	$2.30									
PV of 6th yr. ter. Val. @. 1188%	$36.38									
Sum	$38.68									

Cost of equity for high-growth period (1998–2002) = .05 + 1.5 (.055) = 13.25
Cost of equity for terminal period beyond 2002 = .05 + 1.25 (.055) = 11.88

[a] SG&A, sales, general and administrative; EBIT, earnings before interest and taxes. PV, present value.

INDEX